The New Heaven and New Earth

The New Heaven and New Earth

An Interdisciplinary Comparison between Jürgen Moltmann, Karl Rahner, and Gregory Beale

RAYMOND R. HAUSOUL

Foreword by Gijsbert van den Brink

WIPF & STOCK · Eugene, Oregon

THE NEW HEAVEN AND NEW EARTH
An Interdisciplinary Comparison between Jürgen Moltmann, Karl Rahner, and Gregory Beale

Copyright © 2020 Raymond R. Hausoul. All rights reserved. Except for brief quotations in critical publications or reviews, no part of this book may be reproduced in any manner without prior written permission from the publisher. Write: Permissions, Wipf and Stock Publishers, 199 W. 8th Ave., Suite 3, Eugene, OR 97401.

Wipf & Stock
An Imprint of Wipf and Stock Publishers
199 W. 8th Ave., Suite 3
Eugene, OR 97401

www.wipfandstock.com

PAPERBACK ISBN: 978-1-7252-6283-6
HARDCOVER ISBN: 978-1-7252-6282-9
EBOOK ISBN: 978-1-7252-6284-3

Manufactured in the U.S.A.   04/07/20

But, as it is written,

"What no eye has seen,

nor ear heard,

nor the heart of man imagined,

what God has prepared

for those who love him."

—1 Corinthians 2:9

Contents

Preface ix
Abbreviations xi
Foreword by Gijsbert van den Brink xiii
Abstract and summary xv
1   Introduction and methodology 1
2   Rahner, Moltmann, and Beale on the dialogue between ST and BT 29
3   Karl Rahner's concept on the new heaven and new earth 52
4   Jürgen Moltmann's concept on the new heaven and new earth 96
5   Gregory Beale's perspective on the new heaven and new earth 136
6   Comparison and enrichment 185
7   Conclusion 290
Bibliography 307
Subject Index 337
Author Index 339
Ancient Document Index 343

Preface

While I was writing my master's thesis on the message of the land of Canaan in 2013, my attention was drawn to the theme of the new creation. If the former Canaan was potentially the prototype of the coming new heaven and the new earth, it was exciting to discover how this theme of the renewal of the earth evolved in the Bible. Personal preliminary studies on this theme showed me, however, that it was mainly from the field of Biblical Theology (BT) that the theme of the new heaven and new earth was written. The theme itself was treated as a stepmother in Systematic Theology (ST). This brought me to the question of whether it was possible to compare some eschatological concepts from both fields to get a clearer view of the Christian doctrine about the new heaven and the new earth.

I realized several times during my research on the new heaven and the new earth that I stand like a dwarf on the shoulders of giants. In addition to the large number of publications that I worked through, I think of those who motivated me and believed in my capacities for this project. First of all, I would like to thank my promoter, from Systematic Theology, Prof. Dr. Jan Hoek, and my co-supervisor, from Biblical Theology, Prof. Dr. Mart-Jan Paul. In many conversations with them, I was able to taste on a modest scale the richness of an interdisciplinary comparison.

I would also like to thank the many loyal friends who supported the publication of this edition. God knows you and may he also fulfill the desires and needs of your hearts. A word of thanks goes to Jacques Rommel and Kevin Rigolle because both supported me linguistically. Finally, I am indefinitely indebted to my dear wife Belinda and my sons Adriël and Ilja, who often had to miss their father in sports games because I wanted to work on "the new heaven and new earth" again. This work is dedicated to them.

Ypres, Summer 2019
Raymond R. Hausoul

Abbreviations

BT	Biblical Theology
Gr.	Greek
Hebr.	Hebrew
LXX	Septuagint
NT	New Testament
NTBT	Beale, Gregory K. *A New Testament Biblical Theology: The Unfolding of the Old Testament in the New*. Grand Rapids: Baker Academic, 2011.
OT	Old Testament
ST	Systematic Theology

Foreword

This study by the young Belgian theologian Raymond Hausoul operates in a field that for a long time was somewhat in the background of Christian theological reflection, but which has rightly received more attention in recent decades, namely the so-called cosmic eschatology. The writer is concerned with the future of the earth and even of the universe. Or in biblical language: with the new heaven and the new earth. How can we address this notion in a theologically responsible way today? Is there only discontinuity with the here and now, or is there also continuity and perhaps even a restart of earthly life as we know it today? Partly in the light of contemporary ecological problems, this is an appropriate theme. In his detailed and comprehensive research, Raymond Hausoul searches for sustainable answers to the many questions that arise here, which leads to an essential and highly instructive study.

His studies go back to a successfully defended PhD dissertation at the *Evangelische Theologische Faculteit* in Leuven (Belgium). As a result, the author is taking his departure point in the representations of the new creation by two well-known European systematic theologians and a slightly lesser-known American biblical theologian, Karl Rahner, Jürgen Moltmann, and Gregory Beale, respectively. Mainly the choice for the last one is surprising, but it is perfectly justifiable. Gregory Beale is a biblical theologian of the Reformed tradition, who pays great attention to eschatological themes in his work and is therefore influential even outside his circle. The fact that, unlike Moltmann and Rahner, he rejects the historical-critical approach makes the comparative investigation both more complex and more exciting.

Thus, on the one hand, Raymond Hausoul has an intrinsic interest in cosmic eschatology—an interest that is also evident in his study of God's future for the animals (*Gods toekomst voor dieren—God's future for animals*, 2019) that has so far not been translated into English. On the other hand, he also has a more methodical aim. He has begun to relaunch the conversation between biblical scholars and systematic theologians, which is often hindered by far-reaching specialization, and explores where it can lead.

Raymond Hausoul also briefly includes in his reflections the debate on the relationship between Christian eschatology and contemporary scientific cosmology. This is of great significance for the viability and persuasiveness of systematic theological discourse. The Christian narrative is a story of hope and expectation amid secular narratives about an imminent *Big Rip* or *Big Chill* of our solar system. However, in order not to leave it unreal and ethereal, this story needs to be critically-constructively linked to these existing science-fed narratives. Just as Reformed theology today will have to relate to influential biological theories such as the neo-Darwinian synthesis, it will also have to connect to leading cosmological theories that define the public debate. This book takes this aspiration seriously.

From the analyses of Karl Rahner, Jürgen Moltmann, and Gregory Beale as from their mutual comparison, this book argues that the new creation should be thought of as a glorification and perfection of the original creation. There is thus no annihilation and novel creation to be expected, because in the midst of break-up and discontinuity there will also be continuity. This conclusion is shared by many who have dealt with this subject. But the author concretizes it in a whole number of detailed observations that challenge systematic theology to process biblical material more adequately and, conversely, challenge biblical theology to become aware of its often hidden dogmatic assumptions. This raises some questions for Moltmann and Rahner because of the role that extra-biblical concepts play in their thinking (e.g., the *zimzum* idea in Moltmann and the way evolutionary theories are processed in Rahner). However, questions are also asked in the direction of Beale, primarily because of his non-reflected anthropocentrism.

Although Raymond Hausoul doesn't even mention it that way in this publication, I find it interesting that he also—and maybe even especially?—is bridging the gap between an orthodox reformed approach (represented here by Beale) and the more *mainstream* Christian theology we find in Moltmann and Rahner. Raymond Hausoul shows that both theological traditions have something to say to each other, and in doing so, overcomes caricatures that are quite common. Moreover, in his final chapter, he zooms out and compares his conclusions to treatments of the new heaven and the new earth in ten recent dogmatic studies from various parts of the (Western) world. This tour shows that there is still some work to be done in the field of cosmic eschatology. In this way, Raymond Hausoul's study stimulates and challenges us to take up this work, following up on his fascinating explorations in this book.

GIJSBERT VAN DEN BRINK
Professor of Theology and Science
Vrije Universiteit Amsterdam

Abstract and summary

In theology, there is a growing appreciation for the interdisciplinary conversation. This dissertation examines how the systematic-theological representations of the new heaven and earth of Rahner and Moltmann can be critically compared with the biblical-theological perspective of Beale on this matter in a methodically responsible way. It will explore in an exemplary way what an interdisciplinary comparison between experts in Systematic Theology (ST) and Biblical Theology (BT) can yield in the theological discourse of the new heaven and the new earth. It reveals that Beale's BT makes unconscious hermeneutical choices in its research and that Rahner's and Moltmann's ST common uses biblical "proof texts," without adequately taking the biblical context into account. Furthermore, it becomes constantly visible how both disciplines complement, challenge, and encourage each other on micro- and macro-level. Chapter 7 closes the inquiry of this dissertation with a structured conclusion about the methodical observations in the interdisciplinary comparison and the resulting value of this research.

1 INTRODUCTION AND METHODOLOGY

Today there is a growing interest in the interdisciplinary dialogue between academic disciplines. In theology, this desire relates to the dialogue between Systematic Theology (ST) and Biblical Theology (BT). However, within academic publications, an exemplary development of how the methodological gap between ST and BT can be bridged remains. Systematic theologians and biblical theologians write individual chapters in common publications, with no attempt to bridge this gap and carry a visible dialogue with each other in these. An inquiry into a possible comparison between experts in ST and BT that is methodologically responsible can be a significant contribution to addressing this gap.

This dissertation provides a new contribution to this by examining how, through a critical interdisciplinary comparison, the systematic-theological representations of Rahner and Moltmann on the new heaven and new earth can interact with the biblical-theological perspectives of Beale. It will so serve as an exemplary exploration of what a comparison between both theological disciplines can bring to the theological topic of the new heaven and new earth. In addition, this dissertation proposes a substantial contribution to the academic inventory of the cosmic eschatology of Rahner, Moltmann, and Beale in regard to the new heaven and earth. From the research question, the dissertation is structured as follows:

Chapter 1 contextualizes the research question of the dissertation, offers an overview of recent publications on the subject and includes a justification of methodology and assumptions. Chapter 2 investigates how Rahner, Moltmann, and Beale estimate an interdisciplinary conversation between ST and BT. The individuality of these academic disciplines and the enrichments and dangers of a dialogue between the ST and BT are discussed. Chapters 3 to 5 contain a hermeneutical-theological analysis of Rahner's, Moltmann's, and Beale's reflections on the new heaven and the new earth. In addition to their differences in approach and execution, the core elements of the three theologians in their own approach to the subject are investigated. Chapter 6 examines how a critical interdisciplinary comparison between Rahner's, Moltmann's, and Beale's eschatology can be methodically conducted in a responsible way. From the chosen methodology therein, a first critical comparison is held on hermeneutical choices which the interlocutors make. After this, a second comparison is undertaken which focuses on the substantive choices Rahner, Moltmann, and Beale make in their talk about the new heaven and earth. This visualizes to which extent an interaction between ST and BT can be of value in the theological debate about the new heaven and earth. In chapter 7, the dissertation will be closed with a conclusion about the methodical observations in the interdisciplinary comparison and the resulting added value.

2 RAHNER, MOLTMANN, AND BEALE ON DIALOGUE BETWEEN ST AND BT

Chapter 2 presents the attitudes of Rahner, Moltmann, and Beale facing an interdisciplinary conversation with the other field presented. This chapter shows their individual attitudes towards this and mentions the enrichments and dangers they a priori observe in a dialogue between ST and BT. The chapter demonstrates that all three theologians are in favor of such a dialogue when it is developed on an equal level. Their own enrichments, which they see in the dialogue between ST and BT, can be summarized as follows: the dialogue between ST and BT offers (1) inspiration by new insights; (2) awareness of one's own presuppositions; (3) enhancements from the overall theological picture; (4) relevance of the Bible and the Christian faith. Although Rahner, Moltmann, and Beale place different accents in their objectives of ST and BT, they agree both that ST deals with subjects from the Christian creed and social questions thereabout, while the BT describes the biblical storyline. It will also be demonstrated that for all of them, the Bible is a basic source in the reflection about faith in the dialogue between BT and ST. On the question of the authority of the Bible, they think differently.

3 KARL RAHNER'S PERSPECTIVE ON THE NEW HEAVEN AND NEW EARTH

Chapter 3 offers a new contribution to the study of Rahner's eschatology by analyzing and profoundly systematizing Rahner's thoughts on cosmic eschatology. The investigation into this shows how Rahner stresses in his hermeneutical principles that the future is only realized by God's absolute intervention. From this, responsible discourse on eschatology is only possible if it departs from the salvation which has already been achieved by Christ. For Rahner, the glorified and resurrected Christ constitutes the objective beginning of the new creation.

In his reflections on the new creation and on the interpretation of the biblical data about this, Rahner remains reluctant. At the same time, he emphasizes that the format and the content of the biblical imagery should not be separated. In his reflection on matter, Rahner presents the tangible and intangible as an inseparable unity. The history of the cosmos is therefore inextricably linked with the history of mankind. In Rahner's elaborations of this, Christ's resurrection stands in the midst and is very important when it comes to the reflection of the future resurrection. Christ's resurrected body is a unique and radical transformation of his crucified body. From this paradigm, Rahner speaks about the ultimate future resurrection of the body that humanity will receive. But he also insists that this does not mean that the resurrected body consists of the same identical atomic matter as the crucified body. With regard to time, Rahner sees eternity as the fruit of the personal history of human beings. Eternity as an infinite continuation of time or as an absence of time is rejected by him. Finally, Rahner stresses in his theocentric perspective on the new creation that in the *visio beatifica* the knowing of God remains an ongoing process in which the Creator and his creation will pervade each other in the same way as God's spirit permeates the Christian today.

4 JÜRGEN MOLTMANN'S PERSPECTIVE ON THE NEW HEAVEN AND NEW EARTH

Chapter 4 analyzes Moltmann's eschatology on the new heaven and earth. This chapter is unique in its comprehensiveness. In Moltmann's theology, eschatology stands in a central middle and cosmic eschatology is leading in this. The various hermeneutical principles that determine Moltmann's eschatology are analyzed and systematized in this chapter. It explains how Moltmann's eschatology is christologically determined. The crucifixion and resurrection of Christ are, according to Moltmann, related to the discontinuity and continuity between this creation and the new creation. The resurrection of Christ thereby anticipates what will take place between the present and the eschatological horizon. The doctrines of salvation and of creation are closely connected with this horizon. Out of this, history can be distinguished in three phases: *creatio originalis*, *creatio continua*, and *creatio nova*.

With regard to time and space, Moltmann says that God has confined himself to form a *nihilum*, in which he created the world. This *nihilum* makes creation imperfect and points to the future redemption. Despite recognizing positively that earthly historical time (*chronos*) causes the *creatio orginalis* to move to the *creatio nova*, he emphasizes the negativity of *chronos* because it is connected with the *nihilum*. Therefore, in the new creation, eonic cycle time will exist, which never perishes and glorifies all times throughout history. Also, on space (*topos*), Moltmann thinks both positively and negatively. On the one hand, space offers creation protection, but on the other hand, it makes a distance between creation and Creator. In the new heaven and earth, that distance disappears and God pervades all living space (*perichoresis*).

In his view on matter, Moltmann sees in Christ's Incarnation and resurrection a testimony to the redemption and renewal of the material. The matter of God's whole creation will be renewed and completed in the eschatological moment. The creation will be then changed into an eternal dwelling place for the triune God and will participate eternally in the trinitarian life. Moltmann recognizes various anticipations during this *creatio continum* on the coming new creation. These are images and metaphors which give us an idea of the new heaven and earth. They bring two facets forward: the absence of the current negativity and the presence or reminder of the current positivity.

5 GREGORY BEALE'S PERSPECTIVE ON THE NEW HEAVEN AND NEW EARTH

Chapter 5 analyzes Beale's perspective on the new heaven and earth. Because this has not yet been comprehensively done, this chapter constitutes a first scientific contribution to Beale's eschatology of the new creation. First, it examines the hermeneutical principles in Beale's BT. His methodical form and his focus on the biblical storyline from protology to eschatology are discussed. After this, it looks at the substantive themes that empower Beale's BT. Central to this, Beale has the idea that (1) the story of creation reveals God's plan for this creation, (2) Eden is the prototype of God's new creation, and (3) the history of salvation is continuously accompanied by references to this beginning. Beale also emphasizes that Christ's resurrection constitutes the beginning of God's new creation in Christ. From this, Beale concludes that the Christian has already been spiritually resurrected in the life of the new creation. The physical resurrection thereby remains outstanding. This will happen at Christ's second coming. For that moment, the Spirit is preparing Christians as first fruits. A glimpse of that blessed future can be seen in the creation story of Genesis when it testifies of God walking on earth and of the peace that humanity in the new creation is allowed to receive.

6 CRITICAL COMPARISON

Chapter 6 provides a critical interdisciplinary comparison between Rahner's, Moltmann's, and Beale's theological speaking on the new heaven and the new earth. This answers the research question of this dissertation. In the beginning, it reminds the reader of the openness for dialogue between ST and BT, which the three theologians recognize. From there, it establishes a comprehensive methodology for the interdisciplinary comparison that this chapter presents. In a hermeneutical and substantive critical comparison, it will examine to what extent the BT or ST of the respective theologians can have any significance for the other in talking about the new heaven and the new earth. This hermeneutical interaction reveals how Beale's BT unconsciously takes some important decisions from ST when it comes to the realization of the future. It also shows that Rahner's distinction between "eschatology" and "apocalypse," and his exegesis of Mark 13 is inaccurate. In addition, all three theologians complement each other well in their perspective on protology and eschatology. They positively challenge each other to reflect critically on the origins of evil, and on the permanent impact evil has on God's original creation. Further, both systematic theologians stimulate in their theological perspectives Beale's BT to an examination of the biblical images which are connected with the topic of cosmic eschatology, and they also request from his BT a theological investigation of the resurrection stories of Jesus Christ.

After the hermeneutical comparison, the substantive comparison reveals how the spiritual renewal, which Beale's BT stresses, and the physical renewal, which Rahner and Moltmann both emphasize in their ST, can be brought together. This ensures that a strict separation between the tangible and intangible aspects of the resurrection is avoided. It also shows the balance which is necessary between the continuity and discontinuity of this creation and new creation. Also, Moltmann's and Beale's contributions about space are brought in juxtaposition so that they complement and challenge each other. This interdisciplinary comparison can potentially result in a further investigation of the contrasts and similarities in the biblical imagery about the new heaven and earth. Also, they may be further examined in BT to illustrate how God's plan for this creation is related to his own being. Finally, the substantive comparison brings the question of the meaning and implication of certain biblical words for time forward. This interdisciplinary investigation, therefore, shows that both the ST and BT should be aware that their reflection on time and eternity is often more affected by an extra-biblical philosophy than by the Bible itself.

7 CONCLUSION

The conclusion of this dissertation brings the methodical observations in the interdisciplinary comparison to our attention. Of significance is the awareness of (1) the significance of the theological approach which the conversation partner applies, (2) the own hermeneutical grid, (3) the uniqueness and equality of both disciplines, and (4) on their own contributions to theology. The interdisciplinary comparison is from this perspective, valuable. It makes both disciplines aware of their presuppositions and shows how both are related to the complete field of theology. ST and BT are in fact, an integral part of the same whole. Although both operate in a different way within theology, they search for the same reliable, authentic Christian theology.

This chapter speaks also of the significance of the interdisciplinary comparison on the theme of the new heaven and earth. In addition to the aforementioned hermeneutical awareness, it will be shown that this interdisciplinary investigation between experts on ST and BT about the new creation does not have to focus primarily on providing concise "proof texts," but should be seen in a mutual exchange of wider theological themes, which recommends new sub and main themes. From this perspective, the dialogue between the ST of Rahner and Moltmann on the new heaven and earth, and the BT of Beale on the same topic, has an added value for both disciplines. In the midst of this dissertation stands thereby the essential question of continuity and discontinuity between this creation and the new creation. We conclude from the separate analyses of Rahner, Moltmann, and Beale, as from the interdisciplinary comparison between them that the new creation is not a *restitutio in integrum* or a *renovatio* of the current creation (continuity), and that it also should not be seen as an *annihilatio mundi* (discontinuity). Rather, the new heaven and the new earth represent a change, glorification, and completion of the original first heaven and earth which God created. There is both a fundamental continuity and a radical discontinuity between the current life in Christ today and the future life in God in the new creation. So the future involves both a radical break with a subsequent *novum* and a process-based transformation and renovation, which transcends our thinking. However, the eschatological perspective on the ultimate arrival of the triune God to this creation urges us to take God's creation seriously. From the results of this research, there are still major challenges in the dialogue between ST and BT on the topic of the new heaven and earth. But at the same time, the Christian testimony may continue to witness that God, for his creation, offers not a hopeless end, but rather an endless hope.

1

Introduction and methodology

1.1　PURPOSE OF THE INVESTIGATION

This dissertation investigates how two systematic-theological designs on eschatology and a biblical-theological design can be of significance for theological discussion about the new heaven and the new earth. The concrete research question is:

> How can comparison between Karl Rahner's and Jürgen Moltmann's systematic theological designs on eschatology and Gregory Beale's biblical-theological design be of significance in a theological dialogue concerning the new heaven and the new earth?

In literature, the importance of such an interdisciplinary dialogue between representatives from the discipline of ST and that of the BT has already been mentioned several times (cf. §1.2.4).[1] To ascertain its relevance, it is important to compare the designs of different professional experts from theological disciplines. This dissertation does not offer an independent systematic-theological or biblical-theological design concerning the new heaven and new earth. To begin with, this seems too pretentious and, moreover, it would ignore the core of the research question, which is to get a closer look at the way interaction between well-known designs on the part of ST and BT take shape, as well as which potentials of an interdisciplinary dialogue are as yet unused.

In this thesis, Rahner, Moltmann, and Beale are chosen, and their different theological designs are compared. Through this comparison, systematic-theological and biblical-thematic reflections on the new creation can be linked. In this way, a careful comparison reveals how an interdisciplinary comparison can increase the

---

1. Vanhoozer, "Theology of the New Testament," 28; Wilkinson, *Eschatology*, 24–26, 54–57; Mühling, *Grundinformation*, 305–14; Turner and Green, "New Testament," 1–22; Goldingay, "Biblical Narrative," 123–42; O'Collins and Kendall, *Bible for Theology*, 2; Mildenberger, *Prolegomena*.

understanding of three separate designs from different denominational, cultural, and disciplinary areas, and at the same time shows how each design is limited and how a comparison can lead to enrichment on the subject of the new heaven and the new earth.

1.2   THE RELATIONSHIP BETWEEN BT AND ST

In the past, a strict separation between BT and ST has often been made.[2] The Dutch theologian Kees van der Kooi writes:

> They are households next to each other, while at most in the kitchen, the housemates look over a shoulder with surprise at what the other brews. . . . Most practitioners of dogmatism are already happy when they have some overview of their own field. . . . A simple appeal to exegetical results and biblical theology, as it seemed to be for former generations, seems to be definitely over.[3]

As a result, the fields of BT and ST have little in common with each other. But we also discover in our society that there is an appreciation for the interdisciplinary discussion.[4] This also has its influence on the dialogue between BT and ST. As a result of the demand for a responsible interdisciplinary dialogue, the desire to bridge the gap between ST and BT has therefore grown over the past decades. Kevin Vanhoozer already stated in 2014:

> There are encouraging signs that the two disciplines, after generations of wandering in the wilderness in isolation from one another, are each approaching the Promised Land of interdisciplinary partnership.[5]

This will lead both disciplines to a cycle of mutual influence and enrichment. The same thought can be found with Markus Mühling when he pleads for more interaction between BT and ST in his reflection on the new creation.[6] This motivates the

---

2. See detailed: Den Hertog and van der Kooi, *Tussen leer en lezen*; Van der Kooi, "Van binnenuit," 30–49. See for further definition and introduction in these professional fields: Klink and Lockett, *Understanding Biblical Theology*; Barr, *Concept*, 1–17; Van den Brink and van der Kooi, *Dogmatiek*, 28–32; Guarino, *Foundations*; Kamphuis, "Systematische theologie," 59–71; Fischer, *Protestantische Theologie*; Gunton, "Historical and Systematic Theology," 3–20.

3. Van der Kooi, "Van binnenuit," 32: "Het zijn huishoudingen naast elkaar, terwijl de huisgenoten hoogstens in de keuken over een schouder met bevreemding toekijken wat de ander brouwt . . . [D]e meeste beoefenaren van de dogmatiek zijn al blij wanneer ze enigszins het eigen veld overzien. . . . Een eenvoudig beroep op exegetische resultaten en bijbelse theologie, zoals dat voor vroegere generaties leek te zijn weggelegd, lijkt definitief voorbij." See also, Van den Brink and van der Kooi, *Dogmatiek*, 491–92.

4. Repko et al., *Introduction*, 3–22, 63–85; Schmidt, "Box," 39–49; Moran, *Interdisciplinarity*, 3–12, 188–92.

5. Vanhoozer, "Theology of the New Testament," 28. Cf. Green, "Scripture and Theology," 23–43; Goldingay, "Biblical Narrative," 123–42; Nineham, *Use and Abuse*, 214–32.

6. Mühling, *Grundinformation*, 305–14. See also, Wilkinson, *Eschatology*, 24–26, 54–57.

research to compare two systematic-theological theologians and a biblical theologian and to find out what the added value of this comparison may be.

The interdisciplinary discussion involves two different disciplines that enter into dialogue with each other. This societal tendency is a reaction to a reduced approach of the individual sciences. On the one hand, a reduction can cause one's own professional research to deepen and, on the other hand, can cause the research to overlook contextual elements and underestimate the complexity of the subject.[7]

In this dissertation, an interdisciplinary comparison is chosen between two theologians from the ST field and one theologian from that of the BT. Such a comparison between ST and BT is not new (see §1.5). Therefore, the synopsis below provides an overview of the relationship between ST and BT in Western theology.

1.2.1 General developments

What in Western theology today has been divided into ST and BT belonged together until the seventeenth century.[8] Judaism and Christianity traditionally used the Bible in the reflection on religious subjects. Despite the differences in hermeneutical association with the Bible, there was a dialogue between biblical exegesis and Christian faith. While theology held on to this dialogue globally, German universities in the Enlightenment opted for a separation between the two.[9] In the context of this separation, Jürgen Moltmann and Karl Rahner developed their theology. Furthermore, the growing gap between biblical sciences and systematic theology also influenced American theology in the middle of the twentieth century, within the context in which Gregory Beale found himself. A more detailed description of the manner in which the separation between BT and ST took place is of importance for a better understanding of the positions of the three theologians to whom our investigation is addressed. That is why we give brief attention to this development in the next section.

1.2.2 The time after the Enlightenment

During the Enlightenment, a shift occurred within German academic theology in the use of the Bible within ST. Through the strong emphasis on the intellect, an increasing tension arose between faith and reason.[10] Systematic theology, which set the tone at theological faculties, often wanted to interpret the Bible from certain philosophical frameworks. In contrast to this rationalistic approach, others insisted on the traditional method of relating Christian faith to biblical texts as authentication (*dicta*

---

7. See for theology, Fredericks, "Religious Studies," 161–74.

8. See detailed, Zwiep, *Tussen tekst en lezer*, 2:2–268; Hauser and Watson, *History of Interpretation (Medieval-Reformation)*; Bray, "Church Fathers," 23–40.

9. Stylianopoulos, "Biblical," 555–57.

10. Kraus, *Biblische Theologie*; Merk, *Biblische Theologie*.

probantia). So, the Bible was used to demonstrate the super-temporal truths of one's own systematic-theological positions.[11]

This maintenance of the Bible in ST caused a rivalry between those above rationalistic and traditional approaches. Systematic theologians wanted to free dogmatics from the ties of confessionalism, and biblical scholars wanted to get rid of every dogmatic harness. The Bible could not be a paper papal for ST and ST should not be a dictatorship for the interpretation of the Bible. Around the year 1745, the need for privatization of the professional disciplines with their methodical distinction became apparent in German theology.[12] A striking point in this development was the inaugural speech of Johann Gabler (1753–1826) *Oratio de justo discrimine theologiae biblicae et dogmaticae regundisque recte utriusque finibus*, held on 30 March 1787 at the University of Altdorf. Gabler proposed to separate biblical exegesis and Christian faith from each other. This was the birth-hour of biblical theology (BT). Incidentally, Gabler was not the first to introduce a division between biblical exegesis and Christian faith. His contribution was mainly that he made a methodical distinction between the two, which officially created the field of BT and the separated field of ST.[13]

Gabler considered BT as a historical-descriptive discipline that reconstructed what the biblical writers meant to say at the time and ST as a didactic-normative discipline that addressed the question of the relevance of faith. Gabler's vision turned out to be ground-breaking, with the result that from then on ST in Western Europe was mainly concerned with the Christian faith tradition, in consultation with contemporary philosophy. In distinction, BT dealt with the biblical testimony. In Gabler's performance, she adopted the contours of the historiography of religion and wanted to describe historically-objectively what faith meant at the time.[14]

1.2.3 Developments up to the twenty-first century

In the two centuries that followed, rational Enlightenment thinking would not only characterize the theology of German universities.[15] This way of thinking also influenced Anglo-Saxon countries. For example, Walter Brueggemann mentions the later biblical-theological works of the Germans Walther Eichrodt and Gerhard von Rad.[16]

---

11. See for example, Hülsemann, *Vindiciae Sanctae*; Schmidt, *Collegium Biblicum*.

12. Den Hertog and van der Kooi, "Problemen op tafel," 11; Kraus, *Biblische Theologie*, 17; Merk, *Biblische Theologie*, 20.

13. Gabler, *Kleine theologische Schriften*, II:179–198. He followed strongly, Zachariae, *Biblischer Theologie*. See detailed, Niebuhr and Böttrich, *Gabler*; Sandys-Wunsch and Eldredge, "Gabler," 133–158 (esp. 150).

14. Gabler, "Oration," 495–96.

15. For a historical overview see, Steinberg, "Korte geschiedenis," 21–49; Rosner, "Biblical Theology," 3–11.

16. Brueggemann, *Theology*, xv; Von Rad, *Theologie*; Eichrodt, *Theologie 1: Gott und Volk*.

As was to be expected, the sharp separation between ST and BT gradually caused an increasing distance between these two disciplines. A fruitful exchange was often lacking. In the twentieth century, the artificial separation that Johann Gabler made between a prescriptive ST and a descriptive historically-objective BT was for many the core problem of this lack of exchange.[17] The objective neutrality that the BT received as a label turned out to be a myth. Also, within the field of BT scholars read the texts from their own context, as recipients and not as senders. There is no purely objective exegesis that can be considered completely neutral and value-free. Objective neutrality in BT, which works purely historically-descriptive, turns out to be impossible. The explanation of what a text meant is colored by the presuppositions of the scholar in the present.[18]

This is reflected in the pluralism of concepts that exist within BT. James Barr and Gerhard Hasel map out the most important concepts within BT and provide a critical reflection on their methodical-hermeneutical choices.[19] These concepts can be divided into three main paradigms: (1) a systematic approach, (2) a historical approach, and (3) a canonical literary approach.[20] The systematic approach usually works with a theological center and often places questions from ST in the foreground of BT.[21] The historical approach often concentrates on the question of how the Israelite religion and the biblical texts originated from a historical-critical analysis.[22] The literary-canonical approach raises the question of how literary stylistic tools can be used to communicate the testimony of OT and NT and attaches importance to the Bible as a canonical collection of equivalent books.[23] The biblical theologian will, in describing the testimony of the OT and NT, choose one of these paradigms and also make his choices in the field of selection, delimitation, accentuation, and ranking.[24] A further distinction between these different concepts within BT is the development of both a historical-critical and a historical-canonical analysis of the BT. While the historical-critical approach focuses primarily on the historical development of religions and the evolutionary development of their teachings, the historical-canonical approach rather accepts the testimony of the Bible as authentic. In both cases, it concerns choices in methodology.[25]

17. Steinberg, "Korte geschiedenis," 24; Barr, *Concept*, 6, 15; Brueggemann, *Theology*, 13–15; Hasel, "Relationship," 113–14; Gaffin, "Systematic Theology and Biblical Theology," 283.

18. Grenz and Franke, *Beyond Foundationalism*; Kelsey, *Proving Doctrine*, 202–3; Bultmann, "Voraussetzungslose Exegese," 149; Gaffin, "Systematic Theology and Biblical Theology," 283; Warfield, "The Idea of Systematic Theology," 65–68, 73–74.

19. Barr, *Concept*; Hasel, *Theology*.

20. Steinberg, "Korte geschiedenis," 29–48; *Die Ketuvim*, 20–57; Rendtorff, *Canonical Hebrew Bible*, 1–4.

21. For example, Vriezen, *Hoofdlijnen*; Eichrodt, *Theologie 1: Gott und Volk*; *Theologie 2: Gott und Welt*; *Theologie 3: Gott und Mensch*; Köhler, *Theologie*.

22. For example, Gerstenberger, *Theologies*; Von Rad, *Theologie*. For a historical perspective based on a more historical-canonical approach, see Waltke, *Old Testament Theology*; Kaiser, *Theology*.

23. For example, Koorevaar and Paul, *Theologie*; Rendtorff, *Canonical Hebrew Bible*.

24. Steinberg, "Korte geschiedenis," 29.

25. Brueggemann, *Theology*, 13.

The same will be the case with different systematic-theological designs. Because ST has a less fixed method than BT, there is a greater variety of methods available.[26] Traditionally, ST divides itself into the following main paradigms: (1) kerygmatic-confessional approaches, (2) philosophical-hermeneutical approaches, and (3) more current-free approaches.[27] The kerygmatic-confessional approach offers an analytical-systematic deepening of the articles of faith and wants to articulate, clarify, and proclaim the Christian creed. The philosophical-hermeneutical approach responds to the contemporary thinking climate and its specific questions to Christian doctrine. It often gives an apologetic answer.[28] In this approach, there is also the weak or deconstructivist theology that distances itself from all metaphysics and emphasizes the human interpretation, in which the "being" is explained, and the radical theology that states that "being" precedes our understanding, and therefore is more than just interpretation, even if it is only interpreted accessible.[29] The more current-free approaches came to the forefront from the nineteenth century through the increasing specialization within ST and the practice of ST as an end in itself with its issues.[30]

For a study that wants to compare designs from the two disciplines of ST and BT, it is important to take into account the above variations. A comparison of a systematic-theological design with a BT historical-thematic design will be different from a comparison of a systematic-theological design with a BT literary-canonical design. In a confrontation with the differences, the theologian's own determination also comes into sharp focus. Here, hermeneutical questions come to the forefront. In this dissertation, we must take these presuppositions into account. Also, it will become apparent in this writing that Rahner is mainly in the philosophical-hermeneutical approach, that Moltmann does not want to limit himself to one concept of ST, and Beale uses his BT mainly from a systematic-historical paradigm.

1.2.4 Importance of a dialogue

It was gradually confirmed that both ST and BT are not completely neutral. Human theories are always influenced by their presuppositions. Ludwig Wittgenstein and Hans-Georg Gadamer separately demonstrated, from their philosophy, that no one can be fully objectively disconnected from their own context, i.e., their tradition, culture,

---

26. Tillich, *Systematic Theology 1*, 34; Van den Brink and van der Kooi, *Dogmatiek*, 30. See for a historical overview of the developments within ST, Webster, "Introduction," 3–6; McGrath, *Christian Theology*, 143–44; Van Genderen and Velema, *Dogmatiek*, 29–33; Pannenberg, *Systematische Theologie 1*, 27–28; Weber, *Grundlagen*, I:87–181; Wentsel, *De openbaring (ST2)*, 2:407–624.

27. Webster, "Introduction," 9–10; Muis, "Dogmatiek," 84–86; Grudem, *Systematic Theology*, 21–23.

28. Tillich, *Systematic Theology 1*, 30–31, 35–38.

29. Schaafsma et al., "Vervreemding," 13–16, 19–22.

30. Van den Brink and van der Kooi, *Dogmatiek*, 26; Erickson, *Christian Theology*, 656; Berkhof, *Christelijk Geloof*, 88. See for an overview, Ford and Muers, *Modern Theologians*; Moltmann, *Erfahrungen*, 171–259.

class, sex, history, etc.[31] Every reading of a text is framed in a confessional and contextual way. We read the Bible from our own experiences, expectations, and assumptions. Even in translating the Bible, one's theology plays a role in the choices we make.[32] Several researchers approach a text in different ways: historical-critical, historical-canonical, literary, symbolic, depth-psychological, societal-critical, feminist, etc.

This realization does not mean that humankind is surrendered to absolute arbitrariness and that universal statements can no longer be made. Rather, the contextual definition of the research makes it clear that every theological statement has its own "grammar" and is subjectively determined.[33] The theologian cannot be fully objectified and, as a reader, remains involved in the interpretation process with his subjective input. From this, theologians like Stephen Fowl and Christopher Spinks conclude that the Bible has no definite meaning, but that it unfolds continuously in the translation.[34] On the other hand, Arie Zwiep calls for vigilance against postmodern relativism that leaves the question of truth unanswerable and leaves no room for revelation.[35] The abandonment of any claim to truth would go beyond what is customary in modern scientific theory. Krzysztof Burdzy and Peter Novick thus point out that, even in modern theology, the realization that the practice of science is paradigm dependent is no reason to say that modern science is at the mercy of absolute arbitrariness.[36]

If there are different contextual approaches next to each other, this does not mean that the Bible text has been deprived of its original meaning. It is enriching when people from different cultures and situations read the same biblical story. While individual theological reflection often works as a mirror, dialogue offers the advantage of openness to other elements in the object under investigation. In the words of Ludwig Wittgenstein, "One learns the game (life and meaning) by watching how others play."[37]

Recently, for example, all kinds of Bible comments have appeared that were written from African, Asian, feminist, apologetic, or one of many other backgrounds.[38] This joint intercultural reading of the Bible can be a catalyst for new, cross-border forms of dialogue and identity building. For this reason, the ST may not withdraw into its discipline. It has to take up the challenge to be practiced in close relation with reading the Bible and also with the discipline of the biblical sciences which deals with

---

31. Gadamer, *Wahrheit und Methode*, 293–326; Wittgenstein, *Philosophische Untersuchungen*. Cf. Thiselton, *Two Horizons*, 293–326, 357–438.

32. De Vries, "Vertalingen kiezen," 43.

33. Zwiep, "Onderweg," 38; Westermann, "Zur Frage," 14–15.

34. Fowl, *Theological Interpretation*; Spinks, *Bible and the Crisis*, 66.

35. Zwiep, "Onderweg," 50.

36. Cf. Burdzy, *Search for Certainty*; Novick, *Noble Dream*.

37. Wittgenstein, *Philosophical Investigations*, 23.53.

38. Adeyemo et al., *Africa Bible Commentary*; Ngewa, *Africa Bible Commentary Series*; Nicholls, *Asia Bible Commentary*; Sakenfeld, *Reading the Bible as Women*; Kroeger and Evans, *IVP Women's Bible Commentary*; Cabal, *Apologetics*. For several perspectives together, see Patte, *Global Bible Commentary*.

the study of the Bible.[39] We are not considering here an explanation with the exegeses of individual Bible texts that ST likes to use as "proof texts," as was often the case in the past. The Bible was then nothing more than a collection of isolated texts that could be used at random in the ST. In this way, little justice was done to the own genres and purport of these biblical texts.[40] When we talk about a close relationship between ST and the discipline of the biblical sciences, we think mainly of an interdisciplinary relationship between ST and a responsible theological interpretation of the Bible, as it largely takes place in BT. Although BT has been viewed critically, because of its methodical variation, it can lead to valuable insights into ST. After all, in theological reflection, BT gives the ST an awareness of what the relevant biblical texts, which serve to substantiate certain doctrinal positions, mean in their context. This diversity of biblical texts and different theological perspectives is not something that we need to eliminate or neutralize. Rather, it shows the richness of biblical perspectives on the path God is following with this creation.

Therefore, ST and BT should be engaged in an interdisciplinary discussion in which there are continuous interaction and mutual influence between equivalent subjects. In this way, they can be held accountable by each other for the theologies they have formed. It is from this background that this dissertation investigates how the design of a biblical theologian and the designs of two systematic theologians can enrich each other in an interdisciplinary comparison of the new heaven and the new earth.

1.3 THE SUBJECT OF A NEW HEAVEN AND NEW EARTH

The expectation of a new heaven and earth already manifests itself in the OT: "For I am about to create new heavens and a new earth; the former things shall not be remembered or come to mind" (Isa 65:17, cf. 66:22).[41] The NT echoes this hope and speaks twice about a new heaven and a new earth, "We wait for new heavens and a new earth, where righteousness is at home" (2 Pet 3:13), "Then I saw a new heaven and a new earth; for the first heaven and the first earth had passed away, and the sea was no more" (Rev 21:1).

In church history, the Creed of Nicea-Constantinople is the oldest confession, mentioning the hope for the new creation. At the end of it, we find, "and life in the coming empire" (καὶ ζωὴν τοῦ μέλλοντος αἰῶνος). Apart from this concise formulation, there is little or no reference to the new heaven and earth in the confessions of the early church, while other eschatological subjects are mentioned. Although the

---

39. Reynolds et al., *Reconsidering*; Bockmuehl and Torrance, *Scripture's*; Den Hertog and van der Kooi, *Tussen leer en lezen*; Green and Turner, *Between*.

40. Van den Brink and van der Kooi, *Dogmatiek*, 33, 35, 486.

41. All Bible references are from New Revised Standard Version (NRSV).

subject of the new heaven and the new earth is discussed several times in the Bible, it is less at the center of theological attention.[42]

In Christian theology, in recent decades, the question arose to (re)discover the Christian hope for the new creation in its integrity and individuality. Tom Wright, Richard Bauckham, and others contributed from the discipline of New Testament studies,[43] Alister E. McGrath, Colleen McDannell, Bernhard Lang and others from the perspective of historical theology,[44] Walter Brueggemann, Hendrik J. Koorevaar, Mart-Jan Paul made contributions to this from their reflections on the place of the earth and the land in the department of Old Testament,[45] and Gregory Beale, Thomas Schreiner, and Richard Middleton did so from a biblical-theological field of expertise.[46]

This interest in the new creation is less present in the field of ST. This interest in the new creation is less present in the field of ST. If you look at some of the dogmatism on this subject, you will discover that the starting points for the theme of the new heaven and earth remain concise and rather form an appendix.[47] It is admittedly true that many people place Ernst Troeltsch's words from 1916:

> A modern theologian says, "the eschatological office is mostly closed nowadays."[48]

As opposed to those of Hans Urs von Balthasar:

> If the word of Troeltsch could apply to 19th-century liberalism, "The eschatological office is usually closed," on the contrary, it has been working overtime since the turn of the century.[49]

---

42. McDannell and Lang, *Heaven*, 47–358; McGrath, *Christian Theology*.

43. Wright, *Surprised by Hope*; Wright, *New Heavens, New Earth*; Bauckham and Hart, *Hope against Hope*.

44. McGrath, *Heaven*; McDannell and Lang, *Heaven*.

45. Koorevaar and Paul, *Land*; Brueggemann, *Land*. See also my own contributions about this topic, Hausoul, "Land Ahead!"; "Land"; *Boodschap*.

46. Middleton, *New Heaven*; Schreiner, *King*; Beale, *New Testament*.

47. Concise are, Culver, *Systematic Theology*, 1155–56; Grudem, *Systematic Theology*, 1158–64; Van den Brink and van der Kooi, *Dogmatiek*, 639–40, 673–78; Wohlmuth, *Mysterium*, 224–33; Schwarz, *Eschatology*. More expanded are, Van de Beek, *God doet recht*, 83–95; Hoek, *Hoop*, 262–74; Pannenberg, *Systematische Theologie 3*, 625–53; Moltmann, *Kommen*, 287–350.

48. Troeltsch, *Glaubenslehre*, 36: "Ein moderne Theologe sagt: 'das eschatologische Bureau sei heutzutage zumeist geschlossen.'" Troeltsch gives the following reason for this statement, "Immer unerträglicher wird für das sittliche Gefühl der Lohn- und Strafgedanke. Das Jenseits kann nichts anderes sein als das allmähliche Hervortreten der Folgen, die das höhere Leben zeitigt, und ein immer tieferes Hineinwachsen ins göttliche Geisterreich"—"The idea of pay and punishment is becoming increasingly unbearable for the moral feeling. The afterlife can be nothing else than the gradual emergence of the consequences of the higher life and an ever deeper growing into the divine spiritual realm."

49. Von Balthasar, "Eschatologie," 403: "Wenn für den Liberalismus des 19. Jahrhunderts das Wort von Troeltsch gelten konnte: 'Das eschatologische Bureau ist meist geschlossen', so macht dieses im Gegenteil seit der Jahrhundertwende Überstunden."

The New Heaven and New Earth

Nevertheless, the eschatological office that deals with cosmic eschatology is still closed to a large extent. In any case, overtime is not yet an issue. Matthias Remenyi writes:

> As a rule, the hope of a new heaven and earth is rather a stepchild of the eschatological discussion.[50]

Gottfried Bachl makes the same judgment, "The cosmic dimension has always been overshadowed by anthropocentric interest."[51] And Jürgen Moltmann writes, "in our theological tradition eschatology has always been limited to an *individual eschatology*."[52] Karl Rahner asks the question about the twentieth century:

> If this epoch does not come to an end and a new one is slowly coming up, which will have a more direct relationship to the cosmic and human-historical e[schatology] of Christianity from the implications of its own overall human dynamics for the future.[53]

Therefore, interdisciplinary research with contributions from systematic-theological and biblical-theological perspectives offers the possibility to make a personal contribution to the study of the new creation.

The choice to use the term "new creation" for the new heaven and the new earth in this dissertation is in line with a broad theological tradition that refers to the various Judaeo-Christian representations on this theme. Also, "new creation" refers to the late-Jewish and early Christian use of terminology to the renewal of humanity.[54] Christian eschatology uses the term "new creation" for both fields of meaning. Second Corinthians 5:17 emphasizes that "if anyone is in Christ, there is a new creation" (εἴ τις ἐν Χριστῷ, καινὴ κτίσις; cf. Gal 6:15). From a semantic point of view, this terminology around "new creation" also occurs in the case of cosmic renewal or "new heavens and a new earth" (οὐρανὸν καινὸν καὶ γῆν καινήν; 2 Pet 3:13; Rev 21:1).[55]

Therefore, traditionally eschatology distinguishes between the individual or personal renewal of humanity to "new creation" and the collective or cosmic renewal of this creation to "new creation." These are not two independent events. The completion of humans as individuals takes place within the great process of the completion

---

50. Remenyi, *Um der Hoffnung*, 419: "In der Regel ist es vielmehr so, dass die Hoffnung auf einen neuen Himmel und eine neue Erde eher ein Stiefkind der eschatologischen Diskussion darstellt."

51. Bachl, *Eschatologie*, I:18: "Die kosmische Dimension liegt seit eh und je im Schatten des anthropozentrischen Interesses."

52. Moltmann, "Liebe," 837: "in unserer theologische Tradition war die Eschatologie immer auf eine *Individualeschatologie* beschränkt worden."

53. Rahner, "Eschatologie (SM)," 1185: "ob diese Epoche nicht zu Ende geht und langsam eine neue heraufkommt, die von den Implikationen ihrer eigenen gesamtmenschlichen Zukunftsdynamik ein unmittelbareres Verhältnis zu der kosmischen und menschheitsgeschichtlichen E[schatologie] des Christentums haben wird."

54. Jackson, *New Creation*; Hubbard, *New Creation*.

55. Van den Brink and van der Kooi, *Dogmatiek*, 648; Jackson, *New Creation*, 7–10; Mell, *Neue Schöpfung*, 1–4.

of creation as a collective. Notwithstanding this dual use of "new creation" for both anthropological and cosmological modification, the term in this dissertation refers to the collective cosmic renewal of current creation and thus to the promised "new heaven and earth."

1.4 CLARIFICATION OF CHOSEN THEOLOGIANS

It is not feasible to treat a large number of theologians in-depth in a dissertation. Because this dissertation is written by the discipline of ST, a comparison was chosen between two systematics and one biblical theologian, who all focus extensively on the theme of the new heaven and the new earth in several publications.

To minimize the influence of the interdisciplinary discussion on the subject, it was decided not to choose representatives from the same tradition. The criterion for the selection is that the theologians have dealt with the theme in detail. This led us to choose the Protestant Jürgen Moltmann (b. 1926), the Roman Catholic Karl Rahner (1904–1984), and the Reformed Gregory Beale (b. 1949). Although the choice of these three theologians is partially subjective, it is also objectively justifiable. The following considerations will demonstrate this.

1.4.1 Jürgen Moltmann

Regarding the choice of the theme of the new heaven and the new earth, I chose to bring together theologians from recent history, who are more or less influential in the recent discussions about the new heaven and the new earth. A choice for theologians from the distant past could have been made as well, as long as they had sufficient attention for the theme of the new heaven and the new earth.

As we have already noted, only a few systematic theologians from the last century were profoundly into cosmic eschatology (§1.3). Despite the golden age of eschatology at the beginning of the twentieth century, the results of the concise research on the new heaven and the new earth were mainly described regarding discontinuity. For this reason, many people followed in the footsteps of Rudolf Bultmann in opting for a consistent, coexisting eschatology in the here and now.[56] Theological reflections on the new heaven and earth did not go much further than the statement that the new life would manifest itself in a new form of reality that could only be speculated on in the present.[57]

This changed in the second half of the twentieth century. In particular, this was achieved through the *Theology of Hope*, with which the name Jürgen Moltmann was associated. His *Theologie der Hoffnung* (1964) caused a renaissance in eschatological

---

56. Bultmann, *Geschichte*, 181; "Eschatologie," 134–52.

57. Schwöbel, *Gott in Beziehung*, 437; McDannell and Lang, *Heaven*, 307–52; Müller-Goldkuhle, *Eschatologie*.

thinking and radically broke with Bultmann's purely existentialist eschatology. Christian-oriented eschatology had to be fundamentally revised.

> Therefore, a right theology would have to be considered in terms of its future goal. Eschatology should not be their end, but their beginning.[58]

Although speaking of cosmic eschatology in *Theologie der Hoffnung* remained sketchy, the reflection on the new creation received greater attention in Moltmann's later works.[59] A breakthrough in this respect was *Das Kommen Gottes* (1995). From that moment on, this hermeneutical principle continued to work out for Moltmann and ensured that he also reflected extensively on cosmic eschatology. The consideration that Moltmann, as a current systematic from the Protestant tradition, has thought extensively about the new creation, justifies the choice for him in this research.

1.4.2 Karl Rahner

From Roman Catholic sources, Karl Rahner called for a new eschatological reflection on the new creation.[60] Herbert Vorgrimler expressed this in 2004:

> In his reflections on eschatology, Karl Rahner confronted a topic around which today's systematics have come a long way, probably also out of fear of the hard questions that arise here, How can "eternal life" be thought of? Or can it even be "imagined"?[61]

These methodical questions in Rahner's eschatology created a fruitful dialogue with various movements, such as the theology of liberation, ecological theology, the theology of universal redemption, and interreligious dialogue.[62] This included the interaction with Moltmann's *Theologie der Hoffnung*, of which elements recur in Rahner's conception of the "absolute future."[63] Nevertheless, each theologian developed his own eschatology and laid a new foundation within his own tradition. Many of Rahner's ideas, which were controversial at the time, are now commonplace and still determine

---

58. Moltmann, *Theologie*, 12: "Eine rechte Theologie müßte darum von ihrem Zukunftsziel her bedacht werden. Eschatologie sollte nicht ihr Ende, sondern ihr Anfang sein." See also, Pannenberg, *Theologie und Reich Gottes*, 9–29.

59. Sicouly, *Schöpfung*, 40–51 (esp. 50).

60. Rahner, "Ewigkeit," 422–23.

61. Vorgrimler, *Karl Rahner: Gotteserfahrung*, 275: "Karl Rahner stellte sich in seinen Überlegungen zur Eschatologie einem Thema, um das heutige Systematiker einen großen Bogen machen, wohl auch aus Scheu vor den harten Fragen, die sich hier stellen: Wie lässt sich 'ewiges Leben' denken? Oder lässt es sich gar 'vorstellen'?"

62. Díaz, *Being Human*; Ludlow, *Universal*; Dupuis, *Christian Theology*.

63. Rahner, *Theologie der Zukunft*, 561–79.

eschatological thinking in Catholic circles.[64] This justifies the choice of Rahner in this dissertation.

The decision to place Karl Rahner's eschatology alongside that of Jürgen Moltmann is not an exceptional one. Edward Schillebeeckx already did this in a presentation of his own eschatological hermeneutics. Also, this was partly done in the dissertations of Pablo Sicouzy and Matthias Remenyi, who both focused on Moltmann's eschatology.[65] This is understandable for those who realize that Jürgen Moltmann and Karl Rahner, from their German-Western European background, were in broad-oecumenical dialogue and exercised great influence in their own church traditions with their research on cosmic eschatology.[66]

1.4.3 Gregory Beale

Anyone who wants to compare a systematic theologian with a biblical theologian about the theme of the new heaven and the new earth will benefit if the biblical theologian shows a great interest in this subject. In BT, the American Gregory Beale is well known for his attention to the theme of the new creation. Although less prominent than Rahner and Moltmann, he is notable for choosing the new creation as the core theme of his BT in a wide range of publications.

From the table of contents of his main work, *A New Testament Biblical Theology* (NTBT), it appears that this theme intersperses his entire biblical-theological exposition. The terms "Eschatological" and "New Creation" are found in almost all twenty-eight chapter-titles of this book, which is more than a thousand pages in length. This leads Howard Marshall to note in his review of NTBT that:

> [n]ot since *An Introduction to the Theology of the New Testament* by Alan Richardson (1958) has there been such a deluge of eschatological expressions.[67]

For Beale, the Bible has a development towards the future new creation, which influences every other subcategory of biblical speech. Beale sees eschatology not only as one of many options for examining the Bible but also as the center from which Christian faith can best be understood.[68] Also worth mentioning is his *The Temple and the Church's Mission* (2004), in which Beale works out a BT of the temple, as a concept that develops throughout the history of salvation and flows into the new heaven and earth. Therefore, eschatology and new creation are at the heart of his work. According

---

64. Purcell, "Rahner," 195–210; Endean, "Has Rahnerian Theology a Future?," 281–96.
65. Schillebeeckx, "Hermeneutische beschouwingen," 40, 47–48 (Rahner), 44–45, 51n5 (Moltmann); Sicouly, *Schöpfung*; Remenyi, *Um der Hoffnung*.
66. Moltmann, *Weiter Raum*, 18, 22; Rahner, "Erfahrungen," 113–15.
67. Marshall, "Review."
68. Beale, *New Testament*, 18, 58; "Eden," 5–31; "Eschatological," 11–52.

to Beale, BT paid too scant attention to this eschatological perspective. Afterward, this conclusion was confirmed and adopted by many biblical theologians.[69]

In addition, Beale's ideas are gaining increasing recognition in BT. During the writing of this dissertation, the biblical-theological monographs *A New Heaven and a New Earth* by Richard Middleton and *Making All Things New* by Benjamin Gladd and Matthew Harmon were published. Both works are strongly based on Beale's ideas.[70] Because of its strong connection with the theme of the new creation, Beale's design is best suited to be placed in a dialogue about the new heaven and the new earth alongside the publications of the systematics Jürgen Moltmann and Karl Rahner.

At the same time, the choice for Beale also presents challenges. Beale's BT is characterized by an American historical-canonical approach to the Bible, which is largely lacking in German theology. Moltmann and Rahner will be more familiar with a historically critical approach to the Bible. However, this diversity can serve as an advantage and provides a representation of the current reality in which theologians consult each other's sources across continents and work together on different projects. Anyone who investigates the possibility of a comparison between designs from ST and BT within the same theological-cultural context is under the suspicion of having chosen suitable concepts in advance to facilitate the possibility. In this dissertation, we want to avoid this by choosing three theologians primarily on the basis of their attention to the theme of the new heaven and the new earth. This implies that the necessary continental differences in the practice of theology must also be taken into account in the critical equation (ch. 6).

1.5   RECENT PUBLICATIONS AND OWN CONTRIBUTIONS

Investigations into a fruitful dialogue between the ST and the BT, by comparing different theological concepts, have already taken place on different topics. However, such an evaluation was not yet focused on an academic study on reflection on the subject of the new heaven and new earth. The overview below provides a list of recent publications that are closely related to this research. The choice was made for classification into two categories: (1) publications on an interdisciplinary comparison between a systematic and a biblical theologian; and (2) publications on the new creation of Moltmann, Rahner, and/or Beale. The listed works have been ranked on the basis of their relevance to their own research question.

---

69. Beale, *New Testament*, 17–19. See with references to Beale, Schreiner, *King*, xiii; Alexander, *From Eden*; Maddox, "Nurturing the New Creation," 24.

70. Middleton, *New Heaven*; Gladd and Harmon, *Making All Things New*.

1.5.1 Interdisciplinary comparisons between ST and BT

1.5.1.1 *Patricia Sharbaugh (2008)*

In her dissertation *Uncovering the Roots of the Crucified God: How Walter Brueggemann's Old Testament Theology Challenges and Contributes to Jürgen Moltmann's and Jon Sobrino's Interpretation of the Cross*, Patricia Sharbaugh chooses a comparison of three theologians.[71] After a short introduction (1–14), she analyzes in chapter 2 Brueggemann's *Old Testament Theology* (15–93), and in chapter 3, the thinking of Jürgen Moltmann and Jon Sobrino (94–157). Chapter 4 ultimately focuses on the question of the differences and similarities between the three theologians (158–210). In response to the research question, Sharbaugh concludes that Moltmann and Sobrino recognize a theological crisis in the cross of Christ that lies at the root of many questions about suffering and God's promises. This is in accordance with Brueggemann's theology, which refers to the human experience of suffering and the relationship with God's covenant.

With regard to the methodology used, it is remarkable that Sharbaugh pays twice as much attention to Brueggemann as to the other two theologians. In chapter 4 she focuses in detail on the general question of the influence of the OT in the theology of Moltmann (159–172) and Sobrino (173–179), and then briefly discusses the conversation that her research question is about in a nutshell (180–210). This conversation is mainly framed by Sharbaugh's own reflections on the proposals of Brueggemann, Moltmann, and Sobrino. A comparison between the three theologians is practically non-existent. What has been announced several times as "conversation,"[72] appears to be Sharbaugh's own analytical reflection on different interpretations of crucifixion.

1.5.1.2 *The Two Horizons Commentary (2005–)*

Since 2005 the first parts of *The Two Horizons Commentary* have been published.[73] The purpose of this sequence is to connect a BT with a current ST. This is done by (1) exploring the interpretative meaning of a biblical book; (2) linking current theological themes in the same biblical book and placing them in a biblical-theological framework; and (3) linking the message of the biblical book with current systematic and practical-theological issues.[74]

Despite the desire to bring BT and ST into a conversation, in the parts published so far (OT: nine volumes volumes, NT: seven volumes), the biblical-theological and

---

71. Sharbaugh, *Uncovering*.

72. Sharbaugh, *Uncovering*, v, xii, 11, 14, 43, 158, 173, 180, 187.

73. Green and Turner, *Two Horizons New Testament Commentary*; McConville and Bartholomew, *The Two Horizons Old Testament Commentary*. In mid-2016, the editors of the NT parts were taken over by Wall and Fowl, *Two Horizons New Testament Commentary*.

74. Turner and Green, "New Testament," 2–3.

systematic-theological contributions appear only in separate chapters, side by side. There is no effective conversation or a critical comparison between BT and ST. In addition, twelve of the published volumes in this series have been written by one person. These authors—like the editorial board of the series—are from the field of biblical studies, which means that the systematic-theological part is often not in-depth. A representative from the ST is missing in these parts. For the parts written by both a biblical scholar and a systematic theologian, this is less the case. However, a disadvantage remains that the two disciplines remain juxtaposed in these publications, each with their own chapters. The interaction between the concepts of the BT and ST remains in the background.

1.5.1.3 Michael Gilbertson (2003)

In his dissertation *God and History in the Book of Revelation: New Testament Studies in Dialogue with Pannenberg and Moltmann*, Gilbertson concentrates on the question in which way the eschatology of Jürgen Moltmann and Wolfhart Pannenberg corresponds with the explanation of the biblical book of Revelation.[75] After it has been demonstrated that both systematics make their dependence on biblical-apocalyptic tradition (1–19), but that their ST takes little or no account of a BT (20–44), Gilbertson investigates how his own interpretation of space and time in Revelation (45–142) can enrich both theologians (143–200). In this last part, he is focusing on the core question of dialogue. Gilbertson observes that Moltmann's and Pannenberg's eschatology show continuity and discontinuity with his personal analysis of Revelation. However, the dialogue remains fragile. Methodically the question arises whether Gilbertson should not have chosen a biblical theologian who had already investigated the theology of Revelation.[76] Now Gilbertson's research on Revelation takes up twice as much space as the dialogue with the systematics, which is his main concern in the research question.

1.5.2   Investigations on the new heaven and earth

1.5.2.1 Matthias Remenyi (2010)

Matthias Remenyi investigates the hermeneutical principles of Moltmann's eschatology in *Um der Hoffnung willen: Untersuchungen zur eschatologischen Theologie Jürgen Moltmanns*. He first discusses the fundamental hermeneutical issues (19–180) and subsequently focuses on hermeneutical issues in Moltmann's individual (181–285),

---

75. Gilbertson, *God and History*.

76. For example, Bauckham, *Theology of Jürgen Moltmann*. Bauckham is also inspired by Moltmann, see Bauckham, *God Will Be*; *Theology of Jürgen Moltmann*. The same criticism applies to, Wilkinson, *Eschatology*.

historical (286–294), and cosmic eschatology (395–458). Although Remenyi starts with an analysis of 1 Corinthians 15, which according to him "von geradezu systembildender Relevanz für das Gesamt seiner [Moltmanns] Theologie erweist"—"of almost system-forming relevance for the whole of his [Moltmann's] theology" (12), he does not return to this issue at a later stage. Moltmann's interaction with BT remains virtually untouched because Moltmann's further analysis is based solely on the field of systematics.

1.5.2.2 Günter Thomas (2009)

In 2009, the evangelical theologian Günter Thomas published his postdoctoral thesis *Neue Schöpfung: Systematisch-theologische Untersuchungen zur Hoffnung auf das "Leben in der zukünftigen Welt."*[77] In this extensive work, he investigates in which way five German Protestant theologians, namely Karl Barth (124–212), Wolfhart Pannenberg (213–284), Eberhard Jüngel (285–314), Jürgen Moltmann (315–343), and Dietrich Bonhoeffer (344–382), talk about the new creation. Although Moltmann wrote most extensively about new creation among these five theologians, Thomas consciously chooses to devote only twenty-eight pages to this theologian. The reason for this is that his own theological vision is already in line with Moltmann's perspective.

1.5.2.3 Pablo C. Sicouly (2007)

In his *Schöpfung und Neuschöpfung: "Neuschöpfung" als theologische Kategorie im Werk Jürgen Moltmanns*, Pablo C. Sicouly pays attention to the question of whether there is any consistency in Moltmann's speaking about the new creation.[78] After analyzing the theme of the new creation in Moltmann's publications from between 1968 and 1999 (35–136), Sicouly concentrates on Moltmann's dialogue partners (137–268), in order to demonstrate in a personal synthesis that Moltmann's speaking about the new creation has remained consistent (269–356). Because all the attention is focused on the key question, "Is there consistency in Moltmann's speaking about the new creation?," Sicouly devotes brief attention to the hermeneutical assumptions Moltmann makes and his handling of BT.

1.5.2.4 Harald Fritsch (2006)

In his *Vollendende Selbstmitteilung Gottes an seine Schöpfung: Die Eschatologie Karl Rahners*, Harald Fritsch analyzes the eschatology of Rahner.[79] After an analysis of

---

77. Thomas, *Neue Schöpfung*.
78. Sicouly, *Schöpfung*.
79. Fritsch, *Selbstmitteilung*.

Rahner's historical background (31–99), Fritsch evaluates Rahner's hermeneutics (100–333) and his theological statements on death (334–395), resurrection (396–439), judgment (440–489), return (490–500), and completion (500–512). The research into the new heaven and earth with Rahner is still limited, and the relationship with the BT is absent.

1.5.3 The contribution of this dissertation

This review of recent publications provides the first indications of the extent to which an interdisciplinary comparison between different designs from the ST and BT in relation to the subject of the new heaven and the new earth can be relevant. A methodically justified comparison between a systematic theologian and a biblical theologian was only achieved concisely. By critically comparing the systematic theological representations of the new creation with Rahner and Moltmann with the biblical-theological perspectives of Beale, an exemplary exploration is performed, which can result in a possible interaction between two concepts from ST and one from BT. So, the question of the present research is consciously formulated as:

> How can comparison between Karl Rahner's and Jürgen Moltmann's systematic theological designs on eschatology and Gregory Beale's biblical-theological design be of significance in a theological dialogue concerning the new heaven and the new earth?

1.6 METHODOLOGICAL APPROACH

Two subquestions arise from the research question: (1) How do the three aforementioned theologians see an interdisciplinary dialogue between ST and BT; and (2) how do they speak about the new heaven and the new earth? These subquestions lead to the following division of this dissertation,

Chapter 1 contextualizes the subject and the research question of the dissertation. In addition to an overview of recent publications within the research field, it also contains an account of methodology and presuppositions.

Chapter 2 examines the position of the theologians in question with regard to interdisciplinary dialogue versus the other field of study. In relation to the research question, it is important to know to what extent Rahner and Moltmann are prepared to compare their concepts with a design from BT, and to what extent Beale is prepared to do so with the domain of ST. The comparison made between the three concepts of the new heaven and the new earth can be more strongly defended if Rahner, Moltmann, and Beale also emphasize the importance of such interdisciplinary research. The individuality of the disciplines and the profits and dangers which the three theologians see in a dialogue between the ST and BT, thus become visible.

Chapters 3 to 5 contain a hermeneutical-theological analysis of Rahner's, Moltmann's, and Beale's reflections on the new heaven and the new earth. The order in which the theologians are discussed is chronologically determined by their year of birth: Rahner (1904), Moltmann (1926), Beale (1949). We will consciously examine all three theologians independently in order to avoid that one of them determines the system of coordinates for the other. The personal approach and accentuation in the reflection on the same subject can thus be made visible. In addition to the differences in approach and elaboration, it emerges that there are several core elements in their own thematic approach to the subject. For this reason, the theological concepts, accents, and hermeneutical presuppositions are systematically checked. After all, the reconstruction, analysis, and reflection of this are together at the service of the sub-question, "How do these theologians speak about the new heaven and earth?"

Chapter 6 contains the nucleus of this dissertation. It includes a critical comparison of Rahner's, Moltmann's, and Beale's concepts about the new heaven and the new earth. As such, this chapter answers the research question by bringing the results of all the previous chapters into interaction with each other. Based on the methodology chosen at the beginning of this chapter, an initial critical comparison will be carried out. The hermeneutical choices that the three theologians make individually are central to these decisions. Next, a second critical comparison will be made about the theologians' substantive choices about the new heaven and earth. Hereby it becomes visible in an evaluative way what an interaction between two systematic theological concepts and a biblical-theological concept can yield in the theological discourse about the new heaven and the new earth.

Chapter 7 concludes the dissertation by offering a conclusion of the methodical observations that have emerged in the critical comparison. The added values of the interdisciplinary comparison between a BT design and two ST designs, in the discussion about the new heaven and new earth, are taken into account.

1.7 SYSTEMATIC-THEOLOGICAL FOUNDATION

1.7.1 The justification for the hope

1.7.1.1 *Stimulated by the Christian confessions*

Anyone who speaks of the hope of a new creation of heaven and earth—either from a systematic-theological or from a biblical-theological point of view—will be suspicious of engaging in speculation and thus moving beyond the realm of scientific reflection. Eschatology, including cosmic eschatology, has to justify itself methodically for its scientific incitements. Does the fact that people are constrained to allow us to talk about a future state of affairs that cannot be extrapolated from empirical developments?

Many people answer this question in the negative: only the present can be meaningfully spoken of; the hereafter can only be speculated and imagined.[80]

However, Christian eschatology, which has the courage to speak of futures, knows itself well grounded in and directed at God's promises about the redemption and restoration of this cosmos. Despite the fact that the eschaton is still in the offing, this grounding in God's promises makes it possible to talk about it in anticipation. In this regard, faith extrapolates in its own way the experience that the manner in which God has fulfilled promises gives ground to expect God to continue to fulfill his promises in the future.[81]

Christian hope is not moldy or empty. The hope itself (*spes qua*) is never completely undetermined. It is always oriented towards a substantive expectation (*spes quae*) that is known and hence partly determined. Hope that is completely unspecified and unfocused remains an empty, purely formal concept that is contentless and meaningless "non-sens." The "hope for" must be filled with a concrete perspective. This perspective is born from the experience of salvation here-and-now, in Christ and by the Spirit.[82]

Christian eschatology derives perspective and support from God's omnipotence and faithfulness to his promise. That does not make Christian hope irrational. It is not a product of one's own religious-ideological illusion, but a supra-rational fact. After all, it is based on nothing but God, "who gives life to the dead and calls into existence the things that do not exist" (Rom 4:17). Christian hope is based on the omnipotence and faithfulness of God. It considers this not only as a metaphysical axiom but also as a point of belief that entails the idea of future hope. With this, Christian hope is not anthropocentric, but theocentric and develops from the expectation that is based on God's faithfulness. As a consequence, it has been subjected to theological analysis. This analysis is fundamental in order to ensure, in a disciplined manner, that Christian hope maintains a balance between a presumptuous all-knowledge and a hopeless non-knowledge.[83] Gerrit Berkouwer warns, "How will one not have to be wary here of constructions and postulates that far exceed the boundaries of the biblical-eschatological testimony!"[84] However, he immediately admits to this:

---

80. Abraham, "Eschatology and Epistemology," 582–84.

81. Thiselton, *Last Things*, 12; Pannenberg, *Theology and the Philosophy of Science*, 309–10; Berkhof, *Gegronde verwachting*, 15–26; Moltmann, *Theologie*, 16, 20.

82. Remenyi, "Hoffnung, Tod und Auferstehung," 81; Smith, "Determined Hope," 207. Against, Bornkamm et al., *Christliche Hoffnung*, 62.

83. Thiselton, *Last Things*, 21; Abraham, "Eschatology and Epistemology," 589, 593; Polkinghorne, *God of Hope*, xvii; Hoek, *Hoop*, 31; Schwarz, *Eschatology*, 245.

84. Berkouwer, *Wederkomst*, 1:266: "Hoe zal men hier niet op z'n hoede moeten zijn voor constructies en postulaten, die de grens van het bijbels-eschatologisch getuigenis ver overschrijden!"

> Yet this insignificant danger zone should not stop us from doing so, because both the Old and the New Testament talk about the new earth in a remarkably explicit way.[85]

In several areas, Christian tradition pays attention to the new creation. It is no accident then that cosmic eschatology concentrates on this theme. Although the future is still hidden (1 John 3:2), it is possible to see a glimpse of it from afar (Heb 11:13). Whoever dismisses biblical expression of this as blurry can also apply the same reasoning to other theological subjects, such as the Trinity or Incarnation. That is why Nicholas Lash says too little when he says:

> the Church alone knows that we know absolutely nothing about our absolute or ultimate future except that we *have* a future in the mystery that we call God.[86]

If the church only knows this about the future, she is left with nothing but silence about every representation of what the character of that future will be. Meeting the call to account for the hope that is given to her (1 Pet 3:15) is then practically impossible.[87]

1.7.1.2 *Grounded on the Resurrection*

Anyone who seeks a solid foundation for his or her hope must realize that this foundation must be able to withstand even death. Otto Pesch writes:

> Either there is hope for humans, which has a reason, which even death, yes the total death of humanity cannot harm—or the life of humans is so hopeless that we can only strive to do the just nearest and all that is possible for us.[88]

An important argument to express Christian hope about the new creation is the resurrection of Christ and the faith in a God who remains faithful to all promises. The unique testimony of Christ's physical resurrection and glorification is, in the Christian tradition, the beginning of the hope for a genuine new creation; it "is the linchpin; it is the foundation, content, and goal of Christian hope."[89] Andreas Lindemann writes, "Only from Easter shines a light that does not make the hope of overcoming the

---

85. Berkouwer, *Wederkomst*, 1:266: "Toch mag deze allerminst denkbeeldige gevaren-zône ons er niet van terughouden, omdat op een opvallend expliciete wijze zowel in het Oude als in het Nieuwe Testament over de nieuwe aarde wordt gesproken."

86. Lash, *Theology on the Way*, 194.

87. Hughes, "Crossing," 105.

88. Pesch, *Frei sein aus Gnade*: "Entweder gibt es für den Menschen eine Hoffnung, die einen Grund hat, dem selbst der Tod, ja der totale Tod der Menschheit nichts anhaben kann—oder das Leben des Menschen ist so hoffnungslos, dass wir uns nur noch bemühen können, das gerade Nächstliegende und uns Mögliche möglichst gut zu tun."

89. Remenyi, "Hoffnung, Tod und Auferstehung," 90: "ist Dreh- und Angelpunkt, sie ist Grund, Inhalt und Ziel der christlichen Hoffnung."

border of death look completely absurd."⁹⁰ In the resurrection, Christian hope finds a solid foundation that is so strong that not even death—which normally makes most of the human hope questionable—can stand up to it. Of course, this does not prove the resurrection or the existence of God. Whether God's existence cannot be confirmed theologically or philosophically. However, those who are willing to have faith in the testimony of the New Testament, which states that God did not leave Christ in the tomb and raised him from dead, will find sufficient motivation in this to speak of a future hope which extends beyond the border of death. He can testify with Paul, "Christ has been raised from the dead, the first fruits of those who have died" (1 Cor 15:20) and speak with Peter of "a living hope" (1 Pet 1:3). This Christian hope of the resurrection does not pass by death but through death. It is based on what is already the reality for those who trust God.

1.7.1.3 Reflections from theology

Traditionally, theologians have indicated that in eschatology, different theological lines converge. This is also the case with cosmic eschatology, which relates to a new heaven and earth. For this reason, this theme deserves a deeper logical-analytical reflection. Of course, this must be done accurately. Human representations must be strictly tested in the theological discipline. The theologian cannot afford to make a fabulous representation of the new creation. At the same time, he must not abuse this caution by stating that Christian-theological science is ignorant on this subject. After all, Christian tradition has various interpretations and representations of the new creation that can be subjected to further investigation.

According to Jürgen Moltmann, a tension similar to the one that occurs when talking about the hereafter also occurs in historical research.⁹¹ Just as history examines, interprets, and reinterprets the past on the basis of current data, eschatology does so for the future on the same basis of current data. Both are restricted as they cannot travel forwards or backward in time with a "time machine." Therefore, the discussion of the new creation is not a flight from reality, but a critical analysis of what is said in this reality about that new creation.

1.7.2 Theology and cosmology

1.7.2.1 Alienation between theology and cosmology

During the last few centuries, a long-standing division between faith and natural science has resulted in Christian eschatology only focusing on the so-called individual

---

90. Lindemann, *Korintherbrief*, 343: "Nur von Ostern her leuchtet ein Licht, das die Hoffnung auf Überwindung der Todesgrenze nicht als gänzlich absurd erscheinen lässt."

91. Moltmann, *Kommen*, 319.

eschatology.⁹² The future of the cosmos stood in the shadow of the individual's anthropocentric interest. Therefore, questions about the future of the cosmos were left to the fields of cosmology, astrophysics, and other natural sciences. The rise of the philosophy of the Enlightenment strongly contributed to this division, arguably more than science. From that perspective, it was commonly assumed that theology was mainly focused on the meaning of life and on the relationship between God and humanity, while natural sciences had to deal with the laws of material existence. The outcome of these differences only increased the gap between both disciplines.

In the past decades, theology has rediscovered the field of cosmic eschatology. Those who proclaim that the prospect of Christian cosmic eschatology is an entirely different creation than the current one, give cause for a persistent breach between theology and natural science. In that case, eschatology expresses itself in terms of absolute discontinuity—which will evoke critical questions from many theologians. However, anyone who rejects absolute discontinuity between this creation and the new creation, and leaves openness for a particular form of continuity has to recognize that there is much common ground between theological and physical sciences. This new creation then stands in relationship with the creation we face today.

This does not mean that a Christian–eschatological cosmology would be a replacement for an empirical cosmology or *vice versa*. Every branch of science will be held accountable. In Christian theology, this requires responsive reflections of the biblical confession of hope. Christian faith in God's promises chooses to confess God as Creator and Redeemer of this creation. However, Christian eschatology refers to the future, which professes the same reality that natural science is currently investigating. Therefore, alienation between the discipline of theology and other scientific fields should be avoided.

Because of the growing interest in the theme of the new heaven and the new earth, theologians today recognize more than ever that theology and natural science should not be disintegrated.⁹³ In the interdisciplinary dialogue, both are needed. The universe, with its interwoven structure of time, space, and matter is too complex to be contained to one science. We all look to reality from a different perspective with our presuppositions. Therefore, dialogue and cross-fertilization between various natural sciences and theology should offer an advantage for both fields of research.⁹⁴ This could lead to new scientific proposals and research questions that are useful for both disciplines.

---

92. See detailed: Hausoul, "Theology and Cosmology," 324–36.

93. Polkinghorne, *Science and Religion*; Pannenberg, *Theology of Nature*; Russell, "Cosmology and Eschatology," 563–80; Peters et al., *Brücken bauen*; Müller, *Kosmologie*.

94. Pannenberg, *Theology of Nature*, 26–27; "Die Frage," 118–19; Wilkinson, *Eschatology*, 95–116; Moltmann, *Erfahrungen*, 68–84.

The New Heaven and New Earth

1.7.2.2 Creation doomed to die

A harmonious consonance between the field of theology and that of natural sciences can be found partly in the shared awareness of both disciplines, that not only human life is mortal and finite at this time, but also that future life in the universe is doomed if no intervention takes place. In one hypothesis, the cosmos decelerates exponentially, the expansion of the universe finally comes to a standstill, and the universe collapses through a contraction. This would result in a so-called *Big Crunch*, the reverse of a *Big Bang*. A second hypothesis is that the universe would continue to cool down to the maximum cooled status of 0 Kelvin, due to further expansion. That would be a so-called *Big Chill* or *Big Freeze*; in both cases, life would no longer be possible. Both hypotheses were changed after scientific research discovered that the universe was not slowing down, but accelerating. The cause of this was to be explained by stipulating the existence of "dark energy" not yet empirically discovered. If the universe continued to expand rapidly, it would eventually lead to all elements being pulled apart. That would produce a so-called *Big Rip*.

In all the final scenarios which the scientific cosmology currently has to offer, there is a radical bankruptcy for any evolutionary optimism. John Polkinghorne correctly states: "the universe is condemned to ultimate futility, and humanity wants to have a transient episode in its history."[95]

1.7.2.3 Challenges for Christian theology

Even though a meltdown or other life-threatening end of the cosmos is still far in the future, theology is currently seeking answers to the question of God's intention with this cosmos? The discipline of natural science is unable to respond to this question. The scientist recognizes the limits to his own discipline. When it comes to the future of the present universe, physics–empirical research only predicts scenarios of disasters. But it is also known in Christian doctrine that God's promises often radically contradict what can be expected from creation. This calls on faith to put all expectations on God and to hold on to God in confidence, even if it radically contradicts the expectations in this world. The resurrection of Jesus Christ, the anchor of Christian hope, makes this most visible.

The Christian feels this tension between the expected reality and the promises of God when it comes to the future of creation. Traditionally, the old Creed of Nicene–Constantinople mentions the hope of the new creation: "and life in the coming empire" (καὶ ζωὴν τοῦ μέλλοντος αἰῶνος). Anyone who holds on to any form of physical continuity between this creation and the new creation is challenged by this perception. If the cosmic expectations of current scientists become a reality (*Big*

---

95. Polkinghorne, *Faith of a Physicist*, 162; e.g., Russell, "Cosmology and Eschatology," 565; *Time in Eternity*.

Crunch, Big Chill, or *Big Rip*), the continuity of this creation towards the new creation would not be possible and every hope of an eternal physical future for this creation is no more than vain talk.[96] What remains are conditions for heavenly non-material spirits, like they were confessed in ancient Greek sagas about Mount Olympus. The biblical expectations that are presented in an earthly and concrete way would then only be feasible. God would have to create a new creation from nothing (*ex nihilo*), as this creation originated from nothing in Genesis 1. In such a new heaven and earth, which is created *ex nihilo* we should not expect "resurrected bodies." It would only contain "new bodies" (*ex nihilo*). The biblical hope of resurrection and the statement that "creation itself will be set free from its bondage to decay and will obtain the freedom of the glory of the children of God" (Rom 8:21) would not happen. For this earth would perish and receive no freedom of corruption or participation in the glory of the children of God.

Often, critical reflections on the final scenarios from the field of natural sciences led humans towards a rejection of the ancient biblical and Christian expectations of the future. An example of this can be found with the biochemist Arthur Peacocke. He calls on natural sciences not to waste their time by engaging in a dialogue with theological reflections on the future:

> All speculation on detailed scenarios of this consummation, the theological exercise called "eschatology," surely constitutes a supreme example of attempting to formulate a theory underdetermined by the facts. As such, it seems to be a fruitless and unnecessary exercise.[97]

According to Peacocke, Christian faith is about God and about the birth, resurrection, and glorification of Jesus. Although Peacocke was a progressive leader in the interdisciplinary dialogue between theology and natural sciences, he opted not to enter into detailed and extended dialogue concerning the relationship between eschatology and cosmology. Peacocke chooses the proposition that theology and natural sciences speak of two different worlds. This kind of posture brings us back to the position in which no further thought is given to the possibility of an enriching dialogue between eschatology and scientific cosmology.[98]

1.7.2.4 *A lack of awareness of the bodily resurrection*

Although dialogues between natural sciences and theology have been taking place on an increasing scale for more than fifty years, there is comparatively little attention

---

96. Tanner, "Eschatology," 222; e.g., Macquarrie, *Principles*, 351–62.
97. Peacocke, *Paths*, 48.
98. Russell, "Cosmology and Eschatology," 563; "Bodily Resurrection," 3–7; Polkinghorne, *Science and the Trinity*, 144; *End of the World*; Ellis, *Far-Future*.

for bodily resurrection.[99] While Christians mostly believe in a certain form of resurrection, it is the confession of the bodily resurrection that often separated minds. But without a bodily resurrection, the physical part of God's creation would be seen as a temporary decor, without any additional future.

The biblical testimony stands opposed to that. From the beginning, God has a higher purpose in mind and bears witness to a new heaven and a new earth. The followers of Jesus are adamantly observing that the heavenly Messiah became a physical human, died physically on the cross, and rose physically from the dead. Jesus did not have a false body, and the resurrection of his physical body was acknowledged by many (1 Cor 15:13–14).

The missing emphasis of the holistic physical resurrection in Christian doctrine gives reason to ignore the biblical revelation of a renewal of the universe. But it is from the resurrection of Jesus Christ that eschatology dares to speak of the new creation in terms of both continuity and discontinuity.

At the same time, we must acknowledge that natural sciences also rely (unconsciously) on various philosophical, metaphysical assumptions. In the past, natural scientists often had difficulties recognizing this in their own field. The physicist, cosmologist, and astrobiologist Paul Davies gave his praised introduction to cosmological research the apt subtitle: *Speculating about the Fate of the Cosmos*.[100]

Today, experts from natural sciences realize that their research is less "exact" than they pretended it to be in the nineteenth century. After physics had its peak in the nineteenth century, it was still assumed that in a few years there would be nothing more to discover. The world at that time was thought to be completely charted by the discoveries of natural sciences. That attitude would change because of the numerous discoveries of Albert Einstein. Further discoveries made it clear that natural science had certainly not mapped the cosmos sufficiently. This field of research faced great challenges and was confronted with laws that challenged each other. A well-known example is the relationship between the general theory of relativity and quantum physics. Despite the fact that both are valid, they are mutually exclusive. This is still the situation at the moment, although the discipline of natural sciences holds on to the fact that these two laws offer the best formulations about reality today. Also, science nowadays is still positively critical of its own explanations about the future of the universe. As the theologian, the natural scientist knows the advantages and challenges in her or his field. Today, in our society, there is a strong encouragement to avoid isolation and work more interdisciplinary as a scientist.[101]

---

99. Wilkinson, *Eschatology*, 49.

100. Davies, *Last Three Minutes*.

101. Repko et al., *Introduction*, 3–22, 63–85; Schmidt, "Box"; Moran, *Interdisciplinarity*, 3–12, 188–92; See also: Kärkkäinen, *Creation*, 123.

1.7.2.5 *Resurrection as groundwork for an open system*

Theologians emphasized that all theological reflections on eschatology find their foundation in the confession of the resurrection of Jesus Christ.[102] Stimulated by this transcendent and immanent event from God's faithfulness as Creator and Savior, it is possible to make statements about the future.[103] This includes the future of the cosmos. Based on the empty grave, Christian doctrine teaches that God is engaged in this creation and that death does not get the last word. In the Gospels of the New Testament, the resurrection stories of Jesus Christ show that there is continuity between the present perishable body and the imperishable resurrection body (*ex vetere*) as well as space for discontinuity, by speaking about a transformed glorified resurrection body (*theosis*). It is important to find a healthy balance between both: continuity and discontinuity. Resurrection and glorification of the creation belong together in Christian confessions.

Based on the Christian faith in a bodily resurrection, it is possible that there is openness between theologians and physicists for a common dialogue.[104] The resurrection testifies that creation is not a closed system that does not permit external *anticipation*. God can *anticipate* in this cosmos in a special way, as it happened at the resurrection of the Son, and nowadays through the innovative power of the Spirit. From the resurrection of the Son, the renewal of the Spirit, and the eschatological speech, there is common ground on which the discipline of theology and that of the natural sciences can enrich each other in their professional reflections.

This understanding would permit questions of mutual interest to enter the dialogue between natural sciences and theology in a reflection on the new heaven and the new earth: Are there theological indications for new laws of nature that God realizes in the new creation?[105] For example, can we deduce "new" laws from the biblical miracles? To what extent does general relativity, which relates matter, space, and time in physics, remain in the theological speech about the new heaven and the new earth?[106] To what extent is not matter, but "information" the fundamental component of the universe?[107] Where is a transformation of physical laws forced into the testimony of a new creation?[108] What ensures us that the cosmos with all its complex data, despite the

---

102. Thiselton, *Last Things*, 12; Remenyi, "Hoffnung, Tod und Auferstehung," 90; Lindemann, *Korintherbrief*, 343.

103. Russell, *Cosmology*; "Cosmology and Eschatology," 564; "Entropy," 463; Clayton, "Eschatology as Metaphysics," 128–49; Polkinghorne, *God of Hope*, 12, 94–95; O'Donovan, *Resurrection*, 14, 31.

104. Wilkinson, *Eschatology*, 107.

105. Russell, *Time in Eternity*, 51, 81, 181; Wilkinson, *Eschatology*, 51.

106. Kim, "Christian Hope," 159; Polkinghorne, *Science and the Trinity*, 156; *God of Hope*, 100, 117–20.

107. Kauffman, *At Home in the Universe*; Wheeler, "Information, Physics, Quantum," 309–36.

108. Wilkinson, *Eschatology*, 109; Russell, "Bodily Resurrection," 3–30; Murphy, "Resurrection Body," 202–18.

already present "decay," will remain intact so that life is guaranteed? To what extent is there a metaphorical relationship between entropy and evil and between entropy and renewal?[109] Does the new creation also know the law of entropy and the second law of thermodynamics, or can these laws be lifted into a perfect creation?[110] If they are still present: can heavenly bodies, such as the sun or the stars, continue to convert energy into heat eternally without their energy source running out, and do the elements also remain eternally, without decay in their core? When these laws are lifted: How can an abolition of such laws prevent the continuity between this creation and the new creation from being lost so that in Christian speaking there can only be a future creation *ex nihilo*? Does today's creation already contain sufficient physical conditions and characteristics that also remain in the new creation and may only need to be transformed into a continuum (so, no discontinuity)? These kinds of questions challenge the theological-cosmological reflection on the expectation of the new heaven and earth.

The dialogue between both disciplines can lead to a fruitful result in speaking about the current and the new creation based on these kinds of questions. Both disciplines should not be isolated in their own research but may meet each other as equal partners in dialogue. The extent to which these metaphysical presuppositions are even theological or anti-theological can then be discussed.

The natural sciences are, in turn, served if theology not only provides them with devotional publications on the new creation but also examines this topic in academic reflections on the new heaven and the new earth. This kind of interdisciplinary dialogue will make it possible to provide a common theological-scientific contribution to the Christian hope for a new cosmos. Doing so, theology and science can actually advance to a point where the above-mentioned questions can be seriously tackled.

Therefore, it may be a desideratum that, as a result of the responsibilities in this dissertation, the dialogue between natural sciences and Christian-theological cosmic eschatology may also increase.

---

109. Nürnberger, "Eschatology and Entropy," 970–96; Russell, *Cosmology*, 226–46; "Entropy," 449–68.

110. Wilkinson, *Eschatology*, 113; Russell, *Cosmology*, 226–72.

2

Rahner, Moltmann, and Beale on the dialogue between ST and BT

This chapter investigates how the theologians referred to perceive an interdisciplinary dialogue with other disciplines. The three drafts drawn up by the chosen theologians relating to the new heaven and the new earth could be defended more strongly if they emphasized the importance of such an interdisciplinary research. The critical comparison undertaken in this dissertation can then consider the arguments for and against an interdisciplinary dialogue put forward by Rahner, Moltmann, and Beale. This does justice to the individuality and accentuations that the three theologians possess in their own field of study. This chapter thus reveals the enrichments and dangers that they a priori observe in a dialogue between ST and BT. This indicates how meaningful the other discipline is to the systematic or biblical theologian.

Like elsewhere in this dissertation, this chapter methodically chooses to discuss the three theologians separately and in chronological order. This prevents us from defining the correlational character of each theology. At the end of the chapter, you will find a summary of the outcome that the theologians hope to achieve from an interdisciplinary dialogue, fully taking into account the respective characteristics of their own discipline.

2.1 RAHNER ON THE INTERACTION WITH BT

2.1.1 Call for dialogue

The distinction made by German universities between BT and ST, which occurred during the Enlightenment, did not go unnoticed by Rahner (§1.2.3). As was to be expected, this sharp separation caused an enormous distance between the two disciplines as time went by. A fruitful exchange was often lacking. Rahner acknowledges this alienation and writes that it seems that many Catholic theologians look at their colleagues in other theological disciplines with suspicion. He clarifies that a dialogue between the field of BT and that of ST is to be welcomed. After all, BT and ST express the same reality and can positively enrich each other.[1] Here we will examine what exactly that enrichment, in Rahner's view, consists of.

2.1.1.1 Call for ST to engage in dialogue with BT

In his speech *Exegese und Dogmatik* to his fellow dogmatists, Rahner states, "So, Dear friend, be honest, you understand exegesis less than would be desirable."[2] In this respect, Rahner does not consider the systematic theologian to be an expert when it comes to the interpretation of the Bible. ST has little insight into what exactly happens in the discipline of biblical studies. This guarantees the required distance between ST and BT. Little or no consideration for each other. Rahner acknowledges that this also applies to himself. Too often, the Catholic dogmatist is satisfied with an ecclesiastical "proof" from the Christian tradition. A reference to *Enchiridion Symbolorum, Definitionum et Declarationum de Rebus Fidei et Morum* by Heinrich Denzinger and Peter Hünermann or to an encyclical will then be considered sufficient.[3]

Rahner believes this has led to the impoverishment of theology. It is the responsibility of the dogmatist to listen by all means to the Scriptures.[4] BT offers a great enrichment for the ST because it helps to discover the Bible in a fresh and new way. In doing so, it provides the ST with new insights that can help to clarify and amplify its own dogmatic thinking. Rahner's personal conviction is that the Bible, as a *norm non normata*, is the only inspired and infallible main source of Catholic doctrine.[5] By consulting each other's publications, representatives of both disciplines can create a clear and more balanced theology, which can enrich both sides. Grounded in the Bible as the primary source, BT and exegesis can contribute to the understanding of Catholic doctrine, "Dogmatics working with biblical theology will draw new insights from Scripture, which are often not actually new, but rather present the old as a novelty."[6] Rahner acknowledges that not everything that is being said about certain contemporary subjects of faith has been well thought out nor worked out. This proved not to be feasible, since the Bible itself, as the source of Catholic theology, is a fruitful and inexhaustible work. With this Rahner recognizes how BT is of great value in its

---

1. Rahner, "Exegese," 82, 87, 96; "Biblische Theologie," 449, 451; Rahner and Vorgrimler, "Biblische Theologie," 51.
2. Rahner, "Exegese," 93: "Also: Lieber Freund, sei ehrlich, Du verstehst von Exegese weniger, als wünschenswert wäre." See also, Rahner, "Dogmatischen Schriftbeweis," 3.
3. Rahner, "Exegese," 94; "Dogmatischen Schriftbeweis," 2.
4. Rahner, "Dogmatischen Schriftbeweis," 3.
5. Rahner, "Heilige Schrift," 115, cf. 111–113; "Exegese," 93–94; "Inspiration," 721.
6. Rahner, "Dogmatischen Schriftbeweis," 3. "Bibeltheologisch arbeitende Dogmatik wird aus der Schrift neue Erkenntnisse schöpfen, die oft nicht eigentlich neu sind, sondern ein Altes als neu Erkanntes darstellen." See also, Rahner, "Biblische Theologie," 451.

effort to map the rich biblical content. The dogmatist may be inspired by BT on the basis of that awareness. Processing the results of BT may become a natural task for any dogmatist.

Rahner praises the *Theologie des Alten Testaments* of the Roman Catholic Paul Heinisch,

> The structure remains, more than with the modern Protestant theologies of the Old Testament, in the vicinity of the structure that is common in dogmatics today.... In any case, it will help the dogmatic scholar to express the Bible better in his scholarship than before.[7]

Rejecting such interaction between ST and BT is not an option for Rahner. Where BT is missing as an equal interlocutor in ST, ST remains too multi-faceted, too imprecise, and too general.[8] This inaccuracy occurs because ST distances itself too much from the Bible as its main source. However, for Rahner, it is actually the church that reads, preaches, and advises to think and act from within the biblical revelation. This means that the dogmatist also reflects on the doctrine of faith from this context. Rahner does not want to restrict himself to Roman Catholic theology. The evangelical Protestant theologian is also welcome to participate in the dialogue.[9] For Rahner, this is above all true that the Bible is the direct source from which ST should draw from. Rahner finds it unacceptable that ST only sees the Bible as a *fons remotus* to which just some references are made. In that case, the biblical revelation tends to be reduced to a footnote. Rahner wants the ST to adopt biblical thinking and hopes that the BT will be able to accommodate the ST in this. There can be no ecclesiastical dogmatic subject based solely on oral tradition (*depositum fidei*) without a biblical foundation.[10]

2.1.1.2 *Call to BT to enter into dialogue with ST*

Rahner also urges the biblical scholar as an exegete not to restrict the research to merely philological textual explanations. For Rahner, a biblical explanation is more than text analysis. The research of the biblical scholar should also be related to the broader biblical-theological and Catholic tradition of faith. Rahner argues that the exegete builds up and not just dismantles, and strives to positively demonstrate the harmony or challenges between its own discipline and the established dogmatism.[11] Biblical studies must be careful not to degenerate into a mere foundation of the

---

7. Rahner, "Rezension: Heinisch," 44, "Der Aufbau bleibt mehr als bei den modernen protestantischen Theologien des AT in der Nähe des Aufbaus, der heute in der Dogmatik üblich ist . . . Dem Dogmatiker wird es jedenfalls dazu helfen daß die Bibel in seiner Wissenschaft besser als bisher zu Worte kommt."

8. Rahner, "Dogmatischen Schriftbeweis," 3; "Heilige Schrift," 115, 120; "Exegese," 88.

9. Rahner, "Prinzipien," 403.

10. Rahner, "Heilige Schrift," 114–19.

11. Rahner, "Prinzipien," 116; "Exegese," 87–90.

traditional Catholic tradition of faith. This can be a major problem for Catholic biblical studies, where faith is linked to age-old traditions and customs. The discoveries in biblical studies can then be reduced to proof of what has already been proven. In that case, there will be no more innovation in the research. Rahner wants to avoid this and encourages the biblical scholar to be inspired again and again by the fresh and inexhaustible source of the Bible. It is the ST, in turn, who can sensitize the BT to the dogmatic premise it carries with it. To make it easier to recognize these presuppositions, the believing Catholic exegete may not, for example, immediately ignore historical-critical research. Like Protestant exegesis, it must be used to arrive at new and old insights. Rejection is only necessary if certain methodical assumptions are incorrect or implausible. The exegete must work in such a conscientious manner and should not see it as his main task to accept alleged certainties thoughtlessly or to disprove them without a valid reason.[12]

In this way, ST and biblical studies should perform their research separately, and not operate in the form of submission to the other. Because of this, Rahner chooses to place both subjects next to each other at the same level. The primary task of BT is to take stock of the source data from the Bible. It portrays the message of the Bible in a responsible manner. If this happened more often, it would eliminate the danger that the biblical equinox could only be understood as a philological discussion.[13]

In summary, the interrelationships and enrichment, which Rahner sees in an interdisciplinary dialogue between BT and ST, can be summarized as follows,

1. For BT and ST, the Bible is the primary source (*norma non normata*).

2. ST and BT are equivalent and cover their own field of expertise.

3. ST reflects on the Christian doctrine of faith as it has been established and confessed over the centuries.

4. BT reflects on the biblical revelation, what it means, and what it entails for today's Christian doctrine of faith.

5. BT can enrich the ST by making it aware of the biblical testimony. Where this is lacking, Rahner sees the risk of lack of clarity, inaccuracy, and/or imbalance in ST.

6. BT can enrich ST by making it aware of the biblical-theological storyline. This prevents ST from basing itself on loose biblical texts instead of on the overall picture of biblical revelation.

7. ST can enrich BT by making it aware of its own dogmatic and confessional presuppositions.

---

12. Rahner, "Exegese," 92, 102; "Biblische Theologie," 451.
13. Rahner, "Dogmatischen Schriftbeweis," 3.

2.1.1.3 Rahner's own handling of BT

In Rahner's own works, there is no application of his own plea for interaction between ST and BT. Also, Harald Fritsch and Wolfhart Pannenberg note that the concretization and thematization from the biblical data in Rahner's eschatology are simply non-existent.[14] In talking about the new heaven and the new earth, the systematic theologian limits himself to his own field of study. Biblical-theological reflections do not take place anywhere. There are thus no concrete examples of how to bridge the gap between BT and ST when talking about the new creation. Rahner confines himself only to refer to the significance of the synthesis between BT and ST. He sees himself as the first recipient of the call to take greater account of BT in his work in ST. At the same time, this does not mean for Rahner that the dogmatic or systematic theologian must be fully qualified in the field of BT. After all, there are limits to one's own discipline that must be respected. Rather, he calls for attention to be paid to the interdisciplinary dialogue between them.

2.1.2 Rahner's view on the Bible

Anyone who theologically reflects on the Bible does so from a certain attitude towards the Scriptures. This attitude can be different for Rahner than for Moltmann or Beale. When a critical comparison is made between the systematic and biblical scholar, it is essential to examine the attitude of the persons concerned. In the previous section, we observed that Rahner established that a historically critical interpretation of the Bible could lead to different results in theology than a historically-canonical interpretation of the Bible. The choices made in this respect will lead to different results in theological research. From this observation, the question must be addressed of what Rahner's own view of the Bible is.

2.1.2.1 The Bible as reliable and primordial

Rahner traditionally follows the Council of Trent in his conceptions of the Bible. This Council confessed that God's Spirit inspired all books of the Bible.[15] God is the initiator and inspires the one who writes the Bible. The confession speaks of both a human and divine writer, without one lifting the other.

From this balance, between God's and human's responsibility, Rahner rejects a theory of verbal inspiration that implies or assumes a mechanical dictate. The full recognition of the human writer explains the historical and theological specificity of the books of the Bible. At the same time, it offers the possibility to develop a BT that

---

14. Fritsch, *Selbstmitteilung*, 131; Pannenberg, *Systematische Theologie 3*, 586–87.
15. Denzinger and Hünermann, *Enchiridion*, 1501; Rahner, "Schriftinspiration," 3–58; "Über die inspiration," 209–15.

takes into account this specificity of the books of the Bible.[16] From this background, Rahner classifies the Bible, as far as its essential content is concerned, as historically reliable. The Bible is inspired and free of error. It is the primary source of Christian dogmatism. However, this does not mean that the exact historicity of each verse has been determined. For example, the statements of Jesus in the NT cannot be typified as summarized "sound recordings" (*Bandaufnahmen*). However, they do give a reliable picture of what Jesus really meant to say.[17]

2.1.2.2 *God's revelation and canon formation*

When it comes to the question of God's revelation and canon formation, Rahner remains somewhat cautious. This theological question is part of the subjects that have not been adequately reflected in history.[18] However, Rahner does point out that Christian theology cannot limit the inspiration of God to the books of the OT and NT alone. The general revelation of God also permits that in the past, God's Spirit inspired other people who were not connected to the distinctive people of God. The supernatural revelation of salvation applies to all men and is not limited only to Jewish people. However, God emphasizes that this does not mean that the inspired general revelation is of equal value to the particularly inspired revelation of God in the Bible, where OT and NT are equal.[19]

Rahner states that God's revelation reached its climax and endpoint from the coming of Christ and the mission of the apostles. The revelation in Christ can only be surpassed by the revelation of the triune God, who completes Christ's work of salvation in the eschaton. In this respect, the revelation of God was concluded with the death of the apostles. After absolute salvation has been given by them in Christ, there can be no new supreme revelation. The biblical canon is rounded and is considered to be of God's will. It is a standard and a source for all times, as was already the case in the early church.[20]

At the same time, Rahner is cautious about equating the confession of absolute rounding with the extent of the books of the Bible as we know it today. He encloses the possibility that a certain document is still missing from the Bible. If today the church were to discover an unknown work from apostolic times and unanimously acknowledged it as the legitimate expression of primeval Christianity, this document would be part of the absolute rounding off of the canon. Nothing would change in the doctrine of a closed canon. However, the church should acknowledge that she overlooked one of the inspired writings over the course of various centuries. Because of this attitude,

---

16. Rahner, "Inspiration," 718–20.
17. Rahner, "Exegese," 95, 99–102; "Heilige Schrift," 112.
18. Rahner, "Inspiration," 720.
19. Rahner, "Inspiration," 716, 720. See also, Neufeld, "Schrift," 244.
20. Rahner, "Inspiration," 721, 724.

the canon can never be considered complete. The church, as an organ, always retains the right to recognize certain books as canonical at a later date and to add them to the already recognized biblical books.[21]

There would be more to say about this, but our research does not require it. It is sufficient to point out here that Rahner's view of the formation of the Bible may differ from that of Beale in various places. The comparison between the three theologians in chapter 6 will have to clarify this concretely.

2.2 MOLTMANN ON THE INTERACTION WITH BT

2.2.1 BT as an interlocutor

In contrast to Rahner, Moltmann did not write a separate work in which he reflected on a possible dialogue between ST and BT. This does not mean that Moltmann is completely silent on this issue. From his biographical background and various remarks in his works, it is possible to determine how he appreciates the relationship between ST and BT. We will clarify this in the paragraphs below and analyze the potential enrichment that such a dialogue, according to Moltmann, can bring.

2.2.1.1 *The rediscovery of biblical hope*

During his academic studies in Göttingen, Moltmann was influenced by the former Old Testament scholar Gerhard von Rad (1901–1971). In later times the influence of the New Testament scholar Ernst Käsemann (1906–1998) was added. Both of them gave Moltmann's theology a solid foundation in BT.[22] According to Moltmann, the philosophical influences of Immanuel Kant (1724–1804) and Georg Hegel (1770–1831) in the nineteenth century meant that theologians began to base Christian eschatology primarily on philosophical thoughts. That is why Moltmann's *Theologie der Hoffnung* accused the eschatology of Karl Barth and Rudolf Bultmann of being too strongly existentially focused on the present and not enough on the biblical description of the coming of YHWH, the God who gives and fulfills all promises.

It is always ultimately an influence of Greek thought and questioning when one understands the revelation of God, which is witnessed in the biblical writings, as "epiphany of the eternal presence." This is more the God of Parmenides than the God of Exodus and the resurrection.[23]

---

21. Rahner, "Inspiration," 724.
22. Moltmann, *Weiter Raum*, 103; *Erfahrungen*, 16.
23. Moltmann, *Theologie*, 74, "Es ist letztlich immer ein Einfluß griechischen Denkens und Fragens, wenn man die Offenbarung Gottes, die in den biblischen Schriften bezeugt wird, als 'Epiphanie der ewigen Gegenwart' versteht. Das bezeichnet eher den Gott des Parmenides als den Gott des Exodus und der Auferstehung." See also, Moltmann, *Theologie*, 11, 22–27, 49–50, 95–214, 127, 142–44, 274; "Richtungen," 37.

The Bible was Moltmann's book of hope.[24] The true language of Christian eschatology did not lie in the Greek logos, but in God's promises expressed in Israel's hope and experience. In his theology, Moltmann emphasizes these biblical hopes and promises and sees them in relation to God's intervention in this creation (cf. §4.2.3). The promise and hope of the kingdom determine the perspective on the history of salvation and reveal God's being. For this purpose, Moltmann relies on BT,

> Now it is the newer Old Testament theology which has demonstrated that the words and propositions of "God's revelation" in the Old Testament are consistently connected with propositions of "God's promise." . . . Therefore the question arises to systematic theology whether the leading understanding of the revelation of God does not have to be dominated by nature and the direction of this promise.[25]

In this respect, Moltmann points out that Israel's faith distinguished itself from other religions in that it addressed the God of promise, while others were directed towards the gods of revelation. Faith and promise relate to each other. Just as the promises come from God's being, so God is revealed in the promises. Moltmann relies on reformed theology for this purpose.[26]

After the rediscovery of biblical-theological eschatology, Moltmann was given the time to develop a ST of hope, based on the outstanding fulfillment of the biblical promises and looking to the promised world of God.[27] With this in mind, Moltmann followed in the footsteps of his former Old Testament teacher, Gerhard von Rad.[28] This methodical approach led him, in comparison with Barth and Bultmann, to reflect more strongly on Christian eschatology from a biblical-theological framework. However, Moltmann did not limit itself to this framework.[29] The BT was rather regarded as a respected interlocutor alongside many others in systematic reflection. For Moltmann, the fact that eschatological incitements in those days began to be limited to the mere processing of exegetic and dogmatic insights and, for example, were no longer taking philosophy into account at all, was not seen as a desirable development, but as an impoverishment.[30]

---

24. Moltmann, *Gospel of Liberation*, 30.

25. Moltmann, "Aufgaben," 22, "Nun hat aber gerade die neuere alttestamentliche Theologie gezeigt, daß die Worte und Sätze vom 'Offenbaren Gottes' im Alten Testament durchgängig mit Sätzen der 'Verheißung Gottes' verbunden sind. . . . Es stellt sich von daher die Frage an die systematische Theologie, ob das sie leitende Verständnis der Offenbarung Gottes nicht von der Art und der Zielrichtung der Verheißung beherrscht sein muß." See also, Moltmann, *Theologie*, 36. Contra, Chung, "Moltmann on Scripture," 3, which completely omits Moltmann's focus on the biblical promises.

26. Moltmann, *Theologie*, 36–37.

27. Moltmann, "Richtungen," 44; "Aufgaben," 22–23; *Theologie*, 34–36, 101–2.

28. See also the more than twenty-five references to Gerhard von Rad in, Moltmann, *Theologie*, 337. See also, Meeks, *Origins*, 63–73.

29. Williams, "Moltmann," 77–80; Bauckham, *Moltmann*, 6–7.

30. Moltmann, "Richtungen," 44; "Aufgaben," 22–23; *Theologie*, 34–36, 101–2.

At the same time, he warns that dealing with BT should not degenerate into fundamentalism or historicism. Central to this is the biblical testimony of the gospel. For example, in a discussion between Thomas Aquinas and Joachim of Fiore, Moltmann points out that not the doctrine of the church nor the experience of history, but the gospel, as it is testified in the Old and New Testaments, should be a judge.[31] Moltmann also writes critically about the relationship between exegesis and preaching,

> Only when the coercion to preach arises from exegesis, does preaching lose the taste of deliberate manipulation and is the preaching determined by the Word and not by the preacher's present ecclesial or inner situation.[32]

On the other hand, it is the modern ST that, by asking the right critical questions, can make BT aware of its own hermeneutical-methodical assumptions in the theological statements it makes.

2.2.1.2 *Christian theology and BT*

Moltmann would later point out on several occasions that a Christian theology had to be rooted in a BT, "Christian theology must be biblical theology."[33] Otto Weber (1902–1966) was an example to Moltmann in this respect, as he created a unity between BT and ST in his *Grundlagen der Dogmatik*.[34]

In post-Enlightenment modern theology, this biblical-theological thinking, together with the practice of biblical exegesis, stood in the background (§1.2). Theology was rather a philosophy of religion, and the interpretation of the Bible was limited to historical exegesis, "the hermeneutic bridge over the 'nasty wide ditch' (Lessing) of history, was missing."[35] Those who were involved as biblical scholars were occupied with old biblical truths that had almost lost all relevance to current systematic-theological thinking. This phenomenon meant that for many people, the Bible remained an unknown book. The Christian tradition did not expect anything new from it. Moltmann regrets this and observes,

---

31. Moltmann, *Geschichte*, 182; "Christliche Hoffnung," 243; "Aufgaben," 22; *Experiment Hoffnung*, 21.

32. Moltmann, "Verkündigung als Problem," 113, "Nur wenn sich aus der Exegese die Nötigung zur Predigt ergibt, verliert das Predigen den Beigeschmack gewollter Manipulationen und wird die Predigt vom Wort bestimmt und nicht von der gegenwärtigen kirchlichen oder inneren Situation des Predigers."

33. Moltmann, *Erfahrungen*, 87; *Experiment Hoffnung*, 17, "Christliche Theologie muß biblische Theologie sein."

34. Moltmann, *Weiter Raum*, 55; *Erfahrungen*, 87.

35. Moltmann, *Weiter Raum*, 136, "die hermeneutische Brücke über den 'garstigen breiten Graben' (Lessing) der Geschichte, fehlte."

> Without biblical theology, theology cannot be Christian theology. Therefore, we should do everything to encourage theologians and Christians to study the Bible. But that will only be possible if you read the Bible with new eyes.[36]

In the latter case, BT was able to help. It can see to it that ST can once again see the relevance and topicality of the Bible.

With this in mind, Moltmann warmly welcomes an interdisciplinary discussion between ST and BT. For him, systematic theology is only a contribution to the greater theological whole. This makes the dialogue with other theological disciplines a must.[37] Theological faculties should not only train their students in one specific field, such as historical theology, practical theology, systematic theology, or biblical studies; they should also emphasize the unity of theology by demonstrating an interdisciplinary conversation.[38] This attitude of Moltmann—which we also encounter with Rahner—stimulates this dissertation, in which exemplary reflection is provided on the relevance of a dialogue between the field of ST and that of BT.

In his conversation with Richard Bauckham, Moltmann also points out that the interaction between dogmatics and biblical exegesis must occur even more. Doing so, he expresses his belief in a unity of theology in its various disciplines.[39] This interactive dialogue, to which Moltmann refers, also takes place implicitly and explicitly in his works. We see an example of this in his talk about the new heaven and earth in *Das Kommen Gottes* (§4.7.5). There Moltmann bases his firmly on biblical-theological analyses by Richard Bauckham.[40] The interrelationships and enrichments that Moltmann sees in the ST-BT dialogue can thus be summarized as follows,

1. The Bible is the primary source of Christian faith.

2. ST and BT are equivalent to each other.

3. ST reflects on biblical hope from a Judaeo-Christian point of view.

4. BT investigates what the biblical text means.

5. ST and BT can both enrich each other by making each other aware of Judaeo-Christian hope. Moltmann sees the danger of extra-biblical philosophical thinking that takes the place of God's promises where this is lacking.

6. BT can enrich ST by making it aware of the topicality of the biblical-theological storyline for today.

36. Moltmann, "Aufgaben," 20.

37. Moltmann, *Erfahrungen*, 13, cf. 66, 107, 120–125. With reference to, Kraus, *Systematische Theologie*.

38. Moltmann, "Aufgaben," 23.

39. Moltmann, "Bible," 232. See also Moltmann's reaction to Bertold Klappert, "Antwort Jürgen Moltmann," 139.

40. Moltmann, *Kommen*, 341n111.

7. BT can enrich ST by offering it the central themes in the Bible as core elements in the biblical revelation.

8. ST makes BT aware of its hermeneutical-method assumptions in the statements it makes.

2.2.2   Moltmann's view on the Bible

The influence of a person's view of the Bible in theological thinking and, thus on interdisciplinary dialogue was already pointed out in Rahner's analysis (§2.1.2). The following paragraphs may clarify the extent to which Moltmann's view of the writing differs from that of Rahner. However, we note that Moltmann mainly has parallels with Rahner. The main reason for this divergence of views is probably the separate cultural and confessional development they experienced.

2.2.2.1   *The Bible as a conversation partner*

Though Moltmann is attentive to biblical expressions, he questions the idea of the Bible as an infallible standard. It is useful to elaborate on Moltmann's thinking on this since it is precisely Beale who follows this approach, and it also echoes—to a lesser extent—in Rahner's view of Scripture. When studying the Bible, Moltmann clearly experienced God's truth but rejected naive biblicism. Anyone who turns the Bible into a foundation deprives it of its own progress. The Bible is not an immobile and solidly founded book. It is a book that is in motion and has a history of progress that leads to the future fulfillment of God's promises. In history, the word of God withdraws from any human authority that wishes to have it and to enshrine it in law.[41] For those familiar with Moltmann's theology, this perspective is in line with his aversion to the historically established (*futurum/chronos*) and his plea for the developing positive that is historically irreplaceable (see §4.2.2).

For Moltmann, the Bible nevertheless remains an important interlocutor in his theological adventures. It testifies to God's central message and human participation in that message. The Bible is thus both the word of God and a testimony of human faith. The latter allows us also to make critical remarks on the Bible text, where it goes against God's central message. According to Moltmann, the dialectic process between the church and the Bible is also reflected in church history. While the early church was guided by the biblical books of the OT, she did not hesitate to write her own testimony about the central message in later biblical books that would ultimately form the NT.[42]

Moltmann finds a central biblical-theological main motive in 1 Corinthians 15:20–28. In his works, he constantly refers to these verses, especially 1 Corinthians

---

41. Moltmann, *Erfahrungen*, 122–23, 127; "Aufgaben," 20–21.
42. Moltmann, *Erfahrungen*, 128–35; *Kommen*, 23; *Trinität*, 38, 261.

15:28 being mentioned the most.⁴³ In his dissertation on Moltmann's eschatology, Matthias Remenyi devotes a separate chapter to this biblical passage, because according to him, it is "of almost system-forming relevance to the whole of his theology."⁴⁴ However, Moltmann's strength lies more in the theological reflection from these and other biblical statements than in its exegetical reflection. So he doesn't dwell on relevant biblical texts and the complex exegetic issues that come along with them. His own interpretations are then associated with biblical texts with no further hermeneutical-executive justification. For this reason, Richard Bauckham writes, "what little exegesis he sacrifices tends to be remarkably ignorant and incompetent."⁴⁵ In addition to several examples, Bauckham refers to Moltmann's expressions on Revelation 21:5,

> It is not, "Behold, I create" (Hebrew: barah), but, "I make (Hebrew: asah) everything new." The divine "making" is the shaping and shaping of what is "created."⁴⁶

Bauckham notes that this text in Revelation is written in Greek rather than Hebrew. It uses ποιέω—a word that the Septuagint uses to translate the Hebrew בָּרָא into Genesis 1:1. In addition, Revelation 21:5 is biblical-theological more in relation to Isaiah 65:17, where בָּרָא is also found. Bauckham concludes that Moltmann's explanation "requires an exegesis that no hermeneutic, however pre-modern or post-modern, could conceivably support."⁴⁷

In a short article, Moltmann responds to this criticism as follows, "Only a mind fixated on 'disciplined exegesis' can read—and misunderstand—my theological text in this way."⁴⁸ For Moltmann, theology is not under the authority of texts or the dictatorship of exegesis. Theology is not a comment on biblical texts, and biblical texts are not a replacement for theological reflection. For Moltmann, asking whether a theological statement is in accordance with the Bible is only a remnant of an old doctrine of verbal inspiration.⁴⁹

In his reactions to this criticism from Bauckham, Moltmann makes a remarkable difference from his own former statements. Earlier, we saw that according to him, BT is not hierarchically superior to ST and ST is not hierarchically superior to BT; both are equally important in order to achieve a complete theological result (cf. §2.2.1).

---

43. References and allusions to 1 Cor 15:28 can be found in, Moltmann, *Kommen*, 131; *Weg Jesu*, 204; *Geschichte*, 290; *Trinität*, 119; "Rechtfertigung," 172; "Richtungen," 37; *Kirche*, 47–48; *Theologie*, 140–50; *Reich Gottes*, 19.

44. Remenyi, *Um der Hoffnung*, 12, "inherited itself from the geradezu systembildender Relevanz für das Gesamt seiner Theologie." See also, Remenyi, *Um der Hoffnung*, 19–65; Bauckham, *Theology of Jürgen Moltmann*, 162, 244.

45. Bauckham, "Time," 25–26.

46. Moltmann, *Kommen*, 299, "Es heißt nicht: 'Siehe, ich schaffe' (hebräisch: barah), sondern: 'ich mache (hebräisch: asah) alles neu'. Das göttliche 'Machen' ist Formen und Gestalten dessen, was 'geschaffen' ist."

47. Bauckham, "Time," 180n52.

48. Moltmann, "Bible," 232.

49. Moltmann, "Bible," 230.

The danger of manipulating the biblical text in homiletically-systematic reflection, as mentioned there, is absent for Moltmann when he describes the relationship between the biblical text and the systematic reflection in his response to Bauckham. This is an inconsistency in Moltmann's methodology that requires alertness. After all, the way in which he deals with biblical texts runs the risk of allowing the Bible to become changeable for its own benefit. In an interdisciplinary comparison between Moltmann's ST and BT, this comes to light and raises justifiable critical questions.

From these methodological points of view, Moltmann's approach to the Bible text can be described as ad hoc and eclectic. Bible texts are not binding standards but open discussion partners, who support and encourage theological reflections,

> Taking account of exegetical discipline, I can develop my own theological relationship with the biblical texts, for theology is not a commentary on the biblical writings ... the disciplined exegesis tells us what the text meant for the author and the people he was addressing in his own time; but the theological reflection is supposed to say what it means today if we place it in the context of *our* own time.[50]

Moltmann clearly separates biblical studies from ST. He does so in the spirit of Johann Gabler's (1753–1826) definition (§1.2.2). By doing so, he creates the same dangerous distinction between ST and BT as the modern Enlightenment did. According to Moltmann, this phenomenon caused the Bible to become a grey, meaningless ancient book for many people. In those days, ST focused more on the hope of the philosophers than on the biblical hope (§1.2). Moltmann's autobiography (2006) places this danger in the foreground so that this attitude towards Bauckham's remark comes over as strange in 1999.

Specifically, Moltmann states in this context that he is not an exegete, but a theologian who understands the biblical text merely as a partner in dialogue.[51] The biblical text is an inspiration for his theological reflection and should not become an authoritarian regulation.[52] Only what is related to the central message of hope is important to Moltmann. This choice will influence a comparison between Moltmann's ST and a BT, so it is important to go further into this and see how Moltmann sees that central message concretely. After all, we realize that Moltmann's works, unlike Rahner's, are characterized by a great deal of attention to biblical texts. This makes Moltmann a much-loved theologian in evangelical-reformation circles.[53] Simultaneously we will see that critical voices can also be heard about the question of whether Moltmann's view of writing is truly as evangelical as it seems to be in the eyes of some (cf. §2.2.2.3).

---

50. Moltmann, "Bible," 230.
51. Moltmann, "Bible," 231–32.
52. Moltmann, *Erfahrungen*, 17.
53. Van den Brink, "Geboeid door Moltmann," 48–57; Müller-Fahrenholz, *Phantasie*; Bauckham, *Theology of Jürgen Moltmann*.

The New Heaven and New Earth

The ambiguities in this respect must be taken into account if we want to compare Moltmann's ST with Beale's BT, which was written from a reformed perspective. For that reason, we will dwell longer on Moltmann's view of Scripture than on the view of Rahner or Beale.

2.2.2.2 *The central message of hope*

When Moltmann concretely speaks about the central message of the Bible, he connects OT and NT and attaches equal values to both of them. In this respect, Moltmann differs from Rahner, who mainly highlights the discontinuity and elevates the NT above the OT. For Moltmann, continuity between OT and NT is more important than discontinuity. Only in the kingdom of God, the new creation to which both Testaments point, are the Scriptures fulfilled. For too long, Christians have confined themselves only to the message of the New Testament. Beale's BT agrees with that basic attitude and gives a detailed account of how God's desires for creation in the OT and NT are realized and fulfilled.

For Moltmann, the focus of the OT is on God's covenant promises with Israel, which point to God's plan of salvation for all peoples, and yes for all creation. God's universal promises are central to the NT. These find an eschatological beginning in the work of Christ and God's Spirit. Following the example of the biblical theologians Gerhard von Rad and Ernst Käsemann, Moltmann connects the Old Testament promises with the future of Christ's death and resurrection. This connection bears witness to the continuity of God's promises to the patriarch Abraham, which is adequate for everyone through the work of Christ, and to the discontinuity of the recipients of these promises, in that they were first directed primarily at Israel in the OT and then universally extended to all creation. For Moltmann, the center of the Bible is thus the rebirth of all things in the new creation. As far as texts are in accordance with these central basic truths from the OT or NT, they are "holy" and proclaim the gospel to humanity. It follows that a quotation from the Bible is not yet a guarantee for the truth of a particular theorem.[54]

Sung Chung criticizes this attitude when it comes to applying it in evangelical circles,

> it is inappropriate for evangelicals to identify a theme or a text as "the matter of Scripture" which regulates the canonicity of other biblical themes and texts.[55]

According to Chung, this method is not in line with Jesus' own choice to quote one biblical text in the wilderness against the devil. In this situation, Jesus recognizes every

---

54. Moltmann, *Erfahrungen*, 123, 127, 138–39; *Gekreuzigte Gott*, 243; *Theologie*, 131–134, 146, 261, 247n136. See also, Von Rad, *Theologie*, I:120.

55. Chung, "Moltmann on Scripture," 10.

bible verse as the word of God and as a whole that cannot be broken. God's word is not a fallible human testimony.

Chung overlooks the fact that Moltmann only indicates the way in which biblical texts can be recognized as canonical. This authority of the biblical text is in line with the process of canon formation. From this point of view, Moltmann distinguishes between texts that are in accordance with the central message of the OT and NT and texts that are not. This maintenance of a so-called open canon goes too far for Chung. At the same time, Chung, from his own evangelical background, makes a hierarchical distinction between central themes and peripheral themes in the Bible. The fact that one Bible text gives no guarantee about the truth is also recognized by him when it concerns a text that is separate from the context. For Moltmann, that context is the central message of the OT and NT. If a text does not comply, it will be downgraded.

This methodology requires vigilance. Moltmann's idea of an open canon contains hermeneutical circular reasoning. He recognizes texts as canonical on the basis of the central message and he recognizes the central message on the basis of canonical texts. For Moltmann, this means that the canon formation process remains open. What corresponds with the central message receives the hallmark "holy,"

> For factual reasons, one can consider with Luther the Epistle of James a "strawy epistle" and prefer to reject the apocalypse, but one can also use non-biblical texts corresponding with the "cause of Scripture" for preaching.[56]

Moltmann's basic attitude towards an open and closed canon is linked to his choice of an open promise (see §4.2.3). He turns his back on closed or rigid promises. God is faithful to all the promises and transcends them,

> because in all fulfilments the promise, and what is still in it, does not yet become congruent with reality and therefore remains constantly surplus.[57]

Israel's new experiences broaden the horizon of its promise. Prophets interpret unfulfilled events as possibilities for expansion and broaden God's covenant with Israel to include the nations. This process of reinterpretation and universalization will reach a climax if, in these promises, cosmic creation fully participates in eschatological history.[58]

---

56. Moltmann, *Erfahrungen*, 130, "man kann aus sachlichen Gründen mit Luther den Jakobusbrief für eine 'strohene Epistel' halten und die Apokalypse am liebsten ausscheiden, man kann aber auch der 'Sache der Schrift' entsprechende außerbiblische Texte zur Predigt verwenden." See also, Moltmann, *Theologie*, 260.

57. Moltmann, *Theologie*, 94, "weil in allen Erfüllungen die Verheißung, und was noch in ihr steckt, noch nicht mit der Wirklichkeit deckungsgleich wird und darum ständig überschüssig bleibt." See also, Moltmann, *Theologie*, 100, 103.

58. Moltmann, *Gekreuzigte Gott*, 100; *Theologie*, 112–20, 123–24.

2.2.2.3 Differences with evangelicalism

In the previous section, we saw that Moltmann's view of writing was criticized by a conservative-evangelical and -reformed perspective. Moltmann saw the Bible too much as a noncommittal interlocutor and did not take it sufficiently seriously as an absolutely fundamental authority. With the words of Kevin Gilbert,

> Moltmann's view of the place of Scripture as a source of theology falls outside the scope of an Evangelical method. It is not that inerrant, authoritative, primary source by which all theological statements can be judged as true or false.[59]

On the contrary, Moltmann saw in this evangelical fundamentalist reaction a movement that did injustice to the Bible by seeing it as an infallible paper pope. Fundamentalism and evangelicalism are the same for Moltmann. Incidentally, this does not do justice to the distinction between the two categories. According to Moltmann, fundamentalism or evangelicalism do not argue but simply put forward propositions. It does not require insight but submission. Evangelicalism is often about the power struggle between God's word and the "spirit of the time." For Moltmann, this movement originated as a pietistic reaction to the theological *Zeitgeist* of the early twentieth century, which was imbued with historical-critical rationalism and demythologization principle.[60] For Moltmann, we need not only a demythologization of the Bible but even more its "de-historicization" in order to free it from the shackles of the past and to discover the future in it.[61]

From an evangelical point of view, there is interference with this kind of conclusion of Moltmann on the one hand, while on the other hand supporters of this movement welcome Moltmann's interaction with the biblical text. In Moltmann's many references to biblical texts, evangelicals see their own hermeneutical principle, which consists of relating theological statements to biblical speech.[62] Moltmann distinguishes himself from Rahner in this respect. Although his terminology sounds strongly orthodox, this does not necessarily mean that his conclusions are as well. For the elaboration of his own theological ideas, he claims too much freedom in dealing with the biblical text.

Because Moltmann does not always clearly explain the concepts he uses, many evangelical and reformer readers turn away from him. Several researchers have already wondered whether Moltmann's theological methodology is a reliable option for evangelicals at all.[63] Because his thinking is mainly progressive and exploratory,

---

59. Gilbert, "Theological Method," 176.

60. Moltmann, *Gott im Projekt*, 189–90, 194–97; "Fundamentalisme," 93, 96; "Theology in Germany," 196; *Gekreuzigte Gott*, 13.

61. Moltmann, *Experiment Hoffnung*, 21.

62. Gilbert, "Theological Method," 173–75; Jansen, "Moltmann's View," 285.

63. Chung, "Moltmann on Scripture," 1–16; Gilbert, "Theological Method," 164; Clutterbuck, "Jürgen Moltmann," 489–90.

the answer is both a "yes" and a "no." While evangelicals can find their way back to much of Moltmann's theological reflection, they also tend to reject other parts as too liberal. Precisely because evangelical theology, unlike Moltmann, emphasizes divine revelation, there must be cautiousness to categorize Moltmann within an evangelical tradition.[64] We will take this into account in the critical comparison between Rahner, Moltmann, and Beale in this dissertation.

2.2.3 Plea for dialogue

The above-mentioned choice for an open canon and a central normative message does not mean that Moltmann has abandoned the importance of thorough exegesis. In his biography, he acknowledges that studying for the exam that followed his doctoral thesis opened his eyes to the exegetical gaps in his own theology.[65] Elsewhere he wrote,

> When I asked myself what I would like to have done differently and at which points I have to admit that my critics are right, then I have to name exegesis first.[66]

Responsible exegesis is indeed important to better understand the biblical theologian as an interlocutor. Moltmann declares that he refrains from listening to exegetical-hermeneutical discussions from the seventies onwards,

> I found it rather inconvenient to listen to the biblical texts. In Germany, historical and theological exegesis diverged. . . . At a loss, I must have found my own post-critical and "naive" relationship to the biblical writings and tried to make my "own verse" on the texts.[67]

That is why Moltmann, as a systematic theologian, welcomes the fact that Richard Bauckham, as a New Testament scholar and exegete, also examines his theological exhibitions exegetically, "I am grateful to Richard Bauckham for reading my theological exposition exegetically too. . . . For the full multiplicity of standpoints, we need more cross-readings."[68] This theological interdisciplinary dialogue is also the focus of this dissertation.

---

64. Gilbert, "Theological Method," 164. See further for the determination of the nature of evangelical theology, Demarest, "Systematic Theology," 1064–66; Bruce, "Interpretation," 565–68; Grenz, "Theology and Piety," 151.

65. Moltmann, *Weiter Raum*, 60.

66. Moltmann, "Adventure of Theological Ideas," 104.

67. Moltmann, *Erfahrungen*, 16, "Ich empfand sie eher als hinderlich, auf die biblischen Texte zu hören. In Deutschland traten die historische und die theologische Exegese auseinander. . . . Ratlos geworden, habe ich dann wohl ein eigenes, nachkritisches und 'naives' Verhältnis zu den biblischen Schriften gefunden und versucht, mir meinen 'eigenen Vers' auf die Texte zu machen."

68. Moltmann, "Bible," 232.

2.3 BEALE ON THE INTERACTION WITH ST

2.3.1 ST as an interlocutor

In chapter 1.2, we have already pointed out that the question added value of BT for ST is historically obvious. Jürgen Moltmann and Karl Rahner took this question into account in their methodical reflection on theology. The question of the added value of the ST for BT is less obvious. In a personal letter, in which I asked Beale about his own reflection on the importance of the dialogue between BT and ST, he replied, "I never did this, though I came close in my introduction to my NT Biblical Theology."[69] However, a reflection on the value of the dialogue between BT and ST is not taking place there. Beale only discusses the differences which, according to him, exist between BT and ST. With this, he wants to clarify his own biblical-theological approach. In later correspondence with Beale about the comparison between his BT and Rahner's and Moltmann's ST in this dissertation, he further writes, "Your project sounds very interesting."[70] Although his reactions to this remain brief, it can be concluded that he himself is not opposed to it. However, this subject of interdisciplinary dialogue is not a priority for Beale.

In this context, we can also point to Beale's special publication on the question of the reliability of the Bible. In this, as a biblical theologian, he enters into conversation with the systematic theologian Andrew McGowan, who states that the Bible is God-inspired and yet can contain errors.[71] From various parts of the text in the book of Revelation—about which Beale wrote a huge commentary in the series of *New International Greek Testament Commentary* (NIGTC, 1999)—Beale shows that the views of McGowan on the reliability of the Bible are exegetical and biblical-theologically untenable. For this, Beale uses various biblical texts from Revelation as a basis to disprove McGowan's vision. However, this example illustrates that Beale's publications deal with the conversation with systematic theologians. But there is no broad interaction with McGowan's ST. In his publications, Beale prefers to stay within his own field of expertise.

When it comes to the dialogue between BT and ST, it should be noted that Beale refers several times to his great example, the biblical theologian Geerhardus Vos, who recognized early on in the reformed tradition that BT and ST can work in a complementary way and need not be in conflict with each other. Vos even described ST as "the crown which grows out of all the work that Biblical Theology can accomplish."[72] We saw in the previous chapters that Rahner and Moltmann rejected such a hierarchical view of the ST over the BT. Both subjects were of equal standing and deserved equal respect. In the case of Beale, this hierarchical distinction does not come back

---

69. Beale to Hausoul, "Re: Question."
70. Beale to Hausoul, "Trialogue."
71. Beale, "Can the Bible," 1–22.
72. Vos, "Idea," 23–24.

either. In line with Vos, he does characterize BT as a "(historical) storyline" and ST as a "category" or "circle" (§5.2). The storyline places the biblical data in a broader organic context and prevents Christian doctrine from being founded only on isolated "places of proof." This attention to the biblical drama has also grown within ST in recent decades, partly due to the influence of postliberalism (§5.2.1.2).

Due to the influence of Vos, Beale's *A New Testament Biblical Theology* (2011, abbr. NTBT) has a strong systematic-theological structure. Although the biblical-theological storyline is primary to Beale, he divides his argument into categories that remind us of the classical categories of ST. In particular, his extensive reflections on justification and reconciliation (§5.6.4) and on the *Church and Israel* (§5.8) fit into the field of ST rather than in the field of BT. Nevertheless, Beale wants to draw attention to this, so that biblical-theological enrichment also takes place with respect to these themes.[73] The structure of his BT is thus strongly determined by the traditional systematic-theological accents.

Furthermore, the structure of Beale's BT is also determined by the main theme. This main theme is the eschatological renewal, the new creation, or the founding of God's kingdom. As an eschatological fact, it determines the theological outlines of the Bible. Beale derives this main theme from the biblical storyline that he develops in his BT.[74] This approach ensures that ST and BT are conceptually related in their methodical thinking. This methodical approach and the choice of the relevant main theme of the innovation is not only a characteristic of Beale's NTBT. It can be found in most of his works, whether it be *The Temple and the Church's Mission*, *We Become what we Worship* or *Hidden but Now Revealed*, each time the biblical unfolding of these subjects is central to Beale. This is most evident in his NTBT, which is regarded as the *magnum opus* for Beale. Finally, in this main work, too, ST provides the filter of the new creation from which Beale describes the biblical-theological narrative lines. Beale also states that ST

> should integrate the inaugurated aspect of eschatology more into the discussion of other NT doctrines, even if they still put a section of consummative eschatology as the last chapter.[75]

Despite the fact that he only explicitly refers to ST in his *NTBT*,[76] his thinking is nevertheless strongly determined by reformed theology. However, it is impossible to escape such a systematic paradigm in BT. The awareness of this rather shows that even the biblical scholar consciously or unconsciously derives its advantages and prejudices from what ST does. Just as it is impossible to design a BT without systematic categories, neither can a ST be developed without some kind of a biblical-theological

---

73. Beale, *New Testament*, 6n16.
74. Beale, *New Testament*, 6, 8, 18, 21, 23, 296, 578.
75. Beale, *New Testament*, 18.
76. Beale, *New Testament*, 204.

storyline. It is important to consider this in more detail in the comparison and to point out where BT (unconsciously) makes it clear that systematic theological thinking in its field forms part of the basis. For the moment, it is sufficient to conclude that Beale also sees in his theological research an enrichment in the research into a comparison between a subject from BT and ST.

This can be summarized as follows,

1. The Bible is the primary source of the Christian faith.
2. ST and BT are equivalent to each other, and both have their own field of expertise.
3. ST reflects on Christian doctrine from thematic circles.
4. BT investigates how biblical themes develop in the Bible and concentrates on the biblical storyline.
5. BT can enrich ST by making it aware of the biblical-theological storyline and its continuity and development.
6. ST can enrich BT by offering it the central themes of the traditional orthodox Christian confessions as core elements for structuring the biblical storyline.
7. BT can enrich ST by making it aware where it leaves the biblical testimony and threatens to degenerate into inaccuracy or blurring.

2.3.2 Beale's view on the Bible

Because Beale is mainly occupied with BT and exegesis, it is easy to gain insight into his dealings with the Bible. His handling of the biblical text can be described as "canonical, genetic-progressive . . . exegetical, and intertextual."[77] Methodically, Beale focuses mainly on the overall biblical revelation and pays less attention to the uniqueness, structure, and religious-cultural background of the separate biblical books. An exception to this is his analysis of the Psalms, where the structure of the Bible book is used by Beale to develop the storyline and message.[78] Elsewhere, this attention for the separate structure and the methodical reflection on the question of how a BT can do justice to this shape and structuring of the various books of the Bible is lacking. Beale's work focuses on the bigger picture, the central message of the OT and NT. It is thus particularly important in his BT to examine how the testimony of each book of the Bible is related to the overarching narrative of the OT and NT. This storyline is one of continuity for Beale. Like Moltmann, he considers the OT and NT to be equivalent and consequently examines in his BT how the various core issues develop in the testimony of the OT and NT.

77. Beale, *New Testament*, 15.
78. Beale, *New Testament*, 73–81.

In his publications, Beale also points out several times that he sticks to the divine inspiration of the OT and NT.[79] This means that Beale is part of the orthodox evangelical-reformed tradition for whom the infallibility of the Bible and its authority as God's word and guideline are of crucial importance. This choice is also reflected in the titles that some of his publications bear. For example, in *The Erosion of Inerrancy in Evangelicalism* (2008), he pleads for the unity of the Bible and a fundamental attitude towards God's word as it can be found in the Chicago declaration.[80] Veli-Matti Kärkkäinen appreciates the new insights and discoveries that Beale presents in his *A New Testament Biblical Theology* (2011), but at the same time characterizes Beale's method as an "ultra-conservative approach to critical questions of biblical scholarship."[81]

According to Kärkkäinen, Beale's methodology leads to the fact that a large number of biblical interpreters leave his publications untouched. Beale himself describes his methodical approach to the Bible as a method that combines grammatical-historical exegesis with a canonical-contextual exegesis.[82]

In §1.4.3, we already noted that the orthodox evangelical-reformed background of Beale could be a challenge in comparison with the more progressive systematics Rahner and Moltmann. Therefore, we take the critical note of Kärkkäinen seriously in this study by taking into account that Rahner and Moltmann will also make similar remarks about Beale's interpretation of the Bible. Nevertheless, it will only be the comparison itself that shows the extent to which Beale's conservative attitude influences the dialogue between BT and ST.

2.4 CONCLUSION

1. All three theologians see the Bible as a primary source of reflection on the Christian faith. But, to the question concerning the authority of the Bible in theological research, they think differently.

2. Although the question of interdisciplinary research is still relatively new, all three theologians are in favor of a dialogue between ST and BT. Also, all emphasize that the two disciplines can be distinguished, but cannot be separated from each other. ST indirectly influences BT, and BT does so in the case of ST. The two disciplines are equally adjacent to each other and methodically form their own entity.

3. All three theologians place their own specific accents in their description of what ST and BT are doing. Together they conclude that ST is occupied with the

---

79. Beale, *New Testament*, 223–24; "Can the Bible," 19–22; *Temple*, 26. See in detail, Beale, *Erosion*, 13–160, 223–66.
80. Beale, "Can the Bible," 21; *Erosion*, 19–22, 267–80.
81. Kärkkäinen, "Bookreview: The Temple," 46.
82. Beale, *We Become*, 23.

topics of the Christian confession. It thinks in terms of the major themes that the church has traditionally embraced as Christian faith and is committed to the current questions that society asks the church. The BT understands its task as describing what the biblical storyline is and how it develops (Beale). According to Rahner, BT should also examine the relevance of the biblical revelation for today and should not only deal with the historical significance of the text (see also, Moltmann).

4. In conclusion, the enrichment or the positive meaning Rahner, Moltmann, and Beale show in a well-functioning dialogue between ST and BT can be summarized with the following keywords and descriptions,

    a. *Inspiration*—BT enriches ST by clarifying and enriching its systematic-theological research with new insights, and ST enriches BT by providing core elements of Christian faith that can methodically inspire the biblical theologian and deepen its own theological research.

    b. *Awareness*—BT enriches the ST because with its interpretation of the biblical testimony it indicates where the systematic (unconsciously) uses extra-biblical ideas and ST enriches BT by showing what the hermeneutical, methodical, or dogmatic-confessional presuppositions are that the biblical theologian (unconsciously) takes into account in his interpretations and where the limits of the objective in his own field are thus exceeded.

    c. *Overall view*—BT enriches ST by showing it the great storyline, the associated central subjects, and the resulting overall picture of biblical revelation. ST enriches BT by accentuating Jewish tradition or Christian doctrine. This can serve as a benchmark to emphasize the core elements in the storyline even more.

    d. *Actuality*—BT can enrich ST by showing it the topicality of the biblical-theological storyline for today, and ST can enrich BT by showing it the relevance of social questions to Jewish tradition or Christian faith teaching in the past and present.

5. Rahner follows the Council of Trent in the views on the Bible and sees God's Spirit as initiator and inspirer of the biblical books. Though the Bible is inspired and free of error, for Rahner, this does not mean that each verse is characterized by historical accuracy.

6. Rahner defends the possibility that some documents are still missing in the Bible and that they can still be discovered and recognized as canonical.

7. According to Moltmann, OT and NT are God's infallible word and humanly fallible testimony of faith. Both can support ST with their own equivalent message.

The canon of the Bible cannot be fixed in a fundamentalist way because of the open promise of God and is therefore open to editorial scrutiny.

8. Beale's explanation of the Bible can be typified as canonical-contextual. He follows the conservative explanation in critical issues concerning the authenticity of the Bible texts and rejects freer views on the infallibility or authenticity of the Bible.

3

Karl Rahner's concept on the new heaven and new earth

This chapter will analyze Rahner's thoughts on cosmic eschatology systematically. Little research has been conducted to date on Rahner's eschatology visible through the number of dissertations written. This chapter, however, is an original contribution (see §3.1).

At a structural level, the main focus of this chapter is the analysis of Rahner's hermeneutic principles (§3.2). Rahner's choices herein form the basis of his further eschatology. After this, we will look at Rahner's views concerning the new heaven and the new earth (§3.3). Subsequently, his specific geo- and anthropocentric speeches are discussed with regard to matter (§3.4) and time (§3.5). The order of these sections corresponds to Rahner's order of publication. Finally, §3.6 illustrates Rahner's theocentric perspective, elaborates on his view on the new creation, and finishes the chapter with a conclusion (§3.7).

3.1   INTRODUCTION

3.1.1   Quantity and productivity

Karl Rahner (1904–1984) is one of the greatest German theologians of the twentieth century.[1] The six-part edition *Sämtliche Werke* (1995–2015)[2] contains his complete oeuvre and shows that Rahner's theology is still relevant. Regularly important

---

1. Recent biographical data can be found with: Vorgrimler, "Karl Rahner," 215–84; Lehmann, "Rahner," 805–8; Neufeld, *Brüder*. According to Rahner, an autobiography would never be published (Rahner, "Erfahrungen," 105). As an introduction to Rahner's thinking, see among others: Batlogg, *Denkweg*; Schulz, *Karl Rahner begegnen*. For a critical look at Rahner: Felsinger, "Karl Rahner," 205–15; May, *Glaube*.

2. Rahner, *Sämtliche Werke*.

theological works appear which refer to this Catholic theologian.³ What Rahner left behind in his work, is astonishing. At the end of his life, his bibliography contained more than four thousand contributions. This oeuvre can be reduced to 1,700 if we leave out all translations, re-publications, and similar texts,⁴ but in any case, it demands respect. For Alister McGrath, this gigantic production can only be understood from the fact that Rahner published a lot of essays.⁵ This statement is put into perspective by the German translation of McGrath's *Christian Theology*: several of Rahner's essays are as voluminous as a normal monograph.⁶

Formally speaking, Rahner's texts have an experimental character. They are challenging preliminary designs rather than detailed studies. This does not mean that these designs are theologically primitive. Although Rahner's work makes no philosophical claim—with the exception of his dissertation *Geist in Welt* (1939)⁷—his style of writing contains a philosophical-exploratory dimension, which is fully at the service of his complex theological labyrinth formulations, with which readers of Rahner are familiar. Rahner himself sees his theology as "Thinking reflection on those data which are already given in the general faith consciousness and in the general school theology."⁸ The term "school theology" refers here to the neo-scholastic or the neo-Thomistic, which developed after the revival of Thomism by the encyclical *Aeterni Patris* (1879) of Pope Leo XIII.

3.1.2 Criticism of eschatology

In his critical reflection on Neo-Scholasticism, Rahner states that there is still a lot of work to be done within the field of eschatology.⁹ Among other things, he misses in the field of eschatology: (1) a well-considered hermeneutics of eschatological statements; (2) a theology of natural and salvific history; and (3) a reflection on the relationship between protology and eschatology.¹⁰ In his article *Eschatologie*, he also turns against

---

3. See for an overview of the secondary literature on Rahner: Universitätsbibliothek Freiburg im Breisgau, "Karl Rahner Sekundärliteratur."

4. Batlogg and Raffelt, "Lebenswerk," 35–36. See for a complete overview: Raffelt, "Bibliographie."

5. McGrath, *Christian Theology*, 109.

6. McGrath and Wiese, *Der Weg*, 125.

7. Rahner, *Geist in Welt*.

8. Rahner, "Gnade als Mitte," 120: "denkerische Reflexion auf jene Daten, die im allgemeinen Glaubensbewußtsein und in der allgemeinen Schultheologie schon gegeben sind."

9. Rahner, "Über den Versuch eines Aufrisses," 246. Cf. "Theologie und Anthropologie," 55. Gisbert Greshake later points out that these operations have been largely completed: Greshake, "Eschatologie," 865.

10. Rahner, "Eschatologie: Theologisch," 1095–98. Later he repeated this view: Rahner, "Überlegungen zur Methode," 109–10; "Die Herausforderung," 32–33; "Eschatologie (SM)," 1186–88; "Theologie und Anthropologie," 55, 64–65.

the tendency in the ST to see general eschatology as a mere appendix to individual eschatology.[11]

This criticism is not mild. For Michael Schmaus (1897–1993), an advisor of the *Lexikon für Theologie und Kirche*, Rahner goes too far. In a letter to Herbert Vorgrimler (January 19, 1959), Schmaus states that the article *Eschatologie* is not sufficient for the research done in the field of eschatology. If no changes are made, he threatens to cancel his participation in the complete series.[12] For Rahner, this attitude of Schmaus is exaggerated. He defends himself in a letter to the editor-in-chief Remigius Bäumer (February 13, 1959):

> If one looks at an average (also very good) school theology, one notices that most of the topics demanded here are actually not dealt with. Where, for example, is there a fundamentally thematically developed hermeneutics of eschatological statements?[13]

If his article does not appear in the lexicon, he will resign, Rahner states resolutely. After several conversations during spring 1959, he no longer has to amend his article, and Schmaus adjusted his critical attitude.[14]

3.1.3 Rahner's own contributions

His plea for a revised and modernized eschatology initially led Rahner to write his own systematic-eschatological overview. Together with the Swiss theologian Hans Urs von Balthasar (1905–1988), he designed the first proposal of an extensive scientific ST during summer 1939. The following eschatological themes would be addressed:[15] the doctrine of completeness, the eons, the theology of the apocalypse, the completeness of the world, the last things, the dialectics between the individual and general eschatology, and the dialectics between this world and the new creation.

Rahner officially published this proposal in 1954 and the eschatological section contained a detailed overview in which the following elements were discussed under the heading "the new eon": time change, material change, the definitive of the spirit, the definitive of the new eon.[16] Despite the fact that from 1941 onwards, there were

---

11. Rahner, "Eschatologie (SM)," 1094. Cf. "Über den Versuch eines Aufrisses," 447; *Grundkurs*, 426; Phan, *Eternity*, 19–23, 215–21.

12. See for this writings: Vorgrimler, "Editionsbericht," 45, 49.

13. Vorgrimler, "Editionsbericht," 49–50: "Wenn man eine durchschnittliche (auch sehr gute) Schultheologie anschaut, merkt man, daß die meisten der hier geforderten Themen tatsächlich nicht behandelt werden. Wo gibt es denn z.B. eine grundsätzlich thematisch entwickelte Hermeneutik der eschatologischen Aussagen?"

14. Vorgrimler, "Editionsbericht," 50–51.

15. Rahner, "Über den Versuch eines Aufrisses," 23.

16. Rahner, "Über den Versuch eines Aufrisses," 447. Hans Urs von Balthasar later criticized this proposal (Von Balthasar, "Größe und Last," 533).

contractual agreements with publisher Herder about this dogmatics, called *Handbuch der katholische Dogmatik*, Rahner later abandoned the plan to write it. His own overall eschatological overview remained unprocessed. Though he did not leave a pure synopsis of his eschatology, its contours can be developed on the basis of Rahner's numerous contributions to eschatology. He speaks of the hermeneutics of eschatological statements, dying and death, purgatory, the resurrection of the body, judgment, eternity and time, the second coming of Christ, and the new creation.[17]

For Rahner, speaking about hope is traditionally one of the most important subjects in theology. Just as for Jürgen Moltmann and Gregory Beale, eschatology is not a defined subject at the end of ST (§1.4). Eschatology is a formal-structural principle of theological statements:

> We understand the history of salvation and revelation only if we live and hear it as the history of the growing radicalism of the promise of salvation. We understand Jesus Christ as the Incarnate Word of God only when we believe him as the one who will "come again," who is the future and thus the Word of God's absolute self-commitment to the world.[18]

Due to the fact that the population's knowledge and interest in this matter declined sharply in these days, Rahner often expresses himself extremely cautiously in his comments on eternal life and provides extensive justification for his hermeneutics.[19] Peter Phan sees a total coherence in Rahner's eschatology. Only over time, there is a gradual development from an existentialist to an interpersonal accentuation.[20]

In the past, several theses have already described Rahner's eschatology. Nevertheless, the research into the new creation remained brief.[21] The following more extensive research into Rahner's thoughts on cosmic eschatology, which is based on the building blocks he himself provides for this purpose, is thus legitimized.

---

17. See i.e., Rahner, "Auferstehung (STh)," 211–25; "Prinzipien," 401–28; "Leben der Toten," 429–37; *Auferstehung*; "Christentum," 159–79; "Kirche," 348–67; "Über das christliche Sterben," 273–80; *Glaube*, 13–14; "Frage," 519–40; "Ewigkeit," 422–32; "Fegfeuer," 435–49. See also the works of Rahner in the Bibliography of this book.

18. Rahner, "Frage," 520–21: "Wir verstehen Heils- und Offenbarungsgeschichte nur dann, wenn wir sie leben und hören als die Geschichte der wachsenden Radikalität der Verheißung des Heiles [sic!]. Wir erfassen Jesus Christus als das fleischgewordene Wort Gottes nur dann, wenn wir ihn glauben als den, der 'wiederkommen' wird, der also der Zukünftige und so das Wort der absoluten Selbstzusage Gottes an die Welt ist." Cf. "Ewigkeit," 422; "Christentum," 159.

19. E.g., Rahner, "Ewigkeit," 422.

20. See in detail: Phan, *Eternity*, 26–39, 201, 209–210.

21. Worth mentioning are: Fritsch, *Selbstmitteilung*, 501–11; Fletcher, *Steigerung*, 110–39; Ludlow, *Universal*, 275–77; Geister, *Aufhebung*, 59–121; Murphy, *Critical*; Phan, *Eternity*, 201–10; Schmidt, *Eschatologie*, I:369–372.

3.2 HERMENEUTIC PRINCIPLES

For the field of eschatology, Rahner's article *Hermeneutics of Eschatological Assertions* is of inestimable value. Wolfhart Pannenberg describes it as the "most important contribution of contemporary theology to an anthropological justification and interpretation of eschatological statements."[22] Here Rahner shows that the ancient biblical worldview causes profound difficulties for eschatological statements. His discussion of the associated gaps can be summarized in seven main theses. In order to better understand his eschatological thinking about the new creation, it is essential to highlight these hermeneutical starting points.

3.2.1 Theses 1–3: Direction, the source of revelation and limitations

3.2.1.1 Thesis 1: Eschatology is about the future

According to Rahner, eschatological statements always focus on the future in a strictly chronological-empirical sense and are inextricably linked to the Christian creed. History is focused on a decisive end so that an existential demythologization of eschatological statements can be categorically rejected because it leads to an absolute existentialism and a de-eschatologization. Rahner's fifth thesis clarifies this and mentions that demythologization forgets,

> that human beings exist in true temporality, directed towards what is really still outstanding in the future, and live in a world which is not only abstract existence, but must attain salvation with all its dimensions (thus also the non-existential temporality, thus also the profane temporality).[23]

What "demythologization" exactly means in this context is missing from this explanation. Mainly the term gets a negative connotation (§3.3.4.2).[24] Peter Phan argues that Rahner's demythologization criticism concretely opposes Rudolf Bultmann. Rahner mentions Bultmann several times by name in the context of this subject.[25] However,

---

22. Pannenberg, *Systematische Theologie 3*, 585: "wichtigsten Beitrag der gegenwärtigen Theologie zu einer anthropologischen Begründung und Interpretation eschatologischer Aussagen." Interaction with Rahner's eschatological principles will be found at: Fritsch, *Selbstmitteilung*, 91–121; Phan, *Eternity*, 67–76; Pannenberg, *Systematische Theologie 3*, 585–86; Moltmann, "Methoden," 54; Berkhof, "Over de methode," 480–91.

23. Rahner, "Prinzipien," 404: "daß der Mensch in echter, auf wirklich noch ausständig Zukünftiges gerichteter Zeitlichkeit existiert und in einer Welt lebt, die nicht nur abstrakt Existenz ist, sondern mit allen ihren Dimensionen (also auch der nicht existentialen, also auch der profan-zeitlichen Zeitlichkeit) das Heil erlangen muß."

24. See also: Rahner, "Perspektiven," 550; "Auferstehung (STh)," 213, 217.

25. Phan, "Eschatology," 178. See also: Fritsch, *Selbstmitteilung*, 124; Koch, "Weltende," 149. References to Bultmann can be found at: Rahner, "Kirchliche Christologie," 198; "Künftige Wege," 51–53; "Theologie und Anthropologie"; "Dogmatische Fragen," 160; "Eschatologie: Theologisch," 1096; "Theos," 154.

it is important that Rahner himself nuances this statement because Bultmann mainly advocates an exclusively present eschatology.[26]

3.2.1.2 *Thesis 2: God reveals the future to humans*

For Rahner, it is undeniably established in Christian doctrine that God reveals knowledge about the future of humanity. The human openness to this revelation is at the heart of the theological understanding of historicity (*Geschichtlichkeit*). Rahner already philosophically and theologically analyzes this openness in his *Hörer des Wortes*. But there is also a human limitation present here: God can only reveal what a person can absorb. Humans do not *a priori* determine this absorption limit for themselves. It is God who meets humans and determines their final demarcation.[27]

With these thoughts, Rahner emphasizes that hermeneutical principles about eschatological statements should inherently develop with the word of God, by being confronted and criticized through it. Eschatological statements should be anchored in the Bible. Anyone who unilaterally invokes God's word and denies any hermeneutic principle is deceiving himself because he/she also maintains an (unspoken) hermeneutic principle. After all, any interpretation of eschatological statements is subjected to certain hermeneutical presuppositions.[28]

3.2.1.3 *Thesis 3: Limits within eschatological speaking*

In his third thesis, Rahner mentions two elements that delimit the space in which eschatological statements take place: (1) bounded in the revelation of the day of completion; and (2) bounded by the human historicity. Both are fundamental to the fourth and fifth thesis.

3.2.1.3.1 Limited in the revelation of the day of completion

Building upon Mark 13:32 and Acts 1:7, Rahner points out that not only the time of the completion day is hidden to humans, but even any data ontologically related to this completion day. The completion itself is still hidden for humanity. If this were not the case, the Christian existential characteristics of "faith" and "hope" would be superfluous. The Christian has no unambiguous perspective on what the future looks like. There is an irreconcilable and irremovable dialectic tension between *revealed* and *hidden* in eschatological statements. Revelation brings the *hidden* only from the state of unfamiliarity into the state of familiarity, as *revealed* and *known hidden*. At the same

---

26. Rahner, "Eschatologie: Theologisch," 1096. Cf. Fritsch, *Selbstmitteilung*, 69–71, 103.
27. Cf. Rahner, *Hörer*, 172..
28. Rahner, *Grundkurs*, 415; "Überlegungen zur Methode," 110; "Prinzipien," 407, 427.

time, what is revealed remains not completely understandable or comprehensible. Rahner calls this the "hidden character" of completion.[29] William Thomson rightly writes that Rahner's future is characterized as "uncontrollable and hidden yet also present, something we really look forward to, something in the presence of which we hope, dare, trust, and surrender ourselves."[30]

This hidden presence of completion is essential for Rahner. In *Frage nach der Zukunft* he clarifies this even more. The Christian theologian who takes the gospel seriously should always keep in mind that scientifically we cannot say anything about God's future (*docta ignorantia futuri*). Because of this, God, who is the "absolute future," can be distinguished from the socializable evolutionary and within-worldly future. There is a "wise ignorance of the future, the resolute engagement with the unplanned, the conviction that the venture into the open is not a dull remnant of irrationalism that is slowly dispelled, but a lasting existential and a moment at the dignity of human freedom."[31] From the relativization of one's own within-world future and the utopian longing, transformed by absolute hope, for a different (un-feasible, non-evolving, non-mechanical) absolute future, humans create for themselves a better within-world future, which they eventually exchange over time for an even better utopian within-world future.[32] In this process, humankind keeps its "yes" to creation in balance with its "yes" to its absolute future. The future kingdom of God cannot be simplistically planned by people from world history and does not only come from outside. It realizes itself as the act of God, which can be understood as the self-transcendence of world history. At the same time, human beings adhere to the principle of the *docta ignorantia futuri*. If humans were to understand, grasp, and calculate the future, this would bring the aforementioned utopian development process to a standstill. Then the presence of the human well-thought-out inner-world condition would be a realization and completion of the absolute future. Only a consistent adherence to the principle of the *docta ignorantia futuri* keeps humanity from this and makes it permanently critical of any utopian-inner-world design.[33]

However, this does not mean that humans continue without purpose. The critical note on the present is linked to positive *designs* of the future. It should be emphasized that these are *designs*. The future can only be sketched and not deterministically

29. Rahner, "Prinzipien," 418–19; "Christentum," 164.

30. Thompson, "Hope for Humanity," 158.

31. Rahner, "Frage," 536: "weise Nichtwissen der Zukunft, das entschlossene Sicheinlassen auf das Ungeplante, die Überzeugung, daß das Wagnis ins Offene nicht ein trüber Rest von Irrationalismus, der langsam ausgeräumt wird, sondern ein bleibendes Existential und ein Moment an der Würde der Freiheit des Menschen ist." Cf. "Christentum," 162. In Rahner's talk about this inner-world future, his resistance against Marxism, which thinks it can make the future its own, also plays an important role: "Marxistische," 77–88.

32. Rahner, "Frage," 526–27, 536–40; "Marxistische," 80–82; "Christentum," 159; "Prinzipien," 413. Rahner possibly derives the Latin terminology from Nicholas of Cusa (1401–1464). Cf. Edwards, "Resurrection," 369.

33. Rahner, "Frage," 538.

recorded as a building plan. Otherwise, this would endanger the freedom of the history of humanity. Rahner is categorical in this: "Who rejects the *docta ignorantia futuri* in such a way, is actually no longer a Christian."[34] In speaking of the absolute future, there must be a healthy balance between Christian reflection on God's future and the venture into the unknown. From this hermeneutical principle, a concrete understanding of what eternity, the glorified body, or the fellowship with all redeemed means is precluded. However, it remains possible to talk about these matters in an idea-based manner. Rahner thus advocates a precise distinction between content and form of eschatological statements.[35]

3.2.1.3.2 Limited by the human Geschichtlichkeit

Just like all physical creation, humans are subjected to time and space. Yet humanity knows something like *Geschichtlichkeit* (historicity). Humans are able to remember the past and to live with expectations for the future. This makes us unique and helps us to understand ourselves better (*Selbstverständnis*).[36] Because people are versatile, their expectations are also versatile. Their hope is thus focused on total salvation and not reduced to just the partial aspects of it. For Rahner, the latter is important:

> Where it would be overlooked that also in the question of salvation humans belong to their physical, spatiotemporal, bodily existence and that therefore the condition of humans and thus also that of their one and whole perfection must always be stated, then humans and their self-understanding would be mythologized in truth.[37]

Through the historicity of humanity, Rahner thus realizes that memories and expectations permanently influence a human's life and speech.

---

34. Rahner, "Frage," 538–39: "Wer so die docta ignorantia futuri ablehnt, ist eigentlich kein Christ mehr."

35. Rahner, "Ewigkeit," 430; "Prinzipien," 410. Cf. "Eschatologie: Theologisch," 1097.

36. Rahner, "Prinzipien," 410–11. Rahner's choice of words is a strong reminder of Martin Heidegger. This relationship between Heidegger and Rahner is a research question in itself. See: Rahner, "Erinnerungen," 34; "Introduction," 152–71. Karl Lehmann states: "The discipleship of Rahner from M. Heidegger is undeniable and repeatedly admitted by himself," in: Lehmann, "Karl Rahner," 161. In addition, Max Müller can be quoted: "Karl Rahner has never been Heidegger's 'pupil' (not even in his early work 'Geist in Welt') in the sense as if there had been a content-related (thus 'material') agreement and commonality of any kind; but the manner ('formaliter' thus) in which Heidegger's thinking took place has had the strongest effect on him," in: Müller, "Geist in Welt," 30–31. See further: Adams, "Eschatology," 292–98; Lehmann, "Philosophisches," 18–19; Muck, "Heidegger," 257–59; Hurd, "Heidegger and Aquinas," 132.

37. Rahner, "Prinzipien," 411: "[W]o übersehen würde, daß zum Menschen auch in der Heilsfrage seine physische, raumzeitliche, leibhaftige Existenz gehört und immer auch von daher die Verfassung des Menschen und also auch die seiner einen und ganzen Vollendung ausgesagt werden muß, da würde der Mensch und sein Selbstverständnis in Wahrheit mythologisiert."

The New Heaven and New Earth

3.2.2 Theses 4–5: Starting points

3.2.2.1 Thesis 4: Determined in terms of content by current Christology

Rahner's fourth thesis builds on his third thesis and focuses on the content of eschatological statements. In terms of content, eschatological statements only reveal what is necessary for a current understanding. They are not fully understood and comprehensible apocalyptic reports of the future, because of this conflict with the hidden character of the completion day (thesis 3a). These are statements about the future of the present, in which humans reflect on their self-understanding (thesis 3b). Precisely, because of the intrinsic relationship of being human, these statements do not remain alien or unprecedented. As a result, the future to which eschatological statements point must be truly present and thus ex-istence.[38] By placing apocalyptic negatively against eschatology, Rahner wants to avoid any speculative talk about the future. Apocalyptic is for him subjective utopia; eschatology, on the other hand, is objective in nature.

This leads Rahner to the statement that eschatological statements are limited to God's completion of humanity in salvation, which we already have hidden in Christ. Without wishing to elaborate a detailed foundation, Rahner recognizes all eschatological statements in Christian faith, such as the completion of the individual, humanity, and the world. All this, as a totality in Christ's resurrection, finds its new beginning in the present history. The salvation of all creation is permanently founded and brought about by the resurrection of the Messiah.[39] This makes the christological approach an important principle for the interpretation of eschatological statements. It should be noted that in Roman Catholic dogmatics, of which Rahner is a representative, soteriology is also embedded in Christology. It is related to the embedding of ecclesiology in Christology, and of soteriology and pneumatology in ecclesiology.

3.2.2.2 Thesis 5: Starting from a christological present

Like the fourth, the fifth thesis also builds on the third thesis. Rahner focuses here on the starting point (*Quelle*) from which eschatological statements originate and states that this starting point lies in current experience. This explains why the growth in clarity and scope of eschatological statements is inherent in the progress of salvation history. Again Rahner warns that eschatology is not an apocalyptic report of the future in the present. They are statements from the present to the future (thesis 3b): "Impression (*Einsage*) from the present into the future is eschatology, expression

---

38. Rahner, "Prinzipien," 407–8, 412–14, 418–19, 426. Cf. Rahner, *Grundkurs*, 414–15; "Eschatologie (SM)," 1187; "Überlegungen zur Methode," 110; "Parusie," 124; "Prinzipien," 413; *Grundkurs*, 414.

39. Rahner, "Prinzipien," 413, 414n11; *Grundkurs*, 426; "Christentum," 159; "Eschatologie: Theologisch," 1096. Cf. Vorgrimler, *Karl Rahner: Gotteserfahrung*, 424.

(*Aussage*) from the future into the present is apocalyptic."[40] He strongly emphasizes that apocalyptic "impression" is only fantasy or gnostic because it assumes that the future already exists in an over-temporal existence and only from there projects its content into this creation.[41]

If such an apocalyptic *Einsage* were true, it would have to be explained: (1) what would ultimately be the importance of such reports for the present; (2) how and if such a clearly defined report of the future can still offer openness to the future; and (3) why this report then comes to us in the form of various images or metaphors that correspond with each other in terms of content, but not in terms of forms of representation.[42] In this way, Rahner clearly separates eschatology from apocalyptic.

It should be emphasized that Rahner's fifth thesis does not focus on the content of eschatological statements (thesis 4) but on their starting point. The content of eschatological speech lies in the future; its starting point lies in the present. This implies that for Rahner eschatological statements about our eschatological existential situation (*eschatologische Daseinssituation*) are based on the completed work of Christ in the present and aims at the completion in the future. Humankind does not create this perspective on the future from its own experiences or worldview; it is given to it in faith by the word of God. This divine word is also connected with God's self-meditation (*Selbstmitteilung*) in Christ. Eschatological statements are inextricably related to the Person of Christ and his benefits to humans. They do not primarily inform about what is to come but interpret the present tense in the light of the Coming. Jesus Christ is the high point of eschatological revelation.[43] On the basis of this principle, Rahner interprets all conversations about eschatological completion as a transposition of Christology and anthropology. That Christology is central to this is evident from his choice to see Christian anthropology and Christian eschatology as sub-areas of it.[44]

In contrast to the demythologization that leads to absolute abstract existentialism (cf. thesis 1), Rahner clings to a concrete existence of humanity that in its completion, does not merge into an unknown mystical dimension. From this conviction, it is true that "there can be no eschatological statements that cannot be traced back to the Christian existence as it is now."[45] That does not in any way mean that the future is completely unknowable now. After all, that would lead to "de-eschatologization."

---

40. Rahner, "Prinzipien," 418: "Aus-sage von Gegenwart in Zukunft hinein ist Eschatologie, Einsage aus der Zukunft heraus in die Gegenwart hinein ist Apokalyptik." Cf. Rahner, "Prinzipien," 414–15; *Grundkurs*, 416.

41. Rahner, "Prinzipien," 418–19.

42. Rahner, "Prinzipien," 408, 416–17, 419, 423–24.

43. Rahner, "Prinzipien," 414–17. Cf. Rahner, "Eschatologie: Theologisch," 1096; "Überlegungen zur Methode," 110; "Dogmenentwicklung," 23–24; Vorgrimler, *Karl Rahner: Gotteserfahrung*, 99.

44. Rahner, "Prinzipien," 415–16; "Grundsätzliche," 406–10.

45. Rahner, "Prinzipien," 418: "es keine eschatologische Aussagen geben könne, die nicht auf die über diese christliche Existenz, so wie sie jetzt ist, zurückgeführt werden können." Cf. Rahner, "Prinzipien," 404–5, 411.

Rahner only argues that the future should manifest itself from the point of departure of the present. In a footnote, he briefly refutes the assumption that Jesus is an exception to this and that he would have had complete knowledge about the future.[46] A year later, during a guest lecture in Trier, Rahner would discuss this issue in more detail (December 9, 1961). He states that Christ did not receive his knowledge about the future from outside or through a *visio beatifica* as *Einsage*, but that this knowledge originated from within. This explains why the day of completion is also unknown to Jesus (Mark 13:32; cf. Matt 24:36) and why his wisdom could increase (Luke 2:52). Also, Jesus' eschatological proclamation is thus *Aussage* (expression) from his own experience in the present. Only in the awareness that he brought salvation and judgment in Person did Jesus' conviction exceed the expectations of his time.[47]

In Rahner's thinking, the present and the future are inextricably linked when it comes to eschatological statements. Eschatology is, therefore, more than a theoretical rational matter. It is necessary to allow the free choices of faith of humans to exist. The future is not merely an open possibility, but God has promised the future in Christ's kingdom of blessings. Humankind accepts this from a responsible, active relationship with God. This shows that eschatology may not be an appendix at the end of ST, but that it influences the whole of Christian theology or at least acts as a formal structural principle of all theological statements.[48]

3.2.3 Thesis 6: Consequences

Starting from the five theses mentioned, Rahner formulates in random order five (sub)theses, which together form his sixth thesis.

1. Heaven and hell are not at the same level: Because eschatological statements are based on God's grace in our time (theses 4–5), salvation and rejection are not on the same level. Primarily, eschatology speaks of Christ's blessing, completing grace. Heaven and hell should, therefore not receive the same weight in dogmatic thinking.[49]

2. Eschatology involves the individual and the collective: Eschatology involves the individual and the collective: Because Rahner assigns a place to the human being as an individual and the world as a totality within God's plan of salvation (cf. thesis 4), eschatology must be both individual and universal. Eschatology must be integral because individual eschatology and cosmological eschatology speak

---

46. Rahner, "Prinzipien," 416, 419n13.
47. Rahner, "Dogmatische Erwägungen," 223, 231, 234–44.
48. Rahner, "Frage," 520; *Grundkurs*, 414.
49. Rahner, "Prinzipien," 421–22; "Ewigkeit," 432; *Grundkurs*, 418.

of the same reality. Every individual is inextricably linked to the whole cosmos and everything that lives on it as a totality.[50]

3. Short and long-term expectations: For Rahner, it is pointless to make a distinction between a short and long-term expectation of the day of completion. Because eschatological statements are *Aussagen* from the present, they influence the near-present (short-term expectation) and the distant future (long-term expectation). From this perspective, they are of existential significance for the present. Those who lose sight of the latter lose the relevance of the eschatological statement for the present. On the other hand, anyone who only emphasizes the relevance for the present and sees eschatological statements exclusively as existential, "de-eschatologizes" humanity in the present (cf. thesis 5).[51] Marie Murphy wrongly concludes from this that Rahner argues for a realized eschatology: "Rahner's eschatology must be understood not only as an extension of his Christology but also as a realized eschatology."[52] However, Rahner does not argue for a realized eschatology, but for an eschatology that speaks from the present about future states of affairs and at the same time is also relevant to the present.[53]

4. Christ as a hermeneutical principle: Because eschatological statements are Christian-soteriologically determined in terms of both content and point of departure, Jesus Christ is the hermeneutical principle for the understanding of all eschatological statements (cf. theses 4–5). What cannot be interpreted from a christological-soteriological perspective, for Rahner, is "not a genuine eschatological statement, but fortune-telling and apocalypticism, or a misunderstood way of speaking, which does not see the Christological meaning."[54] The expectation of salvation focuses on the completion of the work of the risen Christ.

5. Eschatology is determined by Christ's salvation: With the help of Christology and principles of historical theology, Rahner observes that history has an end, in which the contrast between Christ and the world intensifies, and in which total history ends in God's final victory. Completion of this world thus means: (1) God's judgment, because completion is based on God's freedom; (2) Christ's return and judgment, because completion is the completion of Christ's blessed salvation; (3) individual judgment, because people do not lose their being and function; (4) general judgment, because the world is more than the sum of individuals; and (5) resurrection of the body and glorification of the world, because

---

50. Rahner, *Grundkurs*, 426; "Prinzipien," 423; "Eschatologie: Theologisch," 1098.
51. Rahner, "Prinzipien," 424; "Eschatologie: Theologisch," 1096.
52. Murphy, *Critical*, 194–95; *New Images*, 73.
53. See explicitly: Rahner, "Letzte Dinge," 221–22.
54. Rahner, "Prinzipien," 425–26: "keine echte eschatologische Aussage, sondern Wahrsagerei und Apokalyptik, oder eine nicht verstandene Redeweise, die das christologisch Gemeinte nicht sieht." Cf. "Ewigkeit," 432.

completion is the completion of Christ's resurrection.[55] In all this, the christocentric character of Rahner's eschatological speaking is clearly evident.

3.2.4 Thesis 7: Distinction of content and form

In thesis 3a, Rahner argues for a precise distinction between content and form of eschatological statements.[56] He elaborates on this in his seventh thesis. Form and content can be distinguished but cannot be separated. Eschatological statements are never myth- or imageless.[57] Every thought is an image; there is no "understanding" without images. Visual speech, therefore, remains indispensable.

Anyone who relates several eschatological statements about a subject to each other ensures that content and form are easier to distinguish. Other forms make the same content easier to imagine. At the same time, the content still does not allow itself to be squeezed out of the form. The speech does not lose the image. For this reason, eschatology continues to refer to the old biblical representations. Eschatology also continues to refer to the old sources.[58] Determining whether an interpretation of the imagery is correct is therefore, only possible for Rahner by examining to what extent the interpretation contradicts the general ecclesial doctrine that is laid down in confessions. If this is impossible, it must be examined whether the statement is derived from Christian anthropology and Christology, on which eschatology is based.[59] With this thesis, Rahner gives limited freedom to research into eschatological imagery.

3.2.5 Conclusion

In conclusion, Rahner states that his theses are the starting point for further research. The theologian should examine to which basis his own binding eschatological statements can be reduced. He should determine whether and how this starting point is related to his own christological, soteriological, or anthropological design, and from there transpose it to the eschatological completion of salvation. The connections between these four loci are important to Rahner. Finally, the hermeneutical principle necessary for the interpretation of biblical and systematic eschatology can be deduced from this. To those who are skeptical about this hermeneutical principle, Rahner poses at the end of his argument the provocative question of whether they can name an eschatological statement that is not related to Christology, soteriology, and/or anthropology.[60]

---

55. Rahner, "Prinzipien," 425–26.
56. Rahner, "Prinzipien," 410; "Eschatologie: Theologisch," 1097.
57. Rahner, "Prinzipien," 426–28; *Hörer*, 201–2.
58. Rahner, "Prinzipien," 427.
59. Rahner, "Prinzipien," 427–28.
60. Rahner, "Prinzipien," 510; "Eschatologie (SM)," 1191.

3.3 SPEAKING ABOUT THE NEW CREATION

3.3.1 Reticence without silence

Rahner remains cautious in his concrete descriptions of the hereafter. According to him, it is impossible to form an image of the new heaven and earth without degenerating into apocalyptic improbabilities. It is precisely the latter, based on his hermeneutic principles that he wants to avoid (theses 4–5; §3.2.2).[61] Eternal life, the salvation of time, the glorified body, the eternal union of all saints, and so on, cannot be imagined in concrete terms. Any attempt to do so is limited to imagery. Whoever claims to be able to give a concrete photograph of the new creation sounds as absurd as a caterpillar who claims to know what it means to be a butterfly. Whoever thinks that the current life in the new creation will have a continuation, such as a reunion of friends, a feast and jubilation, has to admit that his ideas will probably not endure the radical caesura which death brings with it. Rahner mainly lacks in these banal descriptions of the new heaven and the new earth the direct seeing of God, the highest love, the infinite knowing, and the authenticity of eternal life.[62]

Yet his reticence does not end in silence. In his concise publication *Über die Theologische Problematik der "Neuen Erde,"* Rahner focuses primarily on this theme.[63] This decision is in accordance with Vatican II, which in *Gaudium et Spes* speaks of the "new earth" as the transformation of this earth (*transformatio mundi; universum transformandi*) and as God's eschatological gift that is not only the result of human effort. At the same time, Rahner acknowledges that this theme, with its important question about the relationship between Christian-eschatological hope and the human ideology of the future, has not yet been elaborated in-depth. For this reason, his publication on this subject begins with all kinds of questions for the reader: Does the new earth descend from heaven or does humanity realize it from time? Can our responsibility for the earth in the hereafter be distinguished from the "heavenly father city" in the hereafter? Is the earth only the temporary "material" that humanity cultivates for the lasting good deeds in the new creation? Are we contributors to this new creation if we are righteous, loving, and obedient to God's creative task? Or is what humanity is processing no more than fuel for the future world fire?[64]

Rahner answers these questions from a middle position: the Kingdom of God comes to us from above, but is not separate from the present history. Absolute and inner world future do not go together (cf. §3.2.1.3); immanent and transcendent completion does. As he writes elsewhere: "The transcendent accomplishment of

---

61. Rahner, *Grundkurs*, 428; "Neue Erde," 589; *Auferstehung*, 23.
62. Rahner, "Erfahrungen," 118; "Ewigkeit," 430; "Diskussionsbeiträge Zeitbegriff," 238; "Verborgener Sieg," 154; "Auferstehung (STh)," 220, 222–23.
63. Rahner, "Neue Erde," 580–92.
64. Vaticanum II, *Gaudium et Spes*, §38–39; Rahner, "Neue Erde," 586; "Immanente," 597.

personal freedom is the only true immanent accomplishment."[65] This history remains imperfect and is unable to change its finiteness into permanence. What is permanent, however, is the fruit of the love that grows in this finite history.

3.3.2 Christological perspective: matter and time

As can be expected by virtue of his hermeneutical principles, Rahner connects his speaking about the new earth with Christ. Christ is not just an *Exemplarursache* ("specimen cause") of the resurrection of all things. As the first definitively glorified Risen One, he is the objective and decisive beginning of the glorification of the world.[66] During a meditation on Silent Saturday, Rahner declares:

> Christ is already in the midst of all the poor things on this earth that we cannot leave because she is our mother. He is in the nameless wait of all creatures who, without knowing it, wait for the participation in the transfiguration of his body.[67]

At Easter, the eschatological final comes into being. It is "the perfection of the world into the God who really becomes everything in everyone through the event of Easter, which has already begun, but is still perfected in us."[68]

From this hermeneutical principle, Rahner denies any separation between "soul" and "body" in the eschaton. Even after his resurrection, Jesus of Nazareth remains the eternal Godmind: "his humanity is not only the one rewarded with glory, but it remains his own above all."[69] Matter has an eternal future in God's plan of salvation and does not disappear in the eschaton as "superfluous." Christian faith, in the midst of all pessimism, declares that there is hope for the matter. Thanks to God's grace, this evolving world will also have an ultimate intimacy with God. Christ's resurrection in the history of salvation makes an irreversible beginning that finds its purpose in the final intimacy between Creator and creation. In several other works, Rahner explores this hermeneutic principle in more detail. Because of the core value, this has in Rahner's thinking about the hereafter, this subject of matter deserves further investigation (§3.4).

---

65. Rahner, "Immanente," 598: "Die transzendente Vollendung einer personalen Freiheit ist die einzig wahre immanente Vollendung" Cf. Rahner, "Immanente," 603; "Neue Erde," 588–90; "Christentum," 174; Rahner, "Kirche," 366.

66. Rahner, "Auferstehung (SM)," 421–23; "Dogmatische Fragen," 167; "Auferstehung (STh)," 222.

67. Rahner, "Verborgener Sieg," 156: "Christus ist schon inmitten all der armen Dinge dieser Erde, die wir nicht lassen können, weil sie unsere Mutter ist. Er ist im namenlosen Harren aller Kreaturen, die, ohne es zu wissen, harrt [sic!] auf die Teilnahme an der Verklärung seines Leibes."

68. Rahner, "Dogmatische Fragen," 171: "die Vollendung der Welt in den Gott hinein, der wirklich alles in allen wird durch das Ereignis von Ostern, das schon begonnen hat, aber sich in uns noch vollendet."

69. Rahner, "Neue Erde," 590: "seine Menschheit ist nicht nur die mit Glorie belohnte, sondern sie bleibt vor allem seine eigene."

Another element that emerges from Christ through this same hermeneutic speaking is Rahner's vision of history, eternity, and time. Because Jesus is a participant in history during his life and death on earth, the permanent final goal of his life is not outside, but in history: "So then history itself must have a final meaning if morality is to have such a meaning."[70] Death radically changes the concrete history:

> For because death is the end of time as its perfect validity and therefore eternity, that which "follows" death (and resurrection as an essential moment in this death) is exactly that which occurs in death as the final. And vice versa: What happens here is the final and thus the true and forever real and active.[71]

From this, Rahner deduces that humans, together with their lived life history, find God as a conclusion. The individual history of life and the collective history of family and community remain "saved" and recognizable.[72] Although Rahner only touches on this briefly in his publication on the new earth, he elaborates on his views on history, time, and eternity in other works. Just like Rahner's idea about matter and the hereafter, this subject of eternity and time deserves further investigation (§3.5).

3.3.3 Protological perspective

In his publication about the new earth, Rahner briefly refers to the commission that God gave humanity in Genesis 1.[73] The question arises to what extent this commission makes humans responsible for the realization of the ultimate new earth. Rahner himself points out that this task implies that the future of the earth is not separate from that of human history: "Humankind itself creates them as the completion of God's creation entrusted to it in a historical becoming,"[74] and for humanity, it holds: "that he has a respective world at his disposal, which he must take over in freedom."[75]

Although Rahner repeatedly points to the need for a deep reflection on the relationship between eschatology and protology, this reflection is lacking in his own works. All that remains is a slight touch of the subject, the basic tone of which is: "the

---

70. Rahner, "Neue Erde," 590: "Somit muß also die Geschichte selbst eine endgültige Bedeutung haben, soll das Sittliche eine solche haben."

71. Rahner, "Dogmatische Fragen," 169: "Weil nämlich der Tod das Ende der Zeit als ihre vollendete Gültigkeit und darum Ewigkeit ist, ist das, was 'nach' dem Tod (und der Auferstehung als wesentlichem Moment an diesem Tod) folgt, genau das, was im Tod als Endgültiges sich ereignet. Und umgekehrt: Was sich hier ereignet, ist das Endgültige und so das wahrhaft und für immer Wirkliche und Wirkende." Cf. Rahner, "Neue Erde," 589–90.

72. Rahner, "Neue Erde," 589–91.

73. Rahner, "Neue Erde," 586, 591.

74. Rahner, "Neue Erde," 586: "der Mensch selbst schafft sie als die ihm aufgetragene Vollendung der Schöpfung Gottes in einem geschichtlichen Werden."

75. Rahner, "Prinzipien," 423: "daß ihm eine jeweilige Welt verfügt ist, die er in Freiheit übernehmen muß."

relationship between protology and e[schatology] remains unreflected."[76] Also, in one of his contributions to two encyclopedias on protology, he only mentions the need for such reflection.[77] In his article on *Schöpfungslehre* we learn:

> For the doctrine of creation must not only and primarily consider the beginning of the reality different from God as a temporal individual moment, but creatureliness as the lasting basic relationship of humans to God; yes, the doctrine of creation would thus be the first piece of such a formal and fundamental theology at all ... the doctrine of creation is thus, seen in this way, a formal moment in a doctrine about the history of salvation and thus the doctrine of the condition of the possibility of an eschatological completion. Insofar as spirit and matter are included in the history of salvation, both of which have the same beginning and the one goal, the doctrine of creation has not only to make the difference between matter and spirit but its unity in origin and goal.[78]

The *Urgeschichte* ("pre-history") is also *Übergeschichte* ("meta-history") by Rahner. In his general talk about matter, it also appears that Rahner considers protological-eschatological thinking of great importance, although he lacks a specific effect of this (cf. §3.4.1).[79] Apart from the fact that a protology, which takes matter into account, influences eschatological speech, Rahner says nothing about the relationship between protology and eschatology.

Rahner connects protology with Christology. The former must be subordinate to the latter: the protology must focus on Christology so that the cosmic aspect in Christology does not fade away. Christ is the beginning and triumph in God's plan of salvation. Rahner also sees this relationship between protology and the inter-worldly future, which humanity creates or evolves from creation (cf. §3.2.1.3).[80] But in speaking about the absolute future, there is no such explicit connection that points to the completion of a protological principle. Only speaking on the basis of the "now" with

---

76. Rahner, "Eschatologie (SM)," 1186: "das Verhältnis von Protologie und E[schatologie] bleibt unreflektiert."

77. Rahner, "Protologie (SM)," 1353–54; "Protologie (LThK)," 181; "Eschatologie: Theologisch," 1095.

78. Rahner, "Schöpfungslehre," 471–72: "Denn die S[chöpfungslehre] muß nicht nur u. in erster Linie den Anfang der von Gott verschiedenen Wirklichkeit als zeitl. Einzelmoment bedenken, sondern die Geschöpflichkeit als bleibendes Grundverhältnis des Menschen zu Gott; ja die S. wäre so das erste Stück einer solchen formalen u. fundamentalen Theologie überhaupt.... S. ist also, so gesehen, ein formales Moment an einer Lehre über die Heilsgeschichte u. somit die Lehre von der Bedingung der Möglichkeit einer eschatolog. Vollendung. Insofern in der Heilsgeschichte Geist u. Materie einbegriffen sind, die beide denselben setzenden Anfang u. das eine Ziel haben, hat die S. nicht nur den Unterschied von Materie u. Geist, sondern ihre Einheit in Ursprung u. Ziel zu machen."

79. Rahner, "Grundsätzliche," 418–20; "Protologie (SM)," 1355.

80. Rahner, *Grundkurs*, 183, 194; "Frage," 523–24; "Christologie im Rahmen," 227–41; "Schöpfungslehre," 472.

regard to the "later" emphasizes Rahner on account of his hermeneutics.[81] The question of whether God's future is completely separate from God's beginning is thus insufficiently addressed.

3.3.4 The imagery of the eschaton

In his *Theologische Prinzipien der Hermeneutik Eschatologischer Aussagen* Rahner briefly talks about the use of eschatological imagery (§3.2.4). In his writings, he returns several times to the use of these images in eschatology. Rahner recognizes that reflection on the way one deals with imagery is important in correctly speaking about eschatology. According to him, too few theologians in the field of eschatology have thought about the interpretation of biblical imagery.[82] Because the research into this also touches the field of BT, this subject deserves our attention in the study of the relation between BT and ST in speaking about the new creation. We focus here on Rahner's hermeneutical-methodological handling of the biblical imagery and on the imagery he himself uses in speaking about the new creation.

3.3.4.1 *Unity in diversity*

With regard to the new creation, Rahner is aware that the biblical images of this are multiple:

> Scripture describes the content of the blessed life of the dead in thousands of images: as rest and peace, as a banquet and glory, as being at home in the Father's house, as the kingdom of the eternal reign of God, as the community of all the blessed, as the inheritance of the glory of God, as a day without downfall, as saturation without annoyance.[83]

From the broad variation in the biblical images of the hereafter, Rahner emphasizes in his own question about the use of imagery that the biblical imagery should not be regarded as a picture postcard of the eschaton: "A harmonizing balance of the pictorial elements on their level is . . . completely superfluous and not at all in the sense of writing."[84] However, Rahner does not see any contrasts in these diverse images. The

---

81. Rahner, "Prinzipien," 412–26.

82. Rahner, "Theologie und Anthropologie," 55. As an example Rahner mentions someone who claims that, on one hand, the trumpet of the archangel does not consist of tubular material and, on the other hand, that the trumpet gives a material sound (64–65).

83. Rahner, *Grundkurs*, 423: "Die Inhaltlichkeit des seligen Lebens der Toten beschreibt die Schrift in tausend Bildern, als Ruhe und Frieden, als Gastmahl und Herrlichkeit, als Daheimsein im Vaterhaus, als Reich ewiger Gottesherrschaft, als Gemeinschaft aller selig Vollendeten, als Erbschaft der Herrlichkeit Gottes, als Tag ohne Untergang, als Sättigung ohne Überdruß." Cf. Rahner, *Auferstehung*, 23; "Auferstehung (STh)," 216.

84. Rahner, "Auferstehung (STh)," 219: "Ein harmonisierender Ausgleich der Bildelemente auf ihrer Ebene ist . . . völlig überflüssig und gar nicht im Sinn der Schrift." Cf. "Prinzipien," 416.

variety in biblical images shows the rich diversity of the future. Unity in the diversity of biblical imagery should be sought.[85]

3.3.4.2 *De-mythologization of imagery*

Because Rahner pays attention to form and content in eschatological statements (§3.2.4), he rejects Rudolf Bultmann's demythologization idea in his methodical handling of biblical imagery (§3.2.1). Although the biblical books carry an antique and dated worldview, it is impossible for Rahner to remove the image from the imagery. Anyone who thinks that this is possible by demythologizing the metaphors does not realize,

> that he has no reason to demythologize and that such demythologization is basically nothing other than his own . . . the justified method which is badly applied in concrete terms, because one rightly throws out the bathwater and wrongly throws out the baby. This criticism of the schemes of ideas is constantly unfinished, for it can always only be done with the help of other "ideas."[86]

In short: those who demythologize replace the original imagery with new imagery of their own. In this way, Rahner is in line with his hermeneutical principle, mentioned in §3.2.4, which distinguishes form and content but never separates them. Every abstract speech ultimately remains a speech in image and likeness.[87]

Michael Barnes and Anne Carr rightly ask themselves, just as we do (see §3.2.1), what exactly Rahner means when he maintains the term "demythologize."[88] The term "myth" is a vague term in theology. Rudolf Bultmann also uses it to refer to the religious fabrications that are part of the biblical text. By removing the "myths" from the text, the "true essence" of the text emerges.[89] Rahner does not think in this direction when he speaks of "demythologizing." He warns against this because this conception of "myth" reduces the form and content of imagery to human fantasies.[90] For Rahner, the "myth" is therefore rather the metaphor itself that serves to proclaim deeper theological truths in such a way that it transcends the listener's own reality. According to

---

85. Rahner, "Prinzipien," 417; "Auferstehung (STh)," 218.

86. Rahner, "Auferstehung (STh)," 217: "daß er keinen Grund hat zu entmythologisieren und daß eine solche Entmythologisierung im Grund nichts anderes ist als seine eigene . . . berechtigte Methode, die konkret schlecht angewendet wird, weil man mit Recht das Bad ausschüttet und mit Unrecht das Kind dazu. Diese Kritik der Vorstellungsschemata ist dauernd unabgeschlossen; denn es kann immer nur mit Hilfe anderer 'Vorstellungen.'"

87. Rahner and Vorgrimler, *Wörterbuch*, 103; Rahner, "Prinzipien," 426; "Auferstehung (STh)," 218.

88. Barnes, "Karl Rahner," 24; Carr, *Theological Method*, 188, 217, 265.

89. Bultmann, *Jesus*, 20. Cf. Johnson, *Origins*.

90. Rahner, "Theologie und Anthropologie," 58; "Prinzipien," 418; Rahner and Vorgrimler, *Wörterbuch*, 291.

him, "demythologization" in the positive sense of the word only serves to grasp the content of ancient imagery.[91] Because Rahner uses the term "demythologize" both positively and negatively several times in his works, this can cause confusion for the reader.[92] The context should then decide whether Rahner opposes demythologization, as Bultmann defends it, or whether he speaks of his own conception of positive demythologization.

3.3.4.3 Conflicting methodological signals

Rahner's approach to demythologization is in keeping with his plea not to separate content and form in imagery. Speaking in images remains insurmountable in human language. Rahner realizes that in many situations, it is impossible to distinguish between form and content at all. Images and content then fully permeate each other. In such situations, a Christian theologian must adhere to biblical speaking. A strict separation between image and speech is impossible at such moments. This makes the biblical imagery a permanent form of speaking about the reality of the new creation. God's absolute future can only be spoken of in images and parables.[93]

Anyone who wants to talk about the content of biblical images should compare several eschatological images about the same themes with each other and with the complete Christian doctrine of faith (thesis 7): "each one is not only understandable in the context of the other but even in its content it cannot be clearly distinguished from the other."[94] Rahner also finds this principle in the Bible, where writers build on previous revelations and reveal new relationships between them.[95]

He does not arrive at a clear own interpretation of the individual biblical images. Despite his remark, "Sacred Scripture is the inexhaustible source of all theology, without which theology would have to become sterile."[96] He shows in his writings the influence of his philosophical training and the way Roman Catholic dogmatics practiced theology during his days. A reference to a biblical text remains a rarity, despite the call of Vatican II to make drastic changes to it.[97] This partly leads to the fact that Rahner's own thoughts about the new creation are little filled with the dynamics of

---

91. Rahner, "Zu einer Theologie des Todes," 181–99; "Christentum," 174; Rahner and Vorgrimler, *Theological Dictionary*, 303.

92. Barnes, "Karl Rahner," 24–45. E.g., Rahner, "Auferstehung (STh)," 217.

93. Rahner, "Christentum," 173; "Prinzipien," 410, 426–28; "Eschatologie: Theologisch," 1079; "Auferstehung (STh)," 217–18; "Auferstehung (STh)," 216–17.

94. Rahner, "Letzte Dinge," 221: "jede ist nicht nur im Zusammenhang met de anderen verständlich, aber läßt sich sogar in ihrem Inhalt nicht absolut eindeutig von einer anderen absetzen." Cf. Rahner, "Auferstehung (STh)," 219.

95. Rahner, "Christentum," 174; "Prinzipien," 403, 427–28.

96. Rahner, "Schriftbeweis," 486: "[d]ie Heilige Schrift ist ja die unerschöpfl[iche] Quelle aller Theologie, ohne die die Theologie steril werden müßte."

97. Vaticanum II, *Dei Verbum*, §21–26; Vaticanum II, *Optatam Totius*, §16.

the biblical imagery. In his talk about cosmological eschatology, Rahner is even very skeptical about the biblical images. This is especially the case in his talk about time and eternity. Then the biblical images of the new creation stand in the same line for him as the imaginative representations of Dante Alighieri's (1265–1321) long poem *La Divina Commedia*.[98]

In his treatise on the resurrection, Rahner shows only a brief example of his methodical principle. This concerns the representation of the trumpet sound and the graves that open up when the resurrection takes place. There is no fear of apostasy for those who think about the tone in which the archangel blows the trumpet or how the relationship between the broadcasting of angels fits in with biblical-eschatological speaking. It is possible to interpret statements such as these as imagery and, at the same time, respect God's power over death.[99]

In conclusion, it can be said that Rahner's reservation with the integration of imagery in ST at the same time aggravates the methodical approach he proposes with regard to biblical imagery. First, he states that the multifaceted imagery entails a lack of clarity and warns against interpreting these images concretely in dogmatic reflection.[100] The latter stems from his hermeneutical principle that eschatological statements can be separated from apocalyptic (§3.2.2). The imagery is, therefore too concrete to be used objectively.[101] Second, Rahner encourages the reader to reflect methodically on how to deal with imagery and to integrate it into an eschatological design. After all, imagery is much richer than abstract language and offers an advantage because it can be interpreted in many ways. Several images thus enrich speaking about the eschaton. It is important for Rahner that ST "through true biblical theology is a visualizing under Scripture."[102] In this way, the reader receives the contradictory signal from Rahner that he should, on the one hand, integrate imagery into the Christian doctrine of faith and, on the other hand, that he should not do so.

3.4 MATTER AND SPIRIT IN THE ESCHATON

In his eschatological reflections, Rahner turns against the idea that creation is only a stage on which the drama of God and humanity takes place:

> Christianity knows no history of spirit and existence which would simply be the overcoming and repulsion of the material, for which the history of the cosmos would at most offer the external stage on which the drama of the personal spirit and its gift for God would take place in such a way that, when the

---

98. Rahner, "Ewigkeit," 430.
99. Rahner, "Auferstehung (STh)," 218–19.
100. Vorgrimler, *Karl Rahner: Gotteserfahrung*, 271.
101. Rahner, "Prinzipien," 427.
102. Rahner, "Schriftbeweis," 487: "durch echte Biblische Theologie ein Sichstellen unter der Schrift ist."

play has happened, the actors will leave the stage and the stage itself, dead and empty, would be left to its own devices.[103]

The history of the earth or cosmogony is inextricably linked to the history of mankind. For this reason, Rahner's interpretation of matter—in the context of the eschaton—is important in his deeper analysis of the new heaven and earth.

3.4.1 Creation as a planned design

3.4.1.1 *Call for an anthropocentric turnaround*

In his works, Rahner points out that an anthropological foundation is necessary for systematic theology. In his theological works, anthropological reflection dominates. This is most frequently expressed in *Theologie und Anthropologie, Grundsätzliche Überlegungen zur Anthropologie und Protologie im Rahmen der Theologie* and *Überlegungen zur Methode der Theologie* and in the chosen pattern of *Grundkurs des Glaubens*.[104]

Hans Urs von Balthasar saw in this emphasis the danger of an anthropological reduction.[105] Rahner clarifies, however, that he does not want to be an "anthropocentric theologian." Rather, he wants to characterize himself as a theologian who advocates that God is the most important in this world, that humanity exists for God's sake, and that God may love God in such a way that humanity forgets itself.[106]

This impetus should result that theology once again began to question the essence of humanity. Rahner hoped that the theology of the twentieth century would experience an anthropocentric turnaround and would thoroughly rethink the common anthropocentric approach. Modern anthropocentrism found its foundation in Enlightenment thinking. As a result, the contemplation of humanity became detached from the contemplation of God. During the Enlightenment, there was a fierce criticism of Judeo-Christian anthropocentrism, and a radical reinterpretation of humanity as the bearer of God's image and reality as a whole took place.[107] Rahner seriously questioned this modern anthropocentric approach and its rejection of what was

---

103. Rahner, "Christentum," 172: "Das Christentum kennt keine Geschichte des Geistes und der Existenz, die einfach die Überwindung und Abstoßung des Materiellen wäre, für die die Geschichte des Kosmos höchstens äußerlich die Bühne böte, auf der sich das Drama des personalen Geistes und seiner Begabung mit Gott derart abspielen würde, daß, wenn das Stück geschehen ist, die Spieler die Bühne verlassen und diese selbst, tot und leer, sich selbst überlassen bliebe." Cf. Rahner, "Diskussionsbeiträge Raum und Zeit," 266; *Grundkurs*, 427–28; "Einheit von Geist und Materie," 338–39; "Immanente," 605; "Schöpfungslehre," 474.

104. Rahner, *Grundkurs*; "Überlegungen zur Methode"; "Grundsätzliche"; "Theologie und Anthropologie."

105. Von Balthasar, *Glaubhaft ist nur die Liebe*, 19–32.

106. Imhof and Biallowons, *Karl Rahner: Im Gespräch*, 2:166.

107. Rahner, "Anthropologie," 180. Cf. Losinger, *Anthropological Turn*, xxii, 6; Weger, *Karl Rahner*, 40; Möller, *Chance*, 22–32.

theological. According to him, anthropology and theology were inextricably linked. Both were concerned with the essential existence of humankind.

Rahner, therefore, describes his systematic theology as "transcendental anthropology."[108] From this basic attitude, he states that a correct understanding of theocentrism can only develop in an anthropocentrism that finds its starting point in the grace that God communicates in Christ. However, in the context of our research into Rahner's vision of the new heaven and the new earth, it is less relevant to discuss this anthropological perspective in detail here. Therefore, the above suggestions are sufficient to elaborate on Rahner's further reflection on matter and spirit and their relation to the eschaton.[109]

3.4.1.2 A positive view of creation

The eschatology of Rahner is characterized by a positive view of creation. Creation is not a superfluous product of chance but a God's design. Rahner's sermon on Romans 8 is entitled: "Creation is designed such that it fits us" (*Die Schöpfung ist entworfen, dass sie zu uns passt*). Whoever sees the world as God's creation acknowledges that it was constructed according to a unique, universal, and meaningful plan. Although Rahner has an anthropocentric elaboration of this planning of creation, the cosmological perspective of the new heaven and earth also emerges, when he writes: "Everything suffers as it were after the birth pangs of the new and completed creation."[110] This idea is enclosed in the preached biblical section (Rom 8:19–23) and is borrowed from Henri de Lubac by Rahner.[111] In this preaching, however, the relation between the present creation and the new creation remains off the radar. Rahner only notes that humankind in slavery is subject to the present time (see further §3.5).[112]

Besides the anthropocentric purpose, this creation has also a theocentric purpose: God is given in love to creation through creation. Grace and Incarnation are part of creation and are not external additions to it. The creation of creation was "from the beginning a moment at the more comprehensive and radical will of God . . . to communicate himself to the non-divine other."[113] Creator and creation are different

---

108. Rahner, "Gnade als Mitte," 83; "Transzendentaltheologie," 324–29; "Überlegungen zur Methode," 96. Cf. Bokwa, *Christologie*; Schaeffler, *Wechselbeziehungen*, 187–228; Muck, *Transzendentale Methode*; Rahner, *Grundkurs*, 223–25; "Theologische Dimension," 390; "Überlegungen zur Methode," 96; "Anthropozentrik," 632–34.

109. See: Brett, *Theological Notion*; Losinger, *Anthropological Turn*; Fischer, *Mensch als Geheimnis*; Eicher, *Anthropologische Wende*.

110. Rahner, "Schöpfung," 112: "Alles leidet gleichsam nach die Geburtswehen der neuen und vollendeten Schöpfung." See for the first one: "Schöpfung," 110, 113.

111. Cf. Klein, "Karl Rahner on the Soul," 4–5.

112. Rahner, "Schöpfung," 110.

113. Rahner, "Christologie im Rahmen," 231: "von vornherein ein Moment an dem unfassenderen und radikaleren Willen Gottes . . ., sich selbst dem nichtgöttlichen anderen mitzuteilen" Cf. Rahner,

but not separate in this respect. There is no question of deism. God is much more the One who undertakes a journey with this creation to which God wants to be given as triune God.[114] We already saw that impetus in Rahner's talk of a transcendental anthropocentric theology (§3.4.1.1).

3.4.1.3 Rejection of any dualism

Rahner turns sharply against any dualism that separates God and creation. He disputes any (neo)platoons or gnostic thinking that does not offer any room in advance for matter in the eschaton. For God, as Creator is the source of heaven, earth, spirit, and matter, as Genesis 1 suggests.[115] In the eschaton, the material creation, which God created as good, does not disappear. Who confesses this idea,

> loves "the Absolute," but not the God who is the Creator of heaven and earth. One basically hates the created real, because it is not that which is inherently unconditional. It is called the relative, the contingent, that which, in relation to God, can only be determined negatively, the mere delimitation of the per se infinite Being, on which it depends alone. It forgets that precisely this condition is the unconditionally beloved of the unconditionally beloved, that it, therefore, has a validity that makes it more than mere runaway, to a dissolving before God, that this created "unconditionally" forbids us (in spite of all philosophy, which has not yet been baptized enough), that it is also merely in relation to God purely negatively.[116]

Such a separation between the immaterial and the material is non-Christian and as odious as a polytheism that worships created powers and forces as divine. The God who is proclaimed by the Christian is a God-with-creation who shows his unconditional love for this creation and does not leave or remove it godless, as Gnosticism does.[117]

"Buch Gottes," 278–91; "Eigenart," 185–94; *Grundkurs*, 196–97; "Über das Verhältnis," 336–40; "Scholastischen Begrifflichkeit," 360, 374.

114. Rahner, "Eigenart," 189–92.

115. Rahner, "Leib," 407–8, 420; "Einheit von Geist und Materie," 338; *Auferstehung*, 27; "Eschatologie: Theologisch," 1094; "Auferstehung (STh)," 224.

116. Rahner, "Ewige Bedeutung," 53–54: "liebt 'das Absolute', aber nicht den Gott, der Schöpfer [des] Himmels und der Erde ist. Man haßt im Grunde das geschaffene Wirkliche, weil es nicht das von sich aus Unbedingte ist; man nennt es das Relative, das Kontingente, das, bezogen auf Gott, nur negative Bestimmbare, die bloße Eingrenzung des an sich unendlichen Seins, auf das es allein ankommt, und vergißt, daß eben dieses Bedingte das unbedingt vom Unbedingten Geliebte ist, daß es daher eine Gültigkeit hat, die es zu mehr macht als zum bloß Verläufigen, zu einem sich vor Gott Auflösenden, daß dieses geschaffen Unbedingte uns verbietet (trotz aller Philosophie, die auch bei uns noch nicht genug getauft ist), es auch bloß in bezug [sic!] zu Gott rein negativ zu werten."

117. Rahner, "Theologische Bemerkungen," 231; "Immanente," 609; "Einheit von Geist und Materie im christlichen Glaubensverständnis," 183–84, 187–95; "Ewige Bedeutung," 54.

For Rahner, the created reality also has a material glorification and transformation that will last forever. The world:

> [I]s in eternity also the perfection of the spirit and the expression of this perfected spirit. Therefore, it participates in its final lot "transfigured," as we say. And that is why we confess that the end will be a new heaven and a new earth.[118]

That is why we acknowledge that the end will be a new mold and a new honor. Thus, matter also shares in God's eschatologically consuming work and does not vanish from view. The world knows no end of itself. It knows only one end of contemporary history. As a world, it shares in the completion of the mind. This was already mentioned by Rahner in his hermeneutical principles, when he wrote about the eschatology of the completion of humanity in the resurrection (§3.2.2). World history, as we know it today with its struggles and difficulties ends, while the world itself enters into glorification.

3.4.2 Unity of matter and spirit

3.4.2.1 *Unappetizing affiliation*

In Rahner's thinking, mind and matter form a complex inextricable unity with each other. The mind is so connected to matter that any dualism is inadmissible. A human cannot be split forever into a separate soul and a separate body. Despite the duality between mind and matter, it concerns two aspects of the same reality that are next to each other and not opposite each other. When natural science or materialism states that humans consist only of matter, they forget that humans are also thinking, recognizable subjects with their own consciousness. If idealism, on the other hand, reduces humankind to an in-itself formed abstract spiritual subject, it forgets that humankind as such only understands itself from the time, space, and matter around it. The smallest "spiritual" thought or the most sublime act of choice does not ignore the human matter. Physicality is therefore not "something" that comes to the mind. Physicality is the concrete presence of the mind itself in space-time.[119]

Here the question arises how this idealistic view of the body, as an expression of the mind, can then be related to Rahner's view that the mind originates from the material existence of humanity. Elsewhere Rahner points out that human consciousness

---

118. Rahner, "Christentum," 173: "ist auch in Ewigkeit in der Vollendung des Geistes der Ausdruck dieses vollendeten Geistes und nimmt darum "verklärt" wie wir sagen, an seinem endgültigen Los teil. Und darum bekennen wir daß das Ende ein neuer Himmel und eine neue Erde sein wird." Cf. "Theologie der Hoffnung," 575; "Immanente," 605; "Neue Erde"; "Fest," 180; "Kirche," 348; "Schöpfungslehre," 474.

119. Rahner, "Naturwissenschaft," 61–62; "Theologische Bemerkungen," 315; "Immanente," 605; *Auferstehung*, 20; "Auferstehung (STh)," 219–23; "Prinzipien," 423.

originates from a material evolution process. Because humans can primarily be characterized as "spirit," matter can be described as "frozen spirit" (*gefrorener Geist*) and the spirit is transcendental elevated above matter.[120] Because matter is connected to the mind, it can thus develop and complete itself.

Rahner further clarifies this by characterizing matter as "not being given to itself" (*das sich selbst nicht gegebene Sein*), while spirit stands for "being given to itself" (*Sein in Selbstbesitz*). God the absolute Spirit who produced matter, also created matter because of the spirit contained in it. So the spirit did not enter matter through a later intervention of God. From the beginning, it was already contained in the created matter. The spirit is, therefore not a stranger in creation. Every human experiences how his mind and body originate from the primitive materials of a sperm cell and egg cell.[121] Rahner extrapolates this thought about humanity to all matter because evolution does not make a difference between humans, animals or other matter in terms of developmental origin. His vision of matter is therefore anthropocentric oriented from his transcendental anthropocentric approach (§3.4.1.1). He does see the present evolutionary coherence of spirit and matter in connection with God.[122]

3.4.2.2 *Eschatological postulate*

With regard to the eschaton, this inseparable connection between matter and spirit means that in materiality and immateriality, humanity has only one ultimate goal and one final completion. Even after death, the soul is not separated from matter. It remains fully connected with this creation. The immortality of the soul can, therefore also be characterized as the biblical hope for the resurrection of the body. At the same time, however, Rahner emphasizes that death encompasses the whole human being in soul, spirit, and body. The deceased is then focused on God and connected with all creation.[123]

This conscious choice of Rahner to link matter and spirit inseparably turns radically against the idea that humans exist only immaterially forever. He wants to prevent that "the 'soul' is ascribed a perfection par excellence, which is completely independent of the future fate of the body."[124] Who dies is not torn from creation, either if he or she is absorbed into creation. In conclusion, Rahner states:

---

120. Rahner, "Leib," 422; *Hörer*, 71; "Hominisation," 48, 52–53, 57; "Anthropozentrik," 632–33.

121. Rahner, "Naturwissenschaft," 47–48; "Theologische Bemerkungen," 318; "Hominisation," 51–52, 59–61, 79–80, 83–85, 88; "Geheimnis des Lebens," 171–84; "Christologie innerhalb," 183–221; "Christentum," 173; *Auferstehung*, 23–24. Cf. Aquinas, *Summa*, I.76.1–3; Edwards, "Relationship," 8.

122. Rahner, "Einheit," 337–40.

123. Rahner, *Grundkurs*, 191; "Leib," 418; "Abgestiegen ins Totenreich," 148; "Einheit von Geist und Materie im christlichen Glaubensverständnis," 185–214; *Auferstehung*, 27; "Christentum," 173; *Zur Theologie des Todes*, 148–420.

124. Rahner, "Zwischenzustand," 459: "der 'Seele' für sich eine Vollendung schlechthin zugesprochen wird, die vom noch künftigen Schicksal des Leibes völlig unabhängig ist." Cf. *Zur Theologie des Todes*, 22.

> So we Christians are the most sublime materialists: we cannot and must not think of the perfection of the spirit and of reality at all unless we also think of the permanence of matter and its perfection.[125]

Michael Barnes recognizes that the way Rahner speaks about this relationship between spirit and matter is in line with the biblical speaking about the future kingdom and the new heaven and earth. Rahner cannot say anything concrete about this final completion of spirit and matter. He bases this, without further explanation, on 1 Corinthians 15:35–36,[126] and justifies it elsewhere with the words: "because every inner-worldly perfection could only be the perfection of finiteness, as not absolute perfection at all."[127] Here again, appears the hermeneutical distinction that Rahner makes between the inner world and the absolute future (§3.2.1.3). According to Rahner, 1 Corinthians 15:44 points out that every human being will experience a radical change in this process. This radical change is necessary to inherit the new heaven and the new earth. However, it is nothing less than death at the core of our being.[128] By dying, however, humans are not alienated from the cosmos. From the christological-soteriological transposition, Rahner concludes that humans ultimately do not become *a-cosmic*, but *all-cosmic*.[129]

3.4.3 Christ's physical resurrection

3.4.3.1 *Christ's eternal humanity*

In his reflection on Christ's humanity, Rahner points out that most eschatologies of his time pay little or no attention to the lasting significance of this issue for eschatology. Everything that can be said about God in the context of the eschatological completion is mainly focused on the *visio beatifica*. Only mysticism seems to reflect on Christ's eternal humanity. Rahner thus appeals not only to question the place of Christ's humanity in the past but also its place in the present and future.[130] For himself, it is clear that Christ is eternally human and thus remains connected with matter: "we must not think of the eternally perfected Logos of God for all eternity except as the one who is corporeal in materiality,"[131] and: "the *visio beatifica*, the direct vision of God, is based

---

125. Rahner, "Fest," 180: "Wir Christen sind also die sublimsten Materialisten: wir können und dürfen uns keine Vollendung des Geistes und der Wirklichkeit überhaupt denken, außer wir denken auch die Bleibendheit der Materie und ihre Vollendung."

126. Rahner, "Immanente," 609.

127. Rahner, "Christentum," 173: "weil jede innerweltliche Vollendung nur die Vollendung aus Endlichkeit sein könnte, als gar nicht absolute Vollendung wäre."

128. Rahner, *Auferstehung*, 25–26.

129. Rahner, "Christologie innerhalb," 198; *Zur Theologie des Todes*, 22–26.

130. Rahner, "Ewige Bedeutung," 50, 55–58; "Auferstehung (SM)," 422.

131. Rahner, "Fest," 180: "wir dürfen uns den ewig vollendeten Logos Gottes auch in alle Ewigkeit nicht denken außer als den in Materialität hinein Verleiblichten." Cf. "Leib," 410.

on a grace which would not exist and probably could not exist except for the fact that the Logos of God became and remained flesh."[132] This implies that Christ's matter also receives its place before God in glorification. In Christ, everything finds its eternal completion. From this framework, the Messiah is representative of all creation "so that all that is still outstanding is only the execution and revelation of that which took place in the resurrection."[133] The final perfection of matter happens in and through the finished work of the glorified and risen Christ.

3.4.3.2 Glorified matter and space

While Rahner confesses the physical resurrection of Christ, he states that this resurrection body is not in the coordinate system of our visible space and time of creation. Therefore, only they see Christ to whom the Risen One reveals himself; he remains hidden from the others.[134]

At the same time, Rahner wants to avoid the idea that the risen person is separate from creation and overcomes the limits of creation. Christ remains conceivable in spatial terms even after his resurrection. The same applies to Mary in the Catholic doctrine of faith. Christ and Mary, after their glorification through their matter, remain subject to space (see Rahner's quote in §3.2.1.3.2). Human beings in the eschaton, therefore, possess a glorified body and live on in a space that is dissimilar to and incompatible with the space known to us. Rahner describes this new reality as a new heaven or earth.[135]

3.4.3.3 Christ and the new creation

In Rahner's reflection on Christ's eternal humanity, the above-mentioned position of Jesus, with regard to the new creation, also emerges. Through the physical resurrection, Jesus of Nazareth is the Firstborn of the new creation. Matter and spirit are also inextricably linked here: "Christianity confesses the resurrection of the flesh, saying that in the last, there is only one story and one end of all."[136]

---

132. Rahner, "Leib," 417: "die visio beatifica, die unmittelbare Schau Gottes, basiere auf einer Gnade, die es gar nicht gäbe und vermutlich auch gar nicht geben könnte außer dadurch, daß der Logos Gottes Fleisch geworden und geblieben ist."

133. Rahner, "Auferstehung (SM)," 420: "so daß alles noch Ausständige nur die Durchführung und Enthüllung des in der A[uferstehung] Geschehenen ist." Cf. *Grundkurs*, 183; "Eschatologie: Theologisch," 1097; "Ewige Bedeutung," 56.

134. Rahner, *Auferstehung*, 14–15, 24–25; "Auferstehung (STh)," 216.

135. Rahner, "Prinzipien," 411. Cf. "Theologische Bemerkungen," 238; *Auferstehung*, 24–25; "Auferstehung (STh)," 223–24; "Assumpta-Dogmas," 239–40.

136. Rahner, "Christentum," 173: "Das Christentum bekennt die Auferstehung des Fleisches und sagt damit, daß es im letzten nur eine Geschichte und ein Ende von allem gibt" "Dogmatische Fragen," 166–67; "Ewige Bedeutung," 57.

Rahner realizes how much criticism there is of the confession of such a material resurrection. The truth of Jesus' physical resurrection is sometimes avoided by orthodox Christians as it is by heretics. It is actually the same as it was then: "when they heard of the resurrection of the dead, some mocked. However, others said, 'We will hear you again about this'" (Acts 17:32).[137] Rahner turns against Hellenistic soul-body dualism and, echoing Tertullianus, calls the "flesh" the pivot of salvation: *caro cardo salutis*. While the resurrection of this "flesh" forms a fundamental basis in the Christian faith, the discussion about it remained limited in many theological reflections.[138]

For Rahner, however, Christ's resurrection is a metaphor for the completion of human history and material creation. When you look at the Risen One, you get a representation of your own future resurrection through this Firstborn. Rahner emphasizes that the resurrection body of Christ is a unique and radical transformation of the crucified body. It is not simply a resuscitation of a dead body. The resurrection does not lead to the continuation of an earthly existence that ends with death. Rahner, therefore, rejects the idea that the identity of the resurrection body is guaranteed only on the basis of identical materiality.[139] Such a replacement of matter does not even occur during normal human growth. The matter of the human body alternates itself with a similar and not identical matter. Old cells make way for new cells. According to Rahner, this means that finding a dead body in a grave does not necessarily rule out the possibility of a resurrection. Rather, the resurrection body shows the eschatological victory of God's grace in this world, in a different mode. Like the risen Christ, the resurrection body of a human being is freed from all the physical limitations of this existence (*Dasein*).[140] At the same time, Rahner also wants to ensure that the belief in a resurrection should not be dismissed as mythology. He does this by pointing out that the biblical statements about eternal life and the resurrection of the dead are only possible if there is a similar identity between this life and the resurrection life. A mythologization of these biblical statements would be in danger of making the Bible claim the opposite. In Christian doctrine, there is also an apotheosis of matter.[141]

Christ's resurrection is of crucial importance to Rahner. If Christ had not risen from the dead, the kingdom of God would still not have had a beginning. It would have been a kingdom that could only be hoped for. Rahner, therefore, emphasizes that the completion of all things began with the breakthrough and victory of the resurrected

---

137. Rahner, *Auferstehung*, 3; "Auferstehung (STh)," 213.

138. Rahner, "Erfahrungen," 116–17; "Zwischenzustand," 460–61; "Leib," 414; *Auferstehung*, 3–5; "Dogmatische Fragen," 158–59; Rahner, "Auferstehung (STh)," 214–15. Cf. Tertullian, *Carnis Resurrectione*, 8.

139. Rahner, *Grundkurs*, 262; "Zwischenzustand," 461, 465–66; "Intellektuelle," 74–75. See as criticism: Felsinger, "Karl Rahner," 209.

140. Rahner, "Zwischenzustand," 462; "Anthropologie," 344; *Auferstehung*, 10–11; "Auferstehung (STh)," 223.

141. Rahner and Rawer, "Weltall," 74–75.

Christ, who will soon be completed.¹⁴² Whoever turns his eyes to the risen Christ is encouraged to accept his own resurrection as a fact. For his resurrection includes the final completion of all humankind before the God who gives eternal life. The person is completed in his totality with spirit, soul and body, immaterial, and material. The transfiguration of the last days, therefore, means the resurrection of the individual human being and a new earth and a new heaven. That which is created by God, accepted in Christ's Incarnation and glorified by Christ's resurrection, is also in us towards final completion. Christ is thus God's instrument in the transformation of *all* creation.¹⁴³

Rahner adds this relationship between Christ's resurrection and the resurrection of all things to the idea of the goodness of creation and the inviolability of matter and spirit. Nevertheless, his elaboration lacks a further reflection on what Christ's role as first born brings with it in terms of specific representations for the new cosmos or new creation. He himself acknowledges this:

> We cannot concretely imagine how such permanence and transfiguration of matter should actually look for all eternity. However, we have to love our corporeality and its worldly environment in such a way that we must not be prepared to think of ourselves differently of eternity also in the permanent materiality of the accomplished.¹⁴⁴

3.5 TIME AND ETERNITY IN THE ESCHATON

In his discourse on time, Rahner blames Christian theology for not thinking enough about this subject. Neither in eschatology nor in any other dogmatic locus, time as a systematically defined subject is central, while the NT has a great diversity of concepts for time (e.g., καιρός, χρόνος, αἰών, ἡμέρα, τέλος, etc.).¹⁴⁵ What can be said in systematic theology about "time" is diffuse among systematics and spread over their reflections from protology to eschatology.

---

142. Rahner, "Auferstehung Jesu," 421; "Parusie," 123; "Dogmatische Fragen," 166–67; "Auferstehung (STh)," 222. For the historical reliability of Christ's resurrection, see Rahner, *Auferstehung*, 13–15. Cf. Felsinger, "Karl Rahner," 208, who recognizes a denial of Christ's resurrection by Rahner. Thus Rahner writes in Rahner, *Grundkurs*, 263 that "Jesus in den Glauben seiner Jünger hinein aufersteht"—"Jesus resurrected into the faith of his disciples." In the context of this quotation, however, it is the effect of the resurrection that is at stake, not the resurrection itself: "Aber dieser Glaube, in den Jesus hinein aufersteht, ist nicht eigentlich und direkt der Glaube an die Auferstehung"—"But this faith, into which Jesus rises, is not actually and directly faith in the resurrection" (263). See also: Rahner, "Auferstehung Jesu," 350.

143. Rahner, "Leib," 426; "Auferstehung Jesu," 344–47, 350; "Fest," 180–81; *Auferstehung*, 20, 26–27; *Zur Theologie des Todes*, 20–23; "Auferstehung (STh)," 219, 222–24.

144. Rahner, "Fest," 180: "Wir können uns zwar nicht konkret vorstellen, wie eigentlich für alle Ewigkeit eine solche Bleibendheit und Verklärtheit der Materie aussehen soll. Aber wir haben diese unsere Leibhaftigkeit und ihre weltliche Umwelt so zu lieben, daß wir in Ewigkeit nicht bereit sein dürfen, uns anders als die auch in der bleibenden Materialität Vollendeten zu denken."

145. Rahner, "Theologische Bemerkungen," 303–5.

According to Rahner, theologians often accept the "vulgar" concept of time as self-evident and only reflect ontologically on time from a view that is primarily connected to the Greek movement model (κίνησις).[146] "Who once writes a theology of the concept and understanding of time?" he asks.[147] Even today, interest in this subject is limited, although the number of dogmatics dealing with the concept of time is increasing.[148] Finally, Rahner did not design a comprehensive theology of the concept of time either. However, he did briefly develop some important elements for this.[149] They are fundamental to his thinking about time and eternity and therefore deserve our attention.

3.5.1 Perishable world time and eternal salvation time

3.5.1.1 *Two categories*

Traditionally, Rahner follows the Christian confession that creation has a beginning and end in time. He rejects a beginningless creation or eternal return of all things. In freedom, people determine their history. In that history, it is not possible to repeat things randomly or to change situations that have come to an end. In freedom, a person must realize that history has an end. When that end comes, the current state of creation becomes the "fullness of time" (καιρός).[150]

Rahner divides our known history of time into two categories: (1) negative transitory time, which subjects people as slaves and which Christ redeems, and (2) positive salvation time, wherein what remains eternal for people takes place. So the same time has a good and a bad side: as a time of decay on one side and time of permanence on the other side. Rahner does not answer the question of what this contrast brings about. Can time itself be classified as negative, or is only the transience that accompanies time negative? In the end, Rahner acknowledges that God gives meaningful content to time and history. Through the Incarnation, God the Son undergoes his own history in time. Truth and time meet in this and reveal that time determines not only the physical-material reality but also that of the mind. This also creates two categories: transient time and salvific time. To what extent these can be distinguished from each other precisely, remains as unclear with Rahner as the distinction between the

---

146. Rahner, "Theologische Bemerkungen," 305.

147. Rahner, "Über den Versuch eines Aufrisses," 21: "Wer schreibt einmal eine Theologie des Zeitbegriffs und Zeitverständnisses?"

148. E.g., Mühling, *Grundinformation*, 78–100; Wohlmuth, *Mysterium*, 49–74; Moltmann, *Kommen*, 307–20; *Gott in der Schöpfung*, 116–52; Pannenberg, *Systematische Theologie 3*, 625–53. For the history of this, see the detailed research: Jager, *Eeuwige leven*.

149. Mainly this happens in: Rahner, "Ewigkeit," 422–32; "Theologische Bemerkungen," 302–22; "Trost der Zeit," 169–88.

150. Rahner, "Theologische Bemerkungen," 303; "Theologie der Freiheit," 31–54; "Immanente," 593–609; "Trost der Zeit," 169–88.

physical-material and the mind (§3.4.2). In any case, Rahner concludes that through the Incarnation, transient time does not permanently dominate human history. Through the Incarnation, salvation time triumphs over transient physical-material time.[151]

3.5.1.2 The confession of creation in and with time

The distinction between salvation time and world time also arises from Rahner's interpretation of the traditional Christian creed: creation has a beginning. World time is thus finite in terms of the past. But how can the limits of this world time, or real-time, be imagined? "Can the *finiteness* of the set of time be otherwise real than by being thought (and so is) as part of a larger set of time that is as real as it is itself, which *ex supposito* should not be?"[152] Each time fragment is thus part of a larger time fragment that is also part of another larger time fragment.

Rahner illustrates this: If a clock runs synchronously with our world time, the defined clock time shows the defined world time. There are then two possibilities:

1. If this clock belongs to creation and is, therefore, part of it, it only measures changes *in* world time. What happens outside creation, it does not measure, because it is part of creation.

2. If the clock is separate from creation, it forms its own "creation," of which it can still be proved that the time measurements of both "creations" are relationally connected. It is theoretically possible that there is an infinite time next to a finite time.[153]

An alternative to this illustration is to determine the beginning of creation by adding delimited units of time with its unique events. But what determines the minimum size of such a unit of time? If units of time can be infinitely reduced, it is impossible to arrive at an absolute unit with which to calculate. Therefore theologians conclude too quickly from natural science that time is easy to measure. But natural science limits time to the relational relation of mutual subjects and does not absolute its view. In natural science *time spacing* is the only thing that matters as a phenomenon of time. A theory of relativity, therefore, makes no difference between past or future, although both are a characteristic of the time we observe. Natural science does not answer the question of the ontology of time.[154]

---

151. Rahner, "Theologische Bemerkungen," 304. For the first also see: "Schöpfung," 110.

152. Rahner, "Theologische Bemerkungen," 308: "Kann die Endlichkeit der Zeitmenge anders real sein als dadurch, daß sie gedacht wird (und so ist) als Teil einer größeren Menge von Zeit, die genauso real ist wie sie selbst, was doch ex supposito nicht sein darf?"

153. Rahner, "Theologische Bemerkungen," 309.

154. "Diskussionsbeiträge Raum und Zeit," 260–61; Rahner, "Theologische Bemerkungen," 310; "Schöpfungslehre," 474. See also: Rolf, "Zeit und Ewigkeit," 121.

Rahner *a priori* chooses to distinguish time phenomena from total world time. He interprets the church dogma, which states that the world was created *in* and *with* time, as a contextual statement of faith that focuses only on the time of salvation. This dogma calls upon humanity to accept salvation in this time as a definitively irreversible free choice.[155] However, the idea that time and history only begin from the fall is unacceptable to Rahner. The fall and the guilt before God do not bring time in. For Rahner, such a thought is even "gnostic heresy."[156]

3.5.1.3 World time and human perception of time

Because every person receives a limited time in freedom, Rahner states that the person acknowledges something of an inner, experienceable, and immediately verifiable, qualified temporality of the human being. This lifetime is linear: despite the fact that his organic death contributes to the emergence of new forms of life, humans experience their life as an irreversible history, starting with the first choice of freedom and ending with death. With this, the time of the individual human being in terms of freedom of action forward and backward is limited. Conscious knowledge of this beginning and end makes people realize that they have a brief part in the history of the universe with which they interact.[157] The spirit and matter of humankind as a unity are inextricably linked to this creation through this moment of time. We must always speak collectively and individually, spiritually and bodily just as in anthropology as well as in eschatology.[158] The temporary material world is not merely a static stage of human history (§3.4.1).

Rahner then wonders whether he should not extrapolate this human sense of time to world time. If this creation forms the space and the inner moment of individual human history, it cannot dissolve its own temporality at the beginning and end. Because of the unbreakable relation between humankind and creation, an eternal creation is impossible. Creation is *Umwelt* ("Environment") and *Mitwelt* ("fellow world") of humanity. Rahner does not exclusively understand this extrapolation. Theologically it is possible to reach this conclusion in other ways as well.[159]

How to interpret world time in isolation ontologically remains a question. Despite all the scientific-objective measurability of time between relational subjects, the above-mentioned world and human time can only be experienced in the

---

155. Rahner, "Theologische Bemerkungen," 311–12; "Diskussionsbeiträge Zeitbegriff," 239.

156. Rahner, "Diskussionsbeiträge Zeitbegriff," 233–34.

157. Rahner, "Diskussionsbeiträge Raum und Zeit," 261; *Grundkurs*, 416, 420; "Theologische Bemerkungen," 312–14, 317; "Christentum," 166. Cf. Heidegger, *Sein und Zeit*, 374.

158. Rahner, "Theologische Bemerkungen," 314: "wir müssen immer kollektiv und individuell, geistig und leibhaftig genauso wie in der Anthropologie auch in der Eschatologie reden." Cf. *Grundkurs*, 418.

159. Rahner, "Theologische Bemerkungen," 313. Rahner refers to: Kern, "Theologischen Auslegung," 519–29.

human-subjective inner consciousness. The essence of world time thus transcends the objective field of work, which natural science researches. The quality of the objectively experienced can never be isolated in a single act because the act of reflection on it itself is again subject to the same condition and carries the reflected quality in itself.[160]

That excludes in advance an objective ontological speaking about world time. Yet even natural science is inseparable in the transcendental. Just as physics finds a new moment in time after each moment in time, it speaks from metaphysics about the finiteness of time. Both observations are not in conflict with each other. Where this seems to happen, there is an apparent observation of the transcendent in physics (*Schein des transzendentalen*), which arises because a found data is too quickly wrongly extrapolated to generality.[161]

3.5.2 Speaking of world time, salvation time, and eternity

3.5.2.1 *Salvation time and world time as transposition*

From his thinking about world time and human time, Rahner concludes that Christian theology primarily starts from salvation-historical time, which begins with the first choice of freedom and ends with death. From there, it looks at all other elements of time. Extrapolation from salvation time to world time should be thought through as adequately as an extrapolation from scientific time to general time. The time phenomenon can be distinguished from the time being.

Rahner transposes his talk about salvation time and world time further from his views on spirit and matter.[162] Like matter "not being given to itself" (*das sich selbst nicht gegebene Sein*), spirit is "being given to itself" (*Sein in Selbstbesitz*, §3.4.2). Likewise, physical time is "not being given," because it is not permanent. Physical time comes, goes, and lifts itself up with this. This is different with salvation time. For Rahner, salvation time is given "to be." It is connected with the "spirit of freedom" that makes it permanent. So the physical time that comes and goes continues. Forward and backward, it has no beginning or ending point because of the *sich selbst nicht gegebene Sein*. Only if it forms part of the temporary history of freedom or the history of salvation is physical time permanent.

At the same time, Rahner states from this transposition that physical time and salvation time are not separate. Just as grace presupposes the physical world to be

---

160. Rahner, "Theologische Bemerkungen," 316. In 1967, Karl Rahner referred extensively to these limitations of the natural sciences, so that even the scientific community today has to respect traditional culture in addition to its scientific and technical knowledge: "Diskussion," 36. Cf. "Selbstverständnis," 102–47.

161. Rahner, "Theologische Bemerkungen," 316–17. With reference to: Kern, "Theologischen Auslegung," 519–29; Kant, *Kritik der reinen Vernunft*, A293–298/B349–355. See also: Freyer, *Zeit*, 319–22, 345.

162. Rahner, "Theologische Bemerkungen," 318.

operative, the supernatural concept of grace-time presupposes the profane concept of time. Just as grace realizes itself in the physical world, "time of grace" realizes an open time of freedom and hope in this world that allows the utopian. Rahner does want to prevent theology, as a sovereign queen, from ignoring the results of natural science:

> Christianity is not really a castle of truth with innumerable rooms which one must inhabit in order to be "in the truth," but *an* opening which leads from all individual truths (and even errors) into *the* truth.[163]

3.5.2.2 World time, salvation time, and God's eternity

Another question Rahner asks himself is how the salvation and world time relate to God's eternity. Scholastic scholars saw God's eternity as "eternal continuation" without beginning and end (*tota simul*). The concept of "continuation" was unavoidable. Only from time concepts is it possible to speak of eternity knowledge (*In cognitionem aeternitatis oportet nos venire per tempus*).[164] Rahner sees this as an opportunity to speak about God's eternity, as it is done in God's free personal revelation (*Selbstmitteilung*).[165] While speaking of God and time is connected with God's immutability, the Incarnation of God the Son speaks of God's infinity and immutability and of God's experience of time and change. With the Incarnation, God's own time becomes part of world time. As a result, time sets itself apart from eternity, but eternity does not set itself apart from time.[166]

From this perspective, time is characterized as a modality of loving freedom. It is καιρός: a uniquely privileged "now" in which God is revealed to humanity. Through this act of God, time finds an enrichment. The neutral homogeneity of this physical world time is the condition for God's freedom of love to manifest itself in the "here and now" of this time frame.[167] It is in this time of events that people can choose God. That is a privileged καιρός: "A Now of Eternity is within you that no longer has any Nothingness behind and in front of it; it has already begun to gather your earthly moments into itself."[168]

---

163. Rahner, "Intellektuelle," 67: "Das Christentum ist eigentlich kein Schloß der Wahrheit mit unzählig vielen Zimmern, die man bewohnen muß, um "in der Wahrheit" zu sein, sondern die eine Öffnung, die aus allen Einzelwahrheiten (und sogar Irrtümern) in die Wahrheit führt." Cf. "Naturwissenschaft und Theologie," 67–68; "Diskussionsbeiträge Zeitbegriff," 239.

164. Aquinas, *Summa*, I.10.1c.

165. Rahner, "Theologische Bemerkungen," 320–21.

166. Rahner, "Theologische Bemerkungen," 321.

167. Rahner, "Theologische Bemerkungen," 322.

168. Rahner, *Kleines Kirchenjahr*, 10: "Ein Jetzt der Ewigkeit ist in dir, das kein Nicht mehr hinter und vor sich hat; das hat schon begonnen, deine irdischen Augenblicke in sich hineinzusammeln." Cf. "Trost der Zeit," 174.

3.5.2.3 Dimming eternity performances

Because Rahner typifies general-traditional representations of eternity as inadequate and obscured, he argues in favor of working with (limited) representation models. A description of what eternal life ultimately is can only be given with difficulty and imperfectly. Nevertheless, with his *Ewigkeit aus Zeit* (1979) he hopes to show that in the present time the Christian may experience something of eternity.

In his talk about eternity performances, Rahner turns against the idea of eternity as a perpetual continuation of time. It is this very idea that causes many to mock "eternal life":

> The one who simply lets time go beyond the death of a person and lets the "soul" continue in this time, so that new time becomes, instead of times being suspended in finality, today brings himself into insurmountable difficulties of thought and also of the existential execution of what is really meant by Christianity.[169]

Such an eternity performance can give rise to the idea that eternity will eventually become boring. After all, an eternal church service full of praise and worship is perceived by many as unpleasant. Rahner also points out that when time goes on indefinitely, "heaven" never reaches a completed "end point." Eternity then is "eternally in the making" or "eternally coming" without ever arriving. Negatively Rahner sees that with the damnation of the walking Jew Ahasuerus who walks the earth forever and finds no rest.[170]

In this way, Rahner describes an eternity consisting of infinitely further time as a negative and evil thing. In an infinitely continued time, as we know it now, every new time moment overcomes and destroys the previous one. This triumph and destruction are what Rahner calls negative. In conclusion, he can only establish: "One sees how dangerous and perishable the idea of eternity as the endless passing of time is."[171] Eternity then is nothing more than tyranny, an eternal hell.

---

169. Rahner, *Grundkurs*, 266–67: "Wer die Zeit einfach über den Tod des Menschen hinaus und in dieser Zeit die 'Seele' weiterdauern läßt, so daß neue Zeit wird, anstatt daß die Zeiten in Endgültigkeit aufgehoben sind, der bringt sich heute in unüberwindliche Schwierigkeiten des Gedankens und auch des existenziellen Vollzugs des christlich wirklich Gemeinten." Cf. Rahner, *Grundkurs*, 419, 427; "Ewigkeit," 423–24; "Theologische Bemerkungen," 321; "Auferstehung Jesu," 422; *Auferstehung*, 26; "Christentum," 171; "Dogmatische Fragen," 169. See also: Rahner, *Grundkurs*, 416, 419, with allusions to Feuerbach, *Gedanken über Tod*. For a further explanation of the issue that Karl Rahner briefly raises, see: Schärtl, "Der Tod," 139.

170. Rahner, "Ewigkeit," 424; "Christentum," 166. This legend story became known through the English monk and chronicler Matthaeus Parisiensis in 1228 and found further spread from there: Westphalus (pseudoniem), *Ewigen Juden*; Vermeylen, *Wandelende Jood*. See for further research:Tilly, "Der Ewige Jude," 289–303; Hasan-Rokem and Dundes, *Wandering Jew*.

171. Rahner, "Ewigkeit," 425: "Man sieht, wie gefährlich und verderblich die Vorstellung einer Ewigkeit als endloses Weitergehen der Zeit ist." Cf. Rahner, *Grundkurs*, 419–20.

A different path is to perceive eternity as a permanent eternal "now" that knows no time. Rahner is rather brief about this and wonders whether this model is legitimate because it is not sufficiently proven. Is there anything "permanent" if there is no "then"? In the current situation, this cannot be established; everything that is and remains continues over time. The proposal for an eternity of the eternal "now" also falls short for that reason. Rahner sees a way out of this dilemma, between eternity as progressing time and eternity as permanence without succession, in the human experience of time, in which he distinguishes three rare permanent "situations" that do not immediately perish or be redeemed and from which it is possible to reflect on time and eternity.[172] We will consider these three frames of reflection in more detail below.

3.5.3 Three lasting situations about time and eternity

3.5.3.1 *Historical moments*

The first framework for reflection on time and lasting eternity Rahner sketches as follows: Many experience time as a sequence of moments that together form a long chain, without beginning or end. Each moment dissolves the preceding one and makes way for a new moment. Yet we realize that something lasting exists in these separate and alternating moments of time. About these "lasting moments," we write coherent histories that do not pulverize into a cloud of dust of purely separate independent moments.[173]

Time and eternal permanence are thus at stake. Although every moment in history is delineated, binding factors in all moments connect the whole into one entity. These connecting factors cannot be of the same quality as what makes time go by flashing and re-extinguishing moments of time. That which "forms" history is thus separate from the time that shatters itself: "Even in the actual temporal there is more than time, a lasting one at least, which unites time into historical forms of time."[174] Here Rahner's philosophical conviction of an imperishable super temporary substance resounds.[175]

3.5.3.2 *Thoughts and their connecting factor*

The second framework for reflection on time and lasting eternity is the human spirit that unites past, present, and future as one entity and total time. We combat the

---

172. Rahner, *Grundkurs*, 419–20; "Ewige Bedeutung," 425–30.
173. Rahner, "Ewigkeit," 426. Cf. Freyer, *Zeit*, 319–20.
174. Rahner, "Ewigkeit," 427: "Schon in eigentlich Zeitlichem steckt mehr als Zeit, ein Bleibendes mindenstens, das Zeit zu geschichtlichen Zeitgestalten eint."
175. Cf. Freyer, *Zeit*, 327.

alternation of separate moments in time by forming one larger time total from minuscule events.[176]

Anyone who objects to the fact that this one great time total is only a thought about the time span of a person who moves on in real-time is contradicted by Rahner on the basis of the philosophy that it is precisely this thought formation, which is meaningful and truly stationary in time, that is more than the element of real-time that evaporates and wavers. Because a "thought about the time span" is possible, this proves precisely that it is not subject to the lapse of time. If that were the case, such a thought would not be possible and would immediately flow away in time. What constitutes the whole of history can thus be distinguished from the time that shatters itself. The thought formed is ontologically not part of the quality of delving and passing the time. The temporary consists of more than time. It also contains a supertemporality that is permanent and unites time into a historical unity.[177]

3.5.3.3 *Personal choices and their permanence*

As a final framework for reflection on time and enduring eternity, Rahner points to freedom of choice. A person remains responsible for all his choices. What happens is not rotatable or tends to disappear in time: "Freedom is always absolute, is the yes that knows about itself and wants to be valid as true forever."[178] It is not possible to evade responsibility with time. Time can heal, but not erase. Time is an open time of decision, of hope, of the unforeseen as space for action, which creates the possible from the utopian and thus creates time. The choices made are—if repentance and reversal are lacking—irrevocable in that respect. This forms true eternity in time, which is definitive and unchanging.[179]

3.5.4 Speaking of eternity

3.5.4.1 *Temporary incomprehensibility*

All three frameworks of reflection, which Rahner mentions, clarify that not everything that people experience is temporal-perishable. There is a simultaneous existence of permanent validity and advancing time. For Rahner, an eternity proposal that allows time to end in "nothing" or that time to progress eternally is incompatible with the Christian belief in eternal life. According to the Bible, eternity brings the

---

176. Rahner, "Ewigkeit," 427–28; "Prinzipien," 410–11.
177. Rahner, "Ewigkeit," 427–28.
178. Rahner, "Trost der Zeit," 186: "Freiheit ist immer absolut, ist das Ja, das um sich weiß und als wahr für immer gültig sein will." Cf. *Grundkurs*, 422.
179. Rahner, "Theologische Bemerkungen," 320; "Ewigkeit," 429; *Grundkurs*, 422; "Trost der Zeit," 173–74.

temporariness of all humankind home to final completion. This statement of faith already becomes a reality in faith in the resurrection of Christ.[180]

Despite these biblical references, the hermeneutical principle of the hidden character resounds in Rahner's talk of time and eternity, which states that everything ontologically related to the day of completion is unknown to humans (thesis 3a; §3.2.1.3). Revelation brings the hidden from the state of unfamiliarity into the state of fame as the revealed and known hidden that at the same time remains incalculable and insurmountable. Rahner limits his concrete speaking about time and eternity in the hereafter by typifying it as:

> Unknown, the unimaginable and actually only know that it is filled with the incomprehensibility of God and his love. . . . If we accept the incomprehensibility of our eternal life for ourselves now and still hope and trust, then we have done enough.[181]

From this position, he sees the Christian life as the life of faith and hope, which is still waiting for the final and, therefore cannot yet show itself triumphantly. It is only possible to talk about this in an idea-based way, or to say it with Rahner: in form, but not in content (§3.2.4).

3.5.4.2 *Eternity as completed time*

From his talk about time and eternity, in the human responsibility for one's own free choices, Rahner shows that eternity is a fruit of one's own personal history, which each person shapes from his own freedom. This fruit of time no longer continues in eternity, but is dissolved from time and remains in freedom forever.[182] Aware of the scope of this idea, one recognizes the impact of each free decision.

Nor does Rahner fail to point out in this context God's love which overcomes in Christ and which is the cause and the guarantee that humanity has a future *from* this transient and fast-paced time. Eternity is not directly related to human events. It lifts them up and disengages itself from them. Eternity is not outside, above, or next to time. It takes place *in* and *from* time: "the present is thus deeply carried by the future itself, our perfection (as a process) is the "perfection of perfection" which already exists and yet happens (*quoad nos*)."[183] Lifetime can thus be seen as a river of life that

---

180. Rahner, "Ewigkeit," 430; *Grundkurs*, 423. See also: Tillich, *Systematic Theology 3*, 420.

181. Rahner, "Ewigkeit," 430: "Unbekannte, das Unvorstellbare und wissen eigentlich nur, daß es erfüllt ist von der Unbegreiflichkeit Gottes und seiner Liebe. . . . Wenn wir so die Unbegreiflichkeit unseres ewigen Lebens für uns jetzt annehmen und dennoch hoffen und vertrauen, dann haben wir genug getan." Cf. "Frage," 536–40; "Prinzipien."

182. Rahner, "Ewigkeit," 430–31; *Grundkurs*, 420–23; "Auferstehung (SM)," 422; "Trost der Zeit," 183.

183. Rahner, "Immanente," 602: "die Gegenwart ist also im tiefsten getragen durch die Zukunft selbst, unsere Vollendung (als Vorgang) ist die 'Vollendung der Vollendung,' die schon existiert und

makes many detours but does not lose any water when it eventually flows into the eternity sea. In that respect, there is a "resurrection of time" *in* eternity.[184] For Rahner, the Johanneum theology is in line with this: "This fulfilling message of the gospel contains a multiple. Eternity as the fruit of time is a coming before God."[185] For Rahner too, the "past" of the Spirit is not what *was*, but what *is* and *remains*. Time is needed to provide eternity and freedom. The "one-way" human history (cosmic, individual history, history of Jesus, etc.), which is carried out in freedom and action, contains at its end "more" than this beginning.[186] Rahner has anchored this christologically:

> If we look forward from the correct interpretation of the death of Christ and do not understand what "comes after" death as an event that in a continuing time only follows the event of death, but as the timeless finality of this very temporal life that is truly consummated by death itself, then we will not be able to understand what "comes after" death as an event that only follows the event of death in a continuing time, but as the timeless finality of this very life that is really consummated by death itself.[187]

Because people think in terms of time, they get into trouble when talking about this. Rahner thus argues for a demythologizing contemplation of time: death—and not afterward—definitively "fixes" what happens through spirit and freedom in time. This "fixed" then stands as a permanent eternity against the representation of eternity as infinitely continuing open time or eternity as eternal "now."[188]

3.6 THE VISIO BEATIFICA

3.6.1 Theo-centrism

Besides the geo- and anthropocentric approaches to the new creation, which are especially visible in Rahner's vision of matter and time, he also attaches value to its theocentric aspects. God wants to communicate with creation. That is God's most important goal. Everything else is secondary to this.[189] For Rahner, the afterlife is more than an intellectual contemplation of God's glory. It is more than that we will see

---

sich dennoch ("quoad nos") ereignet." Cf. Phan, *Eternity*, 53–58.

184. Rahner, "Trost der Zeit," 178, 187.

185. Rahner, *Grundkurs*, 423: "Diese erfüllende Botschaft des Evangeliums beinhaltet ein Mehrfaches. Die Ewigkeit als Frucht der Zeit ist ein Kommen vor Gott." Cf. "Trost der Zeit," 187–88.

186. Rahner, "Trost der Zeit," 329.

187. Rahner, "Dogmatische Fragen," 169: "Wenn wir von der richtigen Interpretation des Todes Christi aus vorwärtsblicken und das, was 'nach' dem Tode kommt, nicht verstehen als ein Ereignis, das in einer weiterfahrenden Zeit sich nur an das Ereignis des Todes anschließt, sondern als die sich ausgezeitigt habende Endgültigkeit eben dieses zeitlichen, durch den Tod selbst wirklich vollendenden Lebens."

188. Rahner, *Grundkurs*, 420.

189. Rahner, "Auferstehung (STh)," 219–20; "Über das Verhältnis," 336.

the infinity of absolute reality, the inaccessible light, the incomprehensibility that is infinitely blessed life face to face. It is also a personal participation of humanity in the grace of God. In concrete terms, this means that this future must also result in God in the completion of eternal life.[190]

In this Rahner takes into account Christ's eternal mediatorship. Also, in eternity, people see the Father only through the Son. Rahner speaks more about seeing the Trinity, Father, Son, and Spirit, than about seeing God as one. The *visio beatifica* then is the fulfillment of God's self-communication through the Son and the Spirit in grace.[191]

3.6.2 Continuing knowledge of God

Rahner writes about the ultimate relationship between the triune God and humanity "that all speaking can only be the last moment before that blessed silence which also fills the heavens of the clear vision of God face to face."[192] In this way, he excludes the possibilities that in the hereafter, people know and understand God completely. With the *visio beatifica* and the ultimate participation of humanity in the grace of the triune God, knowing God remains an ongoing process. Never do the saints reach a complete knowledge of God, because "the finite spirit can only recognize the infinite being of God in a finite way: *Videt infinitum, sed non infinite.*"[193] The *visio beatifica* does not eliminate the limited knowledge of God, but only the absolute separation between humanity and God. Caution is advised with the proposition that this limited knowledge is negative. Rahner criticizes the Greek ideal that makes knowledge the measure of all things. A philosophy of the person and of the freedom of the finite being, of history and of decision, could show relatively easily that the essence of the self-execution of the finite person in the historical decision of freedom necessarily includes the risk, the passage into the open, the trust in the unseen, the concealment of the origin, and the concealment of the end, i.e., a certain way of not knowing.[194]

---

190. Rahner, *Grundkurs*, 423; "Frage," 526–27; "Christentum," 172; "Eschatologie: Theologisch," 1097. Cf. Phan, "Eschatology," 188–89.

191. Rahner, "Dreifaltige Gott," 378–82; "Ewige Bedeutung," 57–58.

192. Rahner, "Erfahrungen," 107: "daß alles Reden nur der letzte Augenblick vor jenem seligen Verstummen sein kann, das auch noch die Himmel der klaren Schau Gottes von Angesicht zu Angesicht füllt."

193. Rahner, "Dogmatische Erwägungen," 341: "der endliche Geist kann die unendliche Wesenheit Gottes nur auf endliche Weise erkennen: Videt infinitum, sed non infinite." Cf. Ott, *Eschatologie*, 27; Aquinas, *Summa*, I.12.7.

194. Rahner, "Dogmatische Erwägungen," 230.

3.6.3   Perichoresis

In addition to the above elements, the hereafter is also characterized by the radical-definition of God's self-communication to this world. He is the "transcendent" perfection and can and wants so as God to be the "immanent" perfection and the "immanent" principle of the movement towards this one real and only fulfilling perfection: God—all in all. A separation between Creator and creation is impossible at that stage of the *visio beatificia*. God then is everything in all. Rahner sees this in the life of Jesus Christ, the One who was perfectly human and perfectly God. He notes that in Western theology, there is little attention for this relationship between God and creation in the eschaton, while it is present in traditional Christology. According to Rahner, one reason for this difference lies in the fact that Western theology has focused too much on God's transcendence. God's immanence was largely ignored.[195]

Rahner's ideas about perichoresis are criticized by Morwenna Ludlow. According to her, Rahner's transcendental immanent speaking tends to be pantheistic.[196] However, this criticism does not take into account that Rahner opposes not unification but a distinction against a separation between Creator and creation. Creator and creation intrude upon each other in the eschaton in the same way as God's Spirit in principle, permeates the Christian in this time. It is, therefore, more than just a perfect relationship between creation and Creator. What is central to Rahner here is rather a complete reflection of God's reality in creation. From that framework, it becomes clear why Rahner connects God's transcendence with full immanence.

3.7   CONCLUSION

1. In Rahner's theology, eschatology receives a large amount of attention. In particular, his hermeneutical principles regarding eschatological statements are of relevance here. For the theme of the new heaven and the new earth, he calls for attention, but he himself remains reserved in concrete descriptions about this.

2. From his omniscience, God reveals the future to humans. According to Rahner, this happens partly in hidden form, which means that the future cannot be planned by a person within the world, but can only be realized in this history by God's absolute future.

3. Rahner juxtaposes eschatology with apocalyptic. Apocalyptic wants to capture the future and ignores the hidden character of eschatological statements. Eschatology speaks of the future from the revelation in the present. It does so from what has already been revealed through the work of Christ in this creation.

---

195. Rahner, "Welt," 75, 79; *Grundkurs*, 428–29; "Frage," 526; "Immanente," 609. Cf. Petty, *Faith*, 94–106.

196. Ludlow, *Universal*, 227.

Apocalyptic, on the other hand, wants to make statements from the future into the present, which for Rahner is subjective-utopian.

4. Rahner rejects the demythologization of eschatological imagery because it is impossible to remove the image from the imagery. Who demythologizes replaces the original imagery with a new imagery. However, demythologization can help improve understanding of the essential content of the imagery.

5. Rahner distinguishes between content and form and realizes that different forms have a clarifying effect on the same content and build on earlier revelations. Rahner further emphasizes that form and content are inseparable. Speech does not lose its image.

6. From his methodical rejection of apocalyptic reportage-eschatology, Rahner remains skeptical about using biblical images in speaking about the new heaven and the new earth. Biblical imagery is not a picture postcard of the eschaton. Variation differences mainly show the diversity of the future.

7. For Rahner, the material and immaterial forms are an inseparable unity. Also, matter has an eternal future in God's plan of salvation. The history of the cosmos is inextricably linked to the history of humanity. Rahner turns sharply against any (neo)platoon or gnostic thinking that does not offer space to matter in the eschaton.

8. Jesus Christ is for Rahner the hermeneutical principle to understand eschatological statements. As the first glorified Risen One, Christ is the objective beginning of world glorification. Christ is the eternal human who remains connected with matter and space even after his resurrection.

9. Christ's resurrection from the dead is of crucial importance to Rahner as a metaphor for his own future resurrection. The resurrection body of Christ is a unique and radical transformation of the crucified body. Rahner hereby rejects the idea that the identity of the resurrection body is only guaranteed if it consists of exactly the same identical cell matter. However, Rahner lacks a further concrete conclusion about the future resurrection body from the resurrection body of Christ the Firstborn.

10. Through the Incarnation, the two categories arise: "fleeting time" and "salvific historical time." The specific distinction between the two is unclear when we look at Rahner's writings. Although the material world has a "fleeting time," it is not a static stage, but an *Umwelt* and *Mitwelt* for people. Yet its "fleeting time" perishes if it is not part of the salvation-historical time. Through the Incarnation, God's own time even becomes part of world time. That leads Rahner to contrast time with eternity, but not to contrast eternity with time.

11. The representation of eternity as an infinitely progressing time is for Rahner as negative as an eternity in which time is absent. At the same time, he realizes that not everything that exists in this time is transient. On the contrary, he imagines eternity as the fruit of his own personal history, which a person freely fills in with his own responsibility. Eternity thus only absorbs what was fruitful for God in human history. The rest of human time is released further as eternity begins.

12. Rahner attaches importance not only to the geo- and anthropocentric aspects but also to the theocentric aspects of the new heaven and earth. In the *visio beatifica*, knowing God remains an ongoing process. According to Rahner, in the new creation, God will be everything in everything. Creator and creation then permeate each other in the same way as God's Spirit permeates the Christian now in time.

4

Jürgen Moltmann's concept on the new heaven and new earth

This chapter offers an analysis of Moltmann's vision on the new heavens and the new earth. Because Moltmann's conceptions of the new heavens and the new earth have already been examined and described in greater detail by other authors than the conceptions of Rahner's (cf. §1.5.2), the original contribution of this chapter consists mainly of providing a complete overview. The following structure is chosen for this chapter: After a brief introduction (§4.1), various hermeneutic principles are discussed that determine Moltmann's eschatology (§4.2). Afterward, his concepts about time and space in the new creation are examined (§4.3–4.4). This choice was made because Moltmann, in his *Das Kommen Gottes*—the work that systematically brings his eschatology together—devotes a separate chapter to these two subjects in the elaboration of his cosmic eschatology.[1] Then, in §§4.5–4.6, the themes of matter and of God's dwelling are discussed because they are closely connected with Moltmann's thinking on the new creation, and he mentions them several times in his argument. In the following section (§4.7), attention is paid to the various anticipations of the new creation that Moltmann acknowledges in the Bible. Besides the image of the cosmic temple, which he elaborates at the end of his chapter on cosmic eschatology in *Das Kommen Gottes*, the images that Moltmann treats elsewhere in his works are also discussed here. The chapter ends with a conclusion (§4.8).

---

1. Moltmann, *Kommen*, §IV.3–4.

4.1 INTRODUCTION

4.1.1 Greatness and fame

Jürgen Moltmann (b. 1926) is a renowned systematic theologian.[2] His works are fascinating because of his extensive knowledge and clear wording. In total, he published more than five hundred titles.[3] A main work is his early trilogy, which highlights the basic questions of hope and is written programmatically: *Theologie der Hoffnung—Theology of Hope* (1964) highlights the eschatological orientation of theology; *Der gekreuzigte Gott—The Crucified God* (1972) highlights the crucified Christ as the pivotal point and criterion of hope; and *Kirche in der Kraft des Geistes—The Church in the Power of the Spirit* (1975) accumulates both works from an ecclesiological-pneumatological point of view.[4] His later six-part series *Systematischen Beiträge zur Theologie* is also well-known: *Trinität und Reich Gottes—The Trinity and the Kingdom* (1980); *Gott in der Schöpfung—God in Creation* (1985); *Der Weg Jesu Christi—The Way of Jesus Christ* (1989); *Der Geist des Lebens—The Spirit of Life* (1991); *Das Kommen Gottes—The Coming of God* (1995); *Erfahrungen theologischen Denkens—Experiences in Theology* (1999). In all these works, Moltmann develops the complexity and relevance of speaking about the new creation.[5]

While Moltmann writes in a German Protestant context, his biography and publications bear witness to an openness to other traditions and movements: Roman Catholic, Eastern Orthodox, and liberation theology, as well as influences from the charismatic movement, are reviewed. His experiences with the struggle and suffering of global Christianity and political commitment further influence his theological-ecclesiological framework.[6]

4.1.2 Eschatological orientation

For Moltmann, eschatology is the root of all theology. It is not an end treatise or a loose appendage that degenerated into apocryphal insignificance, but the central guideline within systematic theology: "Christianity is completely and not only in the appendix eschatology. It is hope, prospect, and orientation forwards."[7]

---

2. See for biographical data: Moltmann, *Weiter Raum*. A recent introduction to Moltmann's thinking is offered by: Welker, *Theologische Profile*, 235–89; Müller-Fahrenholz, *Phantasie*; Bauckham, *Theology of Jürgen Moltmann*.

3. See for a complete overview: Wakefield, *Jürgen Moltmann*, 29–194.

4. See Moltmann's own words about this trilogy: Moltmann, *Weiter Raum*, 101–6, 185–91, 196–99, 274; "Christian Eschatology," 260; *Trinität*, 11.

5. See detailed: Sicouly, *Schöpfung*; Häring, "Schöpfungstheologie," 182.

6. Cf. Hennecke, "Related," 292–309.

7. Moltmann, *Theologie*, 12: "Das Christentum ist ganz und gar und nicht nur im Anhang Eschatologie, ist Hoffnung, Aussicht und Ausrichtung nach vorne." Cf. "Is the World," 129–38.

The New Heaven and New Earth

Eschatology is the refrain that resounds in all the theological compositions, and from *Theologie der Hoffnung* (1964) makes its way in Moltmann's publications. Along the way, it finds its synthetic climaxes in such major works as *Das Kommen Gottes* (1995) and *Ethik der Hoffnung* (2010). The theme "new creation" is given an eminent place in this. Moltmann turns his back on modernity that views universal eschatology unilaterally as mythology and restricts Christian eschatology to existential interpretations of individual death. Individual eschatology must go hand in hand with cosmic eschatology.[8]

Moltmann owes his choice to see eschatology as a central guideline in Christian theology, mainly to the three-volume publication *Prinzip der Hoffnung* by the Jewish neo-Marxist philosopher Ernst Bloch (1885-1977).[9] This philosopher argued that the true "Genesis" is not at the beginning, but at the end of history. From this influence, Karl Barth wrote a letter in November 1964 asking the critical question to Moltmann whether *Theologie der Hoffnung* is not a baptized version of Bloch's *Prinzip der Hoffnung*.[10] While Bloch is only mentioned eight times in *Theologie der Hoffnung*,[11] Moltmann does not deny that this philosopher inspired him to write this work: "I did not want to imitate Ernst Bloch's *Principle of Hope*. . . . I wanted a parallel action in theology on the theological premises of Jews and Christians."[12]

Moltmann is critical of Bloch. Bloch's ontology of the "not yet" offers no foundation for hope because it must irrevocably change into an ontology of the "not-anymore."[13] Later Barth writes to Moltmann about his own eschatological development: "You know that I was once about to move in this direction, but then I kept my hands off it."[14] Moltmann recognizes this development in Barth's commentary on the Letter to the Romans (1919) and the contacts with Christoph Blumhardt, whom Barth called "the theologian of hope."[15]

Other criticisms of Moltmann's work originated from his positive references to Marxism and socialism and the ongoing dialogue with the neo-Marxist ideology-critical *Frankfurter Schule*. Paul Enns criticizes: "Moltmann is more indebted to Karl

---

8. Moltmann, *Erfahrungen*, 59; *Sprache*, 137–38.

9. Bloch, *Prinzip Hoffnung*. Cf. Moltmann, *Weiter Raum*, 84; *Erfahrungen*, 90; *Kommen*, 13, 48–51, 80–82; *Umkehr*, 9–10; *Im Gespräch*; *Experiment Hoffnung*, 49; *Theologie*, 313–34. See also: Hryniewicz, *Challenge*, 14; Adams, "Eschatology," 298–303; O'Collins, "Principle," 129–44.

10. Barth, *Briefe 1961–1968*, 273. Cf. Moltmann, *Weiter Raum*, 114–15; *Geschichte*, 174.

11. Moltmann, *Theologie*, 12, 70, 189, 222, 241, 242[2x], 309.

12. Moltmann, *Theologie*, Vorwort (1997): "Ich wollte Ernst Blochs "Prinzip Hoffnung" nicht nachahmen. . . . Ich wollte eine Parallelhandlung in der Theologie auf den theologischen Voraussetzungen von Juden und Christen."

13. Moltmann, *Kommen*, 42n58.

14. Barth, *Briefe 1961–1968*, 276: "Sie wissen, dass ich einst auch im Begriff war, in dieser Richtung vorzustoßen, dass ich dann aber die Hände davon gelassen habe."

15. Moltmann, *Weiter Raum*, 114–15; *Anfänge*, 1:37–49.

Marx for his theology than to the teachings of Scripture."[16] What Enns and others overlook is that Moltmann uses his Marxist statements to reveal gaps in the capitalist market system. Moltmann sees capitalist ideologies as a religious form in all aspects of life.[17]

In addition, Moltmann denounced socialism, which "is thoroughly discredited by his Stalinist and post-Stalinist practices" early on.[18] Moltmann doubts the idea that socialism is better than capitalism: "The kingdom of God can be socialism, but socialism is not yet the kingdom of God."[19] In his later works, these references to Marxist ideas become less numerous.

4.1.3 Theology as an adventurous journey

Moltmann has little interest in methodological issues. Rather, he is interested in the revision and innovation of the theological content. For him, the exercise of theology means going on a journey of adventure or discovery. It is walking on a "public road" and not defending "castles of dogmatics": "The path came into being when I walked. And, of course, my walking attempts are personal-biographical, political-contextual, and determined by the historical *kairos* in which I live."[20]

Kevin Gilbert reflects critically on this methodical approach. From the words "[A]lways using the same method leads to rigidity on the part of the author and to weariness in the reader," which is only used in the English introduction of Moltmann's work, Gilbert concludes that Moltmann deliberately uses a proliferation of methods.[21] But that is not what Moltmann means. The context clarifies that he only states that his earlier trilogy is written from one theological focus (§4.1.1). About his *Systematischen Beiträge zur Theologie,* he says that these:

> [N]o longer presented the whole of theology in a single focus but now viewed *my "whole" as a part* belonging to a wider community and as my contribution to theology as a whole.[22]

---

16. Enns, *Moody Handbook*, 630. Cf. Walton, "Moltmann," 153.

17. Moltmann, *Gott im Projekt*, 141.

18. Moltmann, *Gekreuzigte Gott*, 14: "durch seine stalinistische und nachstalinistische Praxis gründlich diskreditiert ist."

19. Moltmann, *Gekreuzigte Gott*, 296: "Das Reich Gottes kann Sozialismus sein, aber damit ist der Sozialismus noch nicht das Reich Gottes." Cf. "Auferstehungshoffnung," 117; "Hoffnung und Entwicklung," 61.

20. Moltmann, *Erfahrungen*, 11: "*Der Weg entstand erst im Gehen.* Und meine Gehversuche sind natürlich persönlich-biographisch, politisch-kontextuell und durch den geschichtlichen Kairos, in dem ich lebe, bestimmt." Cf. *Wie ich*, 30; *Kommen*, 14; *Geschichte*, 233; *Umkehr*, 154.

21. Gilbert, "Theological Method," 167; Moltmann, *Trinity*, vii.

22. Moltmann, *Trinity*, vii.

There is no deliberate, methodical proliferation here. It is the focus from which Moltmann operates theology, which he broadens. As a theologian, he is by no means unique in this respect.[23]

Nevertheless, it cannot be denied that Moltmann sees theology as an experimental thinking and formulates it as proposal, in which an overarching methodology remains shrouded in mist: "This may explain to some extent the variety of influences and my reactions that may have irritated some of the doctoral students who were involved with my theology."[24] This irritation is actually audible among critics who describe Moltmann's theology as interwoven with inconsistencies, vagueness, and unorthodox content wrapped in orthodox terminologies.[25]

In this way, Józef Niewiadomski sees Moltmann's remarks about the new creation as inconsistent and ambiguous.[26] Pablo Sicouly investigates this and concludes that Niewiadomski's criticism is unjustified.[27] However, in the development of Moltmann's theology, there are changes in emphasis on the new creation.

Whereas in earlier works, the divine is central, later the new creation is at the center, and the term "kingdom of God" is mainly linked to social eschatology.[28] Although many people investigated Moltmann's eschatological thinking in different areas, his research into the new creation remained comprehensive.[29] The following research into his thoughts on cosmic eschatology, based on building blocks he himself provides for this purpose, is thus legitimized.

4.2 HERMENEUTICAL PRINCIPLES

In 1999, after more than thirty-five years of theological impact, Moltmann published his *Erfahrungen theologischen Denkens* as a contribution to theological methodology and hermeneutics. However, this does not in any way mean that he did not previously consider methodically-hermeneutic issues.[30] Rather, the theological content and not the hermeneutic reflection were his main focus. The reason for this was Moltmann's

---

23. Cf. Bauckham, "Moltmann's Eschatology," 301.

24. Moltmann, *Geschichte*, 231: "Das mag die Vielfalt der Einflüsse und meiner Reaktionen ein wenig erklären, die manche Doktoranden, die sich mit meiner Theologie beschäftigten, irritiert haben mag."

25. See: Gilbert, "Theological Method," 164, 178; Clutterbuck, "Jürgen Moltmann," 489–505; Schweitzer, "Consistency," 197–208; Ahlers, "Theory," 236; Vroom, *De Schrift alleen?*, 166.

26. Niewiadomski, *Zweideutigkeit*, 10–12, 53, 127, 153.

27. Sicouly, *Schöpfung*, 128–29, 354–59, 367–70; Remenyi, *Um der Hoffnung*, 96–99, 451; Tang, *God's History*, 89–90; Bauckham, *Theology of Jürgen Moltmann*, 4–5, 23, 33–35, 214; Momose, *Kreuzestheologie*, 40–41.

28. Thomas, *Neue Schöpfung*, 317.

29. See in particular: Thomas, *Neue Schöpfung*, 315–43; Sicouly, *Schöpfung*; Niewiadomski, *Zweideutigkeit*; Remenyi, *Um der Hoffnung*, 395–458; Bauckham, *God Will Be*, 49–76, 155–226; *Theology of Jürgen Moltmann*, 1–46.

30. With regard to eschatology, see for example: Moltmann, *Weiter Raum*, 106–10; "Methoden."

choice to see theology as an adventure (§4.1.3). Although this conceals his hermeneutical principles in many respects, they are, at the same time, not inconsistent or completely hidden.[31] In this context, it is important to reflect on various elements that keep recurring in Moltmann's theological reflection.

4.2.1 "Theology of Hope" and "Theology of the Cross"

4.2.1.1 A circular movement between eschatology and Christology

In his thinking, Moltmann abandons the Cartesian method of "yes or no" and "this or that." On the contrary, he develops a methodology of relationships, communities, and transitions. In this way, he centralizes the collective and subordinates the modern individualizing to it. He also connects Christology and eschatology in such an inextricable way: "There is no Christology without eschatology and no eschatology without Christology."[32]

Christian eschatology speaks of *Christ's* coming. Christ is the heart of world history. The death of Christ on the cross is the crossroads of all Christian theology.[33] Moltmann's book *The Crucified God*, therefore, bears the subtitle *The Cross of Christ as the Foundation and Criticism of Christian Theology*.

Through the cross, God reveals his glory in suffering.[34] Christian theology is a reaction to the cry of Jesus: "My God, my God, why have you forsaken me?" (Mark 15:34). Either all theology ends with that question, or Christian theological life begins with it.[35] Moltmann chooses the latter. For him, cross and resurrection are inextricably linked. If that were not the case, there would be no continuity between this creation and the new creation.[36] Christ's resurrection already bears witness to this new era. Christology is thus the beginning of eschatology and eschatology, the completion of Christology. Whoever denies Christ's resurrection denies his Christianity:

> Christianity stands and falls with the reality of the resurrection of Jesus from the dead by God. . . . Christian faith that is not the faith of resurrection can neither be called Christian nor faith.[37]

---

31. Cf. Gilbert, "Theological Method," 168.

32. Moltmann, "Christliche Hoffnung," 247: "Es gibt keine Christologie ohne Eschatologie und keine Eschatologie ohne Christologie." Cf. *Geschichte*, 137; *Weiter Raum*, 275–76, where Moltmann calls this the central thesis of his theology of hope.

33. Moltmann, *Gekreuzigte Gott*, 189; *Wie ich*, 28; *Weg Jesu*, 344–50; *Umkehr*, 101, 136; *Perspektiven*, 137, 142; *Theologie*, 13.

34. Moltmann, *Gekreuzigte Gott*, 197.

35. Cf. Moltmann, *Weiter Raum*, 29, 41; *Wie ich*, 22; *Kommen*, 12; *Gekreuzigte Gott*, 10; *Theologie*, 16.

36. Moltmann, *Ethik*, 58–59; *Theologie*, 200.

37. Moltmann, *Theologie*, 150: "Das Christentum steht und fällt mit der Wirklichkeit der Auferweckung Jesu von den Toten durch Gott. . . . Christlicher Glaube der nicht Auferstehungsglaube ist,

The New Heaven and New Earth

Despite the fact that Christ's resurrection is historical without equal, "founds," "enlightened," "interrogates," and "transforms" this event the future. For Moltmann, Christ's resurrection is the anticipation, prolepsis, or preview (*Vorschickung*) of the new creation. Through this event, the new creation is already visible in the present.[38] What happened to Christ is thus a type for all who died. Christ is the "Author of life" and "Firstborn" of the new creation that overcame death (cf. Acts 3:15; 26:23; Col 1:18).[39] It is only in the new creation, however, that mankind will perfectly recognize who Christ really is.[40]

4.2.1.2 Resurrection: eschatological or historical?

Nevertheless, Moltmann's hermeneutical choices do not allow this belief in revolt to be seen historically. It is an eschatological event that provides insight into what creation can hope for:

> Whoever calls the resurrection of Christ, like his death on the cross, "historic" overlooks the new creation that begins with it and misses the eschatological hope.[41]

Nothing in the present or past is therefore definitive. In Moltmann's case, the "historical" is connected with the perishable, while the "eschatological" is connected with the imperishable. Thus the cross and the resurrection relate to each other as death and life. This negative view of what is "historical" is extensively addressed in our reflection on time when we look at Moltmann (§4.3). It forms the foundation of Moltmann's opinion that the resurrection is not a static historical fact. Christ's resurrection can only be understood from the perspective of the future, all-encompassing resurrection.[42]

This is where a circular movement arises, which knows no future without resurrection and no resurrection without a future, or: no Christology without eschatology and no eschatology without Christology. Moltmann thus rejects a purely linear forward-thinking from Christ's resurrection to the future of all things as too one-sided. His strong emphasis on the eschatological threatens to endanger him in purely linear backward thinking: from the future to Christ's resurrection. This leads to critical remarks about Moltmann's contempt for the historical resurrection.[43]

---

kann darum weder christlich noch Glaube genannt werden." Cf. *Theologie*, 15–16; *Weg Jesu*, 12, 279.

38. Moltmann, *Kommen*, 46; "Richtungen," 36; *Theologie*, 163.

39. Moltmann, *Kommen*, 86, 96, 156; *Weg Jesu*, 264–65, 343; "Hoffnung und Entwicklung," 62.

40. Moltmann, *Gekreuzigte Gott*, 103.

41. Moltmann, *Weg Jesu*, 236: "Wer die Auferstehung Christi wie seinen Kreuzestod 'historisch' nennt, übersieht die neue Schöpfung, die mit ihr beginnt, und verfehlt die eschatologische Hoffnung." Cf. *Kommen*, 156; "Resurrection," 52.

42. Moltmann, *Weg Jesu*, 68; "Resurrection," 50–52; *Theologie*, 183.

43. Pannenberg, *Systematische Theologie 3*, 580n53; Williams, "Moltmann," 82; Park, "Christian Hope," 168.

Although Moltmann confesses Christ's resurrection in his works,[44] we come across a gap in his methodology. This gap is partly reinforced by the English translations in which Moltmann's nuance does not resonate sufficiently. This is how R. A. Wilson and John Bowden translate the German statement: "Die Auferweckung Jesu von den Toten durch Gott spricht noch nicht 'die Sprache der Tatsachen', sondern erst die Sprache des Glaubens und der Hoffnung, d.h. Die 'Sprache der Verheißung,'"[45] as follows: "The resurrection of Jesus from the dead by God does not speak the 'language of facts,' but only the language of faith and hope, that is, the 'language of promise.'"[46] Because *noch nicht* has not been translated and *erst* is incorrectly translated with "only," Moltmann seems to deny the resurrection as a fact. It is this mistranslated statement that Randall Otto upholds when he accuses Moltmann of fickle vagueness in speaking about the resurrection.[47] If Otto had used the original German edition, he would not have come to that conclusion. He would then have discovered that Moltmann only indicated that the actual visibility of the new life that brings about Christ's resurrection is still lacking. It concerns the "still remaining difference between the experienced 'unredeemed world' and the belief in the preempted reconciliation."[48] Stephen Williams' comment that Moltmann does not testify of an empty grave anywhere is also unjustified.[49] We find it that Moltmann talks about this several times. According to him, the fact that the tomb of Jesus was empty is one of the best-asserted facts.[50] Christ's resurrection thus took place, but its effects are not visible in the past and present. This speaking in terms of anticipation of the future leads Moltmann not to characterize the testimony of the resurrection as a human projection, but to classify it as a real vision.[51] So, it is understandable that these ambiguities in Moltmann's vision of the resurrection should be criticized. Moltmann's rejection of the "historical" in the history of salvation means that the resurrection of Christ cannot be verified and remains a mysterious event for humanity today. Although Moltmann still speaks of an empty grave, the question remains what relevance this has for him as "evidence" for the resurrection.

---

44. Moltmann, *Sein Name*, 56; *Kommen*, 339; *Weg Jesu*, 279; *Theologie*, 146, 150, 183; Moltmann-Wendel and Moltmann, "Mit allen Sinnen," 24.

45. Moltmann, *Gekreuzigte Gott*, 160: "Die Auferweckung Jesu von den Toten durch Gott spricht noch nicht 'die Sprache der Tatsachen', sondern erst die Sprache des Glaubens und der Hoffnung, d.h. Die 'Sprache der Verheißung.'"

46. Moltmann, *Crucified God*, 173.

47. Otto, "Resurrection," 83, 85.

48. Moltmann, *Gekreuzigte Gott*, 160: "noch bleibende Differenz zwischen der erfahrbar 'unerlösten Welt' und dem Glauben an die zuvorgekommene Versöhnung."

49. Williams, "Moltmann," 82.

50. Moltmann, *Kommen*, 339; *Sein Name*, 31, 33, 36–37, 40; *Weg Jesu*, 237–68.

51. Moltmann, *Sein Name*, 51–54; *Weg Jesu*, 236, 239, 242; *Trinität*, 102, 100–101; *Gekreuzigte Gott*, 150–57; *Perspektiven*, 10–29; *Theologie*, 162.

4.2.1.3 Resurrection: the beginning of a new era

In Moltmann's eschatological and christological speaking, the new creation is central. Whoever speaks of Christ must do so from the eschatological horizon of the new creation, the redemption of creation in the new heaven and earth. With this statement, Moltmann radically opposes the idea that all the promises of God are fulfilled in the present: "With the resurrection of Jesus, not everything has happened yet."[52] Aaron Park overlooks this element: "[Moltmann's] views agree to look at Christian hope in the light of a future which transcends chronological time and can be grasped only in its dialectical, or existential, relation to history."[53] For Moltmann, the resurrection is precisely the beginning of the fulfillment of the promise. However, its completion does not take place completely in this time, as existentialists claim, but in the time of new creation: "Neither does history devour eschatology (Albert Schweizer), nor does eschatology devour history (Rudolf Bultmann)."[54] In this way, Moltmann turns his back on social individualism, and by focusing on the cosmological transformation from Christ's work, he enriches Christian eschatology.[55]

4.2.2 Adventus and futurum

In his talk about the future, Moltmann distinguishes between *adventus* and *futurum*.[56] *Adventus* anticipates what is due. *Futurum* points to what extrapolates from what is and was. *Futurum* is the calculable transient future, *adventus* is the hoped imperishable future of God. *Futurum* does not bring a *novum* and only develops the historical potential. *Adventus* points to the definite and permanent arrival of the other, new and changing that was not before. Moltmann, therefore, describes *adventus* as the equivalent of παρουσία and *futurum* as the equivalent of φύω.[57] This distinction between *adventus* and *futurum* makes "futuristic eschatology" a *contradiction in terminis*. Eschatology is only possible from the *adventus* or παρουσία that looks forward to the arrival of the permanently coming.[58]

---

52. Moltmann, *Theologie*, 147: "Mit der Auferweckung Jesu ist noch nicht alles geschehen."

53. Park, "Christian Hope," 168, 171.

54. Moltmann, *Theologie*, 150: "Weder verschlingt die Geschichte die Eschatologie (Albert Schweizer), noch verschlingt die Eschatologie die Geschichte (Rudolf Bultmann)." Cf. *Theologie*, 132–33, 137–43, 208; *Kommen*, 24–39; *Weg Jesu*, 339–42.

55. Moltmann, "Rechtfertigung," 172; *Gemeinde im Horizont*, 33–34.

56. E.g., Moltmann, "Liberation," 265; *Kommen*, 42–44; *Weg Jesu*, 229, 341, 345; *Gott in der Schöpfung*, 143–47; "Hoffnung und Entwicklung," 64–67; "Antwort auf die Kritik der Theologie der Hoffnung," 210–12. Jürgen Moltmann points out at note 11 on page 210, that he already found this linguistic distinction in others, such as: Brunner, *Das Ewige*, 26n1.

57. Moltmann, *Kommen*, 42; *Weg Jesu*, 179–80; *Gott in der Schöpfung*, 143; "Richtungen," 36.

58. Moltmann, *Gott in der Schöpfung*, 144; "Hope," 209.

From this theoretical distinction between *adventus* and *futurum* follows the distinction between extrapolation and anticipation. Extrapolation indicates the future from the present and the past, while anticipation is the knowledge of the future that influences the present and the past. Moltmann thus turns against eschatology, which stems from the analytical-theological extrapolation of God's salvific history into the present and the past, because it is in danger of degenerating into speculation or of concealing a true expectation of the future.[59]

4.2.3   God's promises and the people

4.2.3.1 *Human promises and God's promises*

Moltmann does not base his eschatology on predictions, trend analyses, or extrapolations, but on God's promises.[60] The first categories speak ambiguously about the future. They only influence the subjective present of their followers. They do not fulfill themselves and, at most passively, act as *self-fulfilling* or *self-destroying prophecy*.[61] God's promises are at odds with this. It sounds clear, and what God says is guaranteed to happen. In his promises, God commits himself and is faithful to himself.[62]

In his *Theology of Hope*, Moltmann went back on these promises of God by starting from God's promise history.[63] He discovered that God's promises looked forward to the future and that the present only anticipated this future. This led to its elaboration in 1972 of the Jewish concept of *Sjechina* (§4.7.2). From the NT, this would ultimately be the promise of the resurrection world that lights up in Christ.[64]

4.2.3.2 *Resurrection as a living hope*

Moltmann's works connect the living hope of today with the expectations of the hereafter. From the resurrection of the crucified Christ, life in history becomes a mission. God's promises open the eyes of humanity to what is realizable. From God's *promissio* follows the *missio* of the church, which is called to live in anticipation of the new creation.[65]

The salvific meaning of the resurrection includes not only the forgiveness of sins but also being raised for the sake of justification. Christ's resurrection makes possible

---

59. Moltmann, "Methoden," 52–53; "Hoffnung und Planung," 251–68. Against: Berkhof, "Over de methode," 480–91.
60. See already: Moltmann, *Theologie*, 92–93.
61. Moltmann, *Erfahrungen*, 92.
62. Moltmann, *Erfahrungen*, 93, 96–99, with reference to: Weber, *Treue Gottes*, 99–112.
63. Moltmann, *Weiter Raum*, 106–7; *Erfahrungen*, 94–96; *Theologie*, 94–95, 101–39.
64. Moltmann, *Erfahrungen*, 86.
65. Moltmann, *Weiter Raum*, 109; *Erfahrungen*, 105–6; *Kirche*; *Theologie*, 250–79, 229–312.

the realization of righteousness, rebirth, a new creation, and fulfillment of the spirit in this creation.[66] In the power of rebirth, the church bears witness in the present to the living hope by being a foretaste of the new creation. We will return to this later in §4.7.4. Here it is only mentioned that this anticipation of the church is fundamental for Moltmann's theology. A theology of hope should be related to a life of hope. Moltmann emphasizes this methodically because many have too often isolated both from each other.[67]

4.2.4 Creation and salvation

4.2.4.1 *Three creation phases: originalis, continua, nova*

In his remarks on "creation," Moltmann uses the phases *creatio originalis, creatio continua*, and *creatio nova*—concepts that traditionally include the terms *regnum naturae, regnum gratiae*, and *regnum gloriae*. Together, these three phases form one progressive history of God and creation.[68] God begins his history with this creation from *creatio originalis*. Even before the fall, protology and eschatology were linked together. Moltmann quotes the biblical theologian Ludwig Köhler: "To the beginning corresponds an end, to creation corresponds the perfection, to the 'very good' here corresponds the 'quite glorious' there."[69] This relationship between protology and eschatology does not imply that the *creatio nova* is a restored *creatio originalis*. It is a completed transformation of the *creatio originalis*. Although the original creation is good, it is the beginning of a creative process that finds its salvation, fulfillment, and completion in the new creation.[70] It is precisely Genesis 1:28 that shows that in the *creatio originalis*, humans have a mission that remains to be realized. Therefore, the "it was very good" (Gen 1:31) encompasses the entire creative process from the first unfinished and temporary creation (*creatio originalis*) to the deified and eternal creation (*creatio nova*).[71]

The *creatio orginalis* is followed by the *creatio continua*, characterized by transience and death, which speak of the imperfect and unfinished. Yet the redemption that takes place in it is also part of creation. Salvation and creation belong together. Creation must not be reduced to the beginning. In redemption, creation also has its

---

66. Moltmann, *Erfahrungen*, 104–6.
67. Moltmann, *Erfahrungen*, 58–59, 90, 123.
68. Moltmann, *Gott in der Schöpfung*, 20, 68–69; "Schöpfung," 127. *Theologie*, 123–24. For a critical discussion, see: Lønning, "Schöpfungstheologie," 207–23.
69. Moltmann, "Schöpfung," 124; Köhler, *Theologie*, 74: "Dem Anfang entspricht ein Ende, der Schöpfung die Vollendung, dem 'sehr gut' hier das 'ganz herrlich' dort." Moltmann, *Kommen*, 290; *Weg Jesu*, 105n35; "Schöpfung," 125–26.
70. Moltmann, *Kommen*, 109, 290–91; *Geschichte*, 166; *Weg Jesu*, 307; *Gott in der Schöpfung*, 53–55, 68–69; *Trinität*, 116, 228–29; *Theologie*, 123.
71. Moltmann, *Kommen*, 109, 290–91, 304; *Weg Jesu*, 307; *Trinität*, 116, 228–29; *Gott in der Schöpfung*, 53–55, 68–69; "Schöpfung," 128, 134; *Theologie*, 123.

role.⁷² Moltmann sees this connection between creation and salvation in the proclamation of the NT, which speaks of "creating" (καλέω), "awakening" (ἐγείρω), and "making alive" (ζῳοποιέω; cf. Rom 8:11). As acts of salvation, they are related to the new creation that begins with the resurrection of Christ and completes the creation process in the *creatio nova*.

4.2.4.2 The teaching of zimzum

Another facet that typifies Moltmann's theology is the doctrine of the so-called *zimzum* (צמצום), which has its roots in the teachings of the Kabbalist mystic Isaac ben Salomo Luria Ashkenazi (1534–1572).⁷³ It states that God limited his eternity and omnipresence to produce a separate space-time for creation. Through God's self-restraint, an "empty space" was created (חלל הפנוי), a chaos or *nihil*, in which God realized this creation (*creatio in nihilo*). Because of this *nihil*, creation is imperfect and focused on its future completion. This nihil is characterized by Moltmann as *Gottverlassenheit*—Godforsakenness, *Hölle*—Hell, and *absoluter Tod*—absolute death, which threatens this creation.⁷⁴

4.2.4.3 No Gnostic Redemption Myth

In his discourse on *creatio originalis*, *continua*, and *nova*, Moltmann shows an unassailable relationship between complete creation and complete salvation. He fiercely opposes anthropocentric thinking. Christians should not think from the perspective of anthropocentrism but from that of Christocentrism, which simultaneously offers space to the whole cosmos. Not only humans but also nature shares in God's salvific history.⁷⁵ Moltmann thus rejects a limitation of salvation to only the immaterial as gnostic ideas. Christian eschatology should not be redemption *out of* creation, but the redemption *of* creation.⁷⁶ Although the first heaven and earth perish (Rev 21:1–4), there comes no completely different heaven and earth in their place. God would contradict himself if he did not deliver everything he created. Eschatology is tuned by protology (*incipit vita nova*). The *creatio ex nihilo* finds its perfection in the eschatological *creatio ex vetere*.⁷⁷

---

72. Moltmann, *Kommen*, 109–10; "Schöpfung," 126.

73. For further information, see: Grözinger, *Mittelalterlichen Kabbala*, 626–27, 811–16; Bauke-Ruegg, *Allmacht Gottes*, 172–77.

74. Moltmann, "Gottes Selbstbeschränkung," 76–78; *Kommen*, 291, 310, 326–27; *Weg Jesu*, 352; *Gott in der Schöpfung*, 98–105; *Trinität*, 124; "Schöpfung," 52.

75. Moltmann, *Weg Jesu*, 298–300; *Gott in der Schöpfung*, 45, 149–50, 195; *Trinität*, 123; *Sprache*, 137.

76. Moltmann-Wendel and Moltmann, "Mit allen Sinnen," 24; Moltmann, *Kommen*, 15, 151, 284–85, 297; *Weg Jesu*, 286, 307, 320; *Gott in der Schöpfung*, 105, 240, 285.

77. Moltmann, *Kommen*, 292, 297.

Related to this is also the resurrection of the body. A human being is both immaterial and materially related to creation (see §4.5). Where attention for material salvation is lacking, a gnostic myth of salvation arises: "Whoever eschatologically teaches the 'destruction of the world' wants to reverse creation and seems to be fascinated more by nothing (*Nichts*) than by existence (*Dasein*)."[78] After the church had broadly accepted the (neo)platonic ideas about divine transcendence and the sublime nature of the invisible spiritual world from the time of Justin Martyr (±114–165) onwards, a later rediscovery of the biblical hope brought the inaccuracies of this to light. As a result, a renewed eschatology reveals a much more realistic and dynamic future for this creation. A cosmic eschatology is thus indispensable for Moltmann because of the relationship between creation and salvation. Eschatology without cosmology, deforms itself into pure gnostic immaterialism. Moltmann turns against this and thinks the new creation from a cosmological theocentrism.[79]

4.2.4.4 Continuity and discontinuity

Moltmann is aware of the traditional diversity in speaking about continuity and discontinuity between this creation and the new creation. While orthodox Lutheranism taught the total destruction of this creation, the early church and reformed tradition chose the total change of this creation, and orthodox theology emphasized its glorious deification.[80]

In his early years, Moltmann mainly emphasized the absolute *novum* of the new creation. No future could be expected from this ephemeral history. History could not produce a *novum ultimum*. Only what transcended death and conquered could be a *novum ultimum*.[81] Later Moltmann nuanced this: "these two apocalyptic eons are not two different divine creations which exclude one another. They are *two world times* of God's *one same* creation."[82] Whoever waits for the new creation does not expect another creation (cf. §2.2.2.1). The afterlife is not separate from our time. On the other hand, the new creation does not originate from within the old creation (*futurum*) but enters the old creation (*adventus*). The *creatio ex nihilo* completes itself in the *creatio ex vetere*. The new creation is this creation, which is purified, cleansed, transformed, and glorified.[83] In addition to the apocalyptic "flesh and blood cannot inherit the

---

78. Moltmann, *Kommen*, 297: "Wer eschatologisch die 'Weltvernichtung' lehrt, der will die Schöpfung rückgängig machen und scheint mehr vom Nichts als vom Dasein fasziniert zu sein." Cf. *Kommen*, 69–71, 112, 277, 285–86; *Weg Jesu*, 216, 262, 286–96.

79. Moltmann, *Kommen*, 47–64, 285; *Geist des Lebens*, 101–6; *Gott in der Schöpfung*, 47; "Theology in Germany," 202.

80. Moltmann, *Kommen*, 294, 300.

81. Moltmann, *Kommen*, 42–43n58; "Schöpfung," 132; "Theologie in der Welt," 282; *Theologie*, 28–29, 46, 119, 206.

82. Moltmann, "Hope and Reality," 83.

83. Moltmann, *Kommen*, 297–99; "Schöpfung," 66.

kingdom of God" (1 Cor 15:50), there is the messianic kingdom idea: "this perishable body must put on the imperishable, and this mortal body must put on immortality" (v. 53).[84] There are continuity and discontinuity between *finis* and *telos*. This is less expressed in the concept of *transformatio*. Moltmann thus has a strong preference for the orthodox theology of the deification of creation.[85] He decides that the Lutheran idea of world-destruction is based on a one-sided cross-theology, while the orthodox idea of deification is based on a theology of resurrection. Yet *reductio in nihilum* and *elevatio ad Deum* belong together. While the new rejects what goes against her, the old brings back what went wrong and was well renewed and broadened. Moltmann clarifies this from the biblical expressions "new land seizure," "new David," "new covenant," "new exodus," "new temple," "new commandment," "new obedience," "new song," "new people of God," "new creation." In all these expressions, tension can be felt between the truly new and what is already present.[86]

This tension between continuity and discontinuity is illustrated by Moltmann with the resurrection of Christ: (1) the risen Christ "develops" discontinuously in such a way that it does not originate from the crucified Christ; and (2) the risen Christ does not destroy the crucified Christ, but incorporates it into continuity and creates the new one. The crucified Christ is the risen Christ.[87] Resurrection is not restoration, but the anticipation of God's promise. In Moltmann's thinking about the *novum* category, the new thing from the discontinuous perspective is the unexpectedly surprising, and from the continuous perspective the analog known: "It is a universal and final transformation process, not a continuation of world history, nor a destruction of the existence of the world, but a new shaping of its essence."[88] Through the death and resurrection of the cosmos, it reaches the expected new heaven and new earth.[89]

4.2.5 Interpretation of biblical imagery

4.2.5.1 *No conceptual definition*

Speaking about the hoped-for future (*spes quae*) requires a language game of its own, the language of hope (*spes qua*). For Moltmann, this language is not conceptual, as if

---

84. Moltmann, *Erfahrungen*, 51; *Kommen*, 292.

85. Moltmann, *Kommen*, 299, 301.

86. Moltmann, *Kommen*, 45, 297, 301; "Kategorie Novum," 176–77.

87. Moltmann, *Kommen*, 45–46, 297, 301; *Weg Jesu*, 280–81; *Trinität*, 138–39; "Kategorie Novum," 176–77.

88. Moltmann, *Wissenschaft*, 66: "Es handelt sich um einen universalen und endgültigen Transformationsprozess, nicht um eine Fortsetzung der Weltgeschichte, aber auch nicht um eine Vernichtung des Daseins der Welt, sondern um die neue Formgebung ihres Soseins." Cf. "Kategorie Novum," 178–79.

89. Moltmann, *Kommen*, 287.

it definitively records, concludes, and understands everything.[90] The language of hope looks forward to what has not yet been realized, what is possible, and promised. God's great promises do not correspond to the experienced reality and reach forwards in the future. The language of hope thus opens the present to the reception of the future possible and frees it from the rigid past. The latter explains to Moltmann why promise texts cannot be summed up with a single adequate interpretation. Interpretation cannot capture and exhaust pledges in a conceptual way. It is merely an idea of the promise that is contained in the text and can offer added value in meaning.[91] While the language of hope is not conceptually defined, it is possible to speak about it in metaphors.

4.2.5.2 Metaphors and concepts

Metaphors are ambiguous and create surprise effects. Concepts are unambiguous and always mean the same thing. Whoever defines conceptually, delimits, and bounds to distinguish sharply. Anyone who speaks metaphorically breaks down boundaries and opens up to several interpretations. In both cases, the basis lies in an image of thought. Concepts and metaphors arise from experiences (Immanuel Kant).[92] However, like concepts *enclose*, metaphors *unlock*.

Metaphorical language is open towards the future. It is provisional, experimental, indirect, iconoclastic, and changeable. Metaphors from the experiential creational world, offer imaginative aspects about the unreachable divine world that transcends one's own perception. Metaphorical language speaks through images, analogies, and comparisons. It in itself forms a concise resemblance that formally includes the form "as if."[93]

According to Moltmann, the danger of concepts is that they become rigid and become idols. This explains why, for example, conceptual speaking about God is impossible. An "understood" God would only be a dead idol, which we humans have in our "grip." The danger of metaphors is that they obscure the ultimate view of the matter: "A metaphor only begins to shine when not everything is metaphorical."[94]

4.2.5.3 Continuity and discontinuity

In the biblical imagery of the new heaven and earth, Moltmann recognizes two hermeneutic facets. There is the absence of the current negativity and the presence or

---

90. Moltmann, *Erfahrungen*, 100.
91. Moltmann, *Erfahrungen*, 102–3.
92. Moltmann, *Erfahrungen*, 150, 156.
93. Moltmann, *Erfahrungen*, 149–51. Cf. McFague, *Metaphorical Theology*, 16–19.
94. Moltmann, *Erfahrungen*, 154: "Ein Metapher beginnt erst zu leuchten, wenn nicht alles metaphorisch ist."

remembrance of the current positivity. From this double paradigm, hope remains realistic and futuristic.[95]

This continuity and discontinuity are necessary for Moltmann. Christian hope that adapts to world domination loses the Crucified One. Hope for God causes a conflict between this age and the age to come, which manifests itself in metaphorical contrast-images, contrast-histories, and contrast-worlds.[96]

But the absence of the negative, which contrasts with Christian hope, also encloses the presence of the positive: "The specific negation of the negative cannot exist on its own. It depends on the anticipation of the positive."[97] With this, Moltmann turns against Emil Brunner, who states that the positive ultimately remains indeterminate in the eschaton.[98] For this, he refers to the biblical prophets who, according to him, represent the new from the pre-anticipated known: a new land conquest, a new Exodus, a new David, a new covenant, the new Mount Zion.[99] Moltmann thus differs from theologians such as Karl Rahner and Hendrik Berkhof who both argue that the biblical-classical prophets represent the new from extrapolation. We will discuss this in more detail in the critical comparison of the perspective of Rahner, Moltmann, and Beale (§6.2.1). For Moltmann, the new thing is the renewal and restoration of what was lost. Moltmann does realize that these images are analogies that point to the future. In the language of hope, it is not about restitution of the past. The future is not a return to prehistoric times. It is a call for a new creation (בָּרָא). It is a fulfillment of what had been anticipated before. The category *novum* dominates eschatological speaking, which manifests itself from Christ's resurrection (§4.2.1).[100]

4.3 HISTORY TIME AND AIONIC TIME

4.3.1 The myth of modern linear time

Moltmann rejects the modern continuous, homogenous view of time as a myth that has dominated human culture since the Enlightenment. Each ancient civilization measured the time phenomenon linear-quantitatively on the basis of days, months, and years in its own way and also took recurring cycle times into account. In modern times linear-quantitative measurement became dominant. Time was a continuously homogeneous process in which the future was an extension of past and present. In Newton's physics, time was roughly a follow-up of causalities. An important role in

---

95. Moltmann, *Erfahrungen*, 62; "Schöpfung," 132.

96. Moltmann, *Erfahrungen*, 61, 162–63.

97. Moltmann, "Schöpfung," 63: "Die bestimmte Negation des Negativen kann nicht für sich allein bestehen. Sie ist auf die Antizipation des Positiven angewiesen." Cf. *Erfahrungen*, 63; "Schöpfung," 132, 138.

98. Brunner, *Das Ewige*, 221.

99. Moltmann, *Kommen*, 45; "Kategorie Novum," 176.

100. Moltmann, *Kommen*, 44–47; "Kategorie Novum," 177–80.

the acceptance of this image of time was the economic importance in the process of progress. This ideology allowed the strongest to grow as the victor from the past and to control the present and future of the world with their own hands.[101]

Influenced by the Jewish philosophers Franz Rosenzweig (1886–1929) and Walter Benjamin (1892–1940), Moltmann opposes this linear, causal, and quantitative view of time because it takes too little account of qualitative differences in time. Moltmann believes that "future" offers possibilities that "past" includes the actual and that "presence" allows realizing the possible.[102] In terms of potential, the future thus transcends the past. Because the future comes into the present and intervenes (*adventus*), the present changes and acquires meaning for the future. The transcendent future, which is above all historical time, is thus the source from which all time modes acquire transcendental-qualitative significance.[103]

This is in contrast to the modernist view of time, which states that the past transcends the future because it determines and quasi-determines it casually. An event in the past is irreversible.[104] This reasoning recalls Moltmann's views on *futurum* (§4.2.2). Past, present, and future do not stand in a simplistic sequence. They form a complex whole.

The term "linear time" only includes individual life events. In a "time network," these life events can be related to each other. In a network, linear and cyclical concepts of time are then combined with each other. Every present is able to grasp the unrealized future of the past. This interaction with the future of the past is important for the future resurrection of the dead from the past.[105]

Moltmann sees a positive and a negative side in the earthly time (*chronos*). Chronos is positive because it is part of the good *creatio orginalis* and sets its positive-constructive movement towards the *creatio nova* in fulfillment of God's promises. At the same time, *chronos* is negative because of her relationship with changeability and transience. In Greek mythology, *Chronos* is the brother of *Thanatos*, death, and devours everything that comes its way, even its own children. While the future can still change the past, the past turns out not to be able to change the future. At the end of the past, there is only universal death, the total absence of all temporary objects and events.[106]

---

101. Moltmann, *Kommen*, 64, 154–55; *Gott in der Schöpfung*, 137–38, 144; "Methoden," 53. See also: Billings, "Natality or Advent," 142; Bauckham, "Time," 158–73.

102. Moltmann, *Erfahrungen*, 40; *Kommen*, 43, 315; *Gott in der Schöpfung*, 144; Ansell, *Annihilation*, 54–144.

103. Moltmann, *Kommen*, 43–44, 316, 319–20; "Christ," 207–8; *Gott in der Schöpfung*, 140–44.

104. Moltmann, *Erfahrungen*, 40; *Kommen*, 43, 311–12, 315–16; *Gott in der Schöpfung*, 145.

105. Moltmann, *Kommen*, 44, 140, 160, 318–19; *Weg Jesu*, 260–63; *Gott in der Schöpfung*, 133, 136, 139, 142.

106. Moltmann, *Sein Name*, 65; *Kommen*, 291, 310–12; *Gott in der Schöpfung*, 144. Cf. Augustine, *City of God*, XI.5.7; XI.13.15. See also: Meijering, *Augustin*, 52–54.

4.3.2 Initial image: From aionic time to transitory chronos time

Just like Augustine, Moltmann does not let time begin before, but with creation (*creatio cum tempore*). He distinguishes the original aionic time in which God creates heaven and earth and the beginning of the transitory earthly time in Genesis 1:5: "And there was evening and there was morning, the first day." This ephemeral happen-time (*chronos*) is characterized by change: past, present, and future. Because something changes, you recognize time. Here Moltmann follows the (neo)platonic trail that connects time with changeability and eternity with immutability.[107]

According to Moltmann, the imperfect *chronos* reflects God's absence. This "temporary" creation is, therefore, a variable creation that does not have perfection and corresponds to an open asymmetrical unbalanced system that is aimed at its future completion. From the conviction that from Genesis 1:5 onwards, there is a distinction between the original aionic time and the transitory earthly event time, Moltmann connects the future eschatological moment with this original aionic time, which he also characterizes as "original moment."[108]

4.3.3 Experiences of eternity

Despite the distinction between aionic time and transitory contemporary historical time, Moltmann argues that it is possible to experience in the *creatio continua* a foretaste of the future aionic time or the future eschatological moment by (1) the present or "now," (2) the *kairosmoment*, and (3) the intense experience of the moment (*Tiefenerfahrung des Augenblicks*).

4.3.3.1 *Present as relative eternity*

In the present historical time, Moltmann recognizes a *Vorher* and *Nachher*, which distinguish future, past, and present. Future and past are times of not being because the earlier is no more, and the later is not yet-not. Only the present is, and Moltmann estimates that to be high. His first reason for this is that the "now" distinguishes and connects past and future. A second reason is that in the "now," the past is experienced through memory and the future through expectation. Thus the present as "now" or "moment" is unique in the earthly time of events and an *Atom der Ewigkeit*: a fragmentary reflection of the "aionic time" in the new creation.[109]

---

107. Moltmann, "Gottes Selbstbeschränkung," 76–78; *Kommen*, 291, 311, 326–27; *Geist des Lebens*, 86; *Weg Jesu*, 353; *Gott in der Schöpfung*, 124–28; *Trinität*, 115, 124; "Schöpfung," 126. Cf. Augustine, *City of God*, XI.6; Plato, "Timaios," 27d. For an overview, see: Schwarzbauer, *Geschichtszeit*, 65–72; Toulmin and Goodfield, *Discovery*, 42–44.

108. Moltmann, *Gott in der Schöpfung*, 86.

109. Moltmann, *Kommen*, 313–14, 319; "Eschatologische Augenblick," 585; *Theologie*, 21–22. Cf. Augustine, *Confessions*, XI.20.26; Plato, "Parmenides," B.8.5.

However, we can only see this moment, in which past, present, and future come together, as a glimpse of aionic time. It can be distinguished from aionic time because it is impossible for the past to remember perfectly, as a film shot does. Memories and expectations remain relative and changeable through experiences in the present.[110] As a result, there is a distinction between the memory and the past as well as between "expectation" and "future." Ultimately, this fragmentary reflection is about a relative eternity that is unable to fully grasp past, present, and future.

4.3.3.2 Quality time of kairos

Above the relative simultaneity in transitory time (*chronos*) by memory and expectation, Moltmann places the quality time (*kairos*). According to Moltmann, *Kairos* is the brother of life: *Zoe*.[111] This is a wordplay because, in Greek mythology, *Zoe* does not occur as the brother of *Kairos*. With this wordplay, Moltmann points out that *Kairos* changes the empty time into a fulfilled life.

Kairos is thus "the right time," "the favorable opportunity," "the once-only opportunity," which is not given a second chance and in which the dark transient time changes into the luminous future moment that is about to arrive.[112] Yet even this *kairos* is not equal to the eschatological moment or the aionic time. If it were so, the moment would find its end in the present. The eschatological moment, however, is not the temporary moment in which past and future stand still. What happens in the present quality time is merely an anticipation of what happens to the dead in the eschatological moment. There is still a similarity and difference.

4.3.3.3 Deep experience of the moment

Above the *kairosmoment* stands the experience of the present as *Tiefenerfahrung des Augenblicks* ("Deep experience of the moment"). That is the paradoxical "eternal now" (*nunc aeternum*). This moment, like an *Atom der Ewigkeit*, interrupts the transitory time and breaks the distinction between past and future. God's presence is then no longer experienced in the temporality but in the timelessness of the mystical *nunc aeternum*. It is an ecstasy moment that takes place and has its own time experience. The *Tiefenerfahrung des Augenblicks* is not only a relative simultaneity of past, present, and future but an absolute present, an *ungeteilte Präsenz im Präsens*—undivided presence in the present tense, a filled moment of life.[113] Whoever isolates himself from God experiences time as impermanence and death as its universal end. Very different

---

110. Cf. Volf, *End of Memory*, 30, 45, 49–56.

111. Moltmann-Wendel and Moltmann, "Mit allen Sinnen," 39.

112. Moltmann, *Kommen*, 320–23; *Theologie*, 39–50. With references to: Kierkegaard, *Begriff Angst*, 94; Bultmann, *Geschichte*, 106; Barth, *Römerbrief*, 481.

113. Moltmann, *Kommen*, 319–20.

is the life experience of someone who experiences the *Tiefenerfahrung des Augenblicks* and receives a taste of eternity. Because this moment is brief, a hunger for eternal life arises as a perfect undisturbed fullness of life.

4.3.4 Reflections: From transient chronos time to aionic time

The eschatological moment eventually leaves the ephemeral past, present, and future and, like the original moment or the aionic time before Genesis 1:5, enters into eternity. In concrete terms, this means that the time in the new creation does not correspond to the transitory chronos time in this creation. This time disappears and makes way for eternity, as it was present for Genesis 1. This creates a mirror image: from aionic time via transitory time back to aionic time.[114]

4.3.5 The aionic time of new creation

4.3.5.1 *God's coming in the new creation*

The change from transient to aionic time occurs because God comes to dwell in his creation. According to the theory of *zimzum*, God then lifts up his self-restraint (§4.2.4.2). Then God is "all in all." This does not mean that the new creation becomes equal to God, but that it participates in the divine life. Moltmann wants to keep a close eye on the separation between God and creation. For God knows an "absolute eternity," while the new creation knows a "relative eternity," which shares in the "absolute eternity" and which traditionally refers to theology as "aionic time." The glorified creation and the glorified humanity remain finite, but not mortal; they remain subject to time, but not to transience.[115]

Through God's presence in the new creation, a profound transformation and transfiguration of time and space take place. The transient time of occurrence makes way for eternity and the limiting space for the ubiquitous creation. Primeval time and space end when creation becomes a temple for God's eternal glory:

> The *temporal creation* then becomes an eternal creation because then all creatures participate in the eternity of God. The *spatial creation* then becomes the omnipresent creation because then all creatures participate in the omnipresence of God. The departure of creation from time into the aion of glory takes place through the annihilation of death and the raising of the dead.[116]

---

114. Moltmann, *Erfahrungen*, 97; *Kommen*, 323; *Weg Jesu*, 353–55; "Eschatologische Augenblick," 586.

115. Moltmann, *Kommen*, 43, 308; "Eschatologische Augenblick," 588; "Schöpfung," 133.

116. Moltmann, *Kommen*, 323–24: "Die *zeitliche Schöpfung* wird dann zu einer ewigen Schöpfung, weil dann alle Geschöpfe an der Ewigkeit Gottes teilnehmen. Die *räumliche Schöpfung* wird dann zur allgegenwärtigen Schöpfung, weil dann alle Geschöpfe an der Allgegenwart Gottes teilnehmen. Der Austritt der Schöpfung aus der Zeit in den Aion der Herrlichkeit geschieht durch die Vernichtung des

4.3.5.2 Aionic time as the end of the time of chronos

At the dawn of Aionic Time, life conquers death. The moment has come for the transient time that it is no longer "time" (χρόνος οὐκέτι ἔσται, Rev 10:6).[117] Chronos, the earthly linear time, the incessantly transitory time of growth and decay, then ceases to exist. This happens on the last day, when the resurrection of the dead takes place, "in a moment, in the twinkling of an eye" (ἐν ἀτόμῳ, ἐν ῥιπῇ ὀφθαλμοῦ ὀφθαλμοῦ, 1 Cor 15:52). Because the dead exist in God's eternal time, their time between death and resurrection is exactly the same as this moment. The last day is thus meant to be "the Lord's day" in terms of content, for which all times exist simultaneously.[118] Also, the resurrection day is equal to the eschatological moment of eternity. In this, Moltmann builds on Luther, who also stated that both the first and the last man were equally close to the day of resurrection: "Therefore the first man Adam is as near to him as the last who is born before the last day. . . . God does not see time by length, but by the cross."[119] The resurrection of the dead happens shortly after death.

When the eternal God dwells on the new earth, the earthly time changes into an "aionic time" that knows no beginning or end, and no sooner or later. God's coming thus happens *in* time and with respect *to* time.[120] Because God's coming puts an end to the process of historical time, it ends the historically transitory chronos time and simultaneously transforms it as a whole into all times. In an instant, the resurrection of the dead occurs. This takes place synchronously (for all people simultaneously), as well as diachronically (for all dead from Adam), at the last moment. The last day is, therefore, more than the last calendar day. It is the time in which all time transforms into the aionic time. All times of history-time come together herein and are changed and glorified incorporated in the time of the new creation.[121]

4.3.5.3 Aionic time as "fullness of times."

For Moltmann, the new creation is still characterized by time, but time without transience. If time was completely lacking, the completion would be considered as "the end of human freedom and the end of God's possibilities. Time would be abolished in eternity and possibilities in reality. But the completion theologically cannot be

---

Todes und die Auferweckung der Toten."

117. Moltmann, *Kommen*, 308; *Weg Jesu*, 351; "Eschatologische Augenblick," 584.

118. Moltmann, *Sein Name*, 65; *Kommen*, 121–24, 307–8.

119. Moltmann, "Liebe," 848: "Darum ist ihm der erste Mensch Adam ebenso nahe als der zum letzten wird geboren vor dem jüngsten Tag. . . . Denn Gott sieht die Zeit nicht nach der Länge, sondern nach der Quere." Cf. Luther, *Luthers Werke*, 14:70; 36:349; 37:151.

120. Moltmann, *Weg Jesu*, 342, 351–52.

121. Moltmann, *Kommen*, 123, 308, 324; *Weg Jesu*, 123, 352–53; "Eschatologische Augenblick," 582.

thought this way."[122] God wants to give creation eternal vitality and not eternal rigidity or stiffening. Aionic time is a "fullness of times," of which the *Tiefenerfahrung des Augenblicks* gives the highest taste. Just as God is "all in all" in the new creation and pervades everything, so too is the aionic time pervading the time of happening. There is an interaction between time and eternity so that it is possible to speak of "eternal time" and "time-filled eternity."[123]

4.3.5.4 Aionic time as cycle time

How can this aionic time of new creation be imagined in concrete terms? The descriptions Moltmann uses for this are multifaceted and abstract: beginning without end, filled time, aionic time, a time filled with eternity, eternal time, time of eternal life, time of eternal vivacity, a circle of time, reversible time. His representation of "reversible time," which replaces this "irreversible time," clarifies most of what he means. For the present creation, the irreversible linear time of becoming and passing away applies. For the future creation, the reversible time of the eons applies.[124]

For Moltmann, aionic time is not an endless linear-homogeneous timeline. It is a cycle time (*Zeitkreis*) in which all times return eternally. Instead of the time experience of the evening and the farewell, there is the experience of the morning and the salutation. For a linear time, reversible time forms dominate closed, symmetrical, and balanced systems. However, these systems do not occur in historical (*geschichtliche*) reality.[125] With the coming of God, there comes a life that does not die any more and a time that does not perish anymore. Moltmann's cycle time is the geometric image of perfection, which also characterized the paradisiacal state. However, this eternal time cycle is different from God's eternity. It is a relative, participatory eternity of God's dwelling.[126]

Because of this cycle time, Moltmann avoids talking about the hereafter as an eternal standstill. In a cycle time, there is a dynamic past and a dynamic future, without these decaying. Eternal life is a full life that has nothing to do with timelessness and death. There is an eye for memory in the cycle time, because

---

122. Moltmann, "Schöpfung," 133: "das Ende menschlicher Freiheit und das Ende der Möglichkeiten Gottes. Zeit würde in Ewigkeit und Möglichkeiten in Wirklichkeit aufgehoben. So aber kann die Vollendung theologisch nicht gedacht werden."

123. Moltmann, *Kommen*, 325.

124. Moltmann, "Eschatological Future," 127; *Kommen*, 324.

125. Moltmann, *Sein Name*, 66; *Science and Wisdom*, 46; *Kommen*, 311, 314, 324–25; *Weg Jesu*, 354–55; "Verschränkte Zeiten," 217.

126. Moltmann, *Erfahrungen*, 107.

> Without memory and without expectation, we would only perceive moments, impressions of moments and snapshots, but no connections. We could not hear any melody or recognize any movement.[127]

Nevertheless, Moltmann urges caution in speaking about future aionic times. There is a danger of wanting to derive all of its expectations from the present so that the future has nothing new in-store.

4.4 SPACE FOR THE NEW CREATION

In 2008 Moltmann pointed out that a reflection on God and space is often lacked in theological studies. Since Augustine, numerous designs have appeared on the subject of "God and time," while the subject of "God and space" remained virtually untouched until the time of Gottfried Leibniz and Isaac Newton.[128] According to Moltmann, space, like time, is not an empty *abstractum*. Both are qualified by what takes place in them. The "now" between past and future is an intersection of space and time. Then the creation stands between past and future, and between space in front of, behind, below, and above itself.

4.4.1 Created negative living space

According to Moltmann, life and space influence and form each other. Each living space has its own specific modus. People move through the wide space, but seek a resting place in the limited and framed space.[129] Moltmann recognizes the importance of this space for creation. From the *zimzum*, he qualifies the space and time in the *creatio orginalis* as negative. God limited himself and created a necessary space-time that served to guarantee distance and freedom of movement between Creator and creation.

If God's glory were absolutely omnipresent, creation would not exist. God must fulfill his glory in order to be accessible to his creatures, for he who sees God must die.[130] For Moltmann, this space (*topos*) is connected with separation and detachment, as is the duration (*chronos*), which is connected with transience.

The fact that God creates space for creation does not mean that it is separate from him. He allows the world that is distinct from him to exist for itself, with itself, and within itself. The space of creation is both outside him because it stands at a distance

---

127. Moltmann, *Kommen*, 317: "[o]hne Erinnerung und ohne Erwartung würden wir nur Zeitpunkte, Augenblickseindrücke und Momentaufnahmen, aber keine Zusammenhänge wahrnehmen. Wir könnten keine Melodie hören und keine Bewegung erkennen." Cf. *Kommen*, 324; *Gott in der Schöpfung*, 133.
128. Moltmann, "God in the World," 371; *Weiter Raum*, 344.
129. Moltmann, "Gott und Raum," 133–34, 137.
130. Moltmann, *Kommen*, 336; "Gott und Raum," 139–41.

from him, and in him because it exists in him. Moltmann supports this with Scriptures such as: "He brought me out into a broad place" (Ps 18:19), "you have set my feet in a broad place" (31:8), "In him, we live and move and have our being" (Acts 17:28), as well as with a quote from *Midrash Rabba Genesis*: "we do not know whether God is the space of his world or whether his world is his space" (II:68.9).[131]

Moltmann concretizes this from the trinitarian perichoresis and the fetus in the uterus as an example and model. The trinitarian perichoresis points to the penetration of the Father, Son, and Spirit, which leads to unity without identification. God gives himself space and forms that space within God. Similarly, the paradoxical is conceivable outside and in God. This double perspective is also evident in the Latin translation of *perichoresis* with *circumincessio* and *circuminsessio*. *Circumincessio* refers to the dynamic penetration, *circuminsessio* to the resting indwelling. Movement and rest are simultaneously present in the Trinity. Every divine Person exists in the other. Father, Son, and Spirit differ from each other in their relations with each other. The example of the fetus in the womb shows that we grow in the womb for nine months and feel the first pain of separation from birth. This is followed by various other living spaces that form humanity and in which we live: the family and society. Each person is thus in relationship to others and forms their living space.[132]

4.4.2 God's "living" in limited space

Although God is infinite and creation is limited, God finds a dwelling place in creation throughout history. This raises the question of whether the space of creation includes God or whether God includes the space of creation. Moltmann follows the rabbinical view that only God encompasses the space for creation and points out the tensions that arise when God is presented in the Bible as the One who chooses to dwell among people (cf. Exod 29:45).[133] How is this possible without God blowing up or destroying creation through God's infinity?

Moltmann mentions two possibilities: (1) Only a part of God dwells on earth, or (2) God chooses to be lowered to live on earth.[134] The second option is found in the Jewish teachings of the *Shekhinah* and the Christian teachings of Christ's Incarnation. Anyone who denies that God is in the space of creation will abolish both the theology of Christ's Incarnation and that of the *inhabitatio* of the Spirit.[135] God makes space for this creation and is present in this space of creation. Equal perichoresis takes place between unequal. God's special presence is then founded in the special act of

---

131. Moltmann, *Kommen*, 328, 331; *Gott in der Schöpfung*, 101.
132. Moltmann, "Gott und Raum," 135–38; *Kommen*, 330.
133. Moltmann, "Gott und Raum," 136.
134. Moltmann, *Kommen*, 331; *Trinität*, 42. Cf. Goldberg, *Untersuchungen*, 333–35; Kuhn, *Gottes Selbsterniedrigung*.
135. Moltmann, "Gott und Raum," 143–44.

descending and self-destruction, which is already beginning in the divine decision to create (*zimzum*). Throughout history, God finds a limited place of residence on earth. God's *Shekhinah* comes to people and leaves people. Since the destruction of the temple in 587 BC, the Jewish people expect the return of the *Shekhinah* in the end times.[136]

Just as the *Tiefenerfahrung des Augenblicks* gives a foretaste of the aionic time, in which God glorifies creation and transforms it into an eternal creation, the stay of the *Shekhinah* in the time of the event gives a foretaste of God's glory, which pervades creation and participates omnipresent in creation.[137]

4.4.3   God's dwelling in the new creation

When God appears in the new creation, not only does temporal time (*chronos*) change into aionic time but also limited-created space (*topos*) changes into omnipresence. A principle for this is Revelation 20:11: "no place was found for them" (τόπος οὐχ εὑρέθη αὐτοῖς).[138]

While Moltmann points out that aionic time is the "fullness of times," in which all times glorify and return perichoretically transformed, he does not speak so of space. He does note, however, that the new creation is imbued with God's eternity and omnipresence (cf. §4.6.3).

The moment God enters this creation, there is no longer any spatial distance between God and creation. From this distance came independence and sin against God. In the new creation, this changes and the creation is absorbed in God's inner presence.[139] The new creation becomes a complete and eternal dwelling place for God's omnipresence.

Just as God chooses to be restricted at the beginning to create space and time for his creation, God removes that restriction at the end, to live in the new creation. Thus, eschatology not only points to what happens later with creation but also to what happens to God. The previews of the new creation in time and space are then fulfilled in the eternal, omnipresent creation. In this omnipresent creation, God allows creation to participate in God's omnipresence and gives *weiten Raum* in which there is no more oppression or distress. This is how the impermanence and detachment of this creation ends, and its eternal presence begins in the omnipresence of God.

---

136. Moltmann derives this idea from the Talmud via Rosenzweig: Neusner, *Megillah*, 29a.
137. Moltmann, *Erfahrungen*, 39; *Kommen*, 323–24, 332, 336–37; *Gott in der Schöpfung*, 101.
138. Moltmann, *Kommen*, 308, 325.
139. Moltmann, *Kommen*, 325–28, 336–37, 345; *Weg Jesu*, 326–28; *Gott in der Schöpfung*, 100–102; *Trinität*, 178.

4.5 MATTER AND SPIRIT IN THE ESCHATON

4.5.1 Hope for matter

Moltmann rejects any gnostic thinking that offers no room for a future of matter (§4.2.4.3). Richard Bauckham notes that Moltmann emphasizes this recovery of the physical, mainly in his talk about the millennium: "It seems that Moltmann now thinks only the millennium, as a this-worldly future prior to the new creation, can supply such motivation and direction."[140] But in his *Kommen Gottes*, Moltmann also pays attention to the material aspect of the new creation.[141] In this context, Bauckham's dichotomy does not follow if he concludes that Moltmann "see[s] the eschaton itself, the new creation, in a more transcendent way, focused on the beatific vision rather than the earthly kingdom of God so that the need for an earthly fulfillment of history has to be met by millenarianism."[142] In *Das Kommen Gottes* Moltmann also opposes the idea of thinking about a non-physical heaven for the blessed in the afterlife. This kind of intangible representation of liberated souls leans more against the conception of Plato than against the teaching of Christ. While the idea of the immortality of the soul relies on something immortal in humanity and accepts death as a liberating friend, the belief in the resurrection of the dead is based on the hope of a God who creates what does not exist and makes the dead alive by overcoming death as the last enemy.[143] Moltmann, following the example of the New Testament scholar Oscar Cullmann, illustrates this with Christ's suffering: his suffering was terrible. He trembled and was disturbed. His soul was mortally saddened when he prayed that the cup might pass (Matt 26:37–39). He died with the complaint, "My God, my God, why have you forsaken me?" (27:46). Jesus did not experience his death as the salvation of the soul from the body. He experienced death as the separation between his whole Person and the living God.[144]

The former (neo)-Platonism, which some church fathers accepted, is not an option for Moltmann. It lacks the biblical fundamental truth of the "resurrection of the dead" (Heb 6:1–3). Resurrection means more than living on after death. It is an event that encompasses life in its entirety: "The apocalyptic symbol of the 'resurrection of the dead' always means the whole dead in person, body, and soul."[145] Resurrection is hope for the lived life. This totality also includes the body that God gave to humans. This is also part of the resurrection because resurrection without a physical resurrection is no

---

140. Bauckham, "Millennium," 135–36.
141. Moltmann, *Kommen*, 294–306.
142. Bauckham, "Millennium," 135n21.
143. Moltmann, *Sein Name*, 73, 78; *Kommen*, 82–83; "Liebe," 841; *Sprache*, 137.
144. Moltmann, "Liebe," 842. Cf. Cullmann, *Unsterblichkeit*.
145. Moltmann, *Weg Jesu*, 279: "Das apokalyptische Symbol der "Auferweckung der Toten" meint immer den ganzen Toten in Person nach Leib und Seele." Cf. *Kommen*, 74–95; *Gott in der Schöpfung*, 170, 250–53.

resurrection.[146] The kingdom of God is therefore not a kingdom localized in heaven, but a kingdom "like in heaven on earth." Moltmann radically rejects any separation between creation and humanity. Creation and humankind are inextricably linked and threatened by the same *nihil*. Both are eagerly awaiting completion.[147]

In Christian faith, it is therefore not about spiritualization, but about enlightenment. Moltmann points out that almost all the ways of God end in this physicality.[148] God created male and female as God's image on earth; God's Messiah became "flesh" and lived physically among the people on earth; God poured out the Holy Spirit on all "flesh" on earth. From that salvific historical perspective, Moltmann rightly asks the question: "How could the history of God with his creatures not end in a resurrection of the flesh and eternal bodily life?"[149] What God universally merges, is in the new creation not reduced to individualism and spiritualism in salvation.

4.5.2 Resurrection of life

In the end, there is a victory of life over death, as the Nicene Creed testifies. Life in the future century is not separate from a place. Resurrection and eternal life are God's promises for the people on this earth. It is death that is conquered as the last enemy and life that conquers (1 Cor 15:26).[150] Because Christ conquered death, humans may hope for a future in which every negative authority and power is destroyed. This also includes the destruction of death, which cuts humanity off from God's promises. This contrast between life and death leads Moltmann to prefer to speak of "resurrection of life," "resurrection of the body," or "resurrection of the flesh" instead of "resurrection of the dead." In support of this, he refers to Paul who, in addition to the "redemption" (ἀπολύτρωσις, Rom 8:23), "change" (ἀλλάσσω, 1 Cor 15:51), and "glorification" (δόξα, Phil 3:21) of the body, speaks of its "life-giving" (ζωοποιέω, Rom 8:11).[151]

Temporally speaking, according to Moltmann, the "resurrection of life" occurs at the completion of creation, in the eschatological moment of eternity (§4.3.5.2). If this were not the case, humanity would be completed separately from creation. The latter is by no means the case. Without new creation, there is no "resurrection of the flesh":

---

146. Moltmann, *Weg Jesu*, 279; "Liebe," 843.

147. Moltmann, *Sein Name*, 73; *Gott in der Schöpfung*, 82, 147–50; *Kommen*, 306; *Theologie*, 60, 195.

148. Moltmann, *Sein Name*, 62–63; Moltmann-Wendel and Moltmann, "Mit allen Sinnen," 24. Cf. Oetinger, "Leib, Soma," 223: "Leiblichkeit ist das Ende der Werke GOttes, wie aus der Stadt GOttes klar erhellet.—Physicality is the end of the works of God, as the city of God clearly illuminates."

149. Moltmann, *Sein Name*, 62–63: "Wie sollte die Geschichte Gottes mit seinen Geschöpfen nicht in einer Auferstehung des Fleisches und einem ewigen leiblichen Leben enden?"

150. Moltmann, *Lebendige Gott*, 58; *Sein Name*, 61, 73; *Kommen*, 83, 86; *Geschichte*, 189; *Gott in der Schöpfung*, 103; "Kategorie Novum," 179; *Theologie*, 17, 333.

151. Moltmann, *Sein Name*, 63; *Kommen*, 122–23; Moltmann-Wendel and Moltmann, "Mit allen Sinnen," 26, 28–29.

> The idea of being resurrected "from this earth" leaves this earth without hope. It is, therefore, better to change this idea and wait for "to be resurrected with this earth."[152]

On the question of what the resurrection body looks like, Moltmann writes: "By the living, lived body we do not mean the deserted body as an object, scientifically objectified organs, and their medical treatment, but the experienced and lived body, with which I am subjectively identical."[153] With this, he points out that the resurrection of the body cannot be reduced to the recovery of molecules and atoms, which disappeared into the earth at death. Resurrection is also more than the return of a dead person to this perishable life. It is about resurrection in eternal life. This differs qualitatively from the transient life to which creation in the *creatio continua* is subjected.[154] At the same time, Moltmann stresses that the resurrection body is similar to this transient body. For Moltmann, sexuality also exists in the physical resurrection body.[155]

4.5.3 Christ: Firstborn of the new creation

Moltmann sees the importance of matter in the new creation in the life of Christ. Already on the mountain of glorification, Christ reveals that bodily matter shares in glorification. According to Moltmann, anyone who reduces the eschaton or hereafter to mere contemplation of God and embraces the gnostic idea of an immaterial future commits an infringement of the biblical Incarnation-Christology.[156] The biblical hope of the God who raises the dead does not reject the material world in which the cross stood.

With the resurrection of Jesus of Nazareth, humanity realizes that Jesus is the Firstborn of the future general and all-encompassing resurrection to which this creation looks forward. It is this hope that leads Paul to conclude that this mortal body afflicts immortality (1 Cor 15:53). Moltmann emphasizes the continuity between the crucified and risen body of Christ:

> I do not believe that an Easter transfigured body has taken the place of the pre-Easter mortal body of the "flesh and blood" of Jesus so that the two must be distinguished.[157]

---

152. Moltmann-Wendel and Moltmann, "Mit allen Sinnen," 25: "Die Vorstellung, '*von* dieser Erde' auferweckt zu werden, läßt diese Erde ohne Hoffnung zurück. Es ist darum besser, diese Vorstellung zu verändern und darauf zu warten, '*mit* dieser Erde auferweckt zu werden.'" Cf. *Kommen*, 124, 302–4.

153. Moltmann, *Sein Name*, 63: "Mit dem lebendigen, gelebten Körper meinen wir nicht den entseelten Leib als ein Objekt, wissenschaftlich objektivierte Organe und ihre medizinische Behandlung, sondern den erfahrenen und gelebten Leib, mit dem ich subjektiv identisch bin."

154. Moltmann, *Kommen*, 123; *Gekreuzigte Gott*, 156–57; "Kategorie Novum," 179.

155. Moltmann-Wendel and Moltmann, "Mit allen Sinnen," 26, 31.

156. Moltmann, *Kommen*, 297, 300.

157. Moltmann, *Sein Name*, 56: "Ich glaube nicht, dass ein österlicher, verklärter Leib an die Stelle des vorösterlichen, sterblichen Leibes aus 'Fleisch und Blut' Jesu getreten ist, so dass man beide auseinanderhalten muss." Cf. *Weg Jesu*, 20; "Hoffnung und Entwicklung," 62.

The New Heaven and New Earth

It is the crucified, dead, and buried body of Christ that God raised from the dead. Without this identity, there is no resurrection. In heaven, there is no other body of Christ than the body that was born to Mary and crucified by Pilate. Thus, according to Moltmann, the resurrection body will also be the resurrection of the old body. He sees a foundation for this in Philippians 3:21, which states that in the future, our humiliated body will be conformed to Christ's glorified body.[158] Moltmann concludes from this: Jesus' crucifixion took place in solitude. His death was exclusive; no one took part. His resurrection is inclusive and available to all. It encompasses all creation and is not geographically time-limited. It is a cosmic event. His resurrection is crucial and forms the beginning of the new heaven and earth.[159]

Without the resurrection of Jesus, there is no hope for a life of resurrection in the new creation. Moltmann, therefore, pleads for the actual historicity of this resurrection, because: (1) the multiplicity and variation in the messages of the resurrection show that the primal congregation did not find it necessary to make mutual agreements about a unity in reporting; (2) the disciples returned to Jerusalem after the apparitions of Christ from Galilee, although this city was hostile to them; (3) the disciples in the hostile city of Jerusalem freely proclaimed the resurrection without anyone being able to contradict them because Jesus' grave would be demonstrably empty for everyone.[160]

Since the resurrection of Jesus, a process of resurrection has been set in motion that leads to the resurrection of all things.[161] The risen Christ, as Firstborn, points to the universal resurrection yet to come, which is the certain consequence of this commitment. Moltmann's universal resurrection is not only about the future resurrection of people, but also about that of other creatures: animals, plants, stones, and everything that is part of the cosmic system: "The resurrected body of Christ, therefore, works as an embodied promise for all creation."[162] Christ's resurrection anticipates the life of the new creation where righteousness dwells and where God's kingdom completes itself. From this perspective, there is no better place for the future kingdom than the place where the cross stood in the earth: creation glorified to new creation. Thus, there is no Christology conceivable without eschatology and no eschatology without Christology (§4.2.1).[163]

---

158. Cf. Moltmann, *Kommen*, 46, 88, 95, 103, 298; *Weg Jesu*, 272; *Gott in der Schöpfung*, 232, 267.

159. Moltmann, *Sein Name*, 60.

160. Moltmann, *Sein Name*, 58.

161. Moltmann-Wendel and Moltmann, "Mit allen Sinnen," 29.

162. Moltmann, *Weg Jesu*, 281: "Der auferweckte Leib Christi wirkt darum wie eine verkörperte Verheißung für die ganze Schöpfung." Cf. *Kommen*, 338.

163. Moltmann, *Weg Jesu*, 176; "Christliche Hoffnung," 247.

4.6 GOD'S INDWELLING IN CREATION

4.6.1 God's indwelling

While Moltmann's *In der Geschichte des dreieinigen Gottes* emphasizes the redemption of creation in God, his *Das Kommen Gottes* emphasizes the glorification of God in the new creation. Traditionally God desires to dwell with people. In the history of salvation this is expressed through God's abode in the tabernacle and temple, the dwelling of God's fullness in Christ (Col 2:9), the dwelling of God's Spirit in the church, the dwelling in God's love (1 John 4:16), and the dwelling of God in the new creation (Rev 21:3).[164] The history of the covenant and God's faithfulness are thus in continuity with the new heaven and earth: the glory of the new creation radiates its light over the present and past.

God's coming to this creation is the eschatological climax of the history of salvation. It transforms the temporary-perishable creation into God's own home. Prehistory and primal space then come to their fulfillment. Creation then forms the temple for God's *Shekhinah* and transforms into an eternally ubiquitous creation, in so far as all creatures participate in God's eternity and ubiquity.[165]

4.6.2 Perichoresis of Creator and Creation

When God dwells in the new creation, a mutual indwelling (*perichoresis*) arises, of God in creation and of creation in God. Moltmann relates this perichoresis to the openness of God:

> The inner-trinitarian relations of the Father to the Son, of the Son to the Father, and of the Spirit of the Father and the Son are so "open" that every created being can find its eternal home in them.[166]

This also results from the idea that God's eternity is not an absence of temporality. By this, God can give fullness to creation, because God is open to the aionic time as cycle time.[167]

Creation ultimately shares in the divine attributes of eternity and omnipresence, as God previously participated in the time of events (*chronos*) and limited space (*topos*). *Chronos* and *topos* end now. Impermanence and distance between Creator

---

164. Moltmann, "Hope and Reality," 84.
165. Moltmann, *Kommen*, 323, 348–50; "Liebe," 839; *Trinität*, 119.
166. Moltmann, "World in God," 38; *Kommen*, 337; *Gott in der Schöpfung*, 96–98, 101; *Trinität*, 73, 122.
167. Moltmann, *Kommen*, 310.

The New Heaven and New Earth

and creation, created by the *nihil*, make way for the eternal presence in God's omnipresence. God's indwelling eternity gives the creation eternal space-time without distress.[168]

Salvation thus points also, besides the relationship with God, to the participation of the redeemed in the eternal inner-trinitarian life of God. Humankind becomes a temple of God, and God becomes their temple: *finitum capax infiniti*. Creation finds space in God in a creative way, just as God finds space in creation in a divine way.[169] The latter was already the case with Jesus of Nazareth. In the Gospel of John, Jesus already says that the Father and the Son will dwell in humanity (Joh 14:23). Later 1 John also mentions such a mutual perichoresis: the person who stays in love stays *in* God and God stays *in* this person (4:16). Paul takes up this idea when he writes that God will be *all in all* (1 Cor 15:28).[170] God comes with glory into creation and pervades everything. As everything then is in God, God then is in everything. Creation then dwells in God by a mutual unanimous permeation. God glorifies humanity according to God's image because humanity will be part of the life and glory of God and thus fulfills its status as creature, for only creation as a whole can become a parable of its Creator.[171] Then the community of God and the community of the world are no longer opposites of each other. The new creation is a complete Kingdom of God, a complete perichoretic unity of Creator and creation (*panentheism*).[172]

In this discourse on mutual perichoresis, Moltmann clings to the unity and diversity of God and creation, of heaven and earth, of person and nature, and of clergy and sensuality.[173] God always remains more than humanity. The ultimate perichoresis happens without creation and Creator mixing or dissolving. Also, in Moltmann's presentation about the time in the new creation, this came to the fore (§4.3.5). The aionic time of the new heaven and earth is not equal to God's absolute eternity. It is a relative eternity connected to creation and participates in divine eternity. Humankind and creation do not deify in the divine life. God does not merge into creation, which would lead to atheism (*finitum non capax infiniti*). And creation does not dissolve in God, which would lead to pantheism. In Christian terms, Moltmann speaks in such a way that God dwells unmixed and undivided in the new creation and that the new creation dwells in God.[174]

---

168. Moltmann, *Kommen*, 337.
169. Moltmann, "World in God," 38, 41.
170. Moltmann, "Schöpfung," 132.
171. Moltmann, *Erfahrungen*, 145. Cf. Moltmann, *Gott in der Schöpfung*, 133.
172. Moltmann, *Sein Name*, 37; *Erfahrungen*, 56.
173. Moltmann, *Sein Name*, 38; *Kommen*, 306.
174. Moltmann, *Kommen*, 325, 337; *Weg Jesu*, 354–56; "Schöpfung," 133.

4.6.3 God's development

From the history of salvation, creation finds its universal destination in the new creation. Moltmann extrapolates this on God's own (salvific) history. The Creator also finds an ultimate destination in the new creation. God's history is in the suffering with and through this creation connected with the future of this creation.[175] Or, as Douglas Farrow summarizes: "a primordial Trinity (God open to the world) is perfected via the economy (God suffering in the world) into an eternal or doxological Trinity (God glorified in the world)."[176]

The new creation serves the justification of God through the glorification of God. God comes to rest in the Sabbath of the new creation. This completes the healing process of creation, to the glorification of God. This gives the new heaven and earth a soteriological end and doxological eternity character.[177]

4.7 ANTICIPATING THE NEW CREATION

Already in the previous chapters, it appeared that Moltmann, in his remarks on the new creation, takes into account biblical premonitions that anticipate this. In *Das Kommen Gottes*, this is evident from the titles: *Die Zukunft der Schöpfung*—The Future of Creation, *Sabbat und Schechina*—Sabbath and Shekhinah, *Der kosmische Tempel*—The Cosmic Temple, *das himmlische Jerusalem*—The Heavenly Jerusalem.[178] Sabbath and *Shekhinah* point to the new creation in the history of salvation and are complemented by the resurrection of Christ, the church as first fruits, and the description of the new Jerusalem. These anticipations are too easily overlooked in studies of Moltmann's eschatology.[179] Yet they form an integral part in Moltmann's talk about the new creation and they clarify his line of thought.

4.7.1 The Sabbath as a promise of new creation

We mentioned earlier the connection Moltmann saw between *creatio originalis* and *creatio nova* (§4.2.4.1). In the *creatio originalis* there is already an anticipation of the new creation. Moltmann explicitly thinks about the relationship between the Sabbath and the Shekhinah.

---

175. Moltmann, *Kommen*, 351–67; *Trinität*, 20–21, 36–76, 175–77.
176. Farrow, "In the End," 436.
177. Moltmann, *Weg Jesu*, 204.
178. Moltmann, *Sein Name*, 97–109; *Kommen*, 287–93, 338–49; *Gott in der Schöpfung*, 281–398.
179. Such silence is striking at Moltmann: Sicouly, *Schöpfung*; Remenyi, *Um der Hoffnung*. For the importance of attention to this, see: Bauckham and Hart, *Hope against Hope*; Hart, "Imagination," 49–76.

While God created two things each day of creation (water above and below the firmament, fish and birds, people and animals, etc.), he created the Sabbath in the singular. The Sabbath thus looks forward to its partner and thus contains a promise for creation. She waits for the coming of God's *Shekhinah* in the *creatio nova*. As the Sabbath stands in time relation to the *Shekhinah*, the *Shekhinah* is in spatial relation to the Sabbath.[180]

By anticipating this promise, the Sabbath in Genesis 1 has no "evening." She only receives her "fulfillment" in God's future Sabbath, where the aionic time reigns.[181] The message of creation in Genesis is the first step on the long staircase of salvation that leads creation into the new creation. From the *creatio originalis* onwards, the Sabbath cyclically breaks through the working time in the *creatio continua*. Moltmann follows the Jewish tradition that every interruption of working time by the Sabbath reminds humanity of God's desire to be present in the creation period.[182] The resulting cycle time breaks through and arranges the irreversible duration and prepares creation for the eschatological new Sabbath. The Sabbath thus bears witness to God's homeless *Shekhinah* at a time when the new Jerusalem is far away.

4.7.2 The Shekhinah in anticipation of the new creation

Related to the theme of the Sabbath is Moltmann's reflection on the *Shekhinah*. From 1972 Moltmann incorporated the concept of the *Shekhinah* into his theology and gradually developed it.[183] In *Gott in der Schöpfung*, for example, he still concentrates mainly on the Sabbath, and only in *Das Kommen Gottes* does he focus attention on the *Shekhinah*.[184]

Through the *Shekhinah*, God becomes a traveling companion and partner of people on their way to the *creatio nova*. God's *Shekhinah* wants to live in the midst of people (Exod 29:45). This is already apparent when the OT refers to God's union with the garden in Eden, the cloud and fire column, the ark of the covenant, the tabernacle, and the temple. With this, God anticipates through his *Shekhinah* already on living in the new heaven and new earth.[185]

Because God created space through zero to create distance and freedom of movement between God and creatures (§4.4), God cannot be absolutely omnipresent

---

180. Moltmann, *Sein Name*, 68; *Erfahrungen*, 40; "Sabbath," 5; *Kommen*, 292–94, 311–12; *Gott in der Schöpfung*, 281–83.

181. Moltmann, *Sein Name*, 73; *Kommen*, 290.

182. Moltmann, "Liberation," 279–80; *Kommen*, 292, 312; *Gott in der Schöpfung*, 158, 291–92, 311–12. Including references to: Spier, *Sabbat*; Rosenzweig, *Stern der Erlösung*, 345; Heschel, *Sabbath*. See in detail the concrete added value of this for the entire creation (rest for people, rest for the land, relation to the Messiah, etc.): Moltmann, "Liberation," 280–89.

183. Moltmann, *Weiter Raum*, 107.

184. Moltmann, *Kommen*, 12–13, 39–41, 287–93, 348–49; *Gott in der Schöpfung*, 20–21, 281–98.

185. Moltmann, "Gott und Raum," 142; *Kommen*, 13.

in this creation. God must be concealed and limited to reside in creation. This will change in the final completion. In the *creatio nova* God will live universally and will continuously eliminate the self-limitation (*Selbsteinschränkung*) during the *creatio continua*. Then God will fill and permeate the space of the new heaven and the new earth (Rev 21:3; §4.6.2). God will then be all in all. The whole creation will then be a space of God, a temple in which God finds a home and may rest.[186]

4.7.3   Christ the Firstborn of the new creation

Moltmann sees in the Incarnation and Resurrection of the Messiah a foreshadowing of the moment when God's *Shekhinah* will dwell in the completed Sabbath period, and this creation will change into the all-encompassing sanctuary of the new creation.[187] Jesus prayed in the vicinity of the Kingdom of God, "Abba, Father." He healed the sick, accepted the rejected and raised the dead. In it, the contours of the new creation were revealed to the people around him.[188] This happened even more clearly in the resurrection of Christ. The resurrection of the Crucified meant a new beginning in this old world (§4.2.1).

The NT testifies that the Risen One is the same as the Crucified One. Christ died and rose from the dead. The disciples perceived the reality of his appearances with all senses. They testified of the new creation that found its beginning in Christ. It was not a resuscitation of Jesus' dead body, a mysterious return of himself, or a continued life as a walking soul. The disciples saw a physical revival of Christ and experienced the presence of his glorified body.[189]

What the disciples experienced is important to Moltmann because it anticipates the new heaven and earth. In the presence of the Risen One, the disciples experienced the new reality as different from the old reality of death and transience. Moltmann recognizes three dimensions:[190]

1. A prospective view: people recognize the Crucified as the "eternal Living" in the light of the new creation.

2. A retrospective view: people recognize the Crucified in the Risen One by the nail wounds, the bread breaking, and the voice.

3. A reflective view: people recognize themselves as heralds of the new creation. The appearance of the Risen One motivates their testimony.

---

186. Moltmann, "Gott und Raum," 141–42; *Kommen*, 292, 333–37.
187. Moltmann, *Weiter Raum*, 107; *Kommen*, 294, 331–32, 335.
188. Moltmann, *Erfahrungen*, 45–46.
189. Moltmann, *Sein Name*, 51–54.
190. Moltmann, *Sein Name*, 53, 69.

The New Heaven and New Earth

Where the life of the Risen One is in continuity with the life of the Crucified One, the future of the Risen One is in continuity with the future of the Crucified One.[191] The concrete consequences of this for the new heaven and earth are not worked out by Moltmann. He does let us realize that there is also a discontinuity between the life of the Crucified and the life of the Risen One.[192] From itself, creation cannot work on the future (*futurum*). Only through the future of God creation is able to produce the new creation (*adventus*, §4.2.2).

4.7.4 Christ's first fruits as an anticipation of the new creation

Further anticipation of the new creation is the church community that experiences and reveals the theological content of hope (§4.2.3).[193] By pointing this out, Moltmann rejects the idea that the new creation only breaks through in eschaton for the first time. The church already realizes today that life in the here-and-now is not separate from life in the hereafter. Already in the *creatio originalis*, the light of the *creatio nova* breaks through. This creation and the new creation are connected. The "future" of the church is founded in this *creatio originalis* because the Coming One is represented in her in his church. There is thus a diachronic breakthrough of the *creatio nova* in this time of events.

In his *Kirche in der Kraft des Geistes*, Moltmann works out this idea in detail. In this, he connects the mission of the Spirit with the mission of Christ and his followers. The Spirit fills this godless world with God's presence and prepares in it the new creation.[194]

Since Pentecost, the church may see itself as a microcosm of God's indwelling that points to God's ultimate indwelling in the macrocosm. By living from the hope of resurrection, the church allows humanity to taste the powers that the coming age brings with it. In its mission, it strengthens the dialogue between the world and the kingdom of God. It quarrels against any presence of the power of *nihil* on earth and gives hope for the redemption of all creation. Just as the Sabbath breaks through the weekly working week and anticipates the new creation, the church may breakthrough that which deviates from that new creation.[195] In this way, the church moves in the direction of the promised. She renounces the original home and the old friendships and calls for release and resourcing. In doing so, she proclaims, in agreement with Romans 8, that there is

---

191. Moltmann, *Sein Name*, 78; *Theologie*, 75, 182, 206.

192. Moltmann, "Kategorie Novum," 179.

193. Moltmann, *Weiter Raum*, 107; *Kommen*, 294, 331–32, 335; *Kirche*, 33–52, 241–51; *Gekreuzigte Gott*, 225; "Resurrection," 58; *Theologie*, 260. See further for the nuance differences in Moltmann's thinking: Vroom, *De Schrift alleen?*, 169–81.

194. Moltmann, *Erfahrungen*, 75; "Hope and Reality," 80; *Kirche*, 153–56.

195. Moltmann, *Sein Name*, 70, 76; "Liberation," 266; *Gott in der Schöpfung*, 82, 220–21; "Auferstehungshoffnung," 111; "Hoffnung und Entwicklung," 64; "Political Hermeneutic," 103. Cf. Bauckham, *Theology of Jürgen Moltmann*, 10.

an order of revolt that runs from Christ to the Christian and then to all creation.[196] In solidarity with Jesus of Nazareth, the church shows the expectation of the new creation in the misery of the present. Just as Christ suffered outside the city, the church outside the city gates suffers, rejected by its opponents. It lives from hope and calls nothing "very good," as long as not everything is "new." Thus the Christian church reveals the contours of the new creation in its own living conditions, as Jesus did.[197]

4.7.5 The heavenly Jerusalem as an image of the new creation

In his reflection on the new heaven and new earth, Moltmann devotes a complete subchapter to the imagery of heavenly Jerusalem (Rev 21–22). In this, he builds on the biblical-theological research of Richard Bauckham.[198] In an analysis of Moltmann's statements about the new creation, this subchapter should not be left out of the equation. However, a representation of this will have to be limited, given Moltmann's detailed and extensive explanation of the visual language. Mainly, for this reason, the relationship between Moltmann's explanation of this biblical imagery and the aforementioned systematic-theological connections in his speech on the new creation will be pointed out.

4.7.5.1 *Jerusalem and Babylon*

Moltmann points out that the earthly Jerusalem was the city where Jesus was tortured and crucified and also the city of hope to which God gave promises and where the Messiah rose from the dead.[199] He thus sees the earthly Jerusalem as the hopeful symbol for the heavenly Jerusalem that will manifest itself from heaven on earth. In Revelation, this heavenly Jerusalem stands opposite the sinful metropolis of Babylon, which Moltmann connects with the Roman Empire, from which Christians must turn away. The heavenly Jerusalem forms the contrast of the godless metropolises of this world.[200]

4.7.5.2 *City garden and garden city*

The imagery of Revelation describes the new Jerusalem as paradise, the holy city, and the cosmic temple. It is the perfect city garden or garden city, in which the joy and beauty of life from the garden in Eden return. This is the river of life and tree of life that remind us of Eden (Rev 22:1–2). Yet for Moltmann, this new Jerusalem is more

196. Moltmann, *Gott in der Schöpfung*, 113, 196–97.
197. Moltmann, *Kommen*, 65–66; "Richtungen," 37; "Resurrection," 59; "Kategorie Novum," 185.
198. Moltmann, *Kommen*, §IV.5 (338–349); 341n111. Cf. Bauckham, *Theology of Revelation*.
199. Moltmann, *Kommen*, 338–39.
200. Moltmann, *Kommen*, 340.

than a return to the former court. Besides the garden, it is also the city that gives humanity its own demarcated space on earth. Moltmann already pointed out the importance of this in his remarks on space (§4.4). The new Jerusalem is thus the image of complete harmony between culture and nature. In his detailed elaboration of this, Moltmann mainly maintains his hermeneutical principle of continuity in relation to the present positive and discontinuity in relation to the present negative (§4.2.5.3).[201]

4.7.5.3 *The glory of God*

According to Moltmann, Jerusalem fulfills the great ideal that determines the expectation of all ancient cities: to be the central place on earth where heaven and earth meet and where God rules. From this ancient desire, this heavenly Jerusalem descends upon a sublime mountain (Rev 21:10). In mythological representations, this was the residence of the gods.

Revelation mentions about this city that God will dwell with men (21:3). This is a central statement in Moltmann's eschatology of the new creation. The most important of the new Jerusalem is God's all-encompassing presence (cf. §§4.4.3; 4.6; 4.7.2).[202] This fulfills God's desire to dwell in creation.

In the center of the city stands the throne of God and the Lamb as a counter-image of the ancient politics of Babylon/Rome. Unlike the throne of the Roman emperor, it is freely accessible to everyone and not surrounded by court officials and bodyguards. In the heavenly Jerusalem, everyone has direct access to the throne. Furthermore, there is no oppression or submission in the city, but the river of life and the tree of life are at the disposal of all (Rev 22:1–2).[203]

However, what is missing in the new Jerusalem is a temple. Moltmann explains this because there is no distance between God and humanity anymore. God is all in all, making the whole of the new Jerusalem the temple city (cf. §4.6). The latter is evident from the materials that appear in the vision of the new Jerusalem.[204]

In the new creation, God's *Shekhinah* becomes omnipresent and crosses all spatial boundaries. Moltmann thinks that the latter is also reflected in the cube shape of the city: width, length, and height are the same. This shape makes the city unique and reminds us of the dimensions of the Most Blessed Sacrament of Solomon's temple (1 Kings 6:17–20). At the same time, Moltmann understands the absence of a separate temple as the absence of religion because the city is the end and fulfillment of religion.[205]

---

201. Moltmann, *Erfahrungen*, 62; *Kommen*, 45–46, 338.
202. Moltmann, *Kommen*, 347.
203. Moltmann, *Kommen*, 343, 349.
204. Moltmann, *Kommen*, 348.
205. Moltmann, *Kommen*, 345.

4.7.5.4 *The peoples as God's people*

God's desire to live on earth, which in the history of salvation mainly applied to Israel and the temple in Jerusalem, has now been extended to all people. What God in Christ and through the Spirit already showed to creation is completed in the new creation. All nations (ἔθνή) will be God's people (λαοὶ). Moltmann emphasizes that the seer in Revelation 21, by using λαός, wants to emphasize that the new Jerusalem is a covenant between mankind and God. This term is normally used only for God's covenant people.[206]

While the city can be measured in different dimensions, the city walls with their gates refer to the inhabitants who are Jews and Gentiles. The twelve gates contain the names of the twelve tribes of Israel (Rev 21:12), and the city walls rest on the foundation stones marked by the names of Jesus' twelve apostles (v. 14). The listed gems also remind us of the breastplate of the high priest. In the new Jerusalem, all nations will be characterized by the presence of these gems. There is no difference in privileges between Israel and the peoples. Both have free access to the city and enjoy the same blessing. The only ones who do not receive access to the city are those who do not change and hold on to the godless power of Babylon.[207]

Whoever rejects Babylon and chooses the new Jerusalem will serve God and the Lamb in this future city, see his face, bear his name on the forehead, and reign with them (22:3–5). Although the Jewish high priest was only allowed to enter the holy of holies once a year, the nations now live continuously before God's face. They walk in God's light and the kings of the earth who subdued Babylon voluntarily come into the new Jerusalem to "bring their glory into it" (21:24). For Moltmann, this means that their cultural treasures are not abolished, but are desired and saved in the new creation.[208]

4.7.5.5 *The holiness of God*

Through God's presence, the new Jerusalem is the holy city. All the unholy remains outside. The gems, pearls, and crystals reflect the light of God's glory. It is a visible sign of God's presence. After all, his light is the source of all light that permeates everything. Moltmann points out that this penetrating light also refers to God, who is all in all and perichoretically permeates the new creation (§4.6.2). The penetrating light dispels the darkness. Chaos powers 'night' and 'sea' disappear in the new creation (Rev 21:1; 22:5). For the new heaven and the new earth, God will wipe away all tears, and death will be lacking, as will suffering, crying, and pain (21:4). Anything that goes against God's will for this creation remains outside the city. However, the new

---

206. Moltmann, *Kommen*, 348.
207. Moltmann, *Kommen*, 343–44, 347.
208. Moltmann, *Kommen*, 346–47.

The New Heaven and New Earth

Jerusalem is not watertight. It is rightly an open city of light, which does not have to close its gates day and night, and where people are welcome.[209]

4.8 CONCLUSION

1. In Moltmann's theology, eschatology is central, while cosmic eschatology is paramount. He concentrates on the revision and innovation of the theological content. The treatment of hermeneutical-methodological issues remains brief.

2. His eschatology is christologically determined. Cross and resurrection show discontinuity and continuity between this creation and the new creation. The crucified Christ rises as the Firstborn of the new creation. Moltmann interprets this primarily as anticipating from the eschatological horizon of the new heaven and new earth to the present.

3. Moltmann's soteriology and the doctrine of creation are connected and distinguish themselves in three phases of history: *creatio originalis*, *creatio continua*, and *creatio nova*. Creatio nova is the completed transformation of the previous two. It is the renewal and restoration of the lost, without being a return to the *creatio originalis*.

4. Through the teaching of the *zimzum*, Moltmann states that God limits himself to producing space-time (*nihil*), in which God forms creation. This divine *nihil* makes the creation imperfect and focused on the future redemption. So there will be continuity and unprecedented novelty (discontinuity).

5. Moltmann indicates both positive and negative the earthly temporal time (*chronos*). It is positive because it moves the good *creatio orginalis* to the *creatio nova*. It is negative because of the connection with the transience from *nihil*. On the contrary, the new heaven and the new earth have an aionic cycle time which brings together and glorifies all history because God's presence transforms and transfigures creation and causes an interaction between time and eternity, a time-filled eternity.

6. Moltmann also refers to the earthly space (topos) as both positive and negative. Like space, it offers protection to people, but it is also characterized by a distance between creation and Creator. Although God's *Shekhinah* finds a residence in the *creatio continua* in the limited-created space, the new heaven and new earth are characterized by God penetrating all living space and destroying every spatial distance between God and creation. The new creation becomes an eternal residence for God's omnipresence.

---

209. Moltmann, *Kommen*, 344, 348; "Schöpfung," 128.

7. Also, Moltmann grants a future to matter in the new heaven and the new earth. Christ's Incarnation and resurrection testify that salvation also includes the renewal of the physical. Humankind, together with heaven and earth, is renewed and completed in the eschatological moment.

8. God will find the ultimate destiny in the new creation through a perichoresis of God in creation and of creation in God. The redeemed participate in the eternal inner-trinitarian life of God and creation then shares in the divine attributes of eternal time and omnipresent space. Unmixed and undivided, God thus dwells in the new creation, and the new creation then dwells in God. This gives a new heaven and earth a soteriological end and doxological eternity character.

9. Moltmann sees the imagery and metaphors about the new heaven and new earth in an idea-based way. Coming from the creational world, they offer idea-moderate components about the unreachable new creation that transcends one's own perception. Herein there are two hermeneutic facets: the absence of the present negativity and the presence or memory of the present positivity.

5

Gregory Beale's perspective on the new heaven and new earth

This chapter analyzes Gregory Beale's perspective on the new heaven and new earth. Due to the fact that Beale's publications are quite recent, there has been no extensive academic research to this point.[1] Herewith this chapter is the first contribution in response to Beale's scientific analysis on the new creation. After a short introduction (§5.1), some hermeneutic principles in Beale's theological thinking are discussed (§5.2). Next, the biblical-theological way Beale speaks about the new creation is mapped out (§§5.3–1.8). The selected sequence is based on the structure of the main parts in Beale's *A New Testament Biblical Theology* (2011). This work contains a detailed presentation of Beale's BT and is typified by him as his *magnum opus*. The last chapter finally draws conclusions from the previous chapters (§5.9).

5.1 INTRODUCTION

Gregory K. Beale (b. 1949) is a professor of NT and BT at Westminster Theological Seminary in Glenside (Pennsylvania).[2] Theologically, Beale is embedded within the orthodox evangelical-reformed tradition. He sees the biblical testimony as a divinely inspired revelation. This revelation professed in the OT reaches its climax in the NT. Beale never gives the impression that there is a human-historical evolution of religion in the Bible or that biblical books were created by long editorial processes. It is possible to characterize his BT, within a large number of biblical-theological currents, as a systematic-canonical approach of the biblical data (cf. §2.3.2). Beale's main publications concentrate on the relationship between OT and NT, and the biblical-theological

---

1. For concise reactions on Beale's work, see: Marshall, "Review"; Henebury, "Review"; Collman, "Review"; Gurtner and Gladd, *From Creation*; Hamilton, "Appreciation," 58–70; Kärkkäinen, "Bookreview: The Temple," 46; Bostock, "Review," 137.

2. Recent brief biographical data can be found at: Gurtner and Gladd, *From Creation*, xiii–xv.

message of the new creation. His more well-known publications include his *Commentary on the Greek text of Revelation* (1999), *The Temple and the Church's Mission* (2004), and *A New Testament Biblical Theology* (2011). Together with Donald Carson, he was also editor-in-chief of the well-known *Commentary on the Use of the Old Testament in the New* (2007).[3]

Beale developed his own BT in *A New Testament Biblical Theology* (NTBT). For about thirty years, he elaborated on its content through lectures, essays, and monographs.[4] Nevertheless, the BT designed by Beale is not just a recycling operation, but rather a synthesis of its earlier publications. This book is one of the highlights of his academic career.[5] Because in NTBT, eschatology and the new creation are at the center, they help to order Beale's theology. Altogether NTBT contains ten main parts, of which nine (part 1–9) follow a specific biblical-theological storyline. These determine the structure of the analysis described in this chapter. Because the last part (part 10) has a summarizing character, I have chosen to add the information of part 10 to the relevant parts of my analysis.

5.2 HERMENEUTICAL PRINCIPLES

5.2.1 Methodical form

5.2.1.1 BT from a biblical storyline

Beale develops his BT in NTBT from the biblical storyline with its great theological themes. All attention is focused on the description of the progress of God's revelation in its continuity and pluriformity. By concentrating on the storyline and not working with a thematic center, Beale wants to avoid putting his own template on the biblical data.[6]

Though Beale mentions his methodical and hermeneutical choices in NTBT several times, there is no broad justification for the way in which he ranks his main parts. The reader has to do with the remark that chapters 3–28 are arranged on the basis of core elements from Genesis 1–3 and Revelation 21–22.[7] It remains unanswered, however, how Beale exactly makes that choice methodically and why one subject precedes another.

Usually, each main part follows the pattern of an analysis of the subject in the OT, Judaism, the NT, and of the church fathers. Striking is Beale's attention to allusions of extra-biblical sources (see §5.2.2.2). It is also striking that Beale pays particular attention to the traditional letters that mention "Paul" in the opening lines and that he looks at everything from the theme of "new creation." The biblical-theological

---

3. Beale and Carson, *Commentary*; Beale, *Temple*; *Revelation*.
4. Beale, *New Testament*, xi, 24.
5. Gurtner and Gladd, *From Creation*, xiii.
6. Beale, *New Testament*, 6, 9, 29, 61, 167.
7. Beale, *New Testament*, 23.

analysis of the biblical storyline and of the biblical testimony about the new creation are thereby mixed up (cf. §5.2.3).

5.2.1.2 *Contemporary Parallels*

Beale acknowledges that his narrative approach in NTBT does not stand alone. He knows he is connected to a growing number of biblical theologians.[8] This attention also connects with the post-liberal desire to listen to the biblical narrative. The narrative should interpret itself (cf. §5.1.4).[9] Before the rise of post-liberalism, attention to this already existed in creeds and reformational works, which were based on the historical framework of creation, fall, and renewal. Thus Beale describes his own BT as a continuation of the research of Geerhardus Vos (1862–1949).[10] Like Beale, Vos sees a progressive organic development of God's revelation in the Bible. Biblical theology is like "nothing else than the exhibition of the organic progress of supernatural revelation in its historic continuity and multiformity."[11]

Beale does not dare to compare his own methodology with that of others. It would lead too far to compare his BT in detail with other proposals.[12] Although Beale frequently refers to sources that correspond with his views, there is usually no interaction with other opinions.[13] For example, an interaction with James Barr concerning the importance of a continuous way of thinking between the OT and NT would have been appropriate in NTBT.[14] It is only in his *Handbook on the New Testament Use of the Old Testament* (2012) that Beale addresses that issue. However, the significance of this for the BT remains limited.[15]

5.2.2 Emphasis on the biblical storyline

The central storylines of the OT and NT form a *Leitmotif* in Beale's NTBT.[16] Almost all main sections start with "The Story of . . ." This is not only the case in part 1 ("Introduction") and part 10 ("Conclusion"). Only part 8 does not start with "The Story of

---

8. Mentioned are among others: Dempster, *Dominion*; Scobie, *Ways*; Dumbrell, *End*.

9. Vanhoozer, *Drama of Doctrine*; Frei, *Types of Christian Theology*, 13–18, 86; Lindbeck, "Scripture, Consensus, and Community," 82–86; *Nature of Doctrine*.

10. Beale, *Handbook*, 20. *New Testament*, 61–62. Biographical data about Geerhardus Vos can be found at: Gaffin, "Vos, Geerhardus"; Dennison, "Life of Geerhardus Vos."

11. Vos, "Idea," 15; cf. 23, 26.

12. Beale, *New Testament*, 87.

13. See: Henebury, "Review."

14. Barr, *Concept*, 375–76.

15. Beale, *Handbook*, 1–40.

16. Beale, *New Testament*, 168.

..." but contains the word "Storyline: The Distinguishing Marks of the Church as Storyline Facets of the End-Time Inaugurated New Creation."

All attention in these stories goes to the message of the canonical bible books. Methodically Beale chooses to determine the meaning of the biblical text first from its own literary context and the preceding salvation history. Only then should attention be paid to the subsequent salvific events. Hermeneutically, his biblical theology is mainly focused more on the story "in the text" than on that "behind the text."[17] Beale rarely deviates from the analysis pattern: Old Testament expectations, salvific-historical development, and final completion of the end time.

The biblical storylines that Beale develops in his BT are based on the OT, which speaks of God's story with humanity in order to establish a kingdom on earth through his word and Spirit from chaos. This story is characterized by God's covenant promises and salvation, which are elaborated in the NT. The NT transforms the Old Testament story into the life of Jesus in which the Spirit fills the fulfillment of God's plan by resurrection. There is then a government of grace that has begun, and that bears both "already" and "not yet" the hallmark of the new creation that glorifies God's name.[18]

5.2.2.1 The importance of protology

In NTBT, Beale pays great attention to the opening chapters of the Bible, Genesis 1–3.[19] The events mentioned herein are the keys to his BT (see §5.3). The latter is shown by Beale through the references from the biblical storyline to Genesis 1–3. Broad attention is paid to the meaning of Adam, who finds his fulfillment in Christ, the perfect Adam, in the Bible. The last Adam succeeded where the first Adam failed. Eschatology is, therefore, in relation to the protology. The goal of God's plan of salvation is the realization of the original plan of Genesis 1–2.[20] For Beale, this is most clearly visible at the end of the Bible. The biblical testimony has its roots in Genesis 1–3 and its completion in Revelation 21–22.[21] We can understand why he pays attention to Genesis 1–3 from his choice to see the new creation as an eschatological realization of the protology.

5.2.2.2 Allusions and thematic parallels in OT and NT

In focusing on the opening part of the Old Testament, Beale's NTBT does not limit itself to the NT. In this publication, he maps out the theological lines that develop from Genesis 1–3 in the biblical history of salvation. From a salvific historical perspective,

17. Beale, *New Testament*, 7, 9, 14, 219.
18. Beale, *New Testament*, 16, cf. 26, 163, 182, 188, 297, 354, 694, 891, 950, 958.
19. Beale, *New Testament*, 29–87.
20. Beale, *New Testament*, 177–78.
21. Beale, *New Testament*, 59, 176.

God's new revelation through Christ is closely related to God's earlier revelation to and through Israel.[22]

Although the title of Beale's BT is *A New Testament Biblical Theology*, the testimony of the Old Testament does not lack in this work either. Beale acknowledges this in his introduction when he describes his book as biblical theology, which includes both OT and NT.[23] Out of the twenty-two index pages with Bible references in NTBT, there are no less than fifteen (70 percent) with references to the OT, of which four (18 percent) to the prophet Isaiah.

Nevertheless, the term "New Testament" is not misplaced in the title of the book. In his works, Beale pays a lot of attention to the OT from where he draws lines to the NT. This ensures that the Old Testament storyline in his BT is related to the testimony of the NT. Beale realizes that each Testament deserves to be heard in its own way. By emphasizing the complete biblical storyline of both the OT and NT, he develops a BT from a canonical perspective that at the same time pays attention to the influence of the OT on the writers of the NT.[24] For Beale, it is certain that the New Testament writers wrote their works from the message of the OT. His elaboration of the New Testament theology is thus based on an in-depth overview of the biblical-theological and eschatological thoughts in the OT, which determine the agenda for the NT.[25]

Beale assumes a strong continuity between the OT and NT. In the subtitle of his BT: *The Unfolding of the Old Testament in the New*, this methodical choice emerges. In his publications, Beale shows his interest in this continuity by pointing out allusions and references from the NT to other texts. In the majority of the cases, this concerns references to ancient Jewish writings (Targum, Mishna, Qumran, Josephus, Philo, etc.), the Greek Septuagint, and the Masoretic Text of the OT. These works are, according to Beale, the commentaries of antiquity that often continue the testimony of possibly even older oral traditions. Because of its frequent use and his alertness to the parallels between the OT and NT, Beale describes himself as someone with a great interest in this phenomenon. He is a maximalist when it comes to finding intertextual connections between OT and NT.[26] For example, Beale frequently refers to verbal parallels in the Bible. In this, he makes little distinction between the Hebrew and Greek texts of the OT or those of the Targum. Beale assumes that the New Testament writers were sufficiently familiar with these underlying parallel texts. It is also striking that his NTBT lacks the necessary reflection on the context and background of the separate biblical books.[27] Beale is particularly interested in the general biblical witness and does not take into account the unique aspects that characterize each book of the Bible.

22. Beale, *Handbook*, 98.
23. Beale, *New Testament*, 1.
24. Beale, *New Testament*, 2, 4–6, 9–10, 15–16.
25. Beale, *New Testament*, 188.
26. Beale, "Inaugural Lectures," 263–93; *Handbook*, 39–40.
27. Cf. Marshall, "Review."

5.2.3 Eschatological orientation

5.2.3.1 *The perspective of the new creation*

Although Beale realizes that he can bring more than one key-theme to biblical theology, the proposals made so far by others before him are too reductionist. Whoever writes a biblical theology based on a number of subjects can overlook important themes. Biblical theology can never fully cover all biblical topics.[28] In §5.2.2, we already indicated that Beale's methodology puts him in a field of tension between the biblical-theological storyline and the subject of the new creation. According to Beale, the latter is the overarching theme in the Bible, which bears witness to a new covenant, a new temple, a new Israel, and a new Jerusalem.[29]

This choice for the central theme of the new creation shows that Beale also has its own center in its BT. In Beale's NTBT, for example, certain theological subjects are missing or come less to the fore. An example of this is the aspect of physical renewal in the eschaton (we will examine this in more detail in the critical comparison §6.3.1.3). Because there is no consensus among biblical theologians about what exactly is the center, the cluster of centers, or the biblical plot of the Bible, important themes in a BT are always underexposed.[30]

In Beale's opinion, the subject of the new creation or kingdom of God begins in the opening part of the Bible. From there, this theme develops and bears its first fruit in the NT. On end, it comes to full completion in the eschaton. According to Beale, most biblical subjects are connected to this ready and not-yet-realized kingdom of the new creation. So, the biblical storyline is viewed from the lens of renewal, a new creation, and completion. Beale already sees in the creation story a first development towards the completed new creation. Various subcategories are also connected with this, such as oppression, resurrection, idolatry, and restoration of God's image, redemption, the work of God's Spirit, the church, and Israel. They determine the main parts of Beale's NTBT. According to him, the traditional doctrines of the Christian faith can be enriched from the eschatological perspective.[31]

The emphasis on this eschatological perspective is evident in NTBT. There is almost no page to be found without a reference to the development or completion of the new creation. Seven of the ten main parts in NTBT contain the term "New Creation." Although for the BT Beale rejects a biblical-theological middle as too reductionist, he himself places the theme of the new creation overarching above his own BT. For Beale,

---

28. Beale, *New Testament*, xii, 86, 168. Cf. Barr, *Concept*, 5; von Rad, *Theologie*, I:128–130; Hasel, *Theology*, 126.

29. Beale, *New Testament*, 58, 165, 357. Cf. "New Testament and New Creation," 159–73; "Eschatological," 11–52.

30. Beale, *New Testament*, 167. Hamilton, "Appreciation," 61–63..

31. Beale, *New Testament*, 775, cf. 15, 23, 188, 228; *1–2 Thessalonians*, 22.

the new creation is the core theme in the Bible, which is realized through Christ's resurrection and enriches all other biblical-theological themes.[32]

For Beale, the terms "new creation" and "kingdom" are synonymous. So, the theme of the new creation is best understood against the background of Adam's kingship (Gen 1–3) and from the realm of God promised to Israel.[33] Furthermore, Beale constantly connects the theme of the new creation with the theme of the resurrection. There are no salvific historical differences between the two concepts. One cannot exist without the other. This is most evident in the storyline of the resurrection (§5.5). It is this eschatological perspective that makes his BT quite unique.

According to Beale, despite the many reconsiderations of eschatology, BT did not pay enough attention to this perspective in the past.[34] Recently this has changed. Bible scholars rediscover the crucial importance of eschatology in biblical testimony.[35] Beale joins this renewed interest and characterizes his biblical theology as a historical milestone. It is a unique contribution in his field that shows the development of the kingdom of the new creation from Eden to its fulfillment in the new heaven and earth.[36]

5.2.3.2 Salvation-historical eschatology

A keyword in Beale's NTBT is the term "eschatology." Eschatology is not just one of many options for Beale to look at the biblical testimony. Rather, it is the center from which all statements of faith can be understood. In this choice, Beale follows the biblical theologian Geerhardus Vos, who characterized eschatology as the "mother of theology in the form of a philosophy of redemptive history."[37] Eschatology is the fundamental issue and not the final chapter of the BT. It is the lens that makes all biblical themes easier to understand. Each of the main theological themes is linked to the new creation. Beale, therefore, also calls on the discipline of the ST to integrate the theme of the new creation and its eschatological development more into its publications.[38]

Beale's use of "eschatology" or "eschatological" does not focus solely on the completion of salvation, cosmic history, Israel's hope, or the individual saints. In the term "eschatology," he thinks more of the "good and not yet" of the new creation in Christ.[39]

---

32. Beale, *New Testament*, xii, 86, 165, 168, 228, 249, 354.

33. Beale, *New Testament*, 171, 429.

34. Beale, *New Testament*, 17, 19, 177–78. However, see as an exception: Goldsworthy, *According to Plan*; Dumbrell, *Search for Order*.

35. Middleton, *New Heaven*; Schreiner, *King*; Wilkinson, *Eschatology*; Mathison, *From Age to Age*; *New Testament Theology*, 41–116; Thielman, *Theology*, 692–94, 698–714; Scobie, *Ways*.

36. Beale, *New Testament*, 13, 16, 20, 23.

37. Vos, "Hebrews, The Epistle of the Diatheke," 193; Beale, *New Testament*, 19, 89, 578.

38. Beale, *New Testament*, 18.

39. Beale, *New Testament*, 177, cf. 17.

The questions that arise by placing emphasis on the "yes" and "no" of the new creation. In Acts 2, Beale sees the descent of the heavenly eschatological temple that descends on earth. Through this event at Pentecost, the followers of Jesus are a temple in the new creation and fulfill God's promise that Israel will return from captivity.[40] Statements such as these led some to the conclusion that NTBT was no more than a broad defense of amillennialism. However, this is incorrect. Despite the fact that Beale thinks from an amillennialistic perspective about the future, the eschatology in his BT cannot be reduced to that.[41] He himself describes his eschatological framework rather as "inaugurated eschatology." His depiction of the way in which the Bible writers speak about the end times shows that the NT, building on the OT, speaks of partial fulfillment of the eschatological promises. The full fulfillment of these promises has yet to happen. With this, Beale, in his eschatological way of thinking, follows the line of Oscar Cullmann (1902–1999), George Ladd (1911–1982), and Donald Carson (1946–).[42]

5.3 PART 1: BIBLICAL-THEOLOGICAL STORYLINE

In chapters 2–6 of NTBT, Beale focuses on the biblical-theological storyline. He continuously connects this with the creation story (Gen 1–3) and the new creation (Rev 21–22).[43] The analysis below focuses on the themes that are related to the new heaven and new earth in Beale's work. Since Beale connects several of these themes with a broad arsenal of biblical texts and he repeats various elements in his BT, the analysis below concentrates on the core texts in his reflection on the new creation.

5.3.1 The mission of Adam in the first creation

5.3.1.1 *The protology in Genesis 1–3*

While Beale is concise about the Old Testament testimony, he spends almost sixty pages on the biblical-theological meaning of Genesis 1–3.[44] This part of the Bible forms an inclusion with the final part in Revelation 21–22 and influences the entire biblical testimony.[45] Beale particularly emphasizes Genesis 1:28. In his NTBT, he refers to this verse more than ninety times. God's command in Genesis 1:28 is for Beale, the hermeneutic principle that returns as a refrain in the Bible (§5.3.2). The five elements in Genesis 1:28 introduce the basic biblical subjects: (1) God's blessing; (2)

---

40. Beale, *New Testament*, 606, 632, 651.

41. For his amillennialism see: Beale, *Revelation*, 979–83.

42. Ladd, *A Theology of the New Testament*, 70; Cullmann, *Heil als Geschichte*; *Christus und die Zeit*; Carson, *John*, 256.

43. Beale, *New Testament*, 88; "Final Vision," 209.

44. Beale, *New Testament*, 29–87.

45. For example, see: Beale, *New Testament*, 59, 176; *Temple*, 81–122; *Revelation*, 1039–1157.

fertility; (3) spreading; (4) submission of the earth; (5) reigning over the earth.[46] As viceroy, humanity represents God's glory on earth. Humankind populates and orders the earth as God did in the garden.[47]

When God, in Genesis 2:15 calls upon man to "preserve and guard" the garden (לְעָבְדָהּ וּלְשָׁמְרָהּ), the core of this basic mission is repeated. Through the term "guarding" (שָׁמַר) Beale sees Adam as a priest-king responsible for the material and immaterial created.[48] Adam receives permission to eat from all trees except the tree of knowledge (v. 16–17). However, the serpent manages to mislead Adam's wife. According to Beale, humans should have judged the serpent by the knowledge tree. This tree points to the judgment between "good and evil" (טוֹב וָרָע; cf. 2 Sam 14:17; 19:35; 1 Kgs 3:9, 28; Isa 7:15–16).[49] However, instead of guarding the court and judging the serpent, humans choose to do the opposite. They eat of the fruit and hand over the authority of creation to the serpent.

5.3.1.2 Fulfillment of the creative task

What would have happened if the first people had remained faithful to God? Beale answers this question from Genesis 1:28 and 2:15. If the people had resisted the serpent and overcome evil, their blessing would have increased, and they would have ruled the whole earth from the garden as *pars pro toto*. By eating from the tree of life, they would live forever and enjoy the peace between Creator and creation.[50]

As the image of God, humankind held the Sabbath day to look ahead to the future eternal rest (cf. §5.8.2). In this rest, humanity would enjoy the relationship between creation and its Creator. The writer's comment on the marriage institution in Genesis 2:24 also made humanity realize that God longed for a deeper relationship with his creation (§5.8.3). In principle, Genesis 1–2 thus already looks ahead to the future blessing of the new creation.[51] It contains the good beginning of creation that has yet to find its completion. According to Beale, the first person could not enter the finished creation directly. His original natural status first had to be transformed into a spiritual status (cf. 1 Kgs 15:46, 50).[52]

---

46. Beale, *New Testament*, 30, 34n19, 46, 478, 623.
47. Beale, *New Testament*, 30–32, 37, 58.
48. Beale, *New Testament*, 32–33, 45; *Temple*, 83–85.
49. Beale, *New Testament*, 35, 69.
50. Beale, *New Testament*, 33–36, 38–40, 262; *Temple*, 66–71, 81–82, 86–87, 116; "Eschatological," 49.
51. Beale, *New Testament*, 41–42, 871–86; *Temple*, 62.
52. Beale, *New Testament*, 44–45.

5.3.1.3 God's compulsion on earth

In his reflection on the story of creation, Beale also reflects on God's presence in the garden. Although Genesis 1–3 does not explicitly speak about God's desire to dwell among people, God YHWH walks in the garden (3:8), and the description of Eden allows us to think of a temple garden (§5.7.3). Later, biblical texts show this by drawing parallels between Eden, Canaan, God's temple, and the new creation (cf. Gen 13:10; Isa 51:3; Ezek 36:35; 47:12; Joel 2:3).[53]

Like Eden, Canaan was fertile (Deut 8:7–10; 11:8–17; Ezek 47:1–12) and characterized itself as God's holy land (Ps 78:54; Zech 2:12). The highest blessing was that YHWH walked there (Lev 26:1–12). God called Israel from Egypt as a "priestly kingdom," where his dwelling would be central (Exod 19:6; 40:34–38). Also, the later monarchy in Israel had to glorify God (1 Sam 12:22; Isa 48:11) by being the light for all nations and by giving space to God's glory on earth (cf. 2 Sam 7:26; Zech 2:5–11).

When Judah failed and went into exile in 587 BC, God's glory also departed from the temple (Ezek 9:3; 10:4,18–19; 11:22–23). The same was repeated in 70 AD. Then Jerusalem and the temple were destroyed again. For Beale, the Old Testament testimony can thus be described as the story of God who progressively realizes the new creation from the chaos on earth. This God does through the word and the Spirit, and through promise, covenant, and redemption.[54]

5.3.2 Adam's commission and the Old Testament

Beale's BT raises the question of how humans could perform God's command in Genesis 1:28. This command was not limited to the time before the "fall." God created the earth with a purpose and connected blessings with the commission in Genesis 1:28. God ensured that the words in Genesis 1:28 are fulfilled.[55] The mission in which Adam failed, thus returns in the OT. Beale borrows central themes that play a role in this from Charles Scobie and Gerhard Hasel: (1) God; (2) Israel; (3) God and humanity; (4) the Torah; (5) election; (6) promise; (7) covenant; (8) God's rule; (9) worship; (10) liberation; (11) Israel and God.[56] Nevertheless, Beale does not want to reduce himself methodically to these themes. They are part of the broader biblical storyline he wants to explore. He looks at the history of salvation from Genesis 1–2.[57]

Paradigmatically Beale recognizes in the history of salvation a recurring cycle of (1) chaos, (2) liberation, (3) commandment, (4) disobedience, and (5) judgment.

---

53. Beale, *Temple*, 66–80.
54. Beale, *New Testament*, 16, 57, 62, 87, 116, 302, 588, 890, 974.
55. Beale, *New Testament*, 34, 36–38.
56. Beale, *New Testament*, 85–87. With references to: Scobie, *Ways*, 93–102; Hasel, *Theology*, 49–63.
57. Beale, *New Testament*, 85, 176–77.

The segments "liberation" and "commandment" contain God's gracious initiative to offer people new opportunities to complete the creative task. But human disobedience always thwarts this desire. Fulfillment remains unfulfilled.[58]

Below we want to show in summary how Beale, from this paradigm, understands the Old Testament storyline. The titles are chosen from the central subjects that Beale addresses in this part.

5.3.2.1 From Eden to Israel's early history

After Eden, God offers people several opportunities to accomplish the mission of creation. So, Genesis 1:28 resonates in the histories of the primal and patriarchal fathers. In this way, Noah, as second Adam after the chaotic waters, enters a renewed creation and receives the same commission as the first Adam (Gen 9:1–2). In later times this commission comes to Israel, which has been liberated from Egypt by YHWH to serve as a royal priesthood family (Exod 19:6). From the chaos of Egypt, YHWH brings them into a land that recalls Eden. There it must obey God to enjoy the eternal blessing. The people sanctify themselves so that God's tabernacle can be in their midst.[59]

The Torah pays special attention to the disobedience that God's judgment brings upon the people. Whoever turns against YHWH cannot inhabit Canaan. Israel's place in Canaan is thus parallel to Adam's place in the garden. As representatives of God, they should realize the commission of creation in Genesis 1:28. Genesis-Exodus thus forms a repeating cycle in which people are given the opportunity to fulfill God's original commission.[60]

Under the leadership of Joshua, Israel enters Canaan. After the basic conquests, we can speak of peace and God's fulfillment (Josh 21:44). God guarantees the fulfillment of the promises he has made. Yet in Israel's early history, this fulfillment does not reach its completeness anywhere. There remains a hope for the completion of the commission of Genesis 1:28.[61]

5.3.2.2 The reign of Solomon

Beale goes into more detail on the kingship of Solomon. This is for him the climax of Israel's Old Testament kingship. Beale sees in its description numerous references to Genesis 1–3. For example, flora, fauna, gold, and precious stones in Solomon's life recall the garden of Eden. Only at the temple and tabernacle, there is more wealth than with Solomon. However, the temple and tabernacle are related to the court (§5.7.3).

---

58. Beale, *New Testament*, 60, 63–64.
59. Beale, *New Testament*, 46–47, 57, 64, 387, 752–54; *Temple*, 94–95.
60. Beale, *New Testament*, 64, 93.
61. Beale, *New Testament*, 64–65.

Solomon's longing for a heart that can distinguish good from evil also recalls the tree of knowledge in the garden (1 Kgs 3:9; Gen 2:9).[62]

In addition, Beale sees several parallels between Adam and Solomon. When Adam, as a king, names the animals, Solomon praises creation in spells and songs (Gen 2:19–20; 1 Kgs 4:33). The expression "of the cattle, and of the poultry, and of the crawling animals, and of the fish," even occurs only in Genesis 1:26, Deuteronomy 4:17–18, and 1 Kings 4:33. Beale, therefore, sees Solomon, like Adam, as priest-king (§5.7.3.2). David was also such a priest-king, because he wore a linen ephod and made sacrifices (2 Sam 6:13–14, 17; 24:25; cf. 1 Sam 2:18, 28; 14:3; 22:18; 1 Chr 15:27). Yet nowhere in the Bible do we hear that Solomon performed a priestly task. Beale realizes this and sees Solomon as a prototype of the coming priest-king, who has all these functions.[63]

5.3.2.3 *The drama of the Psalms*

In his BT, Beale also takes the biblical wisdom literature into account. That choice is not obvious in the BT.[64] According to Beale, Job and Ecclesiastes combat the rationalism that seeks to determine creation in its entirety. In both, however, the theme of God's plan of salvation with the earth is less common. In Psalms, on the other hand, the latter is the case. Beale considers the book of Psalms as a drama that thematizes Adam's commission and its realization. He concentrates mainly on the psalms that open or close a part of the book. Thus Psalm 1 and 2 place the righteous against the wicked. This subject is related to Israel's commission to manage the earth and to bring it into a new creation.[65]

Psalm 8 is also important. This describes the ideal Adam, who faithfully subjects the earth and rules it according to God's standards (cf. Gen 1:28).[66] Psalm 72 goes back to that fulfillment and ends the second part of the book of Psalms. The theme of the new creation is thus given new emphasis and is related to the kingship and to God's covenants. This motif of the kingship returns at the end of the third part of the book (Ps 89: cf. 72:8 // 89:25; 72:5, 7 // 89:36–37). This creates a relationship between the third part of the book and the first three parts of the book of Psalms.[67] Inconsistent is, however, that Beale does not use Psalm 73 but Psalm 72 to form this inclusio. Psalm 73 is the first psalm of the third part of the book of Psalms, while Psalm 72 is

---

62. Beale, *New Testament*, 65–73; *Temple*, 66–80.
63. Beale, *New Testament*, 69–73; *Temple*, 66–93.
64. See: Steinberg, "Korte geschiedenis," 42–43.
65. Beale, *New Testament*, 75–77, 756.
66. Beale, *New Testament*, 262–63, cf. 37–39, 84, 142, 247, 277, 394, 446, 458, 464, 479, 880, 917, 959; *Temple*, 34, 86, 144, 299.
67. Beale, *New Testament*, 78; "Eschatological," 48.

the last psalm of the second part. Beale lacks a motivation to deviate from this book division.

Psalm 90, the psalm that opens part four of the book of Psalms, speaks of God's people who move away from God's blessings (v. 3–6), come under judgment (v. 7–11), and therefore hope for God's blessing (v. 13–17). Psalm 106, the last psalm of the fourth part of the book of Psalms, continues this testimony. Later generations find that they are as sinful as previous generations (v. 6). This opens and closes the fourth part.[68]

The fifth part of the book begins with Psalm 107 and offers an answer to the cry for the liberation of the righteous. It is through disobedience that the people have been brought into captivity. The liberation brings Israel back in a position where it can perform Genesis 1:28.[69]

From Psalm 145 onwards, the psalmist praises God for fulfilling his promises to creation (v. 2, 21). This praise culminates in Psalm 150, which calls on creation to honor God. God is Creator (146:6) and Sustainer (147:4–18). The Lord reigns forever (146:10), administers justice (146:7–9), and frees all the people (146:8; 147:2–6, 12–14; 149:1–9). The blessing of God thus ends in the abundant fertility which humanity receives in the new creation.

5.3.2.4 Israel's major prophets

In his discussion of the great prophets, Beale is concise. He only mentions their warnings of idolatry. If Israel persists in disobedience, it loses. The people pay little heed to these warnings, after which the Bible book of Lamentations complains about the ruined city of Jerusalem.[70]

Yet the great prophets also speak of Israel's liberation and restoration in the new creation (Isa 40–66; Ezek 36–48). Especially Isaiah brings this forward. Zion may know that YHWH will make Canaan equal to Eden. In Isaiah's connection between the Spirit and fertility, Beale recognizes a parallel with the creation story in which the Spirit generates a creation with her fruit-bearing trees (Gen 1:2, 11–12, 29).[71]

5.3.2.5 The time after the exile

While in the biblical book of Daniel, the primary focus is on the ancient history of the world, Daniel 2 and 7 contain prophecies about the future judgment and the establishment of the eternal Kingdom of God. Beale sees herein allusions to Genesis 1:26–28. The Son of Man will be the last Adam to complete God's purpose with this creation.[72]

---

68. Beale, *New Testament*, 79.
69. Beale, *New Testament*, 80.
70. Beale, *New Testament*, 81–82; Cf. *We Become*, 36–140.
71. Beale, *New Testament*, 81–82.
72. Beale, *New Testament*, 83; *Temple*, 144–45.

Beale remains concise about the other books in the Old Testament. Ezra and Nehemiah describe Israel's new start, temple building, and reconstruction of Jerusalem. Haggai and Zechariah encouraged people to persevere in the new circumstances. Israel may know that there will come a time when the temple will be rebuilt, and the people will live in Canaan again. Then comes God's complete blessing upon them, through the coming of the Messiah. Malachi reminds Israel of God's mercy (1:1–5). God comes to the temple and purifies humankind (3:1–4). Whoever repents of sin will be freed and blessed (3:5–18; 4:1–6).[73]

5.3.3 Eschatological storyline

5.3.3.1 *Eschatological purpose of Genesis 1–2*

In his biblical storyline, Beale emphasizes the eschatological importance of Genesis 1–2. In agreement with Meredith Kline, he acknowledges that the situation in Eden has eschatological potential.[74] It reveals God's plan with this creation. If humanity had fulfilled Genesis 1:28, this plan would have known its completion. Adam would then have lived as the perfect priest-king before God (cf. §5.3.1). So, eschatology precedes soteriology. It is the restoration of all things and the completion of the eternal new heaven and earth. Eschatology is, therefore, already present in protology.[75]

From this hermeneutical perspective, salvation is inextricably linked to the completion of Eden in the new cosmos (Isa 65:17; 66:22; Rev 21:1–22:5). The greatest differences between Eden and the new creation are: (1) the victory over evil; (2) the ultimate protection against sin; (3) the protection of physical decay; (4) the protection of the decay of creation; and (5) the eternal relationship between God and humanity.[76]

5.3.3.2 *The last days in OT and Judaism*

In the OT the hope of the fulfillment of God's promises "in the last days" is heard several times (בְּאַחֲרִית הַיָּמִים, Gen 49:1; Num 24:14; Deut 4:30; 31:29; Isa 2:2; Jer 23:30; 30:24; 48:47; 49:39; Ezek 38:14–16; Dan 2:28–29, 45; 10:14; Hos 3:5; Mic 4:1–4). Beale analyzes these texts and sees growth in detail.[77] While the first reference, Genesis 49:1, is still vague, later texts contain more contours that are reminiscent of Eden. Thus, Ezekiel, Daniel, Micah, and Revelation describe the future Kingdom of God and/or

---

73. Beale, *New Testament*, 84–85.
74. Beale, *New Testament*, 85, 88–89, 176–177. See Kline, *Kingdom*, 111, 113.
75. Beale, *New Testament*, 89–90, 115.
76. Beale, *New Testament*, 91, cf. 89.
77. Beale, *New Testament*, 92–112.

The New Heaven and New Earth

Jerusalem as a high mountain (Ezek 40:2; Dan 2:35; Mic 4:4; Rev 21:10). This reminds of the garden in Eden, which was situated on a mountain (Ezek 28:14–18).[78]

For Beale, these statements about the last few days are not merely metaphors. There is evidence of literality, continuity, and discontinuity between the current creation and the future creation. All oppression comes to an end when the final foundation of God's visible rule on earth comes. Then there will be peace between the nations through the coming of God's Spirit. The statements about the last days thus anticipate what God does in the history of salvation and what fills up in the new creation.[79]

Beale sees this expectation recurring in the Jewish writings to which he attaches great importance (§5.2.2.2). They bring more contours to the biblical expectation. With regard to the new heaven and earth, Beale mentions the following parallels between the Bible and the Jewish sources: the destruction of evil; the renewal of the earth; God's promise of resurrection; the Kingdom of God; the Sabbath as a sign of rest; the hope of the righteous; the inheritance; the restoration of humanity; the building of the temple; the coming of the Messiah; harmony and peace in the new heaven and earth.[80]

5.3.3.3 The last days in NT

Also, the NT speaks about the last days. These are often about the end of history (συντέλεια τοῦ αἰῶνός). The future tense (αἰών) is linked to the judgment of evil (Matt 13:39–40, 49; 24:3), the reception of eternal life (Mark 10:30; Luke 18:30) or the resurrection life that "in all times" (εἰς τὸν αἰῶνα) continues (Luke 20:34–35; John 4:14; 6:51, 58), and the Messiah who rules in all times (Luke 1:33; John 12:34; 14:16). God's glory on earth is then no longer limited to the temple but will encompass all creation. Paul refers several times to this "coming age" (εἰς τὸν αἰῶνα). God and his Messiah will then be praiseworthy and receive eternal glory (Rom 1:25; 9:5). At that time, God "who will sustain you to the end, guiltless in the day of our Lord Jesus Christ" (1 Cor 1:8; cf. 2 Cor 1:13).

However, the NT does not use the term "last days" exclusively eschatologically. Thus Jesus applies the promise of the resurrection in Daniel 12:12 to the listeners of his own time: "an hour is coming, and is nowhere" (ἔρχεται ὥρα καὶ νῦν ἐστιν, John 5:25). Peter also interprets the coming of God's Spirit at Pentecost as the fulfillment of Joel and the beginning of Isaiah's prophecy about the end times. The outpouring of the Spirit is an eschatological promise that the church is already experiencing today. The new creation, about which Isaiah 65–66 prophesies, already breaks through in the life of the Christian: "Therefore if anyone is in Christ, he is a new creation. The

---

78. Beale, *New Testament*, 66n91, 74, 619; *Temple*, 75, 146. For a critical reflection on this proposal, see: Block, "Eden," 15.

79. Beale, *New Testament*, 99, 113–14; *John's Use*, 238–42.

80. Beale, *New Testament*, 117–28.

old has passed away; behold, the new has come." (2 Cor 5:17). This new creation is already in the "now" (5:16), in "an acceptable time," "a day of salvation" (6:2), which is a turning point in history. According to the book of Hebrews, we can already taste the powers of the coming age. With the coming of the Spirit, the eschatological time has begun (Heb 6:4; cf. Rom 8:23; 2 Cor 1:21–22; Eph 1:13–14). Christian hope is based on what the Messiah and the Spirit realize in this time (Heb 6:17–20). Christians have already come "to Mount Zion and to the city of the living God, the heavenly Jerusalem" (12:22). Thus the long-awaited city of God is already present because the saints participate in it (cf. 9:8, 23).

Therefore the last days in the NT are connected with past, present, and future. NT eschatology has a two-dimensional nature. It is characterized by both vertical-spatial and horizontal-time elements. The last days have arrived with the coming of Christ and will be completed in the future century.[81]

From this observation, Beale argues for a revision of the idea that eschatology is only one of many NT subjects. The future realization of the new creation is already within reach in all kinds of subjects. The new creation breaks through into the current creation and finds its ultimate fulfillment in the future. There is discontinuity by the removal of the evil that goes against God's plan. Beale also recognizes this discontinuity in 2 Peter 3, which speaks of the new heaven and earth and that "the earth and the works that are done on it will be burn" (v. 10b). Beale takes these words physically and states that the old creation is destroyed, after which the new heaven and the new earth take their place. In this new heaven and earth, the kingdom receives its full fullness (cf. 2 Pet 1:11).[82]

5.3.3.4 *The last days with the apostolic fathers*

Finally, Beale looks at the way the apostolic fathers talk about the last days. They, too, argue that the coming of Christ heralds the beginning of the new creation. Beale refers to the *Letter from Barnabas* (6:5), in which it is stated that God makes the new creation after the model of the first creation.[83] In Christ, the Christian is a new creation. Christ is the representative of the "new man," from whom the identity of the Christian derives.

Despite the fact that the last days of the old creation have begun with Christ's coming and the new creation has also begun, the new heaven and new earth have not yet been fully realized. Christians may know that they are already a new creation in Christ. First, this applies spiritually from their conversion, and later it will also apply physically at the coming resurrection. When this second phase begins, God's

---

81. Beale, *New Testament*, 130–33, 141–44; *1–2 Thessalonians*, 154; "Old Testament Background of Reconciliation," 550–81.
82. Beale, *New Testament*, 130, 144, 155. With reference to: Michaels, "Eschatology," 394–401.
83. Beale, *New Testament*, 157.

5.4 PART 2: STORYLINE OF OPPRESSION

The second main part of NTBT consists of one chapter. It concentrates on the tribulation that God's people will have to endure before the new cosmos breaks through. For this dissertation, only Beale's hermeneutics of the corporative are important from this main part. Beale states that the Son of Man in Daniel 7 refers primarily to God's people and is only secondarily focused on the Messiah. Both subjects are connected. The Messiah represents and embodies Israel as a Son of Man. What the Messiah experiences, is also experienced by those who are connected with him. When he suffers oppression on earth, they also suffer oppression with him (cf. Mark 13; John 16:32–33). The tribulation, over which Daniel 7–11 prophesies, begins with the coming of the Messiah and extends all over the world.[84]

The serpent who deceived the woman in Genesis 3 still wants to deceive God's people (Rev 12). Eve failed in that battle, but Christ overcomes. He is the true Adam and the true Israel. The end time thus results from earlier events. For Beale, the corporative nature of this in the Bible is important. Just as evil tried to deceive Adam, Eve, and Christ, it also wants to deceive the church. The church of Jesus Christ must be aware of this and arm itself against it.[85]

5.5 PART 3: STORYLINE OF THE RESURRECTION

For Beale, the resurrection is a conceptual equivalent of the new creation. Without a physical resurrection, humanity has no part in a future life on earth. That makes the resurrection a crucial topic in Beale's BT. He even sees it as one of the central eschatological themes in the Bible.[86]

5.5.1 Resurrection and renewal in the OT

That the OT count with a future resurrection is especially known from Daniel 12:2. However, Beale already sees a first indication of the resurrection in the name "Eve." Adam gave this name to his wife after disobedience. With this, Adam expressed the

---

84. Beale, *New Testament*, 193–96, 208–18. See the critical note to this effect: Hamilton, "Appreciation," 69.

85. Beale, *New Testament*, 204, 221–24.

86. Beale, *New Testament*, 493, cf. 227, 238, 249, 354.

hope that life would overcome death (Gen 3:15, 20). Later this hope was emphasized in God's character, which longs for life (Deut 32:39a; Isa 25:8; 26:19; Ezek 36:26–35; Hos 13:14). The cosmic renewal is so connected to the earth, which the dead release (Isa 43:18–21; 65:17; 66:22). In the new creation, their age corresponds to that of the trees (Isa 65:22)—an expectation where LXX thinks of the tree of life in Eden.[87]

5.5.2 Resurrection and renewal in the Gospels and the book of Acts

From the NT, Beale's argument about the resurrection focuses primarily on the Gospel of John. This links the resurrection to the "last day" (6:39–54; 11:23–25; 12:48; cf. 5:24–29). John also connects the resurrection with the rebirth, which makes humans a new creation (3:1–15). Terms such as "new creation," "resurrection," and "kingdom of God" are connected here.[88]

Beale is brief about the resurrection in the other gospels. In each of them, Christ's resurrection is the climax. Christ's physical resurrection is the beginning of the new creation that the OT looked for.[89] Already during Jesus' mission on earth, people saw a glimpse of this through the miracles and healings Jesus accomplished. The Messiah turned the curse into a blessing and accomplished what God commanded Adam to do (Gen 1:28). This happened most powerfully in the resurrection. By this, it is revealed that life overcomes death, and there is hope for this creation.

In Acts, it also appears that this theme of the resurrection was important for the first Christians (cf. 2:22–28; 13:34–36; 17:3–7). Through the resurrection, Christ is the Firstborn of the new creation.[90] The followers of Christ have already tasted the first blessings of it in this life. They experience the resurrection of life in a spiritual way. This offers them the guarantee that also the physical body will rise at the end of time, and death will be conquered forever.[91] That the resurrection and the renewal of creation belong together is crystal clear to Beale. He typifies the resurrection body in his NTBT as a newly created body.[92] In an earlier publication, however, he refers to the parallel between Christ's resurrection and our resurrection. Just as Christ rose from the grave, so will the Christians. At the same time, the resurrection body is also a new body because of its imperishability, which contrasts with the old, perishable body.[93] Because Beale does not deal with this issue in his publications, it remains unclear to

---

87. See for various references to the Jewish tradition: Beale, *New Testament*, 229, 231, 252, 877n15, cf. 231–234.

88. Beale, *New Testament*, 237.

89. Beale, *New Testament*, 227, 237. For further information about the resurrection in the Gospels, Beale refers to: Wright, *Resurrection*.

90. Beale, *New Testament*, 248, cf. 241, 247.

91. Beale, *New Testament*, 248.

92. Beale, *New Testament*, 238, cf. 249.

93. Beale, *We Become*, 291–92.

what extent this new body further corresponds with the old body. So the resurrection body can be about a radical renewal of the old body or about the replacement of the old by a newly created body. Beale does not seem to want to commit to a fixed schedule of continuity or discontinuity. In his reflection on the resurrection, he only focuses on Christ. He also points to the apparition of the risen Christ to Saul (Acts 9:22–26). This event underlines Christ's exalted position and Paul's mission to lead humanity into God's new creation. Especially the parallels between this event and Isaiah 42, 43, and 49 lead Beale to the conclusion to see in Saul a servant who identifies with Christ and leads humanity out of captivity.[94] In his BT, Beale, therefore, pays ample attention to the letters written in Paul's name, while other New Testament works are given less attention (§5.2.2.1).

5.5.3 Resurrection and new creation with Paul

As mentioned above, Beale pays much attention in his reflection on the resurrection to the New Testament letters that mention "Paul" as a writer (pages 249–316). Only Philemon is missing. Following the example of Seyoon Kim, Beale thinks that Paul emphasized the theme of the resurrection mainly because of his experience in Damascus. Christ then appeared to Paul in "exalted, reigning, resurrected new-creational form," as he will appear on his return.[95]

5.5.3.1 *The renewal of creation (Romans)*

In the Letter to the Romans, the resurrection is the basis for the new life. Through faith, the Christian experiences the power of resurrection. Christ is raised from the dead to new life by the God "who gives life to the dead" (4:17) and who raised Jesus from the dead (v. 24; 6:4–13). Beale focuses on the renewal of the heart and the resurrection of the body.[96] The people of the OT and Judaism were looking forward to the renewal of all humanity (spirit, soul, and body). The soul also has to go through the resurrection and be renewed.[97] Also, this was the hope that Jesus and his apostles proclaimed. The time would come when creation would be completely renewed.

In Romans 8:18–23, Beale sees parallels with the promise in Ezekiel 36–37.[98] Only in these two biblical texts does the "flesh" contrast with the "spirit," which is renewed by God's Spirit. It is this renewal that makes Christians "first fruits of the Spirit" (Rom 8:23) by identifying with Christ's death and resurrection (v. 33–39). The new life finds its spiritual beginning in the Christians and completes itself physically

---

94. Beale, *New Testament*, 241–47.
95. Beale, *New Testament*, 292; cf. 291–297; Kim, *Origin*.
96. Beale, *New Testament*, 249–59.
97. Beale, *New Testament*, 252, 555, 735, cf. 132–133, 380, 768, 844.
98. Beale, *New Testament*, 252–53, 257.

in the new cosmos. Because of this, the Christians are the first fruits of what is to come (cf. Rom 11:16; 16:5; 1 Cor 16:15; 2 Thess 2:13).

Because Romans 8:29 speaks of Christ as "firstborn," his physical resurrection is the beginning of a greater physical resurrection that is yet to come. Christ's resurrection thus forms the bridgehead to the new creation.[99] Christ as Firstborn and the Christians as "first fruits of the Spirit" give hope to this creation. Paul refers to this in his reflection on the hopeful sighing of creation (Rom 8:19). The order of resurrections is then: (1) Christ, (2) the Christians, and (3) all creation. Beale notes from this sequence that the new cosmos begins with humankind, which is the crown on creation.[100] Beale does not answer the question to what extent the new heaven and new earth are (dis)continuous in this creation. He mentions that the new creation is the "radical destruction of the physical cosmos" and, at the same time, speaks about "a re-establishment of a physically transformed earth."[101] The re-establishment of the physically altered earth thus contains the physically renovated resurrection bodies (cf. 1 Cor 15:20–28).

5.5.3.2 *Christ, Firstborn and last Adam (1 Corinthians)*

With the exception of 6:14 and 9:1, all references to the resurrection in 1 Corinthians are in chapter 15. In this part of the biblical text, Paul defends the resurrection of the physical body by characterizing Christ's resurrection as the Firstborn of the total resurrection. The great event of the resurrection finds its beginning in Christ and its completion in the future.[102]

Beale concentrates on the analogy 1 Corinthians 15 makes between the first and last Adam: "'The first man, Adam, became a living being'; the last Adam became a life-giving spirit" (v. 45). Beale points out the contrasts between the first Adam and the last Adam.[103] He concludes that the first Adam had not yet a glorified immortal body, as was the case with the last Adam. But the first Adam was created to receive this glorified imperishable body. That would have happened if humanity had remained obedient to God's command. The "natural body" would then have changed into a "spiritual body" (§5.3.1.2, cf. 1 Cor 15:24–27 with 15:21–22, 50–57).[104]

While the first Adam failed, Christ fulfilled God's commands. Christ conquered death, which in biblical-theological terms is humanity's ultimate enemy (cf. 1 Cor 15:26).[105] With this, Christ acquired that for which humankind was originally intended.

99. Beale, *New Testament*, 257.
100. Beale, *New Testament*, 30, 80, 257, 322, 450, 777.
101. Beale, *New Testament*, 312.
102. Beale, *New Testament*, 259, 261.
103. Beale, *New Testament*, 44, 87, 262–63, 439, 441.
104. Beale and Gladd, *Hidden*, 133; Beale, *New Testament*, 44, 441.
105. Beale, *New Testament*, 441.

The resurrection body is thus not equal to an old, physically resuscitated body. Christ's risen crucified body has been transformed and glorified into imperishability. That Christ became a "life-giving Spirit" (v. 45) does not mean that he discarded the physical. His resurrection contains both the material and the immaterial.

Through his victory, Christ, the last Adam, can give life to others. This explains why Paul calls the Spirit the "Spirit of Christ." What is at stake is not a return to the situation before the fall in Eden, but a life which was expected already from the story of creation. The resurrection and new creation are thus connected to the kingdom God had in store for Adam.[106]

In his other works, Beale also points out that he sees the resurrection mainly in terms of continuity. The resurrection is about the restoration of the body that is dissolved and not about a body that rises from nowhere. The example herein is for Beale, the resurrection of Jesus Christ: just as the resurrection body of the Messiah was recognized by the relatives, the whole of humanity will recognize each other in the resurrection body. Beale notes, as the greatest difference, that the present body is characterized by impermanence, while the resurrection body will be characterized by imperishability (1 Cor 15:42, 50). This duplicity is important to him and explains the similar tension between the continuity and discontinuity of the new heaven and the new earth.[107]

5.5.3.3 *The cosmic renewal (2 Corinthians)*

Second Corinthians begins with the testimony of the resurrection, which overcomes death and transience and gives life (1:9–10; 2:14–16; 3:3–7). Beale then concentrates on 2 Corinthians 4–5, which refers to a "new creation." In the phrase "let the light shine out of darkness" (4:6), this new creation is connected with the light that shone in the darkness of the first creation (Gen 1:2–3). At the same time, Beale sees in this an allusion to Paul's experience in Damascus and to Isaiah 9:1–2 (LXX).[108]

With Christ, Christians die in the old creation and will rise in the new life of the new creation. The Christian already experiences the power of resurrection today: "Though our outer nature is wasting away, our inner nature is being renewed day by day [ἀνακαινόω]" (2 Cor 4:16). The renewal has begun. Beale connects this to Colossians 3:10 because these are the only two New Testament texts in which ἀνακαινόω occurs: "and have put on the new self, which is being renewed [ἀνακαινόω] in knowledge after the image of its creator."[109] The Christian is renewed daily in the image of the last Adam (cf. Rom 6:4; Eph 2:15).

---

106. Beale, *New Testament*, 262–63.
107. Beale, *We Become*, 292. See Beale and Gladd, *Hidden*, 130.
108. Beale, *New Testament*, 266.
109. Beale, *New Testament*, 269–70.

This daily renewal anticipates 2 Corinthians 5, which the Christian describes as a new creation in Christ: "So if anyone is in Christ, there is a new creation: everything old has passed away; see, everything has become new!" (v. 17). Although physical renewal is still lacking, non-physical renewal has already begun. Already today, God's intervention forms the new creation on earth. It is this renewal that finds its completion in the new heaven and new earth.[110] For Beale the above-quoted verse thus indicates the beginning of the prophetic fulfillment of the new cosmos, of which Isaiah testified (Isa 43, 65–66). Today God's promises are already "yes" and "amen" in Christ (2 Cor 1:20; cf. 7:1).

Beale pleads for the explanation of a cosmological renewal in 2 Corinthians 5:17. In this way, he resisted Moyer Hubbard, according to whom Paul speaks of an anthropological renewal.[111] Following Douglas Moo and Ryan Jackson, Beale finds that Hubbard: (1) underestimates the overlap between anthropological and cosmological renewal; (2) does not see the allusions to Isaiah 65:17 and 66:22 in 2 Corinthians 5:17; and (3) neglects in this context the importance of Christ's physical resurrection (2 Cor 5:15).[112] What Paul writes refers to the beginning of the cosmic resurrection of all things, because both the immaterial and the material are part of this cosmos. In this century, the spirit of a man rises from spiritual death, while in the next century, the body of this man rises from death.[113]

In 2 Corinthians 5:1–10, Paul speaks about the future physical resurrection body. The "earthly tent," the perishable body, will soon be transformed into an "eternal house." There is a resurrection and a transformation of this creation into the new heaven and earth. Following Earle Ellis, the terms "house," "building," "dwelling," and "not made by hand" in verse 1–2, remind Beale of the new creation as a future temple (§5.7).[114] It is the Spirit of renewal who starts building this temple. The Spirit is thus not merely an anticipation or promise of the future. The Spirit is the beginning of this renewal and reveals what God already realizes from above on earth today. The Spirit is thus the firstfruit of the future redemption of the body (Rom 8:23) and of the inheritance that the believer will receive (Eph 1:13–14). In this way, Beale extrapolates events from the present to the future. The work that Christ began on earth finds its fulfillment in the new heaven and earth.[115]

---

110. Beale, *New Testament*, 270, 299–301.

111. Hubbard, *New Creation*, 133–87. See also: Yates, *Spirit and Creation in Paul*, 122–23, 160, 172–73, 176–77.

112. Beale, *New Testament*, 302n3; Moo, "Creation and New Creation," 51–58; Jackson, *New Creation*, 83–149.

113. Beale, *New Testament*, 301.

114. Beale, *New Testament*, 271; *Temple*, 222–27; Ellis, "II Corinthians V," 217–18.

115. Beale, *New Testament*, 272–73.

The New Heaven and New Earth

5.5.3.4 *The Spirit and the fruit of the resurrection (Galatians)*

Galatians contains few references to the resurrection. However, the letter begins with Christ's resurrection (1:1) and ends with reference to the new creation (6:15). Both texts surround and influence the contents of the letter. Beale first focuses on 2:19–20 and 5:24–25, both of which emphasize life through the Spirit. It is God's Spirit who works the new creation and gives the Christian hope for future fulfillment.[116]

Then Beale focuses on Galatians 6:15. This theme of the new creation is connected in this verse with the fruit-bearing by the Spirit in 5:22–26. Also, in the book of Isaiah, the Spirit, and the fruit-bearing are connected (32:15–18a; cf. 4:2–4; 11:1–5; 44:2–4; 61:1–11). The Spirit who works the resurrection also produces the fruit (cf. Ezek 36–37).[117]

From Galatians 6:14–15, Beale deduces that the resurrection life in Christ is not without suffering. Without the cross, there is no resurrection. In concrete terms, for the Christian, this includes the break with the transient and sinful world and the choice for the new world (6:14). Christ's death and resurrection are both connected with the new creation. The Christian life is characterized by suffering and overcoming with Christ.[118]

5.5.3.5 *The light of the risen Christ (Ephesians)*

The Epistle to the Ephesians mentions that Christ's resurrection makes him the ruler of this and the coming age (1:21). For Beale, this is the "already and not yet" government in which Christ, as last Adam, submits everything to himself (cf. Ps 8:6). The Christian is connected with Christ and, together with him, as a new creation, placed in the heavenly realms (Eph 2:6, 10). Christ is thus the new human who represents Jews and Gentiles as one (2:15; cf. 4:22–24).[119]

In this new position, Christians may know themselves constantly renewed, until the day of redemption, when God seals them with the Spirit (4:30). They are light in the Lord (5:8a) and walk in the light (v. 8b) as people over whom Christ will light (v.14; cf. 2 Cor 4:6). They may reflect the light of the Risen One in this dark creation. According to Beale, Paul refers to this theme of light and darkness to the words of rebellion in Isaiah 26:19, 51:17, and 60:1–3.[120] Through Christ's resurrection, people are able to obey God's statutes. In his reflection on the Epistle to the Ephesians, Beale remains brief about the theme of the new creation.

---

116. Beale, *New Testament*, 272, 275, cf. 298, 306.

117. Beale, New Testament, 304–14. See in detail: Beale, "Old Testament Background of Paul's Reference," 1–38.

118. Beale, *New Testament*, 309–10.

119. Beale, *New Testament*, 277–78.

120. Beale, *New Testament*, 278–80.

5.5.3.6 Resurrection daylight (Philippians)

Beale is also concise about the Epistle to the Philippians. He only points to the beginning of the letter, in which Paul reflects on the resurrection from his captivity and expresses his longing for its completion (1:19–22; cf. 2 Tim 4:18). As in the Epistle to the Ephesians, there is a call to be a light on earth (Phil 2:15). Beale sees in this an allusion to Daniel 12:2. Christians bear witness to the resurrection by acting as luminous stars in this world. They look forward in hope to the day of eschatological renewal (Phil 3:10–14).[121]

5.5.3.7 The new creation which is from above (Colossians)

The hymn in Colossians 1:15–20 describes Christ's superiority over the present (v. 15–17) and the new creation (v. 18–20). For Beale, the hymn contains one of the clearest statements that Christ's resurrection is the beginning of the new creation. Paul presents Christ as the last Adam, who is head of both the first and the new creation. The parallels in Colossians 1:15–20 show that the new creation carries the contours of the first creation. It is the last Adam who completes what the first Adam could not accomplish.[122]

By the redemption of Christ, the Christians are part of the new creation (2:10–15). They share spiritually in the resurrection life (3:1) and will later also share physically in it (3:4). Therefore they should walk in the light of the things that are above, where Christ is (3:2). They have discarded the old man with his sinful practices and put on the new man (3:9–10). They see things differently because they are a new creation. With this, they do not remember what was before, but what is to come (cf. Isa 43:8; 65:17). Therefore the new creation is connected in Colossians with the "from above" and not with the "from below."[123]

5.5.3.8 The certainty of the total resurrection (1–2 Thessalonians)

Remembering Christ's resurrection, Paul encourages Christians in Thessalonica that they will rise physically from the dead (1 Thess 1:9–10; 4:14–17; 5:9–10). The epistle concludes, according to Beale, with the prayer that Christians may experience this resurrection: "may your whole spirit and soul and body be kept blameless at the coming of our Lord Jesus Christ" (5:23b). Beale recalls that this preservation is both physical and spiritual. The renewal of the immaterial already began when people came to faith. Furthermore, Beale spends only a short paragraph on the resurrection in 2

---

121. Beale, *New Testament*, 282–84.
122. Beale, *New Testament*, 315–16, 443.
123. Beale, *New Testament*, 287, 302–3.

Thessalonians. In it, he mentions that the letter refers only to the resurrection in 2:1, where Paul repeats what he said in 1 Thessalonians.[124]

5.5.3.9 *The promise of renewal (1 Timothy, 2 Timothy, Titus)*

Beale is also brief about the resurrection in the pastoral letters: 1 Timothy confesses Christ's resurrection (3:16), 2 Timothy repeats the promise of the resurrection life in which Christians share (1:9–14), and for which they suffer (2:2–12). This truth about the resurrection is important to the addressees. Hymenaeus and Philetus had a different doctrine than the apostles (2:17). Titus 1:3 also contains the above promise of the life of resurrection and speaks of rebirth in 3:5. This rebirth refers to the new life that God's Spirit gives to people, and that is intensively connected with the new creation.[125]

5.5.4 Resurrection in the general letters

5.5.4.1 *God's Image Carrier: Jesus, King and High Priest (Hebrews)*

The Epistle to the Hebrews shows that the risen Christ represents God's image, performs the priesthood, and receives dominion over the earth. According to Beale, these elements point back to the first Adam, who served as a priest in Eden. This is because Christ's priesthood follows his description as last Adam (2:6–9, 17).[126] The Epistle to the Hebrews elaborates on this theme in relation to the new creation.

Christ's high priesthood is connected with future salvific goods (9:11; 10:19–21). He became a high priest in the temple of the new creation. Those who identify with Christ come into the presence of God. Beale points out that Jesus Christ is the only access to the new creation. Just as Moses freed the people from Egypt and brought them into Canaan, the Messiah frees his people from the slavery of sin to bring them into the new creation by his resurrection.[127]

5.5.4.2 *Honorations of the new creation (James)*

The Christians to whom James writes may participate in the new creation through rebirth. God brought them forth through the same word with which the Lord brought forth the first creation. They are the first-born of the new creation (Jas 1:18), who bear witness to the coming renewal that all creation will receive later. Beale strongly connects James 1 to Romans 8 (cf. Jas 3:18).[128]

---

124. Beale, *New Testament*, 288, 290.
125. Beale, *New Testament*, 291.
126. Beale, *New Testament*, 318.
127. Beale, *New Testament*, 320–21; "Eschatological," 47.
128. Beale, *New Testament*, 322–23.

5.5.4.3 The land, the temple, and the new creation (1 Peter)

1 Peter also typifies the Christians as firstborns of the new creation. They may know themselves to be born again to a living hope from God and realize that their inheritance is kept safe (1:3–5). This inheritance is an allusion to the land that Israel received. It refers to the imperishable heritage on the new physical earth. The physical resurrection is a part of this.[129]

Next to the image of the inheritance, 1 Peter speaks about the image of the temple. The Christians form a new temple, which refers to the new heaven and the new earth and which is the fulfillment of the old temple.[130] Through Christ's death and resurrection, new life is possible for humanity. This life is characterized by the absence of evil. In the baptism of water, Christians express this new life. Evil is turned back, and new life in Christ is embraced (3:18–21). This brings with it the necessary struggle in life. In the future glory of the new creation, every evil will be absent (Rev 21:1–22:5). Because the Christian realizes this, he or she chooses to turn his or her back on evil already in this time. In this battle, Christians know that they are behaving by God's Spirit and focus on the full fulfillment of the promises of the new heaven and the new earth.[131] 1 Peter 5 thus ends encouragingly with the imperishable and ultimate that the new life brings with it and of which the crown bears witness of glory (v. 4).

5.5.4.4 Discontinuity of the new creation (2 Peter)

In 2 Peter, the resurrection of all things is central. This epistle refers specifically to the promise of the new heaven and earth (2 Pet 3:13; cf. Isa 65:17; 66:22). While Paul places the beginning of the fulfillment of this promise in the present, Peter focuses on its eventual fulfillment in the future. That explains why Peter especially emphasizes the discontinuity between the old and the new creation. Thus there is the idea of melting the cosmic elements through fire (2 Pet 3:10–12). According to Beale, also Paul's talk about the present creation falls within that pattern. Both apostles work in addition to this. Beale illustrates this by pointing out 2 Peter 3:15–16, where the writer refers to the epistles of Paul.[132] The fact that Peter also has an eye for the good order of this renewal is shown by the fact that God's promises already enable the saints today to "become participants of the divine nature" (1:4). The Christians may thus know that they are connected with the new creation that has come with Christ and will be completed by the physical resurrection of all things in the future.

---

129. Beale, *New Testament*, 325.
130. Beale, *New Testament*, 327.
131. Beale, *New Testament*, 302–4, 328–30.
132. Beale, *New Testament*, 301, 312n30.

The New Heaven and New Earth

5.5.4.5 *The last hour of darkness (1–3 John)*

John's letters emphasize that this world perishes and that darkness gives way to light (cf. 1 John 2:8, 17). This light breaks through in the coming of Christ (1:5–7; 2:8). It refers to the breaking down of the new creation in the old creation. According to Beale, we should read these letters in the light of the Gospel of John. He repeats that the "last hour" (1 John 2:18) is related to the promise of the resurrection in Daniel 12:2 (§5.3.3.3). From this background, we should understand John's teaching on being "born of God" as references to rebirth in relation to the new creation (1 John 3:9; 2:29; 4:7; 5:1, 4, 18; cf. John 1:13; 3:3–8).[133]

5.5.4.6 *Christ's Resurrection and the Later Resurrection (Revelation)*

From the beginning, Revelation bears witness to Christ's resurrection. He is the Firstborn of the dead, and Ruler of the earth (1:5; 3:14). Revelation 1–3 represents him as King, Priest, and Judge, elements which, according to Beale, remind us of Genesis 1–2.[134] It is from this position that the promise of eating from the tree of life sounds in Revelation 2:7. This statement connects Beale with the eternal life of the new heaven and earth (cf. 22:2–19) and the reception of the crown of life (2:10–11). God is the Creator and Redeemer who has revealed himself in Christ.[135] Revelation testifies about the resurrection: (1) the believers are connected with the characteristics of Christ (priesthood, kingdom); (2) the resurrection of the believers is connected with Christ's resurrection (6:11; 20:4–6); and (3) the full completion of God's new heaven and earth is near (Rev 20:12–15). Beale also points to the two witnesses in Revelation 11:11–12. According to him, they represent God's people. Their resurrection sees Beale as their justification before the eyes of the oppressors in the end times.[136]

Finally, Beale points to the new heaven and new earth in Revelation 21:1–4. Because the redeemed are in the new creation, Beale concludes that they have received a newly created body. While paying attention to the relationship between Christ's resurrection and the resurrection of believers, he remains silent about the characteristics of the resurrection body and the extent to which this body is equal to our present body. From Revelation 21–22, Beale only lists what Christians will do in the new creation.[137] He also emphasizes the importance of the resurrection for the new creation. The theme of resurrection should not be missing in a BT.[138]

---

133. Beale, *New Testament*, 333–35.
134. Beale, *New Testament*, 335–46.
135. Beale, *New Testament*, 345–48.
136. Beale, *New Testament*, 351; *Revelation*, 596–602.
137. Beale, *New Testament*, 352–53.
138. Beale, *New Testament*, 297–98, 302, 354.

5.6 PART 4-5: NARRATIVE LINE OF IDOLATRY AND SALVATION

5.6.1 Decay and restoration of God's image

Beale's BT pays great attention to hamartiology and soteriology. His story about this also begins in Genesis 1-3. Although Adam had to guard the garden, the serpent was given access to it, and sin, chaos, and disorder entered creation. Instead of being the image of God, humanity has since been formed in the image of idols. It is Christ who redeems and recreates us from this snare (Rom 8:29). Finally, Adam is the image-bearer of God and fills Genesis 1:28. He is the Son of Man from Daniel 7. The term "Son of Man" emphasizes his connection with Adam. He is the last Adam who submits creation to God's glory and gives her the rest of the new creation.[139]

5.6.2 Christ as the true Adam and the true Israel

5.6.2.1 *Christ as last Adam in the Gospels*

Beale shows extensively that the Gospel of Matthew closely links Christ to Adam. As Son of Man, Christ receives all authority on earth in this gospel. He calls upon his disciples to fulfill the great commission to Adam (Matt 28:18).[140] When this task is accomplished, the "rebirth" (παλιγγενεσία) of all things takes place (19:28).

Parallels between Christ and Adam also occur in the other Gospels. Thus the wild animals that Jesus visits after his temptations (Mark 1:13) refer to the future peace between people and animals on earth (cf. Isa 11:6-9; 43:18-19; 65:17-20).[141] Isaiah 65 connects this blessing with the tree of life and the serpent in Eden (vv. 22-25; cf. Gen 3:14, 22). Beale also sees an anticipation of this eschatological harmony in the healings that Jesus accomplishes.[142] Christ overcomes the fallen state of this creation. Whoever is connected to him is not overpowered by death, but rises from the dead, as Christ does, at the future renewal with a perfectly renewed body (Matt 19:28-29; 1 Cor 15:20).

5.6.2.2 *Christ as Israel in the Gospels*

For Beale, Christ is *the* representative of Israel. Just as Adam and Israel are God's firstborn son (Gen 5:1-3; Exod 4:22), so is Christ. In Psalm 80:17, "Son of Man" therefore

---

139. Beale, *New Testament*, 357-60, 362-63, 368-74, 380-86, 389, 391, 393-401, 427; Cf. *We Become*.

140. Beale, *New Testament*, 388-93.

141. Beale, *New Testament*, 393, 418-419, 421, 431. With reference to: Bauckham, "Jesus and the Wild Animals."

142. Beale, *New Testament*, 423.

refers to both Israel and the Messiah (cf. Dan 7). Christ is the true Israel. What Israel could not do, he does. He faithfully fulfills God's mission. As the last Adam and righteous descendant of Israel, Jesus gathers twelve apostles around him. These represent faithful Israel at the micro-level, but the salvation that Christ brings extends to all nations.[143]

Although Beale does not discuss the Gospel of John anywhere in this context, he states that the conclusions he draws about Jesus as the true Adam, Son of God, and representative of Israel also apply to that part of Scripture.[144]

5.6.3   The restoration of God's image in the letters and Revelation

Also, the Epistles describe Christ as the ultimate image-bearer of God. However, it is only Paul who explicitly characterizes Christ as "image of God" and "last Adam." That is why Beale concentrates mainly on this apostle (pages 439–462) and devotes only four pages to the theme of restoring God's image in the general letters and Revelation (pages 462–465).

5.6.3.1   *Christ, the last Adam (1 Cor 15)*

In 1 Corinthians 15, Paul sees Christ as the last Adam to fulfill the commands of the first Adam. As the first Adam produced death and impermanence through his disobedience, the last Adam produced life and imperishability through his obedience (v. 25–27, 54–57). The "first Adam" is thus an antitype of the last Adam. Christ regains, renews, glorifies, and completes the image of God on earth, as the first Adam should have done before.[145]

Beale connects this with Romans 8: Whoever is in Christ is formed to the "image of his Son" (v. 29), receives the adoption as sons (v. 14–15, 19, 23), and the "glory" (v. 17–18, 21, 30). These three terms remind Beale of Adam, who was created as the son of God, to reflect God's glory on earth as God's image-bearer.[146]

5.6.3.2   *Christ, the image of the invisible God (Colossians)*

In Colossians 1, Paul describes Christ as "the image of the invisible God" (v. 15). According to Beale, this is an allusion to Genesis 1:26. References to the commission in Genesis 1:28 also return in Colossians 1:6, 10, 13.[147] Christ is the ultimate image of God that existed before creation and is now revealed. He fills up and restores what God commanded the first human, as it came to light earlier in 1 Corinthians 15. In

---

143. Beale, *New Testament*, 393, 402–12, 416, 422–28, 447, 652–53.
144. Beale, *New Testament*, 437.
145. Beale, *New Testament*, 439–41.
146. Beale, *New Testament*, 442.
147. Beale, *New Testament*, 444–445; "Colossians," 842–59.

Colossians 1:15–18, Christ's position as last Adam is mentioned. Christ is so "before all things" (v. 17a) as "firstborn of all creation" (v. 15). Colossians 1:18–20 also emphasizes Christ's sovereignty over the new creation. He is the glorified image-bearer of God.[148]

In Colossians 3, Paul explains how Christians should become conformed to this image of Christ, the "new man" (cf. 2 Cor 3:18). They came into the sphere of the new creation *in Christ* and fulfilled Adam's commission. Paul explains this with the metaphor that Christians take off their old clothes and put on their new clothes. This refers to their identification with Christ's resurrection and the new creation in Christ (Col 3:10). The metaphor reminds Beale of Genesis 3, in which God replaces Adam's "old" clothing with "new" (cf. Col 3:7).[149]

5.6.3.3 Christ, the Fulfiller of Promises

Beale also sees the theme of sculptural restoration in 2 Corinthians 3:16–4:2 and Philippians 2:5–11. In his discussion of this, however, he does not add anything fundamentally new. Already during the first coming of Christ, it is visible that God is starting a restart on earth, which is in line with Adam's original commission. Jesus and his followers then stand as new image carriers in relation to Adam, the first image carrier.[150]

In his research into the restoration of God's image in the General Epistles and Revelation, Beale's observations on Hebrews 11 and Revelation 21–22 are particularly remarkable. Hebrews 11 testifies that Abraham applied the promises received to the new creation. The book of Revelation then shows that those who bear Christ's name may realize that they are partakers of God's image (Rev 2:17; 3:12). Thus the name of God and the Lamb is written on their foreheads, and they are presented as inhabitants of the new Eden, the new heaven and earth (Rev 21–22). They recover the position that Adam lost before. In that capacity, they know themselves near God and may see God's face and reflect the light of the Lord (21:10–11; 22:4–5).[151]

5.6.4 Justification and reconciliation

Although Beale realizes that one can look at the entire soteriology from the perspective of the new creation, in his BT, he limits himself to justification and reconciliation. The whole can be compared to a bunch of flowers in which each flower is connected to Genesis 1–2, but in which no new information about the new heaven and earth can be found.

148. Beale, *New Testament*, 445–49.
149. Beale, *New Testament*, 445–46, 449–55; "Colossians," 860–63; *Temple*, 30.
150. Beale, *New Testament*, 455–60.
151. Beale, *New Testament*, 463–65.

5.6.4.1 Positional justification as a new beginning (1 Cor 1)

Beale connects the justification of the believer with the expectation of the new creation, which finds its beginning in Christ's resurrection. Being just is, therefore, more than not being guilty. It also points to the position of the Christian *in Christ* (1 Cor 1:30).[152] Christ accomplished what God commanded Adam. As an obedient image-carrier, he reflects the character of the Creator on earth. Therefore, Christ received the blessings that applied to Adam: "And he has put all things under his feet and has made him the head over all things for the church, which is his body, the fullness of him who fills all in all" (Eph 1:22–23).[153]

Christ's physical resurrection means the beginning of a new creation and the dawn of eternal rule. Through the resurrection of Jesus, a new victorious Adam rose, marking the end of the old creation and the beginning of the new creation.[154] Justification is the beginning of the fulfillment of the promise of restoration that creation has been waiting for (cf. Rom 16:25–26).

5.6.4.2 The revelation of justification (Rom 8)

As society rejects God's gospel, the moment will soon come when it will have to acknowledge the effects of that gospel. Beale points to Romans 8, where the life of Christ is connected with that of the Christians. Just as the world rejected Christ, it rejected the Christians. And just as Christ's resurrection confirms the truth of the gospel (cf. Rom 1:4), so does the coming physical resurrection of Christians (8:11, 23, 31–34). It is especially the physical resurrection that justifies the Christian and reveals that the powers of evil have been overcome.[155] Although Christians have received the official position of sonship, this will only become clear later in creation (8:9–10, 18–23). In the end, the world will recognize that Christians *are* righteous in Christ, and it is true: "he also justified; and those whom he justified he also glorified" (v. 30b).[156]

Sonship, justification, and glorification are thus extensions of each other. According to Beale, the future glorification of Christians is also connected with Paul's statements about being co-heir (v. 17), the redemption of creation (v. 21–22), and the final liberation at the resurrection in the glorified body (v. 23). The physical resurrection is the climax of justification. It is opposed to the false evaluation given by the world of the saints (v. 35–36). It is this hope that motivates Christians to accomplish

---

152. Beale, *New Testament*, 469, 472–73, 475–76, 514.
153. Beale, *New Testament*, 478–79.
154. Beale, *New Testament*, 480.
155. Beale, *New Testament*, 499, cf. 497–501.
156. Beale, *New Testament*, 499–501. See already: Vos, *Pauline Eschatology*, 152–54.

God's good pleasure and to reflect the character of the Lord in creation, as it was formerly dedicated to Adam.[157]

5.6.4.3 Reconciliation as the basis for the new creation (2 Cor 5)

In Paul's case, the atonement is also connected with the new creation. In 2 Corinthians 5:17-21, he describes that Christians, through the resurrection of Christ, are part of the new creation.[158] According to Beale, Paul refers to God's promise of restoration in Isaiah 43:18-19. This text is connected with the promise of the new cosmos (60:15-22; 65:17-25; 66:19-24) and the return from exile (43:10; 45:14; 48:18; 52:7; 54:6-8; 57:18-19; 62:12). Creation and redemption terms are linked together. God's salvation for creation is the continuation of his creation in a completely new way. Beale also sees the same relationship in Revelation 4-5.[159]

For the further relationship between Isaiah and 2 Corinthians 5, Beale relies mainly on Carroll Stuhlmueller's research: God removes the iniquities of the people (Isa 43:25), frees them from the bonds of sin (42:6-9; 49:8-9), reconciles himself with the people (1:11, 15; 34:16-17; 56:7; 60:7, 10; 62:4; 66:2) and grants them the peace of new creation through the death of his servant (53:4-12).[160]

From this background, Paul connects the atonement in 2 Corinthians 5 with the new creation, about which Isaiah already spoke.[161] Christians may already participate in this through the forgiveness of sins. However, they should also behave as members of the new creation (2 Cor 5:14-20). Through the resurrection of Christ, they have been reconciled with God and are no longer in a neutral zone. Rather, they show creation the atmosphere of the new heaven and earth, which will soon become omnipresent. Reconciliation is thus part of the subject of the new creation, and Christ is the theological-geographical tipping point from which new creation originates in all of this.[162]

5.6.4.4 The fulfillment of reconciliation (Rev 21-22)

The book of Revelation continues the above-mentioned theme of Isaiah and mentions how Christians still live in captivity (18:2-4; 19:2). This captivity only ends with the arrival of the new heaven and new earth. Beale characterizes this future time as the temple

---

157. Beale, *New Testament*, 500-501, 503, 508.
158. Beale, *New Testament*, 529-30.
159. Beale, *New Testament*, 348, 532-33; *Revelation*, 140, 160, 369.
160. Beale, *New Testament*, 532; Stuhlmueller, *Creative*.
161. Beale, *New Testament*, 533-34.
162. Beale, *New Testament*, 535-37, cf. 544.

of the end time, which is similar to the new Jerusalem, the restored garden of Eden, or the new creation. This recalls the description of the future Jerusalem in Isaiah 62:1–5.[163]

Only in the new creation can we speak of the completed unity between God and humanity (Rev 21:3; cf. Lev 26:11–12, 40–45; Ezek 37:27). In Revelation 21:4 the prophet mentions the fruits of this unity: "he will wipe every tear from their eyes. Death will be no more; mourning and crying and pain will be no more, for the first things have passed away." All these promises have their origin in the book of Isaiah (Rev 21:1 // Isa 65:17; 66:62; Rev 21:4 // Isa 25:8; 43:18; 65:17; Rev 21:5 // Isa 43:19).[164]

In this description of the new Jerusalem as a temple, Revelation 21:9–27 describes the people of God as a glorious city that has the same form as the holiest in the temple. Beale sees parallels with the temple vision in Ezekiel. There is talk of it: God's tabernacle (Rev 21:3; Ezek 43:7; cf. Lev 26:11–12), the taking away of the prophet (Rev 21:10; Ezek 40:1–2; 43:5), God's glory (Rev 21:11; Ezek 43:2–5), twelve city gates (Rev 21:12–13; Ezek 42:15–19; 48:31–34), measuring (Rev 21:15; Ezek 40:3–5), a cube-shaped structure (Rev 21:16; Ezek 45:1–5), illuminated by God (Rev 21:23; Ezek 43:2,5), a spring with living water (Rev 22:1–2a; Ezek 47:1–9), and fruit trees along a river (Rev 22:2b; Ezek 47:12).[165] These parallels lead Beale to see Revelation 21:1–22:5 as the fulfillment of Ezekiel's temple vision.[166]

In this new creation, God's people receive a high priestly function in the Most Holy Place, for they "will see his face, and his name will be on their foreheads" (22:4). In the broken creation, God's presence was primarily geographically limited to the temple in Israel, and Christians form the new temple of the living God. In the new creation, the whole triune God will fulfill his creation. The whole creation then becomes a temple in which the saints are present and see God's face (cf. Ps 11:4–7; 27:4).[167] The water, the river, the tree of life, and the absence of the curse in the new heaven and new earth further remind us of Eden, where humans walked in God's presence. The curse of disobedience is thus lifted in the new heaven and earth. Humanity is placed in a glorified garden, which bears the characteristics of the court in Genesis 2–3. In principle, God's people can already participate in these future blessings today, thanks to the redemptive work of Christ.[168]

5.7 PART 6: STORYLINE OF THE SPIRIT

In his sixth chapter, Beale discusses the relationship between the temple as the prototype of the new creation and the Spirit of God as its processor. Beale shows that in the

---

163. Beale, *New Testament*, 550; *Revelation*, 285–89, 1039–1121.
164. Beale, *New Testament*, 551–52.
165. Beale, *New Testament*, 552–53; *Temple*, 346–53; *Revelation*, 1030–1117.
166. Beale, *New Testament*, 553.
167. Beale, *New Testament*, 553–54, 634–35; *Temple*, 245–68.
168. Beale, *New Testament*, 554.

Gregory Beale's perspective on the new heaven and new earth

Bible and the Jewish tradition, the Spirit is related to the renewal, the establishment of God's dwelling place on earth, and the definitive breakthrough of the kingdom.

5.7.1 The renewal through the Spirit

5.7.1.1 The transformation by God's Spirit

From the beginning, God's Spirit transforms man and earth: "When you send forth your spirit, they are created; and you renew the face of the ground" (Ps 104:30; cf. Pss 1:2; 2:7). The Spirit bestows the eternal life of the kingdom to come (Ezek 36:26–27). Together with others, Beale connects this renewal, about which Ezekiel 36–37 speaks, with the creation of man in Genesis 2.[169] In both: (1) there is first the body; (2) the breath of God's life then enters; and (3) the land in which YHWH places man is connected with Eden (Gen 2:7–8; Ezek 36:35; 37:5, 9). The biblical storyline also connects the redemption of humanity from slavery with the freedom of the Spirit. The exodus from Egypt and the later liberation from exile compare Isaiah with the future liberation from creation. In the new heaven and earth, the liberated nations walk in God's light, and the kings of the earth pay homage to God (Isa 60:1–5; Rev 21:24–26).[170]

5.7.1.2 The Messiah and the Spirit

By the descent of God's Spirit upon Jesus, the Messiah can reveal the kingdom of God to humans, and the new creation breaks through. Beale repeats that the healings that Jesus accomplished were a glimpse of the new heaven and earth that will soon breakthrough on earth (§5.5.2). The coming of Christ marks the beginning of the end of the material and an immaterial curse that came upon creation. The Spirit is the One who transforms the broken creation into the promised new creation and leads humankind out of slavery.[171]

5.7.1.3 Paul and the Spirit

Paul further develops this relationship between God's Spirit and the new creation. In the present brokenness, the Spirit prepares the first fruits of the new cosmos. Paul calls the Christians "first fruits of the Spirit" (Rom 8:23), who are covenants with Christ, the "firstborn" of the new creation (v. 30; cf. 1 Cor 15:20, 23). The new life

---

169. Beale, *New Testament*, 560–62; Jenson, *Ezekiel*, 281–83; Duguid, *Ezekiel*, 69; Block, *Ezekiel 25–48*, 360, 379; Blenkinsopp, *Ezekiel*, 173; Keil and Delitzsch, *Ezekiel, Daniel*, 117–18.
170. Beale, *New Testament*, 566–67.
171. Beale, *New Testament*, 567–74.

The New Heaven and New Earth

given by the Spirit is the beginning of the physical resurrection of creation in the eschaton (Rom 8:18–23).[172]

This position of Christ as Firstborn is also evident from the indication "last Adam" (1 Cor 15:45). It is the last Adam who, like the first Adam, gives life. Christians testify of this new life in the brokenness, as Christ did during his life on earth. Paul calls on them to produce the "fruit of the Spirit" (Gal 5:22)—a theme that only appears in the future perspectives of Isaiah (Isa 32:15; 57:15–19).[173]

5.7.2 Sinai, Zion, and God's temple

In his reflection on the work of God's Spirit, Beale states that God's heavenly tabernacle began to descend on earth at Pentecost. From that moment, God's Spirit came to dwell in people, and the heavenly temple expanded on earth. This went much further than living God's glory in the Most Holy Place. The tabernacle that Israel built with the Sinai was a model of this later revelation. Beale substantiates this from the parallels between God's descend on Mount Sinai and the coming of the Spirit at Pentecost. While in the OT, the Spirit rested only on prophets, priests, and kings, the prophet Joel saw that a time would come when all Israel would receive the Spirit (3:1). Just as God at the time took a part of his Spirit from Moses and laid it upon the seventy elders (Num 11:25), so Christ, as second Moses, distributes his Spirit among his followers (cf. Acts 2:23).[174]

Beale brings Mount Sinai in relationship to the temple. Mount Sinai is the "mountain of God" in the OT, which has parallels with the temple on Mount Zion (Exod 3:1; 18:5; 24:13). Like the temple, Mount Sinai has a threefold division: (1) the mountaintop/most holy, where God was present and where the Ten Words were given/kept; (2) the center of the mountain/Most Holy Place where the elders/priests served; (3) the foot of the mountain/court outside the temple where the people came to the altar of burnt offering (cf. Exod 19:24).[175]

5.7.3 The storyline of the temple

5.7.3.1 God's all-encompassing temple

Beale pays extensive attention to the storyline of the temple in the Bible. Following various ancient sources, he states that Genesis 1–2 consciously describes creation as a cosmic temple to God, of which the later temples that God's people built on earth

---

172. Beale, *New Testament*, 581–82. Cf. White, *Erstlingsgabe*, 189–95.

173. Beale, *New Testament*, 583–88.

174. Beale, *New Testament*, 593–613. Cf. Niehaus, *God at Sinai*, 371; Turner, *Power*, 279–80, 284–85.

175. Beale, *New Testament*, 608–11; *Temple*, 105.

are an image. Beale connects the court with the earth because both are characterized by water (washbasin) and earth (altar). He then connects the Holy Place with heaven, because both are characterized by the lights (sun, moon, stars, menorah). And the Most Holy Place he connects with the invisible creation where God and the angels live because both are hidden from humanity. This background explains to Beale why Revelation 21–22 describes the new heaven and new earth with the characteristics of a gigantic temple.[176]

After Christ's glorification, the Spirit began to form the church as a living temple, so that God could dwell in this creation. As the Spirit lived in Christ, he now lives in the church. The church is thus a temple of God, pointing forward to the new creation, the all-encompassing temple to God. For Beale, the completion of God's temple is thus synonymous with the creation of the new heaven and earth.[177]

Revelation 21–22 describes this new creation in terms of a city garden and temple. This is remarkable for those who think of valleys, mountains, forests, meadows, stars, planets, and other things when using the expression "new earth."[178] The foundations of this cube-shaped city garden recall the foundation of Solomon's temple and the cube-shaped Most Holy Place therein (1 Kgs 5:17; 6:20–22; cf. Isa 54:11–12; Rev 21:16–20).

The new creation is a future global temple. Beale connects Revelation 21–22 with the prophecies of the temple in Ezekiel 40–48. He realizes that some think that Ezekiel speaks of a future physical temple in Israel.[179] For Beale, however, the prophecy in Ezekiel 40–48 can be compared to a father who promised his young son a horse in 1903. If this father gave his son a car in 1925, it would not be a decline or spiritualization of the promise.[180] At the same time, Beale points out that even for those who interpret the temple in Ezekiel 40–48 as a reference to a future physical temple in Israel, the temple will eventually refer to Christ and God's ultimate dwelling in the new creation.[181] It is, therefore, a temple that includes more than one piece of land in Jerusalem. The temple refers to the complete new cosmos. This explains the many architectural parallels between the temple city in Revelation 21–22 and the temple vision in Ezekiel 40–48. What Ezekiel still sees as a spatially-constrained temple, John describes as a literal cosmic temple.[182]

The new cosmos is described in temple terms in Revelation 21–22. After the prophet mentioned in his preamble that he saw the new heaven and new earth (21:1), he calls the new Jerusalem that descends from heaven (v. 2). Then he learns that God's

---

176. Beale, *New Testament*, 614–48; *Erosion*, 164–67, 184–92; "Eden," 5–31; *Temple*, 32–50, 109.
177. Beale, *God Dwells Among*, 139; *New Testament*, 614–15; *Temple*, 25.
178. Beale, *New Testament*, 615–16; *Temple*, 23.
179. See detailed: Beale, *Temple*, 348–53.
180. Beale, *New Testament*, 643.
181. Beale, *New Testament*, 633.
182. Beale, *New Testament*, 615, cf. 634; *Temple*, 346–54.

tent is with men and that God will dwell among them (v. 3). The new cosmos is identified with the new Jerusalem and the eschatological tabernacle.

Only the righteous will enter this city (22:14–15). Nothing that is unclean enters (v. 27). The unjust remain outside the city (v. 11). Beale cannot imagine that these injustices are in the new creation, but not in the city. Earlier, the prophet wrote of the unjust that "their portion will be in the lake that burns with fire and sulfur, which is 'the second death'" (Rev 21:8; cf. 2 Pet 3:13). Whoever is not allowed to enter the city will not be in the new creation, either. The new Jerusalem is thus synonymous with the new cosmos. The city boundaries are equal to the boundaries of creation.[183]

5.7.3.2 Eden and the temple

A connection of the new creation with the new Jerusalem, the temple and the garden extends the biblical storyline. For Beale, the garden in Eden was the first temple on earth. Although it did not contain a building, it was still a sanctuary. He derives observations that point in this direction mainly from Meredith Kline:

1. God walks in Eden (Gen 3:8), as God later walks in the temple (Lev 26:12; Deut 23:15; 2 Sam 7:6–7; Ezek 28:14).

2. God placed Adam in the garden to "guard" it (רָמַשׁ, Gen 2:15), as God later called upon the priests to guard the temple (Num 3:7–8; 8:25–26; 18:5–6; 1 Chr 23:32; Ezek 44:14). Beale points to Ezekiel 28:13, where Adam wears the same gems as the high priest.

3. The tree of life is the model for the temple *menorah* that is shaped like a tree with branches, leaves, and blossoms.

4. The flora that characterizes the court in Eden is found in Solomon's temple (1 Kgs 6:18, 29, 32, 35; 7:18–20).

5. Just as Israel's temple lay on a mountain (Exod 15:17; cf. Ezek 40:2; 43:12) and had its entrance in the east (Ezek 40:6), Eden also lay on a mountain, with its entrance on the east side (28:14, 16).

6. The ark of the covenant is a reminder of the knowledge tree. According to Beale, both touching the ark and eating the tree resulted in death.

7. Just as a river originated in Eden (Gen 2:10), so does a river originate in the temple (Ezek 47:1–12; Rev 21:1–2; cf. Zech 14:8–9). Also, according to later Judaism, several rivers originated from the tree of life in Eden.

---

183. Beale, *New Testament*, 616–17; *Temple*, 24; *Revelation*, 1101–2.

8. Just like the temple, Eden has three areas. Beale compares Eden and its river spring with the Most Blessed Sacred, the court in Eden with the holy and the rest of the earth with the court.[184]

God placed Adam in the garden of Eden to guard this sanctuary. From the moment Adam fails and the unclean serpent dethrones the temple, Adam loses his priestly function. Two cherubs then take over the function of Adam (Gen 3:24). Their function of vigilance returns later when two cherubs have to guard the covenant box.[185]

Ezekiel 40–48 and Revelation 21–22, thus build on the first temple garden. It was this temple garden that Adam had to extend throughout creation (Gen 1:28).[186] From this background, it is understandable that Revelation 21:1–22:5 describes the new creation as a temple in garden format. The garden in Eden was the first universal temple model on earth that served as a prototype for all the later temples of God's people. At the same time, Beale realizes that Eden is not the original prototype of the new creation. It is only one model. The basis of this is God's heavenly temple. It is the prototype that reveals itself on earth.[187] God declared from the beginning that all sanctuaries on earth could not grasp him (Isa 66:1). Just like the later temples, the garden in Eden was too small for God. Only the heavenly sanctuary can serve as the throne of the Lord. It is this sanctuary that God wants to realize in creation. Eden is, therefore, a miniature form of God's eternal cosmic temple.

Because the later temples can be deduced from the garden in Eden, Beale methodically chooses to consistently connect the new creation with the first creation and the temples in history. This makes it possible to receive more insight into the new earth God has in store for his people. This method motivates Beale to follow the development of Genesis 1–2 in the Bible and to analyze it more deeply, in order to be able to make definitive conclusions about the new creation in Revelation 21–22.[188]

5.7.3.3 *The temple in the history of salvation*

Although the patriarchs did not build sanctuaries, they created holy places. The altars they built and sanctified in Canaan were a sign of God's presence in the land. According to Beale, this attitude found its source in God's command to Adam (Gen 1:28). Following Geerhardus Vos, he sees the holy places of the patriarchs as signposts to the future temple, of which the stoneless sanctuary in Eden was the prototype. This

---

184. Beale, *God Dwells Among*, 27–28; *New Testament*, 617–20; "Eden," 7–12; *Temple*, 66–80, 182–83; "Final Vision," 197–200; *Revelation*, 1110–12. Cf. Kline, *Kingdom*, 31–32, 54–56; *Images*, 35–42. See for a critical reflection on this: Block, "Eden," 1–30.
185. Beale, *New Testament*, 618; *Temple*, 70.
186. Beale, *New Testament*, 621–22; *Temple*, 81–82.
187. Beale, *New Testament*, 627; *Temple*, 133–34.
188. Beale, *New Testament*, 622, 641.

The New Heaven and New Earth

background immediately explains why the patriarchs have a tree in most holy places. The tree is reminiscent of the tree of life in the first sanctuary.[189]

Later Israel built a tabernacle and temple for God. They formed a miniature of God's infinite heavenly temple. God wanted to realize this heavenly temple on earth so that all creation became a temple to God. Whenever Israel saw the temple in Jerusalem, it was reminded that God wanted to make all creation his temple. One day the moment would come when the Creator would fill creation with his glory.[190]

Israel served as a light for the world, as did Adam, to spread God's light across the earth. Therefore the prophets characterize Canaan as Eden (Isa 51:3; Ezek 36:35; Joel 2:3). They recalled that God's glory wants to fill the whole earth. God's temple would first include Jerusalem (Isa 4:4–6; 54:2–3, 11–12; Jer 3:16–17; Zech 1:16—2:11), then Canaan (Ezek 37:25–28), and then all the earth (Dan 2:34–35, 44–45; cf. Isa 54:2–3). Then God would be all in all.[191]

Israel denied this and stated that the temple proved that it was walking in God's will as a people. God had chosen them from among the nations to stay with them. Others would experience God's presence only in judgment. This obstinacy caused Israel to lose the temple and the land. Isaiah characterized this loss as a return to the darkness and formlessness at the beginning of creation (Isa 45:18–19; cf. Gen 1:2).

God's grace offered the people a new opportunity. The Lord brought it back from exile to Canaan to build the temple there. This time God pushed back his temple boundaries. The future glory would surpass the former temple of Eden and Jerusalem. This was fulfilled in the coming of Christ. It is the temple to which all previous temples referred and anticipated (John 2:21; cf. 2 Sam 7:12–14; Zech 6:12–13). Jesus is the cornerstone (Matt 21:42; Mark 12:10; Luke 20:17) who "tabernacled" among people (John 1:14). At the same time, Jesus is also the builder of God's temple. By the resurrection, Christ raises God's temple in the form of his own Person.[192]

Christ's death can be interpreted as the demolition of God's old spatially-constrained temple, and his resurrection can be seen as God's omnipresent new temple that encompasses all creation. Through the Spirit, this temple becomes visible everywhere on earth. Hence Paul reminds Christians that they are a temple of God and that God's Spirit dwells in them (1 Cor 3:16; 6:19; 2 Cor 6:16). This is not about metaphorical language. The congregation of God is the beginning of the fulfillment of God's eschatological creation-encompassing temple.[193]

In the new cosmos, God's desire becomes a reality. Then all creation becomes God's dwelling place. The completion of God's creation is thus equal to the completion of God's temple. Revelation 21–22 underlines the importance of this from the visual

---

189. Beale, *New Testament*, 625–26; "Eden," 98; *Temple*, 96–97. Cf. Vos, *Eschatology*, 85–86.
190. Beale, *New Testament*, 627, 630–31. Cf. Beale, *Temple*, 350.
191. Beale, *New Testament*, 172–173, 631.
192. Beale, *New Testament*, 632.
193. Beale, *New Testament*, 635, cf. 633, 638.

language. Whereas God's presence used to be limited to the Most Holy Place, in the eschaton, it encompasses the whole cosmos. Then all humans shall see the face of God (Rev 21:16; 22:4). The terminology in Revelation 21–22 recalls God's earlier desire to walk on earth (Lev 26:12; Ezek 37:27; Rev 21:3).[194]

The essence of the new creation is thus the presence of the glory of God. The glory is then no longer bounded by walls. It is vast throughout creation. Today the congregation can already see a preview of this through the indwelling of the Spirit. It is "built on the foundation of the apostles and prophets, Christ Jesus himself being the cornerstone, in whom the whole structure, being joined together, grows into a holy temple in the Lord. In him, you also are being built together into a dwelling place for God by the Spirit" (Eph 2:20–22; cf. 4:13–16).[195]

5.8 PART 7–9: THE STORYLINE OF THE CHURCH

In the main sections 7–9 of NTBT, Beale focuses on the question of the relationship between the church and the new creation. He sees the church from a covenantal-theological perspective as restored Israel in the end times.[196] An important basis for this is the presupposition of collective solidarity, in which one *pars pro toto* stands for the other. From this approach, Jesus, as an individual, represents the faithful remnant of Israel (cf. §5.4).[197] Christ is the Adam who fulfills the mission to the first Adam. Because Israel also received this call, he is also the new Israel. The church that is *in Christ* is thus the continuation of this new Israel. Beale makes no distinction here between Israel and the church. This does not mean that the church replaces former Israel. Rather, it continues former Israel and completes in Christ what was commissioned of it.[198] For our research into the new heaven and new earth, a detailed substantiation of this is less important. We, therefore, concentrate on chapter 22 in his NTBT, because this is where Beale speaks about the relationship between the church and the land.

5.8.1 Israel's land promise and fulfillment

5.8.1.1 *Immaterial and material fulfillment*

The Old Testament promise of the land is linked to Israel's recovery. Beale calls the Old Testament testimony about this only briefly. He focuses more extensively on the fulfillment of this promise in Christ and the church. Beale does mention, however, that he rejects the idea that Christ, at his return, begins to gather a people (Israel)

---

194. Beale, *New Testament*, 639–40, 647.
195. Beale, *New Testament*, 175, 643–47; *Temple*, 25, 313.
196. See for a critical reflection on this: Henebury, "Review," 13–16.
197. Beale, *New Testament*, 656.
198. Beale, *New Testament*, 653–55; *John's Use*, 242–46.

from all over the world and brings them back to a geographical land on earth. The promised peace is not locked up in the land but in Christ. It is primarily about immaterial blessings in Christ. Beale recognizes that the promise of the land will soon be fulfilled physically in the new heaven and earth. The land in which Israel resided as "new Adam" was thus a foreshadowing of the future land that would encompass the whole new creation.[199] At this time, the only physical fulfillment is the physical resurrection of Christ.

The theme of the country starts in Genesis 1–2. Humans must subdue the earth by broadening the boundaries of Eden and filling the earth with God's glory.[200] This mission was passed on to Israel (§5.3.2). If they succeeded, the land of Canaan would become like Eden (cf. Gen 13:10; Isa 51:3; Ezek 36:35; Joel 2:3). It is Christ, however, who fully fulfills the mission of creation. In his resurrection, the new creation finds its beginning, and at his return, it will be completed both materially and immaterially. On the new earth, the people of God will be like a vineyard that fills the earth with its fruits, as was to be done in Eden at the time (Isa 27:2–6).[201] In Christ, Israel has succeeded in fulfilling Genesis 1:28. Beale emphasizes the fulfillment of this promise from Psalm 2, where YHWH gives the nations to his King (v. 6, 8) as property. It is this King who is the last Adam. "May he have dominion from sea to sea, and from the River to the ends of the earth!" (72:8, cf. §5.3.2.3). In the Jewish tradition, there is thus the conviction that the land that YHWH promised to Abraham will encompass the whole earth. The creation will then be under the authority of God's King, the Messiah, as the above-mentioned psalms already point out (cf. Acts 13:33).[202]

According to Beale, the NT thinks directly of the completion of the new cosmos in the land promise. The promised land finally points to the kingdom of God that the followers inherit from Christ (Matt 5:3, 10). That kingdom is not geographically delineated, although it is also physical and not an "ethereal, heavenly realm" (cf. Isa 60:21).[203]

Beale sees Canaan as an intermediate step in the history of salvation. He points to Paul who writes that Abraham would be "inherit the world [κόσμος]" (Rom 4:13), and not just *of Canaan*. The κόσμος here refers to the new eternal earth. Hebrews 11 also clarifies that the land God promised Abraham was not limited to Canaan. The patriarchs looked forward to "a better country, that is, a heavenly one" (v. 16a, cf. v. 14), that is a "city" that would be realized from heaven on earth (v. 16b). This city is "the city of the living God," "the heavenly Jerusalem," "Mount Zion" (12:22; cf. 13:14). It is no other city than the new earth, as evidenced by the references to the new Jerusalem in Revelation 21:1–22:5. Beale bases his reflection on a lecture by Mark Dubis and clarifies that the theme of the land should be seen in the broader objective of

199. Beale, *New Testament*, 750, cf. 751, 769.
200. Beale, *New Testament*, 751–52.
201. Beale, *New Testament*, 753.
202. Beale, *New Testament*, 755–56.
203. Beale, "Revelation (Book)," 359; cf. *New Testament*, 751, 753, 756–57.

Genesis 1–2. However, this lecture was not held by Mark Dubis, but by Brian Toews.[204] Just like Eden, Canaan also needed to be more than just a piece of land. Both were to function as a sanctuary in which God walked. The temple in Jerusalem was the beginning of this walk of God in Canaan. His presence could not be limited to the space of the Most Holy Place. Once Israel would completely subdue the earth, and God's glory could then extend from the Most Holy Place into all of Jerusalem (cf. Isa 4:4–6; Jer 3:16–17; Zech 1:16–2:11), into all of Canaan (Ezek 37:25–28), and eventually into the whole cosmos (Isa 54:2–3; Dan 2:34–35, 44–45).[205]

Beale thus connects the theology of the earth with the theology of the temple. The testimony of the new heaven and the new earth in Isaiah 65:17–18 and 66:20–22 is contextually connected with the city of Jerusalem, where the temple of YHWH is located.[206] The new earth is the physical completion of the land promise, which also includes the physical resurrection of the righteous. The latter will inherit the new earth where God's glory is omnipresent (cf. Isa 26:15 with Gen 1:28). In *The Temple and the Church's Mission*, Beale examines this relationship between the temple and the new creation in detail. Later, in NTBT, he concentrated mainly on his analysis of Revelation 21–22 and Romans 8.

5.8.1.2 *The land of the temple in Revelation 21–22*

According to Beale, Revelation 21:1–22:5 is the most comprehensive text about the new heaven and the new earth. Here also the land is connected to the temple. While the vision begins with: "Then I saw a new heaven and a new earth" (21:1a), this new cosmos is then described in terms that recall God's temple (21:3, 16–18), Jerusalem (21:2, 10–27), and Eden (22:1–3). Three theological themes are so connected: the court in Eden, God's glory, and Jerusalem.[207]

Beale is supported in this vision by William Davies, who already points out in his book on the land (1974) that the temple, Jerusalem, and Canaan are unbreakable realities in the OT and Judaism. According to him, this unbreakable bond is evident in the fact that Jerusalem can be considered as an extension of the temple, that Jerusalem became the main part of the land, and the land an extension of Jerusalem.[208]

It is God's intention to make the whole creation a sanctuary from the temple in Jerusalem. Humanity was allowed to participate in the realization of this from the beginning. The earth had to be completely subdued to God's glory. However, this did not take place in Eden, Canaan, or Jerusalem. From these events, humans failed and looked ahead to the arrival of the new Adam, who would make the whole cosmos a

---

204. Beale, *New Testament*, 757–58. Cf. Toews, "Land."
205. Beale, *New Testament*, 627, 752–53; *Temple*, 32, 107, 293–95, 338, 352.
206. Beale, *New Testament*, 753–57.
207. Beale, *New Testament*, 758–59; *Temple*, 25.
208. Beale, *New Testament*, 759. Cf. Davies, *Gospel and the Land*, 150–54.

The New Heaven and New Earth

temple to God.[209] The Messiah finally fulfills this longing and fulfills God's promises: "The kingdom of the world has become the kingdom of our Lord and of his Messiah, and he will reign forever and ever" (Rev 11:15b; cf. Ps 2:2, 8). The new heaven and new earth are therefore described as a paradisiacal new Eden, a new Jerusalem, and an all-encompassing temple, filled entirely with God's presence.[210]

5.8.1.3 The land of the temple in Romans 8

Romans 8 is also important to Beale in this context. This chapter speaks of the heirs (κληρονόμος) of Christ (v. 17). Beale connects this to Romans 4:13, where it mentions Abraham as heir of the world. Only these two texts in the Letter to the Romans contain κληρονόμος. The heirs in Romans 8 are connected with Abraham, who is the heir of the world.[211]

Romans 8 connects this heritage with the physical resurrection of the faithful: "the redemption of our bodies" (v. 23). Furthermore, it is related to statements such as: "the glory about to be revealed to us" (v. 18), "the revealing of the children of God" (v. 19), and "the freedom of the glory of the children of God" (v. 21). The resurrection of the righteous is done by analogy with the resurrection of Christ (v. 11). This future resurrection marks the beginning of the establishment of the new heaven and new earth in which "creation itself will be set free from its bondage to decay" (v. 21). From this creation, the Christians are heirs.

Beale also states from the relationship between Romans 4:13-14 and 8:17 that the future hope of the resurrection and renewal is established in the promise that Abraham would "inherit the world" (4:13). As the father of the faithful, Abraham relied on God "who gives life to the dead and calls into existence the things that do not exist" (v. 17). In Romans, Paul only mentions this making alive (ζωοποιέω) of the dead (νεκρός) in Romans 8:11.[212]

Today Christians may possess "the first fruits of the Spirit." Just as Christ rose from the dead and the land promise began to be fulfilled in him, the Spirit in the Christian already makes a beginning with the resurrection and renewal (Gal 3:16). Thus, united with Christ, Christians leave the world behind them to go on their way to the land of promise (v. 29). Already now, they may receive "forgiveness of sins and a place among those who are sanctified by faith" in Christ (Acts 26:18; cf. Col 1:14). They "have come to Mount Zion and to the city of the living God, the heavenly Jerusalem" (Heb 12:22). In Christ, they taste all the blessings of this future inheritance. Old

---

209. Beale, *New Testament*, 759.
210. Beale, *New Testament*, 759-60; *Temple*, 350; "Revelation (Book)," 358.
211. Beale, *New Testament*, 761.
212. Beale, *New Testament*, 761-62.

Testament types of the new creation, such as Jerusalem and the temple, then reach their intended destination (cf. Rev. 21–22).[213]

Beale typifies what God's Spirit began in Christians as a spiritual phase of the resurrection followed by a physical resurrection in the eschaton. The spiritual phase is thus the beginning of the literal fulfillment because the OT predicted the resurrection of the whole human being: spiritually and physically (cf. Dan 12:2).[214] Beale derives the terminological representation of a "spiritual resurrection" from Bruce Waltke, who states: "the New Testament redefines Land in three ways: first, spiritually, as a reference to Christ's person; second, transcendentally, as a reference to heavenly Jerusalem; and third, eschatologically, as a reference to the new Jerusalem after Christ's second coming."[215]

5.8.2 The Sabbath as a sign of the new creation

5.8.2.1 *The calm in the story of creation*

Like Moltmann, Beale also recognizes a relationship between the Sabbath and the new creation. Although Genesis 1–2 does not specifically mention that Adam rested with God on the seventh day, Beale sees in Genesis 2:3 an indication of the weekly rest day in man. Beale does, however, cautiously emphasize that this is his own suggestion. It is also possible that God blessed the seventh day and that only he himself rested on this day.

After God's work reached a peak in the creation of man, he then chose to set aside a unique time for himself on the seventh day in the week of creation and to rest (Gen 2:3a). The whole story of creation focuses on this day of rest. Beale, therefore, finds it plausible to state, in agreement with many others, that Adam, as an image-bearer of God, also rested on the seventh day.[216] Typologically, this day already points forward to the eternal rest of the new creation, in which, just like on the seventh day of creation, there is no more talk of tomorrow and evening and in which God completes his creative work. The seventh day reminds man that life is not aimless. This earthly temporary history, with its fixed weeks, ends in the eternal Sabbath or eschatological rest. In the Bible, the meaning of rest is further developed from the story of creation. As an example of this, Beale mentions the Sabbath and other holidays in the Bible. These are the holy days for YHWH, which also serve to sanctify Israel (cf. Exod 31:14–15).[217]

---

213. Beale, *New Testament*, 765, cf. 762–764, 767–768.

214. Beale, *New Testament*, 768–69.

215. Waltke, *Old Testament Theology*, 560.

216. Beale, *New Testament*, 777–78. Cf. Kline, *Kingdom*, 78; Waltke, *Old Testament Theology*, 67; Cassuto, *From Adam to Noah*, 64, 68; Keil and Delitzsch, *Pentateuch*, 69–70; Wenham, *Genesis 1–15*, 36–38; Brueggemann, *Genesis*, 36; Eichrodt, *Theologie 1: Gott und Volk*, 133; Vos, *Biblical Theology*, 140.

217. Beale, *New Testament*, 777–80.

God thus created not only space but also the time for his creation in Genesis 1–2. Through this time, God wanted to adjust the life of man to the purpose of this creation. This explains why Genesis 1:14 speaks of the lights in the vault of heaven, which apart from separating the day from the night also served as an indication of "seasons, [מוֹעֵד] and for days and years." מוֹעֵד is best translated as "for festivals and [cultic] seasons" and at the same time reminds one of the sanctifications of the day of rest.[218]

5.8.2.2 The Sabbath in Exodus 20 and Hebrews 3–4

After Genesis 2, the rest day did not disappear from the history of salvation. Precisely because on the seventh day, no morning or evening is mentioned, the rest day was historically salvific and continued in the later Sabbath and holidays. Every time Israel held the Sabbath, it remembered God's day of rest after creation and looked forward to the future eternal rest of the new cosmos. Therefore, the Sabbath commandment in the Ten Words begins with "memorial" (זכר, Exod 20:8). As YHWH sanctified the seventh day, he also sanctified the Sabbath (v. 11).[219]

In support of the parallel between the seventh day and the Sabbath, Beale refers to Gerhard Hasel who shows that in the Bible only in Genesis 2:3 and Exodus 20:11 "blessing" (ברך) and "holy" (קדש) occur closely together. From these observations, it is concluded that Genesis 2:3 is a creative commandment that is only repeated in Exodus 20:11.[220] In this way, Israel tried to fulfill God's creative task in the footsteps of Adam. Yet they did not experience the rest promised by God: "For if Joshua had given them rest, God would not have spoken of another day later on" (Heb 4:8). Christ would only fulfill God's creative mission as a faithful Adam and celebrate the Sabbath as God had foreseen. He brought out the true character of the Sabbath.[221]

At the same time, the Hebrew writer acknowledges that the promise of peace is still lacking. Although Christ gives his followers a beginning of that rest, they receive complete rest only in the new creation. According to Beale, Hebrews 3–4 points forward to the future fulfillment of rest. This text also shows that the rest in Genesis 2:2–3 is meant for both God and humanity.[222] The weekly celebration of the Sabbath serves as a sign of future rest in the new heaven and new earth. Beale finds further support for this in the Judeo-Christian tradition. There, too, the rest of the seventh day pointed forward to the eternal future kingdom, in which the righteous would reign together with the Messiah. God's creation plan can be compared to the construction of a cosmic temple complex in which the Creator, as the ultimate King, will rest on his throne. This explains why Israel only had to build God's temple after it had defeated

---

218. Beale's choice of this translation is based on: Rudolph, "Festivals," 23–40.
219. Beale, *New Testament*, 780–81.
220. Beale, *New Testament*, 782. See: Hasel, "Sabbath," 851.
221. Beale, *New Testament*, 782–84.
222. Beale, *New Testament*, 784–88.

God's enemies. Only then could the temple be built and could God rest as sovereign King (cf. 1 Chr 28:2; 2 Chr 6:41; Ps 132:7–8, 13–14; Isa 66:1).[223]

5.8.2.3 The day of rest in the church and its signs

In the interests of peace and quiet, the call to celebrate the weekly Sabbath is still understandable today. Where this peace is celebrated, humanity realizes that a start has been made with immaterial renewal and that the future material renewal is being looked forward to.[224] For Beale, the church is still held to celebrate the weekly Sabbath. He does note that this does not happen on Saturday but on Sunday. However, an exegetical reason for this change from Saturday to Sunday is missing in the NT. According to Beale, it is, therefore, theological in nature. Because Christ rose up on Sunday (Matt 28:1; Mark 16:2, 9; Luke 24:1; John 20:1, 19) and thereby made a beginning with the new creation, the church celebrates the day of rest on Sunday. Although the church has been freed from the Old Testament nationalistic Sabbath laws, it has not been freed from the Sabbath as a creation order. At the same time, Beale realizes that the rest is not limited to the Sabbath Sunday. The peace that Christians receive in Christ can be experienced every weekday. Every day the church may look forward to the final rest that Christ will bring before creation at his coming.[225]

In addition to celebrating peace, Beale sees a reference to the new creation in many other church institutions. Thus, as the church celebrates bread and wine, it remembers its liberation from exile and looks forward to the coming of the Messiah and the completion of the kingdom (1 Cor 11:23–26). Also, water baptism testifies that the Christian has been transferred through Christ from the old sinful world to the new world (Rom 6:4–5, 8–11). Through Christ's work of salvation, man is already being born again to a new creation, just as the whole creation of God will soon be completely reborn to a new creation (Matt 19:27). Beale sees in the word παλιγγενεσία, which the evangelist uses in this verse, an allusion to the earlier renewal of the earth that occurred after the flood and the return of Israel as a born-again people from exile.[226]

5.8.3   The Christian life as a sign of the new creation

5.8.3.1 Rebirth as a new beginning

After having identified themselves with Christ's death and resurrection in their water baptism, Christians accomplish God's will from the power of the life of resurrection. It is the power of God's Spirit who works the renewal in them until the new creation is

223. Beale, *New Testament*, 789, 796.
224. Beale, *New Testament*, 790–91, 798.
225. Beale, *New Testament*, 789, 791–92, 795, 799, 800.
226. Beale, *New Testament*, 803n5, 813, 816–818.

complete. From Romans 5–6, Beale deduces that before their conversion, Christians were part of ancient creation, which was connected with the first Adam, the old man. However, by identifying with Christ in water baptism, Christians now find themselves in a new position. That is the position in the last Adam, Christ, the new man.[227]

Paul also uses this image of the new and old man elsewhere. In the Epistle to the Ephesians, for example, he writes: "to put away your former way of life, your old self, corrupt and deluded by its lusts, and to be renewed in the spirit of your minds, and to clothe yourselves with the new self, created according to the likeness of God in true righteousness and holiness" (4:22–24). According to Beale, this discarding of the old man took place in the past, when the Christian came to faith. By identifying with Christ, a beginning has now been made in the life of humanity with the new creation. This enables Christians to follow God's commandments and statutes and to fulfill the desire of God's heart. The rebirth and renewal of man is an important eschatological concept.[228]

5.8.3.2 Followers of "the Way"

In §5.7.1.1, the biblical-theological theme of the return from exile was already addressed. Beale raises this theme again in his reflections on the term "the way," which outsiders used to refer to Christians (Acts 24:22). With "the Way," Christians characterized themselves as the new Israel of the end times that saw the beginning of the fulfillment of the promise that former Israel would return from exile.[229]

Just as Israel was imprisoned in Babylon in the OT, Revelation 17–18 shows that for the new spiritual Israel, the ungodly religious, economic-political world system is Babylon in the NT. The church lives in exile in this fallen world. The church refuses to be dragged into universal evil and calls to flee from Babylon (18:4). The Christian should make a choice for "the Way" and walk as a righteous one in God's works, which Christ has prepared. In Revelation 21–22 this is emphasized by the fact that those who choose for injustice have no part in the new creation. Beale hereby states that those who are justified, by faith in Christ, must still characterize themselves by good works in order to inherit the new heaven and the new earth. He who obeys this will inherit the new heaven and earth and serve God therein and worship as kings and priests (Rev 22:3–5; cf. 1:6).[230]

---

227. Beale, *New Testament*, 837.
228. Beale, *New Testament*, 237, 839, 844, 856.
229. Beale, *New Testament*, 858.
230. Beale, *New Testament*, 757, 861, 865–70; *Revelation*, 1113–17.

5.8.3.3 Unity between animals, people, and their Creator

For Beale, there is also the peaceful union of Jews and Gentiles in relation to God's new creation. About this union, Isaiah already said in imagery that the wild and domestic animals and people would live together in the end times (11:6–9). This harmony between animals and humans reminds both of the earlier peace in Eden (Gen 2:19–20) and of the coming of the animals to the ark of Noah, to go along to the "new creation" after the flood.[231] According to Beale, this thought from Isaiah 11 is summarized in Isaiah 65:25. Isaiah 66:18–23 then clarifies that a believing remnant of ethnic Israel will connect with the peoples, who are seen as true Israelites (66:20).[232] Beale does not mention his earlier explanation of peace between physical animals (§5.6.2.1).

In the new creation, there will be no more separation between peoples, from the above-mentioned imagery. It will then be there as in the first creation, where this separation was also lacking. At the same time, Beale adds that the new creation is more than a return to the first creation. There is a new creation, which indicates that the first creation is completed in the new creation.[233]

From the unification of people among themselves, Beale then speaks about the unification of man with God. Both the OT and NT already refer to this (cf. Zech 2:10–11; Rev 21:3).[234] In his reflection on this, Beale concentrates mainly on Paul's words in Ephesians 5:32. There the apostle reflects on the institution of marriage in Genesis 2:24 and connects it with Christ and the church. Genesis 2:24 is thus not a continuation of Adam's words, but a comment from the writer, through which he generalizes the principles of the first marriage for each marriage. Every marriage should refer to the mystery of the unification between Christ and the church. This unification will eventually find its completion in the new heaven and new earth when humanity will live in complete unity with God.[235]

5.9 CONCLUSIONS

1. According to Beale, the creation story in Genesis 1–3 contains God's plan with this creation and is the foundation upon which the history of salvation builds. Eschatology is linked to protology.

2. If humanity had fulfilled God's command in Genesis 1:28, the new creation would have come. Then Adam would have become the perfect priest-king on earth. Eschatology precedes soteriology.

---

231. Beale, *New Testament*, 876.
232. Beale and Gladd, *Hidden*, 163, 186–87; Beale, *New Testament*, 876, cf. 651–703; *Temple*, 307.
233. Beale, *New Testament*, 877.
234. Beale, *Revelation*, 1047.
235. Beale, *New Testament*, 880–884, 881n21.

3. The resurrection is central in Beale's BT and is crucial to participate in future life. Beale emphasizes Christ's resurrection and further points out the balance that must exist in speaking about continuity and discontinuity between the present and the new creation. He does not give a concrete interpretation of this.

4. Jesus' life, death, and resurrection herald the beginning of God's new creation. Christ represents Adam and Israel. He faithfully fulfills God's commission from Genesis 1:28.

5. Christ is the Firstborn, and his physical resurrection is the beginning of the renewal of all creation. With Christ, the Christian died before the old creation and had already spiritually risen in the life of the new creation. This spiritual phase precedes the physical phase because the whole person will rise (spiritually and physically).

6. Christ saves humanity from idolatry and purifies it for God. Beale connects reconciliation and justification with the new creation. Christians should be conformed to the image of Christ, the new man. What Christ experienced in blessing and oppression, they also experience. The future resurrection will only reveal that evil has been overcome.

7. Through the Spirit, the believer reveals God's new creation today. Herein humanity follows Christ. The Spirit prepares the first fruits of the new cosmos and lets them produce the fruit thereof.

8. Eden is the prototype of God's temple. Later events refer to this. In concrete terms, Beale thinks of the tabernacle, the temple, Canaan, Christ, and the church. Revelation 21–22 describes the new creation for that reason as a temple and a garden.

9. The story of creation focuses on the day of rest. This day points forward to the eternal rest which the righteous receive in the new creation.

10. Through rebirth and renewal, the church is able to fulfill God's desire. It is characterized as the new Israel, in which Jews and Gentiles live peacefully together.

6

Comparison and enrichment

This chapter offers an answer to the central question of this dissertation:

> How can comparison between Karl Rahner's and Jürgen Moltmann's systematic theological designs on eschatology and Gregory Beale's biblical-theological design be of significance in a theological dialogue concerning the new heaven and the new earth?

As it has become clear from the previous chapters, this chapter opens with an introduction that acknowledges the appreciation for an interdisciplinary comparison between two systematic theologians and one biblical theologian. It extensively determines the methodology that is followed in this dissertation (§6.1). As a result, the critical equation in this chapter is divided into a hermeneutic (§6.2) and a substantive part (§6.3). The hermeneutical comparison is paramount because these choices *a priori* influence a substantive debate. In both parts, we investigate to what extent the ST or BT of Rahner, Moltmann, and Beale can be of significance for the others in a theologically responsible discourse on the new heaven and earth. The results of this chapter are presented in the conclusion (§6.4).

6.1 INTRODUCTION

6.1.1 Openness to dialogue

The importance of a dialogue between systematic theologians and biblical theologians has been pointed out several times in the literature (see §1.2.4). However, publications that attempt to initiate this dialogue do so by placing BT and ST in separate chapters next to each other (cf. §1.5). One chapter then looks at a specific theme from a biblical-theological perspective, while another chapter looks at the same theme from a systematic-theological perspective. However, this method will not lead to a genuine full-fledged dialogue between both disciplines. In the most favorable cases, it is only a writer of one discipline who *imports* elements into his publication from the other discipline.[1]

Nevertheless, it seems obvious that in order to have a dialogue, there should be communication *between* several people or disciplines. After all, without entering into conversation with the other, it is difficult for an individual within a specific discipline to discover what a dialogue with someone from another discipline would reveal.[2] The dialogue requires several people from different fields of expertise at the dialogue table. For that reason, we do not choose in this dissertation to work out a ST or BT of the new heaven and earth ourselves. After all, there would then be no interaction between designs that would receive recognition in the theology. An own systematic or biblical-theological elaboration of the new heaven and earth in a dissertation like this cannot merely appropriate the respect of other theologians. What is needed are responsibly elected representatives from ST and BT. In this dissertation, Rahner, Moltmann, and Beale have been chosen, and a comparison will be made between their designs in order to determine to what extent such research can be of significance for the discipline of ST and BT (§1.4). So, this comparison concentrates on what has been put forward in the previous analyses of the three theologians (chap. 3 to 5). Also, this critical comparison regularly points to various publications that motivate the importance of interaction between BT and ST.

In chapter 2, we concluded that Rahner, Moltmann, and Beale are open to an interaction between the field of ST and BT. ST and BT are not each other's rivals in their perception. Both can be much more significant than has been claimed by certain theologians during the last three centuries (§1.2). All three theologians surveyed even express their appreciation for a dialogue between the two disciplines and point out the enrichment that goes with it. In the analysis of Rahner's and Moltmann's reflections on the new heaven and new earth, we also saw that the biblical data is central in the thinking of both systematics. With Moltmann, this is most visible because of his explicit references to biblical texts. Such as references to Genesis 1, Romans 8, 1 Corinthians 15, Colossians 1, and of course, his biblical-theological analysis of Revelation 21–22. Rahner, on the other hand, is concise in the use of biblical references. However, he refers to many of the texts mentioned above. He realizes that an application of his plea for interdisciplinary interaction between ST and BT was virtually absent from his works. The same goes for Beale. In his BT, biblical texts naturally have a prominent place, and he devotes the necessary attention to various themes that are characteristic of ST without Beale entering into the dialogue with this discipline as such.

In contrast to Beale, Rahner and Moltmann discuss more specifically, the use of an exchange between ST and BT. They show their openness to pay positive-critical

---

1. See next to the in §1.2 mentioned series of *The Two Horizons* still mentioned: Wright, "Letter to the Galatians," 205–36.

2. Cf. Colwill, "Invitation," 139.

attention to the meaning and interpretation of biblical texts. Also, they are open for a corresponding biblical-theological development in the context of systematic-theological reflection. According to Rahner, this openness to an interdisciplinary comparison is not self-evident (see §2.1.1). However, this underlines the importance of the research question of this dissertation.

6.1.2   No methodical landmarks

In a critical comparison of theologians from different disciplines, an underlying dialogue arises between the two fields of work that requires a well-thought-out plan of approach. The academic reflection on such a dialogue now has a rich multidisciplinary legacy with a broad pragmatic-practical history.[3] In this dissertation, we limit ourselves to the main points in this respect. How a dialogue typically proceeds is not fixed and varies per context.[4] William Isaacs identifies four characteristics that are important for the course of the dialogue: (1) respect, (2) listening, (3) authenticity, and (4) openness.[5] These characteristics can partly be reconciled with elements that Moltmann mentions in his reflection on the dialogue with other religions.[6] In this reflection, he mentions first the willingness to engage in dialogue and the interest and openness for the other discipline. After all, this habit makes one's position vulnerable and sees the theology of the other as a possible added value. Moltmann also points out that the dialogue must enable the interlocutors to represent a clear position. Too strong a tendency to relativize one's point of view makes dialogue more difficult.

The need for this sort of open-mindedness also applies to an interdisciplinary equation. The willingness to engage in dialogue with the other discipline was already mentioned in §6.1.1, building on the results of chapter 2. Furthermore, the analysis of Rahner, Moltmann, and Beale in chapters 3–5 revealed that they have their standpoint on the theme of the new heaven and the new earth. These three theologians offer sufficient openness, differences, and interfaces for critical comparison. In this critical comparison, we make a positive contribution to the potential benefits that the disciplines can offer each other. Because of the openness chosen in chapter 2, extensive attention was paid to the question of how Rahner, Moltmann, and Beale would fundamentally view dialogue with the other discipline. From §1.4.3 and especially from Veli-Matti Kärkkäinen's criticism of Beale's orthodox evangelical-reformed perspective on the biblical data (§2.3.2), we acknowledge that this perspective can pose a challenge in a critical comparison with the more progressive systematics Rahner and Moltmann. Therefore, this research takes into account that Rahner's and Moltmann's

---

3. In general, see: Isaacs, *Dialogue*; Bohm, *Dialogue*. Cf. Mansilla, "Learning to Synthesize," 290–300.
4. Colwill, "Invitation," 138; Isaacs, *Dialogue*, 17–48. Cf. Bohm, *Dialogue*, 6–54.
5. Isaacs, *Dialogue*, 83–184.
6. Moltmann, *Erfahrungen*, 30–33.

theology criticizes Beale's vision of Scripture. Where there is no reason to do so in their publications, we conclude from their interest in the dialogue (chapter 2), that they are generally sufficiently open towards each other. So, despite different perspectives, they can be a positive enrichment for each other in listening together to the testimony of Scripture.

At the same time, we acknowledge that for a dissertation that compares different theological designs, it is a particular challenge when the writers of those designs themselves hardly refer to each other's works. That is indeed the case here. Rahner rarely refers to contemporaries in his publications. Also, he does not mention Moltmann anywhere by name and does not know Beale. After all, Rahner died in 1984, when Beale had hardly published yet.[7] Moltmann does not mention Beale either but refers several times to Rahner. The latter, however, does not occur anywhere in his reflections on the new creation.[8] Beale also shows this pattern: nowhere does he refer to Rahner or Moltmann. The only systematics he touches on from the twentieth and twenty-first centuries are Louis Berkhof, Michael Bird, Wayne Grudem, Karl Barth, Cornelius van Til, and Kevin Vanhoozer.[9] In an e-mail correspondence about his knowledge of Moltmann's and Rahner's eschatology, Beale confirms this with the words: "I do not know much about their specific approaches."[10]

This fact carries with it the risk of misinterpretation. This dissertation attempts to avoid the latter by providing a thorough analysis of the positions of the three theologians in the previous chapters, and by having the results of this critical comparison checked by Beale and Moltmann themselves. Given his advanced age and the lack of time on Moltmann's side, the latter was impossible for him. With Beale, it was only possible to correspond to a limited extent. His intensive timetable did not allow him to respond to the content of this study. This means that, despite the choice to tackle this danger conscientiously, the risk of misinterpretations in this dissertation has not disappeared. It is, therefore up to the critics to point out any errors.

6.1.3 Methodical structure

Because Rahner, Moltmann, and Beale understand the importance of a dialogue between ST and BT, but they do not give a practical elaboration of this approach, we will have to choose our methodology in this critical comparison. From the preceding analysis we made of each theologian, it is possible to see what emphasis each of them individually places in their perspective on the new creation. In the conclusions, their hermeneutical choices become visible, and the core elements of their thinking are also discussed. There was a visible relationship between methodology, hermeneutics,

---

7. For an overview of Beale's publications see: Gurtner and Gladd, *From Creation*, 275–80.
8. See, besides this subject: Moltmann, "Christsein," 156–72.
9. See in particular: Beale, *New Testament*, 988–94; *Erosion*, 291–93.
10. Beale to Hausoul, "Trialogue."

and content in the way the three theologians investigated the topic of the new heaven and the new earth (chapter 3–5). We saw that not only ST but also BT has its assumptions. Both disciplines are concerned with the interpretation and thinking from particular perspectives (cultural, confessional, etc.). The hermeneutical choices play an essential role in the theological reflection on the new heaven and the new earth. This also emerged in the analysis of Rahner's, Moltmann's, and Beale's views on the interdisciplinary dialogue (chapter 2). On the one hand, it became clear that ST and BT each have their specific content representations. On the other hand, it emerged that these representations were also determined by the theologian's methodical and hermeneutical choices. Both ST and BT work with presuppositions. It is impossible to avoid this in a theological reflection.[11]

In recent decades, the essential importance of hermeneutics has been stressed several times. In both ST and BT, theologians build on specific presuppositions.[12] In general, however, biblical theologians are often not interested in theological-philosophical paradigms that influence theological reflection. Craig Bartholomew rightly writes:

> Scholars continue to work with philosophical paradigms shaping their work, of course, but generally, they ignore these paradigms with the result that they are hidden from view and their scholarship has the appearance of neutral, objective analysis.[13]

Because these paradigms are cornerstones in one's theology, it is methodically advisable to start our research with a hermeneutical equation. The hermeneutical choices that form the basis for the substantive speaking about the new creation are placed at the forefront of this chapter.

The themes that are addressed in this comparison of the hermeneutical choices are determined based on the analysis of each theologian. This reveals the hermeneutical core points for Rahner, Moltmann, and Beale. For example, in Rahner's and Moltmann's ST, much attention was paid to the hermeneutical principles of eschatological statements (§§3.2; 4.2.1–3). Because their thinking about this strongly determined their eschatological frameworks, attention for this was the main focus of their analysis and will also be the main focus of the comparison below. In §6.2.1, we will investigate to what extent Beale's BT can be of significance in this comparison of the hermeneutic principles of Rahner and Moltmann. Furthermore, the analysis of the three theologians also showed that their reflection about the new creation was determined by the relation between protology and eschatology (§§3.3.3, 4.2.4, 5.2.2). This is the second theme that is addressed in the comparison of their hermeneutics (§6.2.2). Our

---

11. Cf. Mildenberger, *Prolegomena*, 264–77.

12. E.g., Thiselton, *Last Things*, 185–203; *Hermeneutics of Doctrine*, 541–81. Cf. Thiselton, *New Horizons in Hermeneutics*, 1–30; Vanhoozer, *Drama of Doctrine*; *Is There a Meaning?*

13. Bartholomew, "Uncharted Waters," 12.

research will further result in a particular focus on both the origin of evil and the impact of sin in the history of salvation. In the third theme, we will finally discuss the mindsets that Rahner, Moltmann, and Beale use in their perspective on the new heaven and the new earth. In the previous analysis, we already saw that all three theologians acknowledged that the perspective on the new heaven and the new earth was determined by the interpretation of the biblical images and the associated metaphors, combined with the choice of speaking from a Judeo-Christian anthropology or an Enlightenment anthropology and the Christian aspect (§§3.3.2.4, 4.2.5, 5.2.3). These topics will be addressed in a comparison of the hermeneutical aspects in §6.2.

After the critical comparison of hermeneutical assumptions in the three perspectives on the new heaven and earth, there will be a critical comparison of the core elements herein. They were already identified in the analyses earlier on. From these core elements, we choose to determine the themes of this critical comparison. So, we will start with those elements in which there is much overlap between the three theologians. Such an overlap makes comparison easier. From the analyses, it is possible to determine the core themes for the substantive comparison: the future of the physical material and the future of space and time in the new creation. These are themes that partly overlap in the analysis of the three theologians. The table below shows this and lists the relevant chapter in the analysis that focuses on it. The last column shows where the subject concerned is covered in the critical comparison.

Themes	K. Rahner	J. Moltmann	G. K. Beale	*Comparison*
Matter and resurrection	§3.4	§4.5	§§5.5, 5.8.1	§6.3.1
Time and eternity	§3.5	§4.3	§5.8.2	§6.3.3
Space and temple	§3.4.3	§4.4	§5.7.2–3	§6.3.2
God's presence	§3.6	§4.6		§6.3.2
Sin and salvation		§4.2.4	§§5.6, 5.7.1	§6.3.2
Anticipations		§4.7	§§5.3, 5.8.3	§6.3

The choices that are visible in this overview can be substantiated as follows: First, the substantive comparison in §6.3.1 will begin with the core theme of matter and new creation. This is because the amount of attention paid to this theme by the three theologians is almost identical. There is no other theme from the analyses that can be identified where this is also the case. In speaking about space in the new creation, Rahner is very limited, and in speaking about time, Beale is limited.

Next, in §6.3.2, there will be a substantive comparison of the space of the new creation, in which Moltmann and Beale can, in particular, be compared with each other. The subject of God's presence in the new creation will also be discussed. This combination finds its basis in the performances of Moltmann and Beale because they both see in the history of salvation how God wants to live with humans. The living space of humanity and the living space of God are connected and are also related to each other in our substantive comparison. Because Moltmann and Beale affirm that

God's final coming to this creation will remove the brokenness and evil, it was also decided to link the theme of sin and salvation to this core theme.

Finally, in this critical comparison, §6.3.3 will focus on the theme of time and new creation. Because this theme mainly occurs in the ST of Rahner and Moltmann, and because the BT of Beale lacks this defined theme, it is decided to place this topic at the end. The challenge will be to make Beale's BT meaningful for the ST of Rahner and Moltmann in a responsible way.

The purpose of this chapter is to sketch the results that emerge from a comparison of two systematic theologians and one biblical theologian in speaking about the new heaven and the new earth. It can then be determined what this form of interdisciplinary interaction between the BT and the ST can yield for a theologically competent conversation about this topic.

In this comparison between Rahner, Moltmann, and Beale, it is further decided to repeat as little information as possible from the previous chapters. This ensures that the equation does not become a synthesis or addition to the previous analyses. The information from the previous analyses will, of course, be referred to. It should also be mentioned that the critical comparison is not aimed at presenting a new theological perspective of the new creation. The systematic-theological perspectives and the biblical-theological perspective of Rahner, Moltmann, and Beale are critically compared from each other's professional disciplines and assessed for consistency in terms of content. The focus is thus on their differences in content, ambiguities, shifts in emphasis, and the resemblances. From here, the question is answered:

> How can comparison between Karl Rahner's and Jürgen Moltmann's systematic theological designs on eschatology and Gregory Beale's biblical-theological design be of significance in a theological dialogue concerning the new heaven and the new earth?

6.2 HERMENEUTICAL COMPARISON

In the first chapter, we already concluded that the distinction mentioned by Johann Gabler—namely that BT historically-objective described what the Bible writers wanted to say and that ST subjectively considers the relevance of the faith—is not tenable (§1.2). This also came to the fore in the analysis of Rahner's, Moltmann's, and Beale's ideas about the interdisciplinary dialogue (chapter 2) and the analysis of the new creation (chapters 3–5). Based on this, it was decided in the methodical structure of this critical reflection to put the comparison of their hermeneutical choices first. The general objective is to examine to what extent the BT or ST of the theologians concerned can be of significance in the theologically responsible reflection on the new heaven and the new earth.

6.2.1 Transposition and anticipation

Moltmann and Rahner differ as to whether the new creation is a transposition of this creation. According to Rahner, all eschatological speaking starts from the known salvation that God has revealed in Christ (transposition from the initial mode). We can only speak about the future from the salvation already present in Christ. According to him, speaking about the future apart from that is "apocalyptic reportage fantasy." The transposition of the experience of faith in the initial mode reveals the completion mode. This is because the initial mode already *contains* the completion mode (§3.2). According to Moltmann, however, eschatology departs from the future to the present (anticipation). The experience of faith from which we speak of the future does not originate in the past or present, because it is linked to impermanence. From transient times like past and present only *futurum* arises. This *futurum does* not bring a lasting future; it stands up and perishes. Only from the coming, the *adventus* comes the *novum* of the new heaven and new earth. So, the experience of faith *anticipates* only the future (§4.2.2).

Although Moltmann and Rahner acknowledge this methodical difference between themselves, interaction in a dialogue with each other remains limited. Moltmann pays brief attention to Rahner's vision, and Rahner does not react explicitly to Moltmann anywhere.[14] Therefore, in this hermeneutical comparison, we first compare both systematics with each other and later add Beale as a biblical theologian towards this exercise.

6.2.1.1 *Terminology and assumptions*

6.2.1.1.1 EXTRAPOLATION AND TRANSPOSITION

In his reaction to Rahner's hermeneutics, Moltmann notes that Rahner does not speak of a quantitative "extrapolation" as Hendrik Berkhof claims.[15] Rahner acknowledges that the new creation has a different quality than this creation and does not just extrapolate from it. However, Rahner only wants to speak about the new creation from the salvation already present, which humanity already possesses hidden in Christ (§3.2.2).[16] With this, Rahner makes Christology and anthropology the basic principle of any eschatological speaking.[17] This leads Rahner methodically to insufficiently emphasize that God is the source of the new creation. From the analyses in the previous

---

14. Cf. Moltmann, "Methoden," 53–54; *Geschichte*, 162.
15. Cf. Berkhof, *Christelijk Geloof*, 477, 510–12. Wolfhart Pannenberg adopts this vision of Berkhof. The difference between "transposition" and "extrapolation" is too small to give it the weight as Moltmann does. Extrapolation does not have to be purely quantitative, nor can it be in the case of Rahner. See: Pannenberg, *Systematische Theologie 3*, 586n70.
16. Rahner, "Prinzipien," 417.
17. See further: Losinger, *Anthropological Turn*.

chapters, we concluded that Rahner continues to interpret the future from a transposition of what has come to be. Moltmann, on the other hand, wants to interpret what has come as anticipation from the perspective of the future. Moltmann does so without denying that experience of faith can speak of the future. However, according to him, the experience of faith always starts with *adventus*, which is already present in the history of salvation in a christological-pneumatological way. So, the origin and place of the realization differ between both theologians.

Nevertheless, Rahner also has the opinion that the origin of the new heaven and earth is not in the world-evolution or can be planned and realized by human beings. Only God is the eternal "absolute future," that realizes the fullness of the new creation. This "absolute future" cannot be planned. It comes down to the creation and does not arise from an evolutionary development in this world; it is unexpected, unpredictable, and elusive. Thus the "absolute future" is another name for God (§3.2.1.3).

Moltmann also maintains this speaking about God's "absolute future"—a term used by Martin Buber. For Moltmann, however, the following applies: "God's being is not in becoming, but in coming."[18] Moltmann elaborates on the core idea of this statement in his reflections on *adventus* and *futurum*. Quantitative extrapolations about the new creation from within-world developments are therefore misleading for Moltmann. God's absolute future does not evolve from this impermanent creation. In the latter, both systematics are in agreement. So, both turn away from an existential demythologization that leads only to absolute existentialism and a "de-eschatologization" (§§3.2; 4.2).

6.2.1.1.2 POINT OF RECOGNITION AND POINT OF REALIZATION

By emphasizing eschatological speaking from past and present, Rahner places the source of the future's realization in the background. His choice that God is the source of the absolute future and thus of the new creation shows that the source of realization should not be sought within this world. His fifth hermeneutical thesis, about the *Quelle* of eschatological statements, shows this by emphasizing that God comes to this world in Christ as *Selbstmitteilung* (§3.2.2). The source of the future does not lie in these cases of creation. Nevertheless, Rahner interprets eschatological statements as transposable "expressions" (*Aussagen*), while Moltmann interprets eschatological statements as anticipatory "impressions" (*Einsagen*) from God's coming. This places both theologians opposing each other.

According to Moltmann, Rahner swapped the recognition point of salvation (*Erkenntnisgrund*) with its realization (*Realgrund*). We *recognize* what God does from the promises in the past and present, and that these promises *realize* themselves in the future. The recognition is done in the current promises. An "initial mode" today is only possible based on the promises of God. They are given as *Einsage* from the

18. Moltmann, "Progress and Abyss," 13. Cf. *Weg Jesu*, 28–29; Buber, *Werke III*, 756.

future in the here and now. Only by *Einsage* is *Aussage* possible from "initial mode" to "completion mode." Moltmann already makes this clear in his *Theologie der Hoffnung*. Although Rahner used this as a title of his article in 1967, he did not pay any attention to the content of this work.[19] For Rahner, hope remained one of the three New Testament virtues, while it became a central meaning in Moltmann's publications.

Rahner continued methodically, only making theological statements based on *Aussage*. He states:

> Impression (*Einsage*) from the present into the future is eschatology, expression (*Aussage*) from the future into the present is apocalyptic.[20]

Therefore, every responsible reference about the future is an *Aussage* from the past and present. On the other hand, Moltmann emphasizes God's prolepsis in this creation. Every speaking about the future finds its source in God. Without God's *Einsage*, human *Aussage* is impossible. According to Moltmann, not every religious experience can serve as *Aussage* for eschatological statements. It only applies where the future announces itself in principle as *Einsage*.[21] Rahner will agree that God is the source of any eschatological speaking. This is also evident from his second thesis: the source of eschatological speaking lies with God and must be critically observed from the present presence, but also a partial mystery of completion (§3.2.1.2). This is less pronounced in Rahner's later publications. Then speaking from *Aussage* and the rejection of *Einsage* gets all emphasis. God's speaking from the future into the present is thus lacking in Rahner's reflections. His eschatology can be positively-critically challenged by Moltmann's approach since the core of this can be found in Rahner's theology.

6.2.1.1.3 ESCHATOLOGY AND APOCALYPTIC

Rahner's antipathy to *Einsage* arises from his aversion to an eschatology that wants to record the future as a blueprint. This determinism excludes all human freedom and has little use for the present (thesis 3 and 5, §3.2). Rahner describes this kind of eschatology as "apocalyptic" and has few positive words for it.[22] Many have already criticized his negative interpretations of the word "apocalyptic."[23] Moltmann writes: "There is no eschatology without apocalyptic and no apocalyptic without eschatology."[24] This does

---

19. Rahner, "Theologie der Hoffnung," 561–79.

20. Rahner, "Prinzipien," 418: "Aus-sage von Gegenwart in Zukunft hinein ist Eschatologie, Einsage aus der Zukunft heraus in die Gegenwart hinein ist Apokalyptik."

21. Moltmann, "Methoden," 54.

22. Cf. Rahner, "Prinzipien," 418.

23. Fritsch, *Selbstmitteilung*, 131; Edwards, *Messianism*, 227; Geister, *Aufhebung*, 94; Pannenberg, *Systematische Theologie 3*, 585–86; Koch, "Weltende," 162; Phan, *Eternity*, 76; Vorgrimler, *Hoffnung auf Vollendung*, 86–87; Metz, "Hoffnung als Naherwartung," 147–58; Kerstiens, *Hoffnungsstruktur*, 171.

24. Moltmann, "Methoden," 54: "Es gibt keine Eschatologie ohne Apokalyptik und keine

not mean that Moltmann equates eschatology with an apocalyptic prospectus on the hereafter. His concern is that eschatology and apocalyptic together offer a perspective on the absolute future as the fulfillment of God's promises. While Rahner does not want to "de-eschatologize," he "de-apocalyptizes." His characterization of apocalyptic as deterministic futurology is insufficiently substantiated and may create a Babylonian confusion of speech for outsiders.

Nevertheless, Rahner's attitude towards the word "apocalyptic" is decisive when it comes to imagery. He is talking about a *"legitimen Bildersprache apokalyptischen Redens*—legitimate imagery of apocalyptic speech." In this case, the image is also *Aussage*, which takes Christ's preaching on the coming eschaton as reality seriously. It is thus *Aussage* based on Christ's work of salvation in the past and present. The reason behind this is that Christ's resurrection is both the promise and the beginning of the absolute future. However, a positive attitude towards apocalyptic and *Einsage* is nowhere found in Rahner's theology.

Simultaneously, a comparison with Beale's BT shows that exegetical research does not support the distinction Rahner makes between "eschatology," and "apocalyptic."[25] Although "apocalyptic" has a different meaning in Beale's theology, it usually has no negative connotation. In the Bible, the apocalyptic genre is even closely related to the prophetic. Although there is a discussion in BT about what exactly is "apocalyptic," no biblical scholar follows the above-mentioned definition of Rahner. Remarkably enough, Rahner does not follow this himself in his *Kleines theologisches Wörterbuch*. There he chooses for a standard description of "apocalyptic," as BT interprets it.[26] Rahner's interpretation of the term "apocalyptic" in ST can, therefore, confuse BT among readers who are not familiar with his definition. Also, to what extent Beale's BT influences Rahner's, and Moltmann's theological thoughts about *Einsage* and *Aussage*, has not yet been discussed. This question will be addressed next.

6.2.1.2 God's prolepsis in the history of salvation

6.2.1.2.1 JESUS AND THE MYSTERY

From his emphasis on *Aussage*, Rahner sees completion as a qualitative continuation of the present. The knowability of the new absolute future is thus entirely determined by the present and the past. It is not possible that new *Einsage* expands this knowledge. The completion or realization of this future is, of course, still in the future. Rahner only wants to emphasize that the *eschaton* already begins in the present. At the same time, he states that our knowledge of the future is not yet complete. There are things in this creation that humanity has not yet discovered or chosen. This ensures that the

---

Apokalyptik ohne Eschatologie." Cf. "Methoden," 51; Sauter, *Einführung*, 103.
   25. For a discussion of what "apocalyptic" is, see: Beale, *Revelation*, 37–39.
   26. Rahner and Vorgrimler, "Apokalyptik," 27–28.

future remains open to humans so that the future can be filled in freely. Not everything is thus deterministically fixed in Rahner's theology. According to Moltmann, this openness makes this model susceptible to new *Einsage*.[27]

In his hermeneutic principles, Rahner covers himself for such a new *Einsage*. He does this by stating that eventually, also the new in the eschaton reveals itself as *Aussage* from the present and the past (thesis 3). This new one still has a "mystery character." This is the *docta ignorantia futuri*, which recognizes that creation cannot see what God ultimately revealed (thesis 4–6). Whereas Moltmann states that God gives new promises to humanity from the future, according to Rahner, these "new promises" are *discoveries* of what is already hidden as "mystery character" in the present. No new promises are added; new promises are just revealed or simply uncovered. Rahner finds support for this "mystery character" in Mark 13:32. There it appears that Jesus did not receive new *Einsage*. Jesus declares in this biblical text, namely, "ausdrücklich, daß er *weniger* sagt, als er weiß und sagen *kann*—expressly that he says *less* what he knows and *can* say."[28] What Jesus says about the future finds its source only in his relationship with God. God reveals to him secrets that are already known in creation (*visio immediata*).[29] Jesus will not receive any new additional information about the future. God opens the eyes of Jesus to see what has already been revealed about the future but was not seen before. So, there is no new *Einsage*. Only a revelation of the present *Aussage* takes place. Jesus does not know the hour of return because the *Aussage* is still hidden from him.

To what extent can this interpretation of the biblical text be substantiated in comparison with Beale's BT? From the works of Beale, the explanation of Rahner is less evident. Although Beale does not discuss Mark 13:32 separately, he points to this verse when he explains that in Revelation 14:15–16, the Son is informed of the time of return from God's temple.[30] According to Beale, this is new information. However, that pleads against *Aussage* and for *Einsage*. Also, the standard exegesis, which Beale follows in his BT, states that Jesus does not speak in Mark 13:32 of a secret that is known. It speaks about a secret that is still hidden. According to some biblical scholars, the text refers to absolute ignorance and not to a growing insight by the Son.[31] For Beale, there is, therefore, new information that complements what is still missing in Mark 13:32. So, this text cannot serve to support Rahner's rejection of *Einsage*. The text argues for the opposite and makes us aware of Rahner's assumptions about eschatological statements.

Although the future in Rahner's theology is "closed" for new information (*Einsage*), this should not be just a quantitative continuation of the present. Rahner

27. Moltmann, *Geschichte*, 162. Cf. Phan, *Eternity*, 75–76.
28. Rahner, "Prinzipien," 419n13. Cf. Rahner, "Dogmatische Erwägungen," 232.
29. Rahner, "Dogmatische Erwägungen," 237–38, 243.
30. Beale, *Revelation*, 772, with reference to: Holtz, *Christologie*, 132–33; Wilcock, *I Saw*, 136.
31. Gnilka, *Markus*, 206–7; Pesch, *Markusevangelium 1*, 1:310.

emphasizes that God's absolute future for this creation is crucial. The new creation does not "evolve" from *this* creation. This makes it impossible to give a blueprint of the future in which everything is already fixed. Those who already fully understand, comprehend, and calculate the future today would otherwise experience the complete realization of the absolute future (§3.2.1.3). That cannot be the case. A complete understanding is therefore excluded, given that the completion is already present, but not yet fully revealed. The absolute future can only be sketched out and has a "hiddenness character" in the present. For Rahner, a concrete grasp of the new heaven and earth is thus excluded, and only an idea-based speaking remains. A comparison with Beale and Moltmann also explicitly shows that Rahner's emphasis on *Aussage* and the so-called "hiddenness character" is a direct consequence of his rejection of *Einsage* and apocalyptic reportage. BT enriches ST here because, with her interpretation of the biblical testimony, BT indicates where the ST uses (unconsciously) extra-biblical ideas.

6.2.1.2.2 Prophets and the realization of the *novum*

A comparison between Moltmann and Rahner shows that Rahner's emphasis on *Aussage* threatens to de-eschatologize the future. After all, the complete future is already locked up in the present. God's coming adds nothing new to the realization of the new creation. Rahner thus tends to go in the direction of Bultmann's radical existential interpretation, which he precisely rejected in his hermeneutic principles (§3.2.1). According to Moltmann, what Christ has already done is an anticipation of the future. It points ahead to what is yet to come. So, all emphasis is on God's *Einsage*. God's promises do not rule out new prolepsis. The new is separated from the ephemeral past and present. It does not develop by transience, as *futurum* does. Otherwise, the Christian hope of God's prolepsis threatens to disappear in a general human thought that does not take *advent into* account. Rahner pays little attention methodically to the difference between realization and landmark. As we stated above, we *recognize* what God does from the promises in the past and present, and we realize that these promises are *realized* in the future. According to Moltmann, the new is separate from the perishable past and present and does not allow itself to be developed from there (§4.2.4.4).

When Rahner sees the eschaton as an extrapolation of what is already known to be present through God's redemption, Moltmann rejects it. Completion then degenerates into a transient *futurum*. After all, *futurum* only develops the historical potential and brings nothing new (*novum*): "New can . . . not be extrapolated from history. It is anticipated."[32] Just *adventus* refers to the definition-permanent arrival of the other, the new, and the changing that was not before. For Moltmann, *novum* does not originate from the past and present, but from the future into creation. *Adventus*

---

32. Moltmann, "Antwort auf die Kritik der Theologie der Hoffnung," 212: "Neuen kann . . . nicht aus der Geschichte extrapoliert werden. Sie wird antizipiert."

brings the defining and persistent new. The eschaton is possible from the *adventus* or παρουσία that looks forward to the future (§4.2.2).

Moltmann argues that his hermeneutic choices around this matter are anchored in the biblical prophets. They develop their statements about the future not from the transitory present (*Aussage*), but from God's prolepsis of the future (*Einsage*). Although Beale does not deal with this issue in his BT, a comparison from Beale's biblical-theological storyline shows that the prophets receive new revelation from God and build on what God has already revealed to others (§5.3). What was previously revealed by God is repeated and extended by God's new revelation. It was essential to Israel that the prophets did not contradict each other. Every new *Einsage* they proclaimed had to stand in continuity with earlier revelations.

Beale demonstrates this in detail when he describes how the biblical writers relate their proclamations to God's command in Genesis 1:28. In his BT, there is attention for the biblical storyline that runs historically-theologically from Genesis 1–2 to the new heaven and new earth. The basic idea here is that a person faithful to God's command in Genesis 1:28 can realize the new creation. For example, if Adam had condemned the serpent by the tree of knowledge, the new creation would have come about (§5.3.1). Both Rahner and Moltmann will miss God's absolute intervention in this biblical-theological exhibition of Beale. While Rahner still finds a connection with the idea of transposition, Moltmann will turn against this development model, because it hopes that *futurum* will bring a *novelty*. Beale states that humanity can bring the new heaven and new earth by being faithful to God's command in Genesis 1:28. This would be *futurum* in Moltmann's terms and not *adventus*. According to Moltmann, the new can only breakthrough on earth from God's coming. It cannot be achieved from the present or the past. Even Adam could not bring this about without God's prolepsis. For this, Moltmann can also point to Beale's own words:

> That even this prefall condition [of Adam] was insufficient for qualification to "inherit the kingdom of God" (1 Cor 15:50). . . . Adam would have *been rewarded* with a transformed, incorruptible body if he had remained faithful.[33]

So, Beale acknowledges that Adam could not bring the new creation from his position. God's prolepsis was necessary. Beale expresses this by speaking of God's reward for Adam's faithfulness. However, to what extent does this reward leave room for the prolepsis of God, which is separate from humanity and this perishable creation?

From Moltmann's design, Beale's theological thinking can be called up to prudence in relating the fulfillment of the eschatological with obedience to the commission in Genesis 1:28. It is precisely this biblical-theological storyline of idolatry and decay that Beale elaborates. That makes it clear that without God's prolepsis, creation has no hope. In his reflection on 2 Corinthians, Beale himself emphasizes that renewal is not possible without a break. Even the person who is daily renewed (2 Cor 4:16),

---

33. Beale, *New Testament*, 44–45 (italics by me).

does not reach eternity from within himself. There remains a need for God's prolepsis. The salvific line cannot be continued without a struggle in the eschaton.

In comparison with Moltmann's and Rahner's ST, this element will be even more pronounced in Beale's BT. It will reveal the own dogmatic-confessional presuppositions that Beale (unconsciously) incorporates in his interpretation of the biblical text. Beale should, in our opinion, speak more critically in his BT about a development idea from Genesis 1:28. The only thing that Beale himself finds positive about this development is that possibilities are created in which God's new creation can become a reality. This development pushes the history of the world forward in the direction of the new creation that will be realized by God's coming. This can almost be reconciled with Moltmann's idea. The positive thing about the *futurum* is that it opens world history to new (perishable) possibilities and propels it in the direction of a *novum*. Moltmann also sees the past as something negative. There is no hope to be found in the past. Hope comes from the future. This has already been criticized on several occasions.[34] Moltmann is threatening to let hope swallow faith. He seems to reduce the presence of God in history to the God of hope that is at the forefront and coming. It is the God "who was and who is to come" (ἔρχομαι, Rev 1:4), not the God who "will be" (εἶναι). This verse supports Moltmann's separation between the perishable time of the past, present, and future in this old creation on the one hand, and the imperishable future of the new creation on the other.

From Beale's biblical-theological oeuvre, one can argue that Revelation 1:4 describes God from an eternal meta-historical perspective. Therefore, the statement cannot be understood in the sense of two separate time-orders (cf. Rev 16:5). That God is the God who will also be, is also taught in the Jewish tradition when it confesses God as "Jahweh."[35]

Whether Moltmann cares about this exegesis is doubtful, given his earlier reaction to Richard Bauckham (§2.2.2). For him, God is present in the history of salvation, where the future determines the present through anticipation and foreshadowing (*advent*). Through promise and hope, through God prolepsis in the present, it is freed from transitory. God is always self-defeating present in the history of salvation. This limitation makes creation look forward to the ubiquitous coming of God (cf. §4.4). Although this thought explains Moltmann's choice for *Einsage* and his rejection of *Aussage*, it can be concluded from a comparison that Beale will reject this thought. Together with Rahner, it is clear from his eschatological design that in Moltmann's case, God is essentially only at the forefront, and seems to be locked up in a "coming."

---

34. See further: Hausoul, "An Evaluation," 151–52; Thomas, *Neue Schöpfung*, 335, 339; Enns, *Moody Handbook*, 360; Polkinghorne, "Jürgen Moltmann's Engagement," 64.

35. Beale, *Revelation*, 187–88.

The New Heaven and New Earth

6.2.1.2.3 "Already" and "Not Yet"

In his BT, Beale repeatedly emphasizes what God has already accomplished in salvation history. For example, when the Bible speaks of the "last days," it is not exclusively about the end time as the climax of salvation history. The last days start in the first century. Texts like Revelation 1:3 clarify, in relationship with Mark 1:15, Luke 21:8, and Daniel 7:22, that the end of time is already present through the death and resurrection of Christ. With the coming of Christ, time is fulfilled, and God's kingdom finds its beginning on earth.[36] According to Beale, the Greek *kairos* in Mark 1:15 marks a pivot point. This pivotal point is characterized by the fact that something new in the present takes place. At the same time, the kingdom has not yet been fully realized with the coming of Christ. Also, the Messiah still lives in expectation of the completion of God's rule. From Christ's coming, however, the kingdom finds its beginning. Beale and also Rahner thus testify against Moltmann that the resurrection of Christ is a completed *historical* event that influences the future.[37] Moltmann will have difficulty with this because, in his case, the term "historical" is linked to the negative and the transient. While he realizes that the coming of Christ heralds a new era, the kingdom of God remains only "near" (Mark 1:15). The kingdom has been announced, but with that, it has not yet appeared. This is visible in the miracles Jesus does. When Jesus lets people rise from the dead or heals people, it still happens in transience.[38] The healed and resurrected people die later. In Beale's biblical-theological design, the deeds of Jesus already *belong* to the "already" and do not only *point* to this, as is the case in Moltmann's systematic-theological design. For Paul, the day of final salvation has already begun (2 Cor 6:2). From this perspective, Moltmann does not characterize the great deeds of the Messiah enough as anticipations of the liberating "fullness of time," because they are still subject to the "historical," which Moltmann interprets negatively.

According to Beale, responsible speaking about the future starts from the history of the God of Abraham, Isaac, and Jacob, and the Father of Jesus Christ. In the above terminology of *Aussage* and *Einsage* in Rahner's and Moltmann's eschatology, one can conclude from Beale's design that, according to him, the speaking of God is based on the *Aussage* of what God has done through *Einsage* in the past. Moltmann also recognizes that the historical testimony of the OT and NT is the beginning of any responsible speaking about the future (§2.2.1). The Bible bears witness to the God who comes, frees his people and brings them into his glory. Compared to Beale's theological perspective, there are no objections to this. He remarks, however, that the coming of God does not only find its realization in the *eschaton*. Beale shows in his BT how God has been involved in history from the beginning of creation as the God who is above,

---

36. Beale, *New Testament*, 431, 695–96; *Temple*, 169–71.

37. Beale, *Revelation*, 137–138, 182, 185. Cf. *New Testament*, 129–30; Rahner, "Neue Bild," 353; "Dogmatische Erwägungen," 76.

38. Moltmann, *Kommen*, 100; *Gott in der Schöpfung*, 133.

with, in, and below us. With the coming of Christ, all orders have already changed, and the promises of God to Abraham, Isaac, and Jacob are realized. Beale places all emphasis on the real presence of God's new creation in the present time. According to him, various biblical texts support this view (1 Cor 10:11; Gal 4:26–31; Phil 3:20; Heb 12:22; Rev 3:14). What is already real will only become visible to everyone in the final phase of the history of salvation.[39]

Although all three theologians reject an evolution of the transient, Beale, together with Rahner, advocates that God *realizes* the new creation in the old creation today and that the future *reveals* it. With Christ's work of salvation, the drama of world history has, in principle already ended. From then on the new creation is present but still hidden under the "not yet."

If we compare Moltmann's perspective with Beale's idea of such an "already," we can conclude that Moltmann will not follow this idea. Rather, he chooses to see the history of salvation as announcements of promises that only proclaim what has "not yet" happened.[40] Although according to Moltmann, the resurrection of Christ took place in history, he does not see it as "historical," but as "eschatological." The resurrection had an impact on the present but operated *from the* future. If it operated from the past or the present, it would be "historical" and thus belong to the negative transient *chronos* in the present creation which disappears into nothing. The new creation is thus of a different order than the crucifixion, which is transient (§4.2.1). With Moltmann, terms like "new creation," "eschatological," "resurrection," "*advent*," "aionic time," "*novum*," and "immortality" are related to each other and of a different order than the terms "old creation," "historical," "crucifixion," "*futurum*," "*chronos*," and "impermanence," which together form a separate category. This can be seen in Moltmann's biblical-theological contrasts: Adam-Christ, flesh-Spirit, material-heavenly, natural-spiritual, works-faith, this age-the coming age. Beale also uses these contrasts. He shows the continuity that exists between this creation and the new creation. This continuity is lacking in Moltmann's earlier publications because of the strong emphasis he placed on *novum*. In his later works, Moltmann emphasizes more the continuity in his reflection about the new creation as *nova creatio ex vetere*.

With the resurrection, there is hope for the future. For Moltmann, that future does not fill itself in this reality, as Rahner and Beale assume. It marks the beginning of the new *aion* to which humanity anticipates, without the future realizing it and a partial "already" occurring in the "not yet." Where Moltmann speaks of the new creation, there is only anticipation, a foresight, a reflection, a revelation of the future. The clear speaking about the presence of the new creation in the *now* is lacking. According to Rahner and Beale, the resurrection is precisely the realization of an "already" in this present imperfect creation of the "not yet." The effects of the resurrection in the past and present make a statement possible (*Aussage*) about the future. Moltmann, on the

39. Beale, *1–2 Thessalonians*, 18–19; *Revelation*, 298, 300, 310, 544, 978, 1044.
40. Moltmann, "Hope," 210.

other hand, states that it is not the effects of the resurrection, but only the *Erkenntnisgrund* of the "already," which lies in this perishable *aion*. The so-called fulfillment and elaboration of the resurrection (*Realgrund*) lie in the future *aion*. There is only an announcement of the "already" and "not yet" a realization of it. According to Moltmann, speaking of an "already" and "not yet," as was introduced by Oscar Cullmann, is a *Scheinlösung*, because these terms assume that the imperfect creation is of the same order as the new creation.[41] In Moltmann's eschatology, the terms "already" and "not yet" have no place. The realization of the "already" of the new creation is only possible by God's coming in this creation (*advent*). We see in Moltmann's talk about these matters a strong parallel with Luther, who stated that Christians are not yet righteous in reality (*in re*), but already in hope (*in spe*). For Moltmann, too, the new creation is there only in hope, and its realization lies in God's coming.[42]

Nevertheless, Moltmann has no problem quoting the following words by Johann Blumhardt (1805–1880):

> With the resurrection, the purification of the earth from "sin and death" already starts now. The new world of God begins in the middle of the old world.[43]

Moltmann does so without commenting on it. This may give the reader the impression that Moltmann agrees with Blumhardt's representation of the "already" in the "not yet." A broader investigation of Moltmann's thought is necessary to show this is not the case. Other statements made by Moltmann in his later books also give the impression that he pays more attention to the "already." One could think here of a statement such as: "With Christ eternal, fulfilled life already came into this world,"[44] or of the statement: "When a life is lived in the light of the resurrection of Christ, it is recognized that the power of death is broken and the powers of death have lost their right. In the miracle of the resurrection, a life becomes new."[45] Moltmann does not explicitly mention whether that life is new today or whether it is only about the anticipation of the future new. From our research, we will have to choose the latter option. Moltmann does, however, continue to emphasize anticipation. The kingdom of God does not arise from the church or this world, but by the coming of God (*advent*). The church remains only a sign of the kingdom of God. It is the church that paves the way

---

41. Moltmann, *Kommen*, 23, 27–30.

42. Moltmann, *Kommen*, 29, 39, 45–47, 259. Cf. for the terms *in re* and *in spe*: *Theologie*, 80–81; Luther, *Luthers Werke*, II:495; XXVI:227.

43. Moltmann, *Sein Name*, 78: "'Mit der Auferstehung beginnt schon jetzt die Reinigung der Erde vom "Sünden- und Todeswesen." Es beginnt die neue Welt Gottes schon mitten in der alten Welt.'"

44. Moltmann, *Weiter Raum*, 113: "Mit Christus ist ewiges, erfülltes Leben schon in diese Welt gekommen."

45. Moltmann, *Lebendige Gott*, 197: "Wird ein Leben im Licht der Auferstehung Christi geführt, dann wird erkannt, dass die Macht des Todes gebrochen ist und die Mächte des Todes ihr Recht verloren haben. Im Wunder der Auferstehung wird ein Leben neu."

for God's coming, and therefore continually anticipates what is yet to come.[46] After all, it does not become clear from his publications that his ideas about the "already" and "not yet" have changed in recent years.

If Beale describes the entering of the land of Canaan regarding "already" and "not yet," Moltmann will reduce this to just a moment of decision. By entering the land, humanity should only *choose* God's coming from the promises God has given. In Beale's design, God's will in history is not distinguished from God's real presence in the future. Moltmann sees in the latter, precisely the purpose and the realization of the promises (§4.7.2).

Beale's theological perspective, however, turns against Moltmann's accent of a "not yet," because this accent sees the fruit of the resurrection only as a future and overlooks its influential historical realization.[47] From Beale's publications, it can be concluded that he is more likely to be associated with Rahner's design, which states that God's new creation is *developing* in *this* creation. God, the absolute future, is not only eschatologically present in history and the resurrection. It is already historically making a start with the new creation. Thus the Christians are already first fruits of the new creation in this old creation and celestial citizens on earth. Moltmann does not deny the latter in his theology but interprets it as God's intervention (*advent*) in the time that anticipates the coming age. Thus it is not about an already created new creation that develops in the perishable creation.[48] In contrast to Beale's and Rahner's theological perspective, Moltmann's perspective rejects the beginning of the realization of the work of salvation today.

In a critical comparison of the above subject with the three theologians, a difference emerges between speaking about "from" the old creation as development and "in" the old creation as realization. Beale connects this difference with the biblical expressions "from above" and "from below" (§5.5.3.7). Christians are already born again *from above*, looking for what is *above* and expecting the city *from above* in the future. The future is realized *from above* in the old creation and is not realized *from below*, from the old creation. The seer on Patmos sees the new Jerusalem descending *from above* on earth and does not see it developing from the old Jerusalem. The new creation thus finds its source "above" with God, but realizes itself on this earth. In his publications, Moltmann so strongly emphasizes the realization from God's future, that he questions any possible reality which could already happen "from above" in the present. The biblical "from above" is thus translated in his ST as a "from the front" or a "future" that is only present in anticipatory eschatological terms. The difficulty of this comes to the fore in Moltmann's speech about past, present, and future when he has to make a difference between the earthly perishable future (*chronos*) and the absolute enduring future of God (*kairos*). Rahner, in his works, emphasizes more strongly the

---

46. Moltmann, "Progress and Abyss," 18–19; *Kirche*, 198, 206, 214.
47. Beale, *1–2 Thessalonians*, 18–19.
48. Moltmann, "Auferstehungshoffnung," 111. Cf. Molnar, "Function of the Trinity," 676–77.

initial completion, which God develops from the present to the future. However, at this time, Rahner does not mention the source from which this completion is realized. So, the biblical "from above" threatens to be swallowed up by a "from behind" or a "from the present."[49] The difficulty of this arrises in Rahner's eschatology when Moltmann rejects his "present" by the transience, which is associated with this concept. Therefore, time concepts such as past, present, and future are inadequate indications of God's prolepsis in this creation. Moltmann contrasts the theophany of God as the static Being with the principle that God moves dynamically from the future towards us (§4.2.2). Although a biblical expression such as "from above" differs from what develops "from below," incorporation of this terminology in Moltmann's ST may encounter resistance. If this concept of the "from above" were to become less fundamental in Moltmann's ST, a comparison between the two systematics and the biblical theologian could cause this expression to be elaborated even deeper from BT and become more prominent in eschatological speaking. This will help us speak responsibly about the future. ST can thus make BT aware in the interdisciplinary research of the influence these accentuations in biblical speaking have on the systematic reflection of the Christian doctrine of faith.

6.2.2 The relation between protology and eschatology

6.2.2.1 Salvation historical paradigm

All three theologians acknowledge the relationship between protology and eschatology. The new creation is connected with the first creation. This can be understood from the fact that, for example, Revelation 21–22 contains all kinds of reminiscences of Genesis 1–2. Beale draws the attention of his readers to this in detail (§5.3.1). The protology is determined by eschatology. This is also the case for Moltmann. His creation theology is essentially eschatology (§4.2.4). Rahner sees it no differently: protology and eschatology are inextricably linked. Therefore, the progress of salvation history is simultaneously the progress of the first things in the direction of completion (§3.3.3).

From the analyses above, it appeared that Rahner works out this relation between protology and eschatology, the least in his reflection on the new heaven and the new earth. Moltmann and Beale, on the other hand, place the protological testimony of Genesis 1–2 in the center. This testimony contains the essential elements of the later revelation of God. This overlap makes it possible to compare the thinking of both theologians and to examine how their theologies can be of significance to the other. In the reflection on this, we will further investigate how these may also possibly connect with Rahner's theology.

---

49. Cf. Geertsema, *Van boven*.

6.2.2.1.1 Creation in development

As Moltmann thinks from the three-division: *creatio originalis*, *creatio continua*, and *creatio nova*, Beale offers the three-division: *original creation*, *fallen creation*, and *new creation*. Both are convinced that this creation has a good beginning and that this creation finds its completion in the final phase of the new creation. The original creation in Genesis 1 has been focused on its completion from the beginning. That completion is the new creation in which God will dwell universally. The "very good" in Genesis 1:31 does not bear the meaning of "everything is perfect" or "everything is accomplished." Genesis 1 only describes God's beginning with creation. However, Moltmann and Beale do not want that initial phase to be subordinate to the new creation, because it was this original creation with which God wanted to begin.[50]

In their theologies, Moltmann's ST and Beale's BT can complement each other from their field of expertise, by clarifying each other's research with new insights. Beale's theology can be a contribution to Moltmann's theology because it presents the overall picture of the grand storyline of the development of Genesis 1–2 in the history of salvation. Moltmann's theology can be of significance to Beale in this respect because it brings to the fore various accentuations within the Christian doctrine of faith, in the relationship between protology and eschatology.

If we take Rahner into account, we have to conclude that he also sees creation in development. From the general theory of evolution, he states that matter develops into a living organism. For Rahner, the highest self-development in creation is not the new heaven and new earth, but the coming of Christ to this earth.[51] Without this coming, there would be no new creation possible. Rahner, in support of Teilhard de Chardin, characterizes the salvation work of Christ as the triumphant climax of evolutionary world development and victory over evil. The human self-transcendence of the spirit, which originates from matter, comes here to a climax, together with God's communication (§3.4).[52] We will discuss Rahner's choice later in more detail (§6.2.2.2.3).

6.2.2.1.2 God's prolepsis and human faithfulness

In §6.2.1, we saw that Rahner, Moltmann, and Beale all three recognize that the new creation does not develop within the world from the present creation. God's absolute prolepsis remains necessary for this. We concluded that Moltmann emphasizes this more strongly than Rahner and Beale. He combines the trichotomy *creatio originalis*, *creatio continua*, and *creatio nova* with the terms *natura*, *gratia*, and *gloria*.[53] According to Moltmann, nothing good can be developed from the *natura* of the *creatio*

---

50. Moltmann, *Kommen*, 329.
51. Rahner, *Grundkurs*, 183; "Christologie im Rahmen," 235.
52. Cf. Petty, *Faith*, 72–76; Teilhard de Chardin, "Christologie und Evolution," 93–115.
53. Moltmann, *Geschichte*, 164–166.

originalis. The reason for this is that creation has been marked from the beginning by the negative *nihil*. This *nihil* plays a crucial role in Moltmann's protology. It implies that creation looks forward to God's prolepsis from its very beginning (§4.2.4).

According to Beale, the very beginning of creation is not characterized by the negative. His BT clarifies that God's command to humanity in Genesis 1:28 and 2:15 is the excellent and definite beginning of a process that leads to the completion of the new creation. By obedience to God's command, humanity, together with God, would bring the new creation near. Beale then sees the actual realization of this as a gift from God to humans (§5.3.1.2). The entire history of salvation is characterized as one great chain of human attempts to introduce the blessings of the new creation into this creation. Beale's BT tries to give an overall picture of these attempts in the biblical storyline. In it, he continually shows that in the Bible, all human attempts to do so remain fruitless. The only exception to this is Christ. He is the True Adam who accomplishes the new creation. Beale's salvific historical overview is, therefore, characterized as a progress and recovery model.

From Moltmann's theology, Beale's emphasis on human obedience is questionable. The choice of the human being is much decisive in Beale's representation. With Beale, evil only comes into the world through the disobedience of man (Gen 3). This ensures that, in addition to the aspect of progress, attention is also paid to the question of recovery. For Moltmann, a *restitutio in integrum*, as proposed by Beale, is unthinkable. For him, this proposal is elsewhere dismissed as "Greek thinking" and "false Thomism." The glory and holiness of the new creation, as well as God's proximity to it, have never been present in the initial state of creation and cannot possibly be accomplished by grace, church, or humanity.[54] Beale, therefore, expects too much of this creation and tends to give the impression that the new creation is only an "upgrade" of the original creation. According to Beale, if humanity had sinned in Genesis 1–2, there would have been virtually no radical rupture. God would have rewarded Adam, and there would have been a peaceful development from the original creation to the new creation. Compared to Moltmann, Beale, therefore, thinks too much from what he calls *futurum*, and too little from what Moltmann calls *advent*. According to Moltmann, this kind of criticism also applies to Rahner. We have already seen the impact of this choice on the theological thinking of Rahner, Moltmann, and Beale (§6.2.1).

Although Rahner does not speak out directly on the above matters, he also emphasizes the connection between the original, the fallen, and the new creation. Creation not only moves towards God but is also completed by God's prolepsis.[55] In Rahner's hermeneutical principles, this was already apparent because eschatology, anthropology, and soteriology formed a unity. In a critical comparison, we note that Beale's presentation of the situation is mainly in line with Rahner's ST. In Moltmann's terminology, this would mean that *futurum* and *advent* would complement each other.

---

54. Moltmann, *Kommen*, 288–89; *Geschichte*, 163; "Creation and Redemption," 119–20.
55. Cf. Rahner, "Welt," 77–78, 82.

For Moltmann, this representation also starts too much from a restoration principle that is characteristic of Western theology. From this hermeneutic principle, Rahner and Beale argue that salvation comes from impermanent creation, while Moltmann argues for the reality of an imperishable creation that comes only from salvation through God's *advent*.[56] The mission of God's people on earth is, therefore, according to Moltmann, only to anticipate the new creation and never to realize it.

A comparison between the eschatologies of the three theologians studied makes it clear that, according to Moltmann's design, Rahner and Beale want to bring about too much from the fallen state and therefore ignore the state of imprisonment, in which the original creation already exists. Further research on this subject will then have to focus on the crucial question of transposition and anticipation with which we started this comparison of their hermeneutic approaches.

By the research into the relationship between protology and eschatology, Rahner's and Beale's presentations ask Moltmann the question of what, in his opinion, the usefulness of a *creatio continua* is if it rejects a possible developmental history. Why does Moltmann's theological perspective distinguish it from the *creatio originalis*, when the negative *nihil* characterizes both? What determines the demarcation between the two in his theology? According to Moltmann, this difference exists in the fact that in the *creatio continua*, the redemption reveals itself (§4.2.4). From Moltmann's emphasis on *advent*, the continuity in this is just an indication of the future realization of that redemption. Compared to the *creatio nova*, Moltmann's *creatio continua* is more like a *creatio decontinua*. Together with the *creatio originalis*, *the creatio continua* is wholly subjected to the negative that comes with the *nihil*. The optimistic or pessimistic view of the faithfulness of humanity in the history of salvation is determined from the outset. Because of the presence of the *nihil*, Moltmann does not consider it possible that humanity fulfills God's hope for the *creatio nova*. It is only through God's intervention that the new creation is realized. The answer to the previous question about the source of the evil that reveals itself in this *nihil* thus influences the perspective with which we look at the relationship between the present and the new creation.

6.2.2.2 The origin of evil

While all three theologians acknowledge God as Creator and confess in their works that the negative is absent from the new creation because of God's prolepsis, they think differently about the source of evil. The question of this source of evil was not yet addressed in the preliminary analyses. The reason for this was that this question was in the background of the three theologians when they spoke about the new heaven and the new earth. In the earlier analyses we saw that Moltmann's choice for the *nihil* in his theological reflection on the new creation is strongly present (§4.2.4.2) and that Beale also pays ample attention to the theme of decay and idolatry in his biblical-theological

---

56. Moltmann, *Kommen*, 287–88; "Schöpfung," 123–37.

design. With Rahner, the theme of evil is much less common in his reflection on eschatology and the new heaven and the new earth. We will first focus on Moltmann's perspective, then look at Beale's perspective, and finally pay attention to Rahner. The different thoughts of the three theologians on this subject are briefly summarized to focus on the question to what extent a comparison between them on this subject can be of significance for the theme of the new heaven and the new earth.[57]

6.2.2.2.1 MOLTMANN AND THE *ZIMZUM*

Moltmann's rejection of the *creatio originalis* and *creatio continua* as the potential for the development of *creatio nova* is based on his choice of the doctrine of *zimzum* and the corresponding *nihil* (cf. §4.2.4.2). His acceptance of this model determines his full ST. Moltmann sees it as Manichaean to suppose that evil comes from a power other than God.[58] He knows himself inspired by the Christian speaking of "creation out of nothing" (*creatio ex nihilo*) in these notions of the *zimzum*. However, he interprets these words as a creation *in* nothingness (*creatio in nihilo*) because, in the beginning, there is nothing else but God. To create creation, God chooses first to create a "nothing" (*nihil*). In this *nihil,* God creates the world. So, in this *nihil,* God is not present. This means that God must be limited to give this creation its own space. Moltmann describes this *nihil* hence as the negative. It is necessary for God to create this so that the Lord can come to this creation. The later Incarnation is thus not primarily a testimony of God's condescending love to free sinners, but a fulfillment of this world with God's presence. A disadvantage here is that this negative *zero* has its origin in God. Moltmann acknowledges this.[59] By God's actions, a negative *nihil* is created in which the world is created. God is then both the Origin and the Savior of evil, suffering, and injustice. Nevertheless, this testimony is difficult to reconcile with Moltmann's often mentioned idea that the original creation is good (§4.2.4.1).[60]

Later Moltmann states that the *nihil* did not have its negative influence from the beginning. It only gets this when creatures move away from their Creator.[61] However, this addition does not solve the tension mentioned above. According to the teaching of *zimzum*, the *nihil* is *necessary* for God to be able to separate from creation. God's self-restraint creates a creation that, from the very beginning, is in danger of falling into a dark evil thing. The *nihil* offers space both for life—which is created in it by

---

57. For a further deepening of this theme, see: Jhi, *Heil*; Ho-Tsui, *Sünde*; Fritz, "Placing Sin," 294–312; Halloran, "Evolution," 177–93; Grümme, *Noch ist die Träne*; Bauckham, "Theodicy," 83–97; Macek, "Doctrine of Creation," 150–84.

58. Moltmann, *Gott in der Schöpfung*, 100.

59. Moltmann, *Trinität*, 49.

60. Cf. Thomas, *Neue Schöpfung*, 330; Remenyi, *Um der Hoffnung*, 133; Farrow, "In the End," 436–37; Pannenberg, "Anbrechende Zukunft," 78; Molnar, "Moltmann's Post-Modern Messianic Christology," 679; Pannenberg, *Systematische Theologie 2*, 29; Niewiadomski, *Zweideutigkeit*, 98.

61. Moltmann, *Kommen*, 336; *Gott in der Schöpfung*, 101.

creation—and for death, which represents the negative and sin on earth.⁶² Death is thus in the field of tension because it simultaneously appears to be the cause and result of the negative.

In comparison with Beale's theological perspective, Moltmann is critically asked whether this distance between God and creature is necessary. Is not the biblical God everywhere present for all creatures? Does not the psalmist write: "You hem me in, behind and before, and lay your hand upon me" (Ps 139:5)? Beale has much attention in his BT for that proximity to God. This is evident from the emphasis he places on God's desire to live with people, to walk in their midst, and to be present with people as Immanuel. Moltmann's theology, both from ST and BT, can be asked whether this idea of God's necessary self-restraint and the resulting *nihil* does not exclude God from creation. BT can alert ST to this in the case of the three chosen theologians. The teaching of *zimzum* is an unbiblical idea that is not directly reflected in biblical revelation. Moltmann's idea to connect evil with *nihil*, to which creation has been subject from the beginning, has no resonance with Beale. According to Moltmann's views, the interdisciplinary interaction between ST and BT is also significant because it denounces these kinds of ideas in his field of expertise. In §2.2.1, we have seen this already, and it also emerged that Moltmann methodically emphasizes that not human philosophy, but the Bible should be the book of Christian hope. Theologians who wish to engage in Christian theology may, therefore, base their thoughts on God's promises expressed in the hopes and experiences of Israel and the church. From his plea to return to biblical speaking, Beale's theology challenges Moltmann to examine to what extent his teaching of the *zimzum* is biblically justifiable.

Systematic-theologically another question can be asked about this teaching by Moltmann: If God's limitation (*Selbsteinschränkung*) in God's omnipresence is necessary to distinguish between creation and the Creator, does this imply that the distinction in God's *Selbstentschränkung* in the new creation will soon disappear? This would logically lead to the consequence that in the new heaven and on the new earth, the difference between the Creator and creation fades away. When the *nihil* is necessary for the creation to make a difference between the Creator and the creature, it remains a mystery that this is no longer necessary for the new creation.⁶³ The new creation then threatens to merge with the Creator. Although Moltmann explicitly rejects such pantheism, he actively incorporates its essential insights into his theology of the new heaven and earth. This creates the impression that the difference between the Creator and the creatures in the new creation fades away.⁶⁴ We will return to this in the

---

62. Moltmann, *Kommen*, 312.

63. Cf. Bouma-Prediger, "Creation," 80; Deane-Drummond, *Ecology*, 102–3; Larson, *Times of the Trinity*, 142, 149.

64. Moltmann, *Kommen*, 337; *Gott in der Schöpfung*, 101. Cf. Remenyi, *Um der Hoffnung*, 144–46, 441–42; Munteanu, *Tröstende Geist*, 264; Bouma-Prediger, "Creation," 83.

The New Heaven and New Earth

substantive comparison between the three theologians on God and the space of the new creation (§6.3.2).

From Rahner's and Beale's theological point of view, could we possibly, in all these critical notions, ask the legitimate question in which the teaching of *zimzum* gives a better explanation for the origin of evil than the traditional Christian doctrine of creation, which states that God gives space and time to the other next? According to traditional teachings, God must not choose a limitation to create space for creation. There is no question of a *Selbsteinschränkung* of God there. God is prepared to give love space to the other without restricting space.

Moltmann does not respond directly to this question. However, in his writings about the theodicy, he does respond to the traditional explanation. In it, he states from the beginning that every theological explanation of negative suffering is at the same time a motivation for suffering:

> The question of theodicy . . . is the general eschatological question. . . . It is a practical question that can only be answered by the experience of the new world in which "God will wipe away all tears from their eyes."[65]

Answering or dispensing with the question of the theodicy would even abolish Christian eschatology.[66] Even though Moltmann does not give his answer to the question of suffering, it can be said from the perspective of his thinking that he finds it incomprehensible how Beale, together with the church fathers, following Paul, can explain the suffering from the fall: death as punishment for sin. The text in Genesis 1–3 is too factually conceived for Moltmann and thus loses its original symbolic character.[67] At the same time, Moltmann is equally critical of modern explanations that try to explain suffering as a *natural* consequence of finiteness. Death is then immortalized in the order of creation. Moltmann follows both explanations: (1) the modern interpretation, which states that death is not the result of sin in primal history, and (2) the confession of the church fathers that death is part of the elements that God will overcome in the new creation. For Moltmann, death is thus ultimately a temporary characteristic of this "defective creation" that will be definitively removed by God in the new creation.[68] Moltmann remains silent about the further origin of this death.

---

65. Moltmann, *Trinität*, 65: "Die Theodizeefrage . . . ist die umfassende eschatologische Frage. . . . Sie ist eine praktische Frage, die nur durch die Erfahrung der neuen Welt, in der 'Gott abwischen wird allen Tränen von ihren Augen', beantwortet wird."

66. Moltmann, "Richtungen," 45.

67. Moltmann, *Gott in der Schöpfung*, 35–36, 66–68, 200.

68. Moltmann, *Kommen*, 96, 109–10.

6.2.2.2.2 BEALE AND THE TEMPTATION OF THE SERPENT

Unlike Rahner and Moltmann, Beale spends several chapters in his BT on the relationship between themes such as justification, reconciliation, salvation, and the new creation. His choices here explain why Beale chooses discontinuity in the substantive elaboration of the new heaven and the new earth. For Beale, creation is not easy to wash off, to function as a new creation.[69]

When it comes to the theological explanation of evil, we note that Beale limits himself only to the *revelation of* evil in Genesis 3, while Moltmann wants to extend to the time before and asks himself the question of the *origin* of evil. Beale starts from the idea that death and destruction only appeared after the first human disobedience in Genesis 3, where humanity met the serpent in the garden of Eden. By obeying the word of the serpent, humanity brought evil into good creation (§5.3.1). This brought in an absolute state of loss in creation. Beale emphasizes this several times in his BT. God created creation well, without spot or wrinkle, but humans deliberately rebelled against God, making the best into the worst (§5.6). Beale shows how this effect of sin is clearly described in Genesis 3. This part of the Bible does not give us any theoretical reflections on sin. Sin is illustrated there. In the conversation between the woman and the serpent, God's word is distorted, supplemented, and critically questioned.[70]

To what extent Beale considers this testimony of Genesis 1–3 as a historical fact remains unclear. From his reaction to his former Old Testament colleague, Peter Enns, it can be inferred that this biblical text is not only theologically true for him, but is also essential to history. How Beale exactly sees this essentially is not clear in his works. All his attention in his reaction is focused on the relationship between Genesis 1–2 and the temple of God on earth.[71] According to Moltmann's and Rahner's theological reflections, the description of the primal history in Genesis 1–3 is only an allegorical representation.[72] Moltmann, like Beale, does see pride as the original sin; man wanted to be like God.

Beale's BT also lacks an answer to the question of the *origin* of evil. This can give the impression to the ST as an escape route to avoid theological thinking about it. The BT of Beale may challenge the ST of Rahner and Moltmann and go further than primarily referring to Genesis 3. However absurd the evil may be, it requires the sharpest reflection in Christian theology. Traditionally, this theme has been one of the critical questions posed by the Christian doctrine of faith. Moltmann's and Rahner's ST can provide core elements from the doctrine of faith to Beale, to inspire the BT research methodically, and to deepen its content. For Moltmann, the evil that happened

---

69. Beale, *New Testament*, 237, 561, 570, 836, 843.
70. Beale, *New Testament*, 33.
71. Beale, *Erosion*, 29, 74–75, 166, 185–97; *Temple*, 81–122.
72. Moltmann, *Gott in der Schöpfung*, 35–36, 66–68, 200; Rahner and Rawer, "Weltall," 66; Rahner, *Grundkurs*, 120; "Sünde Adams," 261, 264; "Erbsünde und Evolution," 463–65.

in Auschwitz and Hiroshima is too colossal for him to be explained as merely the product of human disobedience in Genesis 3. The evil that took place there can only be understood as "absolute evil," as demonic power that reaches beyond creation.[73] Rahner also goes in that direction and calls the idea that the evil in this creation originates from the freedom of the first creature incomplete.[74]

In a comparison of Rahner's and Moltmann's theological perspectives, a critical note can be placed on Beale's biblical-theological reflections on evil. If Beale in his BT only refers to Genesis 3 as the beginning of evil, he circumvents the essential question of the relationship between God and evil. We have already seen that through the teaching of *zimzum*, Moltmann ultimately also connects evil with God. In Beale's biblical-theological approach, this is missing, and all emphasis in the theological reflection lies in the relationship between humans and evil. However, Beale cannot stop there. A reflection on the origin of evil may also be addressed in his field of expertise.

The question of the cause of evil thus appears to be a fertile ground for an interdisciplinary dialogue between the two disciplines and the question of the intensity of the intrinsic and extrinsic influence of sin on humanity. Genesis 3 begins with the mention of the serpent as "Now the serpent was more crafty than any other wild animal that the Lord God had made" (v. 1). So the snake is an animal made by Jhwh. The essence of the serpent does not tacitly pass by to God. If sin does not belong to the creation and does not come from God's hand, then it seems to have another source. One can then conclude that there are powers against God that penetrate creation. This is in line with the explanation Beale gives to Genesis 2:15. The man had to guard against intruders who approached the garden from outside. The question of the origin and the reason for this evil is thus also pressing Beale's BT.

The question of whether God could not accomplish the new creation without suffering is, therefore, a question for both theological disciplines. Rahner explicitly emphasizes that thinking about this should not be left to ST alone.[75] BT should also be engaged because it reflects on the themes of salvation history. ST can be meaningful here by providing BT with the accentuations of the Christian doctrine so that it can reflect on biblical revelation from the relevant core elements. That Beale is open to these core elements is evident from the structure of his NTBT. Themes such as resurrection, justification, and reconciliation are discussed. For Beale, ST provides BT with different categories that can be thought through from the biblical storyline (§2.3). In this respect, the theme of evil is not a neglected child. Genesis 1–3, the text that Beale places centrally in his BT, confronts BT with other elements that contain a possible threat of evil. In this way, Genesis 1:28 expresses the subjugation of the animal world powerfully. According to Beale, this happens in parallel with the way in which Jhwh

---

73. Moltmann, "Rechtfertigung," 170. Cf. Moltmann, *Gott in der Schöpfung*, 100.
74. Rahner, "Warum?," 457–59.
75. Rahner, "Warum?," 463–64.

subdued the dark chaos.[76] Instead of the peaceful coexistence between humans and animals, this includes animals that threaten humans, and that must be kept under peaceful control. Moltmann's theological views are that Beale can draw attention to in his systematic reflection on this part of the Bible.[77] Furthermore, in the creation of humanity, there is no statement that God saw that it was good. Although creation is "very good" (1:31), it is this from the totality, as Beale himself argues and Moltmann also states several times.[78] In that respect, not only ST is challenged to think from BT about the biblical testimony in Genesis 1–3. We also note that this comparison of theologians from two different disciplines challenges BT to contribute more deeply thematically-exegetically to the question of the origin of evil. Both disciplines raise detailed questions on this subject.

6.2.2.2.3 RAHNER AND THE MYSTERY OF EVIL

The question of how there may be something inherent in creation that destroys God's work is not answered directly in Rahner's publications. According to him, the origin of evil remains a mystery. All he observes is that not understanding the suffering is part of God's incomprehensibility.[79] According to Rahner, the biblical testimony of Genesis 1–3 does not provide an answer either. After all, these biblical chapters are about an allegorical representation of the situation.[80] At the same time, he states in his ST that in the past, there was once an original first sin. According to Rahner, this happened to an unknown "Adam" or even to several "Adams" at once, somewhere in the distant past. Since this first sin, humanity has been *partly* responsible for the fact that ignorance, illness, suffering, and death make their negative entry into this earth.[81]

Rahner consciously speaks here of partial guilt. After all, humans are partly to blame because death in creation already existed before the first sin took place. Even with an initial sinlessness, humans would not have lived forever. So, without original or personal sin, death would also have occurred.[82] Rahner lacks any further substantiation of this statement. His thoughts on this seem to be based primarily on the evolutionary theology he uses in his anthropological speaking (§3.4).[83] We saw that Rahner described Christ's salvation work as the triumphant culmination of

76. Beale, *New Testament*, 32–34.

77. Moltmann, *Gott in der Schöpfung*, 43–44.

78. Beale, *New Testament*, 621; Moltmann, *Kommen*, 109, 290; *Gott in der Schöpfung*, 281–83.

79. Rahner, "Warum?," 451, 462; "Erbsünde und Evolution," 461–64. Cf. Ho-Tsui, *Sünde*, 196–215, 239–242; Jhi, *Heil*, 96–105, 180–188.

80. Rahner and Rawer, "Weltall," 66; Rahner, *Grundkurs*, 120; "Sünde Adams," 261, 264; "Erbsünde und Evolution," 463–65.

81. Rahner, *Grundkurs*, 116, 121; "Dogmatischen Schriftbeweis," 461–64; "Sünde Adams," 272–75; "Eschatologie (SM)," 1007; *Zur Theologie des Todes*, 39.

82. Rahner and Rawer, "Weltall," 67; "Tod," 921.

83. Cf. Halloran, "Evolution," 184.

evolutionary world development and the ultimate victory over evil. When comparing with Moltmann's and Beale's theological views, it is possible to point out to Rahner that this kind of evolutionism always chooses for the victory of the strongest and oppresses the weaker. To what extent can such an evolutionary development of the world still be related to Christ as Redeemer of the weak and poor in spirit? Moltmann writes explicitly:

> A *Christ evolutor* without the *Christ redemptor* is nothing more than a cruel, unfeeling *Christ selector*, a historical judge of the world without mercy on the weak and a breeder of life whom the victims are not interested in.[84]

In this respect, the creation mechanism is in contradiction with the redemption mechanism. Beale will most likely, for biblical-theological reasons, reject this choice for Christ as the climax of evolution. He may also have significant difficulties with Rahner's view that death and suffering were already present on earth before humanity came into being. According to the biblical testimony, sinless man would not taste death and would not know the misery that evil brought with it if he faithfully observed and completed the creation commission in Genesis 1. Then humanity would have received eternal life to its full extent (§5.3.1).

The only thing Rahner wants to be aware of is that death through sin is now entering human life both positively and negatively. At the positive aspect of death, Rahner thinks of the many martyrs who longed to give their lives for Christ. Death was a favorable occasion for them. For others, death was an adverse occasion, since death robbed them of their actual life with God. According to Rahner, humanity thus has a freedom of choice for the death he or she wants to die: (1) death in a life without God, which brings you into emptiness and nullity, or (2) death in a life for God, which brings you into the fullness of life. This makes it not only a destiny but also an opportunity to complete the human condition through an act. Rahner's definition of being human plays an essential role in this view. You are human by leaving yourself behind in every new act and giving up everything you are to become yourself. According to Rahner, the most definitive way in which one gives up oneself is to die.[85]

In comparison with Moltmann's and Beale's theology, it will become clear that they have difficulties with this positive view of death. Critically the question can be asked whether it is not death, but the giving of all life to God, that we should call positive. Death is inflicted on someone in martyrdom. That is not positive. However, to give full life to God, humans make their own choices in their hearts.

Rahner ultimately calls the negative "*ewig unbegreiflich*—eternally incomprehensible" and surrounds the question of suffering from the unfathomable wise care of God.

---

84. Moltmann, *Weg Jesu*, 320: "Ein *Christus evolutor* ohne den *Christus redemptor* ist nichts anderes als ein grausamer, gefühlloser *Christus selector*, ein geschichtlicher Weltenrichter ohne Erbarmen mit den Schwachen und ein Aufzüchter des Lebens, den die Opfer nicht interessieren."

85. Rahner, "Einige Bemerkungen zur Theologie der Erbsünde," 31; "Tod. IV," 224–25; *Zur Theologie des Todes*, 33–34, 39–40, 103–4. Cf. Jhi, *Heil*, 101.

The real answer to the question of suffering comes when we worship God and surrender ourselves to the incomprehensibility of the Lord as the true fulfillment and salvation.[86]

6.2.2.3 *The impact of sin*

In the previous chapter, we saw that Beale pays ample attention to the impact of human disobedience in the history of salvation. It was through this disobedience that evil permeated all creation. With Rahner and Moltmann, this negative aspect is almost entirely missing in their talk about the new heaven and the new earth. Because their choices herein influence the substantive discussion about the continuity and discontinuity between the current creation and the future creation, it is essential to discuss their separate theological reflections on the impact of sin in the history of salvation.

6.2.2.3.1 EXTRINSIC AND INTRINSIC SIN

The theme of sin is not in the foreground of Moltmann's ST. A separate chapter on this subject is even missing from his leading publications. Nevertheless, he points out that sin means that humanity falls into hopelessness and weakness. Sin is where humans shut themselves off from the blessed possibilities God wants to give creatures. According to Moltmann, sin is not the breaking of God's statutes, but the failure to do good, the derailment into despondency, or the following of the *Zeitgeist*. The emphasis is on the inability to do what has been promised. It is impossible for humans to realize in the present state what God desires. Sin is therefore extrinsic: humanity is in a corrupt state of hopelessness and becomes a plaything of evil that prevails mainly outside themselves. In the new creation, this weakness is overcome. Through the power of God's Spirit, humanity anticipates already today in this creation what the biblical hope looks like.[87]

In Beale's BT, this extrinsic emphasis, which Moltmann applies to sin, does not occur. For example, there is no separate chapter on the powers of evil as an external influence. Beale only seems to see that sin has to do with wrong deeds. Sin is the choice from the hearts of humans, the rebellion against God, and thus the voluntary choice for the radical break between the creatures and their Creator. Sin mutilates and destroys creation and ruins it. In this way, Beale focuses on intrinsic loss. Through the first disobedience, humanity has degenerated into corrupt beings who pursue evil *from within*. The external circumstances that Moltmann puts in the foreground in his ST may fuel this, but they do not cancel out his own choice from the human heart. If we start from Beale's biblical-theological perspective, Moltmann's description of sin will be a typical form of utopian thinking. In Moltmann's ST, the sinner gets a lot of opportunities to apologize.

---

86. Rahner, "Warum?," 463–65.

87. Moltmann, *Im Ende*, 106–8; *Kommen*, 103–5; *Weg Jesu*, 148; "Creation and Redemption," 126; *Theologie*, 18, 109–11, 187.

The way Rahner speaks of sin is very similar to Moltmann. Rahner emphasizes the once-only nature of the possibilities a person receives. In freedom, humans must organize their lives in the right way.[88] Humans may freely choose their final destination. In a critical comparison, Rahner's ST is thus challenged by Beale's BT, with the specific question to Rahner to show where he finds this neutral choice for freedom in the biblical testimony. In the Bible, humanity is seen as a slave to sin. Humans use their freedom only to engage in slavery and idolatry. On its own, humans never want to be what he or she is called to.[89] From Rahner's theology, Beale's BT is too negative about humanity. From a radical existential interpretation, Rahner sees humans not as slaves to sin, but as anonymous Christians who, through the discovery of the Christian faith, indeed come to themselves and thus also become genuinely humans. A comparison between all three theologians shows that not only Beale but also Moltmann has trouble with this representation of Rahner. Moltmann then rejects Rahner's choice because: (1) what is characteristic of the Christian threatens to become generally human, and (2) religious freedom no longer seems to exist on earth.[90]

Rahner sees sinfulness primarily as a stain and not directly as a defect. Together with Moltmann, he is less condemning about the individual choice for sin than Beale. That does not mean that Rahner and Moltmann justify sin. Instead, it means that humans are not entirely guilty for the evil and the suffering in creation. For Moltmann, the main cause of this lies in the *nihil*, and for Rahner, the suffering and death are there even before humans were there. Rahner sees sin as a stain that came upon man through Adam's sin. Sin as a stain requires a smaller prolepsis by God than sin as a deficiency. In the case of sin as a stain, the car is dirty and can be washed. A good detergent is needed, but the car is still working. If we see sin as a lack, then something is missing. The car has no engine anymore. Not even a good car wash helps. The vehicle is defective at the heart of its existence.

In comparison, Beale can point out to both systematics that the above images are not in opposition to each other, but are present in the Bible in a complementary way. Humanity is entirely sinful before God. It is precisely the image of baptism that makes it clear that a person should not only be cleaned from the external influences. Even the inside is not in good shape. Humans must be renewed entirely from God. Sin as a blemish is assumed in biblical texts where it is about the cleansing of the sinner. Sin as an irreparable defect is assumed where sin and death are connected. The latter emphasis is consistently present in Beale's BT. Comparison leads to the conclusion that this representation of Beale may challenge the ST of Moltmann and Rahner to further reflect on this presence of sin in the biblical storyline.

In his BT, Beale continually emphasizes the complete loss of humanity. From his field of expertise, he will thus point out that the Bible sees humans as lost creatures

---

88. Rahner, *Grundkurs*, 116.
89. Highfield, "Freedom," 485–505; Phan, "Karl Rahner's Doctrine," 223–36.
90. Moltmann, *Geschichte*, 162–63.

who actively rebel against God's commandments and are mainly led by evil. In his own BT, Beale pays exhaustive attention to this impact of sin on the history of salvation. The liberation of the wicked humanity which, under the power of sin, rejects God and falls into lawlessness by worshipping other gods, is central. From the first human disobedience to God, there has been the urge for idolatry in humans. In the eschaton, all humans stand guilty before God, and a radical purification occurs.[91] This negative vision cannot be related to Moltmann and Rahner. For them, sin is only a shortcoming and not an aggressive act or a power that destroys everything. According to Moltmann, God does not allow this creation to divert from God's intentions. God clings to the creation and the intentions with it.

The evil and sin in this creation are not comparable to rats who enter the warehouse from outside but to empty racks in a warehouse.[92] There is not a "something" called sin, but rather the "nothing." According to Moltmann, this "nothing" is related to the *nihil* and points to the lack of what will be there later. According to Beale, however, the racks in the warehouse have not been emptied because there was a shortage of supply. They are emptily robbed and plundered. It is an aggressive act, which does not have a *nihil* character, but has a disruptive character. To choose for death instead of life is unreal, inexplicable, catastrophic and, given God's intention with humanity and the world, an inalienable debt. Everything is perverted and therefore has a wrong effect.

6.2.2.3.2 Influence of Western theology

In a critical comparison between Rahner's and Moltmann's ST, the question could also arise whether Beale's biblical-theological presentation is sufficiently objective to serve as valid evidence from the Bible. Moltmann's and Rahner's theological reflection could then draw Beale's attention from the ST expertise to the Western systematic-historical influences that his biblical-theological perspective contains. Western theology has always stressed the radical nature of sin and salvation. Eastern theology, on the other hand, places a different accent. It does not see sin, but the impermanence of creation as the fundamental problem. Therefore, rescue is linked to the destruction of the possibility of corruption. For Moltmann, the biblical explanation of Beale will be too systematically colored. His biblical exegesis contains an (unconscious) adoption of Augustine's ST explanation and thinking from the three keywords: misery, salvation, and gratitude. Moltmann's ST can point out to Beale that he takes over this Western Augustinian thinking too quickly in his BT, without taking into account other alternatives from the biblical testimony. Moltmann points out that it is also possible to think of the Jewish explanation that Adam and Eve do not commit the first human sin in the garden of Eden. The first sin is done by Cain in the field when he kills his brother Abel (Gen 4). Another explanation Moltmann quotes from the early church is

---

91. See especially: Beale, *We Become*.
92. This illustration is taken from: Van de Beek, *Lichtkring*, 139.

that sin begins with the rise of the demonic tyrants (Gen 6). According to Moltmann, this demonic event then resonates in Daniel 7 when the writer places the demonic monsters opposite the Son of Man.[93] So, Moltmann is critical of Beale's reformed approach in his BT. Opposite the three keywords: misery, salvation, and gratitude, he places the three keywords: exodus, transit, and entry. For more information about this, Moltmann could refer to his systematic-theological reflection on this Augustinian Calvinist approach.[94]

6.2.2.3.3 Judgment and renewal

Beale's emphasis on the complete depravity of creation through human infidelity to God explains why grace is more than just a love speech to humans. It is a radical liberation of humanity from the realm of darkness. This contrast between light and darkness is one of the reasons why Beale does not see the new creation in direct continuity with this creation. For Beale, sin is a horror that we cannot ignore and that completely bans creation. Evil has a significant influence on this creation and must be radically destroyed by fire. There is a radical discontinuity between this creation and the new creation.

This choice explains why Beale often puts the discontinuity between the current sinful creation and the future sinless creation in the foreground. With Moltmann and Rahner, discontinuity is less apparent in that respect. All their attention is focused on God's salvation, the renewal, and the resurrection of all things. This ensures that their continuity is in the foreground. In Moltmann's case, we see that on the one hand, he acknowledges the impact of the *nihil*, but on the other hand, he insists that God does not give up this creation. The *nihil* disappears, not the creation. A new creation appears from the old creation. God transforms and glorifies this creation. This element of continuity lacks in Beale's biblical-theological reflection on the resurrection. The power of sin is so dominant in his thinking that there is almost no continuity between this creation and the new creation. This is remarkable for those who realize that Beale places great emphasis on the continuity between the OT and NT. It is one of his greatest achievements in the field of BT to make this continuity in the biblical storyline visible in all facets (§5.2.2).

A critical comparison between Moltmann's and Beale's theologies can lead Beale in his BT to make a more apparent distinction between God's judgment of evil, which is linked to discontinuity, and God's renewal and resurrection of the good, which are linked to continuity. Moltmann does this by connecting the cross with all the negative that perishes in the new creation (discontinuity) and by connecting the resurrection with God's radical renewal of the creation that remains (continuity).

---

93. Cf. Moltmann, *Sein Name*, 187; *Kommen*, 113–14; *Geist des Lebens*, 139; *Weg Jesu*, 148–49. With references to: Buber, *Bilder*, 29–44; Pagels, *Adam*, 31–32, 107–11.

94. Moltmann, *Kommen*, 298–99. Cf. Macleod, "Christology," 40.

In his BT, Beale opposes sin several times with the need for rebirth. This is the way of salvation that God offers sinners to escape the temptations of evil. For Moltmann, humans' loss is not due to themselves. The reason for this loss is the negative *nihil*. Although both theologians do not share the same views on sin, Moltmann will agree that humanity is in a state of inadequacy to overcome evil, and that salvation and completion can only be fully expected from God. When it comes to the path of salvation and renewal, Moltmann's comparison with Beale shows that both are in agreement.

Nevertheless, it is striking that Beale's BT says less about this effect of renewal for the meaning of continuity between the current creation and the new creation than about the effect of sin. While emphasizing the sinful apostasy of humanity and thus naming discontinuity, he reflects little on God's triumph over evil and for the concern of the work of God's hands, which maintain continuity. The emphasis Rahner and Moltmann place in their theological views on the triumph of Christ over the powers of evil in their ST challenges Beale's BT not to speak too pessimistically about the continuity between this creation and the new creation. Because of too much emphasis on discontinuity, Beale's theology seems to assume that the Redeemer ultimately failed to save his entire creation. The overemphasis on discontinuity implies that the powers of evil have managed to let creation go to waste. The power of death has nevertheless taken hold of the first creation, and God can do nothing but start again with a new creation.

Moltmann and Rahner, on the other hand, underline in their ST that God's salvation is powerful enough to preserve and redeem creation. God is Creator and Redeemer and not only Creator. The purifying fire will judge evil, but this does not mean that God's creation will come to a definitive end. In union with Christ, the old creation dies to stand up as a new and glorified creation. As the crucifixion indicates the radicalism of sin and judgment, the resurrection indicates the radicalism of grace and glory. As the death of the Messiah testifies to the apostasy of this earth, the resurrection testifies to God's radical acceptance of and love for this creation. This element of the triumph of the work of redemption accomplished by Christ seems to be in the background in Beale's BT because in his speaking discontinuity predominates. In a critical comparison, the systematic-theological perspective of Rahner and Moltmann makes the lack of reflection on this visible in the biblical-theological perspective of Beale.

6.2.3 Frameworks of reference in speaking about the new creation

6.2.3.1 *Visual language and perspective on the new creation*

6.2.3.1.1 Caution and meeting

All three theologians call for caution in their eschatological designs to imagine the new heaven and earth in concrete terms. Such a representation can lead to speculation. The new heaven and new earth cannot be visually imagined and described, as is the case with a painting. According to Rahner, too much concretion is even harmful to eschatology because it threatens to capture the future. For Rahner, the future of creation remains primarily hidden to humans. To imagine it is as absurd as to suppose that a caterpillar can imagine what it is to be a butterfly (§3.3.1).

Moltmann is also reluctant to thematize biblical visions. Although he mentions several biblical images of the new creation, such as the feast, the marriage of the Lamb, and the new Jerusalem, he is careful not to visualize the new heaven and earth in concrete terms. A philosophical-ideal approach to biblical data mainly influences his reflection on this. According to him, a detailed and conceptual description of the hope for the new creation is unthinkable and unpronounceable. After all, the language of hope looks ahead to what has not yet been realized, what is possible and promised. The view of the continuity and discontinuity between this life and life in the future is thus limited. If we interpret the physical visions of the new creation too conceptually, we run the risk of only wanting to indicate the continuity between this creation and the new creation. God's great promises, however, do not correspond to the experiential reality. The language of hope opens the present to God's future and frees it from the rigid past. Otherwise, the new creation seems nothing more than an evolutionary extension of this old creation. A comparison of both theologians with Beale shows that he too is opposed to such an idea of progress in his BT. This aspect was already discussed in §6.2.1.

6.2.3.1.2 DANGER OF IMPOVERISHMENT

The other danger is that the lack of interaction with the biblical imagery impoverishes cosmic eschatology. Rahner acknowledges this and points out that eschatology, in his time, was strongly determined by the prevailing socio-political ideas. The eschatology thus provides an unclear view of the biblical testimony and seems instead to reflect the own social challenges of the moment. The philosophical speaking about the eschaton without any reference to the biblical images or the Christian testimony predominates in these publications. This is very different in the way in which in the past, for example, the early church father Irenaeus of Lyon wrote about the eschaton. According to Irenaeus, the new creation was characterized by the wine that Christ promised to drink again (Matt 26:29), by fields and houses that Christ promised to his followers (19:29), by the prosperity and fertility that YHWH promised to the righteous (Gen 27:28; Isa 26:19; 65:19–23; Ezek 28:25–26), and by peace among the animals (Isa 11:6–10; 65:25). Irenaeus takes all these images physically literally. They are paintings of what is to come. The church father rejects a symbolic interpretation of the imagery by referring to the traditional testimony.[95]

None of the three theologians will follow this interpretation of Irenaeus. Irenaeus' ideas are not enough for the "not yet" in the renewal that the coming of God brings with it. Even though Rahner and Moltmann seem to reject this use of imagery

---

95. Irenaeus of Lyon, *Adversus Haereses*, V.33–35.

in the ST as too literal and concrete, they acknowledge at the same time that there is also a danger of speechlessness herein. The boundaries are then so sharpened that it is impossible to speak concretely about the new creation. This can lead to a new performance: the new creation can only be visualized by the absence of the existing physical reality. In addition to the above call for caution, both systematics thus place a positive concern with the legitimate imagery of the apocalyptic in the ST (cf. §§3.2.4; 4.2.5). In his second hermeneutical thesis, Rahner states that eschatology must be anchored in the Bible (§3.2.1). The biblical images are theologically valuable because of what they say (*content*) and how they say it (*presentation*). From the analysis, we can conclude that Moltmann can confirm this choice. However, a passable path needs to be found between theological speechlessness and biblical representations of things. Eschatological statements are never myth- or imageless. Every thought is an image; there is no "understanding" without "proposals." Therefore, visual speech remains indispensable. Rahner mentions this explicitly, and Moltmann also calls for the language of hope not to be defined conceptually. We need images and metaphors of the eschaton, despite acknowledging its limitations. Rahner repeatedly argues that the biblical imagery should not be stripped of its "speech," as was done by Bultmann's far-reaching demythologization. Theologians should examine these images for their importance for eschatology. Such a schematization of the biblical visions of the new creation, however, is lacking in Rahner's systematic reflections.

Because Moltmann connects cosmological hope with protology, the reading of his works irrevocably reveals images of the new creation that recall the first creation. One could think here of terms such as Sabbath, *Shekhinah*, Eden, and God's walking in the garden. Also, in his ST, Moltmann ventures into a biblical-theological analysis of Revelation 21–22. He bases this on Richard Bauckham's BT and thus shows that speaking in imagery and speaking in concepts are not mutually exclusive. The vision in Revelation 21–22 bears witness to a world that is entirely by God's desire, but that cannot be described without imagery.[96] These kinds of images and metaphors from the experiential world, give us only a limited idea of the future world. This keeps the language of hope open for the future. BT can provide valuable elements for the ST in its interpretation of the biblical images because it can analyze the images in this text in depth from its field of expertise and to place them in the broader thematic context of the biblical storyline. In the following substantive comparison of Rahner, Moltmann, and Beale, about the new heaven and the new earth, this advantage of an interdisciplinary dialogue will be further discussed.

In Beale's NTBT, which concretely focuses on the new creation, there is no profound interaction with the diversity of visual language that the Bible uses in speaking about the new heaven and the new earth. Beale does investigate the central biblical texts about the new creation but does not discuss the material aspects of the new creation. The only image that occupies a central place in his publications is that of

96. Moltmann, *Kommen*, 338.

the temple (§5.8.1). For example, there is no biblical-theological reflection on the following images: the feast on the mountain of YHWH (Isa 25:6–12), life in the future city of Jerusalem (65:17–25), the fertile mountains (Joel 4:18), and the father house (John 14:1–4). In his publications, Beale refers to these images but lacks a profound interaction. From a comparison of Rahner's and Moltmann's designs with Beale's design, it can be concluded that both systematics can jointly point out to Beale that this lack in his design threatens to endanger the theological value of the biblical images. The imagery then merges into a "speech" that is separate from the biblical imagination. The interpreter's explanation replaces the image. This removes the image from its idea-moderate character and records it unambiguously and conceptually. According to Moltmann, this then removes the surprise effect from the image. In this respect, Beale runs the risk in his design of recognizing the provisional and open character of the interpretation of the image. The meaning seems to be enclosed and grasped in the explanation and is no longer open to the new that transcends the known.

From this, Rahner's and Moltmann's ST call for caution not to omit the biblical images in the descriptions of the biblical storyline. The various images deserve to be included here. In his research on the biblical-theological meaning of the temple, Beale refers to the meaning and value of the temple. As such, it stands as an image of the continuity and discontinuity between the present and the new creation. In his elaboration, he tends to ignore the physical elements of the temple image and to conceive it as purely symbolic. Because Beale either does not extensively discuss the biblical-theological meaning of other physical images of the new creation in the rest of his BT, he seems to suggest that on the material level, there is a discontinuity between the current creation and the new creation. In Beale's explanation, the images function only as symbolic descriptions of the new creation. According to him, we should certainly not take them physically literally as foresight for continuity between the current creation and the new creation. In this respect, Beale follows the general explanation of amillennialism, which mainly explains prophetic language symbolically.[97]

A comparison with Moltmann's systematic-theological speaking about this makes us aware that this way of interpreting does not suffice for the material continuity between the present and the new creation. Moltmann's ST can point out to Beale that there may be two hermeneutic facets associated with the explanation of the imagery. There is both the absence of the current negativity and the presence or memory of the current positivity. These two facets concern both the material and the immaterial. The material explanation should not be missing in this for the sake of the possible discontinuity between this and the new creation. If a biblical writer wants to emphasize this discontinuity between both creations, he will do so by using metaphorical contrast images, contrast histories, and contrast worlds. Moltmann sees an example of this in the description of the heavenly Jerusalem as an image of the new

---

97. Cf. Waltke, "Kingdom Promises," 272.

creation that is contrasted with earthly Babylon as an image of the present cases and transitory creation (Rev 18–21, cf. §6.3.2).

The symbolic explanation Beale gives in his BT of the biblical images has consequences for the explanation. A literal physical reading is excluded in advance by Beale. Biblical visions should be understood symbolically. From Rahner's systematic-theological reflection on "imagery," it can be concluded in comparison that this method, followed by Beale, leads to the conclusion that his BT pays little attention to the image itself. The image serves almost exclusively as an allusion or reminder of earlier prophecies. Only "speech" remains of the imagery, while "image" and "speech," according to Rahner, complement each other slightly in the Bible. While Rahner also assumes that the biblical images are not paintings of the hereafter and that they are not entirely literally physically fulfilled, he takes into account that the image still wants to express something of physical reality. He shows this in his reflection on the imagery of the trumpets that sound at the end of time (§3.3.4). It is possible to relate this also to Moltmann's theological approach because he also insists that the new creation is a fulfillment of that which God is already anticipating.

Therefore, in the exegesis, image and speech should not be mutually exclusive. The image remains an image that, in its full richness, refers to a reality that cannot be captured in words. For Rahner, the interpretation of the biblical imagery should be put high on the agenda of a BT that is connected to Christian eschatology. A description of the new creation should examine even more the biblical imagery based on continuity and discontinuity.

Beale shows in his biblical-theological reflection on the temple that discontinuity can also be described. For the ST, it could be enrichment if the BT would investigate the imagery more in this area. The whole of Christian theology is even involved. Whereas official theology fails to implement the visual language sufficiently in its eschatology, popular-theological designs often use this visual language too quickly and thoughtlessly for their representations. A closer examination of these images within the BT could be of great interest to the ST and is to be encouraged.

6.2.3.1.3 Methodical use of visual language

In the methodical handling of biblical imagery, both disciplines could also enrich each other. Because both Beale and Rahner choose to put form and content on an equal footing in their designs, there is a basis for comparison. Both theologians realize that speaking in metaphors is what enriches the theological speaking about the new creation because an image transcends a story in abstract words. The form influences the content, both cognitively and emotionally.[98] In the explanation of the metaphor, the form of the image, and the content of the image should correspond. In the case of

---

98. Rahner, "Prinzipien," 410. Cf. Rahner, "Eschatologie: Theologisch," 1097; Beale, *Revelation*, 55, 68.

a comprehensive agreement, the form is essentially the same as the content, while in the case of a small agreement; only certain elements are derived from the form, which should then reinforce a specific aspect of the content. With openness to interdisciplinary dialogue, Beale could present to Rahner his methodology for interpreting the biblical-theological images.

Beale offers the method to work from the following four divisions in the interpretation of the biblical symbolism and imagery: (1) the description of the vision, (2) the references present in it, (3) the present symbolism in the vision, and (4) the meaning of the vision. For example, the vision of the beast in Revelation 13 refers to one or more persons in history (point 2). The symbolism of the beast indicates a power that resists God and his people in a brutal and demonic way and reminds of the beasts from the visions of the OT (point 3). The meaning of the vision can then be derived from this form (point 4).[99] With this method, the different images in the Bible can be dissected.

Also, Rahner and Beale warn that the images of the visions should not be fused into one image. The images should enrich each other in order to make the different perspectives of reality visible.[100] Beale's BT could be a possible complement for Rahner. His introduction to the explanation of symbols and imagery provides a methodology for dealing with this variation. First, each image should be individually examined intertextually in its biblical context. This research is primarily the responsibility of BT. Where the context in question does not provide clarity, Beale pleads to examine earlier texts intertextually based on parallels or allusions that the image knows. In concrete terms, Beale thinks of the biblical texts, early Jewish and early Christian literature. Many images thus return several times in the history of salvation. These images are part of the confession because of the continuity that lies between past, present, and future.[101] This allows Beale's BT to provide building blocks to the ST of Rahner and Moltmann to allow the biblical imagery to be addressed more in their research and to enrich theologically responsible speaking about the new heaven and the new earth.

6.2.3.2 Anthropology and the cosmos

6.2.3.2.1 Plea for the cosmos

According to Rahner and Moltmann, the belief in God as Creator cannot be reconciled with a hope of an *annihilatio mundi*. Humans are never redeemed *from* creation. Creation is always redeemed *with* humans. This connection is at the forefront of both systematics in their eschatological reflections. This deserves appreciation because

---

99. Beale, *Revelation*, 52–54, 67.

100. Beale, *Revelation*, 57, 66; Rahner, "Prinzipien," 416–17. Cf. Rahner, "Prinzipien," 408, 419, 423–24.

101. Beale, *Revelation*, 55–56.

Western theology in the past mainly emphasized God's way with humanity. The anthropocentrism, strongly inspired by the philosophy of the Renaissance or Enlightenment, ensured that humans saw themselves as autonomous persons when dealing with creation (*human supremacism*). Humanity was created in God's image to rule over nature as the crown of creation. Then humans fell into sin and were redeemed by God *from* this evil and fallen world. This anthropocentrism led to little or no mention of God's relationship with the cosmos in Christian doctrine. Creation was only a temporary set in which the history of God and humanity could take place. This partly explains why ST focused mainly on individual eschatology and shows little interest in cosmic or universal eschatology (§1.3). Moltmann reacts to this attitude and therefore advocates a new cosmological theocentrism, in which humans and nature are part of the same created order and are directed towards God.[102] Rahner and Beale, however, opt for Judeo-Christian anthropocentrism. The awareness of this choice led both Moltmann and Rahner to argue in their works that individual eschatology should be inextricably linked to cosmic eschatology.

6.2.3.2.2 Importance of the cosmos in Genesis 1–2

In §1.4, we already pointed out that all three theologians pay attention to the cosmos. In his BT, Beale explicitly connects the new creation with the kingdom of God and eschatology with protology. The future of this creation is thus locked up in creation from the beginning. God gives this creation a future in which humanity may fulfill the commission of Genesis 1:28. The importance of this for the interdisciplinary dialogue between ST and BT was already evident in the hermeneutical reflection on protology and eschatology (§6.2.2). For Beale, the garden of Eden is the first temple and prototype of the new creation, which is also a temple of God. Adam was placed in this "Temple Garden" and had the responsibility with his wife to expand this sacred space all over the earth by faithfully fulfilling God's commandment in Genesis 1:28. If they and their descendants obeyed this, all creation would become one holy space in which God could dwell.

Despite his biblical-theological emphasis on the importance of the protology and the attention for the whole cosmos, it is striking that Beale's biblical-theological discussion of Genesis 2 mainly starts from an anthropocentric world view strongly inspired by the philosophy of Enlightenment, which takes little or no account of creation as a whole. That tendency is less present in Rahner's theology. Although he sees humanity as the highest "goal" in this creation and pleads for a transcendental anthropocentric theology (§3.4.1.1), he emphasizes in his eschatology that all creation shares in salvation. In comparison with Moltmann's design, the critical note can be placed in the performance of Beale that Genesis 2 was often misused to predatorily subjugate the earth. This caused humanity to place itself too much at the center of the universe

---

102. Moltmann, *Gott in der Schöpfung*, 149.

and forgot that they were part of a greater whole: the creation, the work of God's hands that the Almighty does not want to abandon.[103]

A comparison with Moltmann's design makes Beale (and indirectly also Rahner) aware that already in Genesis 2, it becomes clear that humans are created for the sake of the earth. Because before it is described in Genesis that God made Adam, the writer notes in Genesis 2:5 that there was not yet a human to work the earth.[104] From the great attention Beale pays to the protology of Genesis 1–2 in his publications, it is remarkable that he lacks a discussion of this observation at all. Beale does not look at God's plan with the universe as a whole. Because he takes little account in his BT of the ecological perspective in Genesis 1–2, he ignores the peace rule for all creation in this text. A comparison of this representation of the matter with Rahner's and Moltmann's ST confronts the BT of Beale positively with an eschatological paradigm that strongly argues to realize in an eschatological speech that not only humanity but the whole of creation is redeemed. In this way Moltmann draws the readers' attention to the fact that in Genesis 1 humanity receives the same blessing as animals: "Be fruitful and multiply" (Gen 1:22, 28): "So human beings have in common with animals their living souls, their living space, their food, and the blessing of fertility."[105]

Beale does not discuss this ecological connection between humans and animals further. It is not expressed when either he discusses the prophetic images in Isaiah 11:6–9 and 65:25. Although Beale first relates these texts to the blessing between humans and animals (§5.6.2), he later chooses to symbolically refer to this peace between humans and animals as peace between humans (§5.8.3.3).

On the other hand, Moltmann sees in these descriptions a poetic prelude to the ecological peace that will ultimately reign in all creation. In Christ God reconciles man with nature, as the biblical references to the Sabbath for the animals (Exod 20:10), the Sabbath Year for the land (Lev 25:1–7), and Christ's abode with the animals (Mark 1:13) for Moltmann seem to clarify.[106] With Beale, this cosmic element is missing in its biblical-theological elaboration of salvation and all attention is paid to "the cosmic expansion of temples through the rule of priest-kings in the image of the deity."[107] Only casually does he mention Christ's stay with the animals, but then he does not return to it (cf. §5.8.3.3).

---

103. Moltmann, *Gott in der Schöpfung*, 43–44.

104. Moltmann, *Geschichte*, 177.

105. Moltmann, *Gott in der Schöpfung*, 195: "Mit den Tieren gemeinsam haben die Menschen also die lebendige Seele, den Lebensraum, die Nahrung und den Segen der Fruchtbarkeit." Cf. Moltmann, *Gott in der Schöpfung*, 284.

106. Moltmann, *Weg Jesu*, 332–36, 360; *Gott in der Schöpfung*, 230.

107. Beale, *Temple*, 87–93.

6.2.3.2.3 IMPORTANCE OF ECOLOGY

In the past, Moltmann already expressed similar criticism of Karl Barth's thinking. Barth only relates God's salvation to humanity. This gives the doctrine of creation an anthropocentric character that emerged from the Renaissance or Enlightenment philosophy in time. In contrast to Judeo-Christian anthropocentrism, which accentuates human responsibility for creation, the anthropocentrism of the Enlightenment chooses the vision that the non-human world was created solely for the sake of humanity.[108] Moltmann's same criticism also applies to Beale's theological design. Moltmann can partly be assisted in this by Rahner, who, in his eschatology, also demands great attention for creation as a whole, but elsewhere the anthropocentrism of Enlightenment philosophy seems to follow. The limited attention for the cosmos that Rahner and Moltmann often critically observe among others in their eschatological research shows that Beale in his BT pays attention to the way of God with humans, but takes little or no account of God's way with the rest of creation. Even though Beale strongly links salvation and the associated renewal with the new heaven and the new earth, creation is still too much of a backdrop in his BT. To what extent that decor shares in God's plan for salvation is not discussed with Beale. Rahner and Moltmann warn in their ST that this approach can lead to unconsciously embracing Gnosticism, which denies any hope for the material reality in creation. Therefore, a comparison between Rahner's and Moltmann's ST and Beale's BT makes us aware that the doctrine of soteriology is inextricably linked to the doctrine of eschatological creation, for whom Jesus Christ as the physically resurrected Messiah of the coming empire wants to be taken seriously. Christ is not only the center of humanity but the center of all creation. By him, the first creation is made, and he is also the Firstborn of the new creation, the Alpha, and Omega.

In the interest of this reflection, it is still striking that Beale mentions in his literature list of NTBT the article *Jesus and the Wild Animals (Mark 1:13): A Christological Image for an Ecological Age* by Richard Bauckham. In that article, Bauckham emphasizes that biblical theology should attach more importance to ecology, because:

> [E]schatology as the key concept[s] of biblical theology has at least tacitly endorsed the modern understanding of history as emancipation from nature.[109]

In light of this, the biblical hope sees a future for this creation. That future is connected with the revelation of God's kingdom. Therefore, a cosmic eschatology thinks responsibly about God's creation.

This can be confirmed by the fact that the new interest in ecology during the last decades also brings with it a renewed interest in thinking about the future of creation. According to Kurt Koch, the environmental crisis even forces theology to

---

108. Moltmann, *Geschichte*, 176–77.
109. Bauckham, "Jesus and the Wild Animals," 3.

take into account not only the attention of humans but also the attention for the rest of creation.[110] In our opinion, this should be an attention to the whole in which Christ is central, through which kingdom and king are inextricably linked. In the substantive comparison between the designs of Rahner and Moltmann and the design of Beale, the awareness of this difference in approach will be raised several times.

6.2.3.3 Christ as Firstborn of the New Creation

6.2.3.3.1 Christ, the climax of God's intervention

In their abstract reflections on the new creation, Rahner, Moltmann, and Beale together emphasize the Christian centric speaking. Christ is the hermeneutical principle of all eschatological statements. He is the high point of eschatological revelation. Together they find a basis in this. According to Moltmann and Beale, the risen Christ gives hope to this world. He is the Firstborn of the new creation, and the last Adam represents what the new creation has to offer. That future goes much further than what Adam could realize in primal history. We already saw this when comparing their talk about protology and eschatology (§6.2.2). The future goes far beyond prehistoric times and what is known today. Therefore, what we can say about future completion finds its solid foundation in Christ.

Rahner and Beale even conclude that speaking about the future is only possible from what Christ has already accomplished and given. Eschatological statements should be interpreted centrally from the perspective of Christ. What cannot be interpreted from a Christian-soteriological perspective is for Rahner, not true Christian eschatology, but divination and negative apocalyptic. We have already considered this in §6.2.1.

By comparing the three theologians, it becomes clear that Moltmann will not follow this wording of Rahner and Beale because his ideas expect too much from the past. However, the past and present are decaying. Only the future remains. The resurrection is a hopeful testimony that only the future can provide certainty. According to Moltmann, it bears witness to God's intervention and reveals to the world what the new world, which will soon become a reality, will contain. The resurrection of Christ is thus a fixed point of reference in speaking about the new creation with Rahner, Moltmann, and Beale. This shows that all three theologians emphasize that Christianity is inextricably linked to eschatology. Christ is the heart of world history. There is no eschatology without Christology and no Christology without eschatology (§§3.2.2; 4.2.1). Beale refers several times to Colossians 1, where Christ is described as the head of the body and the Firstborn of the new creation (§§5.5.3; 5.6.3).[111] Through Christ's work of salvation, the question arises as to the future in which God is all in all.

---

110. Koch, "Weltende," 166–165. Cf. Auer, *Umweltethik*.
111. Beale, *New Testament*, 6.

6.2.3.3.2 RESURRECTION AS A FRAME OF REFERENCE

The earlier analyses show how great importance that all three theologians attach to the resurrection. The resurrection of Christ is the beginning of the new creation. The resurrection of Christ testifies that decay and impermanence will come to an end through God's intervention in this creation. Rahner and Moltmann have repeatedly argued in their theological designs for the future to be seen in the same way as what has already happened in Christ. In his words, Beale's eschatology sometimes closely matches this. This is especially the case when it concerns the transformation of this creation in the new creation. Beale then points out that this transformation can be imagined from the example of Christ's death and resurrection. Just as Christ died and rose from the dead in a glorified body, this creation will die entirely and, at the same time, be wholly transformed into the new creation. Beale sees a substantiation of this thesis in the connection that the Bible makes several times between texts about the new creation and texts about the resurrection (e.g., Isa 65:16–17 in 2 Cor 5:14–17 and Col 1:15–18; further: Rom 8:18–23).[112] This will be repeated more than once in the substantive comparison (cf. especially §6.3.1). The resurrection of Christ is thus related to the resurrection of all creation.

6.2.3.3.3 CHRIST'S SERVICE AS A FRAME OF REFERENCE

Another frame of reference that emerges in the individual analyses of the three theologians is the teaching of Christ and the healings he performed. Beale explicitly points out that the many miracles and signs that Jesus did during his service on earth already show a glimpse of the new heaven and new earth (§5.5.2). This is also the idea we find in Moltmann: "Healings in the context of faith are signs of new creation and the rebirth of life."[113]

In Rahner's works, this is not explicitly mentioned. For the others, Jesus' healings are a limited testimony of the new heaven and earth where there will no longer be pain and sorrow. Of course, the theologians mentioned are aware that this is a limited testimony. Jesus healed the sick only temporarily in this transitory world. From this testimony of Christ, however, hope looks forward to the coming of God's imperishable world in which life overcomes, and death is a thing of the past. The BT from Beale and the ST from Rahner and Moltmann stand side by side in this respect and can enrich each other with new insights. Rahner and Moltmann can point to the relevant core elements in Christology, which are of essential importance for eschatology and Beale can investigate these relations from the biblical storyline biblically-theologically and indicate the accentuations which the biblical writers place in them. This agreement

---

112. Beale, *Revelation*, 1040.

113. Moltmann, *Geist des Lebens*, 202: "Heilungen sind im Kontext des Glaubens Zeichen der Neuschöpfung und der Wiedergeburt des Lebens." Cf. Moltmann, *Kommen*, 100; *Weg Jesu*, 124–32.

6.3 COMPARISON OF CONTENTS

After the hermeneutical comparison between Rahner, Moltmann, and Beale, the substantive comparison about theological approaches of the new heaven and earth deserves attention. The methical choices herein have already been described in §6.1.3. In this substantive comparison, we will refer several times to the above-mentioned results from the hermeneutical equation in order to follow the thought patterns of the three theologians more accurately. This comparison aims to re-examine to what extent an interdisciplinary comparison about the new heaven and the new earth can be of significance for a theological conversation on this subject.

6.3.1 Resurrection and matter

Rahner, Moltmann, and Beale underline the meaning of cosmic renewal or resurrection. The analyses of their theological designs show clearly how each of them places its accents. It is also apparent in which way they correspond with each other. A remarkable similarity is that all three theologians choose to see the resurrection of Christ as a hermeneutic starting point for their further speaking about the resurrection.

Furthermore, the analysis shows that Beale, in his reflection on the resurrection and cosmic renewal, pays particular attention to the order that is used in Romans 8 about the resurrection. Beale also mentions the destruction of the cosmos as he sees it announced in 2 Peter 3. Rahner and Moltmann also refer to both biblical texts in the same context. Another core text is 1 Corinthians 15. This chapter is discussed by all three theologians on the question of the continuity and discontinuity of the resurrection body. This makes it easy to compare Rahner, Moltmann, and Beale on the core theme of resurrection and matter.

This chapter first discusses the specific starting points that all three theologians characterize in their talk about the resurrection and the physical renewal (§6.3.1.1). Further, the importance they attach to the total renewal of creation (both material and immaterial) requires attention in this chapter (§6.3.1.2). Moreover, finally, we look into the difference in speaking about the continuity and discontinuity of cosmic renewal (§6.3.1.3). The aim is to examine how diversity in the methodology used by these theologians enriches the perspective on the new heaven and new earth.

6.3.1.1 Starting points for speaking about the resurrection

6.3.1.1.1 CHRIST'S RESURRECTION AS A STARTING POINT

For all three theologians, the resurrection of Christ is the hermeneutical starting point for their further reflection on the universal resurrection. His resurrection from the dead gives hope to this creation and is a paradigm for cosmic renewal. Christ is the Firstborn of the new creation. As a result, his resurrection is a model of how the whole creation will resurrect

In support of this paradigm, Moltmann repeatedly refers to Philippians 3:21. This text declares that our humiliated body will be conformed to Christ's glorified body (§4.5.3). What can be said about this text from a biblical-theological perspective?

Beale quotes Philippians 3:21 six times in his NTBT. Four times this happens about sin and the lack of God's image. The text thus clarifies that it becomes possible through Christ to be confirmed as a human being to God's image.[114] There is a restoration of God's image in man following the example of Christ, the last Adam. In two other places, Beale does not go into the explanation of Philippians 3:21.[115] He discusses this text in more detail in his *We Become what we Worship*. Here too, it is emphasized that this text clarifies first the restoration of God's image in humans.[116] The question of the relationship between Christ's resurrection and the resurrection of all things is only touched upon in passing. Beale only refers to the tension between continuity and discontinuity in speaking about the new heaven and the new earth. On the one hand, he declares that the cosmos is being destroyed (discontinuity), and on the other hand, he insists that it is being renovated (continuity). Furthermore, he states, from the viewpoint of discontinuity, that in the eschaton, the old perishable body makes way for a new imperishable body. The resurrection is thus the new radical beginning that replaces the past. Further analysis of the parallel that Philippians 3 makes between Christ's new body and our resurrection body lacks in Beale. In light of the fact that in his NTBT, he emphasizes the resurrection and focuses on the letters of Paul, the latter is striking. The main reason for this will be that Beale focuses primarily on the already present spiritual renewal so that the physical renewal receives less attention. Rahner and Moltmann, on the other hand, consciously emphasize the physical renewal in their ST as a reaction to an existentialist theology that pays little attention to this aspect.

What is also striking is that the choice to see Christ's resurrection as a paradigm for the resurrection of all things lacks an analysis of the resurrection stories in the gospels by all three theologians. This is particularly remarkable with Beale. While he considers the resurrection as a core theme and places it at the forefront of his NTBT, he does not reflect separately on the continuity and discontinuity of Christ's

---

114. Beale, *New Testament*, 465n65, 460, 880n20, 916.
115. Beale, *New Testament*, 284, 460.
116. Beale, *We Become*, 221, 282, 290–91.

resurrection body according to the gospels. His biblical-theological effect of the resurrection is mainly limited to the letters of Paul. A biblical-theological reflection on the resurrection body of Christ completely lacks in Beale. Such a reflection is only found, albeit to a limited extent, in Moltmann's systematic-theological perspective (§4.5.3). According to my ideas, a biblical-theological analysis of the stories of the resurrection in the gospels could more clearly demonstrate the significance and added value of the hermeneutical choice for Christ's resurrection as a starting point for speaking about the future resurrection of all creation.

6.3.1.1.2 THE SPIRITUAL AND PHYSICAL RESURRECTION

Beale states in his BT that the believer is already a new creation through the death and rise of the Messiah. Renewal has already begun spiritually and will soon be supplemented by physical renewal. Moltmann points out that this talk of an *already realized and completed* "spiritual resurrection" and an *outstanding* "physical resurrection" was mainly put forward by church fathers such as Augustine.[117] This emphasis on the already realized "spiritual resurrection" may even create the impression that the promise of the future resurrection is spiritualized or allegorically explained.

Beale acknowledges this tension in his BT. He solves this by saying that the biblical prophets speak of one resurrection each time and that Jesus reveals these two phases for the first time: "Truly, truly, I say to you, an hour is coming and is nowhere when the dead will hear the voice of the Son of God, and those who hear will live" (John 5:25; §5.3.3). Moltmann also realizes that this biblical text sees eternal life as a new reality of faith and contrasts it with the death of the perishable world.[118] However, in his ST, this element is hardly mentioned, and the emphasis is on *advent* and the unity of man and nature. The consequence of this is already apparent in the comparison of their hermeneutic choices (§6.2.1).

A comparison between the resurrection in Beale's, Rahner's and Moltmann's theological perspective shows that Beale rejects any eschatology that ignores the beginning of the fulfillment of God's promises in the present and considers the "last days" entirely in the status of "not yet" and mere anticipation. Christ's resurrection marks the beginning of the renewal that is already present, that is, the "spiritual resurrection" that is connected with the new life of the already begun "last days." As a result of this methodical choice, the physical resurrection—which is the main focus in Rahner's and Moltmann's theology—is only secondary in Beale's theology. From Beale's design, Moltmann and Rahner can thus be criticized for the fact that in their ST, the present reality of renewal comes under pressure from God's Spirit. Especially

---

117. Augustine, *City of God*, XX.6.2; "Homilies on John," XIX.15. Cf. Moltmann, *Kommen*, 15; Greshake and Kremer, *Resurrectio Mortuorum*, 214.

118. Moltmann, *Kommen*, 101.

in Rahner's ST, the relation with pneumatology is missing in eschatology.[119] As mentioned in the hermeneutical analysis, this is because Moltmann and Rahner react in their ST mainly to an existential interpretation of the biblical hope that has gone too far (§6.2.1).

6.3.1.1.3 ORDER IN THE RESURRECTION

Moltmann and Beale both indicate that in Romans 8, an order in the resurrection becomes visible: from Christ as Firstborn, it goes to the Christian and then to the whole creation. This explains, according to them, why creation looks forward to the revelation of the sons of God (v. 19; §§4.7.4; 5.5.3).

Beale states that renewal begins with humanity for good reason because it is the crown on creation. God created humanity to rule over his creation as viceroy (Gen 1:28). In his biblical-theological discussion on the resurrection in Romans 8, this anthropocentric view emerges. However, it is not limited to that but forms a common thread in Beale's BT. Moltmann contrasts this anthropocentrism with a geo-centrism or cosmological theocentrism, which attaches as much value to nature as to humanity. According to him, this geo-centrism can already be deduced from the beginning of Genesis. Humankind (אָדָם) was formed from the earth in Genesis 2 (אֲדָמָה) and was connected to the earth from the beginning (v. 5, 7). Therefore, Moltmann considers speaking of humanity as the "crown of creation" unbiblical. Instead, God created the world for his glory and placed the Sabbath as the crowning glory of his creation.[120] The term "crown" does not occur in the Bible concerning humans. In Moltmann's view, Beale's anthropocentric approach in his BT is a product of developments in church history rather than the responsible exegesis of the Bible. Creation is not there for the sake of humanity, but it is there *together with* humans, for the sake of God. Although humanity occupies a unique position as the bearer of God's image, humans are not elevated above creation (cf. §6.2.3.2).[121] It remains biblically irresponsible for Moltmann in this way to disconnect the future of man from the future of creation.

In Beale's BT, there is no discussion of Genesis 2 regarding the relationship between humans and the earth. It can also be deduced from Romans 8 that the future glorification of humanity goes hand in hand with the future glorification of creation.[122] The whole cosmos looks forward to God's innovative actions. According to Moltmann, humanity deserves no higher place than nature. It is only a part of the whole cosmos that is renewed by God. The only distinction Moltmann wants to recognize in Romans 8 is that the Christian can already place himself under God's rule

---

119. Cf. Edwards, "Resurrection," 380.

120. Moltmann, *Kommen*, 15–16; *Gott in der Schöpfung*, 45–47, 149–150, 195. Moltmann also mentions Christ as the crown of creation: Moltmann, *Trinität*, 123.

121. Moltmann, *Gott in der Schöpfung*, 44–45, 149, 195, 304. Cf. Moltmann, *Sein Name*, 38–39.

122. Moltmann, *Geschichte*, 189.

in this present creation. The Christian church is thus anticipation of the new heaven and new earth (§4.7.4). From Moltmann's systematic-theological design, it is possible to point out that, in the light of Romans 8:19, Beale should explain the key text of his BT, Genesis 1:28, not as "subdue the earth," but as "liberate creation in relationship with it."[123] The question of how this idea can be brought in connection with Rahner's theology is interesting. Rahner also criticizes anthropocentrism.

Nevertheless, there is a parallel in his ST with the choice of Beale mentioned above. According to Rahner, humans can primarily be typified as "spirit," matter can be described as "frozen spirit" (*gefrorener Geist*), and the spirit is elevated above matter. Rahner states that matter completes itself simultaneously with the mind, and it is not allowed to distinguish between them. Spirit and matter belong inextricably together. Without matter, there can be no completion of the mind (§3.4.2).

A comparison between Rahner's and Beale's theological perspective shows the strong separation Beale makes between a spiritual and material resurrection. However, Beale's references to the miracles which Jesus did on earth already imply that the restoration of creation does not take place in two neatly distinguished dualistic phases (first a spiritual and then a physical phase), but that both phases form a whole and go together. The comparison can thus help to clarify what Beale intends to say about this.

6.3.1.2 Total renewal of creation

6.3.1.2.1 UNITY BETWEEN CREATION AND SALVATION

A comparison from Moltmann's and Rahner's eschatological designs asks the critical question of Beale's design whether the Bible separates the physical and non-physical as much as he does in his BT. And also, whether the Bible has such a strict separation between "spiritual resurrection" and "physical resurrection." There is a danger that the mind will determine matter and Christian thinking will degenerate into dualistic (neo)Platonism or Gnosticism, neither of which attach any value to matter. In their rejection of Gnosticism, Moltmann and Rahner emphasize that God is both Creator and Redeemer. God should not be separated into a *proteros theos*, who created everything at the beginning, and a *deuteros theos*, who in the end is not concerned with what remains and who is concerned only with the salvation of needy souls.[124] There is a unity between creation and salvation and thus attention to the restoration and glorification of all good things God created. All three theologians testify that God cares for creation and continues his creative work after Genesis 1–2. This aspect should not be missing in Beale's BT either. That the Bible begins with the creation in Genesis and not with the redemption in Exodus is of great significance to understand the biblical-theological story that unfolds in the Bible.

---

123. Moltmann, "Schöpfung," 136.
124. Moltmann, *Kommen*, 285.

Rahner and Moltmann thus emphasize in their rejection of Gnosticism that God does not let his creation go to waste, but comes to his goal with the cosmos. So, Christian eschatology needs universal hope that encompasses the whole earth. The Bible does not speak of salvation *from* the physical, but of salvation *of* the physical (§§3.4.1; 4.2.4). However, a further biblical-theological underpinning of this thesis lacks in their works. It is present in Beale's design. Beale points out from texts like Isaiah 43 and Revelation 4–5 that there is a deep relationship between God the Creator and God the Redeemer. For example, in Isaiah 43 different words are used that apply to both God's creation and God's salvation. These include terms such as "create" (אָרָב), "form" (רַצִי), and "make" (הָשָׁע, v. 7). For Beale, this makes it clear that Isaiah 43 is the background for 2 Corinthians 5:17 because the "new creation" is related to the "atonement." The salvation that God offers this cosmos is the continuation of God's creation in a new way (§5.6.4).

6.3.1.2.2 Renewal of all humanity

Although Beale mentions the union of creation and salvation, he emphasizes it much less than Rahner and Moltmann. The fundamental reason for this emphasis among both systematics is that in their field, there is no talk of material innovation, and they consciously react to it. Where this does not happen, it can lead to the systematic theologian running the risk of unconsciously opening up her or his reflections to gnostic system thinking. Beale does not pay special attention to this danger. Although he is aware of the former gnostic influences in church history, he only briefly relates this movement(s) to the question of the resurrection of the physical.[125] On the other hand, he mentions several times that biblical hope implies the resurrection of all humans. Beale describes this whole human being as consisting of mind, soul, and body. The soul also has to go through the resurrection and be renewed. Rahner and Moltmann agree with this. Death touches the whole human being as absolute unity in his person, self-awareness, and freedom. Only through Christ's work of salvation is it possible to overcome death and receive the resurrection of life.[126]

In their ST, both systematic theologians emphasize that the human being consists of a body and a soul that can be distinguished, but that cannot be separated from each other. There is duality, but not dualism or polarity. According to Rahner and Moltmann, the Bible is more about a holistic renewal that encompasses spirit, soul, and body, and that finds its completion in the eschaton. For Rahner, the connection is so secure "that every statement about the body (as the reality of humanity) implies a statement about the soul and vice versa."[127] After death, the soul will not become

---

125. Beale and Gladd, *Hidden*, 257. See further references to gnostic in: Beale, *New Testament*, 338; *Revelation*, 266, 297, 1154.

126. §5.5.3—§3.3.2; 3.4.3; 4.2.4; 4.5.2.

127. Rahner, "Prinzipien," 422: "daß jede Aussage über den Leib (als Wirklichkeit des Menschen)

detached from the cosmos but remains fully connected to this creation. God's work of salvation does not separate the immaterial from the material. According to this ST, humanity remains inextricably linked to the cosmos and will soon stand before God with all the relationships it has in this creation. Body and soul cannot be seen in isolation. The dead will rise with the soul and body to account for their entire lives. The resurrection includes both the material and the immaterial. The one and all human is raised, not just a part of it, as Gnosticism claimed. Moltmann and Rahner explicitly oppose this gnostic idea, which probably also was the reason for writing 1 Corinthians 15 (§§3.4; 4.2.4; 4.5). This emphasis makes us aware of the importance that a biblical-theological reflection on the resurrection of the physical may have in Christian theology. This awareness is currently lacking in Beale's design.

From the emphasis on the unity of the whole human being, Moltmann also resists the idea of an immortal soul. Thinking about the immortal soul celebrates death as a liberator, while biblical speaking about the resurrection sees death as an enemy and does not base itself on an inherent immortal component of being human, but on the merciful reality of God's fidelity (§4.5). In this respect, Moltmann follows Tertullian's criticism of the Hellenistic soul-body dualism. With this, he criticizes those who accepted (neo)Platonism early on and replaced the expectation of the physical resurrection with the idea of an immortal soul. According to Tertullian, this dualism edited that some of his contemporaries began to teach a half resurrection, namely that of the soul alone. Moltmann rejects this, among other things concerning Christ's resurrection. Christian theology must not reduce salvation to the soul. The body also plays a role in the eschaton. Where the resurrection of the physical is lacking, the fundamental biblical truth of the "resurrection of the dead" is ignored in the doctrine of faith.[128] The talk about death as "last enemy" in 1 Corinthian 15:26 is, according to Moltmann, in line with this. Beale also refers in his BT to this biblical text to substantiate that death is the ultimate enemy of humankind (§5.5.3.2). Although he does not explicitly address the question of the immortality of the soul in his design, he concludes from texts such as 1 Corinthians 15:47–50 that Adam's body was perishable from the beginning and could not inherit the realm of God. Adam's body was created "from the dust" and could only receive imperishableness and eternity through the intervention of God.[129] This implies that for Beale humans are mortal from the beginning and that Beale probably rejects the thought of an "immortal soul" as unbiblical. Although he does use the term "souls" (e.g., Rev 6:9), he does not speak of an "immortal soul" anywhere.[130] Consistently he speaks of a resurrection from the dead. Whether or not he consciously avoids the term is not clear from his work.

eine Aussage über die Seele impliziert und umgekehrt."

128. Tertullian, *Carnis Resurrectione*, 34. Cf. *Adversus Marcionem*, 5.10; Irenaeus of Lyon, *Adversus Haereses*, I.24.5; I.27.3; V.2.2; V.3–4.

129. Beale, *New Testament*, 41, 44–45, 439–40, 583, 919.

130. Beale, *New Testament*, 349; *Revelation*, 390.

Seen from Rahner's theological viewpoint, this rejection of the "immortal soul" can be nuanced. According to Rahner, talking about the immortality of the soul is about the same thing as talking about the resurrection of the body (§3.4.2). Moltmann's vision that the immortality of the soul is an unbiblical thought sounds exaggerated. It is remarkable here that Rahner, for his criticism of the lack of reflection on the resurrection of the physical, also refers to *De Carnis Resurrectione* of Tertullian, which is precisely intended to confirm the belief in the physical resurrection (§3.4.3). Rahner mentions the church father Tertullian as a foundation that, after death, the mind remains connected with the matter. However, there is no further biblical-historical reflection on the difference between speaking of "immortality of the soul" and "resurrection of the body." It should be mentioned that Rahner, in his works, uses the term "spirit" rather than "soul," and emphasizes that death encompasses the whole person. In his works, neither does Beale pay attention to the question of the immortality of the soul. Even though the current reflection on the relationship between soul, mind, and body often takes place outside the boundaries of his field of study, we have to acknowledge that these terms are used several times in the Bible. Therefore, a further reflection on the subject is also within the boundaries of BT.

Moltmann further highlights the contrast between life and death in his choice of the expression "resurrection of life." In this, he differs again from Rahner, who sees death from the beginning of humanity as the culmination of completion (§§3.4.3; 4.5.2). Rahner's vision of death as a positive thing is based on the attitude of the godfearing martyrs, who courageously chose death. He distinguishes between death as a passive natural given, caused by negative sin, and death as a personal act, for which the martyr courageously chooses.[131]

In this reflection, Rahner remains the only one of the three who seems to see something positive in death. In his talk about death, Beale joins Moltmann. In his BT, death is the enemy of life, which is overcome by the resurrection (cf. Rev 21:4; 22:3). Death is related to the curse that came into creation through the disobedience of the first man. Nowhere does Beale mention death as a high point of completion. He refers instead to 1 Corinthians 15:26, where death is the ultimate enemy. How Rahner reacts to this text remains unclear in his works.

From Beale's biblical-theological design, the terminology in speaking about the resurrection body can be strengthened in the case of Rahner and Moltmann, from the realization that the expressions "resurrection of the flesh" and "resurrection of the body," which they often use, do not occur anywhere in the NT as such. They are neologisms from the patristic era.[132] By contrast, the NT speaks of the resurrection *of*

---

131. Rahner, *Zur Theologie des Todes*, 73–106.

132. The "resurrection of the flesh" can be found at: Justin Martyr, *Dialogus cum Tryphone Judaeo*, 80.5; Irenaeus of Lyon, *Adversus Haereses*, 1.22.1; 3.16.6; 4.5; 5.2.2; 9.1, 3; 12.1, 4; 13.3, 5; 14.1; 31.2; 33.1; Augustine, *City of God*, 13.23. See on the other hand: Pseudo-Athenagoras, *De Resurrectione Mortuorum*, 25.3.

or *from* the dead (Matt 22:31; Luke 20:35; Acts 4:2; 17:32; 1 Cor 15:12–13; Heb 6:2; etc.). Beale himself mainly uses the term "resurrection of the body."[133] This emphasizes the radical new of the resurrected body. Moltmann and Rahner recognize this aspect of the radically new. This is most evident in Moltmann's eschatology because of its constant emphasis on *adventus*.

6.3.1.2.3 The importance of physical

In their ST, Rahner and Moltmann emphasize the all-encompassing physical resurrection. The incarnated and risen Christ cannot be separated from matter. In a Christian confession, matter cannot be left behind as surplus in future salvation, nor can it disappear into an indefinable black hole. Christian doctrine has an apotheosis of matter. Like systematic theologians, Moltmann and Rahner are aware that this danger of spiritualization has created challenges throughout church history. This problem already occurred in the New Testament era (cf. 1 Cor 15:12; Col 1:22; 2 Tim 2:18). Moltmann points out that sometime later, Irenaeus of Lyon would also oppose gnostic interpretations of his time from the apostolic proclamation.[134] According to Moltmann and Rahner, the lack of further reflection on the renewal of matter meant that theology paid little attention to the new heaven and earth. Where the church ignored the hope of the resurrection of the physical, only hope remained for souls in an immaterial afterlife. Therefore, in their ST, they oppose a purely non-physical view of the future and emphasize the hope of the future resurrection of the body.

A comparison of Rahner's and Moltmann's ST with Beale's BT shows how different the accents are. Although Beale affirms the physical resurrection, the renewal of the material is in the background in his works. One of the few times he elaborates on this is in his talk about the healings and miracles Jesus did during his service on earth. He notes that these show the physical recovery that the new heaven and the new earth bring with them (§5.5.2). We also come across the same thought in Rahner's theology. Where the kingdom of God is proclaimed, God's plan manifests itself with this creation (§3.2). However, the fact that Beale pays little further attention to material renewal is a shortcoming that is all the more remarkable, because God's plan with the physical is also locked up in the creation story placed centrally by Beale (§5.3). For example, when Beale exegetically discusses biblical parts such as Isaiah 65, Romans 8, and Revelation 21–22, the real question of the renewal of the physical is hardly addressed. Anyone who wants to examine Beale's thinking about this in more detail is forced to look for information that occurs casually in his BT.

The historical-systematic background that Rahner and Moltmann sketch in their ST is a possible contribution that could lead to a biblical-theological design of the new

---

133. E.g., Beale, *New Testament*, 121, 159, 227, 230, 252, 580, 848–49, 903, 911, 919, 939.

134. Moltmann, *Kommen*, 176–78. Cf. Irenaeus of Lyon, *Adversus Haereses*, V.1–15; 2.2; 9.4; 32.1–2; 34–35; Daley et al., *Eschatologie*, 108.

heaven and the new earth, as Beale sketches it, emphasizing the biblical hope of physical resurrection. The core texts on the physical resurrection (Acts 17:32; Heb 6:1–3) cited by Rahner and Moltmann could play an essential role in this. In Beale's draft, Acts 17:32 only occurs casually twice in his NTBT and a reference to the physical resurrection in Hebrews 6:1–3 is completely missing. Also, in his further BT, the explicit importance of the physical resurrection in the Bible does not appear anywhere, as it does in Rahner's and Moltmann's designs. This leads us to the conclusion that Beale's BT can be challenged in this area by Rahner's and Moltmann's ST, in order to underline the importance of the apostolic proclamation on this point in the light of the early Christian problems in this respect.

6.3.1.2.4 Continuity and discontinuity

Questioning of the tension between the discontinuity and continuity of the resurrection body, Beale can refer both systematics to the extensive testimony about this in 1 Corinthians 15. The first eleven verses of this chapter focus on the salvific fact of Christ's resurrection. This event is the center of the gospel and offers a parallel with the future resurrection that awaits Christians. We have already seen that Rahner, Moltmann, and Beale, in their eschatological thinking, are in line with this (§6.3.1.1.1). From 1 Corinthians 15:12 onwards, the author then clarifies the nature of the resurrection and removes any misconceptions about it. He uses the illustration of a seed of grain being sown and the grain being harvested to indicate difference and agreement between the present perishable body and the future resurrection body (1 Cor 15:35–38). This illustration shows, according to Beale, that the resurrection is not a restoration. Rahner also refers to 1 Corinthians 15:35–36, where the apostle avoids identifying the resurrection body with the present body and also avoids to dissolve the relationship between the two.[135] The grain does not become a new entity. It is a transformation from the grain to the grain, in which the germ of the grain is preserved and the shape changes. Therefore Paul calls the present ephemeral body a "natural body" (σῶμα ψυχικόν) and the resurrection body a "spiritual body" (σῶμα πνευματικόν; 1 Cor 15:44). Despite the continuity of the word "body," the different adjectives indicate a radical difference between the two bodies and mark the distance and discontinuity between them very clearly. The same is evident in the statement that "flesh and blood cannot inherit the kingdom of God" (v. 50). Beale's biblical-theological perspective supports this idea as he reflects on the resurrection body from Paul's analogy of the seed and the grain. This clarifies that the shape of the old body perishes.[136] As a result, there is continuity in a radical discontinuity. The body that stands up is thus connected to the dead body and at the same time, not equal to the old body. Continuity and discontinuity must remain in a tense relationship. How Rahner deals with this

135. Rahner, "Immanente," 609.
136. Beale, *Revelation*, 1040.

field of tension in his ST contributes to the fact that Rahner's talk about the quality of the rebellious body remains unclear. He concludes from the discontinuity that finding a dead body in a grave does not necessarily exclude that there is a resurrection and he also argues from the continuity that one should not dismiss the belief in resurrection as a myth (§3.4.3). He also concludes from 1 Corinthians 15:35–36 that after death, humanity becomes *all-cosmic* and their bodies then know no more limitations. Beale or Moltmann do not follow this thinking.[137]

Therefore, the new does not mean a return of the old (§5.5.3.2). Moltmann and Rahner are closely linked to Beale's rejection of a renovation. They both state that the resurrection is not a resuscitation of a corpse. The new does not develop from the old without the intervention of God. It is not just the old in a new form. It is, indeed, a *new* creation. This is one of the reasons why Moltmann uses the category *novum* in speaking about the new heaven and the new earth and points out that the biblical writings apply the word "creates" (אָרָב) both to the original creation and the new creation. The future is thus analogous to the past (§§4.2.4; 3.4.3). Neither was the resurrection of Christ resuscitation or restoration of the crucified body. It was a glorified body that stood up. Analogous to this will be the future resurrection body. The molecules of the present body do not cause the continuity between this body and the resurrection body. Instead, the resurrection body is a glorified body that carries the contours of the perishable body. In this way, Rahner and Moltmann emphasize the discontinuity of the resurrection body. Beale, on the other hand, sees the resurrection mainly in terms of continuity. It is about the recovery of a body that has been dissolved. He sees the example of this in Christ's resurrection. As Christ's resurrection body was recognized by the next of kin, all humanity will recognize each other in the resurrection body (§5.5.3.2).

In his talk about the resurrection body, Beale points out as the most significant difference that the current body is characterized by impermanence, while the resurrection body will be characterized by imperishability (1 Cor 15:42, 50). He adds that Paul draws a contrast between the original body of Adam and the new resurrection body of Christ. Even if Adam had remained obedient to God's command, he would not have been able to inherit the realm of God with his "natural body" (§5.5.3.2). This would have required a radical intervention by God. The "spiritual body" bears witness to such radical intervention. According to Beale, there is no development from this brokenness in all speaking about continuity as if the "spiritual body" is already locked in the germ of the "psychological body." We mentioned that facet above all: the new does not *develop* from the old. Old and new creation are antithetical and not complementary to each other. Beale's contrast here between Adam's original body and Christ's resurrection body is parallel to Rahner's emphasis on God's absolute future and Moltmann's plea for *advent*, which also refers to the necessity of God's intervention in this creation (§6.2.1).

137. Rahner, "Christologie innerhalb," 198; *Zur Theologie des Todes*, 22–26.

Rahner, like Beale, refers to Paul's paradoxical statement in 1 Corinthians 15:44, where we hear that an earthly body is sown, but a spiritual body is raised. He concludes from this that every human being must experience a radical change in order to inherit the new heaven and the new earth. This radical change is nothing less than dying in the core of our being (§3.4.2). Rahner's idea that the resurrection body is a profound expression of the spirit that became one with God's Spirit, on the other hand, cannot be related to Beale's design. This statement is strongly determined by Rahner's view on spirit and matter and lacks the necessary biblical-theological foundation. For Beale, attention to radical change is essential and determines the field of tension between continuity and discontinuity of the rebellious body (§5.5.3). Thus he who says: "What we do know is this: when he is revealed, we will be like him," will also have to say in one breath: "what we will be has not yet been appeared" (1 John 3:2).[138]

Because Beale concentrates in his BT on the "spiritual resurrection," the theological field of tension between continuity and discontinuity in speaking about the future resurrection is not elaborated in his BT. Although Beale does mention 1 Corinthians 15 in NTBT, he does not dig out the biblical-theological testimony of the resurrection body. For his further explanation on the issue of continuity and discontinuity, he refers in the discussion of Philippians 3:21 to his comments on Revelation 21:1.[139] In that comment, he makes the field of tension visible again, but he remains unclear about his own choices in this. So the problems are mentioned, but not explored in depth. However, the general field of tension between continuity and discontinuity that the three theologians distinguish in this way is already evident in 1 Corinthians 15.

6.3.1.3 *Continuity and discontinuity in innovation*

6.3.1.3.1 A DIALECTIC SPEAKING IN BEALE'S THEOLOGY

In Beale's work, it remains challenging to find an answer to the question of the degree of continuity and discontinuity between the present and the new heaven and earth. A demarcated chapter on this crucial issue is missing in his BT. Several remarks in his publications make it challenging to place Beale precisely about this topic. For example, in his NTBT of 2011 Beale focuses on discontinuity, while in earlier works (2008) he points out that

> there will be continuity between the old world and the new, since the new is a renovation or renewal of the old (the coming new cosmos is not a "creation out of nothing" [a creation *ex nihilo*]).[140]

---

138. Beale, *New Testament*, 849; Moltmann, *Sein Name*, 71–72, 202.
139. Beale, *We Become*, 292; *Revelation*, 1039–40.
140. Beale, *We Become*, 291.

The New Heaven and New Earth

Now it is possible that over time Beale changed his views on this. However, it is not the case when he speaks in *NTBT* in the same chapter of "the coming future destruction and renovation of the cosmos" and "the eventual destruction and re-creation of the cosmos."[141] Besides talking about the creation of a new cosmos, in response to the destruction of the old cosmos, stands the testimony of the restoration, the renovation, the renewal, and the recreation of the fallen creation. In this way, Beale does not only want to express himself in terms of discontinuity. Despite the discontinuity, the new creation can be identified with the current creation. Concepts like "new creation," "new heaven," or "new heaven and earth," suggest that there is continuity between the current creation and its eventual transformation into the resurrection. This last aspect is primarily found in Beale's biblical-theological reflections on the resurrection, the temple, and the land, about the total renewal of this creation. Beale speaks in terms of continuity. For example, he speaks of the fulfillment of God's plan with this cosmos in the new cosmos and, according to him, the life of resurrection is part of the extensive new cosmos.[142] Through the work of the Messiah, the mission is fulfilled, which God gave to man from the beginning (Gen 1:28). The light of the new creation thus breaks through into the darkness of the old creation since the "spiritual resurrection" of God's people. A visible physical construction of a new cosmos takes place. For Beale, this new cosmos is equal to the long-awaited kingdom of God, which creation had been looking for from the beginning.[143]

This alternating speaking in terms of partial continuity and radical discontinuity does not make it easy to determine Beale's position. Destruction and renewal stand side by side in his work and are alternately addressed in his works, without providing clarity about the dialectic that arises as a result. Where, for example, does Beale see similarity and contrast when he compares the present earth with its material and immaterial aspects with the new earth and its material and immaterial aspects?

A possible direction in which we will have to find the answer to this question seems to be Beale's expectation of a future transformation of creation. He connects this thought of transformation with the biblical speaking of glorification. Beale sees a parallel to this in the resurrection body of Christ. His resurrected body is a glorification of his crucified body.[144] In addition to this glorification on transformation, Beale chooses to talk about the destruction of the current creation. He often equates the end of this world with the downfall of creation and is connected with the cosmic disasters that are coming over the earth. The question then arises how something that has been destroyed can still be transformed without there being a *creatio ex nihilo*. Doesn't the destruction cause the *nihilum*? The discontinuity between the old and the new is thus brought to the fore again in Beale's theology. This ensures that continuity is in the

---

141. Beale, *New Testament*, 817, 819.
142. Beale, *New Testament*, 256. Cf. Beale, *New Testament*, 248, 257, 325, 582, 896, 934.
143. Beale, *New Testament*, 172, 257, 275, 301–2, 333, 877, 913; "Colossians," 845.
144. Beale, *New Testament*, 433. Cf. Beale, *Revelation*, 150.

background. It is possible that a comparison with Rahner and Moltmann could shed more light on this matter. In the future, we will try to do so and investigate to what extent such a comparison between Moltmann's and Rahner's systematic-theological designs and Beale's biblical-theological design can be of significance for the theological speaking about the new heaven and the new earth.

6.3.1.3.2 THE EARTH AND ITS WORKS WILL BURN

Beale repeatedly emphasizes in his BT the sinfulness of man and the need for God's intervention. This ensures that especially the discontinuity in speaking about the new creation is in the foreground. As a result, Beale sees a separation between the present and future cosmos. This old, fallen, and perishable creation falls apart. In his interpretation of Revelation 21:1–8, he points to the contrasts of the "first-second" and the "old-new" creation. A qualitative contrast is made between the "first earth" where iniquity took place and the "new earth" where eternal joy will exist (cf. Isa 65:16–18).[145] These show that there is a radical renewal, a transformation of the cosmic structure. Greek καινός usually indicates a novelty in terms of quality. According to Beale, this does not have to be completely new in time and did not exist before. To indicate something that is entirely new and has never existed before, the Greek uses mainly νέος. Beale points out, however, that the distinction between the two concepts is not consistently applied in the NT so that the context should provide more clarity about the precise intention of the writer. Unlike ourselves, the biblical writers make little use of the word "new." Where this does happen, it is mainly prophetic statements on Ezekiel, Jeremiah, and Isaiah that are related to the "last days" (§5.3.3).[146] This shows the climax of the prophetic message when it bears witness that something new is about to happen. It surpasses the daily routine of all things so much that it reinforces the all-encompassing character of the new creation all the more. We cannot ignore the unimaginable. Already in Revelation 20:11, we hear of the flight of heaven and earth before the first heaven, and the first earth will be renewed (Rev 21:1). In this talk about the new, the biblical writers use the Hebrew בָּרָא, which is usually only reserved for God's creative work. Whereas Moltmann and Rahner talk about a renewal of the present creation, Beale seems to speak mainly about the destruction of the present creation.[147] In his BT, he thus places the discontinuity between this creation and the new creation central. The old and new cosmos are opposite each other. From Christ's first coming, the new creation finds its beginning, and the old creation has begun its destruction. She will eventually find her end with Christ's second coming.

---

145. Beale, *New Testament*, 1041.
146. Cf. Beale, *New Testament*, 81, 347, 550, 676.
147. Cf. Beale, *New Testament*, 172, 175, 178, 301, 331, 352, 419, 627, 633, 642, 763–66, 796, 891, 913.

The New Heaven and New Earth

Because creation is entirely under the spell of evil, this radical discontinuity is inevitable, according to Beale. In Isaiah 65:16–19 and 51:10–11, the emphasis is on the removal of the evil that characterizes this world. The present evil that goes against God's plan is finally radically removed, "the earth and the works that are done on it will be burned up" (2 Pet 3:10b). Then this old creation will be destroyed, and the new creation created. According to Beale, there is a destruction of the present creation and a subsequent *creatio ex nihilo* (§§5.3.3; 5.5.4).[148]

However, in comparison with Rahner's and Moltmann's theology, it can be emphasized that God will not judge and destroy creation as such, but the godless powers in this creation. The discontinuity occurs because creation is not able to produce the new creation. It is evil that goes against God's plan with this creation, which will be removed by fire. In all this, the three theologians realize that this impact of evil in current creation cannot be underestimated. So, it is necessary to have a day of judgment so that the new creation can take its place. Moltmann mentions besides 2 Peter 3:10–12 also the apocalyptic image of the stars falling out of the atmosphere and the powers of the sky being shaken (Matt 24:29).[149] In the writings of Rahner, we also find these representations but lack the references to the specific biblical texts (§3.3.4). All three theologians thus point out that the new creation is not a seamless continuation of this creation. The creation will undergo a radical cosmic transformation. Evil will be removed. That separation will take place entirely to the deepest foundations of this cosmos. Beale focuses most of the three theologians on the aspect of sin. He believes that the impact of sin and death should not be underestimated. This explains why creation in Romans 8 does not sing a cosmic song of praise but expresses itself in sighing and suffering (v. 22). Although Moltmann rarely speaks of sin as such, he also sees in Romans 8 the longing of creation for the power of new creation. A new creation is impossible without the judgment of wickedness. Also, rebirth is impossible without the contractions of the end time.[150] God will not destroy the present creation. The new creation is still this creation but then purified, cleansed, transformed, and glorified. That is why Moltmann does not think of a deathbed, but of a childbed when he says in his New Testament statements about the passing of heaven and earth. The coming judgment that 2 Peter 3 and other New Testament texts describe is seen by him as the contractions of the rebirth of all creation, like the death of the Messiah, formed the contractions of his resurrection. For this, Moltmann refers several times to Matthew 19:28.[151]

In Moltmann's approach, there is no question of an absolutely new creation as a replacement for the current creation (*creatio ex nihilo*). Instead, there is the completion

---

148. Beale, *New Testament*, 65, 238, 268, 286, 309–12, 478, 749, 874, 877, 894–96, 913, 919, 947, 950, 1043; *Temple*, 213; *Revelation*, 175, 398.

149. Moltmann, *Kommen*, 254.

150. Moltmann, *Kommen*, 253; "Auferstehungshoffnung," 106.

151. Moltmann, *Kommen*, 256; *Weg Jesu*, 106.

and recreation of this creation (*creatio ex fatere*). The "new" is the significant difference in the way God is present in his creation (cf. §4.6). For this reason, the NT says that the form of this creation perishes (1 Cor 7:31—a Bible text that Beale does not mention concerning this subject), but that God does not abandon both the material and immaterial work of his hands.[152] The text from Matthew 19:28 is only discussed in Beale in describing the relationship between Christ and the salvation of creation. Partly based on Philo of Alexandria, Beale translates παλιγγενεσία in this verse with "renewal."[153] Beale also recognizes that 2 Peter 3:5–7 relates the new creation to the world after the flood. The flood did not destroy creation. Creation was thoroughly cleaned. The writer of 2 Peter makes a parallel with this when it comes to the future new creation (3:8–13).[154] In it, we see the reality of the curse that came into creation from Genesis 3:17 confirmed. However, in his talk about the new heaven and the new earth, Beale continues to point out the discontinuity because of sin and brokenness. This emphasis on the theme of sin is virtually absent in the ST of Rahner and Moltmann.

This difference partly explains why both systematics see the new creation as a radical renewal and completion of the old creation. Moltmann mainly emphasizes God's faithfulness. His ideas on the new creation are based on God's promises for creation (§4.2.3). According to Moltmann, the biblical prophets only saw the life and survival of Israel threatened. However, they did not say that about the cosmos. Their visions of the future blessed life on earth point to the deep trust they had in God as Creator and Redeemer.[155] If God's first creation perishes through the fall, it will affect God's honor and majesty and mean the devil's victory over God and his plan with the first creation. The fallen creation remains connected with God's original act of creation in Genesis 1–2 and looks forward to her liberation to confess God as Creator and Redeemer.

At the same time, Moltmann states that the new creation is completely new. The new creation is *adventus* of the unexpected and not *futurum* of the expected in an evolutionary sense. Beale's emphasis on this radical presence of sin challenges us to see it more in a perspective of discontinuity. There is a qualitative difference between this creation and the new creation.

6.3.1.3.3 GLORIFICATION OF CREATION

All three theologians agree that glorification is finally mentioned in the talk about the new heaven and the new earth. Moltmann and Rahner do not see the new creation as a repetition or renovation of the current creation. For Moltmann, this kind

---

152. Moltmann, *Kommen*, 295–97.
153. Beale, *New Testament*, 391; 329n36; cf. 170n29.
154. Beale, *New Testament*, 1043.
155. Moltmann, *Kommen*, 302.

of continuity thinking forgets that one should reflect on *creatio nova* from *creatio originalis* rather than *creatio continua*. Support of that relationship can be found in Beale's BT from the references to Genesis 1–2 made in Revelation 21–22.

Moltmann and Rahner also find support in Christ's resurrection for their plea for a radical renewal of this old creation (*creatio ex vetere*). After all, the resurrection body of Jesus Christ was the glorified imperishable crucified body. Beale also sees from the Jewish tradition this parallel of the relationship between the old and new creation and of the relationship between the present body and the future resurrection body.[156] However, he does not work this out anywhere else. This happens in the theological writings of Rahner and Moltmann. What happened to Christ is for their ST, the paradigm with which they not only look at the resurrection body but also at the renewal of heaven and earth. The resurrection of Christ is part of the total cosmic resurrection in which humanity and nature will share. Rahner distinguishes humankind from nature. For example, because, according to him, the animals do not possess a spirit, they cannot complete themselves, nor can they see God in a personal and intellectual way in the eschaton. At the same time, Rahner emphasizes that nature does share in the glorification of creation and does not fade away as an unusable decor (cf. §3.4.2).[157] He remains unclear about the presence of animals in the new creation. Moltmann is more concrete in this respect. According to him, not only humans but also animals, plants, stones, yes, every universal life will rise (§4.5.3). However, he does not offer a critical reflection and substantiation of this idea. However, he does emphasize that the new creation is on the one hand in continuity with the first creation and that at the same time, there is discontinuity through glorification. The new creation is thus the completion of the complete first creation.

A comparison between the three designs shows the hermeneutic difference with Beale. According to Beale, texts such as Isaiah 11:9 and 65:25, which speak of a glorification of the animal world, point in their context instead of a restored relationship between the nations and Israel in the new creation (§5.8.3.3). We have already discussed this in the hermeneutic equation (§6.2.3.2). From what we found there, we can conclude here that Beale, in his BT, omits Bible texts that speak of physical restoration of creation, such as Revelation 5:13, Ephesians 1:10, or Colossians 1:20, every time to discuss the possible renewal or glorification of nature in the new creation. However, Beale emphasizes that although it has its divine origin in heaven, there is a continuity between the physical earth and the future kingdom.[158] The critical comparison with Rahner and Moltmann about resurrection and matter can also, in this case, provide more clarity in the question to what extent the animal and plant world is part of the coming renewal.

---

156. Beale, *Revelation*, 1040; Neusner, *Sanhedrin*, 92a-b.

157. Rahner, "Immanente," 594, 604, 609; "Eschatologie (SM)," 159–60, 163. Cf. Ludlow, *Universal*, 158–59.

158. Beale, *New Testament*, 36, 110–11, 192–96, 398, 428–32; *Revelation*, 611–12.

6.3.2 Eden, Jerusalem, and space

Moltmann and Beale both emphasize a theology of place. While Moltmann systematically speaks of space in biblical terms, Beale presents a salvific-historical line from the garden in Eden to the city-garden in Revelation 21–22. Rahner does not make any concrete statements about this. According to Oren Martin, this is not self-evident either: "[S]ystematic theologies have not traditionally included in their organization a loci [sic] devoted to land."[159] Therefore, in our comparison, mainly Moltmann's and Beale's theology will be compared at the beginning. After this, we will ask ourselves to what extent their reflection can be significant for a proper analysis of Rahner's systematic-theological approach.

In §6.3.2.1, an interdisciplinary comparison regarding the question to what extent space can be imagined as positive and/or negative is started. There, the relationship will be shown between (1) God's presence and the positive, (2) the presence of evil and the negative, and (3) between space and the resurrection body. In §6.3.2.2, we will look at the description of the new Jerusalem in Revelation 21–22. Attention will be paid to the presence and absence of certain elements that are characteristic of the present creation. Finally, §6.3.2.3 focuses on God's coming in this creation and what consequences this has in the representations of space in the eschaton. The objective is to examine how the diversity in methodology used by the three theologians, in the theologically responsible speaking of the new heaven and new earth, can contribute.

6.3.2.1 Eden and the qualified room

For all three theologians, the earth is more than a decor (§6.3.1). Beale and Moltmann testify that space is qualified by what happens inside of it. It is not an empty abstract. Beale describes the garden in Eden as a most sacred space. It is a sanctuary because God walks there (Gen 3:8; §5.7.3). This makes the garden a prototype for all later temples on earth. In his ST, Moltmann connects God's presence in Eden with the presence of God's *Shekhinah* in the history of salvation. The *Shekhinah* is only a part of God's fullness since God can only live fully in the new creation. Only then does the *Selbstentschränkung* of God occur, and the distance caused by the *nihil* between the Creator and his creation will then be removed (§4.6).

From the analysis of Rahner, it is possible to conclude that he does not immediately reject this idea of a qualified space. After all, the concept is closely linked to how he himself looks at the events of Christ. In Christ God, the Son abides among men, and man looks forward to God's coming in this creation. A comparison of Moltmann's systematic-theological and Beale's biblical-theological view of space offers the opportunity to speak in Rahner's design, in addition to the transitory world time and eternal

---

159. Martin, *Bound*, 12n40. As an exception, he only mentions: Rushdoony, *Systematic Theology*, II:957–1018.

salvation time, of transitory world space and an eternal salvation space (cf. §3.5.1). This qualified salvation time and space move towards God's absolute future. We will return to this in §6.3.2.3.

6.3.2.1.1 Negative and positive space

Through Moltmann's integration of the *zimzum,* he sees the space in which creation resides as negative. The *nihil* creates a distance between the Creator and his creation. Moltmann also recognizes a positive space. That is the space that the triune God gives to himself as Father, Son, and Spirit. Neither the Father nor the Son nor the Spirit occupies this space for himself alone. For each of them exists in the Other. Father, Son, and Spirit lovingly give space to each other. There is a question of God's own choice to give room to himself within the Trinity. God's dwelling in the new heaven and earth is thus a reflection of who God is in himself. Not only humanity, but the whole cosmos is thus changed in God's image and likeness. The whole creation becomes the dwelling place of God, just as the Father, the Son, and the Spirit of eternity give space to one another. A comparison of this between Moltmann's and Beale's theology results in the alertness of the larger overall picture in which a theology of Trinity and eschatology are closely linked. Detailed teaching of the Trinity currently lacks in Beale's publications. In his NTBT, for example, there is no chapter devoted to this issue. A dialogue between his BT and Moltmann's ST could make him aware of this and possibly inspire him to develop the relationship between the new creation and Trinity in biblical salvation history. The comparison can be an added value in this respect.

Moltmann and Beale also point out that God aims to live in the middle of the space that the people of Israel occupy. The different temples in the history of salvation are, therefore a foreshadowing of the future, in which creation is a perfect temple place for God's *Shekhinah* (§§4.7; 5.7). In his BT, Beale investigated this theology of the temple and showed that the sanctuary on earth was a model of God's heavenly temple. It was made according to the design that God revealed to man (Exod 25:8–9, 40; 1 Chr 28:19; cf. Ps 78:69, §5.8.1). While God's *Shekhinah* stays in space during the history of salvation, a person receives a taste of how the Creator will infiltrate the entire creation, and everything will be in all.

These thoughts of Beale can be related to Moltmann's vision of the *creatio continua*. In the *creatio continua* there is the *nihil* as negative space between God and his creation and also the positive space of the temple in which God's *Shekhinah* already pervades creation. This interface allows Moltmann's and Beale's theology to be enriched in an interdisciplinary comparison. Beale's BT, for example, can complement Moltmann's perspective from the realization that the holy places of the patriarchs were also signposts to the future temple space, the new creation of which the stoneless sanctuary in Eden was already a prototype. Beale's biblical-theological explanation of Genesis 1–2 as a cosmic temple can be included here as an enrichment of one's systematic-theological speaking about God's *Shekhinah* and the temple in salvific history (§4.6). The moment will come when the Creator will fill the creation with all the glory (cf. §5.7.3). Therefore, the prophets characterize the prophecies of a futuristic Canaan as the fulfillment of Eden. This reminds us that from Canaan, God wants to fulfill the whole earth with all glory. In his BT, Beale repeatedly points to these relationships between God's promises regarding Canaan and his intent with creation, according to Genesis 1–2. A comparison between Moltmann and Beale shows possibilities for how both designs can inspire and complement each other in this. Together with Moltmann, Beale is convinced that in the new creation, the cosmos will be permeated by the triune God and that the triune God will be permeated by the cosmos, without both mergings (*perichoresis*). In this, the now homeless *Shekhinah* finds her resting place. Creation was looking forward to this event from the beginning. Protology and eschatology are also related here (§6.2.2). Then, the space of the *nihil*, which was traditionally needed to make creation, disappears.

Moltmann sees a biblical impulse for the idea that the *nihil* disappears in Revelation 20:11. There we learn that heaven and earth flee from God's throne, because there is no more room for them (τόπος οὐχ εὑρέθη αὐτοῖς, cf. §§4.4.3; 4.6.2). However, a comparison of this statement with Beale's BT makes it clear that this profession of writing cannot be supported biblically-theologically. For in his works, Beale understands the description in Revelation 21–22 as imagery. He recalls earlier texts in Revelation, which speak about the sky that rolls up and about the mountains and islands that are torn from their place (Rev 6:14; 16:20). In the OT, these types of images are used to indicate destruction.[160] Whereas Moltmann thinks of a disappearance of the negative *nihil*, Beale thinks in the direction of complete disappearance of creation.

A comparison between Beale's and Moltmann's model could contribute that Moltmann's distinction between positive and negative space could also be related to the biblical-theological description of the removal of the first people from the garden in Eden (Gen 3). Because humankind failed in the fulfillment of God's command in Genesis 1:28, this earth offers no room for God's presence. Only through God's graceful intervention can God have a limited presence on earth. Beale follows this pattern in his BT. Through the first human disobedience creation (κόσμος, κτίσις) is under judgment and subject to impermanence (Rom 3:6; 8:19–22; 1 Cor 6:2; 7:31). To free humanity from the evil world of today (αἰών), the Messiah died (Gal 1:4). The old creation (κόσμος) is thus crucified (6:14). Jesus Christ brought humanity into a new creation (κτίσις, v. 15; 2 Cor 5:17).

Initially, Moltmann's ST has nothing to say against these statements. However, unlike Beale, Moltmann does choose to relate the impermanence and malice of the world to the *nihil* and not to human failure. The negative is there, according to Moltmann, even before creation is there.[161] In §6.2.2, we already pointed out that this dif-

---

160. Beale, *Revelation*, 1032. Cf. Beale, *Revelation*, 396–99, 844.
161. Moltmann, *Trinität*, 49.

ference challenges their systematic-theological and biblical-theological concepts to reflect more deeply on the question of the origin of evil.

6.3.2.1.2 GOD'S *PERICHORESIS* AND THE NEW CREATION

It can be added in a comparison that Beale's speaking about space can lead to the conclusion that when the Father, Son, and Spirit give space to each other, space in itself is not negative like Moltmann supposes. We see this in Moltmann's description of the *creatio nova*. There the Creator and creation give space to each other and penetrate each other without both merging into each other.

So God does not need a negative *nihil* to give space to others. Because of this, neither must God limit himself to give his creation sufficient space, like the Father, Son, or Spirit will not be limited to give space to each other.[162] Therefore, Moltmann's description of this *perichoresis* within the divinity is not characterized by limitation, distance, and restraint. It is described as a rapprochement, proximity, and participation. It is the opposite of what the Jewish kabbalist doctrine of *zimzum* stands for. Moltmann's systematic reflection on the *necessity* of *nihil* as a negative space can be challenged in this area. To what extent this can be related to Beale's or Rahner's theology cannot be deduced from their works. However, it can be concluded that Beale and Moltmann agree on the need for a radical intervention by God to make the entire creation a place of residence for God. The negative space, which creates a distance between God and people, will then disappear. A comparison between Moltmann's and Beale's design can still use this fact to note that in his biblical-theological reflection on the new heaven and the new earth, Beale places God and creation more strongly opposite each other than is the case with Moltmann.

6.3.2.1.3 SPACE FOR THE RESURRECTION BODY

Closely linked to the theme of qualified space is the theme of space and the resurrection body. However, none of the three theologians elaborates in-depth how risen humans relate exactly to the new space of the new heaven and earth. However, it is clear to them that God's indwelling does not dissolve creation. God gives *Weiten Raum* ("wide space") to the cosmos in which transience and distance will no longer occur. This idea of wide space already comes to the fore from the expression "new earth." Whoever speaks of the new heaven and new earth realizes that heaven and earth are both connected and distinct. Rahner already points out that the term "earth" evokes the connotation of living space. However, he does not reflect on the question to what extent this living space corresponds to the living space as we know it on this earth.[163]

---

162. Cf. Greshake, *Dreieine Gott*, 232–33.
163. Rahner, "Auferstehung (STh)," 219–23. Cf. Ludlow, *Universal*, 229–33; Phan, *Eternity*, 91.

Nevertheless, in a reflection on Christ's resurrection, Rahner does establish that the heaven in which Christ resides after his ascension is a place that is not part of our well-known space or time.[164] However, Rahner does not deal *in concreto* with how the present presence of Christ in heaven applies to the new creation. He remains unclear about this. We find only the statement that incompletion, the whole of creation changes into a new heaven and a new earth.[165] What space is like in that condition is not further discussed.

If we take into account that the physical world also participates in the resurrection (§6.3.1), it means that the new heaven and new earth offer a place to resurrected bodies. New creation then offers both God and humans its full space. This relationship between humanity and the earth is not new. In his reflection on protology, Beale already refers to the biblical-theological relation that exists between humankind and space from the beginning. Already in Genesis 1–2, the motif of the land comes to the fore. Beale presents the earth as a suitable living space for humanity and gives them space in the garden of Eden and the family.[166] This motive of the land influences the biblical-theological explanation. What God does in Genesis 1–2 and how God does it, is a foreshadowing of God's later work in the history of salvation. From this perspective, it is possible to see Genesis 1–2 as a prolepsis of God's work in time and space. Thus in Genesis 1:28, humankind is given the task of populating and subduing the earth. This element comes to the fore again when God places humanity in the garden with the task of working and guarding it. Adam then begins the execution of this by giving names to animals. After human disobedience, this task of working and guarding is reflected in the precepts of God. Israel should be a kingdom of priests, and the church is for God a holy priesthood family (Exod 19:6; 1 Pet 2:5). God's desire is to enter into a relationship with humanity and to walk in the midst of people. From the garden in Eden, this walking of God with humans is a well-known fact. Beale goes into this facet in detail and continuously shows from the BT that in the history of salvation, humankind is given the task to devote the space completely to God in order to make walking with God on earth possible. Humanity has a large share in this by sanctifying and making itself available to build God's temple on earth.

In Moltmann's theology, this human responsibility for sacred space is in the background. In his ST, he focuses on the relationship between space and the Trinity. By doing so, he emphasizes God's present immanence on earth and sets it against the transcendental speaking of God, which separates Creator and creation too much from each other.[167] A comparison shows the difference with Beale, who, in his BT, does not recognize the connection between Creator and creation enough. At the same time, Moltmann can be critically questioned in such a comparison as to whether his

---

164. Rahner, "Auferstehung (STh)," 223–24; "Assumpta-Dogmas," 246–47.
165. Rahner, "Assumpta-Dogmas," 239.
166. Beale, *New Testament*, 880–81.
167. Moltmann, *Gott in der Schöpfung*, 27.

teaching of *zimzum* does not lead to God being seen as absent in this creation because of his self-limitation, and whether this reinforces a purely transcendental speaking about God. Beale's biblical-theological analysis of the temple shows that God is not limited in the history of salvation, but "unbounded" by free will. This happens because God receives more space on earth with time and comes closer to humanity. From this perspective, Beale does not see space as negative in itself. A critical comparison challenges these perspectives and makes us aware of the (unconsciously) chosen patterns among the three theologians.

6.3.2.2 *The new Jerusalem*

Remarkable in Moltmann's ST is that in his *The Coming of God*, he devotes a separate chapter to the biblical vision of the new Jerusalem that descends on earth like a bride in Revelation 21–22 (§4.7.5). This comprehensive attention to BT is unique for a systematic theologian. What does stand out is that the systematic themes to which Moltmann pays attention in his reflection on the new heaven and the new earth do not explicitly return in this biblical-theological chapter. As a result, ST and BT remain two islands that are present in its theology without connection to each other. In a critical comparison with Beale's and Rahner's design, it is evident that Moltmann's attention to this biblical vision especially invites comparison with Beale's design.

The expression "new Jerusalem" reminds Moltmann of both the continuity and discontinuity of the city with the "old Jerusalem." God's promises were traditionally linked to this ancient Jerusalem. From Beale's BT, this idea can be substantiated in detail. The data for this can already be found in his comment on Revelation 21–22. There Beale refers several times to the parallels between these chapters and the Old Testament prophecies about Jerusalem. Thus is there mention of God's bride (Isa 62:5; Rev 21:2, 9); the absence of tears, death, and suffering (Isa 25:8; 35:10; 65:19; Rev 21:4); the precious stones present (Isa 54:11–12, 21; Rev 21:19–20); the gates with guards (Isa 54:11–12; 62:6, 10; Rev 21:12–14); the absence of sun and moon (Isa 60:19; Rev 21:23); the coming of the nations to the city (Isa 2:2, 5; 60:3, 5, 11; Rev 21:24–26); the river of life (Ezek 47:9; Rev 22:1); the tree of life (Ezek 47:12; Rev 22:2); and the new name (Isa 62:2; Rev 22:4).[168] At the same time, Beale also points out that the prophecies about the new heaven and the new earth always mention that the old is no longer remembered (Isa 43:18–19; 65:17; Rev 21:4). From this, he concludes that the new Jerusalem is of a totally different order than the old Jerusalem: "Only an entirely new creation can adequately house the Creator's presence."[169]

At the same time, from Moltmann's and possibly Rahner's design, the question arises for Beale's presentation whether Revelation 21–22 necessarily implies that there is just discontinuity between this creation and the new heaven and the new earth (cf.

---

168. Beale, *Revelation*, 1044, 1069–70, 1083–84, 1088–89, 1094–95, 1121; *Temple*, 132–33.
169. Beale, *Temple*, 136, cf. 141–42.

§6.3.1). The biblical texts that Beale quotes are rather to say that the new creation should not be equated with the circumstances that characterize the current creation. There is a separation between "this age" and "the age to come." The "I am making all things new" in Revelation 21:5 means at the same time that nothing is lost and everything returns in a new glorified form.[170] Precisely the continuity in the imagery of the heavenly and the earthly Jerusalem between the OT and the NT shows that there is a great similarity between the old and the new Jerusalem. Moltmann points out in his ST that the heavenly city of Jerusalem is placed opposite godless Babylon in Revelation 17–18 and Revelation 21–22. Therefore, the new Jerusalem stands not biblically-theologically against the earthly Jerusalem. That will only be the case if "Babylon" is another designation for the earthly Jerusalem. Beale mentions this possibility but denies that this is the case in Revelation. Like Moltmann, he connects Babylon with the godless world on earth.[171] Babylon is characterized as a whore, home of demons, and prison for unclean animals. Jerusalem, on the other hand, is a bride, a dwelling place of God, decorated with genuine gems. The Christian may focus on this heavenly Jerusalem and turn away from wicked Babylon. From the above enumeration, Beale's design can thus be challenged to clearly distinguish between the contrasts and the similarities in the biblical imagery in Revelation 21–22.

6.3.2.2.1 THE REDEEMED AS A TEMPLE CITY

Beale interprets the biblical vision of the new Jerusalem in Revelation 21:10–22:5 as a symbolic description of God's new world. The Jerusalem that descends from heaven is "the bride, the wife of the Lamb" (Rev 21:9), which refers to those who have been redeemed by the Lamb (cf. 21:2, 10). In the vision that the seer describes, these redeemed are represented in the detailed description of the city. After seeing a new heaven and the new earth in 21:1–8, the image in 21:9–22:5 focuses on the relationship that will exist between God and the people in the new creation.

According to Beale, the vision in Revelation 21:2–22:5 is dominated by various symbolic images that all refer to the redeemed people.[172] Together they form God's new temple, which is realized by the Holy Spirit from the day of Pentecost (§5.7). At the same time, we cannot say that the cosmic element is utterly absent from Beale's theological viewpoint. In his comment, Beale points out that Revelation 21:1–5 may refer to the redeemed people in their risen and glorified state. For Beale too, it is certain that the new creation contains more than the risen people. He sees an indication of this in the geographical expression "a new heaven and a new earth" (21:1) and the

---

170. Moltmann, *Sein Name*, 61, 78, 127; *Kommen*, 292; cf. 44–46, 159; *Geist des Lebens*, 125–26; *Weg Jesu*, 40.
171. Beale, *New Testament*, 742; *We Become*, 237–40; *Revelation*, 591, 853, 887–88, 913, 925.
172. Beale, *Revelation*, 1041, 1045, 1062.

The New Heaven and New Earth

fact that all things are created again (v. 5). The new creation will thus also have to offer the possibility for the redeemed to stay in it.[173]

The connection that makes the vision between the redeemed as a bride and the redeemed as the holy city of Jerusalem thus contains a first hint that there will no longer be a physically defined temple in the new Jerusalem (cf. 21:22). Both Moltmann and Beale emphasize this.[174] The new Jerusalem is no longer a delineated sanctuary but forms a cosmic sanctuary within itself. That the new Jerusalem is a temple is further manifested by the fact that God dwells with men (21:3), that the heavenly Jerusalem descends on an exalted mountain (v. 10), and that God's throne is erected therein (21:22; 22:3). God's glory then permeates every space in the new creation. Also, Moltmann and Beale see support for this in the dimensions of the heavenly Jerusalem, the proportions of which recall the dimensions of the Holy Place in the former temple of Solomon. After that, the temple, the Messiah, and the Spirit anticipated, then becomes a reality. God's *Shekhinah* will fill the whole future cosmos.

According to Beale, in Jewish thought, a physically limited temple also brought a separation between Israel and the other peoples. He thus describes these kinds of temples as particularistic, nationalistic institutions.[175] In the new creation, on the other hand, all nations together form God's people. All humanity then stands equal before God. Moltmann also mentions this (§4.7.5). It should be noted that Moltmann is not entirely consistent here. In his reflection on the heavenly Jerusalem, he notes twice that the martyrs would serve God as kings and priests in the new creation, while he, on the other hand, states in his conclusions that there would be no longer a distinction between kings and priests in the new creation.[176] Thus, all people are equal to each other. That there is no longer a distinction between Israel and the nations is also visible in the vision of Revelation 21–22. The names of the Christian apostles on the foundations of the city are inextricably linked with the names of the twelve Israelite tribes on the gates of the city. Humanity stands as one entity before God.

The prophets of the Old Testament thus spoke of the "people" (λαός) among whom God wants to dwell. Beale points out that Revelation 21:3 transforms the "people" (λαός) into a multiple "peoples" (λαοί). This is done to clarify that the prophecies originally directed at Israel are now fulfilling themselves for "every tribe and language and people and nation" (5:9; 7:9). Then will be fulfilled what Genesis 1–2 anticipated and to which the prophets already referred: all creation will become a temple for the Most High (Zech 2:10–11).[177]

This explanation ensures that in the further interpretation of the vision, Beale pays little attention to the glorified space of the new heaven and earth, as it emerges

---

173. Beale, *Revelation*, 1041–42.
174. Beale, *Revelation*, 1048; Moltmann, *Kommen*, 343–44.
175. Beale, *Revelation*, 1047.
176. Moltmann, *Kommen*, 346, 347, 349. Cf. Remenyi, *Um der Hoffnung*, 412n65.
177. Beale, *Revelation*, 1047.

from the spatial images in the vision. It can also be established that the approach that Beale uses is ultimately already pre-programmed by the anthropocentric emphasis that he shows in his BT. This is because it ensures that the blessed salvation that God brings for all creation is not given much attention in his theology. In addition to the image of the city, Revelation 21–22 focuses on the biblical-theological image of the garden that is related to the land. For Moltmann, the city is both a temple and a garden-city. It is God's perfect dwelling place and the completed paradise of creation (§6.2.2). The vision of the new Jerusalem in Revelation 21–22 is reminiscent of a cosmic harmony between nature and culture. The fullness of life is expressed there.

A comparison shows that also in Beale's theology, the redeemed rule in the new creation, like Adam originally did over the first creation (Gen 1:28). The fact that some will reign as special kings is reprehensible for Beale. Adam's original command to rule over the earth did not include the regency over other people. According to Beale, this preferably means that the new heaven and new earth will contain a certain form of matter in which creatures will live, over which humanity reigns. Beale does not clarify exactly what these creatures are. In his further reflection, he remains unclear and leaves all possibilities open. Only once he refers to the Jewish expectation of the new creation in which the animals live together in peace.[178] At the same time, he states that if there are no animals to rule over in the new creation, it is still possible, for example, that God's people will rule over the angels. Beale then supports this thought with the proposition that angels belonged to the creatures of which Adam was commissioned to rule in Genesis 1 and that angels will also continue to exist in the new glorified world.[179] So if there were no animals in the new heaven and the new earth, there is certainly something over which the martyrs could rule as kings. Thus the city fulfills the desire of humanity to build a permanent living space on earth where healing and redemption can be found (§4.7.5). Moltmann has no problem making these ideas of building and further development also part of the new heaven and the new earth. The Christian faith in God's grace and the associated hope of God's kingdom do not constitute an obstacle to the progress and development of the peoples. On the contrary, they provide a framework in which the positive growth of creation is strengthened, confirmed, and stimulated. Christian hope thus becomes a "hope of human hopes."[180]

Beale does not sufficiently capture this social and cultural aspect of blessing in his biblical-theological reflection. While Moltmann, for example, in Revelation 21:24 sees the nations bringing their cultural treasures to the new Jerusalem, Beale sees this only as a symbolic reference to the peoples who bring themselves into the city as worshippers, because the dead are not allowed to take wealth from the old cosmos into the new cosmos.[181] It is remarkable that in his discussion of the relevant Bible

---

178. Beale, *Revelation*, 1120–21.
179. Beale, *Revelation*, 1116–17.
180. Moltmann, "Hoffnung und Entwicklung," 59–60: "Hoffnung der menschlichen Hoffnungen."
181. Beale, *Revelation*, 1095–96; Moltmann, *Kommen*, 347.

The New Heaven and New Earth

text, Beale not only mentions the relationship between God and humankind but also indirectly clarifies what God's people can expect in the new heaven and the new earth.

In the explanation given by Beale of the vision, this element is mentioned several times. Therefore, the question arises whether, after a critical comparison between Rahner, Moltmann, and Beale, systematic speaking about the new Jerusalem and biblical-theological speaking about it cannot be seen as complementary to each other, so that the heavenly Jerusalem is both glorified time and glorified space. The vision in Revelation would then communicate that the new heaven and the new earth are the entrance into a new cosmic space, in which God and creation are in deep mutual relationship with each other. We will return to this in §6.3.3.

6.3.2.2.2 Absence of sea and night

In the biblical descriptions of the new heaven and the new earth we further discover that there will be several things absent that are part of our living space today: (1) the sea (Rev 21:1); (2) tears, death, sorrow, mourning, and grief (Rev 21:4); (3) sinners (Rev 21:8); (4) fear (Rev 21:12); (5) sun and moon (Rev 21:23); (6) night (Rev 21:25); (7) sin and anger (Rev 21:27); (8) sickness (Rev 22:2); and (9) curse (Rev 22:3). When studying what Moltmann and Beale said about these matters (Rahner does not mention them anywhere), it can be concluded that both theologians relate these elements to the absence of evil.

Moltmann connects the forces of destruction with the sea and night.[182] This connection can be confirmed from Beale's BT. In his commentary on Revelation, he points out that the new creation will be characterized by the absence of evil. There will be no more death, suffering, or destruction (Rev 21:4). Beale is the only one of the three theologians who substantiate this relationship in different ways. On the one hand, the connection between the absence of the sea in 21:1 and the absence of death, mourning, lamentation, or trouble in 21:4 already visible in the text by (1) the parallel between "the sea was no more" (ἡ θάλασσα οὐκ ἔστιν ἔτι; v. 1), and "death will be no more" (ὁ θάνατος οὐκ ἔσται ἔτι; v. 4); and (2) the repetition of "passed away" (ἔρχομαι) in: "the first heaven and the first earth had passed away" (Rev 21:1), and "the first things have passed away" (v. 4).

The sea in the book of Revelation is also related to the origin of cosmic evil, the rebellious peoples on earth, the place of the dead, the place of trade, the separation between the peoples, and the elements of unrest. According to Beale, this sea reminds us biblical-theologically of the sea, which was an obstacle for Israel in its exodus and which was drained by God (Exod 14; Isa 51:10–11). According to a Jewish tradition, the drainage of the sea was one of the things God would do in renewing the world.

---

182. Moltmann, *Sein Name*, 187; *Trinität*, 115.

However, for Beale, this does not necessarily mean that the new creation has no physical sea. This testimony is primarily expressed in imagery (§6.2.3.1).[183]

Besides the sea, the city-garden also lacks the night (Rev 21:25; 22:5). Like Moltmann, Beale also sees the night as a reference to the darkness of evil. The prophet already introduced this through the absences above in Revelation 21:1 and 21:4. Opposite the darkness stands the Lamb as God's light. The redeemed shall walk in this city as bearers of the glory of God (Rev 1:4, 20; 21:11–26; 22:5; cf. Isa 60:19). Beale contrasts this description of the new world with the darkness of this fallen world. The darkness in this fallen creation prevents God from living fully on earth. However, in the eschaton, the negative shadows of the old fallen world will disappear. Just like in the absence of the sea, this does not necessarily mean that the new creation no longer has a literal sun or moon. According to Beale, there is nothing definitive about this. Revelation expresses itself in prophetic images, which means that every physical explanation of a text must be viewed with suspicion. Although Beale chooses the figurative-symbolic explanation as standard, he also considers it as possible that the new creation does have skylights such as the sun and the moon, but that God's light surpasses them. It is to be hoped that God will also take over the warmth that the sun gives to creation so that the new earth does not have to be an eternal cold planet. Nevertheless, what the new creation will look like physically cannot be deduced from the descriptions of Revelation 21–22.[184] The metaphor only indicates that humanity will find peace from the past oppressions. God will wipe the tears from the eyes, and death will no longer be there (Rev 21:4). This is the promise that the prophet Isaiah already mentioned (Isa 65:19; cf. 25:8; 35:10; 51:11).[185]

Eventually, we see that everything which, according to Revelation 21–22, is missing in the new heaven and the new earth, can be biblically-theologically related to evil. It is these negative characteristics that are said to be forgotten in the new heaven and the new earth (Rev 21:4). This categorical finding is striking. In a theologically responsible way, it can raise the question of why biblical imagery never lacks the physical world, today's space, or the time we daily experience. If these thoughts can indeed be determined as such from a biblical-theological reflection on the new creation, this would offer added value for the dialogue between BT and ST.[186] In this respect, the biblical-theological conclusions would call for caution on the ST not to conclude too quickly that other elements characteristic of this creation will also be absent from the new creation. It is precisely a statement such as "I am making all things new" (Rev 21:5) and the belief in the resurrection and glorification of all things that make us realize how much data there will be in the new creation, albeit glorified. The choices

---

183. Beale, *Revelation*, 1050–52.
184. Beale, *Revelation*, 1093, 1096, 1115.
185. Beale, *Revelation*, 1041–43, 1049–51.
186. Cf. Vanhoozer, *Drama of Doctrine*, 7, 23–24, 29–30, 74–75, 188–89; Ricœur and Lacocque, *Thinking biblically*, xvi.

made herein determine the emphasis on continuity or discontinuity in speaking about this creation and the new creation. However, these choices originate rather from the philosophical-theological presuppositions that someone has. Therefore, a comparison between Rahner's and Beale's use of eschatological statements critically raises the question of how Beale in his BT ensures that the biblical-theological explanation, which he gives, does not replace the image. This question is even more present in Beale's explanation of the tree of life and the river in Revelation 22. While Beale has no difficulty in assuming that Revelation 21:1, 21:25, and 22:5 describe that the new creation has no physical sea or heavenly bodies, he does not mention this nuance in the explanation of the tree and river.

According to Beale, the absence of the negative means that everything connected with evil will not enter the new creation. As with the tabernacle and the temple complex in Jerusalem, the new creation distinguishes the holy from the profane. Beale emphasizes in his interpretation of Revelation 21–22 that not all people will enter the heavenly Jerusalem. Extensively he points out in his BT the responsibility that each human has towards God. He who does not believe in Christ is excluded from salvation and remains outside the gates of the city. Such a person is forever excluded from God's healings and life-giving presence (Rev 21:8, 27).[187] Moltmann also mentions this aspect. He who clings to the ungodly Babylon does not enter God's holy city. Unlike Beale, Moltmann does not relate this to being eternally separated from God's blessings. He stays within the imagery of the book of Revelation and only points out that those who hold on to the ungodly power of Babylon will not enter holy Jerusalem.[188]

6.3.2.2.3 THE PRESENCE OF WATER AND LIGHT

Besides the absence of sea and night in Revelation 21–22, there are specific elements that are characteristic of creation today. This includes water and light, which are brought to the attention of both Moltmann and Beale. Beale understands the river of life as a symbolic reference to the new life that God's people will get in the eschaton. He connects this image of the river with the prophetic proclamation of salvation and the restoration of Zion. Connected to the river of life is also the description of the temple stream in Ezekiel 47 and the proclamation:

> The mountains shall drip sweet wine, and the hills shall flow with milk, and all the streambeds of Judah shall flow with water; and a fountain shall come forth from the house of the Lord and water the Valley of Shittim because a spring will spring from the house of the Lord (Joel 3:18).

---

187. Beale, *Revelation*, 1059, 1101–2.

188. Further research and the possible choice of the universalism in Moltmann and Rahner goes beyond the scope of this dissertation. See: Ansell, *Annihilation*, 17–53, 145–209, 360–423; Jhi, *Heil*, 39–86, 180–214; Ludlow, *Universal*, 179–89, 237–77.

This imagery of the water from YHWH's temple and the description of the earth that is full of blessing is often mentioned in the Bible (cf. Isa 35:6–9; 41:17–20; 43:18–20). According to Beale, it figuratively bears witness to the vibrant and joyful resurrection life that the saints receive from God in the future.[189] The same explanation is given by Beale when he speaks of the light. Opposite the absence of the night is the Lamb that will be the light of the new creation. Another lighting, such as the sun or a lamp, seems no longer necessary. God will be the light for the new creation and illuminate every corner of it (Rev 22:5).[190] Beale sees in this a symbolic designation of Christ as "the morning star" (Rev 2:28; 22:16) and the Holy Spirit indicated by the "seven torches of fire" (4:5). Sun, moon, and stars in this creation then only form a shadow of God's glory that in the eschaton illuminates the whole creation and changes it into an eternal day (Col 2:16–17).[191]

So, for Beale, the primary rule is that Revelation can be interpreted figuratively-symbolically and that the absence of sun and moon indicates that nothing from this fallen world can prevent God's presence in the new creation.[192] From Revelation 21:23–25, it is possible to conclude that there will be no more physical sun or moon in the new creation. God's own light will replace these lights. At the same time, Beale considers it possible that the sun, moon, and stars will also exist in the new creation and that God's light will far surpass this. A basis for this is found in Beale's biblical statements that the people will fear God "while the sun endures, and as long as the moon, throughout all generations!" (Ps 72:5), that the throne of David will be fixed "as the sun" (89:36) and shall be established forever "as the moon" (v. 38).[193]

In comparison, Moltmann's theology could react to this explanation. This could be done by focusing on the one-sided anthropocentrism that characterizes Beale's interpretation of these images. Because of this, there is just little room for an explanation that has an eye for changes in the cosmos. The center of humanity dominates and limits his exegetical statements. So, in the discussion of the images mentioned above, Beale explains biblical cosmographic descriptions towards anthropological theological statements:

> Elsewhere in the OT, the waters of the new creation are intended not merely to renovate the natural world but to be given to God's people so that they may refresh themselves (Isa. 41:17–20; 43:18–20). The waters of Ezekiel 47 probably function in like manner, just as the healing effect of the leaves is likely not limited to vegetative and animal life but extends to human life as well.[194]

---

189. Beale, *Revelation*, 1049, 1105–7. Cf. Freedman and Maurice, *Midrash Rabbah: Genesis*, 95.1.
190. Beale, *Revelation*, 1115; *New Testament*, 1093; Moltmann, *Sein Name*, 130.
191. Beale, *New Testament*, 1094; *Revelation*, 1067.
192. Beale, *Revelation*, 1115.
193. Beale, *New Testament*, 78.
194. Beale, *Revelation*, 1107.

Also:

> The "luminary" or "star" (ὁ φωστήρ) of Jerusalem, which is compared to the brilliant radiance of precious stones, is another metaphorical way of referring to "the glory of God."[195]

Therefore, Beale lacks a reflection from humankind to the whole of creation. Biblical writers use only the physical-earthly images because they have no other possibilities to present the future realities to their readers.[196] Although Rahner rarely speaks of elements of the new creation in terms of content, he also interprets the physical and earthly imagery in this way. This becomes visible, for example, when he resolutely rejects the idea that heaven is a reunion of families or an eternal banquet. Such concepts only degrade Christian expectations to mere cheerfulness.[197]

In a critical comparison, it can be noted that Beale threatens to overlook the blessing that the coming of God holds in store for *all* creation. "I am making all things new" is then reduced to the renewal of the human being. For the rest of creation, it seems to be only a message of discontinuity. So, Moltmann stresses in his ST that these kinds of images does not speak about a future *after the end* of this world, but about a future *of this* physical-earthly creation. According to him, the Messiah would not be the Messiah of creation if he did not bring a Sabbath for the whole of creation.[198] From Moltmann's perspective, the images refer to all creation, which in eschaton is related to God. In any case, the biblical images cannot necessarily be limited only to the future of human renewal. In that respect, it is possible to interpret the new Jerusalem not only anthropologically. The new creation also incorporates the glorified essential elements of nature. It thus becomes a cosmos in which God is everything in all. There is running water, but it comes from the throne of God and the Lamb. There is light, but that is not that light from the sun, moon, or stars. It is the light of God's glory in which humanity will live forever.

From Rahner's theological approach, it is also possible to place the critical remark in Beale's idea that the biblical-theological explanation herein shows too little variation within the theme of the future relationship between God and his people. There is a lack of a profound elaboration of the uniqueness that the imagery in this relation indicates. Because Beale only briefly refers to the individual images, without analyzing them biblically-theologically, he runs the risk that the future relationship between God and humanity will only be presented from a limited perspective. Also, Beale does not take the image itself into account in his explanation. As a result, the imagery in his BT threatens to be reduced to merely the "anthropological speech" that Beale perceives in it.

---

195. Beale, *Revelation*, 1066.
196. Beale, *Revelation*, 1108.
197. Rahner, "Erfahrungen," 118.
198. Moltmann, *Geist des Lebens*, 67; *Trinität*, 115–16. Cf. Moltmann, *Kommen*, 302.

6.3.2.3 God's relationship with the new creation

6.3.2.3.1 GOD IS COMING IN CREATION

Moltmann and Beale both acknowledge in salvation history that God wants to live with people. They describe how in the early days of the OT, the glory of God remained in the tabernacle and temple, how God's glory lived in Jesus Christ and how God's Spirit lived in the church from Pentecost onwards. All these events look forward to the completion of the future kingdom in which God as Father, Son, and Spirit, will live fully. Then the triune God will be glorified in creation. Creation is thus directed toward the coming of the fullness of God. A comparison between the two shows that not only Beale's biblical-theological and Moltmann's systematic-theological reflections are closely related. Rahner also follows this line of thought. He does so mainly in his reflection on Incarnation and Trinity, rather than in his eschatological reflection on the new creation. Christ's first arrival in Bethlehem already shows that God wants to be connected with this creation.[199]

All three theologians will confirm unanimously that they see the coming of God in creation as the climax of the history of salvation. Moltmann's *The Coming of God* and Beale's *The Temple and the Church's Mission* are structurally focused on this event. Furthermore, in Moltmann's ST the biblical expression that in the future God will be "all in all" (1 Cor 15:28) is a refrain and in Beale's BT everything is focused on the blessing of salvation, which God brings this creation, coming to dwell in its midst. Both theologians show that the new heaven and the new earth are not there for themselves. God's new creation serves to glorify God's history with this creation. Unlike Beale, Moltmann sees the presence of God's glory in the history of salvation only as an anticipation of the future.[200] Beale and Rahner, on the other hand, think from the model of extrapolation (see further §6.2.1). In the latter case, the future indwelling of God in creation is then the completion of what has already begun in the history of salvation. With Rahner, this accent of God's indwelling in the new creation also comes to the fore, although it receives less attention than with Beale or Moltmann (§3.6.3).

If the triune God is fully present in his creation in the eschaton, all creation will become a temple, and the righteous will see God's face. Beale shows that in the history of salvation, people longed to see God's face and thus be able to discover who God was (Exod 33:20). However, even though the righteous Israelite was allowed to meet God in the temple (Ps 27:4) and humanity received a revelation from the invisible God in Jesus of Nazareth (John 1:18), Paul acknowledges that the Christian still looks in a mirror (1 Cor 13:12).[201] Rahner also emphasizes that the longing for seeing God's face was traditionally present in humankind (§3.6). In the new creation, this hope will be fulfilled. The righteous will then worship God with all their hearts and see God's face

---

199. Rahner, *Trinity*, 28, 35, 89.
200. Moltmann, *Trinität*, 43.
201. Beale, *Revelation*, 1113–14.

The New Heaven and New Earth

(Rev 22:2-3). In comparison with Rahner and Beale, Moltmann may emphasize even more that this "seeing of God's face" is more than an intellectual matter. Seeing God points to the most deep-rooted relationship a person may have with the Creator.

In this Moltmann follows Irenaeus, who indicated that those who see God also share in God's glory. This thought was echoed in the early church by Origen (185–254), Lactantius (260–330), and Augustine (354–430).[202] Together with Rahner, Moltmann turns against a static conception of God as an unmoved Mover. This Aristotelian representation of affairs does not offer any room for God's compassion with the creation that manifests itself in the Incarnation, the passion of the cross, and the resurrection. In itself, God does not need creation to be perfect. However, it is the desire of God to share the highest love with others. This leads God voluntarily to create creation. Although this historical-theological analysis is lacking in the theological publications of Beale, he confirms this idea in his comment on wearing God's name on the forehead (Rev 22:4). This indicates the intense relationship that will exist in the eschaton between God and humanity.[203]

6.3.2.3.2 The Image of the City as a Bride

Western theology mainly emphasized, "the seeing of God" (*visio Dei*) in eternity. Moltmann and Rahner add, from Eastern theology, "the unification with God" (*theosis*). Humankind, in the new creation not only knows the forgiveness of sins but may also be a full participant in the divine nature. The unity between God and humanity may reflect the unique ontological unity between the Son and the Father, without eliminating the uniqueness of unity within the Trinity and the distinction between God and humanity. A theocentric and anthropocentric view of the relationship that exists in the new creation between God and humankind complement each other here. Moltmann and Rahner emphasize that this relationship in God is the eschatological goal for which creation aimed at the beginning. In Moltmann's ST, this unification of God is central. It is the moment in which God is ultimate "all in all" (1 Cor 15:28). In the life of the triune God, the Father, the Son, and the Spirit give space to each other and offer an inviting openness to the creation in their relationship (§4.6). That is the ultimate desire of the Trinity. Every glorification of God *through* creation is, therefore, also God's self-glorification *in* creation. Moltmann finishes *The Coming of God* with this self-glorification and self-realization of God.

A comparison between Rahner's and Moltmann's theologies can enable Moltmann to supplement this from the perspective of Rahner. This happens because Rahner mainly connects the idea of this future unification between humanity and God with Christology. In Jesus Christ, we meet someone who is entirely God and fully human, who is at once one and cannot be separated (§3.6.3). From Rahner's view

---

202. Irenaeus of Lyon, *Adversus Haereses*, 4.20.5. Cf. Russell, *Heaven*, 56.
203. Beale, *Revelation*, 1114.

of the relationship between spirit and matter, it is accentuated that God is permeating creation everywhere today. God's Spirit is present in the evolution of life and the completion of the active self-transcendence of matter in spirit. In this way, creation can respond to God's calling. The danger with this is that it unconsciously introduces a pantheism in which creation and God are equal and ultimately saved. Hans Kessler pointed out this danger in Rahner's theology before. Therefore, he added to Rahner's theology the thought that God's Spirit was both immanently omnipresent *in* the creation and transcendently exalted *above* creation.[204]

However, how can the above systematic-theological thoughts be compared with the BT of Beale? His BT lacks terms like *perichoresis*. Beale does describe how the unification between God and creation starts already today through the work of God's Spirit, and from there, continues in the direction of the eschaton. He points to the indwelling of God's Spirit and the accompanying change of humans who are in Christ (2 Cor 3:18). Through the work of the Messiah, humankind no longer stands against God, but already shares in God's life. So, Peter can testify that Christians will participate in the divine nature (2 Pet 1:4, cf. §5.5.4.4). Throughout the NT, the testimony becomes visible that God does not choose to stand beside this creation. God chooses to infiltrate this creation with all glory so that everything may be through him, in him, and to him (§5.7).

It is possible that Beale's interdisciplinary comparison here undertaken may emphasize the above-described relationship between God and this creation even more strongly in the BT from the biblical imagery. This is possible by using the biblical-thematic image of the city, which is decorated like a bride before the Lamb (Rev 21:2). In Beale's theology, this description of the city in Revelation 21–22 is understood as a reference to the relationship between God and the people in the new creation. God has sanctified and prepared these people like a bride for her groom. Therefore, the city that comes from heaven contains the names of both the apostles and the tribes of Israel and is "the bride, the wife of the Lamb" (21:9), dressed in immaculate fine linen (19:7–8).[205]

Now it is remarkable that Moltmann's image of the city as a bride is missing in his theological reflections, even though he refers to the biblical images several times in his ST. In Moltmann's ST, the emphasis is on the city as a garden. By doing so, he emphasizes the relation between eschatology and protology. A comparison with Beale makes us aware of the impact of the image of the bride and the Lamb. Beale explores this theme further by pointing out the biblical-thematic connections that can be made between biblical themes such as marriage, the election of Israel, and priestly service in the temple with the future relationship of God and creation.[206] The element of the new creation as a temple is also mentioned in Moltmann's ST (§4.4). However,

204. Kessler, *Evolution und Schöpfung*, 158–63.
205. Beale, *Revelation*, 941–43, 1045–46.
206. Beale, *Revelation*, 940–41, 944, 1044, 1046.

Beale connects this image of the city as a temple and the image of the city as a bride biblically-theologically with each other and thus emphasizes even more strongly the bond that will exist between God and humanity in the new heaven and the new earth. His reflection from the biblical-theological images of the bride and the city in Revelation 21–22 mentions not only the unity between God and creation but also the unity between people. According to this, the frequent emphasis on the number twelve in Revelation 21–22 refers to the future unity that exists in the new heaven and the new earth between the righteous of Israel and the righteous of the Gentiles.[207]

The analysis also shows that all three theologians agree that this unification does not imply that God and creation merge. God remains God, and creation remains creation. They reject any form of pantheism. At most, there is panentheism: a creation that exists entirely *in* God. There is thus unification, without mixing or separation. God remains transcendent and pervades the glorified creation, which no longer wants to oppose the Creator and is in God (§4.6.2).

Moltmann connects this talk of panentheism with the resurrection body. Through the resurrection, humankind receives its life back. That life is not unlimited or divine. It remains positively limited and created. If that were not the case, humans would be equal to God in the new creation. Humanity would then be omnipresent, eternal, and omniscient. Moltmann opposes this kind of view (§4.5.2). A comparison shows that he will be assisted in this by Rahner, who also mentions this emphasis on the finiteness and creativity of humans and links it to the general confession of Christianity.[208] In the eschaton, God and creation do not merge into one another, nor do they come apart from one another.

It is possible that the term "new heaven" also refers to this new situation between God and creation. However, nowhere is the term concretely explained by the three theologians. It is only related to the "new earth" and conceived as a reference to creation as a totality, the new universe. The ST and the BT could elaborate on this designation and discuss other proposals.[209] This could then possibly offer a broadening of the answer to the question of why heaven also needs renewal and why the new creation ultimately clings to the distinction between heaven and earth.

6.3.3 Sabbath and eternity

Rahner and Moltmann focus, specifically on the question of the relation between time in the present creation and time in the new creation in their eschatology. This is special for those who realize that concept formation over time usually lacks in theology.

---

207. Beale, *Revelation*, 62.
208. Rahner, "Christentum," 165.
209. Thomas, *Neue Schöpfung*, 20.

Wolfhart Pannenberg argues for the importance of this since the time perspective strongly influences Christian theology.[210]

In Beale's theology, these questions about time in the new heaven and the new earth are missing. He classifies the discussion about this as a "philosophical question."[211] This is partly understandable since time is not in the foreground anywhere in the Bible. Therefore, reflection on this subject is not often done in biblical-theological studies.[212] This is also the case in Beale's theological reflection. At the same time, it is unavoidable not to say anything in a BT about the biblical speaking about time and eternity. So, Beale sometimes makes indirect statements in his works about how he imagines the time of the new heaven and the new earth. We will come back to that later.

In this substantive comparison about time and the new creation, we will first compare the theories of Rahner and Moltmann with each other, and from there, we look forward to their different starting points in speaking about time (§6.3.3.1). In the comparison below, their theologies set the accent, and we look further into how Beale's BT can be of significance in this. After that, the dynamics of the new creation will be examined, as represented mainly in Moltmann's aionic cycle time (§6.3.3.2). Finally, the chapter ends in §6.3.3.3 with two questions. The first question focuses on the possible relationship between God's eternity and Christ's resurrection. The second question reflects on the relationship between the time of the new creation and the meaning of the Sabbath as a day of rest in the history of salvation.

6.3.3.1 *Starting points in speaking about time*

6.3.3.1.1 THE FUTURE TENSE AS THE "FRUITS OF THE PRESENT TIME"

In their theologies about the essence of the era of the new creation, Rahner and Moltmann are an extension of each other. For both, the future tense is the "fruits of time" of the present. Rahner sees a continuation of time in eternity as negative. Therefore, he sees the time in the new creation as a completed endpoint. The new heaven and the new earth know no infinite continuation or standstill of time. The time present is there the "determined fruits of time" of what is happening in the present time. In computer language: Eternity is not a *reset* of history, but its final *backup*. Nor should purgatory, assumed by Roman Catholic theology as "one still after death, . . . maturing of the human being," be seen as a further continuation of the time after death.[213] Death remains the absolute end and turns time into the "established fruits of time" (§3.5.2).

---

210. Pannenberg, *Systematische Theologie 3*, 595. Cf. Freyer, *Zeit*, 319.

211. Beale, *Revelation*, 539.

212. Padgett, *God*, 36. E.g., Brettler, "Cyclical and Teleological Time"; Brin, *Concept of Time*; De Vries, *Yesterday*; Barr, *Biblical Words*.

213. Rahner, *Zur Theologie des Todes,* 24: "einer noch nach dem Tode, . . . erfolgenden Ausreifung des Menschen."

How these "fixed fruits of time" can be imagined remains unclear to Rahner, because both the idea of infinite time and that of a lasting advancing time is problematic and is perceived by Rahner as mythology.[214] With Rahner, there is a reticence in speaking about the time-format of the new heaven and the new earth, because, on the one hand, the final fruits of time transcend the present time, while on the other hand the new creation can be imagined in the Bible as a world with endless progressing time.[215]

Unlike Rahner, Moltmann states that the future tense is both ongoing and permanent. It is not linear time, as is the present time, but an eternal cycle time that preserves and saves the fullness of times (§4.3.5).

Rahner and Moltmann thus both reject the idea of an eternal standstill. God's coming brings with it a life that does not die any more and a time that does not perish anymore. Because Rahner does not discuss the idea of eternal cycle time, it remains unclear how he would react to Moltmann's proposal. There is a good chance that he does not find this proposal acceptable, because in the cycle model, too, the outgoing time will be canceled shortly. Although Moltmann also describes this coming and going of time as negative (§4.3.3), he does not incorporate the problem in his proposal of cycle time. The exact reason for this remains unclear. One possibility is that the far-reaching time does not persist, but rises again and again in the cycle.

6.3.3.1.2 The terminology of *chronos, kairos,* and *aiōn*

Moltmann and Rahner both distinguish the negative transient moment from the positive imperishable moment in the present time. With Moltmann, these different moments are distinguished by the terms *chronos* and *kairos*. Moltmann bases his doctrine of time on these Greek terms. *Chronos* is negative and connected to the linear time. It devours the children it produces and does not allow the past to change the future. *Kairos,* on the other hand, is related to the positive opportunity that is permanent. *Chronos*, according to Moltmann, makes a way in the new creation for this glorified, lasting, and renewed aionic time (§4.3.5).

Rahner also describes the positive moment as a fruitful and lasting time or a "something" that does not shatter itself and stands in opposition to slavish time, which subjects human existence to transience. However, for Rahner, it is difficult to speak of an "aionic time." *Aiōn* in the Bible refers to an eternally continuous time that still has a past, present, and future (§3.5.4).[216] According to Moltmann, the positive, fertile, and lasting time or *kairos* in the new creation is glorified and changed in the aionic time. Just as God imbues everything with God in the new creation, the aionic *kairos*-time will also be characterized as a perichoresis of eternity and time. This performance

---

214. Rahner, *Grundkurs*, 266–67; "Zu einer Theologie des Todes," 184–86.
215. Rahner, *Grundkurs*, 420. Cf. Rahner, "Diskussionsbeiträge Zeitbegriff," 241.
216. Rahner, "Ewigkeit," 424.

recalls Plotinus' old statement (±204–270) about "eternity . . . in which the whole is always present," and from which possibly Boëthius' (±480–525) statement was derived: *Aeternitas igitur est interminabilis vitae tota simul et perfecta possessio* ("Eternity is the total and perfect possession of infinite life").[217]

In the book of Revelation, Moltmann finds support for the idea that the earthly linear transitory and destructive time, *chronos*, is absent in the new creation. There an angel swears "that there would be no more delay [χρόνος]" (10:6). On several occasions, Moltmann states with an appeal to this text that *chronos* will eventually come to an end.[218]

From the comparison, it can be concluded that Beale's BT points out that Revelation 10:6 cannot be applied in the technical-philosophical way that Moltmann presents. The text states that God's intervention in history is specific. There is no more delay. The verse does not speak of the abolition of time or an imminent timelessness. Beale notes in his works that this can be deduced from extra-biblical texts, such as 2 Enoch 33:2 and 65:7.[219] There we learn that there is talk of "an infinite time without number, without years, months, weeks, days and hours" (33:2), and that of the future can be said: "then all-time will disappear, so that there are no more years, months, days or hours" (65:7). Only the last text points to the eschaton. However, Beale has no biblical text that supports the abolition of time or an imminent timelessness. This raises the question of a further biblical foundation for the contrast Moltmann creates between *kairos* and *chronos*.

Although Beale in his BT also mentions the concepts *chronos* and *kairos*, he does not indicate any difference between both. According to him, the NT only knows the contrast between "this age" and "the age to come."[220] Like *aiōn*, *chronos* and *kairos* thus carry the neutral meaning of "time" in Beale. It is possible that this equation of concepts happens unconsciously in Beale's case because a doctrine of time in his BT is nowhere dealt with as a separate theme. A more in-depth explanation of the concept of *aiōn* lacks in his works. Beale suffices by noting that the NT repeatedly designates the future new heaven and earth as the future *aiōn* (Luke 20:34–35; Eph 1:21) and that Jesus promises his disciples that he will be with them until the end of the *aiōn* (Matt 28:20). Beale understands this last expression in the traditional sense of "until the end of time."[221] He also realizes that *aiōn* also has the temporal meaning of "forever and ever" or "eternity."[222]

---

217. Plotinus, *Enneads*, 1:III.7.3; Boëthius, *Consolation*, V.6.4. E.g., Jager, *Eeuwige leven*, 43–51.

218. Moltmann, *Kommen*, 308, 313; *Weg Jesu*, 351; "Eschatologische Augenblick," 584.

219. Beale, *Revelation*, 538–39.

220. Matt 12:32; Luke 20:34–35; Eph 1:21 both together. Mark 10:30; Luke 18:30 *kairos* and "coming age." 1 Cor 2:6; 2 Cor 4:4; Gal 1:4; 1 Tim 6:17; 2 Tim 4:10 "present age" and Heb 6:5 "coming age."

221. Beale, *New Testament*, 130.

222. Beale, *New Testament*, 160; *Revelation*, 333, 748.

The fact that Beale does not extensively discuss the possible differences between *chronos* and *kairos* may also be because the contrast which Moltmann makes between the terms does not occur in the Bible.²²³ Moltmann's systematic-theological talk about *chronos* and *kairos* is mainly inspired by Greek mythology and lacks a fixed basis in the Bible or Christian doctrine. A comparison between Moltmann's and Beale's theologies in this area can challenge both disciplines to think more deeply about the relationship between the different biblical concepts of time. From this research, it can be established for the time being that the BT can do this by asking the ST to connect its doctrine of time more with biblical speaking. Also, ST can do this by asking BT to intensively deal with the question of a timeline from a biblical-theological perspective.

Rahner also sees in the latter an essential task for the BT and points out that a multitude of time concepts characterizes the NT. As an example, he mentions the terms: αἰών, αἰώνιος, ἡμέρα, ὥρα, καιρός, ἔσχατος, τὰ τέλη, σήμερον, ἐνεστῶτα-μέλλοντα θάνατος, ἐφάπαξ, νῦν, παραυτίκα, παραυτά, ὥρα, φθορά, νῦν, ἐκθές.²²⁴ What are the possible theological accents of these terms within the biblical testimony?

It may not be easy to derive fixed concepts for time in the new creation from these and other biblical terms for time. Here the BT clashes with the boundaries of its field. Like any other discipline, this has a dynamic movement in which it is hardly possible to keep up with one's literature. That fact brings with it the necessary specialization and makes us realize that it is enriching to work in theology in an interdisciplinary way in a conversation about time. From the perspective of the Bible sciences, the conclusion is growing that intercultural and international cooperation is also necessary for this conversation. For example, Bible scholars such as Bruce Malina and Marc Brettler call for the abstract Western perspective of time not to be automatically projected onto the biblical period.²²⁵ Therefore, an interdisciplinary conversation between the BT and other disciplines in theology is a given because also in the message of the biblical storyline, time plays a role that should not be underestimated. A separate and deeper reflection on this from the discipline of the BT in relation to the other disciplines could mean a significant enrichment for the systematic-theological speaking about time and its relation with the new creation. The Old Testament speaking about the future *'ōlām* or the New Testament speaks about the "old *aiōn*" and the "new *aiōn*," could be sufficient reason for this.²²⁶

For example, the book of Daniel Beale concludes that there are two separate *aiōnen* (Dan 2:7). However, his further reflection on this remains brief. Beale suffices to connect the old *aiōn* with the anger of the present sinful world, from where Christ redeems humankind to bring it into the new *aiōn*, which Beale then conceives as a

---

223. Cf. Craig, *Time*, 16.
224. Rahner, "Theologische Bemerkungen," 304.
225. Malina, "Rhetorical Criticism," 3–24; Brettler, "Cyclical and Teleological Time," 112.
226. E.g., Tomasino, "עוֹלָם," 345–51; Sasse, "Αἰών, Αἰώνιος," 197–209.

reference to the new perfect creation (cf. Gal 1:4; 6:15).²²⁷ A commonly used biblical expression like "the last days" points to the times in the present old *aiōn*, which announce the arrival of the new *aiōn*. The events in these "last days" are thus proto- or semi-eschatological, according to Beale. They lead to the end of the old *aiōn* and bring the events of the new *aiōn* near. In concrete terms, during these "last days," Beale thinks both of the negative oppression and religious persecution of the old *aiōn* and the positive blessings that the righteous in the new *aiōn* experience when God fulfills his promises to them.²²⁸

This contrast between the two *aiōnen* leads Beale to speak several times in his BT about an "end of time" and an "end of history." However, in a comparison between Rahner's and Moltmann's designs, Beale questions what these terms mean for the element of time. An answer to this question could help to deepen the theme of continuity and discontinuity between the current and the new creation, both for BT and ST.

6.3.3.1.3 NEOPLATONISM AND BIBLICAL THEOLOGY

While Rahner and Moltmann refer several times to the biblical testimony on this subject in their speeches on matter and space, they do so less in their speeches on time. In line with others, they choose to use Augustine and Neoplatonist terms such as "eternity," "timelessness," "immortality," "immutability," and "infinity" and to see time as something negative. The Greek philosopher Parmenides (513–448 BC) applied this kind of time thinking to absolute Being.²²⁹ According to him, the highest Being was eternal and without time. The life after death, which, according to Parmenides, included Being, was thus a radical change of the present. Also, according to Augustine, the time belonged to God's good creation and would merge in the eschaton into eternity. The changing time showed humankind that creation was moving toward this unchanging eternity, which was considered the highest perfection. Augustine described this future "paradise of paradises" as the fulfillment of time, the Sabbath of the Sabbath, and the eighth day of creation, on which humanity rested and saw, saw and loved, loved and adored.²³⁰

Moltmann and Rahner adopt this pattern of thought and do not ask critical questions concerning this philosophical conception of time and eternity. For example, they do not ask the question of whether time in itself contains decay or whether it only reveals decay. Both systematics conclude from Neo-Platonism that time is negative. How Rahner and Moltmann know accurately to deduce that linear time no longer occurs in

---

227. Beale, *New Testament*, 310, 905, 907.
228. Beale, *New Testament*, 83, 115–16, 123, 125, 139.
229. Cf. Daley, *Hope*, 88; Augustine, *City of God*, XI.16.21; "Homilies on John," 38.10.
230. Augustine, *Confessions*, VII.11.17; XI.5.7; XI.13.15; *City of God*, XXII.30; Cf. Meijering, *Augustin*, 52–54; Dalferth, *Gedeutete Gegenwart*, 209–10; Ansell, *Annihilation*, 59–64.

the new creation and cannot be liberated and glorified by God, remains unknown.[231] This is remarkable for those who realize that they do pose critical questions to Neo-Platonism from the ST field of expertise, particularly about the future salvation of matter. From the BT point of view, it is usually skeptical about the fact that theologians relate elements of Greek philosophy to the biblical testimony. The choice to speak about time from a Neo-Platonist metaphysical viewpoint then makes the dialogue between ST and BT more difficult. This is even more difficult if ST bases itself entirely on metaphysical ideas about time and no longer relates them to the Bible. In this case, an interdisciplinary conversation between ST and BT is very difficult. Just as we could conclude from Rahner's and Moltmann's theology earlier that Beale's BT thought too much about sin and salvation from Western theology and paid too little attention to biblical speaking about it (§6.2.2.3.2), it is now possible to point out from Beale's theology that Rahner and Moltmann in their ST also reflect too much about time from a Western philosophy and pay too little attention to biblical speaking about it.

From Beale's theological approach, we can further observe that the Bible only connects transience with sin and guilt and thus not with time. God's intervention in time is even described as the "day" or the "light" against the "night" and the "darkness" in which evil manifests itself. A separation between time and eternity is thus alien to the Bible. In Genesis 1–2, it becomes clear that God is even the maker of time. With Rahner and Moltmann, this testimony has no resonance anywhere. Although they pay attention to the relation between protology and eschatology, they connect the time of the eschatological new creation with the original creation. Moltmann only distinguishes the time before and after Genesis 1:5, and Rahner sees God's institution of time in Genesis 1 as part of the history of salvation. This time finally comes to an end. When the history of salvation is completed in the eschaton, time is also completed.[232] A critical comparison between the three theologians exposes this gap and challenges the theologically responsible speaking about the new heaven and the new earth from ST and BT to reflect precisely on time in the context of the relationship between protology and eschatology.

A further basis for Rahner to see the progressing time as negative lies in his choice to be careful in a concrete speaking about the new creation from the experiences of the present creation (§3.3). This emphasis on a discontinuity in speaking about the new creation from the experiences in this creation makes it difficult to imagine the life that comes with the resurrection. If you look positively at the time and assume that time alone reveals and does not work on decay, you can say that in the future, time will continue and create dynamism in the new heaven and the new earth. John Polkinghorne thus opts for the conception of a renewed and glorified linear time when he concludes:

231. Cf. Klappert, *Worauf wir hoffen*, 72–75; von Balthasar, "Some Points of Eschatology," 261n9; Felsinger, "Karl Rahner," 213.

232. Rahner, "Theologische Bemerkungen," 303.

There can be a new kind of time, whose processes will have a different character, one no longer condemned to the thermodynamic drift to the disorder that is characteristic of this present world. I believe that this new time will be linear like the time of the world, and its unfolding development will enable the redeemed to enter into the unending exploration of the riches of the divine nature.[233]

We deliberately call this more detailed here because Rahner seems to appreciate the proposal of an ongoing physical time more in a later phase of his life. He then writes: "perhaps an end of the physical time is not at all implied in Christian eschatology."[234] From Christ's victory over death, Rahner, as a result of this, confesses that God restores and lets rise that which has affected death. The discontinuity is then linked to death and decay, while God, through the resurrection, gives glorified continuity to that which was destroyed by death.

A comparison with Moltmann's theology shows that he also echoes Rahner's negative view of time. In Moltmann's system, the present history (*chronos*) with its past, present, and future is related to mortality, whereas eternity with its immortality is opposed to eternity. A text quoted by Moltmann is 1 Corinthians 15:53: "For this perishable body must put on the imperishable, and this mortal body must put on immortality."[235] In his BT, Beale, on the other hand, repeatedly points out that this verse is related to the future resurrection body that Christians receive. In addition to the physical transformation that takes place at the resurrection, Beale also recognizes a spiritual transformation and sees a parallel with Philippians 3:20–21.[236] Nowhere does he show that this verse also relates to the change of a perishable time into an imperishable time. From this comparison, Beale's perspective takes a critical approach to Moltmann's use of Scripture. However, at the same time, we must add that Moltmann's depiction of a dynamic in the new heaven and new earth does not place time and eternity as tightly against each other as Rahner does. Moltmann ultimately combines his proposal of immortality and dynamism in the new creation in his proposal of cycle time. Because Rahner's extensive contributions on time and eternity and Beale's reflection on the new creation do not mention this concept anywhere, it is not possible to compare their designs on this proposal.

---

233. Polkinghorne, "Jürgen Moltmann's Engagement," 65.

234. Rahner, "Profangeschichte," 13: "vielleicht ist ein Ende der physikalischen Zeit in der christlichen Eschatologie gar nicht impliziert." Cf. "Profangeschichte," 17.

235. Moltmann, *Sein Name*, 65–66; Moltmann-Wendel and Moltmann, "Mit allen Sinnen," 38.

236. Beale, *We Become*, 221–22. Cf. *New Testament*, 45, 440–41; *Revelation*, 1034.

The New Heaven and New Earth

6.3.3.2 *Dynamics of the new creation*

6.3.3.2.1 Linear time, cycle time, and timelessness

Because both systematic theologians emphasize the resurrection of matter, the representation of eternity as "timeless and fixed time" is difficult to accept. Anyone who confesses the belief in a resurrection body thinks in terms of a mobile body and not of an immobile statue. Moltmann seems to acknowledge this and points out the importance of space and time in this creation. This connection between creation and time is important to Moltmann. For example, he says of the intermediate phase between Christ's resurrection and the general resurrection that the deceased have a sense of time in this phase. If this were not so, they would fall out of time and no longer relate to God's time for creation and to Christ's time for humanity. This relationship between the deceased and Christ cannot be rigid. Eternity also knows its time and space. However, Moltmann thinks that time is at death, not our earthly linear time, but a time of love characterized by acceptance, glorification, and solidarity. Therefore, a future of a creature without time and space is inconceivable for Moltmann (§4.3).[237]

It is possible in comparison to respond to this from Rahner's design, by stating that such a representation of eternity seems far too naive. According to Rahner, time cannot be imagined linearly. However, Rahner bases this rejection apologetically:

> If we understand eternity, which is the finality of our life, which arises in time, as the continuation of a time with always new and different periods of time to be filled in anew and different from each other, then, of course, all the half-secure and half-dumb questions arise, from which the half-secure individual of today is tempted to make the belief of eternal life untrustworthy or ridiculous.[238]

According to Rahner, to avoid stupid questions, there should be no linear progressing time in the eschaton. Otherwise, there is a danger that the Christian representation of the new creation will no longer be acceptable to modern people. With Rahner, this choice ensures that he emphasizes that the cosmos is part of the redemption and also that he makes sure not to speak too speculatively about the redeemed cosmos. Shortly before his death, however, he testified to the questions this thought raised:

---

237. Moltmann, "Liebe," 852.

238. Rahner, "Ewigkeit," 424: "Wenn wir die Ewigkeit, die die Endgültigkeit unseres Lebens ist, die in der Zeit entsteht, als Weiterlaufen einer Zeit mit immer neuen und neu auszufüllenden und voneinander verschiedenen Zeitabschnitten verstehen, dann entstehen natürlich all die halbgescheiten und halbdummen Fragen, von denen her der halbgescheite Mensch von heute die Glaubensüberzeugung vom ewigen Leben unglaubwürdig oder lächerlich zu machen versucht ist." Cf. Rahner, "Auferstehung Jesu," 346; Felsinger, "Karl Rahner," 213.

> I confess that it seems a painful, unresolved task to me of today's theologians to discover a better model for this Eternal Life, which excludes these trivializations from the outset. But how? But how?[239]

An accurate reflection on the new creation is then no longer possible in Rahner's theology. From his publications, one can only conclude that he does everything he can to avoid any schematic representation of this.[240] However, from Moltmann's and Beale's theology, the comment can be made with Rahner that the biblical representation of eternity evokes the idea of progressivity and dynamics more than that is the case in his design. Earlier, Denis Edwards reacted to this fact in Rahner's doctrine of time: "Rahner's transcendental philosophy of time and freedom has produced a too-narrow understanding of eternity as definitive and final validity of history rather than as participation in the fullness of divine life."[241]

Life in the new creation cannot be imagined from the Bible as indescribable, timeless, or full-time. Rather, there are images and thoughts reminiscent of an infinite upward linear line.[242] Every movement that goes with it requires time. Where there is no time, there is no sequence. Moltmann is aware of this when he states that without time progress, one cannot sing a song or carry out a thought process (§4.3.5). These considerations explain why he chooses for an aionic cycle time, which allows, that dynamics are present in the new creation and that the time in the new creation does not perish, as is the case with the current *chronos*-period. Now, in comparison with Rahner, it can be concluded that in the past, he also asked critical questions about his thoughts about the dynamics of the resurrection life in the new heaven and the new earth:

> How to "imagine" this corporeality? Whether one can eat and how could this be imagined, if it had happened with the risen Lord, without the wheel of changeableness and transience turning again?[243]

As a result, Rahner remains very reluctant to speak concretely about the new heaven and the new earth. This reticence is characteristic of the time in which Rahner conducted theology.[244] This has changed in recent decades. The former modernism, which

---

239. Rahner, "Erfahrungen," 119: "Ich gestehe, daß es mir eine quälende, nicht bewältigte Aufgabe des Theologen von heute zu sein scheint, ein besseres Vorstellungsmodell für dieses Ewige Leben zu entdecken, das diese genannten Verharmlosungen von vornherein ausschließt. Aber wie? Aber wie?" Cf. Rahner, "Ewigkeit," 432.

240. Rahner, *Grundkurs*, 419; "Trost der Zeit," 180. Cf. Freyer, *Zeit*, 330; Felsinger, "Karl Rahner," 208.

241. Edwards, "Resurrection," 379. Cf. Thompson, "Hope for Humanity," 166.

242. Cf. Hryniewicz, *Challenge*, 27; Bauckham, "Time," 179; Cullmann, *Christus und die Zeit*.

243. Rahner, "Auferstehung (STh)," 216: "Wie man sich diese Leiblichkeit solle 'vorstellen' können? Ob man da noch esse, und wie mann sich das, wenn es beim auferstandenen Herrn geschehen sei, vorstellen solle, ohne daß damit das Rad der Veränderlichkeit und Vergänglichkeit wieder ins Drehen komme?"

244. See detailed: McDannell and Lang, *Heaven*, 307–53.

The New Heaven and New Earth

saw the new creation as timeless, unchanging, and unmoved, was often experienced as too static a representation of the situation. A still rest, in which modern humans enjoy the fruits of earlier work, is no longer of this time. Postmodern humanity finds joy in a progression of growth, discovery, and development:

> Modern people do not wish, like Augustinian humanity, to find in God the rest for their restless hearts; they want ever new worlds for their restless spirits to conquer. If there is "heaven," it should not be the end of the road, weary humanity's homecoming, but rather like struggling over the brow of the hill to find a vast new vista of unexplored country ahead of us.[245]

When it comes to this dynamic relationship between humanity and God, Beale's approach points out that God's people also maintain God's Torah in the new creation. God's commandments will not be undone, and the redeemed will follow the will of God with perfect hearts. Beale bases this on the idea that Adam also kept God's Torah in the garden of Eden and that these statutes of God are eternal and universal. The life of resurrection gives humanity all the blessings of God's kingdom in which the dynamic living relationship with God is the climax. This union that will then exist between God and creation, Beale sees, for example, in the image of the river with the living water (Rev 21:6; 22:1, 17).[246]

Because Beale does not pay specific attention to the question of time in the new heaven and the new earth, it is not easy to come to a comparison with the others. For comparison purposes, there are insufficient interfaces in terms of content. At the same time, it is precisely the awareness of Rahner's and Moltmann's visions of time in the new creation that can, in a comparison, help to ensure that more attention is paid to this in the biblical-theological reflection on the new heaven and the new earth. In this substantive comparison, we will attempt to do so by reflecting on Moltmann's proposal of possible cycle time from the biblical-theological point of view of Beale.

6.3.3.2.2 Biblical theological reflection on a cycle time

In comparison with Beale's design, it is possible to point out that Moltmann's representation of a cyclical time will ultimately not bring innovation to the new creation. It only leads to the endless repetition of the same events over and over again. It then resembles the eternal circle of nature described by Ecclesiastes: the earth (1:4), the fire of the sun (1:5), the air of the wind (1:6), and the water (1:7). Ecclesiastes sees this as tiring. It should be noted that according to Rahner's vision on time and eternity, such a circle was unsatisfactory (§3.5). Also, Ecclesiastes was a favorite book for Rahner

---

245. Bauckham and Hart, *Hope against Hope*, 157.
246. Beale, *New Testament*, 352; *Revelation*, 1056, 1104–6, 1150; *Temple*, 74–75, 196–98.

that inspired him in his thoughts about the new creation in which this eternal wheel of time would be a thing of the past.[247]

However, a comparison with Beale in this area leads to the conclusion that he understands the text in Ecclesiastes in the sense that creation seems to be a prisoner of an eternally closed and repeating cycle.[248] From this point of view, there seems to be more to indicate that humanity ultimately enjoys in the new heaven and the new earth an open linear time that continues, but is not characterized by death or transience. The central question here is, of course, what is more humane and creative in this respect: (1) an ongoing linear time that leaves no trace of suffering or death or (2) a recurring cycle time that does not allow for new situations. Anyone who does not consider the earthly time of events as negative and firmly adheres to a continuity between this and the new creation will instead feel sympathy for the linear time in the new creation. If, on the other hand, you are less concerned about this earthly linear occurrence time and think discontinuously about the new creation, you will prefer to opt for cycle time. However, also with the latter choice, the question can be asked: Does not a recurring moment, however beautiful it may be, also get the effect of an irritating repetition over time? If the latter is the case, the eternal cycle time eventually changes into an eternal prison from which creation no longer escapes. Although all three theologians fully agree that according to the biblical testimony, the transience will perish, this does not mean that linear time will perish. In support of the latter Moltmann refers to the statement in Revelation 10:6: "that there would be no more delay [χρόνος]." In §6.3.3.1.2, we have already seen that Beale, in his BT, resolutely rejects this type of reasoning. According to him, the verse cannot be exegetically interpreted in this way.[249] Richard Bauckham already wrote about this kind of exegetical application in Moltmann's theology: "What little exegesis he sacrifices tends to be remarkably ignorant and incompetent."[250] Moltmann's reflection on this is as follows:

> I am unable to understand why that is not to be the end of time as *chronos*. In the realm of God's eternal presence, *chronos* can surely have just as little power as death. Even if the text has not explicitly formulated that "end of time," which Richard Bauckham evidently has in mind, simple logic tells one that "the end of time has come" once "there is no more time left."[251]

For Moltmann, with the explanation of Revelation 10:6, his model does not expire. From the reflection on *chronos* and *kairos*, one can already deduce that a future for such a *chronos* is not possible.

---

247. Lohfink, "Gegenwart und Ewigkeit," 3–4.
248. Beale, *New Testament*, 384.
249. Beale, *Revelation*, 538–39. See also: Aune, *Revelation 6–16*, 567; Charles, *Revelation*, I:263.
250. Bauckham, "Time," 179. Cf. Moltmann, *Kommen*, 25–26.
251. Moltmann, "Bible," 232.

The New Heaven and New Earth

6.3.3.2.3 The cycle time and the tree of life

From Beale's biblical-theological research into the new heaven and the new earth, it is possible to relate the cycle time, proposed by Moltmann, to the description of the tree of life in Revelation 22 "with its twelve kinds of fruit, yielding its fruit each month" (v. 2). Beale points out in his comment that this concerns twelve different fruits, each month a different fruit.[252] This verse thus indicates that this tree (or: these trees) produces a cycle of twelve different fruits every year. The time in the new creation does not allow for the permanent disappearance of the fruits. The type of fruit that was there last month will return next year. It does not disappear definitively from the stage. The transience then no longer has the last word.

Beale interprets these descriptions of the tree of life in Revelation 22 as symbolism using the earlier description of the garden in Eden (Gen 2:9–10) and the temple description in Ezekiel (Ezek 47:12). According to him, the purpose of this is to point out that the new creation is the restoration, glorification, and completion of the first creation in which God walked. The tree of life in the geographical garden of Eden has been replaced by several trees of life in the new creation. In his BT, Beale makes it clear that this image implies that in the future, God will dwell entirely with his people and give them eternal life. We must then figuratively interpret its description as a reference to the redemption that God grants his people forever by living entirely in the new creation.[253]

Moltmann also acknowledges that the tree of life in the new creation is related to the tree of life in Eden and the temple vision of the prophet Ezekiel. The vision serves in Revelation to point out to readers that this tree of life gives eternal life and healing to God's people (cf. Rev 22:6). Faced with the oppression and subjugation of earthly Babylon, the seer opposes this invigorating source of God's heavenly Jerusalem.[254]

However, when it comes to the description of the time form in this vision, Beale states in his comment that the seer on Patmos, who was familiar with days, months, and years, could not express his vision without the time forms known to us. In support of this thought, Beale refers to the absence of the moon and sun in the new creation (Rev 21:23; cf. 22:5). If there is no more day and night and the moon is absent, then the months cannot be determined. The total of twelve months that the tree bears fruit cannot refer to cycle time. Therefore, the number twelve serves as a symbol that God's salvation will be fully realized in the new creation.[255]

Here, of course, the question arises whether the idea is correct that the biblical writers could only express themselves in the time forms known to us. In Beale's reaction to the theological-philosophical interpretation of Revelation 10:6, he notes that

---

252. Beale, *Revelation*, 1108.
253. Beale, *New Testament*, 345, 620, 935; *Temple*, 326–27, 351, 360; *Revelation*, 1106–7.
254. Moltmann, *Kommen*, 342–43, 345, 349; *Geist des Lebens*, 298.
255. Beale, *Revelation*, 1107–8.

in extra-biblical texts, such as 2 Enoch 33:2 and 65:7, we hear of the abolition of time or a certain timelessness (§6.3.3.1.2). If extra-biblical writers could speak in this way about a different form of time, we could conclude that also the biblical writers, who lived at the same time, could formulate their thoughts in this way.

Now we must indeed be careful to interpret the description of the tree of life in an unsubtle and literal way. After all, an image always has the character of "is" and "is not." It is more a description than a definition. Any claim for completeness in the interpretation of this image must be rejected. That was all we were given in our hermeneutical comparison of both Rahner's and Moltmann's design (§6.2.3.1). However, at the same time, it is striking that none of the three theologians examined in this picture of the tree of life discusses the time aspect involved. Moltmann's reflection on the tree of life in Revelation 22 refers only to Hildegard von Bingen, who also underlines the parallel between the tree of life in Revelation 22 and Genesis 2, assuming that the tree of life in the garden of Eden also knew continuous fertility. According to Hildegard, through human disobedience, winter came into creation and caused the tree of life to wither and to stop bearing fruit permanently. In the new creation, this aridity will come to an end, and creation will again be continuously bearing fruit. The positive metaphors of light, water, and fertility in the Bible indicate, according to Moltmann, that future continuous fertile time.[256] In his further argument, he does not relate this reflection to his talk about time in the new creation. This is striking for those who realize that it is possible to see in the description of the tree of life both a cycle and a linear continuation of time. Both forms of time do not have to exclude each other in this.[257] The proposed time of this vision is then that of a spiral in which fruits return and at the same time, years pass, without the latter implying negative transience. In his reflection on the time in the new creation, John Polkinghorne, based on Moltmann's cycle model, also posited this proposal of the spiral:

> At the very least, the image of the circle, with its overtones of endlessly repeated return, needs to be replaced by that of the spiral, moving ever closer to the heart of encounter with the life and energies of God.[258]

BT could investigate whether and how this systematic-theological representation of the spiral also returns in other images of the new creation (e.g., in Isa 66:22).[259] What forms of time do they present, and to what extent can these representations be used to say anything about the question of how the biblical writers imagine the time of new creation?

---

256. Moltmann, *Geist des Lebens*, 298.
257. Cf. Brettler, "Cyclical and Teleological Time," 111, 118, 124.
258. Polkinghorne, "Jürgen Moltmann's Engagement," 66. Cf. Bauckham and Trevor, "Shape of Time," 46.
259. Brettler, "Cyclical and Teleological Time," 122.

The biblical-theological research into this could help ST in its questions about the time of the new creation. It could critically inquire whether linear time itself is as bad as Rahner and Moltmann suppose. Does not the image mentioned in §6.3.3.2.2.1 that Moltmann gives off the possibility of music in new creation show that the arrival, disappearance, and repetition of different sounds form a beautiful song? If the sounds remained, the song would degenerate into a cacophony.[260] About the biblical images of the new creation, can time not be described as free of all imperfections and limitations? Is the future not rather a time when life will no longer see death, encounter suffering, and love for the goodwill be permanent? Such a perspective on time in the new creation takes into account the positive growth and progress in this creation that has been pointed out several times in the past by theologians such as John Wesley.[261]

6.3.3.3 Christ's resurrection and God's eternity

6.3.3.3.1 GOD'S ETERNITY AND THE TIME OF SALVATION

Moltmann finds a basis for his description of the aionic time in Paul's talk about the indivisible eschatological moment, the atom of eternity (1 Cor 15:52). In that last moment, all the dead rise from the dead simultaneously and are changed. In this way, "all times" stand up to enter eternity together. Therefore, this last day is the end of the time and day on which the *creatio originalis* completes itself. It is the day on which the first creation transforms into the new creation. The transitory earthly time is then over. "All times" then collectively permeate eternity and thus form the glorified time of the new creation. However, the wealth of time is not lost in this. It forms the root and trunk from which the blossoms and fruits of eternity originate (§4.3.5).

In contrast to Moltmann, Rahner separates salvation from eternity. From there, it is questionable whether there is a last-minute *resurrection* of time, as Moltmann suggests. Is there not rather a radical break between the two times? In Moltmann's aionic time concept, this fraction becomes visible in the separation between the negative time mode of *chronos* and the *Tiefenerfahrung des Augenblicks*. In *concrete terms*: How can the process of all historical *chronos*-time come to an end on the one hand, and on the other hand, there is a simultaneous transformation of "all times" into eternity so that it can be a "fullness of times"? A possible answer, based on Moltmann's design, to this question, is that it is not time as such, but God's transcendental future that is the unity and source of all happening time. In the indivisible atom, on the last day, both the presence and the future of God form the unity of "all times."[262] This then implies

---

260. Moltmann, *Kommen*, 317, 324; *Gott in der Schöpfung*, 133. Cf. Polkinghorne, *God of Hope*, 120.

261. Cf. Wesley, *Sermons II, 34–70*, 411–12.

262. Cf. Moltmann, *Kommen*, 316.

that only the time given by God (*kairos*) rises and that the *chronos*-time decays. Moltmann's statement that all times get up should then be put into perspective.

On the other hand, from Moltmann's design, equally critical questions can be asked about Rahner's sharp discontinuity around the linear time in this creation and the time in the new creation. This seems difficult to identify with Rahner's hermeneutic emphasis on *Aussage* and rejection of an *Einsage*. Although Rahner's hermeneutical principles call for caution in the concretization of eschatological statements (thesis 4), his emphasis on *Aussage* also makes one think of continuity from the perspective of time. That continuity is nowhere to be found in Rahner's talk about time. The time filled by God in the present and past appears to have perished forever in the eschaton or exist only in memories of that time in an even more favorable case.

In his reflection on the future tense, Moltmann does clarify that the future aionic tense is not equal to God's absolute eternity. Aionic time is the relative eternity of creation. It is possible that Rahner can join in. Both systematics then choose not to equate the eternity of the new heaven and the new earth with the eternity of God. The new creation has only a relative eternity that shares in God's absolute eternity.[263] Unlike creation, which has a beginning and an end, God's eternity does not know them.

6.3.3.3.2 Christ's incarnation and resurrection and time

Furthermore, Rahner reminds us in his ST that God the Son through the Incarnation has become part of the time. God not only created the time, but God is also part of the time in Jesus Christ. Although God is eternal, God has chosen to be humbled and become eternally human, subject to the time and space of creation. The Incarnation means that space and time become real for God the Son. Rahner is the only one of three theologians who explicitly reflects on this fact. This is special when we realize that the trinitarian aspect of eternity elsewhere in Christian theology is often not sufficiently mentioned.[264] In Protestant theology, it was Karl Barth in particular who pointed out that the risen Christ should also be central in the reflection on the future time and space.[265] When a human connected with Christ enters the new heaven and the new earth, this also means that this human shares with Christ in the eternal trinitarian life of God. The new heaven and the new earth can thus be described as christocentric.

From the concepts proposed by the three theologians on this subject, this connection with Christ could be further elaborated. It could then be investigated how the Incarnation, death, and resurrection of the Messiah can be related to the possible themes of acceptance, transience, and renewal of time.[266] For Rahner, Moltmann, and

263. Rahner, "Ewige Bedeutung," 47; Moltmann, *Kommen*, 308.
264. Cf. Walter, "Ewigkeit," 1084.
265. Barth, *Schöpfung*, 437–511.
266. As a concise example, see: Bauckham and Trevor, "Shape of Time," 47.

The New Heaven and New Earth

Beale, the salvation work of Christ is a turning point in the history of salvation. His coming and resurrection is the core theme of Christian theology. Because Christ is the Firstborn of the first and new creation, he forms the frame of reference in speaking about the new creation (cf. §6.2.3.3). The three theologians do not address the question to what extent it is possible to speak from this framework about the time in the new creation. According to Moltmann, the resurrection does give hope in speaking of the fullness of time, but the realization of this time should be seen eschatologically. It can only be established that the risen Christ is no longer subject to the transient time of this present creation. His resurrection is thus an "eschatological" event. How these thoughts can be related to the biblical rebellion stories as a frame of reference in the systematic reflection on the time in the new heaven and the new earth is not discussed with him.

This idea could be further related to Rahner's emphasis on *Aussage* in terms of eschatological statements. From the christological-soteriological event, it is possible to assume that Christ was time-bound on earth and that this is still the case after his resurrection. Although impermanence left him, he did not leave time. Rahner will point out that the resurrection cannot be described as a "Return to a vital, space-time existence, as we experience it."[267] The way we think about Christ after his death is not the same as how we think about Christ before his death. If so, Rahner believes that the "resurrection" would not mean salvation, but eternal bondage in this fallen condition:

> [R]esurrection does not mean the beginning of a new period of Jesus' life, filled with other new things and continuing the time of Jesus, but just the lasting, saved finality of Jesus' one unique life.[268]

Of course, the correctness of this wording will have to be examined further. The evangelists describe the risen Christ within the known order of time and space. They seem to continue the current time mode in the revolt stories. There is no indication anywhere that the time for the resurrected Messiah has changed. For example, he is present with his apostles in this time mode for forty days after the resurrection. The stories of revolt thus seem to take place in this space and time. The discipline of BT could further investigate these descriptions and possibly enrich systematic-theological speaking about time and eternity. From there, it would then be possible to ascertain to what extent our eternal destiny is already revealed in the description of the risen Christ.

---

267. Rahner, *Grundkurs*, 262: "Wiederkehr in ein vitales, raumzeitliches Dasein, so wie wir es erfahren."
268. Rahner, *Grundkurs*, 262: "Auferstehung bedeutet nicht den Beginn einer neuen, mit anderem Neuen erfüllten, die Zeit weiterführenden Lebensperiode Jesu, sondern gerade die bleibende, gerettete Endgültigkeit des einen, einmaligen Lebens Jesu." Cf. Felsinger, "Karl Rahner," 213.

6.3.3.3.3 THE SABBATH AS A CROWN ON GOD'S CREATION

Moltmann refers several times in his publications to the biblical meaning of the Sabbath. For him, the Sabbath is an essential prelude to the time of rest in the eschaton. This attention for the Sabbath and its relation to the eternal rest of the new creation is also present in Beale. Because Moltmann, in his ST, gives a limited biblical-theological elaboration of the Sabbath and the holidays in Israel, there is a clear interface with Beale's BT. This makes it possible to enrich Beale's elaboration of this with Moltmann's systematic-theological insights about the Sabbath as the feast of creation and the feast of completion in Judaism.

For Moltmann, the Sabbath is vital for a hectic world in which we live as workaholics. A day of rest protects against the commercialization of life. The unrest that arises from imperishableness leaves creation longing for a place of rest and imperishable time where this threat no longer exists. This unrest is recognized in Beale's theology, in his reflection on the Christian as a pilgrim and resident on earth. Only the future resurrection ends this restless pilgrimage, exodus, or exile and brings God's people home to the eternal land of eternal rest.[269] Moltmann also uses these images of pilgrimage, exodus, and exile. He also uses the image of the eternal Sabbath to point out the eternal rest that God wants to give to creation. In a comparison of the three theologians, it is possible to include Rahner in this theme because this silence and rest of the eternal Sabbath seem to correspond with what he calls the incomprehensible "mystery of God," which is characterized by God's silent presence.[270]

Beale sees a reference to that desired rest also at the end of the story of creation and the foundation of God's tabernacle and temple. Both events show that there can be no rest on earth without God's presence. To confirm this, Beale points to other ancient peoples who knew this relationship between rest and temple.[271] Contrary to Moltmann, Beale is concise when it comes to the Sabbath in Genesis 1. One reason for this is that Beale focuses on the biblical-theological theme of the temple. This puts the Sabbath in the background. All attention with Beale is thus focused on the parallels between creation story and sanctuary to show that the description in Genesis 1–2 reminds of a cosmic temple.

Moltmann focuses more than Beale on the Jewish interpretation of the Sabbath and the biblical-theological meaning of the tranquility that is associated with it. He complements these with his systematic-theological reflections. The Sabbath is thus the sign of God's presence in time. It is the dynamic presence of eternity in time that connects beginning and end, thus creating memory and hope.[272] From these biblical and

---

269. Beale, *New Testament*, 939.
270. Moltmann, *Geschichte*, 166.
271. Beale, *Temple*, 60–66.
272. Moltmann, *Kommen*, 292.

The New Heaven and New Earth

systematic-theological considerations, Moltmann, like the Jews, typifies the Sabbath as the "crown of creation."

Beale lacks this Jewish reflection on the meaning of the Sabbath. Although he acknowledges that God blessed the seventh day in the story of creation, especially, he states that this event also refers to man as the crown of creation: "It would border on hermeneutical narrowness not at least to include Adam within the sphere of application of Gen. 2:3."[273] Compared to Moltmann's ST, this approach is too anthropocentric. Not humanity but the Sabbath as God's appointed time is the crown of creation (§6.2.3.2). He is supported by the Jewish tradition and sees the Sabbath in itself as a temple of God: "In the limited temples of the peoples, heaven and earth touch, but in the Jewish Sabbath, time and eternity touch."[274] The goal of creation is not humanity, but the eschatological Sabbath where God can live completely in the creation and can be all in all.

So, Moltmann points out that creation is designed theocentrically and from the Sabbath as the crown on God's first creation looks forward to the coming of God, the Creator, Liberator, and Finisher of this world. Because Israel counts the days with a number, it is continuously on its way to the next sabbatical rest. Every day in Genesis 1 begins with the limited sleep and looks forward to the infinite rest where God dwells. Moltmann finds support for this thought in the church father Irenaeus of Lyon and Hebrews 3–4.[275] Also, the cycle of the Sabbath forms a basis for his idea of eternal cycle time in the new heaven and on the new earth. This eternal cycle time ultimately sanctifies all times from the past and does not let them be lost. It allows movement and lacks wear or aging.

In comparison with Beale's approach, it is clear that he supports the thesis from BT that Hebrews 3–4 refers to a future rest. This could be a welcome addition to Moltmann's proposal, because it is based on that, of course. According to Beale, the future time of rest is a glorification of the present Sabbath time, which humanity has set aside for God since Adam. However, Beale does not give a biblical-theological answer to the question to what extent this future time is qualitatively different from the present time. The only difference the Bible makes is that it considers the Sabbath time sacred and the weekday time profane. In his BT, Beale does not go into this any further. It is ST that tries to answer these questions. An interdisciplinary comparison with Moltmann's and Rahner's ST on this theme makes us aware of this issue and shows the possibility of making a new biblical-theological contribution to it.

An additional difference between Moltmann and Beale is that Beale sees the continuation of the Sabbath in Christian Sunday. The Sabbath made us look back thankfully at creation and salvation. Sunday, as the day of the resurrection, makes us thankfully look forward to the new creation. However, Beale acknowledges in his BT

---

273. Beale, *New Testament*, 777.

274. Moltmann, "Sabbath," 5.

275. Moltmann, *Gott in der Schöpfung*, 233, 285; *Kommen*, 175; Irenaeus of Lyon, *Adversus Haereses*, IV 16.1; V.30.4; V.33.2.

that its choice of Sunday as a replacement day for the Sabbath is not biblically-theological. It is a theological choice for Sunday because this is the Day of Resurrection of the Firstborn of the new creation. Moltmann acknowledges this difference between the Sabbath and the Sunday and writes: "Whereas the Sabbath is a day of thought and thankfulness, the celebration of the resurrection is a day of beginning and of hope."[276] Nevertheless, he shows historically and systematically-theologically how the Sabbath became Sunday and mentions the disadvantages of this choice.[277] Beale, on the other hand, uses the historical and systematic theology in his BT to show that Sunday replaces the Sabbath. Both theologians are opposed to each other at this point. It is not a question of who is right about both. From the research question, we only observe that Beale sees in his BT the need to step partly outside his field of expertise. So, a comparison between Moltmann's ST and Beale's BT about the Sabbath constitutes a strong enrichment for one's own theological responsible speaking about the new heaven and the new earth.

6.4 CONCLUSION

On the research question: "How can comparison between Karl Rahner's and Jürgen Moltmann's systematic theological designs on eschatology and Gregory Beale's biblical-theological design be of significance in a theological dialogue concerning the new heaven and the new earth?" there are several conclusions to be drawn from the above comparison. From the different critical points of hermeneutical and content-related elements, the observations established there can be summarized as follows.

1. Transposition and anticipation

    a. Rahner and Moltmann think the opposite about the point of recognition and realization of the future. Rahner sees the future as a transposition (Aussage) of what christologically, anthropologically, and soteriologically in Christ has already been realized on earth. Moltmann sees the future as an intervention (Einsage) by God's coming (Advent). From a history of salvation, this is only a question of anticipating the future. This puts both systematics opposite each other in the field of ST.

    b. Beale's BT does not mention the issue of transposition and anticipation, but his development model from Genesis 1–2 is mostly in line with Rahner. The comparison makes it clear that in doing so, he still makes his own hermeneutical choice between the two paradigms.

        i. The awareness of this hermeneutical choice inspires the question of whether the divine realizes the present creation "from" or "from outside."

---

276. Moltmann, "Sabbath," 5.
277. Moltmann, *Gott in der Schöpfung*, 294–98. Cf. *Kommen*, 158.

ii. From Beale's theology, ST can refer to the biblical reference to "the new world" and the "from above" that stands opposite the "of this old world." Moltmann's ST replaces this "from above" with a "front" and a "future," while Rahner's ST replaces the above expressions with a "back" and a "past and present."

iii. This comparison may inspire us to further develop this "from above" in BT as a mutual enrichment for the interdisciplinary dialogue on the new heaven and the new earth.

c. Rahner's distinction between "eschatology" and "apocalyptic" is exegetically not tenable from Beale's BT. Neither does Mark 13:32 support Rahner's rejection of Einsage and plea for Aussage.

i. The exegesis of Mark 13:32 instead pleads for Moltmann's ST in which the emphasis is on Einsage.

ii. An interdisciplinary comparison between BT and ST thus shows the presuppositions that the ST uses and indicates where the systematic theologian (unconsciously) puts his extra-biblical ideas in the Bible.

2. Relationship protology and eschatology

a. Beale's BT can be of significance to Moltmann's and Rahner's ST because it presents an overall picture of the biblical storyline that strongly starts from the idea that the beginning and end are connected.

b. Moltmann's ST can complement Beale's BT from the emphasis in ST on protology and eschatology.

c. Although all three theologians acknowledge the evil in the present creation, only Moltmann attempts to demonstrate the origin of this evil. He does this through the teaching of the *zimzum*. Beale and Rahner limit themselves to the thought that evil through the disobedience of humanity got a full (Beale) or strengthened (Rahner) influence in this creation. In an interdisciplinary comparison, all three theologians are positively challenged to reflect critically on their ideas and to fill gaps. ST can mean a lot for BT.

i. Moltmann's ST may be challenged about the question of the necessity and sustainability of the concept of negative *nihil* and *zimzum*.

ii. Beale's BT critically asks Moltmann's ST how the *nihil* in which God is absent fits in with the overall picture of the biblical testimony about God who is near to humans.

iii. On the other hand, Beale's BT is challenged by Moltmann's and Rahner's ST from the question about the *origin of evil* that, according to Beale, is already lurking in Genesis 2:15.

iv. ST and BT ask each other mutually for their answers to the question of whether God cannot achieve the new creation without the suffering.

d. Between Rahner's and Moltmann's ST and Beale's BT, there are significant differences in their own accents that each of them puts in talking about sin and salvation. Beale's BT emphasizes the enormous impact of sin on humanity and focuses on human failure. Moltmann's and Rahner's ST speak more positively about human capacity and see sin as a problem for all creation that is entirely solved by God's intervention.

i. A comparison shows that in his reflection on a current and new creation, Beale pays more attention to the impact of sin and the discontinuity that goes with it than to the renewal through God's triumph and the continuity that goes with it. The ST of Moltmann and Rahner could inspire Beale to pay more attention to continuity.

ii. Also, they inspire each other to think about the relationship between extrinsic and intrinsic sin and thus arrive at a possible total image of it. Moltmann's and Rahner's ST lacks the reflection on biblical texts that point to the intrinsic nature of sin. In Beale's BT, the extrinsic of sin (e.g., the powers of evil as an external influence on man) is missing.

iii. ST can also point Beale to his (unconscious) systematic-theological paradigm of the Augustinian-Calvinist approach to sin.

e. Also, Beale can challenge Rahner's ST to show where he believes the biblical testimony speaks of a free neutral choice in humans.

f. In comparison, BT and ST challenge each other to further reflect on sin in the biblical storyline.

3. Visual language and perspective on the current creation

a. Rahner's and Moltmann's ST encourage Beale's BT to conduct a further biblical-thematic investigation of the biblical images in his field because they believe that the imagery is lacking in the broad theological reflection.

b. Beale's BT can enrich Rahner's and Moltmann's ST from his method of interpreting biblical images.

c. Moltmann's and Rahner's ST make Beale aware of the anthropocentric paradigm that has a little eye for creation outside of humanity and challenges him to a biblical-theological reflection on a possibly holistic, cosmos-encompassing paradigm.

d. Rahner, Moltmann, and Beale recognize the importance of Christ's salvation work as a frame of reference for the new creation. Moltmann's ST challenges Beale's BT to further reflect on the biblical rebellion stories by pointing out the relevant core elements that are important in the relationship between Christology and eschatology.

4. Resurrection and matter

   a. From the comparison, it can be concluded that Beale's BT focuses primarily on spiritual renewal, while Rahner's and Moltmann's ST emphasize physical renewal.

      i. A comparison can be enrichment in this respect by bringing the two accents together and thus avoiding a strict separation between the immaterial and material aspect of the resurrection.

      ii. The rejection of the gnostic in Moltmann's and Rahner's ST can make Beale aware of the importance of the apostolic proclamation of the physical resurrection in his BT in the light of the New Testament problems in this respect.

      iii. From Genesis 1–2, Moltmann and Rahner see humanity and earth in relation to each other. This element is remarkably lacking in Beale's work, although his BT takes the story of creation as its starting point.

   b. Rahner's and Moltmann's ST can inspire Beale to give a biblical-theological reflection on the resurrection stories of Christ. This then offers added value in the choice of their view on Christ's resurrection as a starting point for the theme of the coming resurrection.

   c. The alternating talk about partial continuity and radical discontinuity does not make it easy to determine Beale's position clearly. His choice of words seems contradictory. In his BT, the discontinuity between old and new is in the foreground because of sin and brokenness.

      i. A comparison with Rahner's and Moltmann's ST can have an additional effect here because both emphasize that God does not judge and destroy his creation but the godless powers of evil. This ensures a possible balance in speaking about continuity and discontinuity between this and the new creation.

      ii. From the Jewish tradition, Beale sees a parallel between the old and new creation and the present and future body but does not work it out anywhere in his BT. Because this effect does occur in Rahner's and Moltmann's ST, an interdisciplinary comparison can lead Beale to propose this effect.

5. Eden, Jerusalem, and space

   a. Moltmann's ST and Beale's BT about space can be amply related, complemented, and challenged. Together they offer an opportunity in Rahner's ST not only to talk about fleeting world time and eternal salvation time but also about fleeting world space and eternal salvation space.

   b. Beale's BT supports Moltmann's vision of the *creatio continua*, in which there is both a distance between God and creation and in which there are spaces (temples) in which God permeates creation. In connection with the new creation, both are convinced that the cosmos is permeated by the triune God, and the triune God is permeated by the cosmos, without both merging into one another.

      i. Moltmann's and Beale's perspective on the arrival of the Trinity in this creation can provide a more substantial total picture in Beale's BT in which Trinity doctrine and eschatology are connected.

      ii. How Beale would react to Moltmann's proposal of the *zimzum* cannot be determined from his BT. However, it can be concluded that both agree that God's radical intervention is necessary to make the entire creation of God's dwelling place.

      iii. In comparison, Beale's approach can point out for Moltmann's ST that Revelation 20:11 cannot be used for the proposition that the new heaven and earth no longer contain any space.

   c. Moltmann's theology can point out to Beale that the descriptions in Revelation 21–22 do not necessarily imply that there is only discontinuity between this creation and the new heaven and earth.

      i. This can challenge Beale to analyze from the BT what contrasts and similarities there are in the biblical images about the new heaven and earth.

      ii. In his explanation, Beale pays little attention to the glorified space in the new heaven and earth, which forces itself upon us from the images and visions. His approach is ultimately determined by an anthropocentric emphasis. Beale thus threatens to overlook the blessing that God's coming brings for all creation. The "I am making all things new" is then reduced to the renewal of the human being.

iii. An interdisciplinary comparison with Rahner's and Moltmann's ST can draw Beale's attention to the fact that physical, space, or time is never lacking in biblical imagery.

d. In comparison with Rahner's ST and Beale's BT, Moltmann can emphasize that the future "seeing of God" is more than just an intellectual matter and points to the deep relationship that a person may have with God.

  i. Rahner's ST can challenge Beale to elaborate the different biblical visions about the future relationship between God and his people in his BT.

  ii. Moltmann lacks the image of the city as a bride, even though he refers to biblical images several times in his ST. His ST puts an emphasis on the city as a garden. The comparison with Beale may lead to an addition here.

e. Nowhere is the term "new heaven," explained by Rahner, Moltmann, or Beale. The term is only seen about the "new earth" and understood as referring to creation as a totality, the new universe. A possible investigation into this may imply a broadening of the question of why heaven also needs renewal and why in the new creation, the distinction between heaven and earth is ultimately maintained.

6. Sabbath and eternity

a. An interdisciplinary comparison can deepen the question about the meaning and implication of time terms such as *kairos* and *chronos*. This can then contribute to the theme of continuity and discontinuity between the present and the new creation. It can further challenge ST and BT to reflect precisely over time in the context of the relationship between protology and eschatology.

  i. A comparison makes BT and ST aware of hermeneutical choices and of the influence of Greek philosophy that quickly asserts itself in Christian doctrine.

  ii. Beale's BT can point out to Moltmann in a comparison that Revelation 10:6 does not say in a technical-philosophical way that *chronos* comes to an end, as Moltmann suggests in his approach.

  iii. Rahner's and Moltmann's ST can point out to Beale that his BT thinks too much about sin and salvation from Western theology and pays too little attention to the nuanced biblical talk about it. Beale may point out that Rahner and Moltmann in their ST reflect too much on time from

Western philosophy and give too little attention to biblical speaking about it.

b. In a comparison of Moltmann's design, critical questions can be asked on Rahner's strong emphasis on discontinuity about linear time in this creation on the one hand and time in the new creation on the other hand.

   i. Together with Beale, Moltmann can point out that the biblical representation of eternity evokes the idea of progressiveness and dynamics more than that in Rahner's theology.

   ii. Beale can demonstrate in an interdisciplinary comparison with Rahner's ST that the Gospels describe the risen Christ within the known order of time and space.

   iii. A comparison reveals the connection Rahner makes between Christ and time. It can then be investigated how the Incarnation, death, and resurrection of the Messiah can be related to the possible themes of acceptance, transience, and renewal of time. This is important because, for Rahner, Moltmann, and Beale, the salvation work of Christ is a turning point in the history of salvation.

c. Rahner's and Moltmann's visions of time in the new creation may challenge Beale to pay more attention to this in his BT. Recent developments in the biblical sciences show that an international, intercultural, and interdisciplinary approach offers an advantage.

   i. Moltmann can critically ask Beale the question whether his assertion that the biblical writers could only express themselves in the time forms known to us is not refuted by himself.

   ii. Beale can take advantage of Moltmann's ST about the Sabbath as a feast of creation and as a feast of completion in Judaism. In his BT, Beale does not elaborate on the Sabbath, although he usually pays much attention to the Jewish tradition. An interdisciplinary comparison with Moltmann's ST can make him aware of this issue and be an enrichment.

d. Rahner's ST can challenge Moltmann's ST with the question if there is a resurrection of time in the last moment and not a radical break between the negative time mode *chronos* and the *Tiefenerfahrung des Augenblicks*.

   i. Beale can relate Moltmann's representation of cycle time to the circle of nature described by Ecclesiastes and the eternal circle that characterizes the tree of life in Revelation 22.

7

Conclusion

Chapter 6 of this dissertation offered an answer to the research question. The detailed comparison of the three theologians in that chapter began with a reflection on hermeneutical presuppositions and was followed by a comparison of content. Both clarify to what extent it was possible to bring BT and ST in dialogue with each other in the topic of the new heaven and earth.

This hermeneutical and substantive comparison made us conclude that Moltmann's, Rahner's, and Beale's eschatology of the new heaven and earth are a welcome addition to each other. ST and BT raise both actual questions in this area. A theologically responsible speaking about the new heaven and the new earth is thereby clarified, challenged, and supplemented. This applies to the research into both the hermeneutical and the substantive elements that play a role in the reflection on the theme of the new heaven and earth within the Christian proclamation of faith.

This concluding chapter brings the methodical observations in the critically conducted equation to attention (§7.1) and examines the ultimate significance of this research for the theme of the new heaven and the new earth (§7.2). The chapter concludes with some implications and prospects for further research (§7.3).

7.1 METHODICAL OBSERVATIONS IN THE INTERDISCIPLINARY EQUATION

This dissertation discussed various observations that are primarily known among theologians, but that are rarely addressed in current attempts to compare the fields of BT and ST. Because of the essential significance of these observations in the interdisciplinary comparison between Rahner, Moltmann, and Beale, it is essential to address them in this conclusion first.

7.1.1 Awareness of reaction theology

In the individual analyses of the three theologians, it became visible that all three theologians implicitly react to other theologies in their reflections. Whereas Beale's BT reacts methodically to those who connect eschatology with the end of salvation-history, Moltmann and Rahner react methodically to those who see eschatology fully realized in the present. Although this seems to be mainly in the background in their publications, the interdisciplinary comparison shows that the impact of this reactive attitude in all three theologians is decisive. An interdisciplinary comparison between ST and BT has the advantage that it can serve to make the systematic-theological and biblical-theological lines of thought more visible. This leads to a more responsible speaking about the future from two different disciplines and justifies the methodology of chapter 6, which started the critical comparison with the hermeneutic presuppositions.

7.1.2 Hermeneutical consciousness

By choosing to start with the hermeneutic principles of the three theologians, it is clear from the beginning that ST and BT have no value-free neutrality. Each discipline interprets data based on its assumptions. Chapter 6 compared Rahner, Moltmann, and Beale in-depth about their representations of the new creation. This comparison happened in such a way that not only the hermeneutic pattern of the theologians became visible. Also, various (unconscious) assumptions were revealed. Some of these assumptions arose through the theological path that every theologian took and his personal life experiences.

The hermeneutical choices made by ST and BT in the theological reflection determine the pattern within which the substantive thinking about the new heaven and earth takes place. The awareness of the influence this has on the theological thinking has led each of the three theologians to turn away from the theological choices made by Rudolph Bultmann (Rahner and Moltmann) or by those who only emphasized the "not-yet" of the new creation (Beale). According to the three theologians, a dialogue between ST and BT is valuable in that respect alone. It makes both disciplines aware of their hermeneutic assumptions (§2.4). Every theologian thinks from a particular framework. The influence of that specific framework has several times been highlighted in the interdisciplinary equation. It has become clear that BT also thinks from a framework. This was already apparent from the fact that there is a plurality of methodology in BT. BT does not form a universal unit. Gerard von Rad, the former biblical-theological teacher of Moltmann (§2.2), mentioned this already in his time:

> One cannot say that since its existence Old Testament theology has evolved into one form upon which for a long time a determining force would have emanated in such a way that generations have continued to work on it

and improved it. Instead, the retrospective observer is struck by a lack of continuity.[1]

This statement is still relevant today. Therefore, the choice of a biblical theologian, as well as the choice of a systematic theologian entails a one-sidedness. Other representatives from BT or ST would have a different comparison. This allows us to conclude that the field of BT, like ST, does not look utterly neutrally at the biblical text. However, there is often no reflection on this in publications that want to contribute to the interdisciplinary dialogue (cf. §§1.5; 6.1). In that respect, it is necessary to understand that BT also has an interpretation of the biblical text, which is colored by the researcher's position.

In the interdisciplinary comparison in this dissertation, it is repeatedly concluded that caution is needed in seeing BT *only* as a supplier of "evidence" for ST like Rahner initially proposed (§2.1.1). BT transposes "proof texts" (or better: "the proof of *the Bible*") from the original context to the self-formed biblical-theological interpreted facts. Whoever wants to map out the biblical storyline systematically, sees that the theologian is also in a specific position. So, like ST, BT is only a signpost to Christian truth and cannot be elevated to *norma non normata*. For many theologians, this is only the case for the Bible itself. The critical comparison of both the hermeneutical principles and the differences and similarities in terms of content between the new heaven and the new earth revealed this.

An essential element of BT linked to this is the accountability of the chosen core themes. Where BT does not provide an adequate answer to this question, it tends to ignore its hermeneutical assumptions, which play a role in the choice of its framework. Therefore, the systematic ranking used by BT should be just as justified as the systematic ranking used by ST. However, the analysis showed that Beale only briefly mentioned this. Also, a further reflection on Beale's hermeneutic was less discussed in his BT than in the ST of Rahner and Moltmann. We saw in Beale's theology that BT even worked with systematic-theological presuppositions. The comparison conducted brought with it a hermeneutic awareness of this and showed the consequences of these choices. It revealed that BT, in a dialogue with ST, should do more than provide "evidence."

This leads us to the conclusion that neither discipline can claim to be completely objective. The idea that BT is an "objective" discipline on which a "subjective" ST can be based is unjustified. Both ST, which is challenged by topical questions, and BT, which explains the surviving Bible text, are in a subjective context. In this respect, the relationship between exegesis and theology can be represented in the form of a circle, in which both disciplines influence each other equally. Therefore, a dialogue between

---

1. Von Rad, "Offene Fragen," 289: "Man kann nicht sagen, daß sich die alttestamentliche Theologie seit ihrer Existenz zu einer Form herausgestaltet hat, von der für längere Zeit eine prägende Kraft ausgegangen wäre dergestalt, daß Generationen an ihr weitergearbeitet und sie verbessert haben. Dem rückschauenden Betrachter fällt vielmehr ein Mangel an Kontinuität auf."

the two disciplines constitutes an added value in recognition of these elements. The explanation of individual Bible texts influences the theology in speaking about continuity and discontinuity, which in turn influences the explanation. This makes it all the more important to make a comparison of the hermeneutical presuppositions before an interdisciplinary comparison of substantive aspects is started. Where this happens, the interdisciplinary dialogue acquires added value because the depth of the theme is discussed.

7.1.3 Uniqueness and equivalence

The research conducted above shows that there can be a great diversity in approaches to the interdisciplinary conversation between ST and BT. This argues in favor of allowing both disciplines to coexist as two equal entities in the theological encyclopedia. In the interdisciplinary comparison, it has become apparent that these two entities are connected. The ST indirectly influences BT, and BT does so for its part in ST. Both place different accents in their eschatology, from their perspective on the Christian creed. Together with Rahner, Moltmann, and Beale, we conclude that in an interdisciplinary dialogue between ST and BT, there can be no hierarchy. One discipline cannot and must not be elevated above the other. Not the hierarchy, but the equality within the dialogue is typical of this interdisciplinary encounter. This leads us further to the conclusion that the two disciplines are neither interchangeable nor mutually subjective. ST and BT stand side by side as two interlocutors, without one discipline dissolving itself in the other. The conversation between the two disciplines makes it clear how they have a specific identity and how enriching cooperation is. Although the boundaries of these disciplines are not fixed, the comparison shows several times that Rahner and Moltmann in their ST look at the Christian doctrine from a different focus than Beale does in his BT. At the same time, both disciplines make use of elements that belong to the other discipline. The comparison shows that both disciplines are characterized as follows:

1. BT aims to map the theological message of the Bible. It does this from a systematic framework, by searching for the core elements of the meta-narrative from the perspective of respect for all the books of the Bible. Central to this is the relationship between God and humanity, and between people in the history of salvation. In the elaboration of this objective, it maps out the continuity and discontinuity of the relationship between past, present, and future in the Bible books. A systematic-theological paradigm is recognized in the Bible. Beale's BT takes little account of this paradigm, nor does it offer a comparison with other paradigms that have been mapped by ST. It happens only in his comment on 1–2 Thessalonians. As a result, the choices made by BT in the interdisciplinary dialogue with others are not always transparent. In the above equation, this

becomes visible in the interpretation of biblical texts that speak of a recovery of the animal world. A justification of the biblical-theological explanation of these texts is missing in Beale's BT. His view of this is reduced to the choices he makes *a priori*. The data Beale obtains are only specific Judeo-Christian texts, most of which originate from the time of the NT. This shows that even BT cannot grasp the complete biblical storyline and makes choices from its own confessional or systematic-theological reflections in its field.

2. Another characteristic of ST is that it places the relationship between God and humanity and among people themselves at the heart of salvation history. However, the categories of ST are rather logically hierarchically ordered and less biblical-historical. In contrast with BT, it is more characterized by high alertness to the various theological motives and by the effect of specific biblical texts in the presentations of the Christian doctrine. It focuses on the question of the meaning and influence of Christian doctrine in historical contexts. This includes the question of the meaning and influence of the Bible for the Christian system. BT addresses this question not much. The historical authenticity and authority of the biblical text are only briefly discussed, as is the case, for example, in biblical exegesis. The text is taken as it is. ST, on the other hand, often lacks the question of the relationship between the individual elements of the Christian confession and the biblical storyline. ST thus runs the risk of placing biblical themes in its paradigm, without taking into account the original context in which the theme is addressed. Especially BT can be of importance for ST. The equation shows that interaction between BT and ST can be much more effective if a complete biblical-theological paradigm is taken into account. Beale already indicates this if he finds that ST and BT can complement each other (§2.3.1). This also applies to Moltmann, who appreciates BT and recognizes how it charts the biblical metanarrative theology. Nevertheless, he often uses additional "proofs" in his ST. The biblical storyline in which the relevant "proof text" is to be found is then hardly taken into account. When we talk about *chronos* and *topos,* we see the dangers involved. A positive example of this can be seen in the comparison between Rahner's ST and Beale's BT. Although Beale implicitly rejects Rahner's explanation of Mark 13 (§6.2.1.2.1) in his works, his BT offers a further substantiation of what Rahner is about in that explanation. Herein his biblical-theological paradigm approaches Rahner's interpretation.

In summary, it can be concluded that BT thinks fundamentally from a historical storyline, whereas ST thinks from a logical-hierarchical perspective. This has already been recognized by Beale: BT draws a development line from biblical revelation, while ST thinks from a circle in its field. Not only ST but also BT chooses to relate Christian doctrine to current questions within Christianity.

To clarify it with an image of the clock: ST chooses to take the Bible apart like a clock and divide it into several parts. All hands, large and small gears, and many other elements that belong to the clock are individually examined and studied. It looks at how the gears are connected and how their mechanical movement makes the clock functional. However, BT chooses not to disassemble the clock and to study its elements concerning the whole of the clock. It maps all the hands, large and small gears, and other elements that are considered essential for a clock. Also, BT can help ST to assemble the clock correctly, so that the original watch remains a clock and is not destroyed, while ST can help BT to pay attention to elements in the clock that do not seem to have any particular function at first glance.[2]

Through an interdisciplinary comparison, both disciplines can become more aware of their methodological choices and performances. Respectful interaction with the other can have a fruitful effect in this because it becomes visible where BT or ST decays into a created paradigm that (unconsciously) becomes decisive for the results. Because the research fields of both areas largely overlap, such a conversation is to be encouraged. Whether this interdisciplinary comparison is also of more considerable significance than, for example, that between ST and another discipline in theology is not said. After all, such research falls outside the scope of the research question in this dissertation.

7.1.4 Enrichment of the overall picture

Another advantage of a comparison with the other discipline is that one looks beyond one's boundaries and can thus deepen one's research field in terms of content. We conclude from the interdisciplinary comparison about the new heaven and the new earth that neither the theological discipline of BT nor that of ST is capable of fully embracing the Christian creed. There are always fields of research to be mentioned that one has an eye for, while the other lacks attention for them. The comparison between Rahner's, Moltmann's, and Beale's theology about the new heaven and the new earth shows the necessity to look at the same theme from different perspectives and accentuations.

Where an interdisciplinary conversation with the other discipline is lacking, there is a risk of continuing to walk on well-trodden paths. While modernism was often characterized by in-depth research and a strict differentiation of its discipline, in which the researchers set themselves the goal of knowing more and more about a specific theme, postmodernism rather exposes its limitations. In many cases, the research was so brief that researchers, due to the lack of an interdisciplinary conversation, threatened to overlook the global significance of their research.[3] It is precisely the interdisciplinary exchange between BT and ST that can meet this need by enriching

---

2. This image is derived from: Iwand, *Glauben und Wissen*, 272.
3. Bartholomew, "Uncharted Waters," 11.

each other from the mutual interest in the broader subject. Thus, ST challenges BT to view the biblical storyline with ST-glasses, while BT, in turn, challenges ST to view its presentation of Christian doctrine with BT-glasses.

An interdisciplinary dialogue between the two disciplines can ultimately be of significance here for the whole theology. Moltmann writes, for example, in response to Bertold Klappert's biblical-theological interaction with his works:

> In such a community of theologians, it is shown that theology is not a private event of religious geniuses, but comes from the community of believers and is designed for the community of humans and the conditions of creation.[4]

BT and ST are integral parts of the same whole. Although both practice theology in a different way, they are in the same quest for a reliable, authentic Christian theology.

The interdisciplinary comparison results in new challenges in the research. This brings new questions and new needs to the fore that call for personal reflection from various disciplines. The critical comparison clarifies that neither discipline has the last word. Statements made in BT or ST are provisional and remain open to new insights, while both disciplines simultaneously strive for completeness. The purpose of the comparison is not only to resolve differences and disagreements between disciplines. It also serves to improve the quality of research by accounting for the presuppositions of each theological model. This bears the fruit that theologians become more aware of their religious tradition and theological position and can put their contributions to the total into perspective.

7.2 MEANING FOR THE THEME OF THE NEW HEAVEN AND EARTH

7.2.1 Summary observations

At the beginning of this dissertation, we drew attention to the fact that in the past, a strict separation was often made between BT and ST (see §1.2). In today's society, on the other hand, we see a growing appreciation for interdisciplinary conversation. This social trend is a reaction to an overly reductionist approach to individual sciences. The demand for a responsible interdisciplinary dialogue has, according to some, given rise to hopes of bridging the gap that exists between ST and BT. "There are encouraging signs that the two disciplines, after generations of wandering in the wilderness of isolation from one another, are each approaching the Promised Land of interdisciplinary partnership."[5]

---

4. Moltmann, "Antwort Jürgen Moltmann," 139: "In einer solchen Gemeinschaft von Theologen zeigt sich, daß Theologie keine Privatveranstaltung religiöser Genies ist, sondern aus der Gemeinschaft der Glaubenden kommt und für die Gemeinschaft der Menschen und die Verhältnisse der Schöpfung entworfen wird."

5. Vanhoozer, "Theology of the New Testament," 28.

This mutual rapprochement between ST and BT may also grow in the eschatological reflection on the new heaven and earth.⁶ The research into a cosmic eschatology in ST remained rather brief and was seen as a gap in influential systematic-theological works (see extensively §1.3). This fact justified the research question of this dissertation:

> How can comparison between Karl Rahner's and Jürgen Moltmann's systematic theological designs on eschatology and Gregory Beale's biblical-theological design be of significance in a theological dialogue concerning the new heaven and the new earth?

The relevant analyses of this dissertation examined what Rahner, Moltmann, and Beale had to say as experts in this field. The amount of material about the theme of the new heaven and the new earth that has emerged in the process is already a contribution in itself for those who want to think critically about their cosmological eschatology. However, the objective of this dissertation was not to design such a cosmological eschatology about the new heaven and the new earth. That would be too arbitrary at this stage. Instead, it has investigated to what extent a comparison between Rahner's and Moltmann's ST and Beale's BT can be of significance for a theologically responsible discussion about the new heaven and the new earth. The answer to this question is elaborated in detail in chapter 6, and the conclusion brought together in §6.4. There, an extensive overview was presented of different elements in which Rahner's, Moltmann's, and Beale's theology can be of significance to each other in a theologically responsible speaking about the new heaven and earth. There is no need to repeat the detailed conclusions reached there. In this last chapter, we only want to summarize the data mentioned there. For the sake of completeness, we also repeat the hermeneutical awareness, which we discussed in §7.1:

1. Hermeneutical awareness

    The interdisciplinary comparison brings out mutual hermeneutic awareness in both disciplines. The comparison showed that Beale's BT, in particular, benefited most from this. The results of the research show the impact of existing theological paradigms (e.g., the gnostic) and of the own paradigms in its BT (e.g., Augustinian Calvinistic paradigm, thinking from transposition). Although this hermeneutic consciousness is already strongly present in ST, a comparison with BT can help discover where it derives its thoughts from extra-biblical data.

2. Deepening the content of overlapping themes

    a. Brief additions

    In comparison, Rahner's, Moltmann's, and Beale's theology offer small enrichments for a theological speaking about the new heaven and earth. Here the meaning of BT for ST is higher than that of ST for BT. Beale's BT (1)

---

6. Wilkinson, *Eschatology*, 24–26, 54–57; Mühling, *Grundinformation*, 305–14.

corrects Rahner's and Moltmann's explanation of Mark 13:32, Revelation 10:6, and 20:11; (2) possibly relates the cycle time in Moltmann's model to Revelation 22; and (3) rejects the application of "apocalyptic" in Rahner's ST. Mutually, Moltmann's ST, in particular, appears to have direct significance for Beale's BT in offering small additions. This is done in deepening themes such as Sabbath, space, and protology.

b. Wide additions

For a broad addition, the equation is more suitable. Rahner's, Moltmann's, and Beale's can extensively supplement their eschatology with data from the other about the relationship between protology and eschatology, between continuity and discontinuity and between intrinsic and extrinsic sin. This fact again underpins the conclusion that a dialogue between ST and BT should not primarily focus on providing concise "evidence texts," but on a mutual exchange of broader themes (§7.1.2).

c. Content recommendations for new themes

  i. Recommendations for new sub-themes

  In the comparison undertaken, both fields of study offer mutual new sub-themes in thinking about the new heaven and earth. For example, Beale's biblical-theological reflection on the resurrection lacks a detailed clarification of this: (1) God's plan with *physical* creation; and (2) the descriptions of Christ's resurrection in the Gospels. These sub-themes support ST in its reflection on the new creation. With the doctrine of sin, further additions are possible: (1) God's judgment on evil and the liberation from good creation; and (2) the "from above" in biblical speaking. Beale's BT also challenges Rahner's and Moltmann's ST to a more in-depth investigation into the relationship between sin and new creation.

  ii. Recommendations for new main themes

  In the recommendation of new main themes, Rahner's and Moltmann's ST challenges Beale's BT several times to an in-depth investigation of the biblical images about the new creation. For all three theologians, there is no further attention to the meaning of the term "new heaven" in the expression "new heaven and new earth."

  iii. Recommendations that fall outside the boundaries of the discipline

  The interdisciplinary comparison also raises questions that fall outside the domain of the specific discipline. To be mentioned from Beale's BT: A biblical foundation (1) of the teachings of the *zimzum* (Moltmann) and (2) of the free neutral choice of humans (Rahner). From Rahner's and Moltmann's ST, the following themes will also be discussed: the relationship between Trinity and eschatology, an investigation into time in the biblical narrative, an investigation into suffering, the origin of evil, and the powers of evil.

This research shows that a comparison between ST of Rahner and Moltmann and BT of Beale about their theology of the new heaven and the new earth has added value for both disciplines. Central to this remains the question of continuity and discontinuity between this and the new creation. We conclude that the choices Rahner, Moltmann, and Beale make in their eschatology of the new heaven and the new earth are inextricably linked to this question.

7.2.2 Meaning for the broad cosmic eschatology

Although this dissertation deliberately limits itself to three theologians (§1.5.3), the question is legitimate how the above observations can contribute to the current discussion about the new heaven and the new earth. Therefore, in conclusion, we wish to examine how this dissertation can influence the discussion about the new heaven and the new earth, as we find in recent publications from ST. We focus on ten works. Because this dissertation is written in the Dutch-speaking area of the Netherland and Flanders, we have made a conscious choice for five Dutch-language and five foreign publications.

The Dutch-language systematic-theological publications are: *Christelijke dogmatiek: Een inleiding* (2012) by Gijsbert van den Brink and Cornelis (Kees) van der Kooi, *De toekomst van God: Ontwerp van een eschatologie* (2012) by Willem J. Ouweneel; *God doet recht: Eschatologie als christologie* (2008) by Bram van de Beek; *Hoop op God: Eschatologische verwachting* (2004) by Jan Hoek; and *Beknopte Gereformeerde Dogmatiek* (1992) by Jan van Genderen and Willem H. Velema.

From foreign publications, the first choice was made for the eschatological monographs of two German theologians from ST: *Mysterium der Verwandlung: Eine Eschatologie aus katholischer Perspektive im Gespräch mit jüdischem Denken der Gegenwart* (2005) by Josef Wohlmuth and *Eschatology* (2000) by Hans Schwarz, who was born and worked in Germany. In addition, three publications remain, all written by American theologians, and which also have an impact on the evangelical movement: *Systematic Theology: Biblical and Historical* (2005) by Robert D. Culver; *Systematic Theology: An Introduction to Biblical Doctrine* (2000) by Wayne Grudem; and *Christian Theology* (1998) by Millard J. Erickson.

7.2.2.1 *Perspective for physical creation*

If we compare these theologians with each other, we acknowledge that almost all of them take a future for the earth into account in their eschatology.[7] The only exception

---

7. Van de Beek, *God doet recht*, 83,90; Culver, *Systematic Theology*, 1153; Wohlmuth, *Mysterium*, 231–34; Hoek, *Hoop*, 262–65; Grudem, *Systematic Theology*, 1158; Schwarz, *Eschatology*, 404.

is Millard Erickson. His ST focuses only on heaven and sees it as the place where God wants the believers to have "for all eternity." The emphasis on this future in the heavenly realms is so powerfully present that Erickson radically opposes it to physical life on earth.[8] It is not given why he remains silent in his reflection on the "new earth." That is remarkable for those who realize that earlier in his work, he already referred to the "renewal of the creation" and quotes Revelation 21:1.[9] However, his eschatological reflections no longer speak of a renewal of creation. Cosmic eschatology fades into the background, and only individual eschatology is paramount.

A similar sound can also be found with Jan van Genderen and Willem Velema. In their reformed dogmatics, they call for caution in giving too earthly descriptions of the new heaven and the new earth. This caution also leads them to the fact that the biblical speaking of the "new earth" is mostly absent.[10] The influence of Gnosticism on Christian thinking about the new creation, of which Jürgen Moltmann and Karl Rahner also make us aware, is not sufficiently recognized in this (cf. §§6.2.3.2; 6.3.1). It is now possible that Millard Erickson, Jan van Genderen, and Willem Velema do not have this, because their works are the oldest of the ten chosen publications. The attention for the environment and the growing awareness of God's creation that comes with it only becomes apparent in theology after the beginning of the new millennium. It remains special that in the ten publications I have chosen, only the works of Bram van de Beek and Gijsbert van de Brink and Kees van der Kooi can relate the neglect of physical recovery more closely to the Greek gnostic influences that easily enter the theological thinking about the new creation. They consciously oppose these gnostic tendencies and emphasize that the biblical-eschatological expectation also includes the "new earth."[11]

7.2.2.2 *Perspective for God's complete creation*

Although most of the ten publications reviewed take a future for the earth into account, this does not mean that their elaboration is automatically based on a holistic view of the future. Thus we see that Robert Culver and Wayne Grudem, in their talk about the new heaven and the new earth, pay no particular attention to the all-encompassing holistic meaning of this earthly-concrete perspective.[12] Their talk about this continues to be a one-sided talk about the future of humanity, as we saw at length in this dissertation at Gregory Beale (cf. §6.2.3.2). The holistic approach that Karl Rahner and Jürgen Moltmann point out is entirely lacking here.

---

8. Erickson, *Christian Theology*, 1233–37.
9. Erickson, *Christian Theology*, 1012.
10. Van Genderen and Velema, *Dogmatiek*, 793.
11. Van den Brink and van der Kooi, *Dogmatiek*, 646; Van de Beek, *God doet recht*, 87.
12. Culver, *Systematic Theology*, 1153; Grudem, *Systematic Theology*, 1158.

The situation is different from the work of Bram van de Beek, Jan Hoek, Hans Schwarz, and Josef Wohlmuth. Van de Beek refers to the holistic presentations in the biblical imagery and Hoek writes, in his plea for a holistic approach to the new heaven and the new earth, about God: "It is not for God to take a few fish out of the pond and then ruin the pond itself."[13] Hoek also refers extensively to the moaning of the current creation.[14] From texts like Isaiah 11 and Romans 8, Schwarz and Wohlmuth ask attention for the restoration of the complete creation, in which they explicitly state that this includes both man and animal.[15] The latter choice requires some clarification for most theologians. This is not immediately given by the systematics. In that respect, Schwarz and Wohlmuth differ little from Moltmann. Therefore, it could be meaningful how BT, among others, thinks about the renewal and redemption of flora and fauna. This can be an incentive for ST to broaden its reflections on this.

7.2.2.3 Perspective from the Resurrection

All ten chosen publications recognize that speaking of the future new heaven and new earth is about the complete renewal and resurrection of all things. Gijsbert van den Brink and Kees van der Kooi, Robert Culver, Willem Ouweneel and Hans Schwarz point out that the completion is related to the physical earth-concrete resurrection of Jesus Christ as Firstborn of the new creation.[16] However, it does not come to a further analysis of the rebellious stories of Christ and the speaking therein of the essence of his resurrection body concerning continuity and discontinuity. Robert Culver's speech on the renewal of the earth is limited to a few sketchy references to the resurrection body, and a reference to this fundamental theme for speaking about the future resurrection of all things is absent from Millard Erickson, Jan van Genderen, and Willem Velema. In this dissertation, the impact of the interpretation of the resurrected body on the conversation about the new creation has been argued several times (§§6.2.3.3; 6.3.1.1). It has been noted that the conversation about Christ as the Firstborn of the new creation is the basis for any further reflection on annihilation, renovation, or renewal of creation in the eschaton (§6.3.1.3). From this perspective, it is remarkable that the latter is discussed extensively with the various systematics, while there is no more profound explanation of the relationship between the new creation and the resurrection of Jesus Christ.[17]

---

13. Van de Beek, *God doet recht*, 83, 90; Hoek, *Hoop*, 262: "Het is Hem niet te doen een paar vissen uit de vijver te halen om vervolgens de vijver zelf te gronde te laten gaan."

14. Hoek, *Hoop*, 263–65.

15. Wohlmuth, *Mysterium*, 231–34; Schwarz, *Eschatology*, 404.

16. Van den Brink and van der Kooi, *Dogmatiek*, 675–76; Ouweneel, *Toekomst van God*, 557; Culver, *Systematic Theology*, 1099; Schwarz, *Eschatology*, 403.

17. Ouweneel, *Toekomst van God*, 556–59; Wohlmuth, *Mysterium*, 231–34; Culver, *Systematic Theology*, 1155; Hoek, *Hoop*, 265–75; Grudem, *Systematic Theology*, 1158–60; Van Genderen and Velema, *Dogmatiek*, 794–95.

7.2.2.4 Perspective from the imagery

The observations made in this dissertation encourage systematics to be more inspired by the biblical imagery in their speech about the new creation. In the hermeneutical reflections on this subject, this importance of imagery was already addressed (§6.2.3.1). This fact can, in the present speaking about the new heaven and new earth, mean a significant enrichment. In the introduction, reference was already made to Markus Mühling, who notes that this reflection is often missing in the ST. He, therefore, calls for more interaction with the BT (§1.2).

In all ten publications, the systematics refrain from reflecting on the imagery. This is remarkable because they regularly refer to the influence of biblical themes on speaking about the new heaven and the new earth.[18] A hermeneutic reflection on the use of imagery is not addressed by many either. Willem Ouweneel briefly discusses the difficulty of interpreting the imagery in Revelation 21:1, where the seer states that the sea is absent.[19] Bram van de Beek, Gijsbert van den Brink, and Kees van der Kooi reflect more extensively on biblical imagery. Van den Brink and van der Kooi point out that there are countless images present in the Bible that can be used in speaking about the future for continuity and discontinuity.[20] Bram van de Beek emphasizes that the biblical imagery is earthly concrete and therefore often embarrasses Christians against dissidents.[21] However, he poses the question of whether it is naive to interpret physical elements in the imagery physically-concrete rather than to interpret this spiritual-abstract.[22] Josef Wohlmuth also calls for more attention to the physical elements in the imagery.[23] Hans Schwarz, on the other hand, is more reserved and writes that many of these biblical images sound "Disney-like."[24] At Millard Erickson, this negative attitude is most powerfully present. A physical conception of biblical imagery is already referred to as populism.[25] Matters such as the future heaven banquet, about which Jesus and the prophets speak, can only be understood symbolically. The fact that Jesus also ate solid food with his resurrection body is problematic for Erickson. He solves this by stating that the resurrection body of Jesus was not finished and could therefore still take food: "the transformation of his body was probably not yet completed."[26] After the glorification, this came to an end.

---

18. Van den Brink and van der Kooi, *Dogmatiek*, 674; Culver, *Systematic Theology*, 1108–10; Wohlmuth, *Mysterium*, 224, 227; Van Genderen and Velema, *Dogmatiek*, 794–95.

19. Ouweneel, *Toekomst van God*, 558.

20. Van den Brink and van der Kooi, *Dogmatiek*, 653–54, 674.

21. Van de Beek, *God doet recht*, 84–95.

22. Van de Beek, *God doet recht*, 86.

23. Wohlmuth, *Mysterium*, 224, 227.

24. Schwarz, *Eschatology*, 403.

25. Erickson, *Christian Theology*, 1235.

26. Erickson, *Christian Theology*, 1239.

In Wayne Grudem's design of the new heaven and the new earth, an eschatological reflection from the imagery is most powerfully present. Based on the biblical-material imagery of food, drink, a tree of life, and streets, Grudem concludes that the new creation is more earthly-physical than is often assumed.[27] He warns against interpreting the imagery of the new heaven and the new earth too quickly as merely "symbolic."[28]

Although the reflection of the images in these systematic works is concise, they call upon readers to recognize the added value of imagery for eschatology.[29] However, a more profound interaction or extensive hermeneutical reflection on the imagery of the new heaven and the new earth, as we find it with Karl Rahner, is not possible (§3.2).

7.2.2.5 Perspective from the biblical theology

In the chosen systematic publications, the interaction with the BT is limited to referring to core texts about the new heaven and earth (Isa 65; 2 Pet 3; Rev 21–22). Millard Erickson is an exception here because he lists an extensive repertoire of biblical texts. However, this remains limited to a list in his ST. A more in-depth investigation is absent.[30] An interaction with or reference to BT is missing in the whole among the ten theologians. References are scarce and limited to Bible comments. Exceptions are (1) Millard Erickson, who speaks about the future in terms of the land and the sabbaticals' peace, and (2) Willem Ouweneel, Jan van Genderen, and Willem Velema who present a brief BT of expectation and point to the relationships between Genesis 1–2 and Revelation 21–22.[31]

Now it is not strange that this relationship between ST and BT is missing. This dissertation considered that given as a basis for its research (§1.2). Less obvious is the fact that the hermeneutic reflection, which is inherent to the ST, is only rarely mentioned in speaking about the new heaven and the new earth. It is only Bram van de Beek, Gijsbert van den Brink, and Kees van der Kooi who discuss themes such as the influence of Gnosticism, the debate on extrapolation, and anticipation, the use of the biblical imagery and Christian-centered thinking within eschatology in their ST.[32] This dissertation extensively demonstrates in §6.2 how these and many other observations in the hermeneutical reflection of eschatology are invaluable for the deepening of speaking about the new heaven and the new earth.

---

27. Grudem, *Systematic Theology*, 1161.
28. Grudem, *Systematic Theology*, 1162.
29. Grudem, *Systematic Theology*, 1161–62.
30. Erickson, *Christian Theology*, 1235–41.
31. Ouweneel, *Toekomst van God*, 558, 566–70; Erickson, *Christian Theology*, 1237; Van Genderen and Velema, *Dogmatiek*, 741–42, 794.
32. Van den Brink and van der Kooi, *Dogmatiek*, 640, 646, 653–54.

What is the content of the ten chosen publications about matter, time, and space? If we examine this, it is striking that all works can establish a relationship between the resurrection of Jesus and the restoration of all things. It briefly discusses the discussion of the matter.

Wayne Grudem's reflection on time is based on Revelation 21–22 and Josef Wohlmuth's reflection on heavenly music.[33] Both systematics recognize in their short speech that time is not harmful, but part of God's good creation. Gijsbert van den Brink and Kees van der Kooi, on the other hand, call for caution in their reflection on time. They see in it the danger of too earthly a view in speaking about it. From the biblical imagery, they thus speak more of a "quality category" concerning time than of a "time dynamics" or change in the new creation. However, the difference between the two categories remains vague.[34]

The theme of the space of the new heaven and the new earth can only be found at Bram van de Beek and Millard Erickson. From the hope for the physical resurrection body, both conclude that the new heaven and the new earth also have spatiality. Bram van de Beek writes: "Performing a physical resurrection without relationships and without an environment to live in is hardly a physical resurrection."[35] Millard Erickson has difficulties with his presentation of the situation. The reason for this is his reflections on the physical resurrection body. He states in these reflections that heaven has a different atmosphere than the earth and cannot be compared with this. So, the resurrection body is a "spiritual body." It has primarily a spiritual condition and only secondarily a condition of place and space.[36] In his ST, he wants to concentrate on this primary condition.

7.2.2.6 Form of order sought

We establish that the observations and considerations made in this dissertation can offer added value to ST in its reflection on the new heaven and the new earth. The methodical enrichment that took place between the theologies of Karl Rahner, Jürgen Moltmann, and Gregory Beale can serve as a new approach in an ST that wants to offer more than just a synthesis of Bible references. From the comparison in this dissertation, we establish that we must follow a path that pays attention to both the material and the immaterial in order to arrive at a balanced model for cosmic eschatology. In this way, there remains a balance between a radical discontinuity and a break-free continuity. This choice to keep continuity and discontinuity in balance appears to be more complicated than one might initially think.

---

33. Wohlmuth, *Mysterium*, 228–29; Grudem, *Systematic Theology*, 1162.

34. Van den Brink and van der Kooi, *Dogmatiek*, 678.

35. Van de Beek, *God doet recht*, 83: "Een voorstelling van een lichamelijke wederopstanding zonder relaties en zonder een omgeving om te leven is nauwelijks een lichamelijke opstanding."

36. Erickson, *Christian Theology*, 1239.

From the individual analyses of Rahner's, Moltmann's, and Beale's theological systems as well as from the interdisciplinary comparison we can conclude that the new creation is not a *restitutio in integrum* or *renovatio* of the current creation (continuity) nor should it be seen as an *annihilatio mundi* (discontinuity). Instead, it can be concluded from the research that the new heaven and earth is a change, glorification, and completion of the first heaven and earth created by God. Continuity and discontinuity should not be played off against each other. There is both a fundamental continuity and a radical discontinuity between the present life in Christ and the future life in the new creation. It is clear to all three theologians that the future can be characterized as the radical *novum* and, at the same time, is related to the past and the present so that there can be no question of a *nova creatio ex nihilo*. The future implies both a radical break with a subsequent *novum* and a process-based transformation and renovation that transcends our thinking.

Rahner's and Moltmann's ST can point out to Beale's BT several times that they need to reflect more on the biblical representations that are given to us. These reveal that evil in the present creation will come to its end, without the downfall of the world. The biblical representations also give the impression that the cosmos itself will share in the future resurrection. In this representation, it remains a "seeing in a mirror" and not yet "seeing face to face" (1 Cor 13:12). Especially Rahner's and Beale's theology warn against confusing eschatology with futurology. Despite the value this interdisciplinary comparison of the future new heavens and earth will bring to both disciplines; we will continue to encounter the limits of understanding.

7.3 IMPLICATIONS AND PROSPECTS

In this dissertation of an interdisciplinary comparison between Rahner's, Moltmann's, and Beale's eschatological designs, it was repeatedly expressed that a person's life is strongly influenced by his future expectations. The afterlife draws the afterlife.[37] The Christian hope with his eschatological designs influences the direction of life. Rahner, Moltmann, and Beale are well aware of this in their eschatological designs and demonstrate it by placing eschatology at the heart of their theology. The ultimate coming of the triune God to this creation is the greatest blessing that the Christian creed looks forward to. This eschatological perspective on a history of salvation, in which Creator and creation are "united," encourages us to take God's earth here and now seriously and to treat nature with care. The contemporary attention to ecology is in line with this. The understanding has grown that the new project, which served to subjugate nature and secure the future through technology, has strangulated itself. For some decades now, this social awareness has led to a new reflection within Christian theology on cosmic hope.

---

37. See for example: Beale, *New Testament*, 958–62; Moltmann, *Ethik*; Rahner, "Schöpfung," 108–13.

The New Heaven and New Earth

The eschatological perspective of the Christian faith can thus contribute to the foundation of a contemporary postmodern ecological theology. It calls upon man to anticipate the blessings that God wants to offer his creation through Christ. In Jesus' coming into being we acknowledge God's love for creation, in the crucifixion, we acknowledge God's judgment of evil in this world, and in Jesus' resurrection, we see God's will for the new heaven and earth. This earth on which we live, like us humans, is part of the creation that God formed and which he ultimately frees from all iniquity.

The purpose of this dissertation was to investigate whether an interdisciplinary collaboration between ST and BT was possible or whether collaboration could only take the form of two separate publications in one edition. This dissertation has shown that based on a careful comparison between different theological designs, building blocks are provided that can innovatively enrich the theological reflection on the new heaven and the new earth in a cooperative of BT and ST. From these results, it can finally be concluded that both BT and ST still face significant challenges to further reflect on the theologically responsible speaking about the new heaven and earth. A first orientation has been developed on which to build further in possible cooperation. Challenges have also come to light in the interdisciplinary comparison between BT and ST about the new heaven and earth that we cannot leave behind us if we want to move forward. The office of cosmic eschatology will not yet be closed in either field (see §1.3). At the same time, the Christian testimony may continue to sound that God has not a hopeless end but an endless hope in store for creation.

Bibliography

Abraham, William J. "Eschatology and Epistemology." In *The Oxford Handbook of Eschatology*, edited by Jerry L. Walls, 581–95. Oxford: Oxford University Press, 2008.

Adams, Nicholas. "Eschatology Sacred and Profane: The Effects of Philosophy on Theology in Pannenberg, Rahner, and Moltmann." *International Journal of Systematic Theology* 2, no. 3 (2000) 283–306.

Adeyemo, Tokunboh et al., eds. *Africa Bible Commentary*. Grand Rapids: Zondervan, 2010.

Ahlers, Rolf. "Theory of God and Theological Method." *Dialog* 22 (1983) 235–250.

Alexander, T. Desmond. *From Eden to the new Jerusalem: An Introduction to Biblical Theology*. Grand Rapids: Kregel, 2009.

Ansell, Nicholas. *The Annihilation of Hell: Universal Salvation and the Redemption of Time in the Eschatology of Jürgen Moltmann*. Paternoster Theological Monographs. Milton Keynes: Paternoster, 2013.

Aquinas, Thomas. *Summa Theologiae*. Cambridge: Cambridge University Press, 2006.

Auer, Alfons. *Umweltethik: Ein theologischer Beitrag zur ökologischen Diskussion*. Düsseldorf: Patmos, 1985.

Augustine. *The City of God (De Civitate Dei)*. Edited by Boniface Ramsey. Translated by William S. Babcock. Works of Saint Augustine, I/6–7. Chicago: Encyclopædia Britannica, 2013.

———. *Confessions*. Translated by Thomas Williams. Indianapolis: Hackett, 2019.

———. "Homilies on the Gospel of St. John." In *Augustine of Hippo: Selected Writings*, edited and translated by Mary T. Clark, 262–81. Classics of Western Spirituality. New York: Paulist, 1984.

Aune, David E. *Revelation 6–16*. Word Biblical Commentary 52B. Dallas: Word, 1998.

Bachl, Gottfried. *Eschatologie*. 2 vols. Texte zur Theologie: Dogmatik 10. Graz: Styria, 1999.

Barnes, Michael H. "Karl Rahner and Demythologization." *Theological Studies* 55 (1994) 24–45.

Barr, James. *Biblical Words for Time*. Studies in Biblical Theology 33. London: SCM, 1962.

———. *The Concept of Biblical Theology: An Old Testament Perspective*. Minneapolis: Fortress, 1999.

Barth, Karl. *Der Römerbrief (Zweite Fassung)*. Zürich: Theologischer Verlag, 1922.

———. *Die Lehre von der Schöpfung 1*. Die kirchliche Dogmatik, 3.1. Zollikon-Zürich: Evangelischer Verlag, 1945.

———. *Karl Barth Briefe 1961–1968*. Edited by Hinrich Stoevesandt and Jürgen Fangmeier. 2nd ed. Zürich: Theologischer Verlag, 1975.

Bartholomew, Craig G. "Uncharted Waters: Philosophy, Theology and the Crisis in Biblical Interpretation." In *Renewing Biblical Interpretation*, edited by Craig G. Bartholomew et al., 1–39. Scripture and Hermeneutics Series 1. Grand Rapids: Zondervan, 2000.

Batlogg, Andreas R. *Der Denkweg Karl Rahners: Quellen, Entwicklungen, Perspektiven.* Mainz: Grünewald, 2003.

Batlogg, Andreas R., and Albert Raffelt. "Ein Lebenswerk erschlossen: Zum Stand der Edition Sämtlicher Werke Karl Rahners." In *Was bleibt von Karl Rahner?: Theologische Programmatik für heute und morgen*, edited by Karl Lehmann, 33–52. Rahner Lecture 2009. München: Karl-Rahner-Archiv, 2009.

Bauckham, Richard J., ed. *God Will Be All in All: The Eschatology of Jürgen Moltmann.* Edinburgh: T&T Clark, 1999.

———. "Jesus and the Wild Animals (Mark 1:13): A Christological Image for an Ecological Age." In *Jesus of Nazareth, Lord and Christ: Essays on the Historical Jesus and New Testament Christology*, edited by Joel B. Green and Max Turner, 3–21. Grand Rapids: Eerdmans, 1994.

———. "The Millennium." In *God Will Be All In All: The Eschatology of Jurgen Moltmann*, edited by Richard Bauckham, 123–47. Edinburgh: T&T Clark, 1999.

———. *Moltmann: Messianic Theology in the Making.* Basingstoke: Pickering, 1987.

———. "Moltmann's Eschatology of the Cross." *Scottish Journal of Theology* 30, no. 4 (1977) 301–311.

———. "Theodicy from Ivan Karamazov to Moltmann." *Modern Theology* 4, no. 1 (1987) 83–97.

———. *The Theology of the Book of Revelation.* Cambridge: Cambridge University Press, 1993.

———. *The Theology of Jürgen Moltmann.* Edinburgh: T&T Clark, 1995.

———. "Time and Eternity." In *God Will Be All In All: The Eschatology of Jurgen Moltmann*, edited by Richard Bauckham, 155–226. Edinburgh: T&T Clark, 1999.

Bauckham, Richard, and Trevor A. Hart. *Hope against Hope: Christian Eschatology at the Turn of the Millennium.* Grand Rapids: Eerdmans, 1999.

———. "The Shape of Time." In *The Future as God's Gift: Explorations in Christian Eschatology*, edited by Marcel Sarot and David Fergusson, 41–73. Edinburgh: T&T Clark, 2000.

Bauke-Ruegg, Jan. *Die Allmacht Gottes: Systematisch-theologische Erwägungen zwischen Metaphysik, Postmoderne und Poesie.* Theologische Bibliothek Töpelmann 96. Berlin: De Gruyter, 1998.

Beale, Gregory K. *1–2 Thessalonians.* IVP New Testament Commentary 13. Downers Grove: InterVarsity, 2003.

———. *The Book of Revelation: A Commentary on the Greek Text.* New International Greek Testament Commentary. Grand Rapids: Eerdmans, 1999.

———. "Can the Bible Be Completely Inspired by God and Yet Still Contain Errors?: A Response to Some Recent 'Evangelical' Proposals." *Westminster Theological Journal* 73, no. 1 (2011) 1–22.

———. "Colossians." In *Commentary on the New Testament Use of the Old Testament*, edited by Gregory K. Beale and Donald A. Carson, 841–70. Grand Rapids: Baker Academic, 2007.

———. "Eden, the Temple, and the Church's Mission in the New Creation." *Journal of the Evangelical Theological Society* 48, no. 1 (2005) 5–31.

———. Email to Raymond R. Hausoul. "On Trialogue (Beale, Moltmann, Rahner)." Email, October 9, 2015.

———. Email to Raymond R. Hausoul. "Re: Question during Writing Dissertation on G.K. Beale, J. Moltmann and K. Rahner." Email, September 15, 2014.

———. *The Erosion of Inerrancy in Evangelicalism: Responding to New Challenges to Biblical Authority*. Wheaton: Crossway, 2008.

———. "The Eschatological Conception of New Testament Theology." In *Eschatology in Bible and Theology*, edited by Kent E. Brower and Mark W. Elliott, 11–52. Downers Grove: InterVarsity, 1997.

———. "The Final Vision of the Apocalypse and Its Implications for a Biblical Theology of the Temple." In *Heaven on Earth: The Temple in Biblical Theology*, edited by T. Desmond Alexander and Simon J. Gathercole, 191–209. Carlisle: Paternoster, 2004.

———. *God Dwells among Us: Expanding Eden to the Ends of the Earth*. Downers Grove: InterVarsity, 2014.

———. *Handbook on the New Testament Use of the Old Testament: Exegesis and Interpretation*. Grand Rapids: Baker Academic, 2012.

———. "Inaugural Lectures: The Cognitive Peripheral Vision of Biblical Authors." *Westminster Theological Journal* 76 (2014) 263–93.

———. *John's Use of the Old Testament in Revelation*. Journal for the Study of the New Testament. Supplement Series 166. Sheffield: Sheffield Academic, 1998.

———. "The New Testament and New Creation." In *Biblical Theology: Retrospect and Prospect*, edited by Scott J. Hafemann, 159–73. Downers Grove: InterVarsity, 2002.

———. *A New Testament Biblical Theology: The Unfolding of the Old Testament in the New*. Grand Rapids: Baker Academic, 2011.

———. "The Old Testament Background of Paul's Reference to 'the Fruit of the Spirit' in Galatians 5:22." *Bulletin for Biblical Research* 15, no. 1 (2005) 1–38.

———. "The Old Testament Background of Reconciliation in 2 Corinthians 5–7 and Its Bearing on the Literary Problem of 2 Corinthians 6:14–7:1." *New Testament Studies* 35, no. 4 (1989) 550–581.

———. "Revelation (Book)." In *New Dictionary of Biblical Theology*, edited by T. Desmond Alexander and Brian S. Rosner, 356–64. Downers Grove: InterVarsity, 2000.

———. *The Temple and the Church's Mission: A Biblical Theology of the Dwelling Place of God*. New Studies in Biblical Theology 17. Leicester: Apollos, 2004.

———. *We Become What We Worship: A Biblical Theology of Idolatry*. Downers Grove: IVP Academic, 2008.

Beale, Gregory K., and Benjamin L Gladd. *Hidden but Now Revealed: A Biblical Theology of Mystery*. Downers Grove: InterVarsity, 2014.

Beale, Gregory K., and Donald A. Carson, eds. *Commentary on the New Testament Use of the Old Testament*. Grand Rapids: Baker Academic, 2007.

Berkhof, Hendrik. *Christelijk geloof: Een inleiding tot de geloofsleer*. 7th ed. Nijkerk: Callenbach, 1993.

———. *Gegronde verwachting: Schets van een christelijke toekomstleer*. Nijkerk: Callenbach, 1967.

———. "Over de methode der eschatologie." *Nederlands Theologisch Tijdschrift* 19 (1966) 480–91.

Berkouwer, Gerrit C. *De wederkomst van Christus*. Vol. 1. Dogmatische Studiën. Kampen: Kok, 1961.

Billings, David. "Natality or Advent: Hannah Arendt and Jürgen Moltmann on Hope and Politics." In *The Future of Hope: Christian Tradition amid Modernity and Postmodernity*, edited by Miroslav Volf and William H. Katerberg, 27–48. Grand Rapids: Eerdmans, 2004.

Blenkinsopp, Joseph. *Ezekiel*. Interpretation. Louisville: Westminster John Knox, 1990.

Bloch, Ernst. *Das Prinzip Hoffnung*. 3 vols. Frankfurt am Main: Suhrkamp, 1959.

Block, Daniel I. *The Book of Ezekiel: Chapters 25-48*. New International Commentary on the Old Testament. Grand Rapids: Eerdmans, 1998.

———. "Eden: A Temple? A Reassessment of the Biblical Evidence." In *From Creation to New Creation: Biblical Theology and Exegesis. Essays in Honor of G. K. Beale*, edited by Daniel M. Gurtner and Benjamin L. Gladd, 1-30. Peabody: Hendrickson, 2013.

Bockmuehl, Markus N. A., and Alan J. Torrance, eds. *Scripture's Doctrine and Theology's Bible: How the New Testament Shapes Christian Dogmatics*. Grand Rapids: Baker Academic, 2008.

Boëthius, Anicius M. S. *The Consolation of Philosophy*. Translated by David R. Slavitt. Cambridge: Harvard University Press, 2008.

Bohm, David. *On Dialogue*. London: Routledge, 2004.

Bokwa, Ignacy. *Christologie als Anfang und Ende der Anthropologie: Über das gegenseitige Verhältnis zwischen Christologie und Anthropologie bei Karl Rahner*. Europäische Hochschulschriften. Reihe 23. Theologie 381. Frankfurt am Main: Lang, 1990.

Bornkamm, Günther et al. *Die christliche Hoffnung und das Problem der Entmythologisierung*. Stuttgart: Evangelisches Verlagswerk, 1954.

Bostock, D. "Review: The Temple and the Church's Mission." *Journal for the Study of the Old Testament* 29, no. 5 (2005) 137.

Bouma-Prediger, Steven. "Creation as the Home of God: The Doctrine of Creation in the Theology of Jürgen Moltmann." *Calvin Theological Journal* 32, no. 1 (1997) 72-90.

Bray, Gerald. "The Church Fathers and Biblical Theology." In *Out of Egypt: Biblical Theology and Biblical Interpretation*, edited by Craig G. Bartholomew, 23-40. Scripture and Hermeneutics Series 5. Grand Rapids: Zondervan, 2004.

Brett, Gregory. *The Theological Notion of the Human Person: A Conversation between the Theology of Karl Rahner and the Philosophy of John Macmurray*. Bern: Lang, 2013.

Brettler, Marc. "Cyclical and Teleological Time in the Hebrew Bible." In *Time and Temporality in the Ancient World*, edited by Ralph Mark Rosen, 111-28. Philadelphia: University of Pennsylvania Museum of Archaeology and Anthropology, 2004.

Brin, Gershon. *The Concept of Time in the Bible and the Dead Sea Scrolls*. Studies on the Texts of the Desert of Judah 39. Leiden: Brill, 2001.

Brink, Gijs van den. "Geboeid door Moltmann." *Soteria* 22, no. 2 (2005) 48-57.

Brink, Gijsbert van den, and Cornelis (Kees) van der Kooi. *Christelijke dogmatiek: Een inleiding*. Zoetermeer: Boekencentrum, 2012.

Bruce, Frederick F. "Interpretation of the Bible." In *Evangelical Dictionary of Theology*, edited by Walter A. Elwell, 565-68. Grand Rapids: Baker, 1994.

Brueggemann, Walter. *Genesis*. Interpretation. Atlanta: Westminster John Knox, 1982.

———. *The Land: Place as Gift, Promise, and Challenge in Biblical Faith*. 2nd ed. Overtures to Biblical Theology 1. Philadelphia: Fortress, 2002.

———. *Theology of the Old Testament: Testimony, Dispute, Advocacy*. Minneapolis: Fortress, 1997.

Brunner, Emil. *Das Ewige als Zukunft und Gegenwart*. Zürich: Zwingli, 1953.

Buber, Martin. *Bilder von Gut und Böse*. Köln: Hegner, 1952.

———. *Werke. Band 3: Schriften zum Chassidismus*. München: Kösel, 1963.

Bultmann, Rudolf K. "Die Eschatologie des Johannes-Evangeliums." In *Glauben und Verstehen: Gesammelte Aufsätze. Band 1*, 134-52. Tübingen: Mohr, 1933.

———. *Geschichte und Eschatologie*. Tübingen: Mohr Siebeck, 1964.
———. "Ist voraussetzungslose Exegese möglich?" In *Glauben und Verstehen: Gesammelte Aufsätze. Band 3*, 142–50. Tübingen: Mohr, 1993.
———. *Jesus Christ and Mythology*. New York: Scribner, 1958.
Burdzy, Krzysztof. *The Search for Certainty on the Clash of Science and Philosophy of Probability*. Hackensack: World Scientific, 2009.
Cabal, Ted. *The Apologetics Study Bible*. Nashville: B&H Publishing Group, 2009.
Carr, Anne E. *The Theological Method of Karl Rahner*. Dissertation Series: American Academy of Religion 19. Missoula: Scholars, 1977.
Carson, Donald A. *The Gospel According to John*. Pillar New Testament Commentary. Leicester: InterVarsity, 1991.
Cassuto, Umberto. *A Commentary on the Book of Genesis: Part One: From Adam to Noah*. Jeruzalem: Magnes, 1989.
Charles, Robert H. *A Critical and Exegetical Commentary on the Revelation of St. John*. 2 vols. International Critical Commentary. Edinburgh: T&T Clark, 1920.
Chung, Sung W. "Moltmann on Scripture and Revelation." In *Jürgen Moltmann and Evangelical Theology: A Critical Engagement*, edited by Sung W. Chung, 1–16. Eugene: Pickwick, 2012.
Clayton, Philip. "Eschatology as Metaphysics under the Guise of Hope." In *World without End: Christian Eschatology from a Process Perspective*, edited by Joseph A. Bracken, 128–49. Grand Rapids: Eerdmans, 2005.
Clutterbuck, Richard. "Jürgen Moltmann as a Doctrinal Theologian: The Nature of Doctrine and the Possibilities for Its Development." *Scottish Journal of Theology* 48 (1995) 489–506.
Collman, Ryan. "Review: New Testament Biblical Theology." Accessed May 20, 2015. https://www.academia.edu/7047557/Book_Review_New_Testament_Biblical_Theology.
Colwill, Deborah. "An Invitation to a Dialogue Table: Will You Come and Join Us?" *Christian Education Journal* 12, no. 1 (2015) 137–50.
Craig, William L. *Time and Eternity: Exploring God's Relationship to Time*. Wheaton: Crossway, 2001.
Cullmann, Oscar. *Christus und die Zeit: Die urchristliche Zeit- und Geschichtsauffassung*. 3rd ed. Zürich: EVZ-Verlag, 1962.
———. *Heil als Geschichte: Heilsgeschichtliche Existenz im Neuen Testament*. Tübingen: Mohr, 1965.
———. *Unsterblichkeit der Seele oder Auferstehung der Toten?: Antwort des Neuen Testaments*. Stuttgart: Kreuz, 1963.
Culver, Robert D. *Systematic Theology: Biblical and Historical*. Geanies House: Christian Focus, 2005.
Daley, Brian, et al. *Eschatologie in der Schrift und Patristik*. Handbuch der Dogmengeschichte, 4.7a. Freiburg: Herder, 1986.
———. *The Hope of the Early Church: A Handbook of Patristic Eschatology*. Cambridge: Cambridge University Press, 1991.
Dalferth, Ingolf U. *Gedeutete Gegenwart: Zur Wahrnehmung Gottes in den Erfahrungen der Zeit*. Tübingen: Mohr Siebeck, 1997.
Davies, Paul C. W. *The Last Three Minutes: Speculating about the Fate of the Cosmos*. Science Masters Series. London: Phoenix, 2001.

Davies, William D. *The Gospel and the Land: Early Christianity and Jewish Territorial Doctrine*. 2nd ed. Sheffield: Sheffield Press, 1994.

Deane-Drummond, Celia E. *Ecology in Jürgen Moltmann's Theology*. New York: Mellen, 1997.

Demarest, Bruce. "Systematic Theology." In *Evangelical Dictionary of Theology*, edited by Walter A. Elwell, 1064–66. Grand Rapids: Baker Book House, 1994.

Dempster, Stephen G. *Dominion and Dynasty: A Biblical Theology of the Hebrew Bible*. New Studies in Biblical Theology 15. Downers Grove: InterVarsity, 2003.

Den Hertog, Gerard C., and Cornelis (Kees) van der Kooi. "De problemen op tafel." In *Tussen leer en lezen: De spanning tussen bijbelwetenschap en geloofsleer*, edited by Gerard C. den Hertog and Cornelis (Kees) van der Kooi, 9–17. Kampen: Kok, 2007.

———, eds. *Tussen leer en lezen: De spanning tussen bijbelwetenschap en geloofsleer*. Kampen: Kok, 2007.

Dennison, James T. "The Life of Geerhardus Vos." In *The Letters of Geerhardus Vos*, edited by James T. Dennison, 13–85. Phillipsburg: P&R, 2005.

Denzinger, Heinrich J. D., and Peter Hünermann. *Enchiridion Symbolorum: Kompendium der Glaubensbekenntnisse und kirchlichen Lehrentscheidungen*. Freiburg: Herder, 2009.

De Vries, Lourens. "Vertalingen kiezen en keuzes van vertalingen." In *Naar een nieuwe kerkbijbel: Een handreiking voor het beoordelen van de Nieuwe Bijbelvertaling*, edited by Henk Room and Wolter H. Rose, 35–41. TU-bezinningsreeks 2. Barneveld: De Vuurbaak, 2001.

De Vries, Simon J. *Yesterday, Today and Tomorrow: Time and History in the Old Testament*. London: SPCK, 1975.

Díaz, Miguel H. *On Being Human: U.S. Hispanic and Rahnerian Perspectives*. Faith and Cultures Series. Marynoll: Orbis, 2001.

Duguid, Iain M. *Ezekiel*. NIV Application Commentary. Grand Rapids: Zondervan, 1999.

Dumbrell, William J. *The End of the Beginning: Revelation 21-22 and the Old Testament*. Moore College Lectures. Homebush West: Lancer Books, 1985.

———. *The Search for Order: Biblical Eschatology in Focus*. Grand Rapids: Baker, 1994.

Dupuis, Jacques. *Toward a Christian Theology of Religious Pluralism*. Maryknoll: Orbis, 1997.

Edwards, Denis. *Messianism, Apocalypse and Redemption in 20th Century German Thought*. Edited by Wayne Cristaudo and Wendy Baker. Adelaide: ATF, 2006.

———. "The Relationship between the Risen Christ and the Material Universe." *Pacifica* 4, no. 1 (1991) 1–14.

———. "Resurrection of the Body and Transformation of the Universe in the Theology of Karl Rahner." *Philosophy & Theology* 18, no. 2 (2006) 357–83.

Eicher, Peter. *Die anthropologische Wende: Karl Rahners philosophischer Weg von Wesen des Menschen zur personalen Existenz*. Freiburg: Universitätsverlag, 1970.

Eichrodt, Walther. *Theologie des Alten Testaments. Teil 1: Gott und Volk*. Stuttgart: Klotz, 1968.

———. *Theologie des Alten Testaments. Teil 2: Gott und Welt*. Stuttgart: Klotz, 1964.

———. *Theologie des Alten Testaments. Teil 3: Gott und Mensch*. Stuttgart: Klotz, 1964.

Ellis, E. Earle. "II Corinthians V.1-10 in Pauline Eschatology." *New Testament Studies* 6, no. 3 (1960) 211–224.

Ellis, George F. R. *The Far-Future Universe: Eschatology from a Cosmic Perspective*. Philadelphia: Templeton Foundation, 2002.

Endean, Philip. "Has Rahnerian Theology a Future?" In *The Cambridge Companion to Karl Rahner*, edited by Declan Marmion and Mary E. Hines, 281–96. Cambridge Companions to Religion. Cambridge: Cambridge University Press, 2005.
Enns, Paul P. *Moody Handbook of Theology: Revised and Expanded*. Chicago: Moody, 2008.
Erickson, Millard J. *Christian Theology*. 2nd ed. Grand Rapids: Baker Academic, 1998.
Farrow, Douglas B. "In the End Is the Beginning: A Review of Jürgen Moltmann's Systematic Contributions." *Modern Theology* 14, no. 3 (1998) 425–447.
Felsinger, Horst. "Karl Rahner und die Auferstehung." *Una Voce-Korrespondenz* 16 (1986) 205–15.
Feuerbach, Ludwig. *Gedanken über Tod und Unsterblichkeit aus den Papieren eines Denkers: Nebst einem Anhang theologisch-satyrischer Xenien*. Nürnberg: Stein, 1830.
Fischer, Herrmann. *Protestantische Theologie im 20. Jahrhundert*. Stuttgart: Kohlhammer, 2002.
Fischer, Klaus P. *Der Mensch als Geheimnis: Die Anthropologie Karl Rahners*. Ökumenische Forschungen II 5. Freiburg: Herder, 1975.
Fletcher, Hilde J. *Die Steigerung des Riesigen und das Weltende: Die Eschatologien von Karl Rahner und Paul Schütz im Vergleich*. Europäische Hochschulschriften. Reihe XXIII. Theologie 749. Frankfurt am Main: Lang, 2002.
Ford, David F., and Rachel Muers, eds. *The Modern Theologians: An Introduction to Christian Theology since 1918*. Oxford: Blackwell, 2005.
Fowl, Stephen E. *Theological Interpretation of Scripture*. Eugene: Cascade, 2009.
Fredericks, Sarah E. "Religious Studies." In *The Oxford Handbook of Interdisciplinarity*, edited by Robert Frodeman, 161–74. Oxford: Oxford University Press, 2010.
Freedman, Harry, and Simon Maurice, eds. *Midrash Rabbah: Genesis*. 2 vols. Midrash Rabbah 1–2. London: Soncino, 1983.
Frei, Hans W. *Types of Christian Theology*. Edited by George Hunsinger and William C. Placher. New Haven: Yale University Press, 1992.
Freyer, Thomas. *Zeit—Kontinuität und Unterbrechung: Studien zu Karl Barth, Wolfhart Pannenberg und Karl Rahner*. Bonner dogmatische Studien 13. Würzburg: Echter, 1993.
Fritsch, Harald. *Vollendende Selbstmitteilung Gottes an seine Schöpfung: Die Eschatologie Karl Rahners*. Würzburg: Echter, 2006.
Fritz, Peter J. "Placing Sin in Karl Rahner's Theology." *Irish Theological Quarterly* 80, no. 4 (2015) 294–312.
Gabler, Johann P. *Kleine theologische Schriften: Opuscula academica*. Edited by Theodor A. Gabler and Johann G. Gabler. 2 vols. Ulm: Stettin, 1831.
———. "An Oration." In *The Flowering of Old Testament Theology: A Reader in Twentieth-Century Old Testament Theology, 1930–1990*, edited by Ben C. Ollenburger et al., 492–502. Sources for Biblical and Theological Study 1. Winona Lake: Eisenbrauns, 1992.
Gadamer, Hans-Georg. *Wahrheit und Methode: Grundzüge einer philosophischen Hermeneutik*. 5th ed. Tübingen: Mohr, 1986.
Gaffin, Richard B. "Systematic Theology and Biblical Theology." *Westminster Theological Journal* 38, no. 3 (1976) 281–99.
———. "Vos, Geerhardus." In *Dictionary of Major Biblical Interpreters*, edited by Donald K. McKim, 1016–19. Downers Grove: IVP Academic, 2007.
Geertsema, H. G. *Van boven naar voren: Wijsgerige achtergronden en problemen van het theologische denken over geschiedenis bij Jürgen Moltmann*. Kampen: Kok, 1980.

Geister, Philip. *Aufhebung zur Eigentlichkeit: Zur Problematik kosmologischer Eschatologie in der Theologie Karl Rahners.* Uppsala Studies in Faiths and Ideologies 5. Stockholm: Almqvist & Wiksell International, 1996.

Gerstenberger, Erhard S. *Theologies in the Old Testament.* Minneapolis: Fortress, 2002.

Gilbert, Kevin J. "Jürgen Moltmann's Theological Method: Evangelical Options?" *Restoration Quarterly* 41 (1999) 163–178.

Gilbertson, Michael. *God and History in the Book of Revelation: New Testament Studies in Dialogue with Pannenberg and Moltmann.* Society for New Testament Studies. Monograph Series 124. Cambridge: Cambridge University Press, 2003.

Gladd, Benjamin L., and Matthew S. Harmon. *Making All Things New: Inaugurated Eschatology for the Life of the Church.* Grand Rapids: Baker Academic, 2016.

Gnilka, Joachim. *Das Evangelium nach Markus: Mk 8,27–16,20.* 3rd ed. Evangelisch-katholischer Kommentar zum Neuen Testament, 2.2. Neukirchen-Vluyn: Neukirchener, 1989.

Goldberg, Arnold. *Untersuchungen über die Vorstellung von der Schekhinah in der frühen rabbinischen Literatur: Talmud und Midrasch.* Studia Judaica. Forschungen zur Wissenschaft des Judentums 5. Berlin: De Gruyter, 1969.

Goldingay, John. "Biblical Narrative and Systematic Theology." In *Between Two Horizons: Spanning New Testament Studies and Systematic Theology,* edited by Joel B. Green and Max Turner, 123–42. Grand Rapids: Eerdmans, 2000.

Goldsworthy, Graeme. *According to Plan: The Unfolding Revelation of God in the Bible.* Downers Grove: InterVarsity, 2002.

Green, Joel B. "Scripture and Theology: Uniting the Two so Long Divided." In *Between Two Horizons: Spanning New Testament Studies and Systematic Theology,* edited by Joel B. Green and Max Turner, 23–43. Grand Rapids: Eerdmans, 2000.

Green, Joel B., and Max Turner, eds. *Between Two Horizons: Spanning New Testament Studies and Systematic Theology.* Grand Rapids: Eerdmans, 2000.

———, eds. *The Two Horizons New Testament Commentary.* Grand Rapids: Eerdmans, 2005.

Grenz, Stanley J. "Theology and Piety among Baptists and Evangelicals." In *Southern Baptists & American Evangelicals: The Conversation Continues,* edited by David S. Dockery, 149–62. Nashville: B&H, 1993.

Grenz, Stanley J., and John R. Franke. *Beyond Foundationalism: Shaping Theology in a Postmodern Context.* Louisville: Westminster John Knox, 2001.

Greshake, G., and J. Kremer. *Resurrectio Mortuorum: Zum theologischen Verständnis der leiblichen Auferstehung.* Darmstadt: Wissenschaftliche Buchgesellschaft, 1986.

Greshake, Gisbert. *Der dreieine Gott: Eine trinitarische Theologie.* Freiburg: Herder, 1997.

———. "Eschatologie: Die Geschichte des Traktates." In *Lexikon für Theologie und Kirche.* Band 3, edited by Walter Kasper et al., 3rd ed., 860–63. Freiburg: Herder, 1995.

Grözinger, Karl E. *Von der mittelalterlichen Kabbala zum Hasidismus.* Jüdisches Denken: Theologie, Philosophie, Mystik 2. Frankfurt am Main: Campus, 2005.

Grudem, Wayne. *Systematic Theology: An Introduction to Biblical Doctrine.* Grand Rapids: Zondervan, 2000.

Grümme, Bernhard. *"Noch ist die Träne nicht weggewischt von jeglichem Angesicht": Überlegungen zur Rede von Erlösung bei Karl Rahner und Franz Rosenzweig.* Münsteraner Theologische Abhandlungen 43. Altenberge: Oros, 1996.

Guarino, Thomas G. *Foundations of Systematic Theology.* New York: T&T Clark International, 2005.

Gunton, Colin E. "Historical and Systematic Theology." In *The Cambridge Companion to Christian Doctrine*, edited by Colin E. Gunton, 3–20. Cambridge Companions to Religion. Cambridge: Cambridge University Press, 1997.

Gurtner, Daniel M., and Benjamin L. Gladd, eds. *From Creation to New Creation: Biblical Theology and Exegesis. Essays in Honor of G. K. Beale*. Peabody: Hendrickson, 2013.

Halloran, Nathan. "Evolution and the Nature and Transmission of Original Sin: Rahner, Schoonenberg, and Teilhard de Chardin." *Colloquium* 44, no. 2 (2012) 177–93.

Hamilton, James M. "Appreciation, Agreement, and a Few Minor Quibbles: A Response to G.K. Beale." *Midwestern Journal of Theology* 10, no. 1 (2011) 58–70.

Häring, Hermann. "Schöpfungstheologie: Ein Thema im Umbruch." *Theologischer Revue* 97, no. 3 (2001) 177–96.

Hart, Trevor A. "Imagination for the Kingdom of God?" In *God Will Be All In All: The Eschatology of Jurgen Moltmann*, edited by Richard Bauckham, 49–76. Edinburgh: T&T Clark, 1999.

Hasan-Rokem, Galit, and Alan Dundes. *The Wandering Jew: Essays in the Interpretation of a Christian Legend*. Bloomington: Indiana University Press, 1986.

Hasel, Gerhard F. *Old Testament Theology: Basic Issues in the Current Debate*. 4th ed. Grand Rapids: Eerdmans, 1991.

———. "The Relationship between Biblical Theology and Systematic Theology." *Trinity Journal Deerfield* 5, no. 2 (1984) 113–27.

———. "Sabbath." In *Anchor Bible Dictionary*. Volume 5, 850–56. New York: Doubleday, 1999.

Hauser, Alan J., and Duane F. Watson, eds. *A History of Biblical Interpretation: The Medieval through the Reformation Periods*. Grand Rapids: Eerdmans, 2009.

Hausoul, Raymond R. *De boodschap van de landwet in Leviticus 25–27 in het kader van de landsbelofte in Exodus-Leviticus-Numeri*. Leuven: ETF, 2011.

———. "An Evaluation of Jürgen Moltmann's Concept of Time and Space in the New Creation." *Journal of Reformed Theology* 7, no. 2 (2013) 137–59.

———. "'Land Ahead!': Israel, the Land, and the Christian Inheritance." In *Israel as Hermeneutical Challenge*, edited by Michael Mulder et al. Leiden: Brill, forthcoming.

———. "The Land in the Books of Exodus, Leviticus and Numbers." In *The Earth and the Land: Studies about the Value of the Land of Israel in the Old Testament and Afterwards*, edited by Hendrik J. Koorevaar and Mart-Jan Paul, 65–95. Edition Israelogie 11. Berlin: Lang, 2018.

———. "Theology and Cosmology: A Call for Interdisciplinary Enrichment." *Zygon* 54, no. 2 (2019) 324–36.

Heidegger, Martin. *Sein und Zeit*. Tübingen: Niemeyer, 1967.

Henebury, Paul. "A Review of G. K. Beale, A New Testament Biblical Theology." Accessed June 28, 2016. http://www.spiritandtruth.org/teaching/reviews/paul_henebury/review_of_new_testament_biblical_theology.pdf.

Hennecke, Susanne. "Related by Freedom: The Impact of Third-World Theologians on the Thinking of Jürgen Moltmann." *Exchange* 32, no. 4 (2003) 292–309.

Heschel, Abraham J. *The Sabbath: Its Meaning for Modern Man*. New York: Farrar, Straus & Young, 1951.

Highfield, Ron. "The Freedom to Say 'No'?: Karl Rahner's Doctrine of Sin." *Theological Studies* 56, no. 3 (1995) 485–505.

Hoek, Jan. *Hoop op God: Eschatologische verwachting*. Zoetermeer: Boekencentrum, 2004.

Holtz, Traugott. *Die Christologie der Apokalypse des Johannes*. Texte und Untersuchungen zur Geschichte der altchristlichen Literatur 85. Berlin: Akademie, 1962.

Ho-Tsui, Emmie Y. M. *Die Lehre von der Sünde bei Karl Rahner: Eine werkgenetische und systematische Erschliessung*. Innsbrucker theologische Studien 85. Innsbruck: Tyrolia, 2011.

Hryniewicz, Wacław. *The Challenge of Our Hope: Christian Faith in Dialogue*. Cultural Heritage and Contemporary Change. Washington: Council for Research in Values and Philosophy, 2007.

Hubbard, Moyer V. *New Creation in Paul's Letters and Thought*. Society for New Testament Studies. Monograph Series 119. Cambridge: Cambridge University Press, 2002.

Hughes, Kevin L. "The Crossing of Hope, or Apophatic Eschatology." In *The Future of Hope: Christian Tradition amid Modernity and Postmodernity*, edited by Miroslav Volf and William H. Katerberg, 101–24. Grand Rapids: Eerdmans, 2004.

Hülsemann, Johann. *Vindiciae Sanctae Scripturae per Loca Classica Systematis Theologici*. Lipsiae: Ritzschiano, 1679.

Hurd, Robert L. "Heidegger and Aquinas: A Rahnerian Bridge." *Philosophy Today* 28 (1984) 105–37.

Imhof, Paul, and Hubert Biallowons. *Karl Rahner: Im Gespräch*. Vol. 2. München: Kösel, 1983.

Irenaeus of Lyon. *Adversus Haereses*. Translated by Norbert Brox. 5 vols. Fontes Christiani 8. Freiburg: Herder, 2001.

Isaacs, William. *Dialogue and the Art of Thinking Together: A Pioneering Approach to Communicating in Business and in Life*. New York: Doubleday, 2008.

Iwand, Hans J. *Glauben und Wissen*. Edited by Helmut Gollwitzer. Nachgelassene Werke 1. München: Kaiser, 1962.

Jackson, T. Ryan. *New Creation in Paul's Letters: A Study of the Historical and Social Setting of a Pauline Concept*. Wissenschaftliche Untersuchungen Zum Neuen Testament. 2. Reihe 272. Tübingen: Mohr Siebeck, 2010.

Jager, Okke. *Het eeuwige leven: Met name in verband met de verhouding van tijd en eeuwigheid*. Kampen: Kok, 1962.

Jansen, Henry. "Moltmann's View of God's (Im)Mutability: The God of the Philosophers and the God of the Bible." *Neue Zeitschrift Für Systematische Theologie Und Religionsphilosophie* 36, no. 3 (1994) 284–301.

Jenson, Robert W. *Ezekiel*. Brazos Theological Commentary. Grand Rapids: Brazos, 2009.

Jhi, Jun-Hyung. *Das Heil in Jesus Christus bei Karl Rahner und in der Theologie der Befreiung*. Forschungen zur systematischen und ökumenischen Theologie 116. Göttingen: Vandenhoeck & Ruprecht, 2006.

Johnson, Roger A. *The Origins of Demythologizing: Philosophy and Historiography in the Theology of Rudolf Bultmann*. Studies in the History of Religions 28. Leiden: Brill, 1974.

Justin Martyr. *Dialogus cum Tryphone Judaeo*. Edited by Miroslav Marcovich. Patristische Texte und Studien 47. Berlin: De Gruyter, 2005.

Kaiser, Walter C. *Toward an Old Testament Theology*. Grand Rapids: Zondervan, 1978.

Kamphuis, Barend. "Systematische theologie." In *Gereformeerde theologie vandaag: Oriëntatie en verantwoording*, edited by Ad L.Th. de Bruijne, 59–71. TU-Bezinningsreeks 4. Barneveld: De Vuurbaak, 2004.

Kant, Immanuel. *Kritik der reinen Vernunft*. Stuttgart: Reclam, 1985.

Kärkkäinen, Veli-Matti. "Book review: The Temple and the Church's Mission: A Biblical Theology of the Dwelling Place of God." *International Bulletin of Missionary Research* 30, no. 1 (2006) 46.

———. *Creation and Humanity*. Constructive Christian Theology for the Pluralistic World 3. Grand Rapids: Eerdmans, 2015.

Kauffman, Stuart. *At Home in the Universe: The Search for the Laws of Self-Organization and Complexity*. Cary: Oxford University Press, 2014.

Keil, Carl F., and Franz J. Delitzsch. *Ezekiel, Daniel*. Commentary on the Old Testament 9. Grand Rapids: Eerdmans, 1988.

———. *The Pentateuch*. Commentary on the Old Testament 1. Grand Rapids: Eerdmans, 1988.

Kelsey, David H. *Proving Doctrine: The Uses of Scripture in Modern Theology*. Harrisburg: Trinity Int., 1999.

Kern, Walter. "Zur theologischen Auslegung des Schöpfungsglaubens." In *Die Heilsgeschichte vor Christus. Band 2*, edited by Johannes Feiner and Magnus Löhrer, 464–546. Mysterium Salutis: Grundriss heilsgeschichtlicher Dogmatik. Einsiedeln: Benzinger, 1967.

Kerstiens, Ferdinand. *Die Hoffnungsstruktur des Glaubens*. Mainz: Gründewald, 1969.

Kessler, Hans. *Evolution und Schöpfung in neuer Sicht*. Kevelaer: Butzon & Bercker, 2009.

Kierkegaard, Søren. *Der Begriff Angst*. Hamburg: Meiner, 1984.

Kim, Junghyung. "Christian Hope in Dialogue with Natural Science: John Polkinghorne's Incorporation of Bottum-up Thinking into Eschatology." In *God and the Scientist: Exploring the Work of John Polkinghorne*, edited by Fraser Watts and Christopher C. Knight, 153–74. Ashgate Science and Religion Series. Brookfield: Taylor and Francis, 2016.

Kim, Seyoon. *The Origin of Paul's Gospel*. Grand Rapids: Eerdmans, 1982.

Klappert, Bertold. *Worauf wir hoffen: Das Kommen Gottes und der Weg Jesu Christi*. München: Kaiser, 1997.

Klein, Terrance W. "Karl Rahner on the Soul." *The Saint Anselm Journal* 6, no. 1 (2008) 1–10.

Kline, Meredith G. *Images of the Spirit*. Baker Biblical Monograph. Grand Rapids: Baker, 1980.

———. *Kingdom Prologue: Genesis Foundations for a Covenantal Worldview*. Eugene: Wipf & Stock, 2006.

Klink, Edward W., and Darian R. Lockett. *Understanding Biblical Theology: A Comparison of Theory and Practice*. Grand Rapids: Zondervan, 2012.

Koch, Kurt. "Weltende als Erfüllung und Vollendung der Schöpfung." In *Hoffnung über den Tod hinaus: Antworten auf Fragen der Eschatologie*, edited by Herbert Vorgrimler, 139–79. Theologische Berichte 19. Zürich: Benzinger, 1990.

Köhler, Ludwig. *Theologie des Alten Testaments*. 4th ed. Neue theologische Grundrisse. Tübingen: Mohr, 1966.

Koorevaar, Hendrik J., and Mart-Jan Paul, eds. *The Land and the Earth: Studies about the Value of the Land of Israel in the Old Testament and Afterwards*. Edition Israelogie. Frankfurt am Main: Lang, 2018.

———, eds. *Theologie van het Oude Testament: De blijvende boodschap van de Hebreeuwse Bijbel*. Zoetermeer: Boekencentrum, 2013.

Kraus, Hans-Joachim. *Die biblische Theologie: Ihre Geschichte und Problematik*. Berlin: Evangelische Verlagsanstalt, 1974.

———. *Systematische Theologie im Kontext biblischer Geschichte und Eschatologie.* Neukirchen-Vluyn: Neukirchener Verlag, 1983.
Kroeger, Catherine C., and Mary J. Evans. *The IVP Women's Bible Commentary.* Downers Grove: InterVarsity, 2002.
Kuhn, Peter. *Gottes Selbsterniedrigung in der Theologie der Rabbinen.* Studien zum Alten und Neuen Testament 17. München: Kösel, 1968.
Ladd, George E. *A Theology of the New Testament.* 2nd ed. Grand Rapids: Eerdmans, 1993.
Larson, Duane H. *Times of the Trinity: A Proposal for Theistic Cosmology.* Worcester Polytechnic Institute Studies in Science, Technology, and Culture 17. New York: Lang, 1995.
Lash, Nicholas. *Theology on the Way to Emmaus.* London: SCM, 1986.
Lehmann, Karl. "Karl Rahner." In *Bilanz der Theologie im 20. Jahrhundert: Bahnbrechende Theologen. Band 4,* edited by Herbert Vorgrimler and Robert vander Gucht, 143–81. Freiburg im Breisgau: Herder, 1970.
———. "Philosophisches Denken im Werk Karl Rahners." In *Karl Rahner in Erinnerung,* edited by Albert Raffelt, 10–27. Freiburger Akademieschriften 8. Düsseldorf: Patmos, 1994.
———. "Rahner." In *Lexikon für Theologie und Kirche. Band 8,* edited by Walter Kasper et al., 3rd ed., 805–8. Freiburg: Herder, 1999.
Lindbeck, George A. *The Nature of Doctrine: Religion and Theology in a Postliberal Age.* Philadelphia: Westminster, 1984.
———. "Scripture, Consensus, and Community." In *Biblical Interpretation in Crisis: The Ratzinger Conference on Bible and Church,* edited by Richard J. Neuhaus, 74–103. Encounter Series 9. Grand Rapids: Eerdmans, 1989.
Lindemann, Andreas. *Der Erste Korintherbrief.* Handbuch zum Neuen Testament, 9.1. Tübingen: Mohr Siebeck, 2000.
Lohfink, Norbert. "Gegenwart und Ewigkeit: Die Zeit im Buch Kohelet." *Geist und Leben* 60 (1987) 2–12.
Lønning, Per. "Die Schöpfungstheologie Jürgen Moltmanns: Eine nordische Perspektive." *Kerygma und Dogma* 33 (1987) 207–23.
Losinger, Anton. *The Anthropological Turn: The Human Orientation of the Theology of Karl Rahner.* Moral Philosophy and Moral Theology 2. New York: Fordham University Press, 2000.
Ludlow, Morwenna. *Universal Salvation: Eschatology in the Thought of Gregory of Nyssa and Karl Rahner.* Oxford Theological Monographs. Oxford: Oxford University Press, 2000.
Luther, Martin. *Martin Luthers Werke: Kritische Gesamtausgabe.* 136 vols. Weimarer Ausgabe. Weimar: Böhlau, 1883–2009.
Macek, Petr. "The Doctrine of Creation in the Messianic Theology of Jürgen Moltmann." *Viatorum* 49, no. 2 (2007) 150–84.
Macleod, Donald. "The Christology of Jürgen Moltmann." *Themelios* 24, no. 2 (1999) 35–47.
Macquarrie, John. *Principles of Christian Theology.* 2nd ed. London: SCM, 2003.
Maddox, Randy L. "Nurturing the New Creation: Reflections on a Wesleyan Trajectory." In *Wesleyan Perspectives on the New Creation,* edited by M. Douglas Meeks, 21–52. Nashville: Kingswood Books, 2004.
Malina, Bruce J. "Rhetorical Criticism and Social-Scientific Criticism: Why Won't Romanticism Leave Us Alone?" In *Social World of the New Testament: Insights and Models,* edited by Jerome H. Neyrey and Eric C. Stewart, 3–24. Baker Academic, 2008.

Mansilla, Veronica B. "Learning to Synthesize: The Development of Interdisciplinary Understanding." In *The Oxford Handbook of Interdisciplinarity*, edited by Robert Frodeman, 288–307. Oxford: Oxford University Press, 2010.

Marshall, I. Howard. "Review: A New Testament Biblical Theology: The Unfolding of the Old Testament in the New." *Themelios from The Gospel Coalition*. Accessed June 30, 2016. http://themelios.thegospelcoalition.org/review/a-new-testament-biblical-theology-the-unfolding-of-the-old-testament-in-the.

Martin, Oren R. *Bound for the Promised Land: The Land Promise in God's Redemptive Plan*. New Studies in Biblical Theology. Downers Grove: InterVarsity, 2015.

Mathison, Keith A. *From Age to Age: The Unfolding of Biblical Eschatology*. Phillipsburg: P&R, 2009.

May, Georg. *Der Glaube in der nachkonziliaren Kirche*. Una Voce-Korrespondenz, 13.1/2. Düsseldorf: Una Voce, 1983.

McConville, J. Gordon, and Craig G. Bartholomew, eds. *The Two Horizons Old Testament Commentary*. Grand Rapids: Eerdmans, 2008.

McDannell, Colleen, and Bernhard Lang. *Heaven: A History*. 2nd ed. New Haven: Yale University Press, 2001.

McFague, Sallie. *Metaphorical Theology: Models of God in Religious Language*. London: SCM, 1983.

McGrath, Alister E. *A Brief History of Heaven*. Malden: Blackwell, 2003.

———. *Christian Theology: An Introduction*. 3rd ed. Oxford: Blackwell, 2001.

McGrath, Alister E., and Christian Wiese. *Der Weg der christlichen Theologie: Eine Einfuhrung*. München: Beck, 1997.

Meeks, M. Douglas. *Origins of the Theology of Hope*. Philadelphia: Fortress, 1974.

Meijering, Eginhard P. *Augustin über Schöpfung, Ewigkeit und Zeit: Das elfte Buch der Bekenntnisse*. Philosophia Patrum 4. Leiden: Brill, 1979.

Mell, Ulrich. *Neue Schöpfung: Eine traditionsgeschichtliche und exegetische Studie zu einem soteriologischen Grundsatz paulinischer Theologie*. Beihefte zur Zeitschrift für die neutestamentliche Wissenschaft und die Kunde der älteren Kirche 156. New York: De Gruyter, 1989.

Merk, Otto. *Biblische Theologie des Neuen Testaments in ihrer Anfangszeit: Ihre methodischen Probleme bei Johann Philipp Gabler und Georg Lorenz Bauer und deren Nachwirkungen*. Marburger Theologische Studien 9. Marburg: Elwert, 1972.

Metz, Johann-Baptist. "Hoffnung als Naherwartung oder der Kampf um die verlorene Zeit: Unzeitgemäße Thesen zur Apokalyptik." In *Glaube in Geschichte und Gesellschaft: Studien zu einer praktischen Fundamentaltheologie*, 149–58. Mainz: Matthias Grünewald, 1977.

Michaels, J. Ramsey. "Eschatology in I Peter III.17." *New Testament Studies* 13, no. 4 (1967) 394–401.

Middleton, J. Richard. *A New Heaven and a New Earth: Reclaiming Biblical Eschatology*. Grand Rapids: Baker Academic, 2014.

Mildenberger, Friedrich. *Prolegomena: Verstehen und Geltung der Bibel*. Biblische Dogmatik: Eine biblische Theologie in dogmatischer Perspektive 1. Stuttgart: Kohlhammer, 1991.

Möller, Joseph. *Die Chance des Menschen—Gott genannt: Was Vernunft und Erfahrung heute von Gott sagen können*. Zürich: Benziger, 1975.

Molnar, Paul D. "The Function of the Trinity in Moltmann's Ecological Doctrine of Creation." *Theological Studies* 51, no. 4 (1990) 673–98.

———. "Moltmann's Post-Modern Messianic Christology: A Review Discussion." *The Thomist* 56, no. 4 (1992) 669–93.

Moltmann, Jürgen. "The Adventure of Theological Ideas." *Religious Studies Review* 22 (1996) 102–5.

———. *Anfänge der dialektischen Theologie: Neudrucke und Berichte aus dem 20. Jahrhundert.* Vol. 1. 2 vols. Theologische Bücherei 17. München: Kaiser, 1962.

———. "Antwort auf die Kritik der Theologie der Hoffnung." In *Diskussion über die "Theologie der Hoffnung" von Jürgen Moltmann*, edited by Wolf D. Marsch, 201–38. München: Kaiser, 1967.

———. "Antwort Jürgen Moltmann." In *Worauf wir hoffen: Das Kommen Gottes und der Weg Jesu Christi*, edited by Bertold Klappert. München: Kaiser, 1997.

———. "Auferstehungshoffnung und Befreiungspraxis." In *Zukunft der Schöpfung: Gesammelte Aufsätze*, 105–22. München: Kaiser, 1977.

———. "Aufgaben christlicher Theologie heute." In *Das Experiment Hoffnung: Einführungen*, edited by Jürgen Moltmann, 13–28. München: Kaiser, 1974.

———. "The Bible, the Exegete and the Theologian." In *God Will Be All in All: The Eschatology of Jürgen Moltmann*, edited by Richard Bauckham, 227–32. Edinburgh: T&T Clark, 1999.

———. "Can Christian Eschatology Become Post-Modern?" In *God Will Be All in All: The Eschatology of Jürgen Moltmann*, edited by Richard Bauckham, 259–64. Edinburgh: T&T Clark, 1999.

———. "Christ in Cosmic Context." In *Christ and Context: The Confrontation between Gospel and Culture*, edited by Hilary D. Regan et al., 205–9. Edinburgh: T&T Clark, 1993.

———. "Christliche Hoffnung: Messianisch oder transzendent? Ein theologisches Gespräch mit Joachim von Fiore und Thomas von Aquin." *Münchener Theologische Zeitschrift* 33, no. 4 (1982) 241–60.

———. "Christsein, Menschsein und das Reich Gottes: Ein Gespräch mit Karl Rahner." In *In der Geschichte des dreieinigen Gottes: Beiträge zur trinitarischen Theologie*, 156–72. München: Kaiser, 1991.

———. "Creation and Redemption." In *Creation, Christ, and Culture: Studies in Honour of T. F. Torrance*, edited by Richard W. A. McKinney, 119–34. Edinburgh: T&T Clark, 1976.

———. *The Crucified God: The Cross of Christ as the Foundation and Criticism of Christian Theology.* Minneapolis: Fortress, 1993.

———. *Erfahrungen theologischen Denkens: Wege und Formen christlicher Theologie.* Systematischen Beiträge zur Theologie 6. München: Kaiser, 1999.

———. "Eschatological Future and Aeon in Moltmann's Theology: Antwort von Jürgen Moltmann." In *Sino-Theology and the Thinking of Jürgen Moltmann*, edited by Jürgen Moltmann and Thomas Tseng, 125–28. Internationale Theologie 10. Frankfurt am Main: Lang, 2004.

———. "Der 'eschatologische Augenblick'. Gedanken zur Zeit und Ewigkeit in eschatologischer Hinsicht." In *Vernunft des Glaubens: Wissenschaftliche Theologie und kirchliche Lehre, Festschrift zum 60. Geburtstag von Wolfhart Pannenberg*, edited by Jan Rohls and Gunther Wenz, 578–89. Göttingen: Vandenhoeck & Ruprecht, 1988.

———. *Ethik der Hoffnung.* Gütersloh: Gütersloher Verlagshaus, 2010.

———. *Das Experiment Hoffnung: Einführungen.* München: Kaiser, 1974.

———. "Fundamentalisme en moderne tijd." *Concilium* 28, no. 3 (1992) 91–96.

———. *Der Geist des Lebens: Eine ganzheitliche Pneumatologie*. Systematischen Beiträge zur Theologie 4. München: Kaiser, 1991.

———. *Der gekreuzigte Gott: Das Kreuz Christi als Grund und Kritik christlicher Theologie*. München: Kaiser, 1972.

———. *Die Gemeinde im Horizont der Herrschaft Christi: Neue Perspektiven in der Protestantischen Theologie*. Bekennen und Bekenntnis 5. Neukirchen: Neukirchener, 1959.

———. "God in the World—The World in God: Perichoresis in Trinity and Eschatology." In *The Gospel of John and Christian Theology*, edited by Richard Bauckham and Carl Mosser, 369–81. Grand Rapids: Eerdmans, 2008.

———. *The Gospel of Liberation*. Waco: Word, 1973.

———. "Gottes Selbstbeschränkung und die Geschichte des Universums." In *Wissenschaft und Weisheit: Zum Gespräch zwischen Naturwissenschaft und Theologie*, 68–82. München: Kaiser, 2002.

———. *Gott im Projekt der modernen Welt: Beiträge zur öffentlichen Relevanz der Theologie*. Gütersloh: Gütersloher Verlagshaus, 1997.

———. *Gott in der Schöpfung: Ökologische Schöpfungslehre*. Systematischen Beiträge zur Theologie 2. München: Kaiser, 1985.

———. "Gott und Raum." In *Wo ist Gott?: Gottesräume, Lebensräume*, by Carmen Rivuzumwami and Jürgen Moltmann, 29–41. Neukirchen-Vluyn: Neukirchener, 2002.

———. "Hoffnung und Entwicklung." In *Zukunft der Schöpfung: Gesammelte Aufsätze*, 59–67. München: Kaiser, 1977.

———. "Hoffnung und Planung." In *Perspektiven der Theologie: Gesammelte Aufsätze*, 251–68. München: Kaiser, 1968.

———. "Hope and History." In *Religion, Revolution, and the Future (United States Lectures & Essays, 1967–1968)*, 200–219. New York: Scribner, 1969.

———. "Hope and Reality: Contradiction and Correspondence." In *God Will Be All in All: The Eschatology of Jürgen Moltmann*, edited by Richard Bauckham, 77–85. Edinburgh: T&T Clark, 1999.

———. *Im Ende—der Anfang: Eine kleine Hoffnungslehre*. München: Kaiser, 2004.

———. *Im Gespräch mit Ernst Bloch: Eine theologische Wegbegleitung*. Kaiser Traktate 18. München: Kaiser, 1976.

———. *In der Geschichte des dreieinigen Gottes: Beiträge zur trinitarischen Theologie*. München: Kaiser, 1991.

———. "Is the World Coming to an End or Has Its Future Already Begun?" In *The Future as God's Gift: Explorations in Christian Eschatology*, edited by Marcel Sarot and David Fergusson, 129–38. Edinburgh: T&T Clark, 2000.

———. "Die Kategorie Novum in der christlichen Theologie." In *Perspektiven der Theologie: Gesammelte Aufsätze*, 174–88. München: Kaiser, 1968.

———. *Kirche in der Kraft des Geistes: Ein Beitrag zur messianischen Ekklesiologie*. München: Kaiser, 1975.

———. *Das Kommen Gottes: Christliche Eschatologie*. Systematischen Beiträge zur Theologie 5. München: Kaiser, 1995.

———. *Der lebendige Gott und die Fülle des Lebens: Auch ein Beitrag zur Atheismusdebatte unserer Zeit*. Gütersloh: Gütersloher Verlagshaus, 2014.

———. "The Liberation of the Future and Its Anticipations in History." In *God Will Be All in All: The Eschatology of Jürgen Moltmann*, edited by Richard Bauckham, 265–89. Edinburgh: T&T Clark, 1999.

———. "Liebe—Tod—Ewiges Leben: Entwurf einer personalen Eschatologie." In *Im Angesicht des Todes: ein interdisziplinäres Kompendium. Band 2*, edited by Hansjakob Becker et al., 837–54. Pietas Liturgia 4. St. Ottilien: EOS, 1987.

———. "Methoden der Eschatologie." In *Zukunft der Schöpfung: Gesammelte Aufsätze*, 51–58. München: Kaiser, 1977.

———. *Perspektiven der Theologie: Gesammelte Aufsätze*. München: Kaiser, 1968.

———. "Progress and Abyss: Remembrances of the Future of the Modern World." In *The Future of Hope: Christian Tradition amid Modernity and Postmodernity*, edited by Miroslav Volf and William H. Katerberg, 3–26. Grand Rapids: Eerdmans, 2004.

———. "Rechtfertigung und neue Schöpfung." In *Zukunft der Schöpfung: Gesammelte Aufsätze*, 157–79. München: Kaiser, 1977.

———. *Das Reich Gottes und die Treue zur Erde*. Gespräch 49. Wuppertal: Jugenddienst, 1963.

———. "Resurrection as Hope." In *Religion, Revolution, and the Future (United States Lectures & Essays, 1967–1968)*, 42–62. New York: Scribner, 1969.

———. "Richtungen der Eschatologie." In *Zukunft der Schöpfung: Gesammelte Aufsätze*, 26–50. München: Kaiser, 1977.

———. "Sabbath: Finishing and Beginning." *The Living Pulpit* 7, no. 2 (1998) 4–5.

———. "Schöpfung als offenes System." In *Zukunft der Schöpfung: Gesammelte Aufsätze*, 123–39. München: Kaiser, 1977.

———. *Science and Wisdom*. Minneapolis: Fortress, 2003.

———. *"Sein Name ist Gerechtigkeit": Neue Beiträge zur christlichen Gotteslehre*. Gütersloh: Gütersloher Verlagshaus, 2008.

———. *Die Sprache der Befreiung: Predigten und Besinnungen*. München: Kaiser, 1972.

———. *Theologie der Hoffnung: Untersuchungen zur Begründung und zu den Konsequenzen einer christlichen Eschatologie*. München: Kaiser, 1964.

———. "Theologie in der Welt der modernen Wissenschaften." In *Perspektiven der Theologie: Gesammelte Aufsätze*, 269–87. München: Kaiser, 1968.

———. "Theology in Germany Today." In *Observations on "The Spiritual Situation of the Age": Contemporary German Perspectives*, edited by Jürgen Habermas, 181–206. Studies in Contemporary German Social Thought. Cambridge: MIT, 1984.

———. "Toward a Political Hermeneutic of the Gospel." In *Religion, Revolution, and the Future (United States Lectures & Essays, 1967–1968)*, 83–107. New York: Scribner, 1969.

———. *Trinität und Reich Gottes: Zur Gotteslehre*. Systematischen Beiträge zur Theologie 1. München: Kaiser, 1980.

———. *The Trinity and the Kingdom: The Doctrine of God*. Minneapolis: Fortress, 1993.

———. *Umkehr zur Zukunft*. Gütersloh: Gütersloher Verlagshaus, 1977.

———. "Verkündigung als Problem der Exegese." In *Perspektiven der Theologie: Gesammelte Aufsätze*, 113–27. München: Kaiser, 1968.

———. "Verschränkte Zeiten der Geschichte: Notwendige Differenzierungen und Begrenzungen des Geschichtsbegriffs." *Evangelische Theologie* 44 (1984).

———. *Der Weg Jesu Christi: Christologie in messianischen Dimensionen*. Systematischen Beiträge zur Theologie 3. München: Kaiser, 1989.

———. *Weiter Raum: Eine Lebensgeschichte*. Gütersloh: Gütersloher Verlagshaus, 2006.

———. *Wie ich mich geändert habe*. Gütersloh: Kaiser, 1997.

———. *Wissenschaft und Weisheit: Zum Gespräch zwischen Naturwissenschaft und Theologie*. München: Kaiser, 2002.

———. "The World in God or God in the World?" In *God Will Be All in All: The Eschatology of Jürgen Moltmann*, edited by Richard Bauckham, 35–41. Edinburgh: T&T Clark, 1999.

Moltmann-Wendel, Elisabeth, and Jürgen Moltmann. "Mit allen Sinnen glauben: Auferstehung des Fleisches." In *Leidenschaft für Gott: Worauf es uns ankommt*, 22–43. Freiburg: Herder, 2006.

Momose, Peter F. *Kreuzestheologie: Eine Auseinandersetzung mit Jürgen Moltmann*. Ökumenische Forschungen 7. Freiburg: Herder, 1978.

Moo, Douglas J. "Creation and New Creation." *Bulletin for Biblical Research* 20 (2010) 39–60.

Moran, Joe. *Interdisciplinarity*. 2nd ed. The New Critical Idiom. London: Routledge, 2010.

Muck, Otto. "Heidegger und Karl Rahner." *Zeitschrift für katholische Theologie* 116, no. 3 (1994) 257–269.

———. *Die transzendentale Methode in der scholastischen Philosophie der Gegenwart*. Innsbruch: Rauch, 1968.

Mühling, Markus. *Grundinformation Eschatologie: Systematische Theologie aus der Perspektive der Hoffnung*. Göttingen: Vandenhoeck & Ruprecht, 2007.

Muis, Jan. "Dogmatiek." In *Wat is theologie?*, edited by Willem van Asselt, 75–91. Zoetermeer: Meinema, 2001.

Müller, Helmut A., ed. *Kosmologie: Fragen nach Evolution und Eschatologie der Welt*. Religion, Theologie und Naturwissenschaft 2. Göttingen: Vandenhoeck & Ruprecht, 2004.

Müller, Max. "Zu Karl Rahners 'Geist in Welt.'" In *Karl Rahner: Bilder eines Lebens*, edited by Hubert Biallowons and Paul Imhof, 28–31. Freiburg: Herder, 1985.

Müller-Fahrenholz, Geiko. *Phantasie für das Reich Gottes: Die Theologie Jürgen Moltmanns. Eine Einführung*. Gütersloh: Gütersloher Verlagshaus, 2000.

Müller-Goldkuhle, Peter. *Die Eschatologie in der Dogmatik des 19. Jahrhunderts*. Beiträge zur neueren Geschichte der katholischen Theologie 10. Essen: Ludgerus, 1966.

Munteanu, Daniel. *Der tröstende Geist der Liebe: zu einer ökumenischen Lehre vom Heiligen Geist über die trinitarischen Theologien Jürgen Moltmanns und Dumitru Staniloaes*. Neukirchen-Vluyn: Neukirchener, 2003.

Murphy, Marie. *A Critical Analysis of Karl Rahner's Eschatology*. New York: Fordham University Press, 1988.

———. *New Images of the Last Things: Karl Rahner on Death and Life after Death*. New York: Paulist, 1988.

Murphy, N. "The Resurrection Body and Personal Identity: Possibilities and Limits of Eschatological Knowledge." In *Resurrection: Theological and Scientific Assessments*, edited by Ted Peters et al., 202–18. Grand Rapids: Eerdmans, 2002.

Neufeld, Karl H. *Die Brüder Rahner: Eine Biographie*. Freiburg im Breisgau: Herder, 1994.

———. "Die Schrift in der Theologie Karl Rahners." In *Der eine Gott der beiden Testamente*, 229–46. Jahrbuch für biblische Theologie 2. Neukirchen: Neukircher, 1987.

Neusner, Jacob, ed. *Megillah*. The Babylonian Talmud: A Translation and Commentary 7. Nashville: Hendrickson, 2011.

———, ed. *Sanhedrin*. The Babylonian Talmud: A Translation and Commentary 16. Nashville: Hendrickson, 2011.

Ngewa, Samuel, ed. *Africa Bible Commentary Series*. Grand Rapids: Zondervan, 2009.

Nicholls, Bruce J., ed. *Asia Bible Commentary*. Singapore: Asia Theological Association, 2008.

Niebuhr, Karl-Wilhelm, and Christfried Böttrich, eds. *Johann Philipp Gabler, 1753–1826: Zum 250. Geburtstag*. Leipzig: Evangelische Verlagsanstalt, 2003.

Niehaus, Jeffrey J. *God at Sinai: Covenant and Theophany in the Bible and Ancient Near East*. Grand Rapids: Zondervan, 1995.

Niewiadomski, Józef. *Die Zweideutigkeit von Gott und Welt in J. Moltmanns Theologien*. Innsbrucker Theologische Studien 9. Innsbruck: Tyrolia, 1982.

Nineham, Dennis E. *The Use and Abuse of the Bible: A Study of the Bible in an Age of Rapid Cultural Change*. New York: Barnes & Noble, 1976.

Novick, Peter. *That Noble Dream: The "Objectivity Question" and the American Historical Profession*. Ideas in Context. Cambridge: Cambridge University Press, 2005.

Nürnberger, Klaus. "Eschatology and Entropy: An Alternative to Robert John Russell's Proposal." *Zygon* 47, no. 4 (2012) 970–96.

O'Collins, Gerald. "The Principle and Theology of Hope." *Scottish Journal of Theology* 21, no. 2 (1968) 129–144.

O'Collins, Gerald, and Daniel Kendall. *The Bible for Theology: Ten Principles for the Theological Use of Scripture*. New York: Paulist, 1997.

O'Donovan, Oliver. *Resurrection and Moral Order: An Outline for Evangelical Ethics*. Leicester: Apollos, 2001.

Oetinger, Friedrich Ch. "Leib, Soma." In *Biblisches und emblematisches Wörterbuch*, edited by Gerhard Schäfer and Martin Schmidt, 222–223. Texte zur Geschichte des Pietismus, 7.3.1. Berlin: De Gruyter, 2013.

Ott, Ludwig. *Eschatologie in der Scholastik*. Handbuch der Dogmengeschichte, 4.7b. Freiburg: Herder, 1990.

Otto, Randall. "The Resurrection in Jürgen Moltmann." *Journal of the Evangelical Theological Society* 35, no. 1 (1992) 81–90.

Ouweneel, Willem J. *De toekomst van God: Ontwerp van een eschatologie*. Evangelisch-Dogmatische Reeks 10. Heerenveen: Medema, 2012.

Padgett, Alan G. *God, Eternity, and the Nature of Time*. New York: St. Martin, 1992.

Pagels, Elaine H. *Adam, Eva und die Schlange: Die Theologie der Sünde*. Reinbek: Rowohlt, 1991.

Pannenberg, Wolfhart. "Anbrechende Zukunft: Jürgen Moltmanns Eschatologie." *Evangelische Kommentare* 29 (1996) 76–78.

———. "Die Frage nach Gott als Schöpfer der Welt." In *Kosmologie: Fragen nach Evolution und Eschatologie der Welt*, edited by Helmut A. Müller, 197–208. Religion, Theologie und Naturwissenschaft 2. Göttingen: Vandenhoeck & Ruprecht, 2004.

———. *Systematische Theologie 1*. Göttingen: Vandenhoeck & Ruprecht, 1988.

———. *Systematische Theologie 2*. Göttingen: Vandenhoeck & Ruprecht, 1991.

———. *Systematische Theologie 3*. Göttingen: Vandenhoeck & Ruprecht, 1993.

———. *Theologie und Reich Gottes*. Gütersloh: Gütersloher Verlagshaus Mohn, 1971.

———. *Theology and the Philosophy of Science*. Philadelphia: Westminster, 1976.

———. *Toward a Theology of Nature: Essays on Science and Faith*. Edited by Ted Peters. International Society for Science & Religion Library. Louisville: Westminster John Knox, 2010.

Park, Aaron P. "The Christian Hope According to Bultmann, Pannenberg, and Moltmann." *Westminster Theological Journal* 33, no. 2 (1971) 153–74.

Patte, Daniel, ed. *Global Bible Commentary*. Nashville: Abingdon, 2006.

Peacocke, Arthur. *Paths From Science Towards God: The End of All Our Exploring*. Oxford: Oneworld, 2001.

Pesch, Otto H. *Frei sein aus Gnade: Theologische Anthropologie*. Freiburg: Herder, 1983.

Pesch, Rudolf. *Das Markusevangelium 1: Einleitung und Kommentar zu Kap. 1,1–8,26*. Vol. 1. 2 vols. Herders theologischer Kommentar zum Neuen Testament 2. Freiburg: Herder, 1976.

Peters, Ted et al., eds. *Brücken bauen: Naturwissenschaft und Religion*. Religion, Theologie und Naturwissenschaft 5. Göttingen: Vandenhoeck & Ruprecht, 2006.

Petty, Michael W. *A Faith That Loves the Earth: The Ecological Theology of Karl Rahner*. Lanham: University Press of America, 1996.

Phan, Peter C. "Eschatology." In *The Cambridge Companion to Karl Rahner*, edited by Declan Marmion and Mary E. Hines, 174–94. Cambridge Companions to Religion. Cambridge: Cambridge University Press, 2005.

———. *Eternity in Time: A Study of Karl Rahner's Eschatology*. Selinsgrove: Susquehanna University Press, 1988.

———. "Is Karl Rahner's Doctrine of Sin Orthodox?" *Philosophy and Theology* 9, no. 1/2 (1995) 223–36.

Plato. "Parmenides." In *Kratylos, Parmenides*, translated by Mario Molegraaf. Verzameld Werk 13. Amsterdam: Bakker, 2005.

———. "Timaios." In *Timaios, Kritias*, translated by Hans Warren. Verzameld Werk 10. Amsterdam: Bakker, 2001.

Plotinus. *The Enneads of Plotinus: A Commentary*. Edited by Paulos Kalligas. Translated by Elisabeth K. Fowden and Nicolas Pilavachi. Vol. 1. Princeton: Princeton University Press, 2014.

Polkinghorne, John C., ed. *The End of the World and the Ends of God: Science and Theology on Eschatology*. Harrisburg: Trinity International, 2000.

———. *The Faith of a Physicist: Reflections of a Bottom-up Thinker*. Princeton: Princeton University Press, 1994.

———. *The God of Hope and the End of the World*. New Haven: Yale University Press, 2002.

———. "Jürgen Moltmann's Engagement with the Natural Sciences." In *God's Life in Trinity*, edited by Miroslav Volf and Michael Welker, 61–70. Minneapolis: Fortress, 2006.

———. *Science and Religion in Quest of Truth*. New Haven: Yale University Press, 2011.

———. *Science and the Trinity: The Christian Encounter with Reality*. New Haven: Yale University Press, 2006.

Pseudo-Athenagoras. *De Resurrectione Mortuorum*. Translated by Miroslav Marcovich. Supplements to Vigiliae Christianae 53. Leiden: Brill, 2000.

Purcell, Michael. "Rahner amid Modernity and Post-Modernity." In *The Cambridge Companion to Karl Rahner*, edited by Declan Marmion and Mary E. Hines, 195–210. Cambridge Companions to Religion. Cambridge: Cambridge University Press, 2005.

Rad, Gerhard von. "Offene Fragen im Umkreis einer Theologie des Alten Testaments." *Gesammelte Studien zum Alten Testament* 2 (1973) 289–312.

———. *Theologie des Alten Testaments*. 2nd ed. 2 vols. München: Kaiser, 1992.

Raffelt, Albert. "Bibliographie des Schrifttums von Karl Rahner." *Universitätsbibliothek Freiburg im Breisgau*. Accessed June 30, 2016. http://www.ub.uni-freiburg.de/fileadmin/ub/referate/04/rahner/rahnersc.pdf.

Rahner, Karl. "Abgestiegen ins Totenreich." In *Schriften zur Theologie 7*, edited by Karl Rahner, 145–49. Einsiedeln: Benziger, 1966.

———. "Anschauung Gottes." In *Sacramentum Mundi 1*, edited by Karl Rahner, 159–63. Freiburg: Herder, 1967.

———. "Anthropologie: Theologische Anthropologie." In *Sacramentum Mundi 1*, edited by Karl Rahner, 176–86. Freiburg: Herder, 1967.

———. "Anthropozentrik." In *Lexikon für Theologie und Kirche 1*, edited by Michael Buchberger et al., 2nd ed., 632–34. Freiburg: Herder, 1957.

———. "Auferstehung des Fleisches." In *Schriften zur Theologie 2*, edited by Karl Rahner, 211–25. Einsiedeln: Benziger, 1955.

———. *Auferstehung des Fleisches: Können wir noch daran glauben?* Kevelear: Butzon & Bercker, 1962.

———. "Auferstehung Jesu." In *Schriften zur Theologie 7*, edited by Karl Rahner, 344–52. Einsiedeln: Benziger, 1966.

———. "Auferstehung Jesu: IV. Zur Theologie der Auferstehung Jesu." In *Sacramentum Mundi 1*, edited by Karl Rahner, 420–25. Freiburg: Herder, 1967.

———. "Biblische Theologie: III. Biblische Theologie und Dogmatik in ihrem wechselseitigen Verhältnis." In *Lexikon für Theologie und Kirche 2*, edited by Michael Buchberger et al., 449–51. Freiburg im Breisgau: Herder, 1958.

———. "Buch Gottes—Buch der Menschen." In *Schriften zur Theologie 16*, edited by Karl Rahner, 278–91. Einsiedeln: Benziger, 1984.

———. "Das Christentum und der 'neue Mensch.'" In *Schriften zur Theologie 5*, edited by Karl Rahner, 159–79. Einsiedeln: Benziger, 1962.

———. "Christologie im Rahmen des modernen Selbst- und Weltverständnisses." In *Schriften zur Theologie 9*, edited by Karl Rahner, 227–41. Einsiedeln: Benziger, 1970.

———. "Christologie innerhalb einer evolutiven Weltanschauung." In *Schriften zur Theologie 5*, edited by Karl Rahner, 183–221. Einsiedeln: Benziger, 1962.

———. "Diskussion zu 'Fragment aus einer theologischen Besinnung auf den Begriff der Zukunft.'" In *Der Mensch und seine Zukunft*, edited by Karl Schlechta, 35–38. Darmstädter Gespräch 9. Darmstadt: Neue Darmstädter Verlagsanstalt, 1967.

———. "Diskussionsbeiträge zu 'Theologische Anmerkungen zum Zeitbegriff.'" In *Weisen der Zeitlichkeit*, edited by Görres-Gesellschaft: Institut für die Begegnung von Naturwissenschaft und Theologie, 228–44. Naturwissenschaft und Theologie 12. Freiburg: Herder, 1970.

———. "Diskussionsbeiträge zur Problematik von Raum und Zeit in der Görres-Gesellschaft." In *Verantwortung der Theologie: Im Dialog mit Naturwissenschaften und Gesellschaftstheorie*, edited by Hans-Dieter Mutschler, 258–68. Sämtliche Werke 15. Freiburg: Herder, 2002.

———. "Dogmatische Erwägungen über das Wissen und Selbstbewußtsein Christi." In *Schriften zur Theologie 5*, edited by Karl Rahner, 222–45. Einsiedeln: Benziger, 1962.

———. "Dogmatische Fragen zur Osterfrömmigkeit." In *Schriften zur Theologie 4*, edited by Karl Rahner, 157–72. Einsiedeln: Benziger, 1960.

———. "Der dreifaltige Gott als transzendenter Urgrund der Heilsgeschichte." In *Mysterium Salutis: Grundriss Heilsgeschichtlicher Dogmatik*, edited by Magnus Löhrer and Johannes Feiner, 2:317–401. Einsiedeln: Benziger, 1965.

———. "Die Einheit von Geist und Materie im christlichen Glaubensverständnis." In *Schriften zur Theologie 6*, edited by Karl Rahner, 185–214. Einsiedeln: Benziger, 1965.

———. "Einheit von Geist und Materie." *Neues Forum* 16, no. 160–161 (1967) 337–40.

———. "Einige Bemerkungen zur Theologie der Erbsünde." In *Dogmatik nach dem Konzil: Theologische Anthropologie und Ekklesiologie*, edited by Albert Raffelt, 31–33. Sämtliche Werke, 22.2. Freiburg: Herder, 2008.

———. "Einige Grundsätzliche Bemerkungen zu einem Dogmatischen Schriftbeweis." In *Schriften zur Theologie 12*, edited by Karl Rahner, 2–3. Einsiedeln: Benziger, 1975.

———. "Erbsünde." In *Sacramentum Mundi 1*, edited by Karl Rahner, 1104–17. Freiburg: Herder, 1967.

———. "Erbsünde und Evolution." *Concilium* 3 (1967) 459–465.

———. "Erfahrungen eines katholischen Theologen." In *Vor dem Geheimnis Gottes den Menschen verstehen: Karl Rahner zum 80. Geburtstag*, edited by Karl Lehmann, 105–19. Schriftenreihe der Katholischen Akademie der Erzdiözese Freiburg. München: Schnell & Steiner, 1984.

———. "Erinnerungen im Gespräch mit Meinold Krauss." In *Erneuerung des Ordenslebens: Zeugnis für Kirche und Welt*, edited by Andreas R. Batlogg. Sämtliche Werke 25. Freiburg: Herder, 2008.

———. "Eschatologie." In *Sacramentum Mundi 1*, edited by Karl Rahner, 1184–92. Freiburg: Herder, 1967.

———. "Eschatologie: Theologisch-Wissenschaftstheoretisch." In *Lexikon für Theologie und Kirche 3*, edited by Michael Buchberger et al., 2nd ed., 1094–98. Freiburg: Herder, 1959.

———. "Die ewige Bedeutung der Menschheit Jesu für unser Gottesverhältnis." In *Schriften zur Theologie 3*, edited by Karl Rahner, 47–60. Einsiedeln: Benziger, 1956.

———. "Ewigkeit aus Zeit." In *Schriften zur Theologie 14*, edited by Karl Rahner, 422–32. Einsiedeln: Benziger, 1980.

———. "Exegese und Dogmatik." In *Schriften zur Theologie 5*, edited by Karl Rahner, 82–111. Einsiedeln: Benziger, 1962.

———. "Fegfeuer." In *Schriften zur Theologie 14*, edited by Karl Rahner, 435–49. Einsiedeln: Benziger, 1980.

———. "Fest der Zukunft der Welt." In *Schriften zur Theologie 7*, edited by Karl Rahner, 178–82. Einsiedeln: Benziger, 1966.

———. "Die Frage nach der Zukunft." In *Schriften zur Theologie 9*, edited by Karl Rahner, 519–40. Einsiedeln: Benziger, 1970.

———. *Geist in Welt: Zur Metaphysik der endlichen Erkenntnis bei Thomas von Aquin*. Edited by Johannes B. Metz. 2nd ed. München: Kösel, 1957.

———. *Glaube, der die Erde liebt: Christliche Besinnung im Alltag der Welt*. Herder-Bücherei 266. Freiburg: Herder, 1967.

———. "Gnade als Mitte menschlicher Existenz: Ein Gespräch mit und über Karl Rahner aus Anlaß seines 70. Geburtstages." In *Herausforderung des Christen: Meditationen, Reflexionen, Interviews*, edited by Karl Rahner, 117–53. Freiburg: Herder, 1975.

———. *Grundkurs des Glaubens: Einführung in den Begriff des Christentums*. 10th ed. Freiburg: Herder, 1976.

———. "Grundsätzliche Überlegungen zur Anthropologie und Protologie." In *Die Heilsgeschichte vor Christus*, edited by Johannes Feiner, 406–20. Mysterium Salutis 2. Einsiedeln: Benziger, 1967.

———. "Heilige Schrift und Theologie." In *Schriften zur Theologie 6*, edited by Karl Rahner, 111–20. Einsiedeln: Benziger, 1965.

———. "Die Herausforderung der Theologie durch das Zweite Vatikanische Konzil." In *Schriften zur Theologie 8*, edited by Karl Rahner, 13–42. Einsiedeln: Benziger, 1967.

———. "Die Hominisation als theologische Frage." In *Das Problem der Hominisation: Über den biologischen Ursprung des Menschen*, edited by Karl Rahner and Paul Overhage, 3rd ed., 13-90. Quaestiones Disputatae, 12/13. Freiburg: Herder, 1965.

———. *Hörer des Wortes: Schriften zur Religionsphilosophie und zur Grundlegung der Theologie*. Edited by Albert Raffelt. Sämtliche Werke 4. Freiburg: Herder, 1997.

———. "Immanente und transzendente Vollendung der Welt." In *Schriften zur Theologie 8*, edited by Karl Rahner, 593-609. Einsiedeln: Benziger, 1967.

———. "Inspiration." In *Handbuch theologischer Grundbegriffe 1*, edited by Heinrich Fries, 715-25. München: Kösel, 1962.

———. "Intellektuelle Redlichkeit und christlicher Glaube." In *Schriften zur Theologie 7*, edited by Karl Rahner, 54-76. Einsiedeln: Benziger, 1966.

———. "Introduction au concept de philosophie existentiale chez Heidegger." *Recherches de science religieuse* 30 (1940) 152-71.

———. "Kirche und Parusie Christi." In *Schriften zur Theologie 6*, edited by Karl Rahner, 348-67. Einsiedeln: Benziger, 1965.

———. "Kirchliche Christologie zwischen Exegese und Dogmatik." In *Schriften zur Theologie 9*, edited by Karl Rahner, 197-226. Einsiedeln: Benziger, 1970.

———. *Kleines Kirchenjahr: Ein Gang durch den Festkreis*. Freiburg: Herder, 1981.

———. "Das Leben der Toten." In *Schriften zur Theologie 4*, edited by Karl Rahner, 429-37. Einsiedeln: Benziger, 1960.

———. "Der Leib in der Heilsordnung." In *Schriften zur Theologie 12*, edited by Karl Rahner, 407-27. Einsiedeln: Benziger, 1975.

———. "Letzte Dinge." In *Sacramentum Mundi 3*, edited by Karl Rahner, 220-23. Freiburg: Herder, 1969.

———. "Marxistische Utopie und christliche Zukunft des Menschen." In *Schriften zur Theologie 6*, edited by Karl Rahner, 77-88. Einsiedeln: Benziger, 1965.

———. "Naturwissenschaft und vernünftiger Glaube." In *Schriften zur Theologie 15*, edited by Karl Rahner, 24-62. Einsiedeln: Benziger, 1983.

———. "Das neue Bild der Kirche." In *Schriften zur Theologie 8*, edited by Karl Rahner, 329-55. Einsiedeln: Benziger, 1967.

———. "Parusie: II. Dogmatisch." In *Lexikon für Theologie und Kirche 8*, edited by Michael Buchberger et al., 123-24. Freiburg: Herder, 1963.

———. "Perspektiven für die Zukunft der Kirche." In *Schriften zur Theologie 9*, edited by Karl Rahner, 541-57. Einsiedeln: Benziger, 1970.

———. "Profangeschichte und Heilsgeschichte." In *Schriften zur Theologie 15*, edited by Karl Rahner, 11-23. Einsiedeln: Benziger, 1983.

———. "Protologie." In *Lexikon für Theologie und Kirche 8*, edited by Michael Buchberger et al., 835-37. Freiburg: Herder, 1963.

———. "Protologie." In *Sacramentum Mundi 3*, edited by Karl Rahner, 1353-56. Freiburg: Herder, 1969.

———. "Rezension: P. Heinisch, Theologie des Alten Testaments (1940)." *Zeitschrift für katholische Theologie* 65 (1941) 44.

———. *Sämtliche Werke*. Edited by Karl Lehmann et al. 36 vols. Freiburg: Herder, 1995.

———. "Die Schöpfung ist entworfen, daß sie zu uns passt (Röm 8,18-23)." In *Biblische Predigten*, 108-13. Freiburg: Herder, 1965.

———. "Schöpfungslehre." In *Lexikon für Theologie und Kirche 9*, edited by Michael Buchberger et al., 471-74. Freiburg: Herder, 1964.

———. "Schriftbeweis: II. In der systematische Theologie." In *Lexikon für Theologie und Kirche 9*, edited by Michael Buchberger et al., 486–87. Freiburg: Herder, 1964.

———. "Das Selbstverständnis der Theologie vor dem Anspruch der Naturwissenschaft." In *Theologie und Wissenschaft: Das Selbstverständnis der Theologie vor dem Anspruch der Natur- und Geisteswissenschaft 1*, edited by Erich Kellner, 102–147. Gespräche um Glauben und Wissen 8. München: Paulus-Gesellschaft, 1964.

———. "Die Sünde Adams." In *Schriften zur Theologie 9*, edited by Karl Rahner, 259–75. Einsiedeln: Benziger, 1970.

———. "Theologie der Freiheit." In *Gnade als Freiheit: Kleine theologische Beiträge*, edited by Karl Rahner, 31–54. Herder-Bücherei 322. Freiburg: Herder, 1968.

———. "Theologie und Anthropologie." In *Schriften zur Theologie 8*, edited by Karl Rahner, 43–65. Einsiedeln: Benziger, 1967.

———. "Theologische Bemerkungen zum Zeitbegriff." In *Schriften zur Theologie 9*, edited by Karl Rahner, 302–22. Einsiedeln: Benziger, 1970.

———. "Die theologische Dimension der Frage nach dem Menschen." In *Schriften zur Theologie 12*, edited by Karl Rahner, 387–406. Einsiedeln: Benziger, 1975.

———. "Theologische Prinzipien der Hermeneutik eschatologischer Aussagen." In *Schriften zur Theologie 4*, edited by Karl Rahner, 401–28. Einsiedeln: Benziger, 1960.

———. "Theos im Neuen Testament." In *Schriften zur Theologie 1*, edited by Karl Rahner, 91–168. Einsiedeln: Benziger, 1954.

———. "Tod." In *Sacramentum Mundi 4*, edited by Karl Rahner, 920–27. Freiburg: Herder, 1969.

———. "Tod. IV." In *Lexikon für Theologie und Kirche 10*, edited by Josef Höfer and Karl Rahner, 2nd ed., 221–26. Freiburg: Herder, 1965.

———. "Transzendentaltheologie." In *Herders theologisches Taschenlexikon 7*, edited by Karl Rahner, 324–29. Freiburg: Herder, 1973.

———. *The Trinity*. New York: Herder & Herder, 1970.

———. "Trost der Zeit." In *Schriften zur Theologie 3*, edited by Karl Rahner, 169–88. Einsiedeln: Benziger, 1956.

———. "Über das christliche Sterben." In *Schriften zur Theologie 7*, edited by Karl Rahner, 273–80. Einsiedeln: Benziger, 1966.

———. "Über das Verhältnis von Natur und Gnade." In *Schriften zur Theologie 1*, edited by Karl Rahner, 323–46. Einsiedeln: Benziger, 1954.

———. "Über den Versuch eines Aufrisses einer Dogmatik." In *Schriften zur Theologie 1*, edited by Karl Rahner, 9–47. Einsiedeln: Benziger, 1954.

———. "Über den 'Zwischenzustand.'" In *Schriften zur Theologie 12*, edited by Karl Rahner, 455–66. Einsiedeln: Benziger, 1975.

———. "Über die Eigenart des christlichen Gottesbegriffs." In *Schriften zur Theologie 15*, edited by Karl Rahner, 185–94. Einsiedeln: Benziger, 1983.

———. "Über die inspiration der Schrift." In *Menschsein und Menschwerdung Gottes: Studien zur Grundlegung der Dogmatik, zur Christologie, theologischen Anthropologie und Eschatologie*, edited by Herbert Vorgrimler, 209–15. Sämtliche Werke 12. Freiburg: Herder, 2005.

———. "Über die Schriftinspiration." In *Menschsein und Menschwerdung Gottes: Studien zur Grundlegung der Dogmatik, zur Christologie, theologischen Anthropologie und Eschatologie*, edited by Herbert Vorgrimler, 3–58. Sämtliche Werke 12. Freiburg: Herder, 2005.

———. "Über die Theologische Problematik der 'Neue Erde.'" In *Schriften zur Theologie 8*, edited by Karl Rahner, 580–92. Einsiedeln: Benziger, 1967.

———. "Über künftige Wege der Theologie." In *Schriften zur Theologie 10*, edited by Karl Rahner, 41–69. Einsiedeln: Benziger, 1970.

———. "Überlegungen zur Dogmenentwicklung." In *Schriften zur Theologie 4*, edited by Karl Rahner, 11–50. Einsiedeln: Benziger, 1960.

———. "Überlegungen zur Methode der Theologie." In *Schriften zur Theologie 9*, edited by Karl Rahner, 79–126. Einsiedeln: Benziger, 1970.

———. "Verborgener Sieg." In *Schriften zur Theologie 7*, edited by Karl Rahner, 150–56. Einsiedeln: Benziger, 1966.

———. "Vom Geheimnis des Lebens." In *Schriften zur Theologie 6*, edited by Karl Rahner, 171–84. Einsiedeln: Benziger, 1965.

———. "Warum läßt Gott uns leiden?" In *Schriften zur Theologie 14*, edited by Karl Rahner, 450–66. Einsiedeln: Benziger, 1980.

———. "Welt in Gott: Zum christlichen Schöpfungsbegriff." In *Sein als Offenbarung in Christentum und Hinduismus*, edited by Andreas Bsteh et al., 69–82. Beiträge zur Religionstheologie 4. Mödling: Gabriel, 1984.

———. "Zu einer Theologie des Todes." In *Schriften zur Theologie 10*, edited by Karl Rahner, 181–99. Einsiedeln: Benziger, 1970.

———. "Zum Sinn des Assumpta-Dogmas." In *Schriften zur Theologie 1*, edited by Karl Rahner, 239–52. Einsiedeln: Benziger, 1954.

———. "Zum Verhältnis von Naturwissenschaft und Theologie." In *Schriften zur Theologie 14*, edited by Karl Rahner, 63–72. Einsiedeln: Benziger, 1980.

———. "Zur scholastichen Begrifflichkeit der ungeschaffenen Gnade." In *Schriften zur Theologie 1*, edited by Karl Rahner, 347–76. Einsiedeln: Benziger, 1954.

———. "Zur Theologie der Hoffnung." In *Schriften zur Theologie 8*, edited by Karl Rahner, 561–79. Einsiedeln: Benziger, 1967.

———. *Zur Theologie der Zukunft*. München: DTV, 1971.

———. *Zur Theologie des Todes*. Quaestiones Disputatae 2. Freiburg: Herder, 1958.

Rahner, Karl, and Herbert Vorgrimler. "Apokalyptik." In *Kleines theologisches Wörterbuch*, 10th ed., 27–28. Herderbücherei 108–109. Freiburg: Herder, 1967.

———. "Biblische Theologie." In *Kleines theologisches Wörterbuch*, 10th ed., 51. Herderbücherei 108–109. Freiburg: Herder, 1967.

———. *Kleines theologisches Wörterbuch*. 10th ed. Herderbücherei 108–109. Freiburg: Herder, 1976.

———. *Theological Dictionary*. New York: Herder & Herder, 1965.

Rahner, Karl, and Karl Rawer. "Weltall—Erde—Mensch." In *Christlicher Glaube in moderner Gesellschaft 3*, 34–76. Freiburg: Herder, 1988.

Remenyi, Matthias. "Hoffnung, Tod und Auferstehung." *Zeitschrift für katholische Theologie* 129, no. 1 (2007) 75–96.

———. *Um der Hoffnung willen: Untersuchungen zur eschatologischen Theologie Jürgen Moltmanns*. Regensburg: Pustet, 2005.

Rendtorff, Rolf. *The Canonical Hebrew Bible: A Theology of the Old Testament*. Leiden: Deo, 2005.

Repko, Allen F., et al. *Introduction to Interdisciplinary Studies*. London: SAGE, 2014.

Reynolds, Benjamin E., et al., eds. *Reconsidering the Relationship between Biblical and Systematic Theology in the New Testament: Essays by Theologians and New Testament*

Scholars. Wissenschaftliche Untersuchungen Zum Neuen Testament. 2. Reihe 369. Tübingen: Mohr Siebeck, 2014.

Ricœur, Paul, and André Lacocque. *Thinking Biblically: Exegetical and Hermeneutical Studies*. Chicago: University of Chicago Press, 1998.

Rolf, Kramer. "Zeit und Ewigkeit als Grunderfahrung menschlichen lebens." In *Ewigkeit?: Klärungsversuche aus Natur- und Geisteswissenschaften*, edited by Otfried Reinke, 110–22. Göttingen: Vandenhoeck & Ruprecht, 2004.

Rosenzweig, Franz. *Der Stern der Erlösung*. Haag: Nijhoff, 1976.

Rosner, Brain S. "Biblical Theology." In *New Dictionary of Biblical Theology*, edited by T. Desmond Alexander and Brian S. Rosner, 3–11. Downers Grove: InterVarsity, 2000.

Rudolph, David J. "Festivals in Genesis 1:14." *Tyndale Bulletin* 54, no. 2 (2003) 23–40.

Rushdoony, Rousas J. *Systematic Theology*. 2 vols. Vallecito: Ross House Books, 1994.

Russell, Jeffrey B. *A History of Heaven: The Singing Silence*. Princeton: Princeton University Press, 1997.

Russell, Robert J. "Bodily Resurrection, Eschatology and Scientific Cosmology." In *Resurrection: Theological and Scientific Assessments*, edited by Ted Peters et al., 3–30. Grand Rapids: Eerdmans, 2002.

———. "Cosmology and Eschatology." In *The Oxford Handbook of Eschatology*, edited by Jerry L. Walls, 563–80. Oxford: Oxford University Press, 2008.

———. *Cosmology: From Alpha to Omega: The Creative Mutual Interaction of Theology and Science*. Theology and the Sciences 32. Minneapolis: Fortress, 2008.

———. "Entropy and Evil." *Zygon* 19, no. 4 (1984) 449–68.

———. *Time in Eternity: Pannenberg, Physics, and Eschatology in Creative Mutual Interaction*. Notre Dame, IN: University of Notre Dame Press, 2012.

Sakenfeld, Katharine D., ed. *Reading the Bible as Women: Perspectives from Africa, Asia, and Latin America*. Semeia 78. Atlanta: Scholars, 1997.

Sandys-Wunsch, John, and Laurence Eldredge. "J. P. Gabler and the Distinction Between Biblical and Dogmatic Theology: Translation, Commentary, and Discussion of His Originality." *Scottish Journal of Theology* 33, no. 2 (1980) 133–158.

Sasse, Hermann. "Αἰών, Αἰώνιος." In *Theological Dictionary of the New Testament 1*, edited by Gerhard Kittel and Gerhard Friedrich, 197–209. Grand Rapids: Eerdmans, 1964.

Sauter, Gerhard. *Einführung in die Eschatologie*. Darmstadt: Wissenschaftliche Buchgesellschaft, 1995.

Schaafsma, Petruschka, et al. "Vervreemding en vertrouwen: Over hermeneutiek en theologie." *Nederlands Theologisch Tijdschrift* 67, no. 1 (2013) 3–26.

Schaeffler, Richard. *Die Wechselbeziehungen zwischen Philosophie und katholischer Theologie*. Philosophischen Bemuhungen des 20. Jahrhunderts. Darmstadt: Wissenschaftliche Buchgesellschaft, 1980.

Schärtl, Thomas. "Der Tod und die Ambiguität der Existenz in der Zeit." In *Was uns der Tod zu denken gibt: Philosophisch-theologische Essays*, edited by Michael Böhnke and Thomas Schärtl, 105–48. Pontes 30. Münster: Lit, 2005.

Schillebeeckx, Edward. "Enkele hermeneutische beschouwingen over de eschatologie." *Concilium* 5, no. 1 (1969) 38–51.

Schmidt, Jan C. "Box: Prospects for a Philosophy of Interdisciplinarity." In *The Oxford Handbook of Interdisciplinarity*, edited by Robert Frodeman, 39–49. Oxford: Oxford University Press, 2010.

Schmidt, Sebastianus. *Collegium Biblicum*. 2 vols. Strassburg: Staedelii, 1671.

Schmidt, Wolf-Rüdiger. *Die Eschatologie in der neueren römisch-katholischen Theologie von der Schuldogmatik bis zur "politischen Theologie."* 2 vols. Berlin: Freie Universität Berlin, 1974.

Schreiner, Thomas R. *The King in His Beauty: A Biblical Theology of the Old and New Testaments.* Grand Rapids: Baker Academic, 2013.

———. *New Testament Theology: Magnifying God in Christ.* Grand Rapids: Baker Academic, 2008.

Schulz, Michael. *Karl Rahner begegnen.* Zeugen des Glaubens. Augsburg: Sankt Ulrich, 1999.

Schwarz, Hans. *Eschatology.* Grand Rapids: Eerdmans, 2000.

Schwarzbauer, Fabian. *Geschichtszeit: Über Zeitvorstellungen.* Orbis Mediaevalis 6. Berlin: Akademie, 2005.

Schweitzer, Don. "The Consistency of Jürgen Moltmann's Theology." *Studies in Religion* 22, no. 2 (1993) 197–208.

Schwöbel, Christoph. *Gott in Beziehung: Studien zur Dogmatik.* Tübingen: Mohr Siebeck, 2002.

Scobie, Charles H. H. *The Ways of Our God: An Approach to Biblical Theology.* Grand Rapids: Eerdmans, 2003.

Sharbaugh, Patricia A. *Uncovering the Roots of the Crucified God: How Walter Brueggemann's Old Testament Theology Challenges and Contributes to Jürgen Moltmann's and Jon Sobrino's Interpretations of the Cross.* Pittsburgh: Duquesne University Press, 2008.

Sicouly, Pablo C. *Schöpfung und Neuschöpfung: "Neuschöpfung" als theologische Kategorie im Werk Jürgen Moltmanns.* Konfessionskundliche und Kontroverstheologische Studien 76. Paderborn: Bonifatius, 2007.

Smith, James K. A. "Determined Hope: A Phenomenology of Christian Expectation." In *The Future of Hope: Christian Tradition amid Modernity and Postmodernity,* edited by Miroslav Volf and William H. Katerberg, 200–227. Grand Rapids: Eerdmans, 2004.

Spier, Erich. *Der Sabbat.* 2nd ed. Das Judentum 1. Berlin: Institut Kirche und Judentum, 1992.

Spinks, D. Christopher. *The Bible and the Crisis of Meaning: Debates on the Theological Interpretation of Scripture.* London: T&T Clark, 2007.

Steinberg, Julius. *Die Ketuvim—Ihr Aufbau Und Ihre Botschaft.* Hamburg: Philo, 2006.

———. "Een korte geschiedenis van de discipline van de theologie van het Oude Testament." In *Theologie van het Oude Testament: De blijvende boodschap van de Hebreeuwse Bijbel,* edited by Hendrik J. Koorevaar and Mart-Jan Paul, 21–49. Zoetermeer: Boekencentrum, 2013.

Stuhlmueller, Carroll. *Creative Redemption in Deutero-Isaiah.* Analecta Biblica 43. Rome: Biblical Institute, 1970.

Stylianopoulos, Theodore G. "Orthodox Biblical Interpretation." In *Dictionary for Theological Interpretation of the Bible,* edited by Kevin J. Vanhoozer et al., 554–58. London: SPCK, 2005.

Tang, Siu-Kwong. *God's History in the Theology of Jürgen Moltmann.* Europäische Hochschulschriften. Reihe 23. Theologie 573. Bern: Lang, 1996.

Tanner, Kathryn. "Eschatology without a Future?" In *The End of the World and the Ends of God: Science and Theology on Eschatology,* edited by John C. Polkinghorne and Michael Welker, 222–37. Theology for the Twenty-First Century. Harrisburg: Trinity Press International, 2000.

Teilhard de Chardin, Pierre. "Christologie und Evolution." In *Mein Glaube*, edited by Joseph Bernhart and Ladislaus Boros, 4th ed., 93–115. Werke 10. Olten: Walter, 1988.

Tertullian, Quintus S. P. *Adversus Marcionem*. Translated by Volker Lukas. 2 vols. Fontes Christiani 63. Freiburg: Brepols, 2016.

———. *De Carnis Resurrectione: Treatise on the Resurrection*. Translated by Ernest Evans. London: SPCK, 1960.

Thielman, Frank. *Theology of the New Testament: A Canonical and Synthetic Approach*. Grand Rapids: Zondervan, 2005.

Thiselton, Anthony C. *The Hermeneutics of Doctrine*. Grand Rapids: Eerdmans, 2007.

———. *The Last Things: A New Approach*. London: SPCK, 2012.

———. *New Horizons in Hermeneutics: The Theory and Practice of Transforming Biblical Reading*. Grand Rapids: Zondervan, 1992.

———. *The Two Horizons: New Testament Hermeneutics and Philosophical Description*. Grand Rapids: Eerdmans, 1980.

Thomas, Günter. *Neue Schöpfung: Systematisch-theologische Untersuchungen zur Hoffnung auf das "Leben in der zukünftigen Welt."* Neukirchen-Vluyn: Neukirchener, 2009.

Thompson, William M. "The Hope for Humanity: Rahner's Eschatology." In *A World of Grace: An Introduction to the Themes and Foundations of Karl Rahner's Theology*, edited by Leo J. O'Donovan. Washington: Georgetown University Press, 1995.

Tillich, Paul. *Systematic Theology 1: Reason and Revelation. Being and God*. Chicago: University Press, 1951.

———. *Systematic Theology 3: Life and the Spirit, History and the Kingdom of God*. Chicago: University Press, 1963.

Tilly, Michael. "Der Ewige Jude in England: Die mittelalterliche Cartaphilus-Legende in ihrem historischen Kontext." *Zeitschrift für Religions-und Geistesgeschichte* 47, no. 4 (1995) 289–303.

Toews, Brian. "The Land in Biblical Perspective: The Creation as Hermeneutical Lens." Paper presented at the Annual Meeting of the Evangelical Theological Society, 1–27. November 17, 2005.

Tomasino, Anthony. "מָלוֹא." In *New International Dictionary of Old Testament Theology and Exegesis 3*, edited by William A. VanGemeren, 345–51. Grand Rapids: Zondervan, 1997.

Toulmin, Stephen E., and June Goodfield. *The Discovery of Time*. Chicago: University Press, 1965.

Troeltsch, Ernst. *Glaubenslehre: Nach Heidelberger Vorlesungen aus den Jahren 1911 und 1912*. München: Duncker & Humblot, 1925.

Turner, Max. *Power from on High: The Spirit in Israel's Restoration and Witness in Luke-Acts*. Journal of Pentecostal Theology: Supplement Series. Sheffield: Sheffield Academic, 1996.

Turner, Max, and Joel B. Green. "New Testament Commentary and Systematic Theology: Strangers or Friends?" In *Between Two Horizons: Spanning New Testament Studies and Systematic Theology*, edited by Joel B. Green and Max Turner, 1–22. Grand Rapids: Eerdmans, 2000.

Universitätsbibliothek Freiburg im Breisgau. "Karl Rahner Sekundärliteratur: Homepage der Sammlung." Accessed March 28, 2013. http://dspace.ub.uni-freiburg.de/handle/25/2.

Van de Beek, A. (Bram). *God doet recht: Eschatologie als christologie*. Spreken over God, 2.1. Zoetermeer: Meinema, 2008.

———. *Een lichtkring om het kruis: Scheppingsleer in christologisch perspectief*. Spreken over God, 3.1. Zoetermeer: Meinema, 2014.

Van der Kooi, Cornelis (Kees). "Van binnenuit of van buitenaf: Het schisma rondom bijbel en openbaring." In *Het uitgelezen boek: Opstellen over de omgang met de bijbel als het Woord van God*, edited by Cornelis van der Kooi et al., 30–49. Zoetermeer: Meinema, 1995.

Van Genderen, Jan, and Willem H. Velema. *Beknopte Gereformeerde Dogmatiek*. Kampen: Kok, 1992.

Vanhoozer, Kevin J. *The Drama of Doctrine: A Canonical-Linguistic Approach to Christian Theology*. Louisville: Westminster John Knox, 2005.

———. *Is There a Meaning in This Text?: The Bible, the Reader, and the Morality of Literary Knowledge*. Grand Rapids: Zondervan, 1998.

———. "Is the Theology of the New Testament One or Many?: Between (the Rock of) Systematic Theology and (the Hard Place of) Historical Occasionalism." In *Reconsidering the Relationship between Biblical and Systematic Theology in the New Testament: Essays by Theologians and New Testament Scholars*, edited by Benjamin E. Reynolds et al., 17–38. Wissenschaftliche Untersuchungen Zum Neuen Testament. 2. Reihe 369. Tübingen: Mohr Siebeck, 2014.

Vaticanum II. *Dei Verbum: Constitutio Dogmatica de Divina Revelatione*, 1965. http://www.vatican.va.

———. *Gaudium et Spes: Constitutio Pastoralis de Ecclesia in Mundo Huius Temporis*, 1965. http://www.vatican.va.

———. *Optatam Totius: Decretum de Institutione Sacerdotali*, 1965. http://www.vatican.va.

Vermeylen, August. *De Wandelende Jood*. Bussum: van Dishoeck, 1912.

Volf, Miroslav. *The End of Memory: Remembering Rightly in a Violent World*. Grand Rapids: Eerdmans, 2007.

Von Balthasar, Hans Urs. "Eschatologie." In *Fragen der Theologie Heute*, edited by Johannes Feiner et al., 403–21. Einsiedeln: Benziger, 1957.

———. *Glaubhaft ist nur die Liebe*. 5th ed. Christ heute. Reihe V 1. Einsiedeln: Johannes, 1985.

———. "Größe und Last der Theologie Heute: Einige grundsätzliche Gedanken zu zwei Aufsatzbänden Karl Rahners." *Wort und Wahrheit* 10 (1955) 531–33.

———. "Some Points of Eschatology." In *The Word Made Flesh*, 255–77. Explorations in Theology 1. San Francisco: Ignatius, 1989.

Vorgrimler, Herbert. "Editionsbericht: Das 'Lexikon für Theologie und Kirche.'" In *Enzyklopädische Theologie: Die Lexikonbeiträge der Jahre 1956–1973. Volume 1*, edited by Herbert Vorgrimler, 20–62. Sämtliche Werke 17. Freiburg: Herder, 2002.

———. *Hoffnung auf Vollendung: Aufriss der Eschatologie*. Quaestiones Disputatae 90. Freiburg: Herder, 1980.

———. "Karl Rahner (1904–1984)." In *Theologische Profile im 20. Jahrhundert: Karl Barth—Dietrich Bonhoeffer—Romano Guardini—Karl Rahner*, edited by Michael Kappes, 215–84. Kevelaer: Butzon & Bercker, 2001.

———. *Karl Rahner: Gotteserfahrung in Leben und Denken*. Darmstadt: Wissenschaftliche Buchgesellschaft, 2004.

Vos, Geerhardus. *Biblical Theology: Old and New Testaments*. Grand Rapids: Eerdmans, 1948.

———. *The Eschatology of the Old Testament*. Phillipsburg: P&R, 2001.

———. "Hebrews, The Epistle of the Diatheke." In *Redemptive History and Biblical Interpretation: The Shorter Writings of Geerhardus Vos*, edited by Richard B Gaffin, 161–233. Phillipsburg: Presbyterian and Reformed, 1980.

———. "The Idea of Biblical Theology as a Science and as a Theological Discipline." In *Redemptive History and Biblical Interpretation: The Shorter Writings of Geerhardus Vos*, edited by Richard B. Gaffin, 3–24. Phillipsburg: P&R, 1980.

———. *The Pauline Eschatology*. Grand Rapids: Eerdmans, 1952.

Vriezen, Theodoor Ch. *Hoofdlijnen der theologie van het Oude Testament*. Wageningen: Veenman & Zonen, 1974.

Vroom, Hendrik M. *De Schrift alleen?: Een vergelijkend onderzoek naar de toetsing van theologische uitspraken volgens de openbaringstheologische visie van Torrance en de hermeneutisch-theologische opvattingen van Van Buren, Ebeling, Moltmann en Pannenberg*. Kampen: Kok, 1979.

Wakefield, James L. *Jürgen Moltmann: A Research Bibliography*. ATLA Bibliography Series 47. Lanham: Scarecrow, 2002.

Wall, Robert W., and Stephen E. Fowl, eds. *The Two Horizons New Testament Commentary*. Grand Rapids: Eerdmans, 2016.

Walter, Peter. "Ewigkeit, Ewigkeit Gottes: Systematisch-theologisch." In *Lexikon für Theologie und Kirche 3*, edited by Walter Kasper et al., 3rd ed., 1083. Freiburg im Breisgau: Herder, 1993.

Waltke, Bruce K. "Kingdom Promises as Spiritual." In *Continuity and Discontinuity: Perspectives on the Relationship between the Old and New Testaments*, edited by John S. Feinberg, 263–87. Westchester: Crossway, 1988.

———. *An Old Testament Theology: An Exegetical, Canonical, and Thematic Approach*. Grand Rapids: Zondervan, 2008.

Walton, Robert C. "Jürgen Moltmann's Theology of Hope." In *Liberation Theology*, edited by Ronald H. Nash, 143–86. Milford: Mott Media, 1984.

Warfield, Benjamin B. "The Idea of Systematic Theology." In *Studies in Theology*, edited by Benjamin Warfield, 49–87. New York: Oxford University Press, 1932.

Weber, Otto. *Grundlagen der Dogmatik*. 2 vols. Berlin: Evangelische Verlagsanstalt, 1983.

———. *Die Treue Gottes und die Kontinuität der menschlichen Existenz*. Gesammelte Aufsätze 1. Neukirchen-Vluyn: Neukirchener, 1967.

Webster, John B. "Introduction: Systematic Theology." In *The Oxford Handbook of Systematic Theology*, edited by John B. Webster et al., 1–15. The Oxford Handbooks. Oxford: Oxford University Press, 2013.

Weger, Karl-Heinz. *Karl Rahner: Eine Einführung in sein theologisches Denken*. Freiburg im Breisgau: Herder, 1978.

Welker, Michael. *Theologische Profile: Schleiermacher, Barth, Bonhoeffer, Moltmann*. Edition Chrismon. Frankfurt am Main: Hansisches Druck- und Verlagshaus, 2009.

Wenham, Gordon. *Genesis 1–15*. Word Biblical Commentary 1. Dallas: Word, 1987.

Wentsel, Ben. *De openbaring, het verbond en de apriori's: Deel 2*. Dogmatiek. Kampen: Kok, 1982.

Wesley, John. *Sermons II, 34–70*. Edited by Albert C. Outler. The Works of John Wesley 2. Nashville: Abingdon, 1984.

Westermann, Claus. "Zur Frage einer Biblischen Theologie." In *Einheit und Vielfalt biblischer Theologie*, edited by Ingo Baldermann, 13–30. Jahrbuch für biblische Theologie 1. Neukirchen-Vluyn: Neukirchener, 1986.

Westphalus (pseudoniem), Chrysostomus D. *Volksbuch vom Ewigen Juden*. Leiden, 1602.

Wheeler, John. "Information, Physics, Quantum: The Search for Links." In *Complexity, Entropy, and the Physics of Information*, edited by Wojciech H. Zurek, 309–36. Santa Fe Institute Studies in the Sciences of Complexity 8. Redwood City: Addison-Wesley, 1990.

White, Joel. *Die Erstlingsgabe im Neuen Testament*. Texte und Arbeiten zum neutestamentlichen Zeitalter 45. Tübingen: Francke, 2007.

Wilcock, Michael. *I Saw Heaven Opened: The Message of Revelation*. Bible Speaks Today. Downers Grove: InterVarsity, 1975.

Wilkinson, David. *Christian Eschatology and the Physical Universe*. London: T&T Clark, 2010.

Williams, Stephen. "Jürgen Moltmann: A Critical Introduction." In *Getting Your Bearings: Engaging with Contemporary Theologians*, 75–124. Leicester: Apollos, 2003.

Wittgenstein, Ludwig. *Philosophical Investigations*. Oxford: Blackwell, 1953.

———. *Philosophische Untersuchungen*. Frankfurt am Main: Suhrkamp, 1978.

Wohlmuth, Josef. *Mysterium der Verwandlung: Eine Eschatologie aus katholischer Perspektive im Gespräch mit jüdischem Denken der Gegenwart*. Studien zu Judentum und Christentum. Paderborn: Schöningh, 2005.

Wright, N. Tom. "The Letter to the Galatians: Exegesis and Theology." In *Between Two Horizons: Spanning New Testament Studies and Systematic Theology*, edited by Joel B. Green and Max Turner, 205–36. Grand Rapids: Eerdmans, 2000.

———. *New Heavens, New Earth: The Biblical Picture of Christian Hope*. Cambridge: Grove Books, 1999.

———. *The Resurrection of the Son of God*. Christian Origins and the Question of God 3. London: SPCK, 2003.

———. *Surprised by Hope*. London: SPCK, 2007.

Yates, John W. *The Spirit and Creation in Paul*. Wissenschaftliche Untersuchungen zum Neuen Testament, II:251. Tübingen: Mohr Siebeck, 2008.

Zachariae, Gotthilf T. *Biblischer Theologie oder Untersuchung des biblischen Grundes der vornehmsten theologischen Lehren*. 5 vols. Göttingen: Boßiegel, 1772.

Zwiep, Arie W. "Onderweg naar morgen: Hermeneutische bespiegelingen vanuit een 'postconservative Evangelical' perspectief." In *Tussen leer en lezen: De spanning tussen bijbelwetenschap en geloofsleer*, edited by Gerard C. den Hertog and Cornelis (Kees) van der Kooi, 33–54. Kampen: Kok, 2007.

———. *Tussen tekst en lezer: Een historische inleiding in de bijbelse hermeneutiek: Van moderniteit naar postmoderniteit*. Vol. 2. 2 vols. Amsterdam: VU University Press, 2014.

Subject Index

Absolute future, 12, 58, 59, 68–71, 86–88, 93, 125–126, 193–197, 203, 248, 278–279
Adam, 139–184, 198–206, 213, 216–255, 274, 282
Adventus, 104–105, 108, 112, 130, 192–193, 197–198, 238, 245
Aionic and cyclic time, 113–118, 274–278
Already, not yet, 98–99, 113, 139–144, 158, 200–207, 232–271
Annihilatio mundi, xx, 224, 305
Anthropocentrism, 73–74, 107, 225–234, 259
Anticipation, 27, 96, 102–111, 114, 127–134, 157, 163, 192–204
Apocalyptic, 60, 61, 65, 72, 93–94, 194–195
Astrophysics, 22–28

Babylon, 131–134, 192, 195, 223, 253, 258, 276
    Open/closed canon, 34–35, 42–43, 45
Biblical Theology, primary source, 3–4, 30–34, 38, 44, 48–49, 291
Biblical Theology, birth-hour, 3–4
Bible, narrative/storyline, xvi, xviii, 32, 38–50, 137–149, 169–172, 198, 205–206, 212, 216, 221–222, 229, 268, 284–285, 293–296, 299
Biblicism, 39–42
Big Crunch, Big Chill, Big Freeze and *Big Rip*, 22–28

Canaan, ix, 145–146, 148–149, 160, 173–174, 176–177, 184, 203, 249
Christ as "Risen One," "Crucified One," 66–67, 79–81, 94, 129–130, 158
Christ as First born, 162, 163–164
Christ as Adam/Israel, 139, 142–149, 152–159, 163–167, 170–184, 188, 201, 206, 211, 213, 216–218, 225–228, 231, 236, 240, 251, 255, 274, 282
Christological approach, 66–67
Chronos, xviii, 19, 112–125, 134, 201–203, 266–279, 288–289, 294
Confession, 6–7, 32, 39, 50, 189, 199, 289
Cosmic temple, 96, 113, 170–180, 248, 281

Council of Trent, 33, 50
Covenant, 43, 109, 111, 125, 128, 133, 139, 141, 145, 147, 169, 195
Creatio continua, 106–109, 113, 123, 128–134, 205–208, 246–248, 287
Creatio ex nihilo, 28, 107–108, 208, 241–244, 305
Creatio ex vetere, 107–108, 201, 246
Creatio nova, 106–123, 127–134, 201, 205–208, 246, 250, 305
Creatio originalis, 106–107, 127–134, 205–208, 246, 278
Creation as *Umwelt–Mitwelt*, 84–85, 94
Creed of Nicea-Constantinople, 8–11
Crown of creation, 225, 233, 282

David, 109, 111, 147, 259
De-eschatologization, 56–61, 60–62, 192–193
Demythologization, 56–57, 193
Dialogue BT–ST, general overview, 2–4, 6–8
Dialogue BT–ST, importance, 1–2, 30–32, 47, 50, 185–187, 291.
Dialogue BT–ST, neutrality, 4–6, 46–48, 291
Docta ignorantia futuri, 57–59, 196
Dualism, *See* Gnosticism
Gnosticism, 75–81, 212, 235–236, 241–243

Ecology, 227–228, 305
Enlightenment, 3, 23, 29, 37, 41, 83, 111, 190, 225–227
Eschatological images, 25–28, 44–64, 69–72, 109–11, 131–134, 262–264, 300–302
Eschatology, history of, 42–45
Eternity of God, *See* absolute future
Evangelical-fundamentalism, 44–45, 51
Evangelical-reformed theology, 49, 136, 167
Expression (*Aussage*), 60–62, 195–204, 278–280
Extra-biblical thinking, 38, 50, 137, 197, 267, 277, 284, 297
Extrinsic and intrinsic sin, 212, 215–217, 285, 298

From above, from below, 159, 203–204, 284, 298
Frozen spirit (*gefrorener Geist*), 76–77, 234
Futurum, 39, 104–112, 130, 192–206, 245

Grammatical-historical exegesis, 49

Heavenly/New Jerusalem, 131–134, 151, 176–179, 222, 253–258, 276
Hell, 62–64
Hermeneutic, exegesis and preaching, 37, 43, 45
Hermeneutic, historical-canonical, 4–7, 14
Hermeneutic, historically-critical, xiii, 4–7, 14, 33
Hermeneutic, methodical approaches, 4–6, 46–49
Hermeneutic, eschatological principles, 5, 19–22, 54–64, 102, 137, 188–191, 288–291
Historicism, 35–37

Impression (*Einsage*), 60–62, 193–200, 278–279, 283–284
Incarnation, 279–280
Individual renewal, 30
Infinite time, 83, 86–88, 91–92
Israel, 36, 42–43, 47, 133, 140–149, 152, 161–168, 170–184, 198–209, 245–264, 281–282

Kairos, 99–100, 114–155, 200, 203, 266–269, 275, 279, 288
Kairosmoment, 114–115
Kingdom of God, 77–78, 42–43, 79–81, 97–100, 121–122, 130, 141, 153, 169, 176, 202–204, 225–226, 238–239

Mary, 79, 124
Matter, 66–67, 76–77, 94, 144

Natural science, 22–28, 76, 83–86
Neo-Scholasticism/Thomism, 52–54
Nihil, *See* Zimzim
Novum, 104–105, 108–109, 111, 192, 197–199, 240, 305

Panentheism, 126, 264
Perichoresis, 119, 125–126, 135, 250–266
Philosophy of religion, 37–39
Physical-, salvation-, and world time, 82–88, 271, 287–289
Plato, 121–122

Postliberalism, 39–42, 138
Prophets, 43, 121, 148, 170, 174–175, 197–198, 232, 242, 249, 254, 302
Protology, 67–69, 106–108, 139, 143–144, 149, 188–191, 204–219, 225–226, 284–288, 298

Realized eschatology, 63
Reformed theology, 36, 47
Renewal, 46–48, 159
Renovation, 240–245, 301, 305
Restitutio in integrum, 205–207, 305
Resurrection Body, 155, 231–232, 239–240
Resurrection of Christ, 60, 64–66, 80–81, 94, 101–111, 124, 142, 153–166, 184, 195, 231–246, 251, 265, 272, 278, 286, 298
River of life, 90, 131–132, 168, 172–173, 252, 258, 274
Roman Catholic theology, 12–13, 29–32, 53, 60, 71, 79, 97, 265

Sabbath, 127–128, 179–181, 226, 233–234, 264–283
Selbsteinschränkung, Selbstentschränkung, 128–129, 209–210, 227
Shekhinah, 105, 120, 125–134, 221, 247–254
Son of Man, 148, 152, 163, 218
Space (*topos*), 119–120, 125–126
Spes qua and *spes quae*, 20, 109

Theocentrism, 91–92
Theosis, 27, 66–67, 282
Tiefenerfahrung des Augenblicks, 113–117, 120, 278, 289
Transformation, 27, 45–46, 65, 80–94, 104–116, 134–157, 179, 229, 239, 242–244, 271, 278, 302–305
Transposition, 61, 78, 85, 192–193, 198, 207, 283, 297
Tree of life, 90, 131–132, 168, 172–173, 252, 258, 274

Visio beatifica, 62, 78, 92, 95
Visio Dei, 262–264

Zimzum, 107, 115, 118–120, 134, 208–212, 248–252, 284, 287, 298
Zion, 121, 148–151, 170 176–178, 258

Author Index

Abraham, William, 20
Adams, Nicholas, 59, 98
Adeyemo, Tokunboh, 7
Ahlers, Rolf, 100
Alexander, Desmond, 14
Alighieri, Dante, 72
Ansell, Nicholas, 112, 258, 269
Aquinas, Thomas. *See* Thomas Aquinas
Auer, Alfons, 228
Augustine, 112–113, 118, 217, 232, 237, 262, 269
Aune, David, 275

Bachl, Gottfried, 10
Balthasar, Hans Urs von, 9, 54, 73, 270
Barnes, Michael, 70–71, 78
Barr, James, 2, 5, 138, 141, 265
Barth, Karl, 17, 35–36, 98, 114, 188, 227, 279
Bartholomew, Craig, 15, 189, 295
Batlogg, Andreas, 52–53
Bauckham, Richard, 9, 16, 36, 38, 40–41, 45, 97, 100, 112, 121, 127, 130–131, 163, 199, 208, 221, 227, 273–275, 277, 279
Bauke-Ruegg, Jan, 107
Bäumer, Remigius, 54
Beek, Bram van de, 9, 217 299–304
Benjamin, Walter, 112
Berkhof, Hendrik, 6, 20, 56, 105, 111, 192
Berkhof, Louis, 188
Berkouwer, Gerrit, 20–21
Billings, David, 112
Bingen, Hildegard von, 277
Bird, Michael, 188
Blenkinsopp, Joseph, 169
Bloch, Ernst, 98.
Block, Daniel, 150, 169, 173
Blumhardt, Christoph, 98
Blumhardt, Johann, 202
Bockmuehl, Markus, 8
Boëthius, Anicius, 267
Bohm, David, 187
Bokwa, Ignacym, 74
Bonhoeffer, Dietrich, 17
Bornkamm, Günther, 20

Bostock, D, 136
Bouma-Prediger, Steven, 209
Bowden, John, 103
Bray, Gerald, 3
Brett, Gregory, 74
Brettler, Marc, 265, 268, 277
Brin, Gershon, 265
Brink, Gijs van den, 41
Brink, Gijsbert van den, viii–xiv, 2, 6, 8–10, 299–304
Bruce, Frederick, 45
Brueggemann, Walter, 4–5, 9, 15, 179
Brunner, Emil, 104, 111
Buber, Martin, 193, 218
Bultmann, Rudolf, 5, 11–12, 35–36, 56–57, 70–71, 104, 114, 197, 221, 291
Burdzy, Krzysztof, 7

Cabal, Ted, 7
Carr, Anne, 70.
Carson, Donald, 137, 143
Cassuto, Umberto, 179
Chardin, Teilhard de , 205
Charles, Robert, 275
Chung, Sung, 36, 41–44
Clayton, Philip, 27
Clutterbuck, Richard, 44, 100
Collman, Ryan, 136
Colwill, Deborah, 186–187
Craig, William, 268
Cullmann, Oscar, 121, 143, 202, 273
Culver, Robert, 9, 299–302

Daley, Brian, 238, 269
Dalferth, Ingolf, 269
Davies, Paul, 26
Davies, William, 177
Deane-Drummond, Celia, 209
Demarest, Bruce, 45
Dempster, Stephen, 138
Dennison, James, 138
Denzinger, Heinrich, 30, 33
Díaz, Miguel, 12

Author Index

Donald, Carson, 137, 143
Duguid, Iain, 169
Dumbrell, William, 138, 142
Dupuis, Jacques, 12

Edwards, Denis, 58, 77, 194, 233, 273
Eicher, Peter, 74
Eichrodt, Walther, 4–5, 179
Einstein, Albert, 26
Ellis, Earle, 157
Ellis, George, 25
Endean, Philip, 13
Enns, Paul, 98–99, 136, 199, 211
Erickson, Millard, 6, 299–304

Farrow, Douglas, 127, 208
Felsinger, Horst, 52, 80–81, 270, 272–273, 280
Feuerbach, Ludwig, 87
Fischer, Herrmann, 2
Fischer, Klaus, 74
Fletcher, Hilde, 55
Ford, David, 6
Fowl, Stephen, 7, 15
Fredericks, Sarah, 3
Freedman, Harry, 259
Frei, Hans, 21, 138
Freyer, Thomas, 85, 88, 265, 273
Fritsch, Harald, 17–18, 33, 55–57, 194
Fritz, Peter, 208

Gabler, Johann, 4–5, 41, 191
Gadamer, Hans-Georg, 6–7
Gaffin, Richard, 5, 138
Geertsema, H.G, 204
Geister, Philip, 55, 194
Genderen, Jan van, 299–303
Gerstenberger, Erhard, 5
Gilbert, Kevin, 44–45, 99–101
Gilbertson, Michael, 16
Gladd, Benjamin, 14, 136–137, 155–156, 183, 188, 235
Gnilka, Joachim, 196
Goldberg, Arnold, 119
Goldingay, John, 1–2
Goldsworthy, Graeme, 142
Green, Joel, 1–2, 8, 15
Grenz, Stanley, 5, 45
Greshake, Gisbert, 53, 232, 250
Grözinger, Karl, 107
Grudem, Wayne, 6, 9, 138, 299–301, 303–304
Grümme, Bernhard, 208
Guarino, Thomas, 2
Gunton, Colin, 2
Gurtner, Daniel, 136–137, 188

Halloran, Nathan, 208
Hamilton, James, 136, 141, 152
Häring, Hermann, 97
Harmon, Matthew, 14
Hart, Trevor, 9, 127, 274
Hasan-Rokem, Galit, 87
Hasel, Gerhard, 5, 141, 145, 180
Hauser, Alan, 3
Hausoul, Raymond, 9, 23, 46, 188, 199
Hegel, Georg, 35
Heidegger, Martin, 59, 84
Heinisch, Paul, 31
Hennecke, Susanne, 97
Hertog, Gerard den, 2, 4, 8
Heschel, Abraham, 128
Highfield, Ron, 216
Hoek, Jan, ix, 9, 20, 299, 301
Holtz, Traugott, 196
Ho-Tsui, Emmie, 208, 213
Hryniewicz, Wacław, 98, 273
Hubbard, Moyer, 157
Hughes, Kevin, 21
Hülsemann, Johann, 4
Hurd, Robert, 59

Imhof, Paul, 73
Irenaeus of Lyon, 220, 236–238, 262, 282
Isaac ben Salomo, Luria, 107
Isaacs, William, 187
Iwand, Hans, 295

Jackson, Ryan, 10, 157
Jager, Okke, 82, 167
Jansen, Henry, 44
Jenson, Robert, 169
Jhi, Jun-Hyung, 208, 213–214, 258
Joachim of Fiore, 37
Johnson, Roger, 70
Jüngel, Eberhard, 17
Justin Martyr, 108, 237

Kaiser, Walter, 5
Kamphuis, Barend, 2
Kant, Immanuel, 35, 85, 110
Kärkkäinen, Veli-Matti, 26, 49, 136, 187
Käsemann, Ernst, 35, 42
Kauffman, Stuart, 27
Keil, Carl, 169, 179
Kelsey, David, 5
Kern, Walter, 84–85
Kerstiens, Ferdinand, 194
Kessler, Hans, 263
Kierkegaard, Søren, 114
Kim, Seyoon, 27, 154.

Author Index

Klappert, Bertold, 38, 270, 296
Klein, Terranc, 74
Kline, Meredith, 149, 172–173, 179
Klink, Edward, 2
Koch, Kurt, 56, 194, 227–228
Köhler, Ludwig, 5, 106
Kooi, Cornelis (Kees) van der, 2, 4, 6, 8–10, 299–304
Koorevaar, Hendrik, 5, 9.
Kraus, Hans-Joachim, 3–4, 38
Kroeger, Catherine, 7
Kuhn, Peter, 119

Ladd, George, 143
Lang, Bernhard, 9, 11, 273
Larson, Duane, 209
Lash, Nicholas, 21
Lehmann, Karl, 52, 59
Leibniz, Gottfried, 118
Lindbeck, George, 138
Lindemann, Andreas, 21–22, 27
Lohfink, Norbert, 275
Lønning, Per, 106
Losinger, Anton, 73–74, 192
Lubac, Henri de, 74
Ludlow, Morwenna, 12, 55, 93, 246, 250, 258
Luther, Martin, 43, 116, 202

Macek, Petr, 208
Macleod, Donald, 218
Macquarrie, John, 25
Maddox, Randy, 14
Malina, Bruce, 268
Mansilla, Veronica, 187
Marshall, Howard, 13, 136,140
Martin, Oren, 247
Mathison, Keith, 142
May, Georg, 52
McConville, Gordon, 15
McDannell, Colleen, 9, 11, 273
McFague, Sallie, 110
McGowan, Andrew, 46
McGrath, Alister, 6, 9, 53
Meeks, Douglas, 36
Meijering, Eginhard, 112, 269
Mell, Ulrich, 10
Merk, Otto, 3–4
Metz, Johann-Baptist, 194
Michaels, Ramsey, 151
Middleton, Richard, 9, 14, 142
Mildenberger, Friedrich, 1, 189
Möller, Joseph, 73
Molnar, Paul, 203, 208
Moltmann-Wendel, Elisabeth, 103, 107, 114, 122–124, 271

Momose, Peter, 100
Moo, Douglas, 157, 199
Moran, Joe, 2, 26
Muck, Otto, 59, 74
Mühling, Markus, 1–2, 82, 297, 302
Muis, Jan, 6
Müller, Helmut, 23
Müller, Max, 59
Müller-Fahrenholz, Geiko, 41, 97
Müller-Goldkuhle, Peter, 11
Munteanu, Daniel, 209
Murphy, Marie, 55, 63
Murphy, N, 27

Neufeld, Karl, 34, 52
Neusner, Jacob, 120, 246
Newton, Isaac, 111, 118
Ngewa, Samuel, 7
Nicholas of Cusa, 58
Nicholls, Bruce, 7
Niebuhr, Karl-Wilhelm, 4
Niehaus, Jeffrey, 170
Niewiadomski, Józef, 100, 208
Nineham, Dennis, 2
Novick, Peter, 7
Nürnberger, Klaus, 28

O'Collins, Gerald, 1, 98
O'Donovan, Oliver, 27
Oetinger, Friedrich, 122
Origen, 262.
Ott, Ludwig, 92
Otto, Randall, 103
Ouweneel, Willem, 299, 301–303

Padgett, Alan, 265
Pagels, Elaine, 218
Pannenberg, Wolfhart, 6, 9, 12, 16–17, 20, 23, 33, 56, 82, 102, 192, 194, 208, 265
Park, Aaron, 102, 104
Parmenides, 35, 113, 269
Patte, Daniel, 7
Paul, Mart-Jan, ix, 5, 9
Peacocke, Arthur, 25
Pesch, Otto, 21, 196
Peters, Ted, 23
Petty, Michael, 93, 205
Phan, Peter, 54–56, 91–92, 97, 194, 196, 216, 250
Plato, 113, 121
Plotinus, 267
Polkinghorne, John, 20, 23–25, 27, 199, 270–271, 277–278
Pseudo-Athenagoras, 237
Purcell, Michael, 13

Author Index

Rad, Gerhard von, 4-5, 35-36, 42, 55, 241, 273, 291-292
Raffelt, Albert, 53
Remenyi, Matthias, 10, 13, 16-17, 20-21, 27, 40, 100, 127, 208-209, 254
Rendtorff, Rolf, 5
Repko, Allen, 2, 26
Reynolds, Benjamin, 8
Richardson, Alan, 13
Ricœur, Paul, 257
Rolf, Kramer, 83
Rosenzweig, Franz, 112, 120, 128
Rosner, Brain, 4
Rudolph, David, 180, 291
Rushdoony, Rousas, 247
Russell, Jeffrey, 262
Russell, Robert, 23-25, 27-28

Sakenfeld, Katharine, 7
Sandys-Wunsch, John, 4
Sasse, Hermann, 268
Sauter, Gerhard, 195
Schaafsma, Petruschka, 6
Schaeffler, Richard, 74
Schärtl, Thomas, 87
Schillebeeckx, Edward, 13
Schmaus, Michael, 54
Schmidt, Jan, 2, 26
Schmidt, Sebastianus, 4
Schmidt, Wolf-Rüdiger, 55
Schreiner, Thomas, 9, 14, 142
Schulz, Michael, 52
Schwarz, Hans, 9, 20, 113, 299, 301-302
Schwarzbauer, Fabian, 113
Schweitzer, Don, 100
Schweizer, Albert, 104
Schwöbel, Christoph, 11
Scobie, Charles, 138, 142, 145
Sharbaugh, Patricia, 15
Sicouly, Pablo, 12-13, 17, 97, 100, 127
Smith, James, 20
Sobrino, Jon, 15
Spier, Erich, 128
Spinks, Christopher, 7
Steinberg, Julius, 4-5, 147
Stuhlmueller, Carroll, 167
Stylianopoulos, Theodore, 3

Tang, Siu-Kwong, 100
Tanner, Kathryn, 25
Tertullian, 80, 236-237.
Thielman, Frank, 142
Thiselton, Anthony, 7, 20, 27, 189

Thomas Aquinas, 37, 59, 77, 86, 92
Thomas, Günter, 17, 100, 199, 208, 264
Thompson, William, 58, 273
Til, Cornelius van, 188
Tillich, Paul, 6, 90
Tilly, Michael, 87
Toews, Brian, 177
Tomasino, Anthony, 268
Toulmin, Stephen, 113
Troeltsch, Ernst, 9
Turner, Max, 1, 8, 15, 170

Vanhoozer, Kevin, 1-2, 138, 188-189, 257, 296
Velema, Willem, 6, 299-303
Vermeylen, August, 87
Volf, Miroslav, 114
Vorgrimler, Herbert, 12, 30, 52, 54, 60-61, 70-72, 194-195
Vos, Geerhardus, 46-47, 138, 142, 166, 173-174, 179
Vries, Lourens de, 7
Vries, Simon de, 265
Vriezen, Theodoor, 5
Vroom, Hendrik, 100, 130

Wakefield, James, 97
Wall, Robert, 15
Walter, Peter, 279
Waltke, Bruce, 5, 179, 222
Walton, Robert, 99
Warfield, Benjamin, 5
Weber, Otto, 6, 37, 105
Webster, John, 6
Weger, Karl-Heinz, 73
Welker, Michael, 97
Wenham, Gordon, 179
Wentsel, Ben, 6
Wesley, John, 278.
Westermann, Claus, 7
Westphalus, Chrysostomus, 87
Wheeler, John, 27
White, Joel, 170
Wilcock, Michael, 196
Wilkinson, David, 1-2, 16, 23, 26-28, 142, 297
Williams, Stephen, 36, 102-103
Wilson, R.A., 103
Wittgenstein, Ludwig, 6-7
Wohlmuth, Josef, 9, 82, 299, 301-302, 304
Wright, Tom, 9, 153, 186

Yates, John, 157

Zachariae, Gotthilf, 4
Zwiep, Arie, 3, 7

Ancient Document Index

OLD TESTAMENT/HEBREW BIBLE

Genesis

1–3	137, 139, 142–143, 145, 163, 183, 210–213
1–2	139, 144–145, 149, 162, 165, 170, 173, 176–177, 179–180, 198, 204–206, 211, 225–226, 245–246, 248–249, 251, 254–255, 270, 281–283, 286, 303
1	25, 67, 75, 115, 128, 186, 205, 214, 226, 270, 281
1:1	40
1:2–3	156
1:2	148, 174
1:5	113, 115, 290
1:11–12	148
1:14	180
1:22	226
1:29	148
1:26–28	148
1:26	147, 164
1:28	106, 143–147, 149, 153, 163–164, 173, 176–177, 183–184, 198–199, 206, 212, 225–226, 233–234, 242, 249, 251, 255
1:31	106, 205, 213
2–3	168
2	179–180, 225–226, 233, 277
2:2–3	180
2:3	179–180, 182
2:5	226, 253
2:7–8	169
2:7	253
2:9	147
2:9–10	276
2:10	172
2:15	144, 172, 206, 212, 285
2:16–17	144
2:19–20	147, 183
2:24	144, 183
3	152, 165, 206, 211–212, 249
3:8	145, 172, 247
3:14	163
3:15	153
3:17	245
3:20	153
3:22	163
3:24	173
4	217
5:1–3	163
6	217
9:1–2	146
13:10	145, 176
27:28	220
49:1	149

Exodus

3:1	170
4:22	183
14	256
15:17	172
18:5	170
19:6	146, 165, 251
19:24	170
20	180
20:8	180
20:10	226
20:11	180
24:13	170
25:8–9	248
25:40	248
29:45	119, 128
31:14–15	179
33:20	261
40:34–38	165

Leviticus

25:1–7	226
26:1–12	145
26:11–12	168

Leviticus cont.

26:12	172, 175
26:40–45	168

Numeri

3:7–8	172
8:25–26	172
11:25	170
18:5–6	172
24:14	149

Deuteronomy

4:17–18	147
4:30	149
8:7–10	145
11:8–17	145
23:15	172
31:29	149
32:39a	153

Joshua

21:44	146

1 Samuel

2:18	147
2:28	147
12:22	145
14:3	147
22:18	147

2 Samuel

6:13–14	147
6:17	147
7:26	145
7:6–7	172
7:12–14	174
14:17	144
19:35	144
24:25	147

1 Kings

3:9	144, 147
3:28	144
4:33	147
5:17	171
6:17–20	132
6:18	172
6:20–22	171
6:29	172
6:32	172
6:35	172
7:18–20	172
15:46,50	144

1 Chronicles

15:27	147
23:32	172
28:2	181
28:19	248

2 Chronicles

6:41	181

Psalms

1–2	147
1:2	169
2:2	178
2:6	176
2:7	169
2:8	176, 178
8	147
8:6	178
11:4–7	168
18:19	119
27:4	168, 261
31:8	119
62	147
72	147
72:5	147, 259
72:7	147
72:8	147, 176
73	147
78:54	145
78:69	248
80:17	163
89	147
89:25	147
89:36–37	147
89:36	259
89:38	259
90:3–6	148
90:7–11	148
90:13–17	148
104:30	169
106:6	148
107	148
132:7–8	181
132:13–14	181
139:5	209
145:2	148
145:21	148
146:6	148

146:7–9	148	43:25	167
146:8	148	49:8–9	167
146:10	148	56:7	167
147:2–6	148	45:14	167
147:4–18	148	45:18–19	174
147:12–14	148	48:11	145
149:1–9	148	48:18	167
150	148	49	154
		51:3	145, 174, 176
		51:10–11	244, 256

Ecclesiastes

1–11	147, 274–275, 279
1:4	274
1:5	274
1:6	274
1:7	274

51:11	257
51:17	158
52:7	167
53:4–12	167
54:2–3	174, 177
54:6–8	167
54:11–12	171, 174, 252
54:21	252
57:15–19	170
57:18–19	147
60:1–5	168
60:1–3	158
60:3	252
60:5	252
60:7	167
60:10	167
60:11	252
60:19	252, 257
60:21	176
61:1–11	158
62:1–5	168
62:11	167
62:2	252
62:4	167
62:5	252
62:6	252
62:10	252
65–66	150, 156
65	163, 238, 303
65:16–19	244
65:16–18	243
65:16–17	229
65:17–25	222
65:17–20	163
65:17–18	177
65:17	8, 40, 149, 153, 157, 159, 151, 168, 183, 252
66:18–23	183
65:19–23	220
65:19	252, 257
65:22	149, 153, 157, 161
65:25	220, 226, 246
66:1	173, 181
66:2	167

Isaiah

1:11	167
1:15	167
2:2	149, 252
2:5	252
4:2–4	158
4:4–6	174, 177
7:15–16	144
9:1–2	156
11	183, 301
11:1–5	158
11:6–10	220
11:6–9	163, 183, 226
11:9	246
25:6–12	222
25:8	153, 168, 252, 257
26:15	177
26:19	153, 158, 220
27:2–6	176
32:15–18	158
32:15	170
34:16–17	167
35:6–9	259
35:10	252, 257
40–66	168
41:17–20	259
42	154
42:6–9	167
43	154, 157, 235
43:7	235
43:8	159
43:10	167
43:18–21	153
43:18–20	259
43:18–19	163, 167, 252
43:18	168
43:19	168

345

Isaiah cont.

66:20–22	177
66:20	183
66:22	153, 168, 183, 277

Jeremiah

3:16–17	174, 177
23:30	149
30:24	149
48:47	149
49:39	149

Ezekiel

9:3	145
10:4	145
10:18–19	145
11:22–23	145
28:13	172
28:14–18	150
28:14	172
28:16	172
28:25–26	220
36–48	148
36–37	154, 158, 169
36:26–35	153
36:26–27	169
36:35	145, 174, 176
37:5	169
37:9	169
37:25–28	174, 177
37:27	168, 175
38:14–16	149
40–48	171, 173
40:1–2	168
40:2	150, 172
40:3–5	168
40:6	172
42:15–19	168
43:2–5	168
43:2	168
43:5	168
43:7	168
43:12	172
44:14	172
45:1–5	168
47	258–259
47:1–12	145, 172
47:1–9	168
47:9	252
47:12	145, 168, 252, 276
48:31–34	168

Daniel

2	148
2:7	268
2:28–29	149
2:34–35	174, 177
2:35	150
2:44–45	174, 177
2:45	149
7–11	152
7	148, 152, 163–164, 218
7:22	200
10:14	149
12:2	152, 159, 162, 180
12:12	150

Hosea

3:5	149
13:14	173

Joel

3:1	170
2:3	145, 174, 176
3:18	258
4:18	222

Micha

4:1–4	149
4:4	150

Zechariah

1:16—2:11	174, 177
2:5–11	145
2:10–11	183, 254
2:12	145
6:12–13	174
14:8–9	172

Maleachi

1:1–5	149
3:1–4	149
3:5–18	149
4:1–6	149

NEW TESTAMENT

Matthew

5:3	176
5:10	176
12:32	267

ANCIENT DOCUMENT INDEX

13:39–40	150
13:49	150
19:27	181
19:28–29	163
19:28	163, 244–245
19:29	220
21:42	174
22:31	238
24:3	150
24:29	244
24:36	62
26:29	220
26:37–39	121
27:46	121
28:1	181
28:18	163
28:20	267

Mark

1:13	163, 226–227
1:15	200
10:30	150, 267
12:10	174
13	xix, 152, 294
13:32	57, 62, 196, 284, 298
15:34	101
16:2	181
16:9	181

Luke

1:33	150
2:52	62
18:30	150
20:17	174
20:34–35	150, 267
20:35	238
21:8	200
24:1	181

John

1:13	162
1:14	174
1:18	261
2:21	174
3:1–15	153
3:3–8	162
4:14	150
5:24–29	153
5:25	150, 232
6:39–54	153
6:51	150
6:58	150
11:23–25	153
12:34	150
12:48	153
14:1–4	222
14:16	150
14:23	126
16:32–33	152
20:1	181
20:19	181

Acts

1:7	57
2	143
2:22–28	153
2:23	170
3:15	102
4:2	238
9:22–26	154
13:33	176
13:34–36	153
17:3–7	153
17:28	119
17:32	80, 238–239
24:22	182
26:18	178
26:23	102

Romans

1:4	166
1:25	150
3:6	166
4:13–14	168
4:13	168, 176, 178
4:17	20, 154, 168
4:24	154
5–6	182
6:8–11	181
6:4–13	154
6:4–5	181
6:4	136
8	74, 130, 160, 164, 177, 186, 230, 233–234, 238, 244, 301
8:9–10	166
8:11	107, 122, 166, 178
8:17–18	164
8:17	166, 168, 178
8:18–23	154, 166, 170, 178, 229
8:18	178
8:19–23	74
8:19–22	166
8:19	155, 178, 233
8:21–22	166
8:21	25, 164, 178

347

Romans cont.

8:22	244
8:23	122, 151, 154, 157, 166, 169, 178
8:29	155, 163
8:30	164, 166, 169
8:31–34	166
8:33–39	154
8:35–36	166
9:5	150
11:16	155
16:5	155
16:25–26	166

1 Corinthians

1:8	150
1:30	166
2:6	267
3:16	174
6:2	249
6:14	155
6:19	174
7:31	245, 249
9:1	155
10:11	201
11:23–26	181
13:12	261, 305
15	17, 155–156, 164, 184, 186, 230, 236, 239, 241
15:12–13	238
15:12	238–239
15:13–14	26
15:20–28	39, 155
15:20	22, 163, 169
15:21–22	155
15:23	169
15:24–27	155
15:25–27	184
15:26	122, 155, 236–237
15:28	39–40, 126, 261–262
15:35–36	78, 239–240
15:42	156, 240
15:44	239, 261
15:45	155–156, 170
15:47–50	236
15:50–57	155
15:50	129, 126, 218, 239–240
15:51	142
15:52	116, 278
15:53	129, 143
15:54–57	184
16:15	155

2 Corinthians

1:9–10	156
1:13	150
1:20	157
1:21–22	151
2:14–16	156
3:3–7	156
3:16–4:2	165
3:18	165, 263
4–5	156
4:4	247
4:6	156, 158
4:16	156, 198
5:1–10	157
5:14–20	167
5:14–17	167, 229
5:15	157
5:16	151, 249
5:17–21	167
5:17	151, 157, 249
6:2	151, 200, 249
6:16	174
7:1	157

Ephesians

1:10	246
1:13–14	151, 157
1:21	158, 267
1:22–23	166
2:6	158
2:10	158
2:15	156, 158
2:20–22	175
4:13–16	175
4:22–24	158, 182
5:8	158
5:14	158
5:32	183

Galatians

1:1	158
1:4	249, 267, 269
2:19–20	158
3:16	178
3:29	178
4:26–31	201
5:22–26	158
5:22	170
5:24–25	158
6:14–15	158
6:14	158
6:15	10, 158, 249, 269

Colossians

1	166, 228
3	165
1:6	164
1:10	164
1:13	164
1:14	178
1:15–20	159
1:15–18	159, 165, 229
1:15–17	159
1:15	164–165
1:17	165
1:18–20	159, 165
1:18	102
1:20	246
1:22	238
2:9	125
2:10–15	159
2:16–17	259
3:1	159
3:2	159
3:4	159
3:7	165
3:9–10	159
3:10	156, 165

Philippians

1:19–22	159
2:5–11	165
2:15	159
3	231
3:10–14	159
3:20–21	271
3:20	201
3:21	122, 231, 241

1 Thessalonians

1–5	159–160, 293
1:9–10	159
4:14–17	159
5:9–10	159
5:23b	159

2 Thessalonians

1–3	159–160, 293
2:1	160
2:13	155

1 Timothy

3:16	160
6:17	267

2 Timothy

1:9–14	160
2:2–12	160
2:17	160
2:18	238
4:10	267
4:18	159

Titus

1:3	160
3:5	160

Hebrews

2:6–9	160
2:17	160
3–4	180, 282
4:8	180
6:1–3	121, 239
6:2	238
6:4	151
6:5	267
6:17–20	151
9:8	151
9:11	160
9:23	151
10:19–21	160
11	165
11:13	21
11:14	176
11:16	176
12:22	151, 176, 178, 201
13:14	176

James

1	160
1:18	160
3:18	160

1 John

1:5–7	162
2:8	162
2:17	162
2:18	162
2:29	162
3:2	21, 241
3:9	162
4:7	162
4:16	125–126
5:1	162
5:4	162
5:18	162

1 Peter

1:3–5	161
1:3	22
2:5	251
3:15	21
3:18–21	161
5:4	161

2 Peter

1:4	161, 263
1:11	151
3	230, 244, 303
3:5–7	245
3:8–13	245
3:10–12	141, 161, 244
3:10	151, 244
3:13	8, 10, 161, 172
3:15–16	161

Revelation

1–3	162
1:3	200
1:4	199, 257
1:5	162
1:6	182
1:20	257
2:7	162
2:10–11	162
2:17	165
2:28	259
3:12	165
3:14	162, 201
4–5	167, 235
4:5	259
5:9	254
5:13	246
6:9	236
6:11	162
6:14	249
7:9	254
10:6	116, 267, 275–276, 288, 298
11:11–12	162
11:15	178
12	152
13	224
14:15–16	196
16:5	199
16:20	249
17–18	182, 253
18–21	223
18:2–4	167
18:4	182
19:2	167
19:7–8	263
20:4–6	162
20:11	120, 243, 249, 287, 298
20:12–15	162
21–22	131, 137, 139, 143, 162, 165, 167, 171, 173–175, 177, 179, 182, 184, 186, 204, 221, 238, 246–247, 252–255, 257–258, 263–264, 287, 303–304
21	133
21:1—22:5	149, 161, 168, 173, 176–177, 253
21:1–8	243, 253
21:1–5	253
21:1–4	107, 162
21:1–2	172
21:1	8, 10, 133, , 168, 171, , 241, 243, 253, 256, 257, 258, 300, 302
21:2	171, 252–253, 263
21:3	125, 129, 168, 175, 183, 254
21:4	133, 168, 237, 252, 256–257
21:5	40, 168, 253–254, 257
21:6	274, 276
21:8	172, 256, 258
21:9—22:5	253
21:9–27	168
21:9	252–253, 263
21:10—22:5	253
21:10	132, 150, 168, 253
21:11–26	257
21:11	168
21:12–14	252
21:12–13	168
21:12	133, 256
21:14	133
21:15	168
21:16–20	171
21:16	168, 175
21:19–20	252
21:22	254
21:23–25	259
21:23	168, 252, 256, 276
21:24–26	169, 252
21:24	133, 255
21:25	256–258
21:27	256, 258
22	258, 276–277, 289, 298
22:1–2	131–132, 168
22:1	252, 274
22:2–3	262
22:2	168, 252, 256
22:3–5	133, 182
22:3	237, 254, 256

22:4	175, 252, 262
22:5	133, 257–258, 276
22:6	276
22:11	172
22:14–15	172
22:16	259
22:17	274
22:2–19	162

EARLY JEWISH AND CHRISTIAN WRITINGS

2 Enoch

33:2	267, 277
65:7	267, 277

Letter of Barnabas

6:5	151

www.ingramcontent.com/pod-product-compliance
Lightning Source LLC
Chambersburg PA
CBHW080407300426
44113CB00015B/2427